61676

TIMBER CONSTRUCTION MANUAL

TIMBER CONSTRUCTION MANUAL

A Manual for Architects, Engineers, Contractors, Laminators and Fabricators Concerned with Engineered Timber Buildings and Other Structures

SECOND EDITION
1974

Prepared by
AMERICAN INSTITUTE OF TIMBER CONSTRUCTION
Englewood, Colorado

A WILEY-INTERSCIENCE PUBLICATION

JOHN WILEY AND SONS, INC.
NEW YORK · LONDON · SYDNEY · TORONTO

Published by John Wiley & Sons, Inc. 1954, 1956, 1962,
1965, 1966, 1974 by American Institute of Timber Construction.

Copyright © 1974, by American Institute of Timber Construction.

Library of Congress Cataloging in Publication Data:
American Institute of Timber Construction.
  Timber construction manual.

  "Timber construction standards, AITC 100-72 . . . sixth
edition, 1972," with special t.p. bound in at end.
  1. Building, Wooden—Handbooks, manuals, etc.
I. American Institute of Timber Construction.   Timber
construction standards.   1973.   II.   Title.

TA666.A5   1974   694'.02'02   73-11311
ISBN 0-471-02549-6

Printed in the United States of America
10 9 8 7 6 5 4

PREFACE

The first edition of the AITC *Timber Construction Manual* was published in 1966. Changes in the wood products industry and technological advances and improvements in the structural timber fabricating industry have necessitated this revised edition of the *Manual*.

New lumber sizes and revisions in grading requirements for lumber and glued laminated timber are reflected in this second edition. Improved and refined design procedures are also incorporated.

The *Timber Construction Manual* was prepared by the AITC engineering staff with the guidance of the Institute's Technical Advisory Committee. The valuable assistance provided from many sources in developing technical data for the *Manual* is gratefully acknowledged.

PREFACE TO FIRST EDITION

In recent years, technical developments and the establishment of an engineered timber fabricating and laminating industry have had a profound effect on construction. Long clear spans of timber trusses, girders, arches, and decking are now commonplace. Engineered timber is widely used in such diversified construction as schools, churches, commercial buildings, industrial buildings, residences and farm buildings, highway and railway bridges, towers, theater screens, ships, and military and marine installations.

Modern practices combine engineering, quality control, and careful grading with the use of proper working stresses, dependable adhesives, and efficient mechanical fastenings to produce reliable construction. Laminating with strong, durable adhesives permits the manufacture of curved and variable shaped members and thus increases the versatility of timber construction.

The American Institute of Timber Construction is a nonprofit, technical, industrial association of manufacturers and fabricators who may design, plant laminate, fabricate, assemble, and erect load-carrying sawn and glued laminated timber framing and decking for roofs and other structural parts of schools, churches, commercial, industrial, and other buildings, and for other structures such as bridges, towers, and marine installations.

The American Institute of Timber Construction has developed this *Timber Construction Manual* for convenient reference by architects, engineers, contractors, teachers, the laminating and fabricating industry, and all others having a need for reliable, up-to-date technical data and recommendations on engineered timber construction. The information and the recommendations herein are based on the most reliable technical data available and reflect the commercial practices found to be most practical. Their application results in structurally sound construction.

The *Manual* has been arranged primarily for convenient use by designers, detailers, and fabricators of engineered timber construction. To avoid repetition, material which pertains to more than one area will be found in only one section. Suitable cross references are made in the other pertinent sections.

Information of an engineering textbook nature, such as derivations of formulae, is not included, since the purpose of the *Manual* is to present data for design and construction application by those familiar with engineering procedures.

Part I of the *Manual* contains design data and construction information. Part II contains AITC recommended standards and specifications which will aid the designer in preparing plans and specifications for engineered timber construction.

Material has been compiled from many sources. Where it has been possible to identify the author of the material reproduced, it is used with the author's permission.

Every precaution has been taken to assure that all the data and information included are as accurate as possible. However, the Institute cannot assume responsibility for errors or omissions resulting from the use of this *Manual* in the preparation of plans or specifications. The Institute does not prepare engineering plans.

The work of the preparation of the *Timber Construction Manual* was guided by the AITC Technical Advisory Committee and was carried out by AITC staff engineers and by engineers and technical representatives of AITC member firms.

Suggestions for the improvement of this *Manual* will be welcomed and will receive consideration in the preparation of future editions.

The *Timber Construction Manual* has been adopted by the American Institute of Timber Construction as its official recommendation.

GENERAL NOMENCLATURE

The following abbreviations and symbols are in general use throughout this *Manual*. Deviations from these notations are identified where they occur. Standard detailing symbols are given under "Timber Detailing" in Section 1.

ABBREVIATIONS

Btu	British thermal unit
c–c	center to center
$\mathcal{C}_L$	centerline
cu	cubic
DL	dead load
EMC	equilibrium moisture content
fbm	foot board measure
ft, ft^2, ft^3, ft^4, . . .	feet, square feet, cubic feet, feet to the fourth power, etc.
ga	gage
in., in.^{2}, in.^{3}, in.^{4}, . . .	inches, square inches, cubic inches, inches to the fourth power, etc.
in.-lb	inch-pound
k	kip (one thousand pounds)
lb	pound
lin	lineal
LL	live load
max	maximum
MC	moisture content
min	minimum
mph	miles per hour
NA	neutral axis
o.c.	on centers
pcf	pounds per cubic foot
plf	pounds per lineal foot
pli	pounds per lineal inch
psf	pounds per square foot
psi	pounds per square inch
SL	snow load
sq	square
TL	total load

WL	wind load
yd	yard

SYMBOLS

A	area of cross section
b	breadth (width) of rectangular member
C	coefficient, constant, or factor
C_c	curvature factor
C_d	depth effect factor
C_F	size factor
C_f	form factor
C_s	slenderness factor
c	distance from neutral axis to extreme fiber
D	diameter
d	depth of rectangular member, or least dimension of compression member
E	modulus of elasticity
e	eccentricity
F_b	allowable unit stress for extreme fiber in bending
F_b'	allowable unit stress for extreme fiber in bending adjusted by slenderness factor
f_b	actual unit stress for extreme fiber in bending
F_c	allowable unit stress in compression parallel to grain
F_c'	allowable unit stress in compression parallel to grain adjusted for l/d ratio
f_c	actual unit stress in compression parallel to grain
$F_{c\perp}$	allowable unit stress in compression perpendicular to grain
$f_{c\perp}$	actual unit stress in compression perpendicular to grain
F_r	allowable unit radial stress
f_r	actual unit radial stress
F_{rc}	allowable unit radial stress in compression
f_{rc}	actual unit radial stress in compression
F_{rt}	allowable unit radial stress in tension
f_{rt}	actual unit radial stress in tension
F_s	allowable unit stress in rolling shear (for plywood)
f_s	actual unit stress in rolling shear (for plywood)
F_t	allowable unit stress in tension parallel to grain
f_t	actual unit stress in tension parallel to grain
$F_{t\perp}$	allowable unit stress for tension perpendicular to grain
$f_{t\perp}$	actual unit stress in tension perpendicular to grain
F_v	allowable unit horizontal shear stress
f_v	actual unit horizontal shear stress
G	modulus of rigidity (shear modulus)
$\hbar$	rise

I	moment of inertia
L	span length of beam, or unsupported length of column, ft
l	span length of beam, or unsupported length of column, in.
M	bending moment
m	unit bending moment
P	total concentrated load, or axial compression load
P/A	induced axial load per unit of cross-sectional area
Q	statical moment of an area about the neutral axis
R	radius of curvature
R_H	horizontal reaction
R_V	vertical reaction
r	radius of gyration
S	section modulus
T	total axial tension load
t	thickness
V	total vertical shear
W	total uniform load
w	uniform load per unit of length
Δ_A	allowable deformation or deflection
Δ_a	actual deformation or deflection
Δ_B	actual deflection due to bending
Δ_S	actual deflection due to shear
$\parallel$	parallel
$\perp$	perpendicular
π	pi
$>$	greater than
$\geq$	greater than or equal to
$<$	less than
$\leq$	less than or equal to

CONTENTS

Part II   DESIGN SPECIFICATIONS

INDEX

Part I

DESIGN DATA

SECTION 1
DESIGN CONSIDERATIONS IN
THE USE OF STRUCTURAL TIMBER

GENERAL

The American Institute of Timber Construction has developed this *Timber Construction Manual* for convenient reference by architects, engineers, contractors, teachers, the laminating industry, and other individuals, such as designers, detailers, and fabricators needing reliable up-to-date technical data and recommendations on engineered timber construction.

Before a designer can effectively design a structural system, whether it be a building, bridge, tower, or other type of structure, he must first be familiar with the fundamental characteristics of the building material involved. Therefore, the first section of the *Manual* has been developed to provide basic information related to the use of engineered timber in structural design, such as economy, durability, fire safety, erection, and typical detailing. With an understanding of these characteristics the designer can more effectively apply the detailed design information contained in subsequent sections of this *Manual*.

Designing for Economy

The economic success of the construction of a project may be greatly influenced by design. The designer must recognize that the entire building, not merely one component such as a beam or a truss, should be properly designed and engineered to obtain maximum economy. Standardized structural parts do have their place when used in designs where all components are designed with an eye to structural adequacy, efficiency, and economy. Often, it is less expensive to call for a fabricator's standard glued laminated arch, beam, or truss pattern than for a custom design. However, each structure should be analyzed so that its own requirements for utility and economy will be satisfied and so that it will not be forced arbitrarily to conform with a stereotyped structural framework design.

Standard sizes and grades

The use of standard sizes and grades will result in maximum economy. For glued laminated members, standard section sizes as given in *Standard for Dimensions of Glued Laminated Structural Members*, AITC 113, included in Part II of this *Manual*, are generally most economical. Any length, up to the maximum length limited by transportation and handling restrictions, is available. For sawn lumber, the sizes given in Table 2.17 are more economical than special sizes and special lengths. Lengths are generally available in even 2-ft increments, and there is a limit on the maximum length normally available from local suppliers.

Standard details

Specially designed connecting hardware should be avoided. The industry has perfected a great variety of steel connecting devices that have proved their effectiveness in permanent construction. Typical connection details are given in *Typical Construction Details*, AITC 104, included in Part II of this *Manual*.

Framing systems

A great variety of structural timber framing systems are available. The relative economy of any one system over another will depend on the particular requirements of the specific job. Consideration of the overall structure, intended use, geographical location, required configuration, and other factors plays an important part in determining the framing system to be used on a job. Table 1.1 may be used for preliminary design purposes to determine the economical span ranges for various timber framing systems. It must be emphasized that the table is to be used for preliminary planning purposes only. All systems require a very close analysis before final design.

The following additional considerations, when applied to timber framing system design, tend to reduce costs. Joints as simple and as few in number as practicable should be used, splices being so placed as to minimize design, fabrication, and erection problems. Unnecessary variations in members must be avoided, that is, the identical member design should be used repetitively where practical and the number of different patterns kept to a minimum.

Certain roof profiles will effect the amount and type of load on a structure and may, therefore, effect economy. Better economy usually results from specifying the allowable design stresses rather than the lumber grades to be used. Judicious use of multiple, cantilever, and suspended spans in beams tends to balance positive and negative moments and may lower costs.

Appearance grades

An additional consideration related to economy of design is appearance. AITC has developed specifications for three standard appearance grades of glued laminated members. These are given in *Standard Appearance Grades for Structural Glued Laminated Timber*, AITC 110, included in Part II of this *Manual*. These appearance grades are not related to strength. It is more economical to specify the finish or appearance grade best suited for each job than to require the "premium" appearance grade for all jobs.

Economy through use of standards

What holds true for appearance grades also holds true for all other aspects of timber construction, i.e., the use of standards developed by the industry brings about economical structures.

TABLE 1.1

ECONOMICAL SPAN RANGES FOR VARIOUS TIMBER FRAMING SYSTEMS

A. PRIMARY FRAMING SYSTEMS		
Type of System	Economical Span Range, ft	Considerations
Roof Framing Systems		
Beams		Beam systems are frequently used where a flat or low-pitched roof shape is desired.
Simple spans		
Straight beams		
Glued laminated	10 to 100	
Sawn	6 to 40	
Tapered beams	25 to 100	
Double tapered-pitched beams	25 to 100	
Curved beams	25 to 100	
Cantilever systems		
		Usually more economical than simple spans when span is over 40 ft.
Glued laminated	10 to 90	
Sawn	24	
Continuous spans		
Glued laminated	10 to 50	
Sawn	10 to 50	
Arches		
Three-hinged arches		For relatively high-rise applications.
Gothic	40 to 90	
Tudor	20 to 120	Provides required vertical wall frame.
A-frame	20 to 100	
Three-centered	40 to 250	
Parabolic	40 to 250	
Radial	40 to 250	
Two-hinged arches		For relatively low-rise applications.
Radial	50 to 200	
Parabolic	50 to 200	

TABLE 1.1 (Continued)

A. PRIMARY FRAMING SYSTEMS		
Type of System	Economical Span Range, ft	Considerations
Roof Framing Systems		
Trusses		Provide openings for passage of wiring, piping, etc.
Flat or parallel chord	50 to 150	Low roof profile.
Triangular or pitched	50 to 90	For pitched roofs requiring flat surfaces.
Bowstring (continuous chord)	50 to 200	Provide greatest clearance with least wall height.
Carrying	40 to 60	
Tied arches	50 to 200	Good where no ceiling is wanted; give clear open appearance for low-rise curve; normally more expensive than bowstring; buttress not required.
Dome structures	50 to 350	
Floor Framing Systems		
Beams		
Simple span		
Glued laminated	6 to 40	
Sawn	6 to 20	
Continuous	25 to 40	
B. SECONDARY FRAMING SYSTEMS		
Roof Framing Systems		
Sheathing and decking		
1-in. sheathing applied directly to primary system	1 to 4	Check deflection on spans greater than 32 in.
2-in. roof deck applied directly to primary system	6 to 10	Check deflection on spans greater than 8 ft.
3-in. roof deck applied directly to primary system	8 to 15	2 in., 3 in., and 4 in. decking provide good insulation, fire resistance, appearance; easy to erect.
4-in. roof deck applied directly to primary system	12 to 20	

TABLE 1.1 (Continued)

B. SECONDARY FRAMING SYSTEMS		
Type of System	Economical Span Range, ft	Considerations
Roof Framing Systems		
Plywood sheathing applied directly to primary system	1 to 4	
Stressed skin panels	8 to 40	
Joists with sheathing	16 to 24	
Purlins with sheathing	16 to 36	
Beams	20 to 40	
Floor Framing Systems		
Plank decking		Floor and ceiling in one.
Edge-to-edge	4 to 16	
Wide face-to-wide face	4 to 16	
Joists with sheathing	10 to 24	

Designing for Permanence

Permanent timber structures should be built not only to be structurally adequate but also to be durable with a minimum of maintenance. With proper design, construction, and usage, wood is a permanent construction material. Certain conditions affect durability and maintenance costs. If proper consideration is given them in the design phases of a project, there will be greater assurance that the structure will be durable and that maintenance costs will be low.

Wood-moisture relationships

Dimensional changes in wood result primarily from a gain or loss of moisture. Wood shrinks and swells in a direction perpendicular to the grain and has practically no dimensional change parallel to the grain. Consideration must be given for changes in dimension if there are to be moisture changes.

Once the moisture content has been lowered to the fiber saturation point (approximately 25–30%), further loss of moisture content results in wood shrinkage. This shrinkage continues almost linearly down to 0% moisture content. Eventually, wood assumes a condition near equilibrium with its environment.

Wood absorbs water in free liquid form and as a water vapor, and gives off water again when the humidity of the surrounding air is low. In the course of absorbing water, wood swells and when the moisture content goes above 20% for repeated or prolonged periods, untreated wood is subject to attack by decay fungi. If wood becomes wet after being installed dry, its swelling results in increased dimensions and sometimes in distortion and twisting. If installed wet, wood may dry in service, shrink, with the result of checking, movement, or distortion.

There is a proven performance of indefinitely long service for untreated wood if it is kept below 20% moisture content. When wood is completely subjected to the elements or other conditions of free water or high relative humidity where decay is possible, a preservative treatment is required. The need for preservatively treated wood is a design consideration based on the conditions intended for the wood in service.

Wood-destroying organisms and their control

Mold, stain, and decay. Molds, stains, and decay are caused by microscopic organisms called fungi, which are actually plants. Decay fungi use organic material, such as wood, as food. For growth, they need, simultaneously, food, suitable temperatures (generally 40° to 110°F), sufficient air, and adequate moisture. The elimination of any one of these elements inhibits the development of fungi. Most decay occurs in wood having a moisture content above the fiber saturation point. Because of lack of air, wood that is continually immersed will not decay; and, because of lack of moisture, wood that is continuously dry will not decay. Usually, wood maintained at a moisture content of 20% or less is safe from fungus damage. When other conditions for fungi growth cannot be controlled, decay can be prevented or stopped by poisoning or treating the food, that is, the wood.

Molds and stains are limited to sapwood and are of various colors. Molds generally do not stain the wood but produce surface blemishes varying from white or light colors to black and can easily be brushed off. Fungus stains penetrate the sapwood and normally cannot be removed by scraping or sanding.

Molds and stains should not be considered as stages of decay, since these fungi do not attack the wood substance appreciably. For most uses in which appearance is not a factor, wood is practically unimpaired by stains and molds. Ordinarily, their only effect on strength is confined to those properties which determine shock resistance or toughness. The only danger is that the early stages of decay may also be hidden in the discolored areas of molds or stain.

Decay-producing fungi, under conditions that favor their growth, may attack both heartwood and sapwood. Heartwood is more resistant to attack than is sapwood. Fresh surface growths are usually fluffy or cottony, seldom powdery like the surface growths of molds. The early stages of decay are often accompanied by a discoloration of the wood, which is more evident on freshly exposed surfaces of unseasoned wood than on dry wood. However, many fungi produce early stages of decay that are similar in color to that of normal wood, or they give the wood a water-soaked appearance. Later stages of decay are easy to recognize because the wood has undergone definite changes in color and texture.

Decay from fungi reduces the strength of wood. In later stages, all decay fungi seriously reduce the strength of wood and also its fire resistance.

Brown, crumbly rot, in the dry condition, is sometimes called "dry rot," but the term is incorrect because decay fungi must have some source of moisture for development, even though the wood may have subsequently become dry.

Prevention and Control of Decay. The best assurance of receiving timber free of decay is to purchase timber in grades that exclude decay. Timber to be used where conditions favorable to the growth of decay-producing organisms are unavoidable should be adequately treated with a wood preservative, unless the heartwood of naturally decay-resistant species is available and considered adequate in view of the decay hazard encountered. Where serious decay problems are present in buildings, they are almost always signs of faulty design or construction or of lack of reasonable maintenance. Design and construction principles that will assure long service and avoid decay hazards in buildings include:

1. Positive site and building drainage.
2. Adequate separation of wood from known moisture sources.
3. Ventilation and condensation control in enclosed spaces.

Building sites should always be graded to provide positive drainage away from foundation walls. All stumps, wood debris, stakes, or wood concrete forms should be removed from the immediate vicinity of a building before backfilling and before placing a floor slab.

All exposed wood surfaces and adjoining areas should be pitched to assure rapid runoff of water. Construction details that tend to trap moisture in end grain should be avoided. The prevention of decay in walls and roofs rests largely in designs that prevent the entrance and retention of rain water. A fairly wide roof overhang, with gutters and downspouts that are designed not to clog, is very desirable.

Adequate separation of wood from known sources of moisture is necessary to prevent excessive absorption of moisture and to facilitate periodic inspection. When it is impossible or impractical to provide adequate separation, it is recommended that wood treated with a preservative or naturally durable species be used.

Wood in contact with concrete near the ground should be protected by a moisture-proof membrane, such as heavy asphalt paper. In some cases, preservative treatment of the wood in actual contact with the concrete is advisable. Girder and joist openings in masonry walls should be big enough to assure that there will be an air space around the sides and ends of these wood members; and, if the members are below the outside soil level, moisture-proofing of the outer face of the wall is essential.

Unventilated, inaccessible spaces under buildings should be avoided. In basementless buildings, wetting of the wood by condensation may result in serious decay damage. A crawl space with at least an 18-in. clearance should be left under wood joists and girders. Condensation can be prevented either by providing openings on opposite sides of the foundation walls for cross ventilation or by laying heavy roll roofing or 6-mil polyethylene membrane on the soil.

Porches, breezeways, patios, and other building appendages present a decay hazard that cannot be fully avoided by construction practices. Therefore, it is generally advisable to use wood treated with a preservative.

Sheathing papers in the walls should be of a "breathing" or vapor-permeable type. Vapor barriers, if installed, should be near the warm face of insulated walls and ceilings. (See *ASHRAE* recommendations.) Roofs must be kept tight, and attic cross ventilation is desirable.

Where highly humid conditions are present in buildings, as in textile mills, pulp and paper mills, and cold-storage plants, properly pressure-treated lumber should be used unless the heartwood of naturally decay-resistant species is available and considered adequate in view of the decay hazard encountered.

To supplement good design and construction practices, periodic inspections of a structure will provide assurance that decay-preventive measures are being maintained and that additional decay hazards are not present. It should be emphasized that damage from decay develops slowly. Periodic inspections will, therefore, reveal indications of moisture penetration or condensation, and once they are detected, corrective measures can be taken in time to avoid significant damage.

Insects. In terms of economic loss, the most destructive insect to attack wood buildings is the subterranean termite. In certain localities, nonsubterranean temites are also very destructive. Other insects attack timber buildings, but, ordinarily, these occurrences are rather rare and their damage is slight. In many cases, these insects can be controlled by the methods used for the termites.

Subterranean Termites. The occurrence of subterranean termites and damage caused by them is much greater in Southern states than in Northern states, where lower temperatures do not favor their development (see Figure 1.1). However, damage to individual buildings may be just as great in Northern states as in Southern states.

Subterranean termites develop and maintain in the ground colonies from which they build their tunnels through the earth and around obstructions to get at the wood they need for food. Each colony shuts itself off and lives in the dark; but unless they have a constant source of moisture, the termites will die. The worker members of the colony cause the destruction of wood. At certain seasons of the year, male and female winged forms swarm from the colony, fly a short time, lose their wings, mate, and, if they succeed in locating suitable places, start new colonies. The appearance of "flying ants" or of their shed wings is an indication that a termite colony may be near and causing serious damage. Not all "flying ants" are termites; therefore, suspected insects should be identified before money is spent for their eradication.

Subterranean termites do not establish themselves in buildings by being carried there in lumber, but by entering from the ground nests after the building has been constructed. They must maintain contact with a source of moisture such as the soil. Telltale signs of the presence of termites are the earthen tubes or runways built by these insects over the surfaces of foundation walls to reach the wood above. Another sign is the swarming of winged adults early in the spring or fall. In wood itself, the termites make galleries that follow the grain, leaving a shell of sound wood to conceal their activities. Since the galleries seldom show on the wood surface, probing with an ice pick or knife is advisable if the presence of termites is suspected.

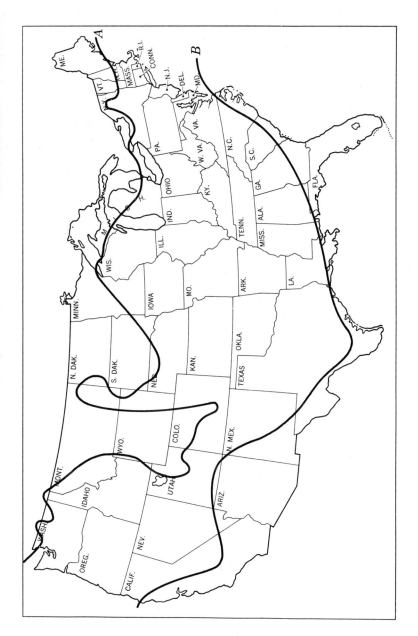

Figure 1.1. LIMITS OF TERMITE DAMAGE. *A,* the northern limit of recorded damage done by subterranean termites in the United States; *B,* the northern limit of damage done by drywood or nonsubterranean termites. Source: *Wood Handbook,* U. S. Department of Agriculture Handbook No. 72, 1955.

Protection and Control. Where subterranean termites are prevalent the best protection is to build so as to prevent their gaining access to the building. The foundations should be of concrete or other solid material through which the termites cannot penetrate. With brick, stone, or concrete blocks, cement mortar should be used, for termites can work through some other kinds of mortar. Wood that is not impregnated with an effective preservative must be kept away from the ground. If there is a basement, it should preferably be floored with concrete. Posts supporting the first-floor beams must be thoroughly treated if they bear directly on the ground or on wood blocking. Untreated posts should rest on concrete piers extending a few inches above the basement floor if that floor is of concrete; if the basement floor is of earth, the concrete piers should extend at least 18 in. above it. If the earth is not excavated beneath the building and if the floor is of wood construction, the floor joists and other woodwork, unless adequately treated with preservative, should be kept at least 18 in. above the earth, and good ventilation should be provided beneath the floor.

Moisture condensation on the floor joists and subflooring which may cause conditions favorable to decay, and thus make the wood more attractive to termites, can be avoided by covering the soil with roll roofing. For buildings with concrete slab floors laid directly over a gravel fill, the soil directly beneath the expansion joints and around utility openings in the floor should be poisoned before the concrete is poured. Furthermore, when insulation containing cellulose is to be used as a filler in expansion joints, it should be impregnated with a chemical toxic to termites. Sealing the top $\frac{1}{2}$ in. of expansion joints and other openings will provide additional protection from ground-nesting termites.

All concrete forms, stakes, stumps, and waste wood should be removed from the building site, because they are possible sources of infestation. In the main, the precautions that are effective against decay are also helpful against subterranean termites.

Where protection is needed in addition to that obtained by structural methods, the soil adjacent to the foundation walls and piers beneath the building should be thoroughly poisoned with a recognized soil poison. A thorough treatment of this kind should provide protection for about 20 years, unless the termites are inadvertently provided with a bridge across the treated soil.

To control termites in a building, one of the main things to do is to break any contact between the termite colony in the soil and the woodwork. This can be done by mechanically blocking the runways from soil to wood, by poisoning the soil, or by both of these methods. Possible reinfestations should be guarded against by frequent inspections for the telltale signs previously given.

Nonsubterranean Termites. Nonsubterranean termites have been found only in a narrow strip of territory extending from Central California around the southern edge of the United States to Virginia (see Figure 1.1). Their damage is confined to an area in southern California and to parts of southern Florida, notably Key West. The nonsubterranean drywood termites are fewer in number, and their depredations are not rapid, but if they are allowed to work unmolested for a few years, they can occasionally ruin timbers with their tunnelings.

Protection and control. In the principal damage areas, careful examination of wood is needed to avoid the occurrence of infestations during the construction of a building. All exterior wood can be protected with an adequate paint film, and unpainted interior wood can be protected by placing fine mesh screen over all holes in the walls or roof of the building. If a building is found to be infested with drywood termites, badly damaged wood must be replaced. Further termite activity can be arrested by approved chemical treatments under proper supervision for safety of people, domestic animals, and wildlife. Where practical, fumigation is another method of destroying insects.

Other Wood-Inhabiting Insects. Large wood-boring beetles and wood wasps infest green wood but may complete their development in seasoned wood. They do not reinfest dry wood. They occur in all forest areas. The borers in timber or lumber can be killed by heating the wood to a center temperature of 130°F for 1 hour or by fumigation. If infested wood is used in constructing a building, the emerging adult borers will chew $\frac{1}{8}$ to $\frac{1}{2}$ in. holes to the surface, penetrating insulation, vapor barriers, siding, or interior surface materials. The surface holes can be plugged and the damaged spots finished or refinished to make them inconspicuous. Since the borers do not reinfest dry wood, extermination treatments are not required in buildings.

Powder-post beetles can infest and reinfest dry wood, reducing it to floury sawdust. The *Lyctus* powder-post beetles, which are encountered most frequently, attack large-pored hardwoods. Their attacks may be recognized by tunnels packed with floury sawdust and numerous emergence holes $\frac{1}{32}$ to $\frac{1}{8}$ in. in diameter. Heat or fumigation treatments will kill the beetles but will not prevent reinfestation. It can be prevented by a surface application of an approved insecticide in a light-oil solution. Any finishing material that plugs the surface holes of wood will also immunize the wood from *Lyctus* attack. Usually, infestations in buildings result from the use of infested wood, and insecticidal treatment or fumigation may be needed to eliminate them.

Carpenter ants chew nesting galleries in wood. The principal species are large dark-colored ants, and many individuals in the colony are $\frac{1}{2}$ in. long. They are distributed throughout the United States. Since the ants require a nearly saturated atmosphere in their nest, an ant infestation may indicate a moisture problem in the wood. Ant infestations may be controlled by insecticides.

Marine borers. Fixed or floating wood structures in salt or brackish water are subject to attack by marine borers. The principal marine borers that cause wood destruction are *Teredoes, Limnoria, Martesia,* and *Sphaeroma.* Almost all these animals attack wood as free-swimming organisms in the early part of their lives. They bore an entrance hole generally at the water line, attach themselves, and grow in size as they bore tunnels into the wood.

Protection and Control. There are no native species of wood in the United States that are naturally resistant to marine borers. The best and only protection is to pressure-treat to heavy retentions of creosote or creosote-coal tar solutions all wood to be used in salt or brackish waters.

Significance of checking

Checking is the result of rapid lowering of surface moisture content combined with differential moisture contents of the inner and outer portion of the piece. As wood loses moisture content to the surrounding atmosphere, the outer cells of the members lose at a more rapid rate than do the inner cells. As the outer cells try to shrink, they are restrained by the inner portion of the member, which has a higher moisture content. The more rapid the rate of drying, the greater will be the differential in shrinkage between the outer and inner fibers and the higher will be the shrinkage stresses.

In sawn lumber and timber, controlling the rate of drying will avoid or minimize checking. Many monumental buildings with great historical value have been constructed in such a way as to exploit the natural beauty of large sawn timbers. In these structures, seasoning checks are accepted as an inherent characteristic of the material.

One of the principal advantages of glued laminated construction is freedom from major checking; however, seasoning checks may occur in glued laminated members for the same reasons as in sawn timbers, but generally to a much lesser degree. When laminated members are glued within the range of moisture content limitations expressed in Voluntary Product Standard PS56-73, *Structural Glued Laminated Timber*, they approximate the moisture content in normal use conditions, thereby minimizing checking that might occur. Moisture content of lumber at the time of gluing is, therefore, of great importance in the control of checking in service. However, serious rapid changes in moisture content after gluing will result in shrinkage or swelling of the wood and may develop stresses in both glued joint and wood that will cause checking. Differentials in the shrinkage rate of individual laminations tend to concentrate shrinkage stresses at or near the glue line. For this reason, when checking occurs, it is usually at or near glue lines. The presence of wood fiber separation indicates adequate glue bond and not delamination.

Structural considerations.

Glued Laminated Timber. In general, checks have little effect on the strength of laminated members. Glued laminated members are made from laminations that are thin enough to season readily in kiln-drying schedules without developing checks. Since checks lie in a radial plane and since the majority of laminations are flat grain, checks are so positioned in horizontally laminated beams that they will not materially affect shear strength. If members are designed with laminations vertical and if checks may affect the shear strength of a beam, their effect may be evaluated in the same manner as for sawn lumber. Seasoning checks in bending members affect the horizontal shear value only. They are usually not of structural importance unless the checks are significant in depth, occur in the mid-height of the member and near the support, and shear governs the design of the members. All these factors must be considered in appraising checks from a structural viewpoint. In general, the reduction in shear strength is directly proportional to the ratio of depth of check to the width of the bending member. Checks in columns are not of structural importance unless the check develops into a split, thereby reducing the l/d of the column. Minor checking may be disregarded, as there is an ample factor of safety in allowable working stresses.

Sawn Lumber and Timber. Checks affect the horizontal shear strength of lumber, and, in establishing basic working stresses, checks are anticipated by a large reduction factor applied to test values in recognition of stress concentrations at the ends of the checks. The published working stress values of horizontal shear for the stress grades are again adjusted for the amount of checking permissible in the various grades at the time of the grading. Since the strength properties of wood increase with dryness, checks may enlarge somewhat with increased dryness from the time of shipment without decreasing shear strength materially. Actually, a fully seasoned timber may be checked in excess of the grade limitations without affecting its adequacy in the structure, because the grading rules are set up with the anticipation that some checking beyond the grade limitations at the moisture content graded may occur with seasoning. This is particularly true if loads producing shear stresses are low. Furthermore, only checks that occur near the supports and in the mid-half of the depth of the member are important to shear strength. In general, the reduction in shear strength is directly proportional to the ratio of depth of check to the width of the bending member.

Even though the grading rules would exclude such a piece, a column may be checked nearly through without having its strength seriously reduced because the main consideration is that the member act as a unit without splitting entirely into two parts for the l/d ratio would then be reduced.

Cross-grain checks and splits that tend to run out the side of a piece, or excessive checks and splits that tend to enter connection areas, may be serious and may require servicing. Details for controlling the effects of checking in connection areas may be incorporated into the design details. To avoid excessive splitting between rows of bolts due to shrinkage during the seasoning period of timbers, the rows of bolts should not be spaced more than 5 in. apart, or a saw kerf, terminating in a bored hole, should be provided between the lines of bolts. Alternatively, the use of two splice plates, one for each row of bolts, rather than a single splice plate, will lessen the probability of splitting. Whenever possible, maximum end distances for connections should be specified to minimize the effect of checks running into the joint area. Some designers require stitch bolts in members with multiple connections loaded at an angle to the grain. Stitch bolts, which should be kept tight, will reinforce pieces where checking is excessive.

The final decision about whether shrinkage checks are detrimental to the strength requirements of any particular structure should be made by a competent engineer experienced in timber construction.

Protection.

Glued Laminated Timber. The application of sealers, paints, and similar protective measures to the surface of the member will retard, but not prevent, checking under extreme conditions. Laminated members to be used under conditions that may produce checking more serious than slight surface checks should receive consideration; sealers and other protection may be required in accordance with *Recommended Practice for Protection of Structural Glued Laminated Timber during Transit, Storage, and Erection*, AITC 111, included in Part II of this *Manual*.

Sawn Lumber and Timber. Because lumber loses moisture approximately 10 times faster through the end grain than through flat grain or vertical grain faces, the application of an end seal to the end grain will help to minimize the shrinkage checks or splits. The extent of checking is related to the steepness of the moisture gradient between the surfaces and the interior of the piece.

Unseasoned lumber should be protected from hot sun and dry winds. Because attic spaces are frequently higher in temperature and lower in humidity than the surrounding atmosphere, they should be properly vented to prevent lumber from rapid drying and resultant checking.

Effects of temperature on wood

The effect of temperature on the dimensional stability of wood is discussed in Section 2. Temperature also has an important effect on the strength of wood.

Allowable unit stress values given in tables in Section 2 apply to glued laminated timber or sawn lumber used under ordinary temperature conditions. Some reduction of stresses may be necessary for members which are subjected to elevated temperatures for repeated or prolonged periods of time, especially where the high temperature is associated with a high moisture content in the wood.

The temperature effect on strength is immediate, and its magnitude depends on the moisture content of the wood and, when the temperature is elevated, on the time of exposure. Under ordinary atmospheric conditions, when wood is exposed to temperatures above normal, if the exposure is for a limited period and the temperature is not excessive, the wood can be expected to recover essentially all its original strength when the temperature is reduced to normal. Experiments indicate that air-dry wood can probably be exposed to temperatures up to nearly 150°F for a year or more without an important permanent loss in most of its strength properties, but while heated its strength will be temporarily reduced compared to its strength at normal temperature.

Tests of wood conducted at about $-300°F$ show that the important strength properties of dry wood in bending and in compression, including stiffness and shock resistance, are much higher at the extremely low temperature than at normal temperature.

The approximate immediate effect of temperature on most of the static strength properties of dry wood (12% MC) within the range 0° to 150°F can be estimated as an increase or a decrease in the strength at 70° of about $\frac{1}{3}$% to $\frac{1}{2}$% for each 1°F decrease or increase in temperature. The change in properties will be greater if the moisture content is high, and less if the moisture content is low. In some geographical locations, fairly high temperatures are commonly experienced but the accompanying relative humidity is ordinarily quite low. Wood exposed to such conditions generally has a low moisture content, and the immediate effect of the high temperature is not so pronounced as in locations where wood has a higher moisture content.

When wood is exposed to temperatures of 150°F or higher for extended periods of time, it is permanently weakened, even though the temperature is subsequently reduced and the wood is used at normal temperatures. The permanent or nonrecoverable strength loss depends on a number of factors, including the moisture content and temperature of the wood, the heating medium and time of exposure, and to some extent on the species and the size of the piece. Glued laminated members are normally cured at temperatures of less than 150°F; therefore, no reduction in their allowable unit stresses due to temperature effects during manufacturing is necessary.

Adhesives used under standard specifications for structural glued laminated members (i.e., casein, resorcinol resin, phenol resin, and melamine resin adhesives) are not affected substantially by temperatures up to those which char wood. The use of other adhesives that might deteriorate at lower temperatures is not permitted by standard specifications for structural glued laminated timber. Low temperatures appear to have no significant effect on the strength of glue joints.

Effects of chemical processes or stored chemicals on wood

Wood is often far superior to many other common construction materials in its resistance to chemical attack. For this reason, wood is used for storage containers for many chemicals, and in processing plants in which structural members are subjected to spillage, leakage, or condensation of chemicals.

Wooden tanks are commonly employed for the storage of water or chemicals that deteriorate other materials. Experience has shown that the heartwood of cypress, Douglas fir, Southern pine, and redwood is the most suitable for water tanks, and that the heartwood of the first three of these species is most suitable for tanks when resistance to chemicals in appreciable concentrations is an important factor. Each of the four species combines moderate to high resistance to water penetration with moderate to high natural resistance to decay and hydrolysis.

Structural members, floors, stairways, catwalks, and docks are frequently exposed to spillage or leakage of chemicals. Volatile chemicals may attack roof supports, ventilating ducts, and stacks in chemical processing plants. Wood should be considered for these applications.

Chemical actions of three general types may affect the strength of wood. The first causes swelling and the resultant weakening of the wood. This action is almost completely reversible; hence, if the swelling liquid or solution is removed by evaporation or by extraction followed by evaporation of the solvent, the original dimensions and strength are practically restored. The second type of action brings about permanent changes in the wood, such as hydrolysis of the cellulose by acids or acid salts. The third type of action, which is also permanent, involves delignification of the wood and dissolving of hemicelluloses by alkalies.

The strength properties of water-swollen wood are, in general, considerably lower, and in some cases more than 50% lower, than those for wood at 12% MC, which is about the average moisture content in normal use. This difference in strength must be taken into account in designing tanks for water and dilute aqueous solutions or other structures in which the wood members are wet for a long time. Alcohols and other wood-swelling organic liquids that do not react chemically with wood reduce its compressive strength proportionally to the extent of swelling. A liquid such as acetone, which swells wood 60% as much as water, causes 60% as much strength loss as is caused by swelling in water. Liquids such as petroleum oils and creosote, which do not cause swelling, have a negligible effect on wood strength. Castor oil hydraulic fluids cause wood to swell to some extent and reduce bending and compressive strength to an extent that depends on the depth of penetration of the fluid and presumably on the degree of swelling of the wood.

Acids have a hydrolytic effect on the cellulose of wood and thus cause some permanent loss in strength. However, most common construction materials corrode in the presence of the same dilute acids to which wood is resistant. When the pH of aqueous solutions of weak acids is above 2, the rate of hydrolysis of the cellulose of wood is small and is dependent on the temperature. A rough approximation of this temperature effect is that, for every 20°F increase in temperature, the rate of hydrolysis doubles. Softwoods, in general, show better resistance to acids than do hardwoods, since they contain somewhat lower percentages of hemicellulose and higher percentages of lignin. Organic acids, such as acetic, formic, lactic, and boric acids, do not ionize sufficiently at room temperature to attack cellulose and thus do not attack wood. Strong acids, such as nitric and hydrochloric acids, and highly acidic salts, such as zinc chloride, tend to hydrolyze wood and cause serious strength loss if they are present in a sufficiently high concentration.

Generally, most acid-resistant paints have not proved very effective for protecting wood in continuous exposure to acids. Tests on small laboratory specimens show that treatment with phenolic resin or furfural alcohol greatly increases the acid resistance of wood, but the difficulty and cost of treating by this method limit its use.

The weakening effect of alkalies appears to be caused by a combination of excessive swelling and of softening and dissolving of lignin and hemicelluloses. Wood offers far less resistance to alkalies than does iron; therefore, wood is seldom used in contact with solutions which are more than weakly alkaline. There is little difference in the resistance of softwoods and hardwoods to alkalies. Alkaline salts, such as sodium carbonate, are quite likely to cause chemical deterioration. Certain alkaline solutions affect wood strength more than do acidic solutions of equal strength.

There are many applications for wood in chemical processing and storage as long as the limits of its chemical resistance with regard to temperature, pH values, type of chemical involved, and type of process are not surpassed. Processes which involve corrosive chemicals at high temperatures are difficult to contain and may permit escape of acidic vapors or gases such as chlorine. Such gases may be absorbed by moisture in the wood, causing gradual loss of strength.

It appears that acids with pH values above 2 and bases with pH values below 10 have little weakening effect on wood at room temperature if the duration of exposure is moderate.

Whenever it is suspected that there is a possibility of chemical attack, an investigation should be made of the chemicals present, including the nature of the chemical, if it is to be in direct contact with the wood, and concentrations in vapor form.

Certain processes produce chemical dusts which tend to accumulate on structural members. Such deposits, if acid in nature, may hydrolyze the wood if they are permitted to remain. Periodic house cleaning will minimize such dangers. The possibility of the existence of conditions favorable to decay are not uncommon in the chemical industry. Waterproof adhesive should be specified and consideration should be given to preservative treatments if the wood moisture content will be above approximately 20% for repeated or prolonged periods.

Protection of fastenings. Fastenings and connections used in untreated timber buildings and structures may be subject to deterioration by corrosion or by chemical attack. Such fastenings and connections should be protected by painting, galvanizing, or plating. In highly corrosive atmospheres, as in chemical plants, it may be desirable to countersink all metal parts into the wood and cover them with hot pitch or tar. In such extreme conditions, the designer should require lumber at or below moisture equilibrium at the time of fabrication to prevent subsequent shrinkage that could open avenues of attack for the corrosive atmosphere.

Iron salts are frequently very acidic and show hydrolytic action on wood in the presence of free water, thus accounting for the softening and discoloration of wood around corroded nails. This action is especially pronounced in acidic woods, such as oak, and in woods containing considerable tannin and related compounds, such as redwood. It can be eliminated, however, by using zinc-coated, aluminum, or copper nails.

Designing for Fire Safety

Neither building materials alone, nor building features alone, nor detection and fire extinguishing equipment alone can provide the maximum safety from fire in buildings. A proper combination of these will provide the necessary degree of protection for the occupants and for the property. Some of the more important design considerations that should be investigated are given below. They are divided into General, Safety to Life, and Safety to Property considerations.

General Considerations

1. The degree of protection needed as dictated by the occupancy or operations taking place in the building.

2. The installation of automatic alarms and/or sprinkler systems.

3. Firestopping and the elimination, or proper protection, of concealed spaces.

4. Separation of areas in which hazardous processes or operations take place, such as boiler rooms and workshops.

Safety to Life Considerations

1. The number, size, type (such as direct to the outside from spaces),

and accessibility of exitways (particularly stairways) and their distance from each other.

2. The installation of automatic alarm systems.

3. Enclosure of stairwells and use of self-closing fire doors.

4. Interior finishes which will assure that surfaces will not spread flame at hazardous rates.

Safety to Property Considerations

1. The installation of automatic sprinkler systems.

2. Proper placement of firewalls and proper protection of openings in them.

3. Interior finishes to assure that surfaces will not spread flame at hazardous rates.

4. Roof venting equipment or provision of draft curtains where walls might interfere with production operations.

Maximum protection of the occupants of a building and of the property itself can be achieved by taking advantage of the fire endurance properties of wood and by giving careful attention to the above-mentioned details that make a building fire-safe, that is, fire-safe rather than so-called "fireproof."

Wood, when exposed to fire, forms a self-insulating surface layer of char and thus provides its own fire protection. Although the surface chars, the undamaged wood below the char retains its strength and will support loads equivalent to the capacity of the uncharred section. Very often, heavy timber members will retain their structural integrity through long periods of fire exposure and still remain serviceable after the surface has been cleaned and refinished. This fire endurance and excellent performance of heavy timber is attributable to the size of the wood members and to the slow rate at which the charring penetrates.

Since size of member is of particular importance with respect to the fire endurance of wood members, building codes specify minimum nominal dimensions for exposed structural members. For fire-resistance classification purposes, buildings of wood construction are generally classified as: *heavy timber construction, ordinary construction,* or *wood frame construction.* *Heavy timber construction* is that type in which fire resistance is attained by placing limitations on the minimum size, thickness, or composition of all load-carrying wood members; by avoiding concealed spaces under floors or roofs; by using approved fastenings, construction details, and adhesives; and by providing the required degree of fire resistance in the exterior and interior walls. *Ordinary construction* has exterior masonry walls and wood framing members of sizes smaller than heavy timber sizes. *Wood frame construction* has wood framed walls and structural framing of sizes smaller than heavy timber sizes. Depending on the occupancy of a building or the hazard of the operations within it, a building of frame or ordinary construction may have its members covered with fire-resistive coverings.

Timber, unlike most other construction materials, is not appreciably distorted by high temperatures; therefore, it is not likely that walls will be displaced or pushed over by expanding members, as often happens with some other materials.

Safety from fire in buildings

Regulations governing the construction of buildings have evolved over the years, mainly as a result of man's attempt to protect himself and his property against the ravages of fire, both from within and from without. The life safety and fire protection provisions found in modern building codes provide what are considered minimum requirements for fire safety, based on experience accumulated from fires and on research in the fire protection field. Such provisions become law when adopted by city councils or similar bodies. Typical provisions are found in all of the four nationally recognized model building codes.

The extent of structural fire endurance desirable beyond building code requirements is a matter of economic balance between the risk inside the building and the available fire protection facilities. Experience indicates that too much emphasis on the fire resistance of the structural frame results in a false sense of security. The emphasis is wrongly placed on so-called "fireproof" buildings rather than on fire-safe buildings. Good building design and adequate structural endurance, plus automatic detection and extinguishing facilities where needed, provide maximum fire safety at minimum cost.

Safety from fire begins with the fire prevention measures that are taken. They include properly designed electrical systems and other services and proper protection around heat sources such as chimneys and furnaces. However, the fire record over the years has shown that most fires have their beginning in the contents of the building rather than in the structure itself. For this reason, fire prevention is related largely to housekeeping and maintenance which are, in turn, directly associated with building administration. Thus, preventing a fire from starting in the first place has little or nothing to do with the structural materials used in the building, and the word "fireproof" as related to structural materials often deludes the building planner and the occupant by giving them an illusory feeling of safety. Because of the combustible nature of the contents of a building, no occupied building is "fireproof."

Even with the best of prevention measures, fires will, and do, start in buildings, perhaps through unforeseeable conditions and events or uncontrollable acts of nature. The first consideration then is the safety of the occupants of the building, and, after their evacuation, the safety of the firemen fighting the fire, and the safety of the property and of adjacent exposed property.

The most important protection factors are the prompt detection of a fire, immediate alarm, and rapid extinguishment of the fire. The fact that there are people in a building is no guarantee that a fire will be discovered promptly. The promptness with which a fire is discovered and the speed with which it is extinguished have an important bearing on life safety and on the extent of damage both to the contents and to the structure. Automatic detectors and extinguishing systems can provide a high degree of protection, but they should not be considered a substitute for other protection measures such as the proper number, location, and enclosure of exitways. The *Life Safety Code*, promulgated by the National Fire Protection Association, is widely used as a guide for safety to life from fire in buildings.

The structural framing of a building, which is the criterion for classifying a building as combustible or noncombustible, actually has little to do with the hazard from fire to the occupants of the building. As stated previously, most fires start in the building contents. Tests have shown that conditions resulting from the burning contents render the inside uninhabitable long before the structural framing becomes involved in a fire. Thus, whether the building is of combustible or noncombustible classification has little bearing on the potential hazard to the occupants. Once a fire starts in the contents, the material of which the building is built can be of significance in facilitating evacuation, fire fighting, and property protection.

The interior finish on the exposed surfaces of rooms, corridors, and stairways is important from the standpoint of its tendency to ignite, flame, and spread fire from one location to another. Some materials, such as paper decorations, exhibit an almost unbelievable rate of flame spread across their surface once they have been exposed to heat and flame. However, the fact that wood is combustible does not mean that it will spread flame at a hazardous rate. In fact, most codes exclude the exposed wood surfaces of heavy timber structural members from flame-spread requirements, simply because wood in such massive form is difficult to ignite and, even with an external source of heat, such as burning contents, resists spreading flame.

Life safety does not end when the occupants of a building have been safely evacuated; it continues as long as the firemen are near or in the building fighting the fire. Fire fighters do not fear the fighting of fires in heavy timber buildings as in buildings of other types of construction. The main reasons are that they do not fear sudden collapse without warning; they can usually ventilate the building; and they can usually fight the fire from within the building or from the top of it, as the nature of the fire requires.

PROPER TIMBER DETAILING

Typical Construction Details

The *Typical Construction Details*, AITC 104, included in Part II of this *Manual*, are recommended as guides and suggestions for architects and engineers to expedite their work and to give greater assurance of high quality with a minimum of maintenance for structures employing engineered timber construction. The details have been compiled from standards developed and used by timber fabricators.

These details are to be used only as guides or suggestions. The drawings are not to scale, and the quantities and sizes of bolts, connectors, and other hardware are illustrative only. The actual quantities and sizes required will depend on the loads to be carried and the size of the members. The architect or engineer must select, modify, and design the details best suited to fit the particular requirements of the job. He should keep in mind ease and economy of assembly and erection.

In the preparation of these details, particular attention has been given to minimizing maintenance and increasing durability through design and construction. Differential movements resulting from dimensional changes are shown. Moisture barriers, flashing, and other features are designated where necessary to avoid moisture or water traps. Durable structures result when these details are incorporated with other good design and construction practices, such as providing adequate roof and site drainage, providing proper protection during construction, and painting or otherwise protecting hardware from corrosion.

When not otherwise detailed, the overall side clearance between non-bearing surfaces of steel assemblies and timber members should be not less than $\frac{1}{8}$ in. Unless shown and required on the shop details, welds should not be located where they will interfere with the assembly of the connection. Hardware and steel accessories should be painted or coated to prevent staining during assembly and erection in work where appearance is a factor.

For additional examples in the design of engineered timber construction, see Section 5 of this *Manual*.

Detailing Symbols

These symbols are intended for large-scale details only. For all symbols, the sizes and quantities required are to be indicated on the drawings. If sizes are mixed, or if these symbols do not provide a clear explanation of the connection, a detail showing the hardware arrangement should be drawn.

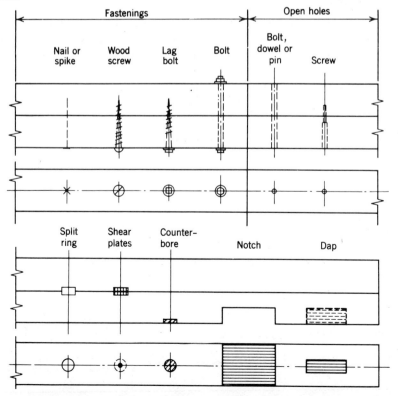

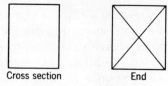

Cross section   End

Glued Laminated or Solid Sawn Members

Detailing abbreviations

Angle(s) (metal section)	$\angle$, $\angle$ s	Malleable iron washer	M.I.
Both sides	B.S.	Mark(ed)	MK
Carriage bolt	C.B.	Mold loft	ML
Centerline	₵	Near side	N.S.
Center-to-center	c–c	Ogee (cast) washer	O.G.
Chamfer	chfr	On centers	o.c.
Channel(s) (metal section)	[, [s	Plate	℔
Counterbore	cbr	Radius	R, rad
Countersink	csk	Steel section	S
Cut washer	C.W.	Shear plate	Sh. Pl.
Diameter	ϕ	Split ring	S.R.
Each side	E.S.	Threaded rod	thrd
Far side	F.S.	Turnbuckle	tbkl
Lag bolt	L.B.	Steel section	W
Lamination	lam	Wrought washer	W.W.
Machine bolt	M.B.		

Welding symbols

These symbols do not explicitly provide for the case that frequently occurs in structural work, that is, duplicate material (such as stiffeners) occurring on the far side of a web or gusset plate. The fabricating industry has adopted this convention; when the billing of the detail material discloses the identity of the far side with the near side, the welding shown for the near side shall also be duplicated on the far side. These symbols have been developed by the American Welding Society.

Arc and Gas Welding Symbols									
Type of Weld						Plug and Slot	Field Weld	Weld All Around	Flush
Bead	Fillet	Groove							
		Square	V	Bevel	U	J			
⌢	△	‖	⌵	⋁	Ⴘ	⊦	▽	●	○	—

Location of Welds		
Arrow (or Near) Side of Joint	Other (or Far) Side of Joint	Both Sides of Joint

1. The side of the joint to which the arrow points is the arrow (or near) side, and the opposite side of the joint is the other (or far) side.

2. Arrow side and other side welds are same size unless otherwise shown.

3. Symbols apply between abrupt changes in direction of joint or as dimensioned (except where all around symbol is used).

4. All welds are continuous and of user's standard proportions unless otherwise shown.

5. Tail of arrow used for specification reference (tail may be omitted when reference not used), for example,C.A. automatic shielded carbon arc; S.A. automatic submerged arc.

6. When only one member of a joint is to be grooved, the arrow points to that member.

7. Dimensions of weld sizes, increment lengths, and spacings are in inches.

ERECTION AND HANDLING OF STRUCTURAL TIMBER

The erection of structural timber framing requires experienced erection crews and adequate lifting equipment to protect lives and property, and to assure that the framing is not improperly assembled or damaged during handling. The unloading and storage of structural timber framing before erection also demand care and good judgment.

The responsibilities of the seller and buyer, when erection is performed by either, are outlined in *Code of Standard Practice*, AITC 106, which is included in Part II of this *Manual*. It is suggested that a shipment of structural timber framing, on receipt at the job site, be checked for tally and damage. The following general considerations apply to erection.

Protection during Unloading

Structural timber framing is subject to surface marring and damage when not properly handled and protected. At the erection site, the following precautions are suggested.

1. Lift members or roll them on dollies or rollers out of railroad cars; do not drag or drop them. Unload trucks by hand or crane; do not dump or drop members.

2. During unloading with lifting equipment, use fabric or plastic belts or other slings which will not mar wood. If chains or cables are used, provide protective blocking or padding.

3. Guard against soiling, dirt, footprints, abrasions, or injury to shaped edges or sharp corners.

Protection during Storage

If structural timber framing is to be stored before erection, it should be placed on blocks well off the ground, and individual members should be separated by strips so that air may circulate around all four sides. The top and all sides of storage piles should be covered with moisture-resistant paper. Clear polyethylene films should not be used because wood members are subject to bleaching from sunlight. Individual wrappings should be slit or punctured on the lower side to permit drainage of water.

Waterproof wrapping paper used for the in-transit protection of glued laminated members should be left intact until the members are enclosed within the building. If wrapping has to be removed at certain connection points during the erection, it should be replaced after the connection is made. If it is impractical to replace the wrapping, all of it should be removed.

Assembly

Trusses are usually shipped partially or completely disassembled and are assembled on the ground at the site before erection. Arches, which are generally shipped in halves, may be assembled on the ground, or connections may be made after the half arches are in position. When trusses and arches are assembled on the ground at the site, they should be assembled on level blocking to permit connections to be fitted properly and tightened securely without damage. The end compression joints should be brought into full bearing, and compression plates installed where specified.

Before erection, the assembly should be checked for prescribed overall dimensions, prescribed camber, and accuracy of anchorage connections. Erection should be planned and executed in such a way that the close fit and neat appearance of joints and the structure as a whole will not be impaired.

Support and Anchorage

The accuracy and adequacy of necessary abutments, foundations, piers, and anchor bolts are the responsibility of the buyer. Before erection begins, all supports and anchors should be complete, accessible, and free of obstructions. The weights and balance points of the structural timber framing should be determined before lifting begins, so that proper equipment and lifting methods may be employed. When timber trusses of long span are raised from a flat to a vertical position preparatory to lifting, stresses entirely different from the normal design stresses may be introduced. The magnitude and distribution of these stresses will vary, depending on such factors as the weight, dimensions, and type of truss. A competent rigger will consider these factors in determining how much suspension and stiffening, if any, is required, and where it should be located.

Bracing

All framing must be true and plumbed. Permanent bracing is bracing so designed and installed as to form an integral part of the final structure. Erection bracing is bracing which is installed to hold the framing in a safe position until sufficient permanent bracing is in place to provide full stability. Proper and adequate temporary erection bracing is introduced whenever necessary to take care of all loads to which the structure may be subjected during erection, including equipment and its operation. This bracing is left in place as long as may be required for safety. Part or all of the permanent bracing may also act as erection bracing. Erection bracing serves to plumb the framing during erection and gives it adequate stability to receive purlins, joists, and roofing materials. It may include sway bracing, guy ropes, tieing off framing nearest to end walls, steel tie rods with turnbuckle takeups, struts, shoes, and similar items. As erection progresses, bracing is securely fastened in place to take care of all dead load, erection stresses, and normal weather conditions. Excessive concentrated construction loads, such as bundles of sheathing, piles of purlins, roofing, or other materials, should be avoided.

Final Alignment

Final tightening of alignment bolts should not be completed until the structure has been properly aligned.

Steel Connections

The field joining, holding, and welding of steel connections are performed according to the requirements for shopwork of such operations, except such requirements as manifestly apply to shop conditions only. Steel connections should comply with the specifications of the American Institute of Steel Construction and of the American Welding Society.

Protection of Field Cuts

All field cuts should be coated with an approved moisture seal if the member was initially coated, unless otherwise specified. All field framing is done in accordance with the requirements of shop practice, except such requirements as manifestly apply to shop conditions only. If timber framing has been pressure-treated, field framing after treatment must be avoided, or, at least insofar as possible, held to a minimum.

Protection against Moisture

During erection operations, all timber framing which requires moisture content control, whether sawn or glued laminated timbers, should be protected against moisture pick-up. Any fabricated structural materials to be stored for an extended period of time before erection should, insofar as is practicable, be assembled into subassemblies for storage purposes.

Removal of Temporary Bracing

Temporary erection bracing should be removed only after all roofing and permanent bracing are installed, the structure has been properly aligned, and connections and fastenings have been finally tightened.

Seasoning Period

Heat should not be fully turned on as soon as the structure is enclosed; otherwise, excessive checking may occur. A gradual seasoning period at moderate temperature should be provided.

SECTION 2
PHYSICAL AND MECHANICAL
PROPERTIES OF WOOD

PHYSICAL PROPERTIES OF WOOD

Physical Structure of Wood

Wood is a cellular organic material made up principally of cellulose, which comprises the structural units, and lignin, which cements the structural units together. It also contains certain extractives and ash-forming minerals. Wood cells are hollow, and they vary from about 0.04 to 0.33 in. in length, and from 0.0004 to 0.0033 in. in diameter. Most cells are elongated and are oriented vertically in the growing tree, but some, called rays, are oriented horizontally and extend from the bark toward the center, or pith, of the tree.

Hardwoods and softwoods

Species of trees are divided into two classes: hardwoods, which have broad leaves; and softwoods or conifers, which have needle-like or scale-like leaves. Hardwoods shed their leaves at the end of each growing season, but most softwoods are evergreens. The terms "hardwood" and "softwood" are often misleading because they do not directly indicate the hardness or softness of wood. In fact, there are hardwoods which are softer than certain softwoods.

Heartwood and sapwood

Looking at the cross section of a log, one may distinguish several distinct zones: the bark; a light-colored zone called sapwood; an inner zone, generally of darker color, called heartwood; and, at the center, the pith.

A tree increases in diameter by adding new layers of cells from the pith outward. For a time, this new layer functions as living cells which conduct sap and store food, but eventually, as the tree increases in diameter, cells toward the center become inactive and serve only as support for the tree. The inactive inner layer is the heartwood; the outer layer containing living cells is the sapwood. There is no consistent difference between the weight and strength properties of heartwood and sapwood. Heartwood, however, is more resistant to decay fungi than is sapwood, although there is a great range in the durability of heartwood from various species.

Annual rings

In climates where temperature limits the growing season of a tree, each annual increment of growth usually is readily distinguishable. Such an increment is known as an annual growth ring or annual ring, and consists of an earlywood and a latewood band.

Earlywood (springwood) and latewood (summerwood)

In many woods, large, thin-walled cells are formed in the spring when growth is greatest, whereas smaller, thicker-walled cells are formed later in the year. The areas of fast growth are called earlywood, and the areas of slower growth, latewood. In annual rings, the inner, lighter-colored area is the earlywood, and the outer, darker layer is the latewood.

Latewood contains more solid wood substance than does earlywood and, therefore, is denser and stronger. The proportion of width of latewood to width of annual ring is sometimes used as one of the visual measures of the quality and strength of wood.

Grain and texture

The terms "grain" and "texture" are used in many ways to describe the characteristics of wood and, in fact, do not have a definite meaning. Grain often refers to the width of the annual rings, as in "close-grained" or "coarse-grained." Sometimes it indicates whether the fibers are parallel to or at an angle with the sides of the pieces, as in "straight-grained" or "cross-grained." Texture usually refers to the fineness of wood structure rather than to the annual rings. When these terms are used in connection with wood, the meaning intended should be defined.

Moisture content

A tree develops functionally in the presence of moisture, and throughout its life the tree remains moist or "green." The amount of moisture in a living tree varies among species, in individual trees within the same species, in different parts of the same tree, and between heartwood and sapwood.

Moisture content (MC) is the weight of the water contained in wood, expressed as a percentage of the weight of the oven-dry wood. (An oven-dry condition is reached when no further loss of weight is experienced on subsequent oven-drying at 214° to 221°F.) As wood loses moisture, the water in the cell cavity is evaporated first. The condition at which the water in the cell cavity has been evaporated but the cell wall is still saturated is known as the "fiber saturation point." This is usually at approximately 30% MC.

Wood in use gives off or takes on moisture from the surrounding atmosphere with changes in temperature and relative humidity until it attains a balance relative to the atmospheric conditions. The moisture content at this point of balance is known as the equilibrium moisture content (EMC). At constant temperature, the equilibrium moisture content depends entirely on the relative humidity of the atmosphere surrounding the wood and the hygroscopicity of the wood or contained materials. (See Table 2.3, which, for practical purposes, applies to the wood of any species.)

Growth characteristics

Wood contains certain natural growth characteristics such as knots, slope of grain, compression wood, and shakes which may, depending on their size, number, and location in a structural member, adversely affect the strength properties of that member. These characteristics are discussed in detail in the *Wood Handbook* of the U.S. Forest Products Laboratory. Structural grading rules take into account the effects of these growth characteristics on the strength of wood in establishing working stress values for stress-graded lumber and glued laminated timber.

Directional properties

Wood is non-isotropic because of the orientation of its cells and the manner in which it increases in diameter. It has different mechanical properties with respect to its three principal axes of symmetry: longitudinal, radial, and tangential (see Figure 2.1). Strength and elastic properties corresponding to these three axes may be used in design.

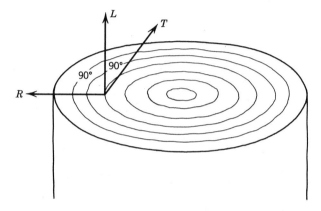

Figure 2.1.   THE THREE PRINCIPAL AXES OF WOOD.
L, longitudinal (parallel to grain); *R*, radial (perpendicular to grain, radial to annual rings); *T*, tangential (perpendicular to grain, tangential to annual rings).

The difference between properties in the radial and tangential directions is seldom of practical importance in most structural designs; for structural purposes it is sufficient to differentiate only between properties parallel and perpendicular to the grain.

Weight and Specific Gravity of Commercial Lumber Species

Table 2.1 gives average weights, in pounds per cubic foot, of various commercial lumber species based on their weight and volume at 12% and 20% MC. It also gives specific gravities based on weight when oven-dry and volume at 12% MC and when green.

For design purposes, it is satisfactory to use weights at 12% MC for glued laminated timber and sawn timber that will remain dry in service. The weight for unseasoned sawn material when it is installed and before it dries in service should be taken at 20% MC for relatively small sizes of less than 3 in. in thickness. The weight based on the equilibrium moisture content with allowance for preservative treatments, if applied, should be employed for unprotected members in exterior or other wet conditions of use. Adhesives used in laminating do not have an appreciable effect on the weight

TABLE 2.1

WEIGHTS AND SPECIFIC GRAVITIES
OF
COMMERCIAL LUMBER SPECIES

Species	Specific Gravity		Weight, pcf	
	Based on Oven-Dry Weight and Volume at 12% MC[a]	Based on Oven-Dry Weight and Volume When Green[b]	Based on Weight and Volume at 12% MC	Based on Weight and Volume at 20% MC
Softwoods				
Cedar				
Incense	0.37	0.35	25.9	27.0
Northern white	0.30	0.29	21.0	22.5
Western	0.35	0.33	24.5	25.5
Western red	0.35	0.33	24.5	25.5
Cypress, Southern	0.46	0.43	32.1	33.7
Douglas fir	0.48	0.45	33.5	35.2
Douglas fir, South	0.46	0.43	32.1	33.7
Douglas fir—larch	0.48	0.45	33.5	35.2
Fir				
Balsam	0.36	0.34	25.2	26.2
Subalpine	0.33	0.31	23.1	24.0
Hemlock				
Eastern—Tamarack	0.43	0.40	30.0	31.4
Mountain	0.45	0.42	31.4	33.0
West Coast	0.45	0.42	29.3	30.7
Hem—Fir	0.42	0.39	26.6	27.7
Larch	0.52	0.48	36.3	37.4
Pine				
Eastern white	0.37	0.35	25.9	27.0
Idaho white (Western)	0.39	0.37	27.2	28.4
Lodgepole	0.42	0.39	29.3	30.7
Northern (jack)	0.43	0.40	30.0	31.4
Ponderosa—sugar	0.41	0.39	29.3	30.7
Southern	0.52	0.48	36.3	37.4
Redwood	0.38	0.36	26.6	27.7
Spruce				
Eastern	0.40	0.38	28.0	29.2
Engelmann	0.34	0.32	23.8	24.7
Sitka	0.40	0.38	28.0	29.2
Hardwoods				
Ash				
Commercial white	0.59	0.54	41.2	42.7
Black	0.48	0.45	33.5	35.2
Beech	0.63	0.57	44.0	44.9
Birch				
Sweet	0.66	0.60	46.1	47.2
Yellow	0.60	0.55	41.9	41.2
Cottonwood, Eastern	0.39	0.37	27.2	28.4
Elm				
American	0.50	0.46	34.9	35.9
Rock[c]	0.63	0.57	44.0	44.9

TABLE 2.1 (Continued)

Species	Specific Gravity		Weight, pcf	
	Based on Oven-Dry Weight and Volume at 12% MC[a]	Based on Oven-Dry Weight and Volume When Green[b]	Based on Weight and Volume at 12% MC	Based on Weight and Volume at 20% MC
Elm (continued)				
Slippery	0.53	0.49	37.0	38.2
Hickory				
Pecan	0.68	0.61	47.5	48.7
Shagbark	0.71	0.64	49.6	50.9
Maple				
Black	0.57	0.52	39.8	40.4
Sugar	0.63	0.57	44.0	44.9
Oak				
Red	0.63	0.57	44.0	44.9
White	0.66	0.60	41.9	47.2
Sweetgum	0.50	0.46	34.9	35.9
Tupelo				
Black	0.51	0.47	35.6	36.7
Water	0.50	0.46	34.9	35.9
Yellow-poplar	0.43	0.40	30.0	31.4

[a]Specific gravity at 12% MC obtained by conversion from specific gravity when green by using Figure 1 of ASTM D2395-69, "Standard Methods of Test for Specific Gravity of Wood and Wood Base Materials."
[b]Specific gravity when green (unseasoned condition) obtained from Tables 1 and 2, ASTM D2555-70, "Standard Methods for Establishing Clear Wood Strength Values." Species combinations show weighted specific gravities for the combinations based on standing volumes shown in Table 4, ASTM D2555 except as noted in footnote[c].
[c]Specific gravities for rock elm obtained from Table 12, *Wood Handbook*, 1955 ed., USDA.

of glued laminated timbers and thus are not considered in determining the weight.

Effect of moisture content

A change in moisture content will result in a corresponding change in the weight of the wood. For a moisture content other than 12 or 20% values for which weights are given in Table 2.1, an intermediate weight should be determined by the designer if this value is critical.

Effect of treatments

Some preservative treatments may add significantly to the weight of wood, depending on the retentions obtained and, in the case of water-borne salts, on the extent to which the wood is seasoned after treatment. Weight increases due to preservative salts are small because retentions of the dry salt are in the range 0.30 to 1.25 pcf. However, some salt treatments are hygroscopic, and wood treated with these salts may tend to increase in moisture content and thus increase in weight during service conditions. In pressure treatments with preservative oils, retentions are higher and the weight increase may be from 5 to 20 pcf or more. For specific values of recommended retentions for various preservatives in different species, see *Treating Standard for Structural Timber Framing*, AITC 109, in Part II of this *Manual*.

Dimensional Stability

Effect of temperature

Wood, like most other solids, expands on heating and contracts on cooling. In most structural designs, the increase of wood in length for a rise in temperature is negligible, and, as a result, the secondary stresses due to temperature changes may, in most cases, be neglected. This increase in length is important only in certain structures that are subjected to considerable temperature changes, or in members with very long spans.

The increase in length per unit of length for a rise in temperature of 1°F is designated the coefficient of linear thermal expansion. It differs in the three structural directions of wood. Radially and tangentially (perpendicular to grain), the coefficient of linear thermal expansion varies directly with the specific gravity of the species. It is in the range of $25 \times 10^{-6} \times$ specific gravity per 1°F for a dense hardwood such as sugar maple to $45 \times 10^{-6} \times$ specific gravity per 1°F for softwoods such as Douglas fir, Sitka spruce, redwood, and white fir. Radial or tangential dimensional changes for common sizes of wood structural members are relatively small. Longitudinally (parallel to grain), the coefficient is independent of specific gravity and varies from 1.7×10^{-6} to 2.5×10^{-6} per 1°F for different species. This is from one-tenth to one-third of the values for other common structural materials and glass. For this reason, consideration must be given to differential thermal expansion of various materials used in conjunction with wood.

The average coefficient of linear thermal expansion for plywood is 3.4×10^{-6} per inch of length or width per 1°F. The coefficient of thermal expansion for thickness is essentially equal to that of solid lumber.

Effect of moisture content

Between zero moisture content and the fiber saturation point, wood shrinks as it loses moisture and swells as it absorbs moisture. Above the fiber saturation point there is no dimensional change with variation in moisture content. The amount of shrinkage and swelling differs in the tangential, radial, and longitudinal dimensions of the piece. Engineering design should consider shrinkage and swelling in the detailing and use of lumber.

Shrinkage occurs when the moisture content is reduced to a value below the fiber saturation point (for purposes of dimensional change, commonly assumed to be 30% MC) and is proportional to the amount of moisture lost below this point. Swelling occurs when the moisture content is increased until the fiber saturation point is reached; then the increase ceases. For each 1% decrease in moisture content below the fiber saturation point, wood shrinks about one-thirtieth of the total possible shrinkage, and, for each 1% increase in moisture content, the piece swells about one-thirtieth of the total possible swelling. The total swelling is equal numerically to the total shrinkage. Shrinking and swelling are expressed as percentages based on the green dimensions of the wood. Wood shrinks most in a direction tangent to the annual growth rings, and somewhat less in the radial direction, or across these rings. In general, shrinkage is greater in heavier pieces than in lighter pieces of the same species, and greater in hardwoods than in softwoods.

As a piece of green or wet wood dries, the outer parts are reduced to a moisture content below the fiber saturation point much sooner than are the inner parts. Thus the whole piece may show some shrinkage before the average moisture content reaches the fiber saturation point.

Table 2.2 gives the average tangential, radial, and volumetric shrinkage values for various species during drying from the green condition to 0% MC. Because the faces of the pieces of lumber are seldom so oriented that the annual growth rings are exactly tangent and radial to the faces of the

TABLE 2.2

SHRINKAGE VALUES OF WOOD BASED
ON DIMENSIONS WHEN GREEN

Species	Percentage of Shrinkage from Green to Oven-Dry Moisture Content		
	Radial	Tangential	Volumetric
Softwoods			
Baldcypress	3.8	6.2	10.5
Cedar			
Alaska	2.8	6.0	9.2
Atlantic white	2.9	5.4	8.8
Eastern red	3.1	4.7	7.8
Incense	3.3	5.2	7.7
Northern white	2.2	4.9	7.2
Port Orford	4.6	6.9	10.1
Western red	2.4	5.0	6.8
Douglas fir			
Coast	4.8	7.6	12.4
Interior North	3.8	6.9	10.7
Interior West	4.8	7.5	11.8
Fir			
Balsam	2.9	6.9	11.2
California red	4.5	7.9	11.4
Grand	3.4	7.5	11.0
Noble	4.3	8.3	12.4
Pacific silver	4.4	9.2	13.0
Subalpine	2.6	7.4	9.4
White	3.3	7.0	9.8
Hemlock			
Eastern	3.0	6.8	9.7
Mountain	4.4	7.1	11.1
Western	4.2	7.8	12.4
Larch, Western	4.5	9.1	14.0

TABLE 2.2 (Continued)

Species	Percentage of Shrinkage from Green to Oven-Dry Moisture Content		
	Radial	Tangential	Volumetric
Pine			
Eastern white	2.1	6.1	8.2
Jack	3.7	6.6	10.3
Lodgepole	4.3	6.7	11.1
Pitch	4.0	7.1	10.9
Pond	5.1	7.1	11.2
Ponderosa	3.9	6.2	9.7
Red	3.8	7.2	11.3
Southern			
Loblolly	4.8	7.4	12.3
Longleaf	5.1	7.5	12.2
Shortleaf	4.6	7.7	12.3
Slash	5.4	7.6	12.1
Sugar	2.9	5.6	7.9
Virginia	4.2	7.2	11.9
Western white	4.1	7.4	11.8
Redwood			
Old growth	2.6	4.4	6.8
Young growth	2.2	4.9	7.0
Spruce			
Black	4.1	6.8	11.3
Engelmann	3.8	7.1	11.0
Red	3.8	7.8	11.8
Sitka	4.3	7.5	11.5
Tamarack	3.7	7.4	13.6
Hardwoods			
Alder			
Red	4.4	7.3	12.6
Ash			
Black	5.0	7.8	15.2
Blue	3.9	6.5	11.7
Green	4.6	7.1	12.5
Oregon	4.1	8.1	13.2
Pumpkin	3.7	6.3	12.0
White	4.9	7.8	13.3
Aspen			
Bigtooth	3.3	7.9	11.8
Quaking	3.5	6.7	11.5
Basswood, American	6.6	9.3	15.8
Beech, American	5.5	11.9	17.2
Birch			
Alaska paper	6.5	9.9	16.7
Gray	5.2		14.7
Paper	6.3	8.6	16.2
River	4.7	9.2	13.5

TABLE 2.2 (Continued)

Species	Percentage of Shrinkage from Green to Oven-Dry Moisture Content		
	Radial	Tangential	Volumetric
Birch (continued)			
Sweet	6.5	9.0	15.6
Yellow	7.3	9.5	16.8
Buckeye, yellow	3.6	8.1	12.5
Butternut	3.4	6.4	10.6
Cherry, black	3.7	7.1	11.5
Chestnut, American	3.4	6.7	11.6
Cottonwood			
Black	3.6	8.6	12.4
Eastern	3.9	9.2	13.9
Elm			
American	4.2	9.5	14.6
Cedar	4.7	10.2	15.4
Rock	4.8	8.1	14.9
Slippery	4.9	8.9	13.8
Winged	5.3	11.6	17.7
Hackberry	4.8	8.9	13.8
Hickory, pecan	4.9	8.9	13.6
Hickory, true			
Mockernut	7.7	11.0	17.8
Pignut	7.2	11.5	17.9
Shagbark	7.0	10.5	16.7
Shellbark	7.6	12.6	19.2
Holly, American	4.8	9.9	16.9
Honeylocust	4.2	6.6	10.8
Locust, black	4.6	7.2	10.2
Madrone, Pacific	5.6	12.4	18.1
Magnolia			
Cucumbertree	5.2	8.8	13.6
Southern	5.4	6.6	12.3
Sweet bay	4.7	8.3	12.9
Maple			
Bigleaf	3.7	7.1	11.6
Black	4.8	9.3	14.0
Red	4.0	8.2	12.6
Silver	3.0	7.2	12.0
Striped	3.2	8.6	12.3
Sugar	4.8	9.9	14.7
Oak			
Black	4.4	11.1	15.1
Bur	4.4	8.8	12.7
Chestnut	5.3	10.8	16.4
Laurel	4.0	9.9	19.0
Live	6.6	9.5	14.7
Overcup	5.3	12.7	16.0
Pin	4.3	9.5	14.5

TABLE 2.2 (Continued)

Species	Percentage of Shrinkage from Green to Oven-Dry Moisture Content		
	Radial	Tangential	Volumetric
Oak (continued)			
Post	5.4	9.8	16.2
Northern red	4.0	8.6	13.7
Scarlet	4.4	10.8	14.7
Southern red	4.7	11.3	16.1
Swamp chestnut	5.2	10.8	16.4
Water	4.4	9.8	16.1
White	5.6	10.5	16.3
Willow	5.0	9.6	18.9
Persimmon, common	7.9	11.2	19.1
Poplar, balsam	3.0	7.1	10.5
Sassafras	4.0	6.2	10.3
Sweetgum	5.3	10.2	15.8
Sycamore, American	5.0	8.4	14.1
Tanoak	4.9	11.7	17.3
Tupelo			
Black	5.1	8.7	14.4
Water	4.2	7.6	12.5
Walnut, black	5.5	7.8	12.8
Willow, black	3.3	8.7	13.9
Yellow-poplar	4.6	8.2	12.7

Source: *Wood Handbook*, U.S. Department of Agriculture.

piece, it is customary, in determining cross-sectional dimensional changes, to use an intermediate or average value between the tangential and radial values. The values in Table 2.2 can be converted to dimensional changes, in inches, by using the formula

$$D_S = \frac{(M_i - M_f)D_i}{\left(\dfrac{30}{T_S \text{ or } R_S}\right) - 30 + M_i}$$

where D_S = shrinkage or swelling, in.
M_i = initial moisture content, % (30% max)
M_f = final moisture content, % (30% max)
D_i = dimension at initial moisture content, in.
30 = fiber saturation point, %
T_S = total tangential shrinkage, %/100
R_S = total radial shrinkage, %/100.

Neither the initial nor the final moisture content (M_i or M_f) can be greater than 30% because that is the moisture content at which, when drying, wood starts to shrink or at which, when absorbing moisture, reaches its maximum dimension.

Values for longitudinal shrinkage with a change in moisture content are

TABLE 2.3

MOISTURE CONTENT OF WOOD IN EQUILIBRIUM WITH STATED DRY-BULB TEMPERATURE AND RELATIVE HUMIDITY

Temperature Dry-bulb, °F	Relative Humidity, Percent																			
	5	10	15	20	25	30	35	40	45	50	55	60	65	70	75	80	85	90	95	98
30	1.4	2.6	3.7	4.6	5.5	6.3	7.1	7.9	8.7	9.5	10.4	11.3	12.4	13.5	14.9	16.5	18.5	21.0	24.3	26.9
40	1.4	2.6	3.7	4.6	5.5	6.3	7.1	7.9	8.7	9.5	10.4	11.3	12.3	13.5	14.9	16.5	18.5	21.0	24.3	26.9
50	1.4	2.6	3.6	4.6	5.5	6.3	7.1	7.9	8.7	9.5	10.3	11.2	12.3	13.4	14.8	16.4	18.4	20.9	24.3	26.9
60	1.3	2.5	3.6	4.6	5.4	6.2	7.0	7.8	8.6	9.4	10.2	11.1	12.1	13.3	14.6	16.2	18.2	20.7	24.1	26.8
70	1.3	2.5	3.5	4.5	5.4	6.2	6.9	7.7	8.5	9.2	10.1	11.0	12.0	13.1	14.4	16.0	17.9	20.5	23.9	26.6
80	1.3	2.4	3.5	4.4	5.3	6.1	6.8	7.6	8.3	9.1	9.9	10.8	11.7	12.9	14.2	15.7	17.7	20.2	23.6	26.3
90	1.2	2.3	3.4	4.3	5.1	5.9	6.7	7.4	8.1	8.9	9.7	10.5	11.5	12.6	13.9	15.4	17.3	19.8	23.3	26.0
100	1.2	2.3	3.3	4.2	5.0	5.8	6.5	7.2	7.9	8.7	9.5	10.3	11.2	12.3	13.6	15.1	17.0	19.5	22.9	25.6
110	1.1	2.2	3.2	4.0	4.9	5.6	6.3	7.0	7.7	8.4	9.2	10.0	11.0	12.0	13.2	14.7	16.6	19.1	22.4	25.2
120	1.1	2.1	3.0	3.9	4.7	5.4	6.1	6.8	7.5	8.2	8.9	9.7	10.6	11.7	12.9	14.4	16.2	18.6	22.0	24.7
130	1.0	2.0	2.9	3.7	4.5	5.2	5.9	6.6	7.2	7.9	8.7	9.4	10.3	11.3	12.5	14.0	15.8	18.2	21.5	24.2
140	0.9	1.9	2.8	3.6	4.3	5.0	5.7	6.3	7.0	7.7	8.4	9.1	10.0	11.0	12.1	13.6	15.3	17.7	21.0	23.7
150	0.9	1.8	2.6	3.4	4.1	4.8	5.5	6.1	6.7	7.4	8.1	8.8	9.7	10.6	11.8	13.1	14.9	17.2	20.4	23.1
160	0.8	1.6	2.4	3.2	3.9	4.6	5.2	5.8	6.4	7.1	7.8	8.5	9.3	10.3	11.4	12.7	14.4	16.7	19.9	22.5
170	0.7	1.5	2.3	3.0	3.7	4.3	4.9	5.6	6.2	6.8	7.4	8.2	9.0	9.9	11.0	12.3	14.0	16.2	19.3	21.9
180	0.7	1.4	2.1	2.8	3.5	4.1	4.7	5.3	5.9	6.5	7.1	7.8	8.6	9.5	10.5	11.8	13.5	15.7	18.7	21.3
190	0.6	1.3	1.9	2.6	3.2	3.8	4.4	5.0	5.5	6.1	6.8	7.5	8.2	9.1	10.1	11.4	13.0	15.1	18.1	20.7
200	0.5	1.1	1.7	2.4	3.0	3.5	4.1	4.6	5.2	5.8	6.4	7.1	7.8	8.7	9.7	10.9	12.5	14.6	17.5	20.0
210	0.5	1.0	1.6	2.1	2.7	3.2	3.8	4.3	4.9	5.4	6.0	6.7	7.4	8.3	9.2	10.4	12.0	14.0	16.9	19.3

not tabulated in Table 2.2, since they are ordinarily negligible. The total longitudinal shrinkage of normal species from fiber saturation to oven-dry condition usually ranges from 0.1 to 0.3% of the green dimension. Abnormal longitudinal shrinkage may occur in compression wood, wood with steep slope of grain, and exceptionally lightweight wood of any species.

The cross-laminated construction of plywood gives it relatively good dimensional stability in its plane. The average coefficient of hygroscopic expansion (or contraction) is about 0.0002 in. per inch of length or width for each 10% change in relative humidity, or 0.2% oven-dry to complete saturation.

The effects of dimensional changes due to a change in moisture content have been considered in the development of the typical construction details given in *Typical Construction Details*, AITC 104, in Part II of this *Manual*.

Thermal Insulation

The rate of heat flow through a material is called its thermal transmission. Thermal transmission through a homogeneous material is termed thermal conductivity, k, and is measured in Btu per hour per square foot per °F temperature difference between the material surfaces per inch of thickness. Thermal transmission through nonhomogeneous material, such as a box section, is designated thermal conductance, C, and is measured across the total thickness of the member. A direct measure of the insulating value of a material is the reciprocal of thermal transmission and is termed resistivity, $1/k$, or resistance, $1/C$. Table 2.4 gives thermal properties and

TABLE 2.4

APPROXIMATE THERMAL PROPERTIES OF COMMON
BUILDING MATERIALS

Material	Thermal Conductivity, k, Btu/hr/ft²/in./°F	Thermal Resistivity, $1/k$, °F/Btu/hr/ft²/in.	Relative Insulating Efficiency (Wood = 100), %
Air	0.168	5.95	476.0
Wood[a] (average for softwoods)	0.80	1.25	100.0
Clay brick	4.8	0.208	16.5
Glass	5.5	0.183	14.7
Limestone	6.5	0.154	12.3
Sandstone	12.0	0.083	6.6
Concrete (sand and gravel)	12.6	0.079	6.3
Steel	312.0	0.0032	0.25
Aluminum	1,416.0	0.000707	0.06

[a]For specific values, see Figure 2.2.

relative insulating efficiencies for common building materials. From the table, it may be seen that solid wood of the species commonly used in construction is markedly superior to other materials in resisting heat transmission.

Thermal conductivity

The thermal conductivity of wood varies with direction of grain; specific gravity; moisture content and distribution; kind, quantity, and distribution of extractives; amount of springwood and summerwood; and features such as checks, knots, and cross grain. Thermal conductivity is approximately the same in radial and tangential directions but is generally about $2\frac{1}{2}$ times greater along the grain. Figure 2.2 may be used to determine

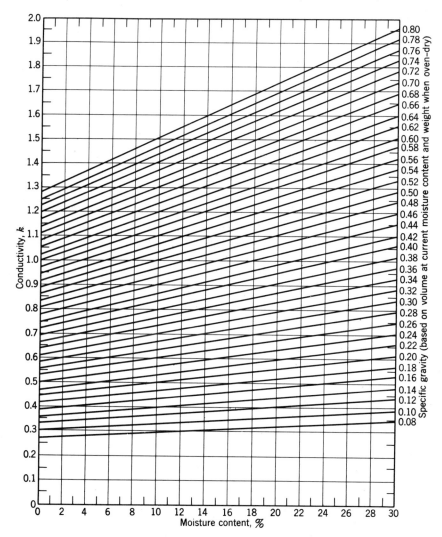

Figure 2.2. THERMAL CONDUCTIVITY VALUES ACROSS THE GRAIN FOR WOOD AT VARIOUS MOISTURE CONTENTS AND SPECIFIC GRAVITIES. Source: *Wood Handbook*, U.S. Department of Agriculture Handbook No. 72, 1955.

thermal conductivity values across the grain for wood at various moisture contents and specific gravities. This figure is based on the formula

$$k = (\text{sp. gr.})(1.39 + 0.028\,\text{MC}) + 0.165$$

where sp. gr. = specific gravity based on volume at current moisture content and oven-dry weight

MC = moisture content, %

Thermal transmission

The overall heat transfer of a member of composite construction can be computed if the conductivity and thickness of the homogeneous materials, the conductance of the nonhomogeneous materials, the surface conductances of both sides of the construction, and the conductances of any contained air spaces are known. The overall thermal transmission, U, of a construction may be computed from the formula

$$U = \cfrac{1}{\cfrac{1}{f_i} + \cfrac{t_1}{k_1} + \cfrac{t_2}{k_2} + \cdots + \cfrac{1}{C_1} + \cfrac{1}{C_2} + \cdots + \cfrac{1}{a_1} + \cfrac{1}{a_2} + \cdots + \cfrac{1}{f_o}}$$

where the additional notations are

f_i = inside surface conductance

f_o = outside surface conductance

t_1, t_2, etc. = thicknesses of materials

a_1, a_2, etc. = conductances of air spaces

Accurate values of conductivities and conductances for various materials may be obtained from the *ASHRAE Handbook of Fundamentals* published by the American Society of Heating Refrigerating and Air-Conditioning Engineers, Inc.

Table 2.5 gives example calculations for U values for a typical wall and floor construction taken from the *ASHRAE Handbook of Fundamentals*. For detailed information on the design of heat transmission coefficients see *ASHRAE Handbook of Fundamentals*.

Acoustical Properties

The acoustical properties of a material or a member of composite construction are determined by its sound insulation and sound absorption abilities. Sound insulation abilities are measured in terms of the reduction in intensity of sound when it passes through a barrier. Sound absorption refers to the amount of incident sound on a surface which is not reflected by that surface.

Sound insulation

Sound insulating values for partitions or materials of construction are related to the sound transmission loss for the construction measured in decibels at various frequencies. The insulating values depend on the intensity of sound on the opposite face of a barrier, the mass and stiffness of the material making up a barrier, and the nature of its design and fastenings. Sound insulation may be designed into a barrier by using materials

TABLE 2.5

EXAMPLE CALCULATIONS FOR TYPICAL
COEFFICIENTS OF TRANSMISSION (*U*)

Construction		Resistance (*R*)
(A)	1. Outside surface (15 mph wind)	0.17
	2. Wood siding ($\frac{1}{2} \times 8$), lapped (avg)	0.81
	3. Sheathing, $\frac{1}{2}$ in. asphalt impregnated	1.32
	4. Air space	0.97
	5. Gypsum wallboard	0.45
	6. Inside surface (still air)	0.68
$U = 1/R = 1/4.40 = 0.23$　　Total $R = 4.40$		
(B)	Winter conditions (heat flow up)	
	1. Top surface, still air	0.61
	2. Linoleum or tile (average value)	0.05
	3. Felt	0.06
	4. Plywood ($\frac{5}{8}$ in.)	0.78
	5. Wood subfloor ($\frac{3}{4}$ in.)	0.94
	6. Air space	0.85
	7. Metal lath and $\frac{3}{4}$ in. plaster (light weight aggregate)	0.47
	8. Bottom surface, still air	0.61
$U = 1/R = 1/4.37 = 0.23$　　Total $R = 4.37$		

with a high mass per unit area, using materials with low rigidity, or using barriers that employ air spaces and that avoid rigid ties from one face to the other. Like most common construction materials, wood alone does not provide good sound insulation but, when combined with other materials in typical constructions, will provide a structural unit of satisfactory sound-insulating ability. Table 2.6 gives transmission loss values for various types of partitions and constructions for frequencies (pitches) from 125 to 4,000 Hz.

The average transmission loss for a barrier is the arithmetic mean of the individual transmission losses as determined at several test frequencies in the range of 125 to 4,000 Hz as shown in Table 2.6. Although the use of an average transmission loss can be utilized to evaluate sound-isolating barriers and thus provide a comparison basis, this approach can prove to be misleading. This is because a relatively high average transmission loss could be determined for a specific barrier because of high individual transmission losses at several frequencies when these frequencies may not be important to the design situation involved.

In an attempt to circumvent the problems related to comparing the sound-insulating capabilities of specific constructions based on average transmission losses, a single number rating system has been developed. This system involves establishing a number called the sound transmission class—STC—by comparing the measured sound transmission loss curves

TABLE 2.6

AIRBORNE SOUND TRANSMISSION LOSSES FOR SOME COMMON BUILDING CONSTRUCTIONS[a]

Type of Construction	Sound Transmission Loss, decibels, for Various Listed Frequencies (in Hz)					
	125	250	500	1,000	2,000	4,000
Single Walls						
2 in. solid gypsum perlite-aggregate plaster (10 psf)	28	30	29	34	40	48
2 in. solid gypsum sand-aggregate plaster (18 psf)	31	32	33	38	45	53
4 in. hollow-core gypsum block, $\frac{5}{8}$ in. sand-aggregate plaster both sides (25 psf)	30	31	33	39	42	46
6 in. hollow-core cinder block, painted both sides (33 psf)	29	31	36	40	46	52
6 in. hollow-core cinder block, $\frac{5}{8}$ in. sand-aggregate plaster both sides (43 psf)	36	33	38	45	50	56
$4\frac{1}{2}$ in. solid brick, plastered both sides (45 psf)	34	35	40	51	57	60
7 in. stone-aggregate concrete, plastered both sides (90 psf)	44	42	52	58	66	70
2 × 4 wood studs, $\frac{1}{2}$ in. gypsum board both sides (6 psf)	20	30	36	41	43	42
2 × 4 wood studs, $\frac{1}{2}$ in. sand-aggregate plaster on $\frac{3}{8}$ in. gypsum lath both sides (16 psf)	27	25	31	44	34	50
$2\frac{1}{2}$ in. wire studs, $\frac{5}{8}$ in. sand-aggregate plaster on a metal lath both sides (19 psf)	26	24	37	31	37	50
$2\frac{1}{2}$ in. wire studs, $\frac{1}{2}$ in. sand-aggregate plaster on $\frac{3}{8}$ in. gypsum lath both sides (12 psf)	26	32	41	45	38	52
Double Walls						
Two separated rows of $\frac{3}{4}$ in. furring channels $2\frac{3}{4}$ in. on center, $\frac{5}{8}$ in. sand-aggregate plaster on metal both sides ($4\frac{3}{4}$ in. total thickness) (17 psf)	29	35	44	43	46	55
$2\frac{1}{2}$ in. wire studs, $\frac{1}{2}$ in. sand-aggregate plaster on $\frac{3}{8}$ in. gypsum lath on $\frac{1}{2}$ in. resilient metal clips both sides (12 psf)	30	37	43	48	43	60
Staggered $3\frac{1}{4}$ in. wire studs, $\frac{1}{2}$ in. sand-aggregate plaster on $\frac{3}{8}$ in. gypsum lath both sides ($5\frac{3}{4}$ in. total thickness) (13 psf)	34	39	44	49	48	60
4 in. hollow-core gypsum block, $\frac{5}{8}$ in. sand-aggregate plaster one side, $\frac{1}{2}$ in. sand-aggregate plaster on $\frac{3}{8}$ in. gypsum lath on $\frac{7}{8}$ in. resilient metal clips second side (26 psf)	25	33	43	48	49	54
Two wythes of plastered 3 in. dense concrete, 3 in. airspace between (bridging in airspace and at edges) (85 psf)	38	40	51	54	57	65
Two wythes of plastered $4\frac{1}{2}$ in. solid brick, 2 in. airspace between (sound-absorbing material in airspace—bridging at edges only) (90 psf)	43	50	52	61	73	78
Two wythes of plastered $4\frac{1}{2}$ in. solid brick, 12 in. airspace between (wythes *completely* isolated) (90 psf)	57	70	83	93	—	—

TABLE 2.6 (Continued)

Type of Construction	Sound Transmission Loss, decibels, for Various Listed Frequencies (in Hz)					
	125	250	500	1,000	2,000	4,000
Floor-Ceilings						
Typical residential floor-ceiling wood finish; and subfloors on wood joists, gypsum lath and plaster below (about 15 psf)	24	32	40	48	51	54
Concrete floor slab, ½ in. plaster finish coat below (about 45 psf)	43	40	44	53	56	58
Wood floating floor of finish; and subfloors on 2 × 2 sleepers on ¾ in. glass fiber blanket on concrete structural slab, ½ in. plaster finish coat below (about 50 psf)	38	48	55	61	59	55
Doors						
1⅜ in. hollow-core wood door, normally hung	5	11	13	13	13	12
1⅜ in. solid wood door, normally hung	10	13	17	18	17	15
1⅜ in. solid wood door, fully gasketed	16	18	21	20	24	26
Specially constructed 2⅝ in. wood door, full double gasketing	20	23	29	23	31	37
Two specially constructed 2⅝ in. wood doors each with full double gasketing, 12 in. airspace between, each door hung on independent wythe of double wall	31	47	43	48	57	66

[a]Source: Acoustical and Insulating Materials Association.

for a partition or barrier with a set of transmission-loss contours of a given shape. This procedure for establishing an STC value is given in ASTM E413-70T, *Tentative Classification for Determination of Sound Transmission Class.* This STC rating then provides an estimate of the relative performance of any given system or barrier in certain common sound insulation problems.

Sound absorption

The effectiveness of any material with respect to absorbing sound is given by its absorption coefficient at the frequency range specified. The sound-absorption coefficient for a material is used to determine the total magnitude of the absorption property of the material that is expressed in the units of sabins. Thus the total sound-absorption capacity of a wall, ceiling, floor, and so forth in sabins is determined by multiplying the sound-absorption coefficient of the material involved by its total area in square feet.

Sound-absorption values for any material may be compared to that of an open window, which is assumed to be the most complete absorber of sound. An open window, 1 ft square, is given a sound-absorption coefficient of unity. A piece of hairfelt of equal area may absorb half as much sound as the open window and, therefore, has a coefficient of 0.50. Sound-absorption coefficients are measured for various frequencies of sound, and the absorption ability of a material may vary widely with differences in frequency. Also, sound-absorption values for wood vary with moisture content, direction of grain, and density. Table 2.7 provides a summary of sound-absorption coefficients for a number of common construction materials and furnishings at various frequencies. These values are not absolute but

TABLE 2.7

SOUND-ABSORPTION COEFFICIENTS
OF VARIOUS BUILDING MATERIALS AND UNITS[a]

Material	Sound-Absorption Coefficients		
	125 Hz	500 Hz	2,000 Hz
Brick wall, painted	0.01	0.02	0.02
Brick wall, unpainted	0.03	0.03	0.05
Carpet, heavy, on concrete	0.02	0.14	0.60
Carpet, heavy, 40 oz hairfelt underlay	0.08	0.57	0.71
Fabrics			
Light, 10 oz/yd^2, hung straight	0.03	0.11	0.24
Medium, 14 oz/yd^2, draped to half area	0.07	0.49	0.70
Heavy, 18 oz/yd^2, draped to half area	0.14	0.55	0.70
Floors			
Concrete or terrazzo	0.01	0.02	0.02
Wood	0.15	0.10	0.06
Linoleum, asphalt, rubber, or cork tile on concrete	0.02	0.03	0.03
Glass, heavy plate	0.18	0.04	0.02
Marble or glazed tile	0.01	0.01	0.02
Plaster			
Gypsum or lime, smooth finish on tile or brick	0.01	0.02	0.04
Same, on lath	0.14	0.06	0.04
Plaster, gypsum or lime, rough finish, on lath	0.14	0.06	0.04
Plywood paneling, $\frac{3}{8}$ in. thick	0.28	0.17	0.10

Sound-Absorbing Units	Sound-Absorption per Unit[b]		
	125 Hz	500 Hz	2,000 Hz
Audience, seated in upholstered seats, per sq ft of floor area	0.60	0.88	0.93
Unoccupied cloth-covered upholstered seats, per sq ft of floor area	0.49	0.80	0.82
Unoccupied leather-covered upholstered seats, per sq ft of floor area	0.44	0.60	0.58
Wooden pews, occupied, per sq ft of floor area	0.57	0.75	0.91
Chairs, metal or wood seats, each, unoccupied	0.15	0.22	0.38

[a]Source: Acoustical and Insulating Materials Association.
[b]Values are in sabins per square foot of seating area, or per unit.

are commonly used to determine the total absorption of sound attributed to a room of a certain construction and occupancy. These data are also used to determine the reverberation time of a room.

Another important acoustical property of wood is that it absorbs low-frequency sounds more readily than high-frequency sounds.

Electrical Properties

The most important electrical properties of wood are its resistance to the passage of an electric current and its dielectric properties. The electrical resistance of wood is utilized in electric moisture meters used to determine moisture content. The dielectric properties of wood are utilized in the high-frequency curing of adhesives in glued laminated members and in the seasoning of wood.

The electrical resistance of wood varies with moisture content, density, direction of travel of the current with respect to the direction of grain, and temperature. It varies greatly with moisture content, especially below the fiber saturation point, decreasing with an increase in moisture content. Electrical resistance varies inversely with the density of wood, although this effect is slight compared to the variance due to moisture content and is greater across the grain than along it. The direct-current electrical resistance of wood approximately doubles for each drop in temperature of 22.5°F, but this relationship varies considerably with the level of moisture content. There is also a variation in electrical resistance between species, which is possibly caused by minerals or electrolytes in the wood itself or dissolved in the water present in the wood.

Metallic salts, such as used in preservative and fire-retardant treatments, may lower the electrical resistance of the wood considerably. Use of wood containing such salts should be avoided for applications where electrical resistance is critical, and in processes involving dielectric heating. Electric moisture meters may give erroneous readings for such wood.

Wood at a low moisture content is normally classified as an electric insulator, or dielectric, rather than as a conductor. A dielectric can be heated by using it as the medium between electrodes carrying charges of oscillating high-frequency electricity or by placing it in an electrical field of like nature. The dielectric constant of wood (the ratio of the capacitance of a wood condenser to the capacitance of a similar condenser employing a vacuum) is proportional to density at a given moisture content. The dielectric constant increases with an increase in either density or moisture content, although variations in moisture content have a greater effect. The dielectric constant parallel to grain is significantly greater than the corresponding constant perpendicular to grain. The constant also decreases with an increase in frequency of the oscillating current.

The power factor of wood is the ratio of the power absorbed in the wood per cycle of oscillation of an electric current to the total apparent power stored in the wood during that cycle. The power factor generally increases with an increase in moisture content. At moisture contents of 0 to 7%, the parallel-to-grain power factors are greater than the corresponding perpendicular-to-grain factors. When the wood is at a moisture content of 15%

or less, the power factor varies with the frequency of the oscillating current and is greater at high frequencies.

Table 2.8 gives the electrical resistance of various species of wood at various moisture contents.

TABLE 2.8

ELECTRICAL RESISTANCE OF VARIOUS SPECIES OF WOOD[a, b]

Species	Electrical Resistance, megohms, for Various Moisture Contents									
	7%	8%	9%	10%	12%	14%	16%	18%	20%	24%
Softwoods										
Cypress, Southern	12,600	3,980	1,410·	630	120	33	11.2	4.6	1.78	0.51
Douglas fir (coast region)	22,400	4,780	1,660	630	120	33	11.2	4.6	2.14	0.60
Fir, white	57,600	15,850	3,980	1,120	180	46	16.6	6.6	3.02	0.86
Hemlock, Western	22,900	5,620	2,040	850	185	51	16.2	6.0	2.52	0.51
Larch, Western	39,800	11,200	3,980	1,445	250	63	19.9	7.6	3.39	0.87
Pine										
Eastern white	20,900	5,620	2,090	850	200	58	19.9	7.9	3.31	0.74
Ponderosa	39,800	8,910	3,310	1,410	300	81	25.1	9.1	3.55	0.87
Southern longleaf	25,000	8,700	3,160	1,320	270	74	24.0	8.9	3.72	0.79
Southern shortleaf	43,600	11,750	3,720	1,350	255	69	22.4	8.7	3.80	0.93
Sugar	22,900	5,250	1,660	645	140	44	15.9	6.6	3.02	0.75
Redwood	22,400	4,680	1,550	615	100	22	7.2	3.2	1.74	0.71
Spruce, Sitka	22,400	5,890	2,140	830	165	44	15.5	6.3	3.02	0.91
Hardwoods										
Ash, commercial white	12,000	2,190	690	250	55	14	5.0	2.0	0.89	0.40
Birch	87,000	19,950	4,470	1,290	200	53	18.2	7.6	3.55	0.95
Gum, red	38,000	6,460	2,090	815	160	45	15.1	6.0	2.63	0.63
Hickory, true		31,600	2,190	340	50	11	3.7	1.5	0.71	0.40
Maple, sugar	72,400	13,800	3,160	690	105	29	10.2	4.5	2.24	0.75
Oak										
Commercial red	14,400	4,790	1,590	630	125	32	11.3	4.6	2.09	0.63
Commercial white	17,400	3,550	1,100	415	80	22	7.2	2.7	1.15	0.44

[a]Source: *Wood Handbook*, U.S. Department of Agriculture.
[b]Average of measurements made along the grain between two pairs of needle electrodes $1\frac{1}{4}$ in. apart and driven to a depth of $\frac{5}{16}$ in., measured at 80°F.

MECHANICAL PROPERTIES OF WOOD

Allowable Unit Stresses for Glued Laminated Timber — Visually Graded

Allowable unit stresses for structural glued laminated timbers based on the use of visually graded lumber are given in Tables 2.9 and 2.10 for softwoods and Table 2.11 for hardwoods. Stresses indicated in these tables are applicable for normal duration of loading and the condition of use specified in the tables. In addition, tabulated allowable unit stresses for bending members are applicable to members 12 in. or less in depth. For members designed for use under conditions other than those specified, the allowable unit stresses given in these tables must be adjusted in accordance with the design requirements and provisions contained on pages **2**-32 through **2**-38. The tables are divided into sections for dry-use and wet-use conditions with the applicable stresses for the conditions of use being shown. Allowable unit stress combinations for dry-use conditions are applicable when the moisture content in service is less than 16%, as in most covered structures. Allowable unit stress combinations for wet-use conditions are applicable when the moisture content in service is 16% or more, as it may be in exterior or submerged construction, and in some structures housing wet processes or otherwise having constant high relative humidities.

Table 2.9 gives stress combinations for softwood timbers stressed principally in bending with the load applied perpendicular to the wide face of the laminations. Stress combinations for members stressed principally in axial tension, axial compression, or loaded in bending parallel or perpendicular to the wide face of the laminations are given in Table 2.10 for softwood species. Table 2.11 contains recommended stress combinations for laminated timbers using visually graded hardwood species.

Requirements for grade of laminations used, slope of grain, tension lamination restrictions, end joint criteria, and manufacturing requirements must be met if the unit stresses given in Tables 2.9, 2.10 and 2.11 are to apply. The requirements for grade of laminations, slope of grain and tension lamination restrictions for softwoods are given in *Standard Specifications for Structural Glued Laminated Timber of Douglas Fir, Western Larch, Southern Pine and California Redwood*, AITC 117, in Part II of this *Manual*.

Similar requirements for hardwoods are contained in *Standard Specifications for Hardwood Glued Laminated Timber*, AITC 119, in Part II of this *Manual*. Other requirements are given in Voluntary Product Standard PS 56–73, *Structural Glued Laminated Timber*, included in Part II of this *Manual*.

The tension parallel to grain and compression parallel to grain stresses given in Table 2.9 are based on the use of laminating stock having the basic slope of grain for the grade specified. If more restrictive slope of grain requirements are used for all laminations in a member, the allowable tension parallel to grain and compression parallel to grain may be increased as provided for in AITC 117. Species other than those included in Tables 2.9, 2.10, and 2.11 may be used if allowable unit stresses are established for them in accordance with the provisions of PS 56.

Allowable Unit Stresses for Glued Laminated Timber — E-Rated and Visually Graded

Allowable unit stresses for softwood structural glued laminated timbers fabricated using laminations that have been both E-rated and visually graded are given in *Standard Specifications for Structural Glued Laminated Timber Using "E" Rated and Visually Graded Lumber of Douglas Fir, Southern Pine, Hem-Fir and Lodgepole Pine*, AITC 120, included in Part II of this *Manual*. The term "E-rated" refers to lumber that has been tested by a nondestructive method to determine the modulus of elasticity of the wood. The

TABLE 2.9

ALLOWABLE UNIT STRESSES (psi) FOR STRUCTURAL GLUED LAMINATED TIMBER FOR NORMAL CONDITIONS OF LOADING, MEMBERS STRESSED PRINCIPALLY IN BENDING, LOADED PERPENDICULAR TO THE WIDE FACE OF THE LAMINATIONS[a,b,c]

Part A   Dry Condition of Use

Combination Symbol	Number of Laminations	Allowable Unit Stresses						
		Extreme Fiber In Bending F_b	Tension Parallel to Grain F_t	Compression Parallel To Grain F_c	Compression $\perp$ to Grain		Horizontal Shear F_v	Modulus of Elasticity E
					Tension Face $F_{c\perp}$	Compression Face $F_{c\perp}$		
Douglas fir and larch								
16F	4 or more	1,600	1,600	1,500	385	385	165	1,600,000
18F	4 or more	1,800	1,600	1,500	385	385	165	1,700,000
20F	4–8[e]	2,000	1,600	1,500	410	410	165	1,700,000
	9–12[d]	2,000	1,600	1,500	450	450	165	1,700,000
	13 or more	2,000	1,600	1,500	385	385	165	1,700,000
22F	4–10[e]	2,200	1,600	1,500	410	410	165	1,800,000
	4 or more	2,200	1,600	1,500	450	385	165	1,800,000
24F	4 or more	2,400	1,600	1,500	450	385	165	1,800,000
26F	4 or more	2,600	1,600	1,500	450	410	165	1,800,000

Note: The 26F combination may not be readily available and the designer should check on availability prior to specifying. Other combinations are generally available from all laminators.

Southern pine

18F	4 or more	1,800	1,600	1,500	385	385	200	1,600,000
20F	8 or more	2,000	1,600	1,500	385	385	200	1,700,000
	7 or more^{d,f}	2,000	1,600	*1,500	450	385	200	1,700,000
22F	4 or more^d	2,200	1,600	1,500	450	450	200	1,700,000
	12 or more	2,200	1,600	1,500	385	385	200	1,700,000
24F	10 or more	2,400	1,600	1,500	385	385	200	1,800,000
	4 or more^d	2,400	1,600	1,500	450	450	200	1 800,000

Note: The 26F combination may not be readily available and the designer should check on availability prior to specifying. Other combinations listed are generally available from all laminators.

26F	11 or more	2,600	1,600	1,500	385	385	200	1,800,000
	11 or more^d	2,600	1,600	1,500	450	450	200	1,800,000

California redwood

16F	4 or more	1,600	1,600	1,600	325	325	125	1,400,000

Note: The 16F combination is generally available. The 22F combination is generally available only in members without end joints and the designer should check with the laminator prior to specifying this stress level.

22F	4 or more	2,200	2,000^g	2,000	325	325	125	1,400,000

Part B   Wet Condition of Use

Combination Symbol	Number of Laminations	Allowable Unit Stresses						
		Extreme Fiber In Bending F_b	Tension Parallel to Grain F_t	Compression Parallel To Grain F_c	Compression ⊥ to Grain		Horizontal Shear F_v	Modulus of Elasticity E
					Tension Face $F_{c\perp}$	Compression Face $F_{c\perp}$		
Douglas fir and larch								
16F	4 or more	1,300	1,300	1,100	260	260	145	1,300,000
18F	4 or more	1,400	1,300	1,100	260	260	145	1,400,000
20F	4–8[e]	1,600	1,300	1,100	275	275	145	1,400,000
	9–12[d]	1,600	1,300	1,100	305	305	145	1,400,000
	13 or more	1,600	1,300	1,100	260	260	145	1,400,000
22F	4–10[e]	1,800	1,300	1,100	275	275	145	1,500,000
	4 or more	1,800	1,300	1,100	305	260	145	1,500,000
24F	4 or more	1,900	1,300	1,100	305	260	145	1,500,000
26F	4 or more	2,100	1,300	1,100	305	275	145	1,500,000

Note: The 26F combination may not be readily available and the designer should check on availability prior to specifying. Other combinations are generally available from all laminators.

Southern pine

18F	4 or more	1,400	1,300	1,100	260	260	175	1,300,000
20F	8 or more	1,600	1,300	1,100	260	260	175	1,400,000
	7 or more[d,f]	1,600	1,300	1,100	300	300	175	1,400,000
22F	4 or more[d]	1,800	1,300	1,100	300	300	175	1,400,000
	12 or more	1,800	1,300	1,100	260	260	175	1,400,000
24F	10 or more	1,900	1,300	1,100	260	260	175	1,500,000
	4 or more[d]	1,900	1,300	1,100	300	300	175	1,500 000

Note: The 26F combination may not be readily available and the designer should check on availability prior to specifying. Other combinations are generally available from all laminators.

26F	4 or more	2,100	1,300	1,100	260	260	175	1,500,000
	11 or more[d]	2,100	1,300	1,100	300	300	175	1,500,000

California redwood

16F	4 or more	1,300	1,300	1,200	215	215	110	1,200,000

Note: The 16F combination is generally available. The 22F combination is generally available only in members without end joints and the designer should check with the laminator prior to specifying this stress level.

22F	4 or more	1,800	1,600[g]	1,600	215	215	110	1,200,000

[a] The tabulated stresses in this table are primarily applicable to members stressed in bending due to a load applied perpendicular to the wide face of the laminations. For combinations and stresses applicable to members loaded primarily axially or parallel to the wide face of the laminations, see Table 2.10.

[b] The tabulated bending stresses are applicable to members 12 in. or less in depth. For members greater than 12 in. in depth, the size factor modifications as given on pages **2**-35 to **2**-38 apply.

[c] The tabulated combinations are applicable to arches, compression members, tension members, and also bending members less than 16¼ in. in depth. For bending members 16¼ in. or more in depth, AITC tension lamination restrictions apply. See *Standard Specifications for Structural Glued Laminated Timber*, AITC 117, in Part II of this *Manual* for specific tension lamination requirements.

[d] This combination requires the use of dense outer laminations.

[e] This combination requires the use of outer laminations with close-grain rate of growth.

[f] Where fewer laminations are required, a combination of a higher allowable unit stress can be selected.

[g] If slope of grain in all laminations is specified to be no steeper than 1 in 20, the tension parallel to grain stress can be increased to 2,200 psi for the dry condition of use and 1,800 psi for the wet condition of use.

TABLE 2.10

ALLOWABLE UNIT STRESSES (psi) FOR STRUCTURAL GLUED LAMINATED TIMBER, FOR NORMAL CONDITIONS OF LOADING, MEMBERS STRESSED PRINCIPALLY IN AXIAL TENSION, AXIAL COMPRESSION OR LOADED IN BENDING PARALLEL OR PERPENDICULAR TO THE WIDE FACE[a]

Part A   Dry Condition of Use

Combination Symbol	Number of Laminations	Tension Parallel to Grain[d] F_t	Compression Parallel to Grain[d] F_c	Extreme Fiber in Bending F_b When Loaded		Compression Perpendicular to Grain $F_{c\perp}$	Horizontal Shear F_v When Loaded		Modulus of Elasticity E
				Parallel to Wide Face[c]	Perpendicular to Wide Face[b,d]		Parallel to Wide Face[c]	Perpendicular to Wide Face[d]	
Douglas fir and larch									
1	All	1,200	1,500	900	1,200	385	145	165	1,600,000
2	All	1,800	1,800	1,500	1,800	385	145	165	1,800,000
3	All	2,200	2,100	1,900	2,200	450	145	165	1,900,000
4	All	2,400	2,000	2,100	2,400	410	145	165	2,000,000
5	All	2,600	2,200	2,300	2,600	450	145	165	2,100,000
Southern pine									
1	All	1,600	1,400	900	1,100	385	165	200	1,500,000
2	All	2,200	1,900	1,550	1,800	385	165	200	1,700,000
3	All	2,600	2,200	1,800	2,100	450	165	200	1,800,000
4	All	2,400	2,100	1,900	2,400	385	165	200	1,900,000
5	All	2,600	2,200	2,200	2,600	450	165	200	2,000,000
California redwood									
1[e]	All	1,800	1,800	1,000	1,400	325	115	125	1,300,000
2[e]	All	1,800	1,800	1,000	1,400	325	115	125	1,300,000
3[e]	All	2,000	2,000	1,400	2,000	325	125	125	1,400,000
4[e]	All	2,200	2,200	2,200	2,200	325	125	125	1,400,000
5[e]	All	2,200	2,200	2,200	2,200	325	125	125	1,400,000

Part B Wet Condition of Use

Douglas fir and larch									
1	All	950	750	1,100	950	260	120	145	1,300,000
2	All	1,400	1,100	1,300	1,400	260	120	145	1,500,000
3	All	1,800	1,450	1,500	1,800	305	120	145	1,600,000
4	All	1,900	1,500	1,450	1,900	275	120	145	1,700,000
5	All	2,000	1,600	1,600	2,000	305	120	145	1,800,000
Southern pine									
1	All	1,300	700	1,000	850	260	145	175	1,300,000
2	All	1,800	1,250	1,400	1,450	260	145	175	1,400,000
3	All	2,100	1,450	1,600	1,700	300	145	175	1,500,000
4	All	1,900	1,500	1,500	1,950	260	145	175	1,600,000
5	All	2,100	1,750	1,600	2,100	300	145	175	1,700,000
California redwood									
1[e]	All	1,500	800	1,300	1,100	215	100	110	1,100,000
2[e]	All	1,500	800	1,300	1,100	215	100	110	1,100,000
3[e]	All	1,600	1,100	1,500	1,600	215	110	110	1,200,000
4[e]	All	1,800	1,800	1,600	1,800	215	110	110	1,200,000
5[e]	All	1,800	1,800	1,600	1,800	215	110	110	1,200,000

[a]The tabulated stresses in this table are primarily applicable to members loaded axially or parallel to the wide face of the laminations. For combinations and stresses applicable to members stressed principally in bending due to a load applied perpendicular to the wide face of the laminations, see Table 2.9.

[b]It is not intended that these combinations be used for deep bending members, but if bending members 16¼ in. or deeper are used, AITC tension lamination restrictions apply. See *Standard Specifications for Structural Glued Laminated Timber*, AITC 117, in Part II of this *Manual* for specific tension lamination requirements.

[c]The tabulated stresses are applicable to members containing three (3) or more laminations.

[d]The tabulated stresses are applicable to members containing four (4) or more laminations.

[e]When used primarily as bending members loaded perpendicular to the wide face of the laminations, combinations 1 and 2 are generally available from most laminators but combinations 3, 4 and 5 are generally available only in laminated members without end joints, and the designer should check with the laminator prior to specifying combinations 3, 4 and 5.

TABLE 2.11
ALLOWABLE UNIT STRESS COMBINATIONS FOR STRUCTURAL GLUED LAMINATED HARDWOOD TIMBER[a]

Part A   Stress Factors for Use in Converting The Stress Module Values of Part B to Allowable Unit Stresses

Species	Extreme Fiber in Bending or Tension Parallel to Grain Factor		Compression Parallel to Grain Factor		Horizontal Shear Factor		Compression Perpendicular to Grain Factor		Modulus of Elasticity Factor	
	Dry	Wet	Dry	Wet	Dry	Wet	Dry	Wet	Dry	Wet
Hickory, true and pecan	3.85	3.10	3.05	2.20	0.26	0.23	0.73	0.49	1.80	1.50
Beech, American	3.05	2.45	2.45	1.80	0.23	0.21	0.61	0.41	1.70	1.40
Birch, sweet and yellow	3.05	2.45	2.45	1.80	0.23	0.21	0.61	0.41	1.90	1.60
Elm, rock	3.05	2.45	2.45	1.80	0.23	0.21	0.61	0.41	1.40	1.30
Maple, black and sugar (hard maple)	3.05	2.45	2.45	1.80	0.23	0.21	0.61	0.41	1.70	1.40
Ash, commercial white	2.80	2.25	2.20	1.60	0.23	0.21	0.61	0.41	1.70	1.40
Oak, commercial red and white	2.80	2.25	2.05	1.50	0.23	0.21	0.61	0.41	1.60	1.30
Elm, American and slippery (white or soft elm)	2.20	1.75	1.60	1.15	0.19	0.17	0.31	0.21	1.40	1.20
Sweetgum (red or sap gum)	2.20	1.75	1.60	1.15	0.19	0.17	0.37	0.24	1.40	1.20
Tupelo, black (blackgum)	2.20	1.75	1.60	1.15	0.19	0.17	0.37	0.24	1.20	1.00
Tupelo, water	2.20	1.75	1.60	1.15	0.19	0.17	0.37	0.24	1.30	1.10
Ash, black	2.00	1.60	1.30	0.95	0.17	0.14	0.37	0.24	1.30	1.00
Yellow-poplar	2.00	1.60	1.45	1.05	0.15	0.13	0.27	0.18	1.50	1.20

Part B   Stress Modules for Use in Computing Allowable Unit Stresses Using the Factors Given in Part A

Combination Symbol	Number of Laminations[b]	Extreme Fiber in Bending Stress Module	Tension Parallel to Grain Stress Module	Modulus of Elasticity in Bending Stress Module	Compression Parallel to Grain Stress Module	Maximum Longitudinal Shear Stress Module	Compression Perpendicular to Grain Stress Module
A	4 to 14	800	800	1,000,000	970	1,000	1,000
	15 or more	800	800	1,000,000	970	1,000	1,000
B	4 to 14	770	800	1,000,000	920	1,000	1,000
	15 or more	800	800	1,000,000	930	1,000	1,000
C	4 to 14	600	750	900,000	860	1,000	1,000
	15 or more	660	780	900,000	870	1,000	1,000
D	4 to 14	450	590	800,000	780	1,000	1,000
	15 or more	520	650	800,000	810	1,000	1,000
E	4 to 14	300	410	800,000	690	1,000	1,000
	15 or more	380	490	800,000	730	1,000	1,000

[a]The tabulated combinations are applicable to arches, compression members, tension members and also bending members less than $16\frac{1}{4}$ in. in depth. For bending members $16\frac{1}{4}$ in. or more in depth, AITC tension lamination restrictions apply in addition to the basic grading requirements specified. See *Standard Specifications For Hardwood Glued Laminated Timber*, AITC 119, in Part II of this *Manual* for specific grading requirements.

[b]When laminations of different thicknesses are used, divide the depth of the member by the thickness of the thickest lamination used and then assume the quotient to be the number of laminations in the member for use in determining the allowable stress.

fabrication of glued laminated timbers utilizing laminations that have been both E-rated and visually graded provides a high degree of predictability with respect to stiffness, and permits the use of higher allowable design values for modulus of elasticity than are permitted when based on a visual-grading basis only.

Allowable Radial Stresses for Glued Laminated Timbers

When curved members are subjected to a bending moment, radial stresses are induced in a direction parallel to the radius of curvature of the center-line of the member (perpendicular to grain). If the moment increases the radius of curvature (makes the member straighter), the stress is tension; if it decreases the radius (makes the member more sharply curved), the stress is compression.

For these members, when the moment causes a stress in tension across the grain, this tensile stress is limited to $\frac{1}{3}$ the allowable unit stress in horizontal shear for Douglas fir and larch for wind or earthquake loadings and for other softwoods for all conditions of loading. The limit is 15 psi for Douglas fir and larch for other types of load. These values are subject to modification for duration of the load. If the calculated stress exceeds these allowable unit stresses, mechanical reinforcing designed in accordance with the procedure on pages **4**-47 to **4**-51 of this *Manual* (or an equivalent design method) should be used and should be sufficient to resist all radial tension stresses.

When the moment is in a direction causing a stress in compression across the grain, this stress is limited to the allowable unit stress in compression perpendicular to the grain for the species involved.

Adjustment of Allowable Unit Stresses for Glued Laminated Timber

Duration of load

Allowable unit stress values given in Tables 2.9, 2.10, and 2.11 apply to glued laminated timber under normal duration of load. These stresses may be used without regard to impact if the stress induced by impact does not exceed the allowable unit stress for normal loading. Normal load duration anticipates fully stressing a member to the allowable unit stress by the application of the full design load for a duration of approximately 10 years (applied either continuously or cumulatively). If the member is designed to be fully stressed by maximum design loads for long-term loading conditions (greater than 10 years either continuously or cumulatively), the allowable unit stresses are taken as 90% of the values tabulated.

For other durations of load, either continuously or intermittently applied, the appropriate factor taken from Table 2.12 or determined from Figure 2.3 should be applied to adjust the tabulated allowable unit stresses. However, these duration of load modifications, including the 0.90 reduction for permanent loading, are not applicable to modulus of elasticity. These provisions are applicable to the modification of the allowable loads for mechanical fastenings when the wood (not the strength of the metal fastening) controls the load capacity.

TABLE 2.12
USUAL DESIGN FACTORS
FOR DURATION OF LOADING

Duration of Load	Factor
2 months (as for snow)	1.15
7 days	1.25
Wind or earthquake	1.33
Impact	2.00

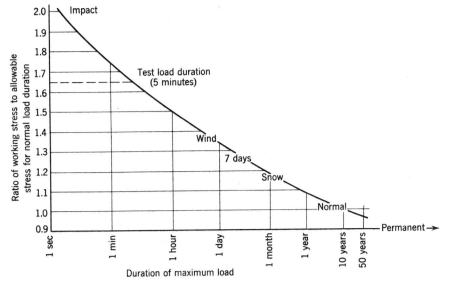

Figure 2.3.   DURATION OF LOAD FACTORS. Derived from Forest Products Laboratory Report No. R1916.

If loads of different durations are applied simultaneously, the size of member required is determined for the total of all loads applied at the allowable unit stress adjusted by the factor for the load of shortest duration in the combination. In like manner, but neglecting the load of shortest duration, the size of member required to support the remaining loads at the stress adjusted by the factor for the load of next shortest duration is determined. By repeating this procedure for all the remaining loads, the size of member required for the controlling duration of load condition is obtained. When the permanently applied load is less than or equals 90% of the total normal load (including the permanently applied load), the normal loading condition will control the size of member required.

Example. Determine the governing loading condition for a 40 ft span glued laminated timber purlin under the uniform loads given.

$$DL = 200 \text{ plf}$$
$$SL \ (2 \text{ months}) = 800 \text{ plf}$$
$$WL = 500 \text{ plf}$$

Assume that half of the snow load will remain when wind load is maximum.

$$S = \frac{M}{F_b} \quad \text{and} \quad M = \frac{wl^2}{8} \quad \text{or} \quad S = \frac{wl^2}{8F_b}$$

$$S = \frac{w(40)^2(12)}{8F_b} = 2{,}400 \frac{w}{F_b}$$

1. From Figure 2.3, it can be seen that wind has the shortest duration of load. For that condition

$$w = \text{WL} + \frac{\text{SL}}{2} + \text{DL} = 500 + 400 + 200 = 1{,}100 \text{ plf}$$

From Table 2.12, duration of load factor for wind is 1.33; thus

$$S = 2{,}400 \frac{1{,}100}{1.33F_b} = \frac{1{,}980{,}000}{F_b}$$

2. Snow has the next shortest duration of load. For that condition

$$w = \text{SL} + \text{DL} = 800 + 200 = 1{,}000 \text{ plf}$$

Duration of load factor for snow is 1.15; thus

$$S = 2{,}400 \frac{1{,}000}{1.15F_b} = \frac{2{,}090{,}000}{F_b}$$

3. For dead or permanently applied load alone

$$w = \text{DL} = 200 \text{ plf}$$

Duration of load factor for permanent load is 0.90; thus

$$S = 2{,}400 \frac{200}{0.90F_b} = \frac{533{,}000}{F_b}$$

Note: As in this example, it is usually quite apparent that dead load alone will not require a section larger than the combination of loadings, and the calculation is, therefore, not normally required.

4. The governing condition occurs in step 2.

Temperature

Allowable unit stress values given in Tables 2.9, 2.10, and 2.11 apply to glued laminated timber used under ordinary temperature conditions. Some reduction of stresses may be necessary for members that are subjected to elevated temperatures for repeated or prolonged periods of time, especially where the high temperature is associated with a high moisture content in the wood. Tests have shown that an increase in strength occurs at low temperatures. See pages 1-16 and 1-17 of this *Manual* for more detailed considerations regarding effects of temperature on strength.

Treatments

Preservative treatments. The allowable unit stress values given in Tables 2.9, 2.10, and 2.11 for glued laminated timber also apply to wood that has been treated with a preservative when this treatment is in accordance with

American Wood-Preservers' Association standard specifications which limit pressure and temperature. Investigations have indicated that, in general, any weakening of timber as a result of preservative treatment is caused almost entirely by subjecting the wood to temperatures and pressures above the AWPA limits rather than by the preservative used. (See *Treating Standard for Structural Timber Framing*, AITC 109, in Part II of this *Manual.*)

Highly acidic salts, such as zinc chloride, if present in appreciable concentrations tend to hydrolyze wood. Fortunately, the concentrations used in wood preservative treatments are sufficiently small that the strength properties other than impact resistance are not greatly affected under normal use conditions. A significant loss in impact strength may occur, however, if higher concentrations are used. Because none of the other common salt preservatives is likely to form solutions as highly acidic as those of zinc chloride, in most cases their effect on the strength of the wood can be disregarded.

In wood treated with highly acidic salts such as zinc chloride, moisture is the controlling factor in the corrosion of fastenings. Therefore, wood treated with highly acidic salts is not recommended for use under highly humid conditions.

Fire-retardant treatments. The allowable unit stresses for fire-retardant treated glued laminated timber treated before or after gluing are dependent upon the species, treatment, and adhesive combinations involved. The effect on strength must be determined for each treatment; the manufacturer of the treatment should be contacted for this information.

Size factor

Allowable unit stresses for glued laminated timbers stressed in bending are dependent on several basic design parameters. The first and most important design condition, from the standpoint of the relative magnitude of the adjustment of allowable stresses, is the size of the member accounting for both the depth of the member (d) and the length of the member (l), with length being considered as a function of the span-to-depth ratio (l/d).

The basic size factor, C_F, can be determined from the relationship:

$$C_F = \left(\frac{12}{d}\right)^{1/9}$$

where C_F = size factor
d = depth of member, in.

This equation is based on the following assumptions being satisfied: that the member is simply supported, that the load is uniformly distributed on the member, and that the span-to-depth ratio (l/d) is equal to 21. This relationship is based on both a theoretical analysis of the failure mechanisms involved in bending members and on empirical testing of results with the previously indicated assumptions forming the basis of the analyses.

This equation obviously results in a C_F of unity when the depth of the member is 12 in. For depths greater than 12 in., this factor imposes a reduction on the tabulated allowable stresses that may be used for design. For depth less than 12 in., a size factor of unity is applicable. For members of variable cross sections such as in tapered beams, d should be taken as that depth at which the stresses are being analyzed.

Table 2.13 presents tabular data for the size factor, C_F in 1 in. increments for members satisfying the basic design assumptions. Sufficient accuracy for intermediate depths may be attained by applying straight-line interpolation.

TABLE 2.13

SIZE FACTORS[a, b, c]

Depth, in.	C_F	Depth, in.	C_F	Depth, in.	C_F
less		33	0.89	57	0.84
than		34	0.89	58	0.84
12	1.00	35	0.89	59	0.84
12	1.00	36	0.88	60	0.84
13	0.99	37	0.88	61	0.83
14	0.98	38	0.88	62	0.83
15	0.98	39	0.88	63	0.83
16	0.97	40	0.87	64	0.83
17	0.96	41	0.87	65	0.83
18	0.96	42	0.87	66	0.83
19	0.95	43	0.87	67	0.83
20	0.94	44	0.87	68	0.82
21	0.94	45	0.86	69	0.82
22	0.93	46	0.86	70	0.82
23	0.93	47	0.86	71	0.82
24	0.93	48	0.86	72	0.82
25	0.92	49	0.86	73	0.82
26	0.92	50	0.85	74	0.82
27	0.91	51	0.85	75	0.82
28	0.91	52	0.85	76	0.81
29	0.90	53	0.85	77	0.81
30	0.90	54	0.85	78	0.81
31	0.90	55	0.84	79	0.81
32	0.90	56	0.84	80	0.81

[a]Applicable to simple span beams, uniformly loaded with an $l/d = 21$.
[b]For conditions of loading other than a uniformly distributed load, the tabulated values for C_F may be adjusted by applying the percentage changes given on page 2-37.
[c]For span-to-depth ratios other than 21, the tabulated values for C_F may be adjusted by applying the percentage changes given on page 2-37.

Figure 2.4 provides a graphical solution of the size effect equation for three loading conditions: a uniformly distributed load, a concentrated point load, and concentrated third point loads. These loading conditions satisfy most commonly encountered design situations. More complex loading conditions can be simulated by one of these basic conditions and still provide sufficient accuracy in the determination of C_F. Percentage changes for C_F for these various loading conditions are given below.

Loading Condition for Simply Supported Beams	Percentage Change
Single concentrated load	+7.8
Uniform load	0
Third point load	−3.2

For span-to-depth ratios other than 21, the percentage changes indicated below can be applied to modify the size factor determined for the basic conditions. For intermediate span-to-depth ratios, use straight-line inter-polation between the values shown.

Span-to-Depth Ratio l/d	Percentage Change
7	+6.3
14	+2.3
21	0
28	−1.6
35	−2.8

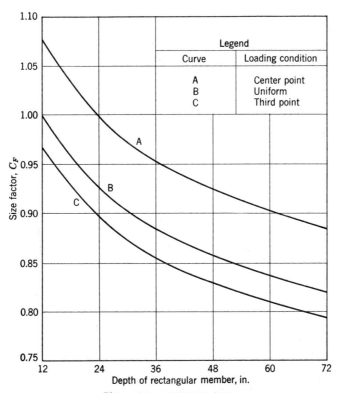

Figure 2.4.   SIZE FACTOR.

For continuous beams and cantilevered members, determine the size factor assuming the members to be equivalent simply supported members with a uniformly distributed load. This will result in a slightly conservative size factor being applied to the design of span types other than simple spans.

The allowable unit bending stress, F_b, is thus modified by applying the appropriate size factor, C_F, to the calculations based on the preceding design considerations in the engineering formulas as follows:

1. Bending members:

$$M = SF_bC_F$$

where M = bending moment, in.-lb
$\quad\ S$ = section modulus, in.^{3}
$\quad\ C_F$ = size factor

2. Members in combined bending and axial compression:
(a) When the bending portion of the combined stress exceeds the compressive portion $(M/S > P/A)$,

$$\frac{M}{SF_bC_F}+\frac{P}{AF'_c} \leq 1$$

where P = axial compression load, lb
$\quad\ A$ = cross-sectional area of member, in.^{2}
$\quad\ F'_c$ = allowable unit stress in compression parallel to grain adjusted for l/d ratios, psi

(b) When the compressive portion exceeds the bending portion of the combined stress $(P/A > M/S)$,

$$\frac{P}{AF'_c}+\frac{M}{SF_b} \leq 1$$

3. Members in combined bending and axial tension:

$$\frac{M}{SF_bC_F}+\frac{T}{AF_t} \leq 1$$

where T = axial tension load, lb
$\quad\ F_t$ = allowable unit stress in tension parallel to grain, psi

Curvature factor

Stress is induced when laminations are bent to curved forms. Although much of this stress is quickly relieved, some remains and tends to reduce the strength of a curved member; therefore, the allowable stress in bending must be adjusted by multiplication by the curvature factor, C_c:

$$C_c = 1-2{,}000\left(\frac{t}{R}\right)^2$$

where t = thickness of lamination, in.
$\quad\ R$ = radius of curvature of inside face of lamination, in.

The ratio t/R may not exceed $1/100$ for hardwoods and Southern pine, nor $1/125$ for softwoods other than Southern pine. The curvature factor is not applied to stresses in the straight portion of a member regardless of curvature in other portions.

Figure 2.5 may be used to determine curvature factors for several different lamination thicknesses.

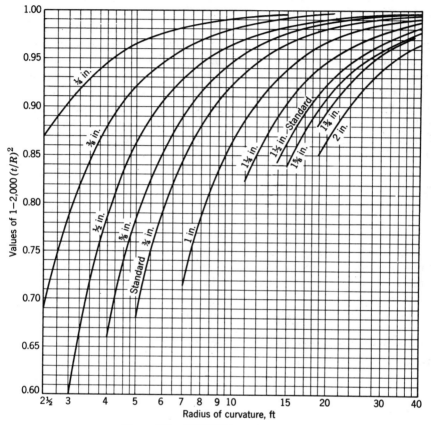

Figure 2.5.   CURVATURE FACTORS.

Modulus of Elasticity

The modulus of elasticity values given in Tables 2.9, 2.10, and 2.11 include deflection due to shear distortion as well as due to bending. In designs where shear deformation is a significant consideration, more refinement may be obtained in design by using the modulus of elasticity parallel to grain, or elastic modulus, E_L, in determining bending deflection; and the modulus of elasticity in shear, or modulus of rigidity, G, in determining shear deflection. Values for E_L and G may be approximated from the formulas:

$$E_L = 1.10E$$

and

$$G = 0.06E_L$$

where E = modulus of elasticity, psi, as given in Tables 2.9, 2.10, and 2.11.

Allowable Unit Stresses for Stress-Graded Lumber

The allowable unit stresses in Table 2.14 apply to sawn lumber under normal duration of load and under continuously dry conditions such as in most covered structures. Stresses for sawn lumber under other conditions of loading and use must be adjusted in accordance with the adjustments and special design considerations on page **2**-40.

Establishment of working stress values. The determination of working stress values for stress-graded lumber involves many factors. Procedures accounting for these factors in establishing design values have been developed through many years of research and are documented and accepted as standard methods.

The recommended design values for visually graded lumber as given in Table 2.14, *Part A*, are established in accordance with ASTM D2555-70, *Standard Methods for Establishing Clear Wood Strength Values* and ASTM D245-70, *Standard Methods for Establishing Structural Grades and Related Allowable Properties for Visually Graded Lumber*, both published by the American Society for Testing and Materials.

For machine stress-rated (MSR) lumber, the modulus of elasticity, E, as given in Table 2.14, *Part B*, is determined by nondestructively testing individual pieces of lumber and then statistically establishing an average E value as tabulated for a given MSR classification. Recommended fiber stresses in bending design values for the various grade classifications tabulated are based on the correlation of the modulus of rupture to modulus of elasticity. Other strength properties for MSR lumber are established in accordance with the applicable provisions of ASTM D245-70.

Adjustment of Allowable Unit Stresses for Stress-Graded Lumber

Moisture content

The allowable unit stress values given in Table 2.14 apply to sawn lumber in continuous dry-use service conditions. For continuous wet-use service conditions, the appropriate factors given in footnotes *f* and *g* of Table 2.14 apply.

Duration of load

For sawn lumber, the appropriate adjustments given under "Adjustment of Allowable Unit Stresses for Glued Laminated Timber — Duration of Load" on page **2**-32 are applied.

Temperature

For sawn lumber, the appropriate provisions given under "Adjustment of Allowable Unit Stresses for Glued Laminated Timber — Temperature" on page **2**-34 are applied.

Treatments

For sawn lumber, the appropriate provisions given under "Adjustment of Allowable Unit Stresses for Glued Laminated Timber — Treatments" on page **2**-34 are applied. In addition, the allowable unit stresses in Table 2.14 should be reduced 10% for lumber pressure-impregnated with fire-retardant chemicals.

TABLE 2.14

ALLOWABLE UNIT STRESSES–STRUCTURAL LUMBER

Part A – Allowable Unit Stresses for Structural Lumber – Visual Grading
(Normal Duration of Loading)

Species and Commercial Grade	Size Classification	Extreme Fiber in Bending, F_b		Tension Parallel to Grain F_t	Horizontal Shear F_v	Compression Perpendicular to Grain $F_{c\perp}$	Compression Parallel to Grain F_c	Modulus of Elasticity E	Grading Rules Agency
		Single-Member Uses	Repetitive-Member Uses						
Balsam fir (surfaced at 15% moisture content. Used at 15% max. MC)									
Select Structural		1,450	1,700	850	65	170	1,200	1,200,000	Northeastern Lumber Manufacturers Association and Northern Hardwood and Pine Manufacturers Association (see footnotes a,b,c,d h and i)
No. 1	2 to 4 in. thick	1,250	1,450	725	65	170	975	1,200,000	
No. 2	2 to 4 in. wide	1,050	1,200	600	65	170	750	1,100,000	
No. 3		575	650	325	65	170	475	1,000,000	
Appearance		1,050	1,250	725	65	170	1,150	1,200,000	
Stud		575	650	325	65	170	475	1,000,000	
Construction	2 to 4 in. thick	750	850	425	65	170	875	1,000,000	
Standard	4 in. wide	425	475	250	65	170	725	1,000,000	
Utility		200	225	125	65	170	475	1,000,000	
Select structural		1,250	1,450	850	65	170	1,050	1,200,000	
No. 1	2 to 4 in. thick	1,050	1,250	725	65	170	975	1,200,000	
No. 2	6 in. and wider	875	1,000	575	65	170	800	1,100,000	
No. 3		525	600	325	65	170	525	1,000,000	
Appearance		1,050	1,250	725	65	170	1,150	1,200,000	

TABLE 2.14 (Continued)

Allowable Unit Stresses, psi

Species and Commercial Grade	Size Classification	Extreme Fiber in Bending, F_b		Tension Parallel to Grain F_t	Horizontal Shear F_v	Compression Perpendicular to Grain $F_{c\perp}$	Compression Parallel to Grain F_c	Modulus of Elasticity E	Grading Rules Agency
		Single-Member Uses	Repetitive-Member Uses						
Balsam fir (surfaced dry or surfaced green. Used at 19% max. MC)									
Select structural	2 to 4 in. thick	1,350	1,550	800	60	170	1,050	1,200,000	Northeastern Lumber Manufacturers Association and Northern Hardwood and Pine Manufacturers Association (see footnotes [a] through [l])
No. 1	2 to 4 in. wide	1,150	1,300	675	60	170	825	1,200,000	
No. 2		950	1,100	550	60	170	650	1,100,000	
No. 3		525	600	300	60	170	400	900,000	
Appearance		1,000	1,150	650	60	170	1,000	1,200,000	
Stud		525	600	300	60	170	400	900,000	
Construction	2 to 4 in. thick	675	800	400	60	170	750	900,000	
Standard	4 in. wide	375	450	225	60	170	625	900,000	
Utility		175	200	100	60	170	400	900,000	
Select structural	2 to 4 in. thick	1,150	1,350	775	60	170	925	1,200,000	
No. 1	6 in. and wider	1,000	1,150	650	60	170	825	1,200,000	
No. 2		825	950	525	60	170	700	1,100,000	
No. 3		475	550	300	60	170	450	900,000	
Appearance		1,000	1,150	650	60	170	1,000	1,200,000	
Select structural	Beams and stringers	1,050	—	700	55	170	725	1,000,000	
No. 1		875	—	575	55	170	625	1,000,000	
Select structural	Posts and timbers	975	—	650	55	170	775	1,000,000	
No. 1		800	—	525	55	170	675	1,000,000	

Grade	Decking (size)									Agency
Select	Decking	1,150	1,300	—	—	—	—	—	1,200,000	NeLMA
Commercial		950	1,100	—	—	—	—	—	1,100,000	
California redwood (surfaced dry or green. Used at 19% max. MC)										
Clear heart structural	4 in. and less thick, any width	2,300	2,650	—	1,550	145	425	2,150	1,400,000	
Clear structural		2,300	2,650	—	1,550	145	425	2,150	1,400,000	
Select structural	2 to 4 in. thick, 2 to 4 in. wide	2,050	2,350	—	1,200	100	425	1,750	1,400,000	
Select structural, open grain		1,600	1,850	—	950	100	270	1,300	1,100,000	
No. 1		1,700	1,950	—	975	100	425	1,400	1,400,000	
No. 1, open grain		1,350	1,550	—	775	100	270	1,050	1,100,000	
No. 2		1,400	1,600	—	800	80	425	1,100	1,250,000	
No. 2, open grain		1,100	1,250	—	625	80	270	825	1,000,000	
No. 3		800	900	—	475	80	425	675	1,100,000	
No. 3, open grain		625	725	—	375	80	270	500	900,000	Redwood
Stud		625	725	—	375	80	270	500	900,000	Inspection
Construction	2 to 4 in. thick, 4 in. wide	825	950	—	475	80	270	925	900,000	Service
Standard		450	525	—	250	80	270	775	900,000	
Utility		225	250	—	125	80	270	500	900,000	(see
Select structural	2 to 4 in. thick, 6 in. and wider	1,750	2,000	—	1,150	100	425	1,500	1,400,000	footnotes
Select structural, open grain		1,400	1,600	—	925	100	270	1,150	1,100,000	[b] through [g])
No. 1		1,500	1,700	—	975	100	425	1,400	1,400,000	
No. 1, open grain		1,150	1,350	—	775	100	270	1,050	1,100,000	
No. 2		1,200	1,400	—	800	80	425	1,200	1,250,000	
No. 2, open grain		950	1,100	—	625	80	270	875	1,000,000	
No. 3		700	800	—	475	80	425	725	1,100,000	
No. 3, open grain		550	650	—	375	80	270	525	900,000	
Clear heart structural	5 by 5 in. and larger	1,850	—	—	1,250	135	425	1,650	1,300,000	
Clear structural		1,850	—	—	1,250	135	425	1,650	1,300,000	
Select structural		1,400	—	—	950	95	425	1,200	1,300,000	
No. 1		1,200	—	—	800	95	425	1,050	1,300,000	
No. 2		975	—	—	650	95	425	900	1,100,000	
No. 3		550	—	—	375	95	425	550	1,000,000	

TABLE 2.14 (Continued)

Species and Commercial Grade	Size Classification	Allowable Unit Stresses, psi								Grading Rules Agency
		Extreme Fiber in Bending, F_b		Tension Parallel to Grain F_t	Horizontal Shear F_v	Compression Perpendicular to Grain $F_{c\perp}$	Compression Parallel to Grain F_c	Modulus of Elasticity E		
		Single-Member Uses	Repetitive-Member Uses							
Douglas fir-larch (surfaced dry or surfaced green. Used at 19% max. MC)										
Dense select structural	2 to 4 in. thick 2 to 4 in. wide	2,450	2,800	1,400	95	455	1,850	1,900,000		West Coast Lumber Inspection Bureau and Western Wood Products Association
Select structural		2,100	2,400	1,200	95	385	1,600	1,800,000		
Dense No. 1		2,050	2,400	1,200	95	455	1,450	1,900,000		
No. 1		1,750	2,050	1,050	95	385	1,250	1,800,000		
Dense No. 2		1,700	1,950	1,000	95	455	1,150	1,700,000		
No. 2		1,450	1,650	850	95	385	1,000	1,700,000		
No. 3		800	925	475	95	385	600	1,500,000		
Appearance		1,750	2,050	1,050	95	385	1,500	1,800,000		
Stud		800	925	475	95	385	600	1,500,000		
Construction	2 to 4 in. thick 4 in. wide	1,050	1,200	625	95	385	1,150	1,500,000		
Standard		600	675	350	95	385	925	1,500,000		
Utility		275	325	175	95	385	600	1,500,000		
Dense select structural	2 to 4 in. thick 6 in. and wider	2,100	2,400	1,400	95	455	1,650	1,900,000		(see footnotes b through i)
Select structural		1,800	2,050	1,200	95	385	1,400	1,800,000		
Dense No. 1		1,800	2,050	1,200	95	455	1,450	1,900,000		
No. 1		1,500	1,750	1,000	95	385	1,250	1,800,000		
Dense No. 2		1,450	1,700	950	95	455	1,050	1,700,000		
No. 2		1,250	1,450	825	95	385	1,050	1,700,000		
No. 3		725	850	475	95	385	675	1,500,000		
Appearance		1,500	1,750	1,000	95	385	1,500	1,800,000		

Grade	Use								Association
Dense select structural	Beams and stringers	1,900	—	1,100	85	455	1,300	1,700,000	West Coast Lumber Inspection Bureau (see footnote b through l)
Select structural		1,600	—	950	85	385	1,100	1,600,000	
Dense No. 1		1,550	—	775	85	455	1,100	1,700,000	
No. 1		1,300	—	675	85	385	925	1,600,000	
Dense select structural	Posts and timbers	1,750	—	1,150	85	455	1,400	1,700,000	
Select structural		1,500	—	1,000	85	385	1,200	1,600,000	
Dense No. 1		1,400	—	950	85	455	1,200	1,700,000	
No. 1		1,200	—	825	85	385	1,000	1,600,000	
Select dex	Decking	1,750	2,000	—	—	385	—	1,800,000	
Commercial dex		1,450	1,650	—	—	385	—	1,800,000	
Dense select structural	Beams and stringers	1,900	—	1,250	85	455	1,300	1,700,000	Western Wood Products Association (see footnotes b through k)
Select structural		1,600	—	1,050	85	385	1,100	1,600,000	
Dense No. 1		1,550	—	1,050	85	455	1,100	1,700,000	
No. 1		1,350	—	900	85	385	925	1,600,000	
Dense select structural	Posts and timbers	1,750	—	1,150	85	455	1,350	1,700,000	
Select structural		1,500	—	1,000	85	385	1,150	1,600,000	
Dense No. 1		1,400	—	950	85	455	1,200	1,700,000	
No. 1		1,200	—	825	85	385	1,000	1,600,000	
Selected decking	Decking	—	2,000	—	—	—	—	1,800,000	
Commercial decking		—	1,650	—	—	—	—	1,700,000	
Selected decking	Decking	—	2,150	(Surfaced at 15% max. MC and used at 15% max. MC)				1,900,000	
Commercial decking		—	1,800					1,700,000	

TABLE 2.14 (Continued)

Species and Commercial Grade	Size Classification	Extreme Fiber in Bending, F_b Single-Member Uses	Extreme Fiber in Bending, F_b Repetitive-Member Uses	Tension Parallel to Grain F_t	Horizontal Shear F_v	Compression Perpendicular to Grain $F_{c\perp}$	Compression Parallel to Grain F_c	Modulus of Elasticity E	Grading Rules Agency
Douglas fir south (surfaced dry or surfaced green. Used at 19% max. MC)									
Select structural	2 to 4 in. thick 2 to 4 in. wide	2,000	2,300	1,150	90	335	1,400	1,400,000	
No. 1/appearance		1,700	1,950	975	90	335	1,150/1,350	1,400,000	
No. 2		1,400	1,600	825	90	335	900	1,300,000	
No. 3		775	875	450	90	335	550	1,100,000	
Stud		775	875	450	90	335	550	1,100,000	
Construction	2 to 4 in. thick 4 in. wide	1,000	1,150	600	90	335	1,000	1,100,000	Western Wood Products Association (see footnotes [b] through [k])
Standard		550	650	325	90	335	850	1,100,000	
Utility		275	300	150	90	335	550	1,100,000	
Select structural	2 to 4 in. thick 6 in. and wider	1,700	1,950	1,150	90	335	1,250	1,400,000	
No. 1/appearance		1,450	1,650	975	90	335	1,150/1,350	1,400,000	
No. 2		1,200	1,350	775	90	335	950	1,300,000	
No. 3		700	800	450	90	335	600	1,100,000	
Select structural	Beams and stringers	1,550	—	1,050	85	335	1,000	1,200,000	
No. 1		1,300	—	850	85	335	850	1,200,000	
Select structural	Posts and timbers	1,400	—	950	85	335	1,050	1,200,000	
No. 1		1,150	—	775	85	335	925	1,200,000	
Selected decking	Decking	—	1,900	—	—	—	—	1,400,000	
Commercial decking		—	1,600	—	—	—	—	1,300,000	
Selected decking	Decking	—	2,050	—	—	—	—	1,500,000	
Commercial decking		—	1,750	—	—	—	—	1,300,000	

(Surfaced at 15% max. MC and used at 15% max. MC)

Allowable Unit Stresses, psi

Eastern hemlock – tamarack (surfaced at 15% moisture content. Used at 15% max. MC)

Grade	Size								Agency
Select structural	2 to 4 in. thick, 2 to 4 in. wide	1,950	2,200	1,150	90	365	1,600	1,300,000	Northeastern Lumber Manufacturers Association and Northern Hardwood and Pine Manufacturers Association (see footnotes b, c, d, h and i)
No. 1		1,650	1,900	975	90	365	1,250	1,300,000	
No. 2		1,350	1,550	800	90	365	1,000	1,200,000	
No. 3		750	850	500	90	365	600	1,000,000	
Appearance		1,400	1,650	950	90	365	1,500	1,300,000	
Stud		750	850	450	90	365	600	1,000,000	
Construction	2 to 4 in. thick, 4 in. wide	975	1,150	575	90	365	1,150	1,000,000	
Standard		550	625	325	90	365	925	1,000,000	
Utility		250	300	150	90	365	600	1,000,000	
Select structural	2 to 4 in. thick, 6 in. and wider	1,650	1,900	1,100	90	365	1,400	1,300,000	
No. 1		1,400	1,650	950	90	365	1,250	1,300,000	
No. 2		1,150	1,300	750	90	365	1,050	1,200,000	
No. 3		675	775	450	90	365	675	1,000,000	
Appearance		1,400	1,650	950	90	365	1,500	1,300,000	

Eastern hemlock – tamarack (surfaced dry or surfaced green. Used at 19% max. MC)

Grade	Size								Agency
Select structural	2 to 4 in. thick, 2 to 4 in. wide	1,800	2,050	1,050	85	365	1,350	1,300,000	Northeastern Lumber Manufacturers Association and Northern Hardwood and Pine Manufacturers Association (see footnotes b through i)
No. 1		1,500	1,750	900	85	365	1,050	1,300,000	
No. 2		1,250	1,450	725	85	365	850	1,100,000	
No. 3		700	800	400	85	365	525	1,000,000	
Appearance		1,300	1,500	875	85	365	1,300	1,300,000	
Stud		700	800	400	85	365	525	1,000,000	
Construction	2 to 4 in. thick, 4 in. wide	900	1,050	525	85	365	975	1,000,000	
Standard		500	575	300	85	365	800	1,000,000	
Utility		250	275	150	85	365	525	1,000,000	
Select structural	2 to 4 in. thick, 6 in. and wider	1,550	1,750	1,050	85	365	1,200	1,300,000	
No. 1		1,300	1,500	875	85	365	1,050	1,300,000	
No. 2		1,050	1,200	700	85	365	900	1,100,000	
No. 3		625	725	400	85	365	575	1,000,000	
Appearance		1,300	1,500	875	85	365	1,300	1,300,000	
Select structural	Beams and stringers	1,400	—	925	80	365	950	1,200,000	
No. 1		1,150	—	775	80	365	800	1,200,000	
Select structural	Posts and timbers	1,300	—	875	80	365	1,000	1,200,000	
No. 1		1,050	—	700	80	365	875	1,200,000	

TABLE 2.14 (Continued)

Species and Commercial Grade	Size Classification	Extreme Fiber in Bending, F_b		Tension Parallel to Grain F_t	Horizontal Shear F_v	Compression Perpendicular to Grain $F_{c\perp}$	Compression Parallel to Grain F_c	Modulus of Elasticity E	Grading Rules Agency
		Single-Member Uses	Repetitive-Member Uses						
Eastern hemlock–tamarack (surfaced at 15% moisture content. Used at 15% max. MC) (cont'd).									
Select	Decking	1,500	1,700	—	—	—	—	1,300,000	NeLMA
Commercial		1,250	1,450	—	—	—	—	1,100,000	
Eastern spruce (surfaced at 15% moisture content. Used at 15% max. MC)									
Select structural	2 to 4 in. thick 2 to 4 in. wide	1,650	1,900	950	70	255	1,350	1,400,000	Northeastern Lumber Manufacturers Association and Northern Hardwood and Pine Manufacturers Association
No. 1		1,400	1,600	800	70	255	1,050	1,400,000	
No. 2		1,150	1,300	675	70	255	825	1,300,000	
No. 3		625	725	375	70	255	500	1,200,000	
Appearance		1,200	1,350	800	70	255	1,250	1,400,000	
Stud		625	725	375	70	255	500	1,200,000	
Construction	2 to 4 in. thick 4 in. wide	825	950	475	70	255	950	1,200,000	
Standard		450	525	275	70	255	775	1,200,000	
Utility		200	250	125	70	255	500	1,200,000	
Select structural	2 to 4 in. thick 6 in. and wider	1,400	1,600	950	70	255	1,150	1,400,000	(see footnotes a, b, c, d, h and i)
No. 1		1,200	1,350	800	70	255	1,050	1,400,000	
No. 2		950	1,100	650	70	255	875	1,300,000	
No. 3		575	650	375	70	255	550	1,200,000	
Appearance		1,200	1,350	800	70	255	1,250	1,400,000	

Allowable Unit Stresses, psi

Eastern spruce (surfaced dry or surfaced green. Used at 19% max. MC)

Grade	Size								Agency
Select structural	2 to 4 in. thick, 2 to 4 in. wide	1,500	1,750	875	65	255	1,150	1,400,000	Northeastern Lumber Manufacturers Association and Northern Hardwood and Pine Manufacturers Association (see footnotes [a] through [i])
No. 1		1,300	1,500	750	65	255	900	1,400,000	
No. 2		1,050	1,200	625	65	255	700	1,200,000	
No. 3		575	675	325	65	255	425	1,100,000	
Appearance		1,100	1,250	750	65	255	1,050	1,400,000	
Stud		575	675	325	65	255	425	1,100,000	
Construction	2 to 4 in. thick, 4 in. wide	775	875	450	65	255	800	1,100,000	
Standard		425	500	250	65	255	675	1,100,000	
Utility		200	225	100	65	255	425	1,100,000	
Select structural	2 to 4 in. thick, 6 in. and wider	1,300	1,500	875	65	255	1,000	1,400,000	
No. 1		1,100	1,250	750	65	255	900	1,400,000	
No. 2		900	1,000	600	65	255	750	1,200,000	
No. 3		525	600	325	65	255	475	1,100,000	
Appearance		1,100	1,250	750	65	255	1,050	1,400,000	
Select structural	Beams and stringers	1,150	—	775	60	255	800	1,200,000	
No. 1		950	—	650	60	255	675	1,200,000	
Select structural	Posts and timbers	1,100	—	725	60	255	850	1,200,000	
No. 1		875	—	600	60	255	725	1,200,000	
Truss	2 to 4 in. thick, 2 to 4 in. wide	1,785	2,050	1,000	65	255	1,200	1,400,000	Northeastern Lumber Manufacturers Association (see footnotes [a] through [i])
1500 f	2 to 4 in. thick, 6 in. and wider	1,500	1,700	1,000	65	255	1,100	1,400,000	
Select	Decking	1,250	1,450	—	—	—	—	1,400,000	
Commercial		1,050	1,200	—	—	—	—	1,200,000	

TABLE 2.14 (Continued)

Species and Commercial Grade	Size Classification	Allowable Unit Stresses, psi							Grading Rules Agency
		Extreme Fiber in Bending, F_b		Tension Parallel to Grain F_t	Horizontal Shear F_v	Compression Perpendicular to Grain $F_{c\perp}$	Compression Parallel to Grain F_c	Modulus of Elasticity E	
		Single-Member Uses	Repetitive-Member Uses						
Eastern white pine (surfaced at 15% moisture content. Used at 15% max. MC)									
Appearance	2 to 4 in. thick	1,100	1,250	725	70	220	1,150	1,300,000	NeLMA and NHPMA
Stud	2 to 4 in. wide	575	650	325	70	220	475	1,000,000	
Construction	2 to 4 in. thick	750	850	425	70	220	875	1,000,000	(see footnotes [b] through [l])
Standard		425	475	250	70	220	725	1,000,000	
Utility	4 in. wide	200	225	125	70	220	475	1,000,000	
Eastern white pine (surfaced dry or surfaced green. Used at 19% max. MC)									
Select structural	2 to 4 in. thick	1,350	1,550	800	70	220	1,050	1,200,000	Northeastern Lumber Manufacturers Association
No. 1	2 to 4 in. wide	1,150	1,350	675	70	220	850	1,200,000	
No. 2		950	1,100	550	70	220	675	1,100,000	
No. 3		525	600	300	70	220	400	1,000,000	
Appearance	2 to 4 in. thick	1,150	1,350	675	70	220	1,000	1,200,000	(see footnotes [b] through [l])
Stud	2 to 4 in. wide	525	600	300	70	220	400	1,000,000	
Construction	2 to 4 in. thick	700	800	400	70	220	750	1,000,000	
Standard		375	450	225	70	220	625	1,000,000	
Utility	4 in. wide	175	200	100	70	220	400	1,000,000	
Select structural	2 to 4 in. thick	1,150	1,350	775	70	220	950	1,200,000	
No. 1		1,000	1,150	675	70	220	850	1,200,000	
No. 2	6 in. and wider	825	950	550	70	220	700	1,100,000	
No. 3		475	550	300	70	220	450	1,000,000	
Appearance		1,000	1,150	675	70	220	1,000	1,200,000	

Classification	Grade								
Beams and stringers	Select structural	1,050	—	700	65	220	675	1,100,000	
	No. 1	875	—	600	65	220	575	1,100,000	
Posts and timbers	Select structural	975	—	650	65	220	725	1,100,000	
	No. 1	800	—	525	65	220	625	1,100,000	
Decking	Select	900	1,050	—	—	—	—	1,200,000	
	Commercial	775	875	—	—	—	—	1,100,000	
Engelmann spruce (Engelmann spruce — lodgepole pine) (surfaced dry or surfaced green. Used at 19% max. MC)									
2 to 4 in. thick / 2 to 4 in. wide	Select structural	1,350	1,550	775	70	195	900	1,200,000	
	No. 1/appearance	1,150	1,300	675	70	195	725/875	1,200,000	Western Wood Products Association (see footnotes b through k)
	No. 2	950	1,100	550	70	195	575	1,100,000	
	No. 3	525	600	300	70	195	350	1,000,000	
	Stud	525	600	300	70	195	350	1,000,000	
2 to 4 in. thick / 4 in. wide	Construction	675	775	400	70	195	650	1,000,000	
	Standard	375	425	225	70	195	525	1,000,000	
	Utility	175	200	100	70	195	350	1,000,000	
2 to 4 in. thick / 6 in. and wider	Select structural	1,150	1,350	775	70	195	800	1,200,000	
	No. 1/appearance	975	1,150	650	70	195	725/875	1,200,000	
	No. 2	800	925	525	70	195	600	1,100,000	
	No. 3	475	550	300	70	195	375	1,000,000	
Beams and stringers	Select structural	1,050	—	700	65	195	650	1,100,000	
	No. 1	875	—	575	65	195	550	1,100,000	
Posts and timbers	Select structural	950	—	650	65	195	675	1,100,000	
	No. 1	775	—	525	65	195	600	1,100,000	
Decking	Selected decking	—	1,300	—	—	—	—	1,200,000	
	Commercial decking	—	1,100	—	—	—	—	1,100,000	
Decking (Surfaced at 15% max. MC and used at 15% max. MC)	Selected decking	—	1,400					1,300,000	
	Commercial decking	—	1,150					1,200,000	

TABLE 2.14 (Continued)

Allowable Unit Stresses, psi

Species and Commercial Grade	Size Classification	Extreme Fiber in Bending, F_b Single-Member Uses	Extreme Fiber in Bending, F_b Repetitive-Member Uses	Tension Parallel to Grain F_t	Horizontal Shear F_v	Compression Perpendicular to Grain $F_{c\perp}$	Compression Parallel to Grain F_c	Modulus of Elasticity E	Grading Rules Agency
Hem-fir (surfaced dry or surfaced green. Used at 19% max. MC)									
Select structural	2 to 4 in. thick 2 to 4 in. wide	1,650	1,900	975	75	245	1,300	1,500,000	West Coast Lumber Inspection Bureau and Western Wood Products Association
No. 1		1,400	1,600	825	75	245	1,000	1,500,000	
No. 2		1,150	1,300	675	75	245	800	1,400,000	
No. 3		625	725	375	75	245	500	1,200,000	
Appearance		1,400	1,600	825	75	245	1,200	1,500,000	
Stud		625	725	375	75	245	500	1,200,000	
Construction	2 to 4 in. thick 4 in. wide	825	975	475	75	245	925	1,200,000	
Standard		450	525	275	75	245	750	1,200,000	
Utility		225	250	125	75	245	500	1,200,000	
Select structural	2 to 4 in. thick 6 in. and wider	1,400	1,650	950	75	245	1,150	1,500,000	(see footnotes ᵇ through ⁱ)
No. 1		1,200	1,400	800	75	245	1,000	1,500,000	
No. 2		1,000	1,150	650	75	245	850	1,400,000	
No. 3		575	675	375	75	245	550	1,200,000	
Appearance		1,200	1,400	800	75	245	1,200	1,500,000	
Select structural	Beams and stringers	1,250	—	750	70	245	900	1,300,000	West Coast Lumber Inspection Bureau
No. 1		1,000	—	525	70	245	750	1,300,000	
Select structural	Posts and timbers	1,200	—	800	70	245	950	1,300,000	
No. 1		975	—	650	70	245	850	1,300,000	
Select dex	Decking	1,400	1,600	—	—	245	—	1,500,000	(see footnotes ᵇ through ⁱ)
Commercial dex		1,150	1,300	—	—	245	—	1,400,000	

Grade	Size classification								Western Wood Products Association (see footnotes [b] through [k])
Select structural	Beams and stringers	1,250	—	850	70	245	900	1,300,000	
No. 1	Beams and stringers	1,050	—	700	70	245	775	1,300,000	
Select structural	Posts and timbers	1,200	—	800	70	245	950	1,300,000	
No. 1	Posts and timbers	975	—	650	70	245	850	1,300,000	
Selected decking	Decking	—	1,600	—	—	—	—	1,500,000	
Commercial decking	Decking	—	1,300	—	—	—	—	1,400,000	
Selected decking	Decking	—	1,750	(Surfaced at 15% max. MC and used at 15% max. MC)				1,600,000	
Commercial decking	Decking	—	1,450					1,500,000	
Idaho white pine (surfaced dry or surfaced green. Used at 19% max. MC)									
Select structural	2 to 4 in. thick 2 to 4 in. wide	1,450	1,650	850	65	240	1,150	1,400,000	
No. 1/appearance	2 to 4 in. thick 2 to 4 in. wide	1,250	1,400	725	65	240	925/1,100	1,400,000	
No. 2	2 to 4 in. thick 2 to 4 in. wide	1,000	1,150	600	65	240	725	1,300,000	
No. 3	2 to 4 in. thick 2 to 4 in. wide	550	650	325	65	240	450	1,100,000	
Stud	2 to 4 in. thick 2 to 4 in. wide	550	650	325	65	240	450	1,100,000	
Construction	2 to 4 in. thick 4 in. wide	725	850	425	65	240	825	1,100,000	
Standard	2 to 4 in. thick 4 in. wide	400	475	250	65	240	675	1,100,000	
Utility	2 to 4 in. thick 4 in. wide	200	225	125	65	240	450	1,100,000	
Select structural	2 to 4 in. thick 6 in. and wider	1,250	1,450	825	65	240	1,000	1,400,000	
No. 1/appearance	2 to 4 in. thick 6 in. and wider	1,050	1,200	700	65	240	925/1,100	1,400,000	
No. 2	2 to 4 in. thick 6 in. and wider	875	1,000	575	65	240	775	1,300,000	
No. 3	2 to 4 in. thick 6 in. and wider	500	575	325	65	240	475	1,100,000	
Select structural	Beams and stringers	1,100	—	750	60	240	800	1,200,000	
No. 1	Beams and stringers	925	—	625	60	240	675	1,200,000	
Select structural	Posts and timbers	1,050	—	700	60	240	850	1,200,000	
No. 1	Posts and timbers	850	—	575	60	240	750	1,200,000	
Selected decking	Decking	—	1,400	—	—	—	—	1,400,000	
Commercial decking	Decking	—	1,150	—	—	—	—	1,300,000	
Selected decking	Decking	—	1,500	(Surfaced at 15% max. MC and used at 15% max. MC)				1,500,000	
Commercial decking	Decking	—	1,250					1,300,000	

TABLE 2.14 (Continued)

Species and Commercial Grade	Size Classification	Extreme Fiber in Bending, F_b		Tension Parallel to Grain F_t	Horizontal Shear F_v	Compression Perpendicular to Grain $F_{\perp}$	Compression Parallel to Grain F_c	Modulus of Elasticity E	Grading Rules Agency
		Single-Member Uses	Repetitive-Member Uses						
Lodgepole pine (surfaced dry or surfaced green. Used at 19% max. MC)									
Select structural	2 to 4 in. thick 2 to 4 in. wide	1,500	1,750	875	70	250	1,150	1,300,000	Western Wood Products Association (see footnotes [b] through [k])
No. 1/appearance		1,300	1,500	750	70	250	900/1,050	1,300,000	
No. 2		1,050	1,200	625	70	250	700	1,200,000	
No. 3		600	675	350	70	250	425	1,000,000	
Stud		600	675	350	70	250	425	1,000,000	
Construction	2 to 4 in. thick 4 in. wide	775	875	450	70	250	800	1,000,000	
Standard		425	500	250	70	250	675	1,000,000	
Utility		200	225	125	70	250	425	1,000,000	
Select structural	2 to 4 in. thick 6 in. and wider	1,300	1,500	875	70	250	1,000	1,300,000	
No. 1/appearance		1,100	1,300	750	70	250	900/1,050	1,300,000	
No. 2		925	1,050	600	70	250	750	1,200,000	
No. 3		525	625	350	70	250	475	1,000,000	
Select structural	Beams and stringers	1,150	—	775	65	250	800	1,100,000	
No. 1		975	—	650	65	250	675	1,100,000	
Select structural	Posts and timbers	1,100	—	725	65	250	850	1,100,000	
No. 1		875	—	600	65	250	725	1,100,000	
Selected decking	Decking	—	1,450	—	—	—	—	1,300,000	
Commercial decking		—	1,200	—	—	—	—	1,200,000	
Selected decking	Decking	—	1,550	(Surfaced at 15% max. MC and used at 15% max. MC)				1,400,000	
Commercial decking		—	1,300					1,200,000	

Allowable Unit Stresses, psi

Mountain hemlock (surfaced dry or surfaced green. Used at 19% max. MC)

Grade	Size / use								Agency
Select structural	2 to 4 in. thick, 2 to 4 in. wide								West Coast Lumber Inspection Bureau and Western Wood Products Association (see footnotes b through i)
No. 1		1,750	2,000	1,000	95	370	1,250	1,300,000	
No. 2		1,450	1,700	850	95	370	1,000	1,300,000	
No. 3		1,200	1,400	700	95	370	775	1,100,000	
Appearance		675	775	400	95	370	475	1,000,000	
Stud		675	775	400	95	370	475	1,000,000	
Construction	2 to 4 in. thick, 4 in. wide	875	1,000	525	95	370	900	1,000,000	
Standard		500	575	275	95	370	725	1,000,000	
Utility		225	275	125	95	370	475	1,000,000	
Select structural	2 to 4 in. thick, 6 in. and wider	1,500	1,700	1,000	95	370	1,100	1,300,000	
No. 1		1,250	1,450	850	95	370	1,000	1,300,000	
No. 2		1,050	1,200	675	95	370	825	1,100,000	
No. 3		625	700	400	95	370	525	1,000,000	
Appearance		1,250	1,450	850	95	370	1,200	1,300,000	
Select structural	Beams and stringers	1,350	—	775	90	370	875	1,100,000	West Coast Lumber Inspection Bureau (see footnotes b through i)
No. 1		1,100	—	550	90	370	750	1,100,000	
Select structural	Posts and timbers	1,250	—	825	90	370	925	1,100,000	
No. 1		1,000	—	675	90	370	800	1,100,000	
Select dex	Decking	1,450	1,650	—	—	370	—	1,300,000	
Commercial dex		1,200	1,400	—	—	370	—	1,100,000	
Select structural	Beams and stringers	1,350	—	900	90	370	875	1,100,000	Western Wood Products Association (see footnotes b through k)
No. 1		1,100	—	750	90	370	750	1,100,000	
Select structural	Posts and timbers	1,250	—	825	90	370	925	1,100,000	
No. 1		1,000	—	675	90	370	800	1,100,000	
Selected decking	Decking	—	1,650	—	—	—	—	1,300,000	
Commercial decking		—	1,400	—	—	—	—	1,100,000	
Selected decking	Decking	—	1,800	(Surfaced at 15% max. MC and used at 15% max. MC)				1,300,000	
Commercial decking		—	1,500					1,200,000	

TABLE 2.14 (Continued)

Species and Commercial Grade	Size Classification	Extreme Fiber in Bending, F_b		Tension Parallel to Grain F_t	Horizontal Shear F_v	Compression Perpendicular to Grain $F_{c\perp}$	Compression Parallel to Grain F_c	Modulus of Elasticity E	Grading Rules Agency
		Single-Member Uses	Repetitive-Member Uses						
Mountain hemlock – hem-fir (surfaced dry or surfaced green. Used at 19% max. MC)									
Select structural	2 to 4 in. thick	1,650	1,900	975	75	245	1,250	1,300,000	Western Wood Products Association (see footnotes [b] through [k])
No. 1/appearance	2 to 4 in. wide	1,400	1,600	825	75	245	1,000/1,200	1,300,000	
No. 2		1,150	1,300	675	75	245	775	1,100,000	
No. 3		625	725	375	75	245	475	1,000,000	
Stud		625	725	375	75	245	475	1,000,000	
Construction	2 to 4 in. thick	825	975	475	75	245	900	1,000,000	
Standard	4 in. wide	450	525	275	75	245	725	1,000,000	
Utility		225	250	125	75	245	475	1,000,000	
Select structural	2 to 4 in. thick	1,400	1,650	950	75	245	1,100	1,300,000	
No. 1/appearance	6 in. and wider	1,200	1,400	800	75	245	1,000/1,200	1,300,000	
No. 2		1,000	1,150	650	75	245	825	1,100,000	
No. 3		575	675	375	75	245	525	1,000,000	
Select structural	Beams and stringers	1,250	—	850	70	245	875	1,100,000	
No. 1		1,050	—	700	70	245	750	1,100,000	
Select structural	Posts and timbers	1,200	—	800	70	245	925	1,100,000	
No. 1		975	—	650	70	245	800	1,100,000	
Selected decking	Decking	—	1,600	—	—	—	—	1,300,000	
Commercial decking		—	1,300	—	—	—	—	1,100,000	
Selected decking	Decking	—	1,750	—	—	—	—	1,300,000	
Commercial decking		—	1,450	(Surfaced at 15% max. MC and used at 15% max. MC)				1,200,000	

Northern pine (surfaced at 15% moisture content. Used at 15% max. MC)

Grade	Size								Grading rules agency
Select structural	2 to 4 in. thick, 2 to 4 in. wide	1,750	2,000	1,050	75	280	1,450	1,500,000	Northeastern Lumber Manufacturers Association and Northern Hardwood and Pine Manufacturers Association (see footnotes b, c, d, h and i)
No. 1		1,500	1,700	875	75	280	1,150	1,500,000	
No. 2		1,250	1,400	725	75	280	900	1,300,000	
No. 3		675	775	400	75	280	550	1,200,000	
Appearance		1,300	1,500	850	75	280	1,350	1,500,000	
Stud		675	775	400	75	280	550	1,200,000	
Construction	2 to 4 in. thick, 4 in. wide	900	1,050	525	75	280	850	1,200,000	
Standard		500	575	300	75	280	550	1,200,000	
Utility		225	275	150	75	280	550	1,200,000	
Select structural	2 to 4 in. thick, 6 in. and wider	1,500	1,750	1,000	75	280	1,250	1,500,000	
No. 1		1,300	1,500	850	75	280	1,150	1,500,000	
No. 2		1,050	1,200	700	75	280	950	1,300,000	
No. 3		625	625	400	75	280	600	1,200,000	
Appearance		1,300	1,500	850	75	280	1,350	1,500,000	

Northern pine (surfaced dry or surfaced green. Used at 19% max. MC)

Grade	Size								Grading rules agency
Select structural	2 to 4 in. thick, 2 to 4 in. wide	1,650	1,850	950	70	280	1,200	1,400,000	Northeastern Lumber Manufacturers Association and Northern Hardwood and Pine Manufacturers Association (see footnotes b through i)
No. 1		1,400	1,600	825	70	280	975	1,400,000	
No. 2		1,150	1,300	675	70	280	775	1,300,000	
No. 3		625	725	375	70	280	475	1,100,000	
Appearance		1,200	1,400	800	70	280	1,150	1,400,000	
Stud		625	725	375	70	280	475	1,100,000	
Construction	2 to 4 in. thick, 4 in. wide	825	950	475	70	280	875	1,100,000	
Standard		450	525	275	70	280	725	1,100,000	
Utility		225	250	125	70	280	475	1,100,000	
Select structural	2 to 4 in. thick, 6 in. and wider	1,400	1,600	950	70	280	1,100	1,400,000	
No. 1		1,200	1,400	800	70	280	975	1,400,000	
No. 2		950	1,100	650	70	280	825	1,300,000	
No. 3		575	650	375	70	280	525	1,100,000	
Appearance		1,200	1,400	800	70	280	1,150	1,400,000	
Select structural	Beams and stringers	1,250	—	850	65	280	850	1,300,000	
No. 1		1,050	—	700	65	280	725	1,300,000	
Select structural	Posts and timbers	1,150	—	800	65	280	900	1,300,000	
No. 1		950	—	650	65	280	800	1,300,000	

TABLE 2.14 (Continued)

Species and Commercial Grade	Size Classification	Extreme Fiber in Bending, F_b		Tension Parallel to Grain F_t	Horizontal Shear F_v	Compression Perpendicular to Grain $F_{c\perp}$	Compression Parallel to Grain F_c	Modulus of Elasticity E	Grading Rules Agency
		Single-Member Uses	Repetitive-Member Uses						
Northern pine (surfaced dry or surfaced green. Used at 19% max. MC) (cont'd.)									
Select	Decking	1,350	1,550	—	—	—	—	1,400,000	NeLMA
Commercial		1,150	1,300	—	—	—	—	1,300,000	
Northern white cedar (surfaced dry or surfaced green. Used at 19% max. MC)									
Select structural	2 to 4 in. thick 2 to 4 in. wide	1,150	1,350	700	65	205	875	800,000	Northeastern Lumber Manufacturers Association (see footnotes b through i)
No. 1		1,000	1,150	600	65	205	675	800,000	
No. 2		825	950	500	65	205	550	700,000	
No. 3		450	525	275	65	205	325	600,000	
Appearance		850	1,000	575	65	205	825	800,000	
Stud		450	525	275	65	205	325	600,000	
Construction	2 to 4 in. thick 4 in. wide	600	675	350	65	205	625	600,000	
Standard		325	375	200	65	205	500	600,000	
Utility		150	175	100	65	205	325	600,000	
Select structural	2 to 4 in. thick 6 in. and wider	1,000	1,150	675	65	205	775	800,000	
No. 1		850	1,000	575	65	205	675	800,000	
No. 2		700	825	450	65	205	575	700,000	
No. 3		425	475	275	65	205	375	600,000	
Appearance		850	1,000	575	65	205	825	800,000	
Select	Decking	975	1,100	—	—	—	—	800,000	
Commercial		825	950	—	—	—	—	700,000	

Allowable Unit Stresses, psi

Size classification	Grade							
Beams and stringers	Select structural	900	—	600	60	205	600	700,000
	No. 1	750	—	500	60	205	500	700,000
Posts and timbers	Select structural	850	—	575	60	205	650	700,000
	No. 1	675	—	450	60	205	550	700,000

Ponderosa pine – sugar pine (ponderosa pine – lodgepole pine) (surfaced dry or surfaced green. Used at 19% max. MC)

Size classification	Grade							
2 to 4 in. thick 2 to 4 in. wide	Select structural	1,400	1,650	825	70	250	1,050	1,200,000
	No. 1/appearance	1,200	1,400	700	70	250	850/1,000	1,200,000
	No. 2	1,000	1,150	575	70	250	675	1,100,000
	No. 3	550	625	325	70	250	400	1,000,000
	Stud	550	625	325	70	250	400	1,000,000
2 to 4 in. thick 4 in. wide	Construction	725	825	425	70	250	775	1,000,000
	Standard	400	450	225	70	250	625	1,000,000
	Utility	200	225	100	70	250	400	1,000,000
2 to 4 in. thick 6 in. and wider	Select structural	1,200	1,400	825	70	250	950	1,200,000
	No. 1/appearance	1,050	1,200	700	70	250	850/1,000	1,200,000
	No. 2	850	975	550	70	250	700	1,100,000
	No. 3	500	575	325	70	250	450	1,000,000
Beams and stringers	Select structural	1,100	—	725	65	250	750	1,100,000
	No. 1	925	—	625	65	250	625	1,100,000
Posts and timbers	Select structural	1,000	—	675	65	250	800	1,100,000
	No. 1	825	—	550	65	250	700	1,100,000
Decking	Selected decking	—	1,350	—	—	—	—	1,200,000
	Commercial decking	—	1,150	—	—	—	—	1,100,000
Decking	Selected decking	—	1,450	(Surfaced at 15% max. MC and used at 15% max. MC)				1,300,000
	Commercial decking	—	1,250					1,100,000

Western Wood Products Association (see footnotes [b] through [k])

TABLE 2.14 (Continued)

Species and Commercial Grade	Size Classification	Allowable Unit Stresses, psi							Grading Rules Agency
		Extreme Fiber in Bending, F_b		Tension Parallel to Grain F_t	Horizontal Shear F_v	Compression Perpendicular to Grain $F_{c\perp}$	Compression Parallel to Grain F_c	Modulus of Elasticity E	
		Single-Member Uses	Repetitive-Member Uses						
Sitka spruce (surfaced dry or surfaced green. Used at 19% max. MC)									
Select structural	2 to 4 in. thick 2 to 4 in. wide	1,550	1,800	925	75	280	1,150	1,500,000	
No. 1		1,350	1,550	775	75	280	925	1,500,000	
No. 2		1,100	1,250	650	75	280	725	1,300,000	
No. 3		600	700	350	75	280	450	1,200,000	
Appearance		1,350	1,550	750	75	280	1,100	1,500,000	
Stud		600	700	350	75	280	450	1,200,000	West Coast Lumber Inspection Bureau (see footnotes [b] through [i])
Construction	2 to 4 in. thick 4 in. wide	800	925	475	75	280	825	1,200,000	
Standard		450	500	250	75	280	675	1,200,000	
Utility		200	250	125	75	280	450	1,200,000	
Select structural	2 to 4 in. thick 6 in. and wider	1,350	1,550	900	75	280	1,000	1,500,000	
No. 1		1,150	1,300	775	75	280	925	1,500,000	
No. 2		925	1,050	625	75	280	775	1,300,000	
No. 3		525	600	350	75	280	500	1,200,000	
Appearance		1,150	1,300	750	75	280	1,100	1,500,000	
Select structural	Beams and stringers	1,200	—	675	70	280	825	1,300,000	
No. 1		1,000	—	500	70	280	675	1,300,000	
Select structural	Posts and timbers	1,150	—	750	70	280	875	1,300,000	
No. 1		925	—	600	70	280	750	1,300,000	
Select dex	Decking	1,300	1,500	—	—	280	—	1,500,000	
Commercial dex		1,100	1,250	—	—	280	—	1,300,000	

Southern pine (surfaced at 15% moisture content, K.D. Used at 15% max. MC)

Southern Pine Inspection Bureau (see footnotes ^{c} and ^{f})

Grade	Size							
Select structural		2,250	2,600	1,350	95	405	1,850	1,900,000
Dense select structural		2,650	3,050	1,550	95	475	2,150	2,000,000
No. 1		1,900	2,200	1,100	95	405	1,450	1,900,000
No. 1 dense		2,250	2,600	1,300	95	475	1,700	2,000,000
No. 2	2 to 4 in. thick	1,350	1,550	775	80	345	975	1,500,000
No. 2 medium grain	2 to 4 in. wide	1,550	1,800	925	95	405	1,150	1,700,000
No. 2 dense		1,850	2,150	1,050	95	475	1,350	1,800,000
No. 3		875	1,000	525	80	345	700	1,500,000
No. 3 dense		1,050	1,200	600	95	475	825	1,600,000
Stud		875	1,000	525	80	345	700	1,500,000
Construction		1,150	1,300	670	75	345	1,300	1,500,000
Standard	2 to 4 in. thick	640	750	375	75	345	1,050	1,500,000
Utility	4 in. wide	300	350	175	75	345	700	1,500,000
Select structural		1,950	2,250	1,300	95	405	1,650	1,900,000
Dense select structural		2,250	2,600	1,500	95	475	1,900	2,000,000
No. 1		1,650	1,900	1,100	95	405	1,450	1,900,000
No. 1 dense		1,900	2,200	1,300	95	475	1,700	2,000,000
No. 2	2 to 4 in. thick	1,150	1,300	750	80	345	1,050	1,500,000
No. 2 medium grain	6 in. and wider	1,350	1,550	900	95	405	1,250	1,700,000
No. 2 dense		1,550	1,800	1,050	95	475	1,450	1,800,000
No. 3		800	900	525	80	345	750	1,500,000
No. 3 dense		925	1,050	625	95	475	875	1,600,000
Dense std. factory		2,200	2,550	1,300	95	475	1,700	2,000,000
No. 1 factory		1,500	1,750	900	95	405	1,150	1,700,000
No. 1 dense factory	2 to 4 in. thick / 2 to 4 in. wide / Decking	1,800	2,050	1,050	95	475	1,350	1,800,000
No. 2 factory		1,500	1,750	900	95	405	1,150	1,700,000
No. 2 dense factory		1,800	2,050	1,050	95	475	1,350	1,800,000
Dense std. factory		1,900	2,200	1,300	95	475	1,650	2,000,000
No. 1 factory		1,350	1,550	900	95	405	1,250	1,700,000
No. 1 dense factory	2 to 4 in. thick / 6 in. and wider / Decking	1,550	1,800	1,050	95	475	1,450	1,800,000
No. 2 factory		1,350	1,550	900	95	405	1,250	1,700,000
No. 2 dense factory		1,550	1,800	1,050	95	475	1,450	1,800,000

TABLE 2.14 (Continued)

Allowable Unit Stresses, psi

Species and Commercial Grade	Size Classification	Extreme Fiber in Bending, F_b		Tension Parallel to Grain F_t	Horizontal Shear F_v	Compression Perpendicular to Grain $F_{c\perp}$	Compression Parallel to Grain F_c	Modulus of Elasticity E	Grading Rules Agency
		Single-Member Uses	Repetitive-Member Uses						
Southern pine (surfaced at 15% moisture, K.D. Used at 15% max. MC) (cont'd)									
Dense structural 86	2 to 4 in. thick	3,000	3,450	2,000	160	475	2,350	2,000,000	Southern Pine Inspection Bureau
Dense structural 72		2,500	2,900	1,650	135	475	2,000	2,000,000	
Southern pine (surfaced dry. Used at 19% max. MC)									
Select structural		2,100	2,400	1,250	90	405	1,600	1,800,000	
Dense select structural		2,450	2,800	1,450	90	475	1,850	1,900,000	
No. 1		1,750	2,000	1,000	90	405	1,250	1,800,000	
No. 1 dense		2,050	2,350	1,200	90	475	1,450	1,900,000	
No. 2	2 to 4 in. thick	1,250	1,450	725	75	345	850	1,400,000	
No. 2 medium grain		1,450	1,650	850	90	405	1,000	1,600,000	
No. 2 dense	2 to 4 in. wide	1,700	1,950	1,000	90	475	1,150	1,700,000	
No. 3		825	950	475	75	345	600	1,400,000	
No. 3 dense		950	1,100	550	90	475	700	1,500,000	
Stud		825	950	475	75	345	600	1,400,000	
Construction	2 to 4 in. thick	1,050	1,200	620	75	345	1,100	1,400,000	Southern Pine Inspection Bureau
Standard	4 in. wide	590	700	340	75	345	925	1,400,000	
Utility		275	325	165	75	345	600	1,400,000	
Select structural		1,800	2,050	1,200	90	405	1,400	1,800,000	(see footnotes c and i)
Dense select structural		2,100	2,400	1,400	90	475	1,650	1,900,000	
No. 1		1,500	1,750	1,000	90	405	1,250	1,800,000	

Grade	Size							Southern Pine Inspection Bureau (see footnotes c and f)
No. 1 dense	2 to 4 in. thick, 6 in. and wider	1,800	2,050	1,200	90	475	1,450	1,900,000
No. 2		1,050	1,200	700	75	345	900	1,400,000
No. 2 medium grain		1,250	1,450	825	90	405	1,050	1,600,000
No. 2 dense		1,450	1,650	975	90	475	1,250	1,700,000
No. 3		725	825	475	75	345	650	1,400,000
No. 3 dense		850	975	575	90	475	750	1,500,000
Dense std. factory	2 to 4 in. thick, 2 to 4 in. wide	2,000	2,300	1,200	90	475	1,450	1,900,000
No. 1 factory		1,400	1,600	825	90	405	1,000	1,600,000
No. 1 dense factory		1,650	1,900	975	90	475	1,150	1,700,000
No. 2 factory		1,400	1,600	825	90	405	1,000	1,600,000
No. 2 dense factory		1,700	1,950	975	90	475	1,150	1,700,000
Dense std. factory	2 to 4 in. thick, 6 in. and wider	1,750	2,000	1,200	90	475	1,450	1,900,000
No. 1 factory		1,250	1,450	825	90	405	1,050	1,600,000
No. 1 dense factory		1,450	1,650	975	90	475	1,250	1,700,000
No. 2 factory		1,250	1,450	825	90	405	1,050	1,600,000
No. 2 dense factory		1,450	1,650	975	90	475	1,250	1,700,000
Dense structural 86	2 to 4 in. thick	2,750	3,150	1,850	150	475	2,050	1,900,000
Dense structural 72		2,300	2,650	1,550	125	475	1,700	1,900,000
Southern pine (surfaced green. Used any condition)								
Select structural	2½ to 4 in. thick, 2½ to 4 in. wide	1,700	1,950	975	80	270	1,050	1,600,000
Dense select structural		1,950	2,250	1,150	80	315	1,250	1,600,000
No. 1		1,400	1,600	825	80	270	850	1,600,000
No. 1 dense		1,650	1,900	975	80	315	975	1,600,000
No. 2		1,000	1,150	575	70	230	550	1,300,000
No. 2 medium grain		1,150	1,300	675	80	270	650	1,400,000
No. 2 dense		1,350	1,500	800	80	315	775	1,500,000
No. 3		650	750	375	70	230	400	1,300,000
No. 3 dense		775	900	450	80	315	475	1,300,000
Stud		650	750	375	70	230	400	1,300,000
Construction	2½ to 4 in. thick, 4 in. wide	850	975	490	70	230	750	1,300,000
Standard		475	550	275	70	230	620	1,300,000
Utility		225	250	125	70	230	400	1,300,000

TABLE 2.14 (Continued)

Species and Commercial Grade	Size Classification	Allowable Unit Stresses, psi							Grading Rules Agency
		Extreme Fiber in Bending, F_b		Tension Parallel to Grain F_t	Horizontal Shear F_v	Compression Perpendicular to Grain $F_{c\perp}$	Compression Parallel to Grain F_c	Modulus of Elasticity E	
		Single-Member Uses	Repetitive-Member Uses						
Southern pine (surfaced green. Used any condition) (cont'd)									
Select structural		1,450	1,650	950	80	270	925	1,600,000	
Dense select structural		1,650	1,900	1,100	80	315	1,100	1,600,000	
No. 1		1,200	1,400	800	80	270	825	1,600,000	
No. 1 dense	2½ to 4 in. thick	1,400	1,600	950	80	315	975	1,600,000	
No. 2	6 in. and wider	850	975	550	70	230	600	1,300,000	
No. 2 medium grain		1,000	1,150	650	80	270	700	1,400,000	
No. 2 dense		1,150	1,300	775	80	315	825	1,500,000	Southern Pine Inspection Bureau
No. 3		575	650	375	70	230	425	1,300,000	(see footnotes ^{c} and ^{i})
No. 3 dense		675	775	450	80	315	500	1,300,000	
Dense std. factory		1,600	—	950	80	315	975	1,600,000	
No. 1 factory	2½ to 4 in. thick	1,150	—	650	80	270	650	1,400,000	
No. 1 dense factory	2½ to 4 in. wide	1,300	—	775	80	315	775	1,500,000	
No. 2 factory		1,150	—	650	80	270	650	1,400,000	
No. 2 dense factory		1,300	—	775	80	315	775	1,500,000	
Dense std. factory		1,400	—	950	80	315	975	1,600,000	
No. 1 factory	2½ to 4 in. thick	1,000	—	650	80	270	700	1,600,000	
No. 1 dense factory	6 in. and wider	1,150	—	775	80	315	825	1,500,000	
No. 2 factory		1,000	—	650	80	270	700	1,400,000	
No. 2 dense factory		1,150	—	775	80	315	825	1,500,000	
No. 1 SR		1,300	—	850	110	270	925	1,600,000	
No. 1 dense SR		1,500	—	1,000	110	315	1,050	1,600,000	

								Western Wood Products Association (see footnotes [b] through [k])
No. 2 SR	5 in. and thicker	1,100	—	725	95	270	675	1,400,000
No. 2 dense SR		1,300	—	850	95	315	775	1,500,000
Dense structural 65		1,650	—	1,100	105	315	1,000	1,600,000
Dense structural 86	2½ in. and thicker	2,200	—	1450	140	315	1,350	1,600,000
Dense structural 72		1,850	—	1250	120	315	1,150	1,600,000
Subalpine fir (white woods) (Western woods) (surfaced dry or surfaced green. Used at 19% max. MC)								
Select structural	2 to 4 in. thick	1,250	1,450	725	60	195	900	900,000
No. 1/appearance	2 to 4 in. wide	1,050	1,200	600	60	195	700/850	900,000
No. 2		850	1,000	500	60	195	550	900,000
No. 3		475	550	275	60	195	350	800,000
Stud		475	550	275	60	195	350	800,000
Construction	2 to 4 in. thick	625	725	375	60	195	650	800,000
Standard	4 in. wide	350	400	200	60	195	525	800,000
Utility		175	200	100	60	195	350	800,000
Select structural	2 to 4 in. thick	1,050	1,200	700	60	195	800	900,000
No. 1/appearance	6 in. and wider	900	1,050	600	60	195	700/850	900,000
No. 2		750	850	475	60	195	600	900,000
No. 3		425	500	275	60	195	375	800,000
Select structural	Beams and stringers	950	—	625	60	195	625	900,000
No. 1		800	—	525	60	195	525	900,000
Select structural	Posts and timbers	875	—	600	60	195	675	900,000
No. 1		725	—	475	60	195	575	900,000
Selected decking	Decking	—	1,200	—	—	—	—	900,000
Commercial decking		—	1,000	—	—	—	—	900,000
Selected decking	Decking	—	1,300	(Surfaced at 15% max. MC and used at 15% max. MC)				1,000,000
Commercial decking		—	1,050					900,000

TABLE 2.14 (Continued)

Species and Commercial Grade	Size Classification	Extreme Fiber in Bending, F_b		Tension Parallel to Grain F_t	Horizontal Shear F_v	Compression Perpendicular to Grain $F_{c\perp}$	Compression Parallel to Grain F_c	Modulus of Elasticity E	Grading Rules Agency
		Single-Member Uses	Repetitive-Member Uses						
Western cedars (surfaced dry or surfaced green. Used at 19% max. MC)									
Select structural	2 to 4 in. thick 2 to 4 in. wide	1,450	1,700	850	75	295	1,250	1,100,000	West Coast Lumber Inspection Bureau and Western Wood Products Association
No. 1		1,250	1,450	725	75	295	975	1,100,000	
No. 2		1,000	1,200	600	75	295	775	1,000,000	
No. 3		575	650	325	75	295	475	900,000	
Appearance		1,250	1,450	725	75	295	1,150	1,100,000	
Stud		575	650	325	75	295	475	900,000	
Construction	2 to 4 in. thick 4 in. wide	750	850	425	75	295	875	900,000	
Standard		425	475	250	75	295	725	900,000	
Utility		200	225	125	75	295	475	900,000	
Select structural	2 to 4 in. thick 6 in. and wider	1,250	1,450	850	75	295	1,100	1,100,000	(see footnotes b through i)
No. 1		1,050	1,250	725	75	295	975	1,100,000	
No. 2		875	1,000	575	75	295	825	1,000,000	
No. 3		525	600	325	75	295	525	900,000	
Appearance		1,050	1,250	725	75	295	1,150	1,100,000	
Select structural	Beams and stringers	1,100	—	675	70	295	875	1,000,000	West Coast Lumber Inspection Bureau
No. 1		900	—	475	70	295	725	1,000,000	
Select structural	Posts and timbers	1,050	—	700	70	295	900	1,000,000	
No. 1		850	—	575	70	295	800	1,000,000	
Select dex	Decking	1,200	1,400	—	—	295	—	1,100,000	(see footnotes b through i)
Commercial dex		1,050	1,200	—	—	295	—	1,000,000	

Allowable Unit Stresses, psi

Grade	Size classification	F_b single-member	F_b repetitive-member	F_t	F_v	$F_{c\perp}$	$F_{c\parallel}$	E	Grading agency
Select structural	Beams and stringers	1,100	—	750	70	295	875	1,000,000	Western Wood Products Association (see footnotes b through k)
No. 1		950	—	625	70	295	725	1,000,000	
Select structural	Posts and timbers	1,050	—	700	70	295	900	1,000,000	
No. 1		850	—	575	70	295	800	1,000,000	
Selected decking	Decking	—	1,400	—	—	—	—	1,100,000	
Commercial decking		—	1,200	—	—	—	—	1,000,000	
Selected decking	Decking	—	1,500	—	—	—	—	1,100,000	(Surfaced at 15% max. MC and used at 15% max. MC)
Commercial decking		—	1,250	—	—	—	—	1,000,000	

Western hemlock (surfaced dry or surfaced green. Used at 19% max. MC)

Grade	Size classification	F_b single-member	F_b repetitive-member	F_t	F_v	$F_{c\perp}$	$F_{c\parallel}$	E	Grading agency
Select Structural	2 to 4 in. thick 2 to 4 in. wide	1,800	2,100	1,050	90	280	1,450	1,600,000	West Coast Lumber Inspection Bureau and Western Wood Products Association (see footnotes b through l)
No. 1		1,550	1,800	900	90	280	1,150	1,600,000	
No. 2		1,300	1,450	750	90	280	900	1,400,000	
No. 3		700	800	425	90	280	550	1,300,000	
Appearance		1,550	1,800	900	90	280	1,350	1,600,000	
Stud		700	800	425	90	280	550	1,300,000	
Construction	2 to 4 in. thick 4 in. wide	925	1,050	550	90	280	1,050	1,300,000	
Standard		525	600	300	90	280	850	1,300,000	
Utility		250	275	150	90	280	550	1,300,000	
Select structural	2 to 4 in. thick 6 in. and wider	1,550	1,800	1,050	90	280	1,300	1,600,000	
No. 1		1,350	1,550	900	90	280	1,150	1,600,000	
No. 2		1,100	1,250	725	90	280	975	1,400,000	
No. 3		650	750	425	90	280	625	1,300,000	
Appearance		1,350	1,550	900	90	280	1,350	1,600,000	
Select structural	Beams and stringers	1,450	—	825	85	280	1,000	1,400,000	West Coast Lumber Inspection Bureau (see footnotes b through l)
No. 1		1,150	—	575	85	280	850	1,400,000	
Select structural	Posts and timbers	1,300	—	875	85	280	1,100	1,400,000	
No. 1		1,050	—		85	280	950	1,400,000	
Select dex	Decking	1,500	1,750	—	—	280	—	1,600,000	
Commercial dex		1,300	1,450	—	—	280	—	1,400,000	

TABLE 2.14 (Continued)

Species and Commercial Grade	Size Classification	Allowable Unit Stresses, psi							Grading Rules Agency
		Extreme Fiber in Bending, F_b		Tension Parallel to Grain, F_t	Horizontal Shear, F_v	Compression Perpendicular to Grain, $F_{c\perp}$	Compression Parallel to Grain, F_c	Modulus of Elasticity, E	
		Single-Member Uses	Repetitive-Member Uses						
Western hemlock (surfaced dry or surfaced green. Used at 19% max. MC) (cont'd)									
Select structural	Beams and stringers	1,400	—	950	85	280	1,000	1,400,000	Western Wood Products Association (see footnotes [b] through [k])
No. 1	stringers	1,150	—	775	85	280	850	1,400,000	
Select structural	Posts and timbers	1,300	—	875	85	280	1,100	1,400,000	
No. 1	timbers	1,050	—	700	85	280	950	1,400,000	
Selected decking	Decking	—	1,750	—	—	280	—	1,600,000	
Commercial decking		—	1,450	—	—	280	—	1,400,000	
Selected decking	Decking	—	1,900	(Surfaced at 15% max. MC and used at 15% max. MC)	—	280	—	1,700,000	
Commercial decking		—	1,600		—	280	—	1,500,000	

Part A — Footnotes Applicable to Visually Graded Lumber

[a]Where Eastern spruce and balsam fir are shipped in a combination, the tabulated values for balsam fir shall apply.

[b]The recommended design values shown in *Part A* are applicable to lumber that will be used under dry conditions such as in most covered structures. For 2 to 4 in. thick lumber the dry surfaced size should be used. In calculating design values, the natural gain in strength and stiffness that occurs as lumber dries has been taken into consideration as well as the reduction in size that occurs when unseasoned lumber shrinks. The gain in load carrying capacity due to increased strength and stiffness resulting from drying more than offsets the design effect of size reductions due to shrinkage. For 5 in. and thicker lumber, the surfaced sizes also may be used because design values have been adjusted to compensate for any loss in size by shrinkage that may occur.

[c]Values for F_b, F_t, and F_c for the grades of Construction, Standard, and Utility apply only to 4 in. widths. Design values for 2 in. and 3 in. widths of these grades are available from Redwood Inspection Service, Southern Pine Inspection Bureau, West Coast Lumber Inspection Bureau and Western Wood Products Association.

[d]The values in *Part A* are based on edgewise use. For dimension 2 to 4 in. in thickness, when used flatwise, the recommended design values for fiber stress in bending may be multiplied by the following factors:

Width, in.	Thickness, in.		
	2	3	4
2 to 4	1.10	1.04	1.00
6 and wider	1.22	1.16	1.11

[e]When 2 to 4 in. thick lumber is manufactured at a maximum moisture content of 15% and used in a condition where the moisture content does not exceed 15% the design values for surfaced dry or surfaced green lumber shown in *Part A* may be multiplied by the following factors:

Extreme Fiber in Bending, F_b	Tension Parallel to Grain, F_t	Horizontal Shear, F_v	Compression Perpendicular to Grain, $F_{c\perp}$	Compression Parallel to Grain,* F_c	Modulus of Elasticity,* E
1.08	1.08	1.05	1.00	1.17	1.05

*For redwood use.

[f]When 2 to 4 in. thick lumber is designed for use where the moisture content will exceed 19% for an extended period of time, the values shown in *Part A* should be multiplied by the following factors:

Extreme Fiber in Bending, F_b	Tension Parallel to Grain, F_t	Horizontal Shear, F_v	Compression Perpendicular to Grain, $F_{c\perp}$	Compression Parallel to Grain, F_c	Modulus of Elasticity, E
0.86	0.84	0.97	0.67	0.70	0.97

TABLE 2.14 (Continued)

gWhen lumber 5 in. and thicker is designed for use where the moisture content will exceed 19% for an extended period of time, the values shown in *Part A* should be multiplied by the following factors:

Extreme Fiber in Bending, F_b	Tension Parallel to Grain, F_t	Horizontal Shear, F_v	Compression Perpendicular to Grain, $F_{c\perp}$	Compression Parallel to Grain, F_c	Modulus of Elasticity, E
1.00	1.00	1.00	0.67	0.91	1.00

hThe tabulated horizontal shear values shown herein are based on the conservative assumption of the most severe checks, shakes or splits possible, as if a piece were split full length. When lumber 4 in. and thinner is manufactured unseasoned the tabulated values should be multiplied by a factor of 0.92.

Specific horizontal shear values for any grade and species of lumber may be established by use of the following tables when the length of split or check is known:

When length of split on wide face is:	Multiply tabulated F_v value by: (Nominal 2 in. Lumber)
No split	2.00
½ × wide face	1.67
¾ × wide face	1.50
1 × wide face	1.33
1½ × wide face or more	1.00

When length of split on wide face is:	Multiply tabulated F_v value by: (3 in. and Thicker Lumber)
No split	2.00
½ × narrow face	1.67
1 × narrow face	1.33
1½ × narrow face or more	1.00

iStress rated boards of nominal 1, 1¼, and 1½ in. thickness, 2 in. and wider, are permitted the recommended design values shown for select structural, No. 1, appearance, No. 2 and No. 3 grades as shown in 2 to 4 in. thick, 2 to 4 in. wide and 2 to 4 in. thick, 6 in. and wider categories when graded in accordance with those grade requirements.

jFor species combinations shown in parentheses, the lowest design values for any species in the combination are tabulated. White woods may include Engelmann spruce, any true firs, any hemlock and any pine. Mixed species may include any Western species.

kWhen decking is surfaced at 15% moisture content and used where the moisture content will exceed 15% for an extended period of time, the tabulated design values should be multiplied by the following factors: extreme fiber in bending, F_b, 0.79; modulus of elasticity, E, 0.92.

Part B – Allowable Unit Stresses for Structural Lumber – Machine Stress-Rated
(Normal Duration of Loading)

Grading Rules Agency Grade Designation	Size Classification	Extreme Fiber in Bending, F_b [d]		Tension Parallel to Grain, F_t	Compression Parallel to Grain, F_c	Compression Perpendicular to Grain $F_{c\perp}$ (Dry)[a]					Modulus of Elasticity, E
		Single-Member Uses	Repetitive-Member Uses			Douglas Fir-Larch	Hem-Fir	Pine[b]	Engelmann Spruce	Cedar[c]	
Western Wood Products Association											
1200f-1.2E	Machine Rated Lumber 2 in. thick or less All widths	1,200	1,400	600	950	385	245	240	195	295	1,200,000
1500f-1.4E		1,500	1,750	900	1,200	385	245	240	195	295	1,400,000
1650f-1.5E		1,650	1,900	1,020	1,320	385	245	240	195	295	1,500,000
1800f-1.6E		1,800	2,050	1,175	1,450	385	245	240	195	295	1,600,000
2100f-1.8E		2,100	2,400	1,575	1,700	385	245	240	195	295	1,800,000
2400f-2.0E		2,400	2,750	1,925	1,925	385	245	240	195	295	2,000,000
2700f-2.2E		2,700	3,100	2,150	2,150	385	245	240	195	295	2,200,000
3000f-2.4E		3,000	3,450	2,400	2,400	385	245	240	195	295	2,400,000
3300f-2.6E		3,300	3,800	2,650	2,650	385	245	240	195	295	2,600,000
900f-1.0E	Machine Rated Joists 2 in. thick or less All widths	900	1,050	350	725	385	245	240	195	295	1,000,000
900f-1.2E		900	1,050	350	725	385	245	240	195	295	1,200,000
1200f-1.5E		1,200	1,400	600	950	385	245	240	195	295	1,500,000
1350f-1.8E		1,350	1,550	750	1,075	385	245	240	195	295	1,800,000
1800f-2.1E		1,800	2,050	1,175	1,450	385	245	240	195	295	2,100,000
West Coast Lumber Inspection Bureau											
900f-1.0E	Machine Rated Lumber 2 in. thick or less All widths	900	1,050	350	725	385	245	—	—	—	1,000,000
1200f-1.2E		1,200	1,400	600	950	385	245	—	—	—	1,200,000
1500f-1.4E		1,500	1,750	900	1,200	385	245	—	—	—	1,400,000
1650f-1.5E		1,650	1,900	1,020	1,320	385	245	—	—	—	1,500,000
1800f-1.6E		1,800	2,050	1,175	1,450	385	245	—	—	—	1,600,000
2100f-1.8E		2,100	2,400	1,575	1,700	385	245	—	—	—	1,800,000
2400f-2.0E		2,400	2,750	1,925	1,925	385	245	—	—	—	2,000,000
2700f-2.2E		2,700	3,100	2,150	2,150	385	245	—	—	—	2,200,000

Allowable Unit Stresses, psi

TABLE 2.14 (Continued)

Grading Rules Agency Grade Designation	Size Classification	Allowable Unit Stresses, psi										
		Extreme Fiber in Bending, F_b [d]		Tension Parallel to Grain, F_t	Compression Parallel to Grain, F_c	Compression Perpendicular to Grain $F_{c\perp}$ (Dry) [a]					Modulus of Elasticity, E
		Single-Member Uses	Repetitive-Member Uses			Douglas Fir-Larch	Hem-Fir	Pine [b]	Engelmann Spruce	Cedar [c]	
West Coast Lumber Inspection Bureau (cont'd)											
900f-1.0E	Machine Rated Joists 2 in. thick or less 6 in. and wider	900	1,050	350	725	385	245	—	—	—	1,000,000
900f-1.2E		900	1,050	350	725	385	245	—	—	—	1,200,000
1200f-1.5E		1,200	1,400	600	950	385	245	—	—	—	1,500,000
1500f-1.8E		1,500	1,750	900	1,200	385	245	—	—	—	1,800,000
1800f-2.1E		1,800	2,050	1,175	1,450	385	245	—	—	—	2,100,000
Southern Pine Inspection Bureau						Southern Pine					
1200f-1.2E	Machine Rated Lumber 2 in. thick or less 2 to 4 in. wide	1,200	1,375	600	950	405	—	—	—	—	1,200,000
1500f-1.4E		1,500	1,725	900	1,200	405	—	—	—	—	1,400,000
1650f-1.5E		1,650	1,900	1,020	1,320	405	—	—	—	—	1,500,000
1800f-1.6E		1,800	2,100	1,175	1,450	405	—	—	—	—	1,600,000
2100f-1.8E		2,100	2,400	1,575	1,700	405	—	—	—	—	1,800,000
2400f-2.0E		2,400	2,750	1,925	1,925	405	—	—	—	—	2,000,000
2700f-2.2E		2,700	3,100	2,150	2,150	405	—	—	—	—	2,200,000
3000f-2.4E		3,000	3,450	2,400	2,400	405	—	—	—	—	2,400,000
3300f-2.6E		3,300	3,800	2,650	2,650	405	—	—	—	—	2,600,000
900f-1.0E	Machine Rated Lumber 2 in. thick or less 6 in. and wider	900	1,025	350	725	405	—	—	—	—	1,000,000
900f-1.2E		900	1,025	350	725	405	—	—	—	—	1,200,000
1200f-1.5E		1,200	1,375	600	950	405	—	—	—	—	1,500,000
1350f-1.8E		1,350	1,550	750	1,075	405	—	—	—	—	1,800,000
1800f-2.1E		1,800	2,050	1,175	1,450	405	—	—	—	—	2,100,000

Part B — Footnotes Applicable to Machine Stress-Rated Lumber

[a]Allowable unit stresses for horizontal shear, F_v (Dry) for all grade designations are as follows:

Douglas Fir-Larch	Hem-Fir	Pine	Engelmann Spruce	Cedar	Southern Pine	Southern Pine KD
95	75	65	70	75	90	95

[b]Pine includes Idaho white, lodgepole, ponderosa or sugar pine.

[c]Cedar includes incense or Western red cedar.

[d]Tabulated extreme fiber in bending values, F_b, are applicable to lumber loaded on edge. When loaded flatwise, these values should be multiplied by the following factors:

Nominal Width, in.	4	6	8	10	12	14
Factor	1.10	1.15	1.19	1.22	1.25	1.28

Source: National Forest Products Association.

TABLE 2.15

ALLOWABLE UNIT STRESSES FOR END GRAIN IN BEARING
PARALLEL TO GRAIN[a]

Species	Glued Laminated Timber and Sawn Lumber 4 in. and Less in Thickness[b] (Seasoned), psi	Sawn Lumber More Than 4 in. in Thickness[c] (Unseasoned), psi
Ash, commercial white	2,060	1,510
Beech	1,790	1,310
Birch, sweet and yellow	1,720	1,260
Cedar, Western	1,570	1,150
Cypress, Southern	1,990	1,460
Douglas fir-larch, dense	2,360	1,730
Douglas fir-larch	2,020	1,480
Douglas fir, South	1,820	1,340
Hem-fir	1,680	1,230
Hemlock, mountain	1,600	1,170
Hickory and pecan	2,050	1,510
Maple, black and sugar	1,710	1,260
Oak, red and white	2,050	1,650
Pine, Eastern white	1,360	990
Pine, Idaho white	1,470	1,080
Pine, lodgepole	1,450	1,060
Pine, Northern	1,570	1,150
Pine, Southern, dense	2,360	1,730
Pine, Southern, medium-grain	2,020	1,480
Pine, Southern, open-grain	1,720	1,260
Redwood, close-grain	2,340	1,720
Redwood, open-grain	1,730	1,270
Spruce, Eastern	1,450	1,060
Spruce, Engelmann	1,170	860
Spruce, Sitka	1,480	1,090
Yellow poplar	1,340	980

[a]These allowable unit stresses apply to the net area in bearing and are subject to adjustments for duration of load. When the stress in end grain bearing exceeds 75% of the adjusted allowable unit stresses, bearing shall be on a metal plate, strap, or other durable, rigid, homogeneous material of adequate strength.
[b]These values based on a maximum moisture content of 19%.
[c]These values should be divided by a factor of 1.10 for members that will remain continuously wet, such as in submerged members.
Source: National Forest Products Association.

Size factor

When the depth of a rectangular sawn lumber beam exceeds 12 in., the allowable unit bending stress, F_b, should be multiplied by the size factor, C_F, as determined from the following formula:

$$C_F = \left(\frac{12}{d}\right)^{1/9}$$

where C_F = size factor

d = depth of member, in.

Adjustment of the allowable unit bending stress for size factor is not cumulative with the adjustment for slenderness factor.

PROPERTIES OF SECTIONS

Table 2.16 gives section properties for structural glued laminated timbers based on industry-recommended standard thicknesses and widths. As far as other considerations permit, the use of standard finished sizes of structural glued laminated timber as indicated in Table 2.16 constitutes recommended industry practice. These standard finished sizes are based upon the lumber sizes published in the American Softwood Lumber Standard, Voluntary Product Standard PS 20-70, which can be used to best advantage for laminating. Other finished sizes may be used to meet the size requirements of a design or to meet other special requirements.

Under recommended industry practice, dimension lumber, surfaced to $1\frac{1}{2}$ in. before gluing, is used to laminate straight members and curved members having a radius of curvature of 27 ft 6 in. or greater. Boards, surfaced to $\frac{3}{4}$ in. before gluing, are used for laminating curved members when the bending radius is too short to permit the use of $1\frac{1}{2}$ in. thick laminations but is not less than 9 ft 4 in. Finished depths of laminated members are, therefore, generally multiples of the $1\frac{1}{2}$ in. or $\frac{3}{4}$ in. net thicknesses. However, other lamination thicknesses may be used to meet special requirements, resulting in finished depths that are not multiples of these net thicknesses.

TABLE 2.16

SECTION PROPERTIES FOR STRUCTURAL
GLUED LAMINATED TIMBER

Number of Laminations		Depth, d in.	Size Factor, $C_F{}^a$	Area, A in.^{2}	Section Modulus, S in.^{3}	Adjusted Section Modulus, $S \times C_F$ in.^{3}	Moment of Inertia, I in.^{4}	Volume per Lineal Foot ft^3
$1\frac{1}{2}$ in.	$\frac{3}{4}$ in.							
$2\frac{1}{4}$ in. WIDTH								
2	4	3.00	1.00	6.8	3.4	3.4	5.1	0.05
	5	3.75	1.00	8.4	5.3	5.3	9.9	0.06
3	6	4.50	1.00	10.1	7.6	7.6	17.1	0.07
	7	5.25	1.00	11.8	10.3	10.3	27.1	0.08
4	8	6.00	1.00	13.5	13.5	13.5	40.5	0.09
	9	6.75	1.00	15.2	17.1	17.1	57.7	0.11
5	10	7.50	1.00	16.9	21.1	21.1	79.1	0.12
	11	8.25	1.00	18.6	25.5	25.5	105.3	0.13
6	12	9.00	1.00	20.2	30.4	30.4	136.7	0.14
	13	9.75	1.00	21.9	35.6	35.6	173.8	0.15
7	14	10.50	1.00	23.6	41.3	41.3	217.0	0.16
	15	11.25	1.00	25.3	47.5	47.5	267.0	0.18

TABLE 2.16 (Continued)

Number of Laminations $1\frac{1}{2}$ in.	$\frac{3}{4}$ in.	Depth, d in.	Size Factor, $C_F{}^a$	Area, A in.^{2}	Section Modulus, S in.^{3}	Adjusted Section Modulus, $S \times C_F$ in.^{3}	Moment of Inertia, I in.^{4}	Volume per Lineal Foot ft^3
8	16	12.00	1.00	27.0	54.0	54.0	324.0	0.19
	17	12.75	0.99	28.7	61.0	60.4	388.6	0.20
9	18	13.50	0.99	30.4	68.3	67.6	461.3	0.21
	19	14.25	0.98	32.1	76.1	74.5	542.6	0.22
10	20	15.00	0.98	33.8	84.4	82.7	632.8	0.23

$3\frac{1}{8}$ in. WIDTH

Number of Laminations $1\frac{1}{2}$ in.	$\frac{3}{4}$ in.	Depth, d in.	Size Factor, $C_F{}^a$	Area, A in.^{2}	Section Modulus, S in.^{3}	Adjusted Section Modulus, $S \times C_F$ in.^{3}	Moment of Inertia, I in.^{4}	Volume per Lineal Foot ft^3
2	4	3.00	1.00	9.4	4.7	4.7	7.0	0.06
	5	3.75	1.00	11.7	7.3	7.3	13.7	0.08
3	6	4.50	1.00	14.1	10.5	10.5	23.7	0.10
	7	5.25	1.00	16.4	14.4	14.4	37.7	0.11
4	8	6.00	1.00	18.8	18.8	18.8	56.3	0.13
	9	6.75	1.00	21.1	23.7	23.7	80.1	0.15
5	10	7.50	1.00	23.4	29.3	29.3	109.9	0.16
	11	8.25	1.00	25.8	35.4	35.4	146.2	0.18
6	12	9.00	1.00	28.1	42.2	42.2	189.8	0.20
	13	9.75	1.00	30.5	49.5	49.5	241.4	0.21
7	14	10.50	1.00	32.8	57.4	57.4	301.5	0.23
	15	11.25	1.00	35.2	65.9	65.9	370.8	0.24
8	16	12.00	1.00	37.5	75.0	75.0	450.0	0.26
	17	12.75	0.99	39.8	84.7	83.8	539.8	0.28
9	18	13.50	0.99	42.2	94.9	93.9	640.7	0.29
	19	14.25	0.98	44.5	105.8	103.7	753.6	0.31
10	20	15.00	0.98	46.9	117.2	114.9	878.9	0.33
	21	15.75	0.97	49.2	129.2	125.3	1,017.4	0.34
11	22	16.50	0.97	51.6	141.8	137.5	1,169.8	0.36
	23	17.25	0.96	53.9	155.0	148.8	1,336.7	0.37
12	24	18.00	0.96	56.3	168.8	162.0	1,518.8	0.39
	25	18.75	0.95	58.6	183.1	173.9	1,716.6	0.41
13	26	19.50	0.95	60.9	198.0	188.1	1,931.0	0.42
	27	20.25	0.94	63.3	213.6	200.8	2,162.4	0.44
14	28	21.00	0.94	65.6	229.7	215.9	2,411.7	0.46
	29	21.75	0.94	68.0	246.4	231.6	2,679.5	0.47
15	30	22.50	0.93	70.3	263.7	245.2	2,966.3	0.49
	31	23.25	0.93	72.7	281.5	261.8	3,272.9	0.50
16	32	24.00	0.93	75.0	300.0	279.0	3,600.0	0.52

$5\frac{1}{8}$ in. WIDTH

Number of Laminations $1\frac{1}{2}$ in.	$\frac{3}{4}$ in.	Depth, d in.	Size Factor, $C_F{}^a$	Area, A in.^{2}	Section Modulus, S in.^{3}	Adjusted Section Modulus, $S \times C_F$ in.^{3}	Moment of Inertia, I in.^{4}	Volume per Lineal Foot ft^3
3	6	4.50	1.00	23.1	17.3	17.3	38.9	0.16
	7	5.25	1.00	26.9	23.5	23.5	61.8	0.19
4	8	6.00	1.00	30.8	30.8	30.8	92.3	0.21
	9	6.75	1.00	34.6	38.9	38.9	131.3	0.24
5	10	7.50	1.00	38.4	48.0	48.0	180.2	0.27
	11	8.25	1.00	42.3	58.1	58.1	239.8	0.29
6	12	9.00	1.00	46.1	69.2	69.2	311.3	0.32
	13	9.75	1.00	50.0	81.2	81.2	395.8	0.35
7	14	10.50	1.00	53.8	94.2	94.2	494.4	0.37

TABLE 2.16 (Continued)

Number of Laminations $1\frac{1}{2}$ in.	$\frac{3}{4}$ in.	Depth, d in.	Size Factor, C_F[a]	Area, A in.^{2}	Section Modulus, S in.^{3}	Adjusted Section Modulus, $S \times C_F$ in.^{3}	Moment of Inertia, I in.^{4}	Volume per Lineal Foot ft^3
	15	11.25	1.00	57.7	108.1	108.1	608.1	0.40
8	16	12.00	1.00	61.5	123.0	123.0	738.0	0.43
	17	12.75	0.99	65.3	138.9	137.5	885.2	0.45
9	18	13.50	0.99	69.2	155.7	154.1	1,050.8	0.48
	19	14.25	0.98	73.0	173.4	169.9	1,235.8	0.51
10	20	15.00	0.98	76.9	192.2	188.4	1,441.4	0.53
	21	15.75	0.97	80.7	211.9	205.5	1,668.6	0.56
11	22	16.50	0.97	84.6	232.5	225.5	1,918.5	0.59
	23	17.25	0.96	88.4	254.2	244.0	2,192.2	0.61
12	24	18.00	0.96	92.3	276.8	265.7	2,490.8	0.64
	25	18.75	0.95	96.1	300.3	285.3	2,815.2	0.67
13	26	19.50	0.95	99.9	324.8	308.6	3,166.8	0.69
	27	20.25	0.94	103.8	350.3	329.3	3,546.4	0.72
14	28	21.00	0.94	107.6	376.7	354.1	3,955.2	0.75
	29	21.75	0.94	111.5	404.1	379.8	4,394.3	0.77
15	30	22.50	0.93	115.3	432.4	402.1	4,864.7	0.80
	31	23.25	0.93	119.2	461.7	429.4	5,367.6	0.83
16	32	24.00	0.93	123.0	492.0	457.6	5,904.0	0.85
	33	24.75	0.92	126.8	523.2	481.3	6,475.0	0.88
17	34	25.50	0.92	130.7	555.4	511.0	7,081.6	0.91
	35	26.25	0.92	134.5	588.6	541.5	7,725.0	0.93
18	36	27.00	0.91	138.4	622.7	566.7	8,406.3	0.96
	37	27.75	0.91	142.2	657.8	598.6	9,126.4	0.99
19	38	28.50	0.91	146.1	693.8	631.4	9,886.6	1.01
	39	29.25	0.91	149.9	730.8	665.0	10,687.8	1.04
20	40	30.00	0.90	153.8	768.8	691.9	11,531.3	1.07
	41	30.75	0.90	157.6	807.7	726.9	12,417.9	1.09
21	42	31.50	0.90	161.4	847.5	762.7	13,348.9	1.12
	43	32.25	0.90	165.3	888.4	799.6	14,325.2	1.15
22	44	33.00	0.89	169.1	930.2	827.9	15,348.1	1.17
	45	33.75	0.89	173.0	972.9	865.9	16,418.5	1.20
23	46	34.50	0.89	176.8	1,016.7	904.9	17,537.6	1.23
	47	35.25	0.89	180.7	1,061.4	944.6	18,706.4	1.25
24	48	36.00	0.88	184.5	1,107.0	974.2	19,926.0	1.28

$6\frac{3}{4}$ in. WIDTH

4	8	6.00	1.00	40.5	40.5	40.5	121.5	0.28
	9	6.75	1.00	45.6	51.3	51.3	173.0	0.32
5	10	7.50	1.00	50.6	63.3	63.3	237.3	0.35
	11	8.25	1.00	55.7	76.6	76.6	315.9	0.39
6	12	9.00	1.00	60.8	91.1	91.1	410.1	0.42
	13	9.75	1.00	65.8	106.9	106.9	521.4	0.46
7	14	10.50	1.00	70.9	124.0	124.0	651.2	0.49
	15	11.25	1.00	75.9	142.4	142.4	800.9	0.53
8	16	12.00	1.00	81.0	162.0	162.0	972.0	0.56
	17	12.75	0.99	86.1	182.9	181.1	1,165.9	0.60
9	18	13.50	0.99	91.1	205.0	202.9	1,384.0	0.63
	19	14.25	0.98	96.2	228.4	223.8	1,627.7	0.67

TABLE 2.16 (Continued)

Number of Laminations		Depth, d in.	Size Factor, C_F[a]	Area, A in.^{2}	Section Modulus, S in.^{3}	Adjusted Section Modulus, $S \times C_F$ in.^{3}	Moment of Inertia, I in.^{4}	Volume per Lineal Foot ft^3
$1\frac{1}{2}$ in.	$\frac{3}{4}$ in.							
10	20	15.00	0.98	101.3	253.1	248.0	1,898.4	0.70
	21	15.75	0.97	106.3	279.1	270.7	2,197.7	0.74
11	22	16.50	0.97	111.4	306.3	297.1	2,526.8	0.77
	23	17.25	0.96	116.4	334.8	321.4	2,887.3	0.81
12	24	18.00	0.96	121.5	364.5	349.9	3,280.5	0.84
	25	18.75	0.95	126.6	395.5	375.7	3,707.9	0.88
13	26	19.50	0.95	131.6	427.8	406.4	4,170.9	0.91
	27	20.25	0.94	136.7	461.3	433.6	4,670.9	0.95
14	28	21.00	0.94	141.8	496.1	466.3	5,209.3	0.98
	29	21.75	0.94	146.8	532.2	500.3	5,787.6	1.02
15	30	22.50	0.93	151.9	569.5	529.6	6,407.2	1.05
	31	23.25	0.93	156.9	608.1	565.5	7,069.5	1.09
16	32	24.00	0.93	162.0	648.0	602.4	7,776.0	1.12
	33	24.75	0.92	167.1	689.1	634.0	8,528.0	1.16
17	34	25.50	0.92	172.1	731.5	673.0	9,327.0	1.20
	35	26.25	0.92	177.2	775.2	713.2	10,174.4	1.23
18	36	27.00	0.91	182.3	820.1	746.3	11,071.7	1.27
	37	27.75	0.91	187.3	866.3	788.3	12,020.2	1.30
19	38	28.50	0.91	192.4	913.8	831.6	13,021.4	1.34
	39	29.25	0.91	197.4	962.5	875.9	14,076.7	1.37
20	40	30.00	0.90	202.5	1,012.5	911.2	15,187.5	1.41
	41	30.75	0.90	207.6	1,063.8	957.4	16,355.3	1.44
21	42	31.50	0.90	212.6	1,116.3	1,004.7	17,581.4	1.48
	43	32.25	0.90	217.7	1,170.1	1,053.1	18,867.4	1.51
22	44	33.00	0.89	222.8	1,225.1	1,090.3	20,214.6	1.55
	45	33.75	0.89	227.8	1,281.4	1,140.4	21,624.4	1.58
23	46	34.50	0.89	232.9	1,339.0	1,191.7	23,098.3	1.62
	47	35.25	0.89	237.9	1,397.9	1,244.1	24,637.7	1.65
24	48	36.00	0.88	243.0	1,458.0	1,283.0	26,244.0	1.69
	49	36.75	0.88	248.1	1,519.4	1,337.1	27,918.7	1.72
25	50	37.50	0.88	253.1	1,582.0	1,392.2	29,663.1	1.76
	51	38.25	0.88	258.2	1,645.9	1,448.4	31,478.7	1.79
26	52	39.00	0.88	263.3	1,711.1	1,505.8	33,366.9	1.83
	53	39.75	0.88	268.3	1,777.6	1,564.3	35,329.2	1.86
27	54	40.50	0.87	273.4	1,845.3	1,605.4	37,367.0	1.90
	55	41.25	0.87	278.4	1,914.3	1,665.4	39,481.6	1.93
28	56	42.00	0.87	283.5	1,984.5	1,726.5	41,674.5	1.97
	57	42.75	0.87	288.6	2,056.0	1,788.7	43,947.2	2.00
29	58	43.50	0.87	293.6	2,128.8	1,852.1	46,301.0	2.04
	59	44.25	0.87	298.7	2,202.8	1,916.4	48.737.4	2.07
30	60	45.00	0.86	303.8	2,278.1	1,959.2	51,257.8	2.11
	61	45.75	0.86	308.8	2,354.7	2,025.0	53,863.7	2.14
31	62	46.50	0.86	313.9	2,432.5	2,091.9	56,556.4	2.18
	63	47.25	0.86	318.9	2,511.6	2,160.0	59,337.3	2.21
32	64	48.00	0.86	324.0	2,592.0	2,229.1	62,208.0	2.25

$8\frac{3}{4}$ in. WIDTH

| 6 | 12 | 9.00 | 1.00 | 78.8 | 118.1 | 118.1 | 531.6 | 0.55 |
| | 13 | 9.75 | 1.00 | 85.3 | 138.6 | 138.6 | 675.8 | 0.59 |

TABLE 2.16 (Continued)

Number of Laminations $1\frac{1}{2}$ in.	$\frac{3}{4}$ in.	Depth, d in.	Size Factor, $C_F{}^a$	Area, A in.^{2}	Section Modulus, S in.^{3}	Adjusted Section Modulus, $S \times C_F$ in.^{3}	Moment of Inertia, I in.^{4}	Volume per Lineal Foot ft^3
7	14	10.50	1.00	91.9	160.8	160.8	844.1	0.64
	15	11.25	1.00	98.4	184.6	184.6	1,038.2	0.68
8	16	12.00	1.00	105.0	210.0	210.0	1,260.0	0.73
	17	12.75	0.99	111.6	237.1	234.7	1,511.3	0.77
9	18	13.50	0.99	118.1	265.8	263.1	1,794.0	0.82
	19	14.25	0.98	124.7	296.1	290.2	2,109.9	0.87
10	20	15.00	0.98	131.3	328.1	321.5	2,460.9	0.91
	21	15.75	0.97	137.8	361.8	350.9	2,848.8	0.96
11	22	16.50	0.97	144.4	397.0	385.1	3,275.5	1.00
	23	17.25	0.96	150.9	433.9	416.5	3,742.8	1.05
12	24	18.00	0.96	157.5	472.5	453.6	4,252.5	1.09
	25	18.75	0.95	164.1	512.7	487.1	4,806.5	1.14
13	26	19.50	0.95	170.6	554.5	526.8	5,406.7	1.18
	27	20.25	0.94	177.2	598.0	562.1	6,054.8	1.23
14	28	21.00	0.94	183.8	643.1	604.5	6,752.8	1.28
	29	21.75	0.94	190.3	689.9	648.5	7,502.5	1.32
15	30	22.50	0.93	196.9	738.3	686.6	8,305.7	1.37
	31	23.25	0.93	203.4	788.3	733.1	9,164.2	1.41
16	32	24.00	0.93	210.0	840.0	781.2	10,080.0	1.46
	33	24.75	0.92	216.6	893.3	821.8	11,054.8	1.50
17	34	25.50	0.92	223.1	948.3	872.4	12,090.6	1.55
	35	26.25	0.92	229.7	1,004.9	924.5	13,189.1	1.59
18	36	27.00	0.91	236.3	1,063.1	967.4	14,352.2	1.64
	37	27.75	0.91	242.8	1,123.0	1,021.9	15,581.7	1.69
19	38	28.50	0.91	249.4	1,184.5	1,077.9	16,879.6	1.73
	39	29.25	0.91	255.9	1,247.7	1,135.4	18,247.5	1.78
20	40	30.00	0.90	262.5	1,312.5	1,181.2	19,687.5	1.82
	41	30.75	0.90	269.1	1,378.9	1,241.0	21,201.3	1.87
21	42	31.50	0.90	275.6	1,447.0	1,302.3	22,790.7	1.91
	43	32.25	0.90	282.2	1,516.8	1,365.1	24,457.7	1.96
22	44	33.00	0.89	288.8	1,588.1	1,413.4	26,204.1	2.00
	45	33.75	0.89	295.3	1,661.1	1,478.4	28,031.6	2.05
23	46	34.50	0.89	301.9	1,735.8	1,544.9	29,942.2	2.10
	47	35.25	0.89	308.4	1,812.1	1,612.8	31,937.7	2.14
24	48	36.00	0.88	315.0	1,890.0	1,663.2	34,020.0	2.19
	49	36.75	0.88	321.6	1,969.6	1,733.2	36,190.9	2.23
25	50	37.50	0.88	328.1	2,050.8	1,804.7	38,452.2	2.28
	51	38.25	0.88	334.7	2,133,6	1,877.6	40,805.7	2.32
26	52	39.00	0.88	341.3	2,218.1	1,951.9	43,253.4	2.37
	53	39.75	0.88	347.8	2,304.3	2,027.8	45,797.1	2.42
27	54	40.50	0.87	354.4	2,392.0	2,081.0	48,438.6	2.46
	55	41.25	0.87	360.9	2,481.4	2,158.8	51,179.8	2.51
28	56	42.00	0.87	367.5	2,572.5	2,238.1	54,022.5	2.55
	57	42.75	0.87	374.1	2,665.2	2,318.7	56,968.6	2.60
29	58	43.50	0.87	380.6	2,759.5	2,400.8	60,019.8	2.64
	59	44.25	0.87	387.2	2,855.5	2,484.3	63,178.1	2.69
30	60	45.00	0.86	393.8	2,953.1	2,539.7	66,445.3	2.73
	61	45.75	0.86	400.3	3,052.4	2,625.1	69,823.3	2.78
31	62	46.50	0.86	406.9	3,153.3	2,711.8	73,313.8	2.83
	63	47.25	0.86	413.4	3,255.8	2,800.0	76,918.8	2.87

TABLE 2.16 (Continued)

Number of Laminations $1\frac{1}{2}$ in.	$\frac{3}{4}$ in.	Depth, d in.	Size Factor, $C_F{}^a$	Area, A in.²	Section Modulus, S in.³	Adjusted Section Modulus, $S \times C_F$ in.³	Moment of Inertia, I in.⁴	Volume per Lineal Foot ft³
32	64	48.00	0.86	420.0	3,360.0	2,889.6	80,640.0	2.92
	65	48.75	0.86	426.6	3,465.8	2,980.6	84,479.4	2.96
33	66	49.50	0.85	433.1	3,573.3	3,037.3	88,438.7	3.01
	67	50.25	0.85	439.7	3,682.4	3,130.0	92,519.9	3.05
34	68	51.00	0.85	446.3	3,793.1	3,224.1	96,724.7	3.10
	69	51.75	0.85	452.8	3,905.5	3,319.7	101,055.0	3.14
35	70	52.50	0.85	459.4	4,019.5	3,416.6	105,512.7	3.19
	71	53.25	0.85	465.9	4,135.2	3,514.9	110,099.6	3.24
36	72	54.00	0.85	472.5	4,252.5	3,614.6	114,817.5	3.28
	73	54.75	0.85	479.1	4,371.4	3,715.7	119,668.3	3.33
37	74	55.50	0.84	485.6	4,492.0	3,773.3	124,653.9	3.37
	75	56.25	0.84	492.2	4,614.3	3,876.0	129,776.0	3.42
38	76	57.00	0.84	498.8	4,738.1	3,980.0	135,036.6	3.46
	77	57.75	0.84	505.3	4,863.6	4,085.4	140,437.4	3.51
39	78	58.50	0.84	511.9	4,990.8	4,192.3	145,980.4	3.55
	79	59.25	0.84	518.4	5,119.6	4,300.5	151,667.3	3.60
40	80	60.00	0.84	525.0	5,250.0	4,410.0	157,500.0	3.65
	81	60.75	0.84	531.6	5,382.1	4,521.0	163,480.4	3.69
41	82	61.50	0.83	538.1	5,515.8	4,578.1	169,610.3	3.74
	83	62.25	0.83	544.7	5,651.1	4,690.4	175,891.5	3.78
42	84	63.00	0.83	551.3	5,788.1	4,804.1	182,326.0	3.83

$10\frac{3}{4}$ in WIDTH

Number of Laminations $1\frac{1}{2}$ in.	$\frac{3}{4}$ in.	Depth, d in.	Size Factor, $C_F{}^a$	Area, A in.²	Section Modulus, S in.³	Adjusted Section Modulus, $S \times C_F$ in.³	Moment of Inertia, I in.⁴	Volume per Lineal Foot ft³
7	14	10.50	1.00	112.9	197.5	197.5	1,037.0	0.78
	15	11.25	1.00	120.9	226.8	226.8	1,275.5	0.84
8	16	12.00	1.00	129.0	258.0	258.0	1,548.0	0.90
	17	12.75	0.99	137.1	291.3	288.4	1,856.8	0.95
9	18	13.50	0.99	145.1	326.5	323.2	2,204.1	1.01
	19	14.25	0.98	153.2	363.8	356.5	2,592.2	1.06
10	20	15.00	0.98	161.3	403.1	395.0	3,023.4	1.12
	21	15.75	0.97	169.3	444.4	431.1	3,500.0	1.18
11	22	16.50	0.97	177.4	487.8	473.2	4,024.2	1.23
	23	17.25	0.96	185.4	533.1	511.8	4,598.3	1.29
12	24	18.00	0.96	193.5	580.5	557.3	5,224.5	1.34
	25	18.75	0.95	201.6	629.9	598.4	5,905.2	1.40
13	26	19.50	0.95	209.6	681.3	647.2	6,642.5	1.46
	27	20.25	0.94	217.7	734.7	600.6	7,438.8	1.51
14	28	21.00	0.94	225.8	790.1	742.7	8,296.3	1.57
	29	21.75	0.94	233.8	847.6	796.7	9,217.3	1.62
15	30	22.50	0.93	241.9	907.0	843.5	10,204.1	1.68
	31	23.25	0.93	249.9	968.5	900.7	11,258.9	1.74
16	32	24.00	0.93	258.0	1,032.0	959.8	12,384.0	1.79
	33	24.75	0.92	266.1	1,097.5	1,009.7	13,581.7	1.85
17	34	25.50	0.92	274.1	1,165.0	1,071.8	14,854.1	1.90
	35	26.25	0.92	282.2	1,234.6	1,135.8	16,203.7	1.96
18	36	27.00	0.91	290.3	1,306.1	1,188.5	17,632.7	2.02
	37	27.75	0.91	298.3	1,379.7	1,255.5	19,143.3	2.07
19	38	28.50	0.91	306.4	1,455.3	1,324.3	20.737.8	2.13

TABLE 2.16 (Continued)

Number of Laminations 1½ in.	Number of Laminations ¾ in.	Depth, d in.	Size Factor, $C_F{}^a$	Area, A in.²	Section Modulus, S in.³	Adjusted Section Modulus, $S \times C_F$ in.³	Moment of Inertia, I in.⁴	Volume per Lineal Foot ft³
	39	29.25	0.91	314.4	1,532.9	1,394.9	22,418.4	2.18
20	40	30.00	0.90	322.5	1,612.5	1,451.2	24.187.5	2.24
	41	30.75	0.90	330.6	1,694.1	1,524.7	26,047.3	2.30
21	42	31.50	0.90	338.6	1,777.8	1,600.0	28,000.1	2.35
	43	32.25	0.90	346.7	1,863.4	1,677.1	30,048.1	2.41
22	44	33.00	0.89	354.8	1,951.1	1,736.5	32,193.6	2.46
	45	33.75	0.89	362.8	2,040.8	1,816.3	34,438.8	2.52
23	46	34.50	0.89	370.9	2,132.5	1,897.9	36,786.2	2.58
	47	35.25	0.89	378.9	2,226.3	1,981.4	39,237.8	2.63
24	48	36.00	0.88	387.0	2,322.0	2,043.4	41,796.0	2.69
	49	36.75	0.88	395.1	2,419.8	2,129.4	44,463.1	2.74
25	50	37.50	0.88	403.1	2,519.5	2,217.2	47,241.2	2.80
	51	38.25	0.88	411.2	2,621.3	2,306.7	50,132.8	2.86
26	52	39.00	0.88	419.3	2,725.1	2,398.1	53,139.9	2.91
	53	39.75	0.88	427.3	2,830.9	2,491.2	56,265.0	2.97
27	54	40.50	0.87	435.4	2,938.8	2,556.8	59,510.3	3.02
	55	41.25	0.87	443.4	3,048.6	2,652.3	62,878.1	3.08
28	56	42.00	0.87	451.5	3,160.5	2,749.6	66,370.5	3.14
	57	42.75	0.87	459.6	3,274.4	2,848.7	69,989.9	3.19
29	58	43.50	0.87	467.6	3,390.3	2,949.6	73,738.6	3.25
	59	44.25	0.87	475.7	3,508.2	3,052.1	77,618.8	3.30
30	60	45.00	0.86	483.8	3,628.1	3,120.2	81,632.8	3.36
	61	45.75	0.86	491.8	3,750.1	3,225.1	85,782.9	3.42
31	62	46.50	0.86	499.9	3,874.0	3,331.6	90,071.2	3.47
	63	47.25	0.86	507.9	4,000.0	3,440.0	94,500.2	3.53
32	64	48.00	0.86	516.0	4,128.0	3,550.1	99,072.0	3.58
	65	48.75	0.86	524.1	4,258.0	3,661.9	103,789.0	3.64
33	66	49.50	0.85	532.1	4,390.0	3,731.5	108,653.3	3.70
	67	50.25	0.85	540.2	4,524.1	3,845.5	113,667.3	3.75
34	68	51.00	0.85	548.3	4,660.1	3,961.1	118,833.2	3.81
	69	51.75	0.85	556.3	4,798.2	4,078.5	124,153.3	3.86
35	70	52.50	0.85	564.4	4,938.3	4,197.6	129,629.9	3.92
	71	53.25	0.85	572.4	5,080.4	4,318.3	135,265.2	3.98
36	72	54.00	0.85	580.5	5,224.5	4,440.8	141,061.5	4.03
	73	54.75	0.85	588.6	5,370.6	4,565.0	147,021.1	4.09
37	74	55.50	0.84	596.6	5,518.8	4,635.8	153,146.2	4.14
	75	56.25	0.84	604.7	5,668.9	4,761.9	159,439.1	4.20
38	76	57.00	0.84	612.8	5,821.1	4,889.7	165,902.1	4.26
	77	57.75	0.84	620.8	5,975.3	5,019.2	172,537.4	4.31
39	78	58.50	0.84	628.9	6,131.5	5,150.5	179,347.3	4.37
	79	59.25	0.84	636.9	6,289.8	5,283.4	186,334.1	4.42
40	80	60.00	0.84	645.0	6,450.0	5,418.0	193,500.0	4.48
	81	60.75	0.84	653.1	6,612.3	5,554.3	200,847.4	4.54
41	82	61.50	0.83	661.1	6,776.5	5,624.5	208,378.4	4.59
	83	62.25	0.83	669.2	6,942.8	5,762.5	216,095.3	4.65
42	84	63.00	0.83	677.3	7,111.1	5,902.2	224,000.5	4.70
	85	63.75	0.83	685.3	7,281.4	6,043.6	232,096.1	4.76
43	86	64.50	0.83	693.4	7,453.8	6,186.6	240,384.5	4.82
	87	65.25	0.83	701.4	7,628.1	6,331.3	248,867.9	4.87

TABLE 2.16 (Continued)

Number of Laminations		Depth, d	Size Factor, $C_F{}^a$	Area, A	Section Modulus, S	Adjusted Section Modulus, $S \times C_F$	Moment of Inertia, I	Volume per Lineal Foot
1½ in.	¾ in.	in.		in.²	in.³	in.³	in.⁴	ft³
44	88	66.00	0.83	709.5	7,804.5	6,477.7	257,548.5	4.93
	89	66.75	0.83	717.6	7,982.9	6,625.8	266,428.8	4.98
45	90	67.50	0.83	725.6	8,163.3	6,775.5	275,510.8	5.04
	91	68.25	0.82	733.7	8,345.7	6,843.5	284,796.9	5.10
46	92	69.00	0.82	741.8	8,530.1	6,994.7	294,289.3	5.15
	93	69.75	0.82	749.8	8,716.6	7,147.6	303,990.5	5.21
47	94	70.50	0.82	757.9	8,905.0	7,302.1	313,902.4	5.26
	95	71.25	0.82	765.9	9,095.5	7,458.3	324,027.5	5.32
48	96	72.00	0.82	774.0	9,288.0	7,616.2	334,368.0	5.38
	97	72.75	0.82	782.1	9,482.5	7,775.6	344,926.3	5.43
49	98	73.50	0.82	790.1	9,679.0	7,936.8	355,704.5	5.49
	99	74.25	0.82	798.2	9,877.6	8,099.6	366,704.8	5.54
50	100	75.00	0.82	806.3	10,078.1	8,264.0	377,929.7	5.60

12¼ in. WIDTH

Number of Laminations		Depth, d	Size Factor, $C_F{}^a$	Area, A	Section Modulus, S	Adjusted Section Modulus, $S \times C_F$	Moment of Inertia, I	Volume per Lineal Foot
8	16	12.00	1.00	147.0	294.0	294.0	1,764.0	1.02
	17	12.75	0.99	156.2	331.9	328.6	2,115.8	1.08
9	18	13.50	0.99	165.4	372.1	368.4	2,511.6	1.15
	19	14.25	0.98	174.6	414.6	406.3	2,953.8	1.21
10	20	15.00	0.98	183.8	459.4	450.2	3,445.3	1.28
	21	15.75	0.97	192.9	506.4	491.2	3,988.6	1.34
11	22	16.50	0.97	202.1	555.8	539.3	4,585.7	1.40
	23	17.25	0.96	211.3	607.5	583.2	5,239.7	1.47
12	24	18.00	0.96	220.5	661.5	635.0	5,953.5	1.53
	25	18.75	0.95	229.7	717.7	681.8	6,728.9	1.60
13	26	19.50	0.95	238.9	776.3	737.5	7,569.4	1.66
	27	20.25	0.94	248.1	837.2	787.0	8,476.5	1.72
14	28	21.00	0.94	257.2	900.4	846.4	9,453.9	1.79
	29	21.75	0.94	266.4	965.8	907.8	10,503.1	1.85
15	30	22.50	0.93	275.6	1,033.6	961.2	11,627.9	1.91
	31	23.25	0.93	284.8	1,103.6	1,026.3	12,829.5	1.97
16	32	24.00	0.93	294.0	1,176.0	1,093.7	14,112.0	2.04
	33	24.75	0.92	303.2	1,250.6	1,150.5	15,476.3	2.10
17	34	25.50	0.92	312.4	1,327.6	1,221.4	16,926.8	2.17
	35	26.25	0.92	321.6	1,406.8	1,294.3	18,464.1	2.23
18	36	27.00	0.91	330.8	1,488.4	1,354.4	20,093.1	2.30
	37	27.75	0.91	339.9	1,572.2	1,430.7	21,813.7	2.36
19	38	28.50	0.91	349.1	1,658.3	1,509.0	23,631.4	2.42
	39	29.25	0.91	358.3	1,746.7	1,589.5	25,545.7	2.49
20	40	30.00	0.90	367.5	1,837.5	1,653.7	27,562.5	2.55
	41	30.75	0.90	376.7	1,930.5	1,737.4	29,680.8	2.62
21	42	31.50	0.90	385.9	2,025.8	1,823.2	31,907.0	2.68
	43	32.25	0.90	395.1	2,123.4	1,911.1	34,239.7	2.74
22	44	33.00	0.89	404.2	2,223.4	1,978.8	36,685.7	2.81
	45	33.75	0.89	413.4	2,325.6	2,069.8	39,244.1	2.87
23	46	34.50	0.89	422.6	2,430.1	2,162.8	41,919.1	2.93
	47	35.25	0.89	431.8	2,536.9	2,257.8	44,712.7	3.00
24	48	36.00	0.88	441.0	2,646.0	2,328.5	47,628.0	3.06

TABLE 2.16 (Continued)

Number of Laminations 1½ in.	¾ in.	Depth, d in.	Size Factor, $C_F{}^a$	Area, A in.²	Section Modulus, S in.³	Adjusted Section Modulus, $S \times C_F$ in.³	Moment of Inertia, I in.⁴	Volume per Lineal Foot ft³
	49	36.75	0.88	450.2	2,757.4	2,426.5	50,667.0	3.13
25	50	37.50	0.88	459.4	2,871.1	2,526.6	53,833.0	3.19
	51	38.25	0.88	468.6	2,987.1	2,628.6	57,127.8	3.25
26	52	39.00	0.88	477.8	3,105.4	2,732.7	60,554.8	3.32
	53	39.75	0.88	486.9	3,226.0	2,838.9	64,115.8	3.38
27	54	40.50	0.87	496.1	3,348.8	2,913.5	67,814.1	3.45
	55	41.25	0.87	505.3	3,474.0	3,022.4	71,651.5	3.51
28	56	42.00	0.87	514.5	3,601.5	3,133.3	75,631.5	3.57
	57	42.75	0.87	523.7	3,731.3	3,246.2	79,755.7	3.64
29	58	43.50	0.87	532.9	3,863.3	3,361.1	84,027.7	3.70
	59	44.25	0.87	542.1	3,997.7	3,478.0	88,449.1	3.76
30	60	45.00	0.86	551.2	4,134.4	3,555.6	93,023.4	3.83
	61	45.75	0.86	560.4	4,273.3	3,675.0	97,752.2	3.89
31	62	46.50	0.86	569.6	4,414.6	3,796.6	102,639.3	3.96
	63	47.25	0.86	578.8	4,558.1	3,920.0	107,685.9	4.02
32	64	48.00	0.86	588.0	4,704.0	4,045.4	112,896.0	4.08
	65	48.75	0.86	597.2	4,852.1	4,172.8	118,270.7	4.15
33	66	49.50	0.85	606.4	5,002.6	4,252.2	123,814.2	4.21
	67	50.25	0.85	615.6	5,155.3	4,382.0	129,527.4	4.27
34	68	51.00	0.85	624.8	5,310.4	4,513.8	135,414.6	4.34
	69	51.75	0.85	633.9	5,467.7	4,647.5	141,476.6	4.40
35	70	52.50	0.85	643.1	5,627.3	4,783.2	147,717.8	4.47
	71	53.25	0.85	652.3	5,789.3	4,920.9	154,138.9	4.53
36	72	54.00	0.85	661.5	5,953.5	5,060.5	160,744.5	4.59
	73	54.75	0.85	670.7	6,120.0	5,202.0	167,535.1	4.66
37	74	55.50	0.84	679.9	6,288.8	5,282.6	174,515.4	4.72
	75	56.25	0.84	689.1	6,459.9	5,426.3	181,685.8	4.79
38	76	57.00	0.84	698.2	6,633.4	5,572.1	189,051.2	4.85
	77	57.75	0.84	707.4	6,809.1	5,719.6	196,611.7	4.91
39	78	58.50	0.84	716.6	6,987.1	5,869.2	204,372.5	4.98
	79	59.25	0.84	725.8	7,167.4	6,020.6	212,333.5	5.04
40	80	60.00	0.84	735.0	7,350.0	6,174.0	220,500.0	5.10
	81	60.75	0.84	744.2	7,534.9	6,329.3	228,871.8	5.17
41	82	61.50	0.83	753.4	7,722.1	6,409.3	237,454.4	5.23
	83	62.25	0.83	762.6	7,911.6	6,566.6	246,247.3	5.30
42	84	63.00	0.83	771.8	8,103.4	6,725.8	255,256.3	5.36
	85	63.75	0.83	780.9	8,297.4	6,886.8	264,480.7	5.42
43	86	64.50	0.83	790.1	8,493.8	7,049.8	273,926.5	5.49
	87	65.25	0.83	799.3	8,692.5	7,214.8	283,592.7	5.55
44	88	66.00	0.83	808.5	8,893.5	7,381.6	293,485.5	5.61
	89	66.75	0.83	817.7	9,096.7	7,550.3	303,603.8	5.68
45	90	67.50	0.83	826.9	9,302.3	7,720.9	313,954.1	5.74
	91	68.25	0.82	836.1	9,510.2	7,798.4	324,534.9	5.81
46	92	69.00	0.82	845.2	9,720.4	7,970.7	335,352.9	5.87
	93	69.75	0.82	854.4	9,932.8	8,144.9	346,406.5	5.93
47	94	70.50	0.82	863.6	10,147.6	8,321.0	357,702.7	6.00
	95	71.25	0.82	872.8	10,364.6	8,499.0	369,239.4	6.06
48	96	72.00	0.82	882.0	10,584.0	8,678.9	381,024.0	6.12
	97	72.75	0.82	891.2	10,805.6	8,860.6	393,054.2	6.19

TABLE 2.16 (Continued)

Number of Laminations		Depth, d in.	Size Factor, $C_F{}^a$	Area, A in.^{2}	Section Modulus, S in.^{3}	Adjusted Section Modulus, $S \times C_F$ in.^{3}	Moment of Inertia, I in.^{4}	Volume per Lineal Foot ft^3
$1\frac{1}{2}$ in.	$\frac{3}{4}$ in.							
49	98	73.50	0.82	900.4	11,029.6	9,044.3	405,337.6	6.25
	99	74.25	0.82	909.6	11,255.8	9,229.8	417,871.5	6.32
50	100	75.00	0.82	918.8	11,484.4	9,417.2	430,664.1	6.38
	101	75.75	0.82	927.9	11,715.2	9,606.5	443,712.2	6.44
51	102	76.50	0.81	937.1	11,948.3	9,678.1	457,024.1	6.51
	103	77.25	0.81	946.3	12,183.7	9,868.8	470,596.7	6.57
52	104	78.00	0.81	955.5	12,421.5	10,061.4	484,438.5	6.64
	105	78.75	0.81	964.7	12,661.5	10,255.8	498,545.9	6.70
53	106	79.50	0.81	973.9	12,903.8	10,452.1	512,927.8	6.76
	107	80.25	0.81	983.1	13,148.4	10,650.2	527,580.3	6.83
54	108	81.00	0.81	992.2	13,395.4	10,850.3	542,512.7	6.89
	109	81.75	0.81	1,001.4	13,644.5	11,052.0	557,720.6	6.95
55	110	82.50	0.81	1,010.6	13,896.1	11,255.8	573,213.9	7.02
	111	83.25	0.81	1,019.8	14,149.9	11,461.4	588,987.6	7.08
56	112	84.00	0.81	1,029.0	14,406.0	11,668.9	605,052.0	7.15

$14\frac{1}{4}$ in. WIDTH

Number of Laminations		Depth, d in.	Size Factor, $C_F{}^a$	Area, A in.^{2}	Section Modulus, S in.^{3}	Adjusted Section Modulus, $S \times C_F$ in.^{3}	Moment of Inertia, I in.^{4}	Volume per Lineal Foot ft^3
9	18	13.50	0.99	192.4	432.8	428.5	2,921.7	1.34
	19	14.25	0.98	203.1	482.3	472.6	3,436.2	1.41
10	20	15.00	0.98	213.8	534.4	523.7	4,007.8	1.48
	21	15.75	0.97	224.4	589.1	571.4	4,639.5	1.56
11	22	16.50	0.97	235.1	646.6	627.2	5,334.4	1.63
	23	17.25	0.96	245.8	706.7	678.4	6,095.4	1.71
12	24	18.00	0.96	256.5	769.5	738.7	6,925.5	1.78
	25	18.75	0.95	267.2	835.0	793.2	7,827.8	1.86
13	26	19.50	0.95	277.9	903.1	857.9	8,805.2	1.93
	27	20.25	0.94	288.6	973.9	915.5	9,860.7	2.00
14	28	21.00	0.94	299.3	1,047.4	984.6	10,997.4	2.08
	29	21.75	0.94	309.9	1,123.5	1,056.1	12,218.3	2.15
15	30	22.50	0.93	320.6	1,202.3	1,118.1	13,526.4	2.23
	31	23.25	0.93	331.3	1,283.8	1,193.9	14,924.6	2.30
16	32	24.00	0.93	342.0	1,368.0	1,272.2	16,416.0	2.38
	33	24.75	0.92	352.7	1,454.8	1,338.4	18,003.6	2.45
17	34	25.50	0.92	363.4	1,544.3	1,420.8	19,690.4	2.52
	35	26.25	0.92	374.1	1,636.5	1,505.6	21,479.4	2.60
18	36	27.00	0.91	384.8	1,731.4	1,575.6	23,373.6	2.67
	37	27.75	0.91	395.4	1,828.9	1.664.3	25,376.0	2.75
19	38	28.50	0.91	406.1	1,929.1	1,755.5	27,489.6	2.82
	39	29.25	0.91	416.8	2,032.0	1,849.1	29,717.4	2.89
20	40	30.00	0.90	427.5	2,137.5	1,923.7	32,062.5	2.97
	41	30.75	0.90	438.2	2,245.7	2,021.1	34,527.8	3.04
21	42	31.50	0.90	448.9	2,356.6	2,120.9	37,116.4	3.12
	43	32.25	0.90	459.6	2,470.1	2,223.1	39,831.1	3.19
22	44	33.00	0.89	470.3	2,586.4	2,301.9	42,675.2	3.27
	45	33.75	0.89	480.9	2,705.3	2,407.7	45,651.5	3.34
23	46	34.50	0.89	491.6	2,826.8	2,515.8	48,763.1	3.41
	47	35.25	0.89	502.3	2,951.1	2,626.5	52,012.9	3.49
24	48	36.00	0.88	513.0	3,078.0	2,708.6	55,404.0	3.56

TABLE 2.16 (Continued)

Number of Laminations $1\frac{1}{2}$ in.	$\frac{3}{4}$ in.	Depth, d in.	Size Factor, $C_F{}^a$	Area, A in.²	Section Modulus, S in.³	Adjusted Section Modulus, $S \times C_F$ in.³	Moment of Inertia, I in.⁴	Volume per Lineal Foot ft³
	49	36.75	0.88	523.7	3,207.6	2,822.7	58,939.4	3.64
25	50	37.50	0.88	534.4	3,339.8	2,939.0	62,622.1	3.71
	51	38.25	0.88	545.1	3,474.8	3,057.8	66,455.0	3.79
26	52	39.00	0.88	555.8	3,612.4	3,178.9	70,441.3	3,86
	53	39.75	0.88	566.4	3,752.6	3,302.3	74,583.9	3.93
27	54	40.50	0.87	577.1	3,895.6	3,339.2	78,885.8	4.01
	55	41.25	0.87	587.8	4,041.2	3,515.8	83,350.0	4.08
28	56	42.00	0.87	598.5	4,189.5	3,644.9	87,979.5	4.16
	57	42.75	0.87	609.2	4,340.5	3,776.2	92,777.4	4.23
29	58	43.50	0.87	619.9	4,494.1	3,909.9	97,746.5	4.30
	59	44.25	0.87	630.6	4,650.4	4,045.8	102,890.1	4.38
30	60	45.00	0.86	641.3	4,809.4	4,136.1	108,211.0	4.45
	61	45.75	0.86	651.9	4,971.0	4,275.1	113,712.2	4.53
31	62	46.50	0.86	662.6	5,135.3	4,416.4	119,396.7	4.60
	63	47.25	0.86	673.3	5,302.3	4,560.0	125,267.7	4.68
32	64	48.00	0.86	684.0	5,472.0	4,705.9	131,328.0	4.75
	65	48.75	0.86	694.7	5,644.3	4,854.1	137,580.7	4.82
33	66	49.50	0.85	705.4	5,819.3	4,946.4	144,028.8	4.90
	67	50.25	0.85	716.1	5,997.0	5,097.4	150,675.2	4.97
34	68	51.00	0.85	726.8	6,177.4	5,250.8	157,523.1	5.05
	69	51.75	0.85	737.4	6,360.4	5,406.3	164,575.3	5.12
35	70	52.50	0.85	748.1	6,546.1	5,564.2	171,835.0	5.20
	71	53.25	0.85	758.8	6,734.5	5,724.3	179,305.0	5.27
36	72	54.00	0.85	769.5	6,925.5	5,886.7	186,988.5	5.34
	73	54.75	0.85	780.2	7,119.2	6,051.3	194,888.4	5.42
37	74	55.50	0.84	790.9	7,315.6	6,145.1	203,007.7	5.49
	75	56.25	0.84	801.6	7,514.6	6,312.3	211,349.5	5.57
38	76	57.00	0.84	812.3	7,716.4	6,481.8	219,916.7	5.64
	77	57.75	0.84	822.9	7,920.8	6,653.5	228,712.4	5.71
39	78	58.50	0.84	833.6	8,127.8	6,827.3	237,739.5	5.79
	79	59.25	0.84	844.3	8,337.6	7,003.6	247,001.0	5.86
40	80	60.00	0.84	855.0	8,550.0	7,182.0	256,500.0	5.94
	81	60.75	0.84	865.7	8,765.1	7,362.7	266,239.5	6.01
41	82	61.50	0.83	876.4	8,982.8	7,455.7	276,222.5	6.09
	83	62.25	0.83	887.1	9,203.3	7,638.7	286,451.9	6.16
42	84	63.00	0.83	897.8	9,426.4	7,823.9	296,930.8	6.23
	85	63.75	0.83	908.4	9,652.1	8,011.2	307,662.3	6.31
43	86	64.50	0.83	919.1	9,880.6	8,200.9	318,649.2	6.38
	87	65.25	0.83	929.8	10,111.7	8,392.7	329,894.6	6.46
44	88	66.00	0.83	940.5	10,345.5	8,586.7	341,401.5	6.53
	89	66.75	0.83	951.2	10,582.0	8,783.1	353,173.0	6.61
45	90	67.50	0.83	961.9	10,821.1	8,981.5	365,212.0	6.68
	91	68.25	0.82	972.6	11,062.9	9,071.6	377,521.5	6.75
46	92	69.00	0.82	983.3	11,307.4	9,272.1	390,104.5	6.83
	93	69.75	0.82	993.9	11,554.5	9,474.7	402,964.0	6.90
47	94	70.50	0.82	1,004.6	11,804.3	9,679.5	416,103.1	6.98
	95	71.25	0.82	1,015.3	12,056.8	9,886.6	429,524.8	7.05
48	96	72.00	0.82	1,026.0	12,312.0	10,095.8	443,232.0	7.12
	97	72.75	0.82	1,036.7	12,569.8	10,307.2	457,227.8	7.20

TABLE 2.16 (Continued)

Number of Laminations 1½ in.	¾ in.	Depth, d in.	Size Factor, $C_F{}^a$	Area, A in.²	Section Modulus, S in.³	Adjusted Section Modulus, $S \times C_F$ in.³	Moment of Inertia, I in.⁴	Volume per Lineal Foot ft³
49	98	73.50	0.82	1.047.4	12,830.3	10,520.8	471,515.1	7.27
	99	74.25	0.82	1,058.1	13,093.5	10,736.7	486,097.1	7.35
50	100	75.00	0.82	1,068.8	13,359.4	10,954.7	500,976.6	7.42
	101	75.75	0.82	1,079.4	13,627.9	11,174.9	516,156.7	7.50
51	102	76.50	0.81	1,090.1	13,899.1	11,258.3	531,640.5	7.57
	103	77.25	0.81	1,100.8	14,173.0	11,480.1	547,430.7	7.64
52	104	78.00	0.81	1,111.5	14,449.5	11,704.1	563,530.6	7.72
	105	78.75	0.81	1,122.2	14,728.7	11,930.2	579,943.1	7.79
53	106	79.50	0.81	1,132.9	15,010.6	12,158.6	596,671.2	7.87
	107	80.25	0.81	1,143.6	15,295.1	12,389.0	613,718.0	7.94
54	108	81.00	0.81	1,154.3	15,582.4	12,621.7	631,086.2	8.02
	109	81.75	0.81	1,164.9	15,872.3	12,856.6	648,779.2	8.09
55	110	82.50	0.81	1,175.6	16,164.8	13,093.5	666,799.8	8.16
	111	83.25	0.81	1,186.3	16,460.1	13,332.7	685,151.2	8.24
56	112	84.00	0.81	1,197.0	16,758.0	13,574.0	703,836.1	8.31
	113	84.75	0.80	1,207.7	17,058.6	13,646.9	722,857.7	8.39
57	114	85.50	0.80	1,218.4	17,361.8	13,889.4	742,218.8	8.46
	115	86.25	0.80	1,229.1	17,667.8	14,134.2	761,922.8	8.54
58	116	87.00	0.80	1,239.8	17,976.4	14.381.1	781,972.3	8.61
	117	87.75	0.80	1,250.4	18,287.6	14,630.1	802,370.6	8.68
59	118	88.50	0.80	1,261.1	18,601.6	14,881.3	823,120.6	8.76
	119	89.25	0.80	1,271.8	18,918.2	15,134.6	844,225.2	8.83
60	120	90.00	0.80	1,282.5	19,237.5	15,390.0	865,687.6	8.91
	121	90.75	0.80	1,293.2	19,559.5	15,647.6	887,510.6	8.98
61	122	91.50	0.80	1,303.9	19,884.1	15,907.3	909,697.3	9.05
	123	92.25	0.80	1,314.6	20,211.4	16,169.1	932,250.8	9.13
62	124	93.00	0.80	1,325.3	20,541.4	16,433.1	955,174.0	9.20
	125	93.75	0.80	1,335.9	20,874.0	16,699.2	978,470.0	9.28
63	126	94.50	0.80	1,346.6	21,209.3	16,967.4	1,002,141.6	9.35
	127	95.25	0.79	1,357.3	21,547.3	17,022.4	1,026,192.0	9.43
64	128	96.00	0.79	1,368.0	21,888.0	17,291.5	1,050,624.2	9.50

^{a}Applicable to simple span bending members, uniformly loaded with an L/d ratio of 21. For other conditions of loading, see page **2-37**.

The industry standard finished widths for glued laminated members correspond to the following nominal widths (which result from nominal lumber widths with an allowance for drying and surfacing).

Nominal Width of Laminating Stock, in.	Net Finished Width of Member, in.
3	2¼
4	3⅛
6	5⅛
8	6¾
10	8¾
12	10¾
14	12¼
16	14¼

Standard widths are most economical because they represent the maximum width normally obtained from the lumber stock used in laminating. Other widths may be used to meet special requirements.

Laminations may be comprised of two pieces side by side when members wider than the lumber stock available are needed. This is generally the case for widths exceeding 12 in. (nominal). Edge joints in adjacent laminations in this type of member must be staggered laterally at least the net thickness of the lamination. If a bending member is horizontally laminated (load acts normal to wide face of lamination), these edge joints need not be edge glued unless torsion is a significant design consideration. However, if the member is vertically laminated (load acts normal to the edge of lamination), edge gluing is required.

Sawn Lumber and Timber

Table 2.17 lists sizes and properties of sections for sawn lumber and timber and includes values for net cross-sectional area, section modulus, moment of inertia, weight per lineal foot, and board measure per lineal foot.

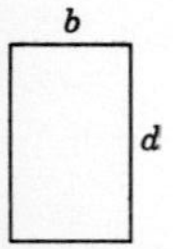

TABLE 2.17

SECTION PROPERTIES FOR SAWN LUMBER AND TIMBER[a,b]

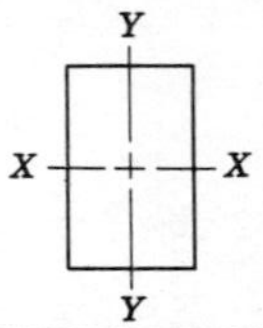

Nominal Size $b \times d$ in.	Standard Dressed Size (S4S) $b \times d$ in.	Area of Section A in.²	X-X Axis Moment of Inertia I in.⁴	X-X Axis Section Modulus S in.³	Y-Y Axis Moment of Inertia I in.⁴	Y-Y Axis Section Modulus S in.³	Board Measure per Lineal Foot	25 pcf	30 pcf	35 pcf	40 pcf	45 pcf	50 pcf
1 × 3	¾ × 2½	1.875	0.977	0.781	0.088	0.234	¼	0.326	0.391	0.456	0.521	0.586	0.651
1 × 4	¾ × 3½	2.625	2.680	1.531	0.123	0.328	⅓	0.456	0.547	0.638	0.729	0.820	0.911
1 × 6	¾ × 5½	4.125	10.398	3.781	0.193	0.516	½	0.716	0.859	1.003	1.146	1.289	1.432
1 × 8	¾ × 7¼	5.438	23.817	6.570	0.255	0.680	⅔	0.944	1.133	1.322	1.510	1.699	1.888
1 × 10	¾ × 9¼	6.938	49.466	10.695	0.325	0.867	⅚	1.204	1.445	1.686	1.927	2.168	2.409
1 × 12	¾ × 11¼	8.438	88.989	15.820	0.396	1.055	1	1.465	1.758	2.051	2.344	2.637	2.930
2 × 3[a]	1½ × 2½	3.750	1.953	1.563	0.703	0.938	½	0.651	0.781	0.911	1.042	1.172	1.302
2 × 4[a]	1½ × 3½	5.250	5.359	3.063	0.984	1.313	⅔	0.911	1.094	1.276	1.458	1.641	1.823
2 × 6[a]	1½ × 5½	8.250	20.797	7.563	1.547	2.063	1	1.432	1.719	2.005	2.292	2.578	2.865
2 × 8[a]	1½ × 7¼	10.875	47.635	13.141	2.039	2.719	1⅓	1.888	2.266	2.643	3.021	3.398	3.776
2 × 10[a]	1½ × 9¼	13.875	98.932	21.391	2.602	3.469	1⅔	2.409	2.891	3.372	3.854	4.336	4.818
2 × 12[a]	1½ × 11¼	16.875	177.979	31.641	3.164	4.219	2	2.930	3.516	4.102	4.688	5.273	5.859
2 × 14[a]	1½ × 13¼	19.875	290.775	43.891	3.727	4.969	2⅓	3.451	4.141	4.831	5.521	6.211	6.901
3 × 4	2½ × 3½	8.750	8.932	5.104	4.557	3.646	1	1.519	1.823	2.127	2.431	2.734	3.038
3 × 6	2½ × 5½	13.750	34.661	12.604	7.161	5.729	1½	2.387	2.865	3.342	3.819	4.297	4.774
3 × 8	2½ × 7¼	18.125	79.391	21.901	9.440	7.552	2	3.147	3.776	4.405	5.035	5.664	6.293
3 × 10	2½ × 9¼	23.125	164.886	35.651	12.044	9.635	2½	4.015	4.818	5.621	6.424	7.227	8.030
3 × 12	2½ × 11¼	28.125	296.631	52.734	14.648	11.719	3	4.883	5.859	6.836	7.813	8.789	9.766
3 × 14	2½ × 13¼	33.125	484.625	73.151	17.253	13.802	3½	5.751	6.901	8.051	9.201	10.352	11.502
3 × 16	2½ × 15¼	38.125	738.870	96.901	19.857	15.885	4	6.619	7.943	9.266	10.590	11.914	13.238

Weight in pounds per linear foot of piece when weight of wood per cubic foot equals:

Nominal	Dressed												
4 × 4	3½ × 3½	12.250	12.505	7.146	12.505	7.146	1⅓	2.127	2.552	2.977	3.403	3.828	4.253
4 × 6	3½ × 5½	19.250	48.526	17.646	19.651	11.229	2	3.342	4.010	4.679	5.347	6.016	6.684
4 × 8	3½ × 7¼	25.375	111.148	30.661	25.904	14.802	2⅔	4.405	5.286	6.168	7.049	7.930	8.811
4 × 10	3½ × 9¼	32.375	230.840	49.911	33.049	18.885	3⅓	5.621	6.745	7.869	8.933	10.117	11.241
4 × 12	3½ × 11¼	39.375	415.283	73.828	40.195	22.969	4	6.836	8.203	9.570	10.938	12.305	13.672
4 × 14	3½ × 13¼	46.375	678.475	102.411	47.340	27.052	4⅔	8.047	9.657	11.266	12.877	14.485	16.094
4 × 16	3½ × 15¼	53.375	1,034.418	135.661	54.487	31.135	5⅓	9.267	11.121	12.975	14.828	16.682	18.536
6 × 6	5½ × 5½	30.250	76.255	27.729	76.255	27.729	3	5.252	6.302	7.352	8.403	9.453	10.503
6 × 8	5½ × 7½	41.250	193.359	51.563	103.984	37.813	4	7.161	8.594	10.026	11.458	12.891	14.323
6 × 10	5½ × 9½	52.250	392.963	82.729	131.714	47.896	5	9.071	10.885	12.700	14.514	16.328	18.142
6 × 12	5½ × 11½	63.250	697.068	121.229	159.443	57.979	6	10.981	13.177	15.373	17.569	19.766	21.962
6 × 14	5½ × 13½	74.250	1,127.672	167.063	187.172	68.063	7	12.891	15.469	18.047	20.625	23.203	25.781
6 × 16	5½ × 15½	85.250	1,706.776	220.229	214.901	78.146	8	14.800	17.760	20.720	23.681	26.641	29.601
6 × 18	5½ × 17½	96.250	2,456.380	280.729	242.630	88.229	9	16.710	20.052	23.394	26.736	30.078	33.420
6 × 20	5½ × 19½	107.250	3,398.484	348.563	270.359	98.313	10	18.620	22.344	26.068	29.792	33.516	37.240
6 × 22	5½ × 21½	118.250	4,555.086	423.729	298.088	108.396	11	20.530	24.635	28.741	32.847	36.953	41.059
6 × 24	5½ × 23½	129.250	5,948.191	506.229	325.818	118.479	12	22.439	26.927	31.415	35.903	40.391	44.878
8 × 8	7½ × 7½	56.250	263.672	70.313	263.672	70.313	5⅓	9.766	11.719	13.672	15.625	17.578	19.531
8 × 10	7½ × 9½	71.250	535.859	112.813	333.984	89.063	6⅔	12.370	14.844	17.318	19.792	22.266	24.740
8 × 12	7½ × 11½	86.250	950.547	165.313	404.297	107.813	8	14.974	17.969	20.964	23.958	26.953	29.948
8 × 14	7½ × 13½	101.250	1,537.734	227.813	474.609	126.563	9⅓	17.578	21.094	24.609	28.125	31.641	35.156
8 × 16	7½ × 15½	116.250	2,327.422	300.313	544.922	143.313	10⅔	20.182	24.219	28.255	32.292	36.328	40.365
8 × 18	7½ × 17½	131.250	3,349.609	382.813	615.234	164.063	12	22.786	27.344	31.901	36.458	41.016	45.573
8 × 20	7½ × 19½	146.250	4,634.297	475.313	684.547	182.813	13⅓	25.391	30.469	35.547	40.625	45.703	50.781
8 × 22	7½ × 21½	161.250	6,211.484	577.813	755.859	201.563	14⅔	27.995	33.594	39.193	44.792	50.391	55.990
8 × 24	7½ × 23½	176.250	8,111.172	690.313	826.172	220.313	16	30.599	36.719	42.839	48.958	55.078	61.198
10 × 10	9½ × 9½	90.250	678.755	142.896	678.755	142.896	8⅓	15.668	18.802	21.936	25.069	28.203	31.337
10 × 12	9½ × 11½	109.250	1,204.026	209.396	821.651	172.979	10	18.967	22.760	26.554	30.347	34.141	37.934
10 × 14	9½ × 13½	128.250	1,947.797	288.563	964.547	203.063	11⅔	22.266	26.719	31.172	35.625	40.078	44.531
10 × 16	9½ × 15½	147.250	2,948.068	380.396	1,107.443	233.146	13⅓	25.564	30.677	35.790	40.903	46.016	51.128
10 × 18	9½ × 17½	166.250	4,242.836	484.896	1,250.338	263.229	15	28.863	34.635	40.408	46.181	51.953	57.726

TABLE 2.17 (Continued)

Nominal Size $b \times d$ in.	Standard Dressed Size (S4S) $b \times d$ in.	Area of Section A in.^{2}	X-X Axis Moment of Inertia I in.^{4}	X-X Axis Section Modulus S in.^{3}	Y-Y Axis Moment of Inertia I in.^{4}	Y-Y Axis Section Modulus S in.^{3}	Board Measure per Lineal Foot	Weight in pounds per linear foot of piece when weight of wood per cubic foot equals: 25 pcf	30 pcf	35 pcf	40 pcf	45 pcf	50 pcf
10 × 20	9½ × 19½	185.250	5,870.109	602.063	1,393.234	293.313	16⅔	32.161	38.594	45.026	51.458	57.891	64.323
10 × 22	9½ × 21½	204.250	7,867.879	731.896	1,536.130	323.396	18⅓	35.460	42.552	49.644	56.736	63.828	70.920
10 × 24	9½ × 23½	223.250	10,274.148	874.396	1,679.026	353.479	20	38.759	46.510	54.262	62.014	69.766	77.517
12 × 12	11½ × 11½	132.250	1,457.505	253.479	1,457.505	253.479	12	22.960	27.552	32.144	36.736	41.328	45.920
12 × 14	11½ × 13½	155.250	2,357.859	349.313	1,710.984	297.563	14	26.953	32.344	37.734	43.125	48.516	53.906
12 × 16	11½ × 15½	178.250	3,568.713	460.479	1,964.463	341.646	16	30.946	37.135	43.325	49.514	55.703	61.892
12 × 18	11½ × 17½	201.250	5,136.066	586.979	2,217.943	385.729	18	34.939	41.927	48.915	55.903	62.891	69.878
12 × 20	11½ × 19½	224.250	7,105.922	728.813	2,471.422	429.813	20	38.932	46.719	54.505	62.292	70.078	77.865
12 × 22	11½ × 21½	247.250	9,524.273	885.979	2,724.901	473.896	22	42.925	51.510	60.095	68.681	77.266	85.851
12 × 24	11½ × 23½	270.250	10,274.148	1058.479	2,978.380	517.979	24	46.918	56.302	65.686	75.069	84.453	93.837
14 × 16	13½ × 15½	209.250	4,189.359	540.563	3,177.984	470.813	18⅔	36.328	43.594	50.859	58.125	65.391	72.656
14 × 18	13½ × 17½	236.250	6,029.297	689.063	3,588.047	531.563	21	41.016	49.219	57.422	65.625	73.828	82.031
14 × 20	13½ × 19½	263.250	8,341.734	855.563	3,998.109	592.313	23⅓	45.703	54.844	63.984	73.125	82.266	91.406
14 × 22	13½ × 21½	290.250	11,180.672	1,040.063	4,408.172	653.063	25⅔	50.391	60.469	70.547	80.625	90.703	100.781
14 × 24	13½ × 23½	317.250	14,600.109	1,242.563	4,818.234	713.813	28	55.078	66.094	77.109	88.125	99.141	110.156

[a]For lumber surfaced 1⅝ in. thick, instead of 1½ in., the area (*A*), moment of inertia (*I*) and section modulus (*S*) about the *X-X* axis may be increased 8.33%.
[b]For members over 12 in. in dimension, check availability with local suppliers. Lengths are generally available in 2 ft increments with a limit on maximum length; check with local suppliers for lengths normally available.

SECTION 3
LOADS

LOADS

LOADS AND FORCES

Structural framing should be designed, as stipulated by the governing building code, to sustain dead load, live load, snow load, wind load, impact load, earthquake load, and any other loads and forces which may reasonably affect the structure during its service life. In the absence of a governing code, the loads, forces, and combination of loads should be in accordance with accepted engineering criteria for the area under consideration.

The design loads and the methods of applying them as given in this section are based on a compilation of the most current data available from the authoritative sources noted herein. These sources include nationally recognized standards, accepted engineering practices, and published material of engineering and research agencies and societies. It is recommended that, in the absence of information considered to be more accurate; these loads be used for design purposes.

DEAD LOADS

Dead load consists of the weight of the appropriate portion of the structural members and all material fastened thereto or permanently supported thereby.

During the life of a building or other structure, additional loads may be applied that actually become dead loads but in all probability are not treated as such in the original design. If it is anticipated that such loads will be added at a later date, modifications should be made in the original design. Consideration should be given to the possible reroofing of the structure, and allowance appropriate to the type of roofing involved should be made.

The actual weights of the various materials and constructions should be used in design if this information is available. In the absence of such values, weights acceptable to the building official may be assumed. In view of the multiplicity of building codes that are in effect in various jurisdictions of the United States, it is not possible to provide tabular dead load data that is acceptable to all code authorities. Table 3.1 gives the approximate weight, in pounds per square foot, of various construction materials. Table 3.2 gives the approximate weight of other materials in pounds per cubic foot.

TABLE 3.1

WEIGHTS OF CONSTRUCTION MATERIALS

The average figures and ranges given in this table are suitable for general use. Specific products may vary considerably from these values; therefore, where available, actual weights listed in manufacturer's catalogs and in various reference books should be used.

Material	Weight, psf		
Ceilings			
Acoustical fiber tile	1.0		
Gypsum ceiling block, 2 in. thick, unplastered	10.0		
Plaster on tile or concrete	5.0		
Plasterboard, unplastered	10.0		
Suspended metal lath and gypsum plaster	10.0		
Floors			
Asphalt mastic, per inch of thickness	12.0		
Cement finish, per inch of thickness	12.0		
Concrete slab, per inch of thickness			
Plain, lightweight	8.5		
Plain, stone aggregate	12.0		
Reinforced, stone aggregate	12.5		
Cork, tile, $\frac{1}{16}$ in.	0.5		
Flexicore, 6 in. slab	46.0		
Gypsum slab, per inch of thickness	5.0		
Hardwood, 1 in. nominal	4.0		
Linoleum, $\frac{1}{4}$ in.	1.0		
Plywood, per inch of thickness	3.0		
Terrazo, 1 in.; 2 in. stone concrete base	32.0		
Vinyl tile, $\frac{1}{8}$ in.	1.4		
Roofs			
Lumber sheathing, 1 in. nominal	2.5		
Plywood sheathing, per inch of thickness	3.0		
Solid timber decking 15% MC	2 in. nom.	3 in. nom.	4 in. nom.
Cedar, Northern white	2.8	4.6	6.5
Cedar, Western	3.2	5.3	7.4
Douglas fir	4.3	7.2	10.1
Douglas fir-larch	4.4	7.3	10.2
Douglas fir-South	4.1	6.8	9.6
Fir, balsam	3.3	5.4	7.6
Fir, subalpine	3.0	4.9	6.9
Hem-fir	3.7	6.2	8.7
Hemlock, Eastern-tamarack	3.9	6.5	9.1
Hemlock, mountain	4.0	6.7	9.4
Hemlock, mountain-hem-fir	3.7	6.2	8.7
Pine, Eastern white	3.3	5.6	8.0
Pine, Idaho white	3.5	5.9	8.2

TABLE 3.1 (Continued)

Material	Weight, psf		
	2 in. nom.	3 in. nom.	4 in. nom.
Roofs (continued)			
Pine, lodgepole	3.7	6.2	8.7
Pine, Northern	4.0	6.7	9.4
Pine, ponderosa-sugar	3.7	6.1	8.6
Pine, Southern	4.6	7.6	10.7
Redwood, California	3.5	5.8	8.1
Spruce, Eastern	3.6	6.0	8.5
Spruce, Engelmann	3.0	5.1	7.1
Spruce, Sitka	3.6	6.0	8.5
Asphalt shingles ($\frac{1}{4}$ in. approx.)	2.0		
Cement asbestos shingles ($\frac{3}{8}$ in. approx.)	4.0		
Cement tile	16.0		
Clay tile			
2 in. book tile	12.0		
3 in. book tile	20.0		
Roman	12.0		
Spanish	19.0		
Ludowici	10.0		
Composition			
Three-ply ready roofing	1.0		
Roofing felt, 3-ply and gravel	5.5		
Roofing felt, 5-ply and gravel	6.5		
Corrugated metal, galvanized			
20 U.S. Std. ga	1.66		
24 U.S. Std. ga	1.16		
28 U.S. Std. ga	0.78		
Decking (nonwood), per inch of thickness			
Concrete plank	6.5		
Insulrock	2.7		
Poured gypsum	6.5		
Tectum	2.0		
Vermiculite concrete	2.6		
Gypsum sheathing, $\frac{1}{2}$ in.	2.0		
Insulation, per inch of thickness			
Expanded polystyrene	0.2		
Fiberglas, rigid	1.5		
Loose	0.5		
Wood shingles, 1 in.	3.0		
Walls and Partitions			
Clay tile, 4 in., load-bearing	23.0		
Clay tile, 4 in., non-bearing	18.0		
Facing tile, 4 in.	25.0		
Glass block, 4 in.	18.0		
Gypsum block, hollow, 4 in.	12.5		
Gypsum block, solid, 2 in.	9.5		

TABLE 3.1 (Continued)

Material	Weight, psf
Walls and Partitions (continued)	
Masonry, 4 in. thick	
Clay brick, medium absorption	39.0
Concrete block, heavy aggregate	30.0
Concrete block, light aggregate	20.0
Concrete brick, heavy aggregate	46.0
Concrete brick, light aggregate	33.0
Plaster	
Solid, 2 in.	20.0
Solid, 4 in.	32.0
Hollow, 4 in.	22.0
Gypsum on wood or metal lath	8.0
Cement on wood or metal lath	10.0
Stucco, $\frac{7}{8}$ in.	10.0
Terra-cotta tile	25.0
Windows, glass, frame, and sash	8.0
Wood paneling, 1 in.	2.5
Wood studs, 2×4	
12 in. o.c.	2.1
16 in. o.c.	1.7
24 in. o.c.	1.3
Plastered one side	12.0

LIVE LOADS

Live load may be defined as the weight superimposed by the use or occupancy of a building or other structure, but excluding wind, snow, earthquake, or dead load.

Floor Live Loads

In the absence of a governing building code, the minimum floor live loads given in Table 3.3, as recommended by the American National Standards Institute, should be used. For occupancies or uses not listed in Table 3.3, minimum floor live loads should be determined in a manner satisfactory to the governing building official.

Floors should be designed to support safely, in addition to the deal load, the uniformly distributed live loads shown in Table 3.3 or a concentrated load as given in Table 3.4, whichever produces the greater stress. Unless otherwise specified, the tabulated concentrated loads are assumed to occupy an area $2\frac{1}{2}$ ft square and are so located as to produce a maximum stress condition in structural members.

For floor live loads of 100 psf or less, the design floor live load on any member supporting 150 ft² or more may usually be reduced at the rate of 0.08%/ft² of area supported by the member, except that no reduction

TABLE 3.2

MATERIAL WEIGHTS[a]

Substance	Weight, pcf	Substance	Weight, pcf
Earth (Excavated)		*Metals and Alloys*	
Clay, dry	63	Aluminum, cast,	165
Clay, damp, plastic	110	hammered	
Clay and gravel, dry	100	Brass, cast, rolled	526
Earth, dry	76 to 95	Copper, cast, rolled	556
Earth, moist	78 to 96	Iron, cast, pig	450
Mud	108 to 115	Iron, wrought	480
Sand and gravel, dry,		Lead	710
loose	90 to 105	Steel, rolled	490
Sand and gravel, dry,		Tin, cast, hammered	459
packed	100 to 120	Zinc, rolled, sheet	449
Sand and gravel, wet	118 to 120		
		Liquids	
Masonry		Gasoline	42
Concrete, plain		Petroleum	54
Cinder	108	Water, fresh	62.4
Expanded slag	100	Water, ice	56
Stone, gravel	144	Water, sea	64
Light aggregate,			
load bearing	70 to 105	*Other Solids*	
Concrete, reinforced		Asphaltum	81
Cinder	111	Glass, common	156
Slag	138	Glass, plate or crown	161
Stone	150	Grain, barley	39
Brick		Grain, corn, rye, wheat	48
Soft	100	Grain, oats	32
Medium	115	Pitch	69
Hard	130	Tar, bituminous	75

[a]For timber weights, see Table 2.1, pages 2-6 and 2-7.

should be made for areas to be occupied as places of public assembly. The reduction should exceed neither N (in percent) as determined by the following formula, nor 60%:

$$N = 23.1 \left(1 + \frac{DL}{LL}\right)$$

where DL = dead load per square foot of area supported by the member
LL = design floor live load per square foot of area supported by the member

For floor live loads exceeding 100 psf, no reduction should be made, except that the design floor live loads on columns may be reduced 20%.

TABLE 3.3

MINIMUM UNIFORMLY DISTRIBUTED LIVE LOADS[a]

Occupancy or Use	Live Load, psf	Occupancy or Use	Live Load, psf
Apartments (*see* Residential)		Residential	
Armories and drill rooms	150	Multifamily houses	
Assembly halls and other		Private apartments	40
places of assembly:		Public rooms	100
Fixed seats	60	Corridors	80
Movable seats	100	Dwellings	
Balconies (exterior)	100	First floors	40
Bowling alleys, poolrooms,		Second floors and	
and similar recreational		habitable attics	30
areas	75	Uninhabitable attics	20
Corridors		Hotels	
First floor	100	Guest rooms	40
Other floors, same as		Public rooms	100
occupancy served		Corridors serving	
except as indicated		public rooms	100
Dance halls and ballrooms	100	Corridors	80
Dining rooms and restaurants	100	Reviewing stands and	
Dwellings (*see* Residential)		bleachers	100
Garages (passenger cars)	50	Schools	
Floors should be designed		Classrooms	40
to carry 150% of the maxi-		Corridors	80
mum wheel load anywhere		Sidewalks, vehicular	
on the floor		driveways, and yards,	
Grandstands (*see* Reviewing		subject to trucking	250
stands)		Skating rinks	100
Gymnasiums, main floors,		Stairs, fire escapes, and	
and balconies	100	exitways	100
Hospitals		Storage warehouses, light	125
Operating rooms	60	Storage warehouses, heavy	250
Private rooms	40	Stores	
Wards	40	Retail	
Hotels (*see* Residential)		First floors, rooms	100
Libraries		Upper floors	75
Reading rooms	60	Wholesale	125
Stack rooms	150	Theaters	
Manufacturing		Aisles, corridors, and	
Light	125	lobbies	100
Heavy	250	Orchestra floors	60
Marquees	75		
Office buildings		Balconies	60
Offices	50	Stage floors	150
Lobbies	100	Yards and terraces,	
Penal institutions		pedestrians	100
Cell blocks	40		
Corridors	100		

TABLE 3.4

CONCENTRATED LIVE LOADS[a]

Location	Load, lb
Elevator machine room grating (on area of 4 in.^{2})	300
Finish light floor plate construction (on area of 1 in.^{2})	200
Garages, passenger cars	See Table 3.3
Office floors	2,000
Scuttles, skylight ribs, and accessible ceilings	200
Sidewalks	8,000
Stair treads (on center of tread)	300

Roof Live Loads

The minimum roof live loads should be as stipulated by the governing building code. Roof live loads used in design should represent the designer's determination of the particular service requirements for the structure,

TABLE 3.5

MINIMUM ROOF LIVE LOADS[a]
(in psf of horizontal projection)

Roof slope	Tributary loaded area in square feet for any structural member		
	0 to 200	201 to 600	Over 600
Flat or rise less than 4 in. per foot / Arch or dome with rise less than $\frac{1}{8}$ of span	20	16	12
Rise 4 in. per foot to less than 12 in. per foot / Arch or dome with rise $\frac{1}{8}$ of span to less than $\frac{3}{8}$ of span	16	14	12
Rise 12 in. per foot and greater / Arch or dome with rise $\frac{3}{8}$ of span or greater	12	12	12

but, in the absence of a governing code, in no case should they be less than the recommended minimum.

Minimum roof live loads for flat, pitched, or curved roofs as recommended by the American National Standards Institute are given in Table 3.5. Roofs should be designed to resist either the tabulated minimum loads, applied as full balanced or full unbalanced, or the snow load, whichever produces the greater stress.

The American National Standards Institute also recommends as minimums design vertical live loads of 60 psf for flat roofs used as sundecks or promenades, and of 100 psf for flat roofs used as roof gardens or for assembly uses. These loads are, in effect, floor live loads and may be treated as such. Roofs to be used for other special purposes should be designed for appropriate loads as approved by the building official.

SNOW LOADS

Basic Snow Loads

Snow loads on roofs vary widely throughout the United States. Factors affecting snow load accumulation on roofs include climatic variables of elevation, latitude, wind frequency and duration of snowfall, roof geometry, and site exposure. In addition, snowfall varies from year to year, and either a mean recurrence interval must be established for design purposes or design should be based on the maximum recorded snow load for which data is available. Snow loads should be as stipulated by the governing building code, but in the absence of such a code, snow loading used for design should be based on local investigation, or by the use of accepted snow load maps.

Before discussing roof loads, it is necessary to consider ground snow loads since these form the basis for determining roof loads. Several researchers and agencies have measured ground snow load distribution and plotted appropriate isogram maps depicting these loads. Figure 3.1 presents maximum snow loads on the ground based on records of the U.S. Weather Bureau. Recent data reported by H. C. S. Thom of the Environmental Data Service, U.S. Department of Commerce, in "Distribution of Maximum Annual Water Equivalent of Snow on the Ground" and published in the *Monthly Weather Review*, Vol. 94, No. 4, 1966, provides snow load maps based on 25-, 50-, and 100-year mean recurrence intervals. In general, the 50-year mean recurrence data as prepared by Thom corresponds generally to the values listed in Figure 3.1 with slightly higher values recorded for the Northeastern states and somewhat lower values plotted for the Western states.

For the Western states, Figure 3.1 indicates that the snow loads for these regions should be established based on local experience. Actual snow pack in these regions of over 700 psf has been recorded and many of the inhabited regions have snow loads of 100, 200, or 300 psf.

L. W. Neubauer, in his paper "Snow Loads on Roofs in Mountain Regions," published in *Transactions*, ASAE, Vol. 12, No. 3, 1969, proposes the

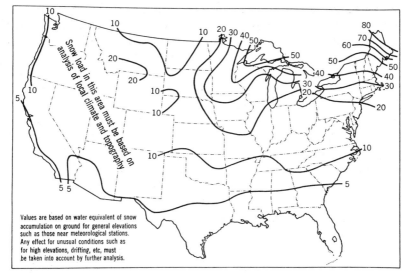

Figure 3.1   SNOW LOAD IN PSF ON THE GROUND, 50-YR MEAN RECURRENCE INTERVAL. Source: U.S. Weather Bureau, Washington, D.C.

use of the following equation to estimate ground snow loads in the Western mountain regions, based on a number of field studies conducted:

$$SL = 2.3 \left(El. + \frac{L}{4} - 8.5 \right)^2$$

where SL = ground snow load, psf
$\quad\quad El.$ = elevation, ft/1,000
$\quad\quad L$ = latitude, degrees

Although this equation is strictly empirical, it should be helpful in estimating snow loads at various elevations and latitudes when satisfactory snow-load maps or data are not available.

Roof Snow Loads

Based on a determination of the ground snow load as specified by the governing building code, through the use of maximum snow load maps such as given in Fig. 3.1, by the use of snow load maps based on a specific mean recurrence interval as developed by Thom, or by the use of an equation such as the one suggested by Neubauer, it is next necessary to determine the actual snow loads to be expected on the roof surface. As indicated, the roof snow load is a function of the geometry of the roof and the exposure to wind forces.

These factors can be accounted for in design by applying appropriate snow load coefficients to the basic ground snow loads. Specific snow load coefficients have been developed to relate roof snow load to ground snow load based on comprehensive surveys of actual conditions. This approach has been adopted by Canada and is included in the National Building Code of Canada.

For the design of both ordinary and multiple series roofs, either flat, pitched, or curved, a basic snow load coefficient of 0.8 should be used to convert ground snow load to a roof snow load. This value should then be increased or decreased if necessary because of specific roof geometry conditions, such as decreasing for roof slopes exceeding 20° and increasing for roofs having valleys formed by multiple series or other similar geometry conditions. When roof slopes exceed 20°, the design load in PSF may be decreased by $(SL/40-\frac{1}{2})$ for each 1° of slope over 20°. Specific coefficients for these roof configurations are given in the *American National Standard Building Code Requirements for Minimum Design Loads in Buildings and Other Structures* by the American National Standards Institute.

For roofs exposed to winds of sufficient intensity to blow snow off, the basic snow load coefficient can be reduced to 0.6. This coefficient is only applicable if (*a*) the roof is not shielded from the wind on any side or is not likely to become shielded by obstructions higher than the roof within a distance of 10*h* from the building ("*h*" is the height of the obstruction above the roof level), and (*b*) the roof does not have any projections, such as parapet walls, which may prevent the snow from being blown off by the wind.

Since unbalanced loading can occur as the result of drifting, sliding, melting and refreezing, or physical removal of snow, structural roof members should be designed to resist the full snow load as defined above distributed over the entire roof area, the full snow load distributed on any one portion of the area, and dead load only on the remainder of the area, depending on which load produces the greatest stress on the member considered. With respect to duration of load, snow load duration is the cumulative time during which the maximum design load is on the structure over its entire life. A *2-month* duration is generally recognized as the proper design level for snow loads. Although some snow remains on roofs for periods exceeding 2 months in a single year, such snow loads seldom approach the design load.

Although the analysis of roofs for snow loading is complex due to the many variables involved, recent technical data developed as discussed in the preceding paragraphs have provided the engineer with sufficient information to make a realistic analysis.

WIND LOADS

General

Designing structures to resist wind loading is, like the analysis for snow loading, a very complex engineering problem. Considerable research has been conducted to evaluate wind effects on various structures that has resulted in the establishment of design pressure coefficients that account for building shape and wind direction. In addition, extensive studies of basic wind velocities related to geographical location have resulted in the development of detailed wind velocity maps for the United States. Other studies of surface resistance relative to the degree of land development and gust characteristics at a given location have provided a method for a further refinement of the basic wind velocity and its effect on structures. However, much work remains to be done to relate further the dynamic behavior of structures to wind forces that are attributable to gusting and turbulence.

The wind load analysis information presented here is intended to provide the engineer with a design procedure that accounts for the basic parameters affecting wind loading of structures. The material has been compiled from a variety of sources, including the *American National Standard Building Code Requirements for Minimum Design Loads in Buildings and Other Structures*, American National Standards Institute; *Wind Forces on Structures*, Paper No. 3269, Final Report of the Task Committee on Wind Forces of the Committee on Loads and Stresses of the Structural Division, ASCE; *New Distributions of Extreme Winds in the United States* by H. C. S. Thom, Vol. 94, ST 7, July 1968, *Journal of the Structural Division*, ASCE; *Strength of Houses*, Building Materials and Structures Report 109, National Bureau of Standards, U.S. Department of Commerce; and *Structural Information for Building Design in Canada*, 1965, Supplement No. 3 to the National Building Code of Canada.

Basic Wind Velocities

Figures 3.2 and 3.3 represent wind probability maps for 50- and 100-year mean recurrence intervals, respectively. These figures provide basic wind velocities for observed air flows in open, level country at a height of 30 ft above the ground. For the design of most permanent structures, a basic wind speed with a 50-year mean recurrence interval should be applied. However, if in the judgment of the engineer or authority having jurisdiction, the structure presents an unusually high degree of hazard to life and property in case of failure, a 100-year mean recurrence interval wind velocity should be used for design. Similarly, for temporary structures or structures having negligible risk of human life in case of failure, a design wind velocity based on a 25-year mean recurrence interval may be used. Additional wind velocity maps for various mean recurrence intervals are given in *New Distribution of Extreme Winds in the United States*, by H. C. S. Thom, Vol. 94, ST 7, July 1968, *Journal of the Structural Division*, ASCE.

Since the wind velocities given in Figures 3.2 and 3.3 are for a height of 30 ft, it is necessary to modify this value for other design heights. An accepted procedure is to apply an exponential formula of the form

$$V_h = V_{30}\left(\frac{h}{30}\right)^{1/x}$$

where V_h = wind velocity at any height

V_{30} = wind velocity at a height of 30 ft

$\quad h$ = height

$\quad x$ = exponent depending upon general site exposure conditions such as follows:

For level or slightly rolling terrain with minimal obstructions such as airports, x may be taken as 7; for rolling terrain with numerous obstructions such as suburban areas, a value of 5 may be assumed; and for urban areas, a value of 3 is recommended.

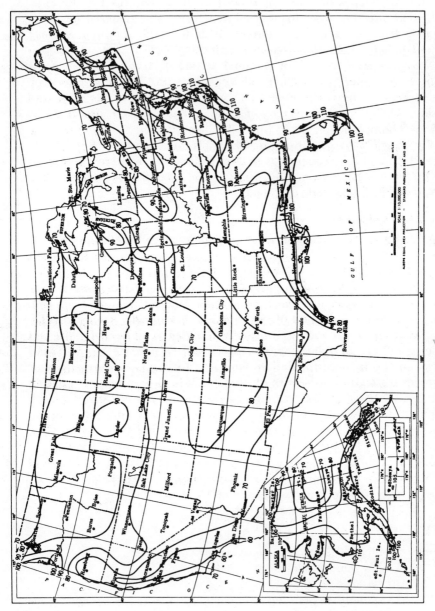

Figure 3.2.   ISOTACH 0.02 QUANTILES, IN MPH: ANNUAL EXTREME-MILE 30 FT ABOVE GROUND, 50-YR MEAN RECURRENCE INTERVAL. Source: *New Distribution of Extreme Winds in the United States*, by H. C. S. Thom, Paper No. 6038, Vol. 94, ST7, July 1968. *Journal of the Structural Division*, ASCE.

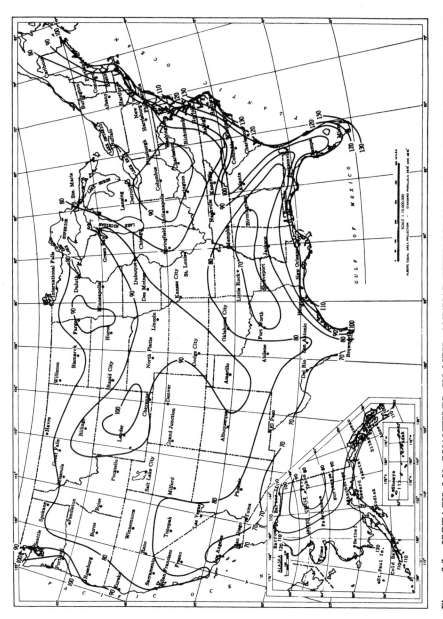

Figure 3.3. ISOTACH 0.01 QUANTILES, IN MPH: ANNUAL EXTREME-MILE 30 FT ABOVE GROUND, 100-YR MEAN RECURRENCE INTERVAL. Source: *New Distribution of Extreme Winds in the United States,* by H. C. S. Thom, Paper No. 6038, Vol. 94, ST7, July 1968, *Journal of the Structural Division,* ASCE.

Thus for open, relatively level areas similar to those from which the data given in Figures 3.2 and 3.3 are derived, the following equation is applicable:

$$V_h = V_{30}\left(\frac{h}{30}\right)^{1/7}$$

This is commonly referred to as the $\frac{1}{7}$th power law for determining wind velocities.

Based on the use of this relationship, Table 3.6 gives wind velocities for various height zones based on multiplying the basic wind velocity obtained from Figure 3.2 or 3.3 by an average correction factor for that height zone.

TABLE 3.6

WIND VELOCITIES CORRESPONDING TO VARIOUS HEIGHTS

Height, h, ft	Approximate Height Zone	Correction Factor[a]	Basic Wind Velocities, mph					
			60	70	80	90	100	110
30	20 to 40 ft	1.00	60	70	80	90	100	110
60	41 to 80 ft	1.10	66	77	88	99	110	121
110	81 to 140 ft	1.20	72	84	96	108	120	132
190	141 to 240 ft	1.30	78	91	104	117	130	143
320	241 to 400 ft	1.40	84	98	112	126	140	154

[a]Based on the relationship $V_h = V_{30}(h/30)^{1/7}$.

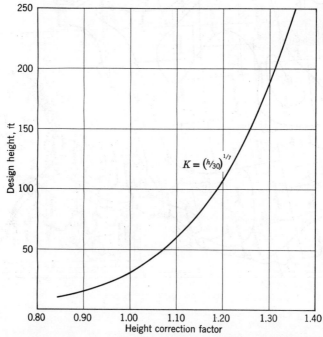

Figure 3.4.   **HEIGHT CORRECTION FACTOR BASED ON 1/7th POWER LAW.**

Similarly, Figure 3.4 can be used to determine a height correction factor based on the $\frac{1}{7}$th power law for any specific height to be analyzed in design.

In addition to adjusting the basic wind velocities for height and site exposure conditions, it is also possible to apply a gust response factor in the determination of design velocity pressures. The concept of determining gust response factors is very complex and the engineer is referred to the following ASCE papers for a detailed analysis of gust loading of structures: *Gust Loading Factors* by Davenport, Vol. 93, ST 3, June 1967, *Journal of the Structural Division*, and *Gust Response Factors* by Vellozzi and Cohen, Vol, 94, ST 6, June 1968, *Journal of the Structural Division*.

As a general guide, the gust response factor is primarily a function of the size and height of the structure and the surface roughness and obstructions existing in the surrounding area. For small-to-medium size structures located in open, relatively level terrain and ranging in height up to approximately 100 ft, a gust response factor of 1.3 is commonly assumed. Similarly, for taller buildings of approximately 400 ft in height, a gust response factor of 1.1 can be used for design purposes.

It is recommended that the designer use a dynamic analysis accounting for wind turbulence and the size and natural frequency of the structure to determine gusting effects on structures greater than 400 ft in height. Therefore, a design wind velocity is determined by modifying the basic wind velocity obtained from either Figure 3.2 or 3.3 for height, site exposure, and the gust effect. For additional information related to the effect of site exposure on wind velocity, the engineer is referred to the *American National Standard Building Code Requirements for Minimum Design Loads in Buildings and Other Structures*, ANSI A 58.1-1972.

Velocity Pressures

For standard air (0.07651 pcf, corresponding to 15°C at 760 mm of mercury) and velocity of wind, V, expressed in miles per hour, the velocity (dynamic) pressure, q, in psf, is given by

$$q = 0.00256V^2$$

Thus the dynamic pressure for any given combination of geographic location, height of structure, and basic wind velocity can be determined by using the design wind velocity in the above equation. Table 3.7 gives velocity pressure values for various heights and basic wind velocities for a site located in open, level terrain. The gust response factor has not been incorporated in this table but can easily be accounted for in a separate calculation by multiplying the tabulated values by the applicable gust response factor.

Therefore, for general design purposes, the effective velocity pressure for any height, h, may be determined from the relationship

$$q_h = (0.00256)(V_{30})^2(h/30)^{2/x}(G_F)$$

where V_{30} = basic wind velocity obtained from Figure 3.2 or 3.3
$\quad\quad h$ = height of building
$\quad\quad x$ = exponent depending upon general site exposure conditions
$\quad\quad G_F$ = gust response factor

TABLE 3.7

VELOCITY PRESSURES,[a] q, CORRESPONDING TO BASIC
WIND VELOCITIES, V

Height,[b] ft	Basic Wind Velocity, mph[c]					
	60	70	80	90	100	110
30	9.2	12.5	16.4	20.7	25.6	31.0
60	11.2	15.2	20.0	25.2	31.2	37.8
110	13.3	18.1	23.8	30.0	37.1	44.9
190	15.6	21.2	27.8	35.1	43.4	52.5
320	18.1	24.6	32.3	40.8	50.4	61.1
510	20.7	28.1	36.9	46.6	57.6	69.7

[a]Velocity pressure based on $q_{30} = 0.00256 V_{30}{}^2$.
[b]Height correction based on $q_h = q_{30}(h/30)^{2/7}$.
[c]From Figure 3.2 or 3.3.

Example. Calculate the effective velocity pressure acting on a permanent structure to be located in relatively open, level terrain near Cheyenne, Wyoming. Assume the design height to be 100 ft and that a 50-year mean recurrence interval wind velocity is applicable.

From Fig. 3.2, a basic wind velocity of 80 mph for a height of 30 ft is applicable for Cheyenne, Wyoming.

Since the height of the structure is 100 ft, and the structure is to be located in relatively open, level terrain, a gust response factor of 1.3 is applied.

Also for this type of site exposure it is recommended that an exponential value of x be taken as 7. The effective velocity pressure for this condition is:

$$q_{100} = 0.00256(80)^2 \left(\frac{100}{30}\right)^{2/7}(1.3)$$

$$q_{100} = 30.0 \text{ psf}$$

Wind Pressure

To determine the design wind pressure distribution acting on a building or structural element, the calculated velocity pressure is multiplied by an appropriate pressure coefficient, C_p. These pressure coefficients thus define the wind pressure acting normally on the surface of a building or element thereof and are dependent upon the external shape of the structure and its orientation with the wind. Pressure coefficients are considered to be either positive, representing a pressure, or negative, indicating a suction force on the structural element being analyzed. Therefore, depending upon orientation to the wind and existence of openings, a building or element may be subjected to a pressure difference between opposite sides or faces and it is thus the total resultant wind pressure that must be accounted for in design.

General Pressure Coefficients

For typical rectangular buildings and other enclosed structures having vertical walls that may have openings for doors and operable windows, for example, design pressure coefficients have been established. These are as given in the following sections.

Internal Pressure Coefficients

The determination of the internal wind pressures acting on a structure or element thereof can be made by applying the following equation:

$$p_i = q_{hi} C_{pi}$$

where p_i = internal wind pressure, psf
q_{hi} = internal effective velocity pressure in psf at height h
C_{pi} = internal pressure coefficient

It is important to note that the internal effective velocity pressure, q_{hi}, as used in this equation, differs from the basic effective velocity pressure, q_h, as previously discussed in that the gust response factor, G_F, need not be applied. This is primarily because the damping provided by restricted exterior openings, as it occurs in most buildings, causes the internal pressures to be less sensitive to gust effects. As a conservative approach, the designer can apply the effective velocity pressure, q_h, in the determination of internal wind pressure values.

Internal pressure coefficients for walls and roofs representing various percentages of wall openings are shown in Figure 3.5. The pressure as determined by using these coefficients is assumed to be uniform on all internal surfaces at a particular building height and is assumed applicable to flat, pitched, or arched roof configurations.

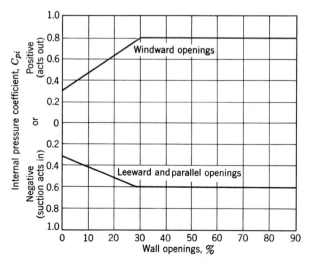

Figure 3.5.   INTERNAL PRESSURE COEFFICIENTS FOR WALLS AND ROOFS.

External Pressure Coefficients

To calculate the external wind pressures acting on a building or structural element, use is made of the following equation:

$$p_e = q_h C_{pe}$$

where p_e = external wind pressure, psf
q_h = effective velocity pressure in psf at height h
C_{pe} = external pressure coefficient

Walls

Average external pressure coefficients as given below should be used for calculating external pressures on wall surfaces of buildings.

Wall location with respect to wind direction	External pressure coefficient C_{pe}
Windward wall	+0.8
Leeward wall	
Height-to-width and height-to-length ratio $\geqslant$ 2.5	−0.6
Other dimensional configurations	−0.5
Parallel wall	−0.7

Roofs

For structures having a flat, pitched, or arched roof, external suction pressure, p_e, based on wind parallel to the surface of the roof can be computed by applying the following external pressure coefficients:

Building configuration (roof parallel to wind direction)	External pressure coefficient C_{pe}
Wall height to least width dimension < 2.5	−0.7
Wall height to least width dimension $\geqslant$ 2.5	−0.8

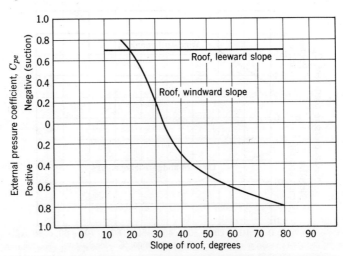

Figure 3.6.   EXTERNAL PRESSURE COEFFICIENTS FOR ROOFS WITH WIND NORMAL TO THE ROOF SURFACE.

The computed external wind pressure as determined by applying the above pressure coefficients is assumed to be uniform over the entire roof surface. For structures having a pitched or sloping roof with the direction of wind acting perpendicular to the ridge of the roof, average external pressure coefficients may be obtained from Figure 3.6 for various roof slopes. For arched roofs with the wind direction perpendicular to the axis of the arch, the external pressure coefficients as indicated for Figure 3.7 are applicable. In the figure shown, N is the ratio of rise to span, h/L.

Roof section	External pressure coefficient C_{pe}
Roof on elevated supports Windward quarter where	
$N < 0.2$:	-0.9
$0.2 \leqslant N < 0.3$:	$6N - 2.1$
$0.3 \leqslant N \leqslant 0.6$:	$2.8N - 0.7$
Center half:	$-N - 0.7$
Leeward quarter:	-0.5
Roofs supported at ground elevation	
$N \leqslant 0.6$	
Windward quarter:	$1.4N$
Center half:	$-N - 0.7$
Leeward quarter:	-0.5

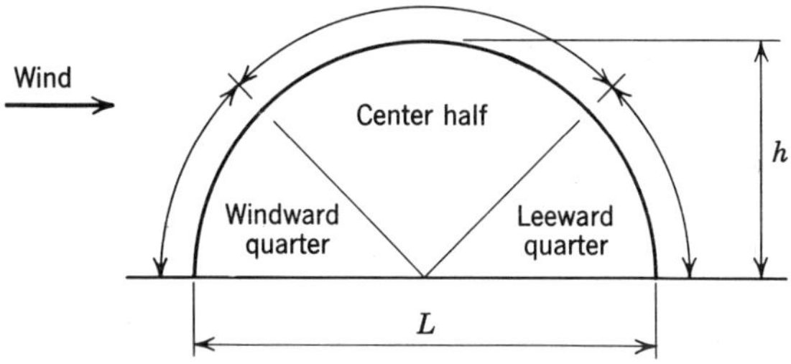

Figure 3.7.   ROUNDED OR ARCHED ROOF.

Local Pressure Coefficients

In determining the local wind pressure acting on ridges, eaves, cornices, and 90° corners of roofs, the external pressure coefficients as given below are applicable.

Roof pitch, θ	Local external pressure coefficients for roofs	
	Ridges and eaves	Corners
0 to 30°	-2.4	$0.1\theta - 5.0$
> 30°	-1.7	-2.0

The pressure determined by applying these coefficients is assumed to act on a strip of width $0.1w$ where w is the least width of the building normal to the ridge. This local pressure is assumed to be applied perpendicularly outward at these locations along the ridges, eaves, and cornices but is not included with the net external pressure when computing total wind loads.

Other Structures

For design information concerning net pressure coefficients to be applied in the wind analysis of special structures such as (*a*) roofs over nonenclosed areas (flat plates), (*b*) chimneys and tanks, (*c*) signs and outdoor display structures, (*d*) trussed towers, and (*e*) tower guys, the designer is referred to *American National Standard Building Code Requirements for Minimum Design Loads in Buildings and Other Structures*, American National Standards Institute.

Bridges and Trestles

The recommendations on wind pressures of the American Association of State Highway Officials for highway bridges or the recommendations of the American Railway Engineering Association for railroad bridges and trestles should be applied for the wind analysis of these structures.

Shielding

No allowance for reductions in those pressures obtained by applying the preceding analyses should be made for the effects of shielding that may be afforded by other buildings, structures, or terrain features. The shielding of one element of a structure on another element of the same structure, however, is applicable (see *Wind Forces on Structures*, ASCE paper No. 3269).

Anchorage

Adequate anchorage of the roof and columns, and of wall and columns to the foundation to resist overturning, uplift, and sliding due to computed wind forces should be provided in all cases.

Wind Pressure Coefficients — Specific Design Cases

The preceding recommendations are of limited use because they do not take into account oblique wind directions, the variation of pressure over the surfaces, or buildings of unusual shape. Table 3.8 gives local wind pressure coefficients for various parts of a building surface and for various wind directions. It also gives internal pressure coefficients which depend on the location of openings. The total force in any direction can be determined by summing the pressures on the appropriate surfaces. The letters *A, B, C,* etc., designate portions of the structure. For example, in the following example, *A* represents the windward wall, *B* the leeward wall, *C* and *D* the end walls (not windward or leeward), *E* and *F* the windward roof slope, and *G* and *H* the leeward roof slope. The pressure coefficients designated C_{pe}^* in Table 3.8 are for the areas *m* and *n*, and they take into account the large local pressure that occur near roof edges. The C_{pe}^* values are to be used in the design of local elements only, not for overall roof wind loading. To obtain the local pressure on the exterior surface, the appropriate factor from Table 3.8 is multiplied by the velocity pressure calculated according to the principles previously discussed.

TABLE 3.8
WIND PRESSURE COEFFICIENTS[a]

CLOSED BUILDINGS												
Structure	α	External Pressure Coefficient, C_{pe}								Internal Pressure Coefficient, C_{pi}		
		A	B	C	D	E	F	G	H	Openings Uniformly Distributed	Openings Mainly on Side		
											A	B	C
House Roofs 0° to 10° h:b:L = 1:1:1	0°	0.9	−0.5	−0.6	−0.6	−0.7	−0.7	−0.5	−0.5	±0.2	0.8	−0.4	−0.5
	15°	0.8	−0.5	−0.7	−0.5	−0.7	−0.6	−0.5	−0.6	±0.2	0.7	−0.4	−0.6
	45°	0.5	−0.5	0.5	−0.5	−0.8	−0.5	−0.5	−0.4	±0.2	0.4	−0.4	0.4
	45°	For m, $C_{pe}^* = -1.2$; for n, $C_{pe}^* = -0.8$											
House h:b:L = 2.5:2:5	0°	0.9	−0.5	−0.7	−0.7	−0.6	−0.6	−0.5	−0.5	±0.2	0.8	−0.4	−0.6
	45°	0.6	−0.5	0.4	−0.5	−0.9	−0.7	−0.6	−0.7	±0.2	0.5	−0.4	0.3
	90°	−0.5	−0.5	0.9	−0.4	−0.8	−0.2	−0.8	−0.2	±0.2	−0.4	−0.4	0.8
	45°	For m, $C_{pe}^* = -1.5$											
House h:b:L = 2.5:2:5	0°	0.9	−0.5	−0.7	−0.7	−0.6	−0.6	−0.5	−0.5	±0.2	0.8	−0.4	−0.6
	45°	0.6	−0.5	0.4	−0.4	−0.4	−0.5	−0.6	−0.7	±0.2	0.5	−0.4	0.3
	90°	−0.5	−0.5	0.9	−0.4	−0.7	−0.2	−0.7	−0.2	±0.2	−0.4	−0.4	0.8
	45°	For m, $C_{pe}^* = -1.2$											
House h:b:L = 2.5:2:5	0°	0.9	−0.5	−0.8	−0.8	0.3	0.3	−0.6	−0.6	±0.2	0.8	−0.4	−0.7
	45°	0.6	−0.5	0.4	−0.4	0.3	−0.1	−0.5	−0.6	±0.2	0.5	−0.4	0.3
	90°	−0.5	−0.5	0.9	−0.4	−0.8	−0.2	−0.8	−0.2	±0.2	−0.4	−0.4	0.8
	75°	For m, $C_{pe}^* = -1.2$											
Closed hall Roofs 0° to 3° h:b:L = 1:4:4	0°	0.9	−0.3	−0.4	−0.4	−0.8	−0.8	−0.3	−0.3	±0.2	0.8	−0.2	−0.3
	15°	0.8	−0.3	−0.1	−0.5	−0.7	−0.8	−0.2	−0.3	±0.2	0.7	−0.3	−0.2
	45°	0.5	−0.4	0.5	−0.4	−0.9	−0.6	−0.6	−0.3	±0.2	0.4	−0.4	0.4
	15°	For o, side C, $C_{pe}^* = -0.8$											
	45°	For m, $C_{pe}^* = -2.0$; n, $C_{pe}^* = -1.0$											
Closed hall h:b:L = 1:8:16	0°	0.8	−0.5	−0.5	−0.5	0.2	0.2	−0.6	−0.6	±0.2	0.7	−0.4	−0.4
	45°	0.5	−0.5	0.4	−0.3	0.1	−0.1	−0.8	−0.5	±0.2	0.4	−0.4	0.3
	90°	−0.3	−0.3	0.9	−0.3	−0.5	−0.1	−0.5	−0.1	±0.2	−0.2	−0.2	0.8
	10° and 90°	For m, $C_{pe}^* = -1.0$											

[a]Source: *Wind Forces on Structures*, Paper No. 3269, Final Report of the Task Committee on Wind Forces of the Committee on Loads and Stresses of the Structural Division, American Society of Civil Engineers.

TABLE 3.8 (Continued)
WIND PRESSURE COEFFICIENTS[a]

OPEN AND CLOSED BUILDINGS

Structure	α	A	B	C	D	E	F	G	H	J	K
		External Pressure Coefficient, C_{pe}									

Building open on one side Roof 30°, $h{:}b{:}L = 1{:}2{:}4$

(I) One Long Wall Open

	α	A	B	C	D	E	F	G	H	J	K
	0°	0.8	−0.5	−0.7	0.8	0.8	−0.7	−0.3	0.8	−0.4	0.8
	45°	0.7	−0.6	0.4	0.6	0.8	−0.4	−0.2	0.6	−0.7	0.7
	60°	0.3	−0.7	0.7	0.3	0.4	−0.4	−0.3	0.2	−0.6	0.2
	180°	−0.5	0.9	−0.8	−0.5	−0.5	−0.8	−0.4	−0.5	−0.2	−0.5

(II) One End Wall Open

	α	A	B	C	D	E	F	G	H	J	K
	0°	0.9	−0.7	−0.7	−0.4	−0.7	−0.8	−0.2	−0.7	−0.4	−0.7
	45°	0.5	0.7	0.8	−0.5	0.7	−0.4	−0.3	0.7	−0.6	0.8
	60°	0.1	0.9	0.9	−0.6	0.9	−0.4	−0.3	0.9	−0.7	0.9
	90°	−0.5	0.8	0.8	−0.5	0.8	−0.3	−0.4	0.8	−0.4	0.8

Buildings open on two sides Roofs 30°, $h{:}b{:}L = 1{:}2{:}4$

(I) Two Long Walls Open

	α	A	B	C	D	E	F	G	H	J	K
	0°		−0.2	−0.7	−0.7	−0.2	0.4	−0.9	−0.5	−0.8	
	45°		0.5	−0.4	0.5	−0.4	0	−0.3	−0.6	0	
	60°		0.7	−0.6	0.5	−0.4	−0.3	−0.1	−0.7	−0.3	

(II) Two End Walls Open

	α	A	B	C	D	E	F	G	H	J	K
	0°	0.9	−0.7	−0.7	−0.4			−0.2	−0.7	−0.4	−0.7
	45°	0.5	−0.4	−0.1	−0.8			−0.3	−0.4	−0.8	−0.3
	60°	0.3	−0.2	0.1	−0.5			−0.3	−0.1	−0.8	0.1

	60°	End Det, C = 0.7, D = −0.6; End Det, E = 0.6, F = −0.8

Closed buildings with roof vents Roofs 20°, $h{:}b{:}L = 1{:}4{:}8$
$h' = 0.5h$

	α	A	B	C	D	E	F	G	H	J	K	F & J Open	F & J Closed	F Only Open	J Only Open
												Internal Pressure Coefficient, C_{pi}, with Vents			
	0°	0.8	−0.5	−0.7	−0.7	−0.2	0.6	−1.0	−0.6	−0.5	−0.6	−0.2	±0.2	0.5	−0.4
	45°	0.4	−0.5	0.4	−0.5	−0.3	0.2	−1.3	−1.4	−1.0	−0.7	−0.5	±0.2	0.1	−0.9
	90°	−0.4	−0.4	0.8	−0.3	−0.4	−0.2	−0.3	−0.3	−0.2	−0.4	−0.3	±0.2	−0.2	−0.2

	0° and 45°	For m, $C_{pe}{}^* = −1.2$; n, $C_{pe}{}^* = −2.4$

[a]Source: *Wind Forces on Structures,* Paper No. 3269, Final Report of the Task Committee on Wind Forces of the Committee on Loads and Stress of the Structural Division, American Society of Civil Engineers.

TABLE 3.8 (Continued)
WIND PRESSURE COEFFICIENTS[a]

TALL BUILDINGS, ROOFS, AND PASSAGEWAYS

Structure	α	External Pressure Coefficient, C_{pe}								Internal Pressure Coefficient, C_{pi}				
		A	B	C	D	E	F	G	H	Openings Uniformly Distributed	Openings Mainly in			
											A	B	C	Roof EF
Tall buildings closed Roofs 0° to 15° A:b:L = 2.5:1:1	0°	0.9	−0.6	−0.7	−0.7	−0.8	−0.8	−0.8	−0.8	±0.2	0.8	−0.5	−0.6	
	15°	0.8	−0.5	−0.9	−0.6	−0.8	−0.8	−0.7	−0.7	±0.2	0.7	−0.5	−0.8	
	45°	0.5	−0.5	0.5	−0.5	−0.8	−0.7	−0.7	−0.5	±0.2	0.4	−0.4	0.4	
	45°	For m, $C_{pe}{}^{*}=-1.0$; n, $C_{pe}{}^{*}=-0.8$												
Tall buildings closed, A:b:L = 2:1:2	0°	0.9	−0.5	−0.8	−0.8	−1.0	−1.0	−0.5	−0.5	±0.2	0.8	−0.4	−0.7	
	45°	0.6	−0.5	0.4	−0.4	−0.3	−0.4	−0.5	−0.6	±0.2	0.5	−0.4	0.3	
	90°	−0.6	−0.6	0.9	−0.4	−0.7	−0.5	−0.7	−0.5	±0.2	−0.5	−0.5	0.8	
	0°	For m, $C_{pe}{}^{*}=-1.2$												
Shed roof h:b:L = 1:2.4:12	0°	0.9	−0.5	−0.6	−0.6	−0.5	−0.5	−0.5	−0.5	±0.2	0.8	−0.4	−0.5	−0.4
	45°	0.5	−0.6	0.4	−0.4	−1.2	−0.7	−1.1	−0.7	±0.2	0.4	−0.5	0.3	−0.8
	90°	−0.4	−0.3	0.9	−0.2	−0.3	0	−0.3	0	±0.2	−0.2	−0.1	0.8	0
	180°	−0.4	0.8	−0.7	−0.7	0.1	0.1	0.2	0.2	±0.2	−0.3	0.7	−0.6	0
	45°	For m, $C_{pe}{}^{*}=-1.4$												
Peaked roof h:b:L = 1:1:5	0°	0.9	−0.5	−0.6	−0.6	0.6	0.6	−0.5	−0.5	±0.2	0.8	−0.4	−0.5	0.5
	45°	0.5	−0.8	0.4	−0.5	0.2	−0.1	−1.0	−0.8	±0.2	0.4	−0.7	0.3	0
	90°	−0.4	−0.4	0.9	−0.3	−0.4	0	−0.4	0	±0.2	−0.1	−0.1	0.8	−0.1
	180°	−0.5	0.9	−0.6	−0.6	−0.5	−0.5	−0.1	−0.1	±0.2	−0.4	0.8	−0.5	−0.4
	45°	For m, $C_{pe}{}^{*}=-1.3$												
Closed connecting passage between large walls h:b:L = 1:1:10 Access doors closed	0°	0.8	−1.2	−1.4	−1.5					−0.5	0.7	−1.1	−1.3	

[a]Source: *Wind Forces on Structures*, Paper No. 3269, Final Report of the Task Committee on Wind Forces of the Committee on Loads and Stresses of the Structural Division, American Society of Civil Engineers.

3-26 *Timber Construction Manual*

TABLE 3.8 (Continued)
WIND PRESSURE COEFFICIENTS[a]

SHELTER ROOFS

Structure	α	A	B	C	D	J	K	L	M
		External Pressure Coefficient, C_{pe}				End Surfaces			
Roof + 30° $\alpha = 0°\text{-}45°$, A-D full length $\alpha = 90°$, A-D part length L' 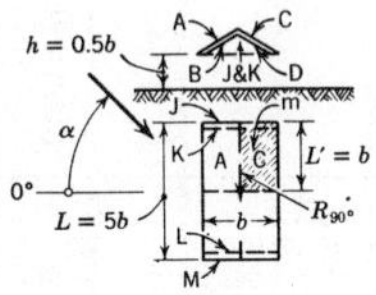	0°	0.6	−1.0	−0.5	−0.9				
	45°	0.1	−0.3	−0.6	−0.3				
	90°	−0.3	−0.4	−0.3	−0.4	0.8	−0.4	0.3	−0.3
	45° 90°	For m, $C^*_{pe,\text{top}} = -1.0$; $C^*_{pe,\text{bottom}} = -0.2$ Tangential acting friction, $R = 0.05q:L:b$							
Effect of trains or stored material **Roof + 30°** $\alpha = 0°\text{-}45°\text{-}180°$ A-D full length $\alpha = 90°$, A-D part length L' 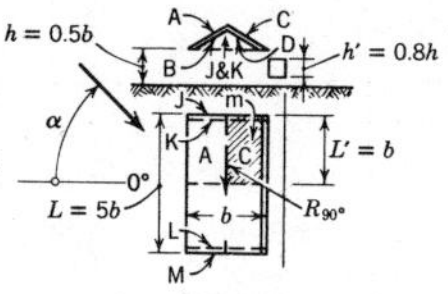	0°	0.1	0.8	−0.7	0.9				
	45°	−0.1	0.5	−0.8	0.5				
	90°	−0.4	−0.5	−0.4	−0.5				
	180°	−0.3	−0.6	0.4	−0.6				
	45° 90°	For m, $C^*_{pe,\text{top}} = -1.5$; $C^*_{pe,\text{bottom}} = 0.5$ End surface friction load, see above							
Roof + 10° $\alpha = 0°\text{-}45°$, A-D full length $\alpha = 90°$, A-D part length L' 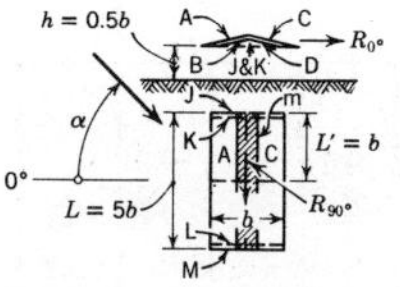	0°	−1.0	0.3	−0.5	0.2				
	45°	−0.3	0.1	−0.3	0.1				
	90°	−0.3	0	−0.3	0	0.8	−0.6	0.3	−0.4
	0° 0° and 90°	For m, $C^*_{pe,\text{top}} = -1.0$; $C^*_{pe,\text{bottom}} = 0.4$ Tangential acting friction, $R = 0.1q:L:b$							
Effect of trains or stored material **Roof + 10°** $\alpha = 0°\text{-}45°\text{-}180°$, A-D full length $\alpha = 90°$, A-D part length L' 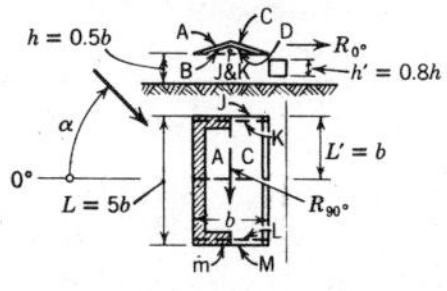	0°	−1.3	0.8	−0.6	0.7				
	45°	−0.5	0.4	−0.3	0.3				
	90°	−0.3	0	−0.3	0				
	180°	−0.4	−0.3	−0.6	−0.3				
	0° 0° and 180°	For m, $C^*_{pe,\text{top}} = -1.6$; $C^*_{pe,\text{bottom}} = 0.9$ End surface friction load, see above							
Roof − 10° $\alpha = 0°\text{-}45°$, A-D full length $\alpha = 90°$ A-D part length L' 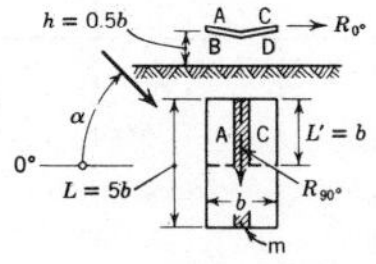	0°	0.3	−0.7	0.2	−0.9				
	45°	0	−0.2	0.1	−0.3				
	90°	−0.1	0.1	−0.1	0.1				
	0° 0° and 90°	For m, $C^*_{pe,\text{top}} = 0.4$; $C^*_{pe,\text{bottom}} = -1.5$ Tangential acting friction, $R = 0.1q:L:b$							
Effect of trains or stored material **Roof − 10°** $\alpha = 0°\text{-}45°\text{-}180°$, A-D full length $\alpha = 90°$, A-D part length L' 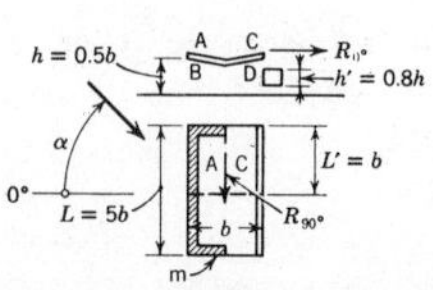	0°	−0.7	0.8	−0.6	0.6				
	45°	−0.4	0.3	−0.2	0.2				
	90°	−0.1	0.1	−0.1	0.1				
	180°	−0.4	−0.2	−0.6	−0.3				
	0° 0° and 180°	For m, $C^*_{pe,\text{top}} = -1.1$; $C^*_{pe,\text{bottom}} = 0.9$ Tangential acting friction, $R = 0.1q:L:b$							

^aSource: *Wind Forces on Structures*, Paper No. 3269, Final Report of the Task Committee on Wind Forces of the Committee on Loads and Stresses of the Structural Division, American Society of Civil Engineers.

TABLE 3.8 (Continued)
WIND PRESSURE COEFFICIENTS[a]

ROOFS AND GRANDSTANDS

Description	α	___ External Pressure Coefficient, C_{pe} ___												Internal Pressure Coefficient, C_{pi} Openings Uniformly Distributed	Openings Mainly in		
		A	B	C	D	E	F	G	H	J	K	L	M		A	B	C
Sawtooth roof Friction in wind direction $R_a = 0.1q{:}b{:}L$ $h{:}b{:}L = 1{:}4{:}5$	0°	0.9	−0.3	−0.4	−0.4	0.6	−0.6	−0.6	−0.5	−0.5	−0.4	−0.3	−0.3	±0.2	0.8	−0.2	−0.3
	45°	0.5	−0.4	0.5	−0.3	0.2	−0.8	−0.5	−0.4	−0.2	−0.4	−0.2	−0.5	±0.2	0.4	−0.3	0.4
	90°	−0.4	−0.4	0.9	−0.3	−0.3	−0.4	−0.4	−0.4	−0.4	−0.4	−0.4	−0.3	±0.2	−0.3	−0.3	0.8
	180°	−0.3	0.9	−0.3	−0.3	−0.2	−0.3	−0.3	−0.4	−0.4	−0.6	−0.6	−0.1	±0.2	−0.2	0.8	−0.2
	0° and 180°	For m, $C_{pe}^{*} = -1.3$; n, $C_{pe}^{*} = -2.0$															
Flat roof $h{:}b{:}L = 1{:}3{:}4$	0°	0.9	−0.5	−0.6	−0.6	−0.8	−0.8	−0.4	−0.4	−1.0	−0.4	−0.5	−0.5	±0.2	0.8	−0.4	−0.5
	45°	0.5	−0.5	0.5	−0.4	−0.6	−0.5	−0.5	−0.5	−0.5	−0.5	−0.5	−0.5	±0.2	0.4	−0.4	0.4
	90°	−0.5	−0.5	0.9	−0.4	−0.8	−0.4	−0.8	−0.4	−0.4	−0.4	−1.0	−0.4	±0.2	−0.4	−0.4	0.8
	0° and 90°	For m, $C_{pe}^{*} = -1.1$; n, $C_{pe}^{*} = -1.5$															

Description	α	A	B	C	D	E	F	G	H	J	K	L	M	With Windows and Doors Closed	A with Window Y open	C with All Gates Open	C with only Gate X Open
Hanger arch roof Smooth surface $h{:}b{:}L = 1{:}12{:}12$ $r = 5/6b$ $Y = 0.1b$ $X = 0.1b$	0°	0.7	−0.2	−0.3	−0.8	−0.1	−0.5	−0.8	−0.8	−0.4	−0.1			±0.2	0.4	−0.1	−1.5
	30°	0.6	−0.3	0.2	−0.4	−0.1	−0.4	−0.7	−0.9	−0.7	−0.4			±0.2	0.7	0.6	0.7
	90°	−0.3	−0.3	0.9	−0.3							−0.8	−0.7	±0.2	−1.0	0.8	0.4
	30°	For m, $C_{pe}^{*} = -1.8$ with $C_{pe,min}^{*} = -2.5$ N = −0.5; O = −0.3; P = −0.1; Q = −0.1															

Description	α	C_{pe} at top and bottom of roof								C_{pe} at front and back of wall						
		A	C	E	G											
Grandstands open three sides Roof 5°	0°	−1.0	0.9	−1.0	0.9	−0.7	0.9	−0.7	0.9	0.9	−0.5	0.9	−0.5			
	45°	−1.0	0.7	−0.7	0.4	−0.5	0.8	−0.5	0.3	0.8	−0.6	0.4	−0.4			
	135°	−0.4	−1.1	−0.7	−1.0	−0.9	−1.1	−0.9	−1.0	−1.1	0.6	−1.0	0.4			
	180°	−0.6	−0.3	−0.6	−0.3	−0.6	−0.3	−0.6	−0.3	−0.3	0.9	−0.3	0.9			
	45°	For m_D, $C_{pe,top}^{*} = -2.0$; $C_{pe,bottom}^{*} = 1.0$														
	60°	For m_W, $C_{pe,K}^{*} = -1.0$; $C_{pe,J}^{*} = 1.0$														
	90°	Tangential acting friction, $R_D = 0.1q{:}b{:}L$; $R_W = 0.1q{:}h{:}L$														

Smooth closed reservoir

$$F_D = (P_i - P_a)A, \text{ in which } P_i = \text{working pressure, } A = \tfrac{\pi}{4}d^2, \; P_a = C_{pe}\,q,$$

and $C_{pe} = -1.0$

Source: *Wind Forces on Structures,* Paper No. 3269, Final Report of the Task Committee on Wind Forces of the Committee on Loads and Stresses of the Structural Division, American Society of Civil Engineers.

TABLE 3.8 (Continued)
WIND PRESSURE COEFFICIENTS[a]

CYLINDERS, CHIMNEYS, TANKS, AND SPHERES						

				Value of h/d		
				1	7	25
Structure		α	Sphere	Value of L/d		
				2	14	50
				Value of C_{pe}		
Cylinder, surface load Smooth surfaces / Sphere, surface load Smooth surfaces		0°	1.0	1.0	1.0	1.0
$\Delta P = P_i - P_e$ $P_e = C_{pe}q$ $P_i = C_{pi}q$ $d\sqrt{q} > 2.3$ lb$^{\frac{1}{2}}$		15°	0.9	0.8	0.8	0.8
$\Delta P = P_i - P_e$ $P_e = C_{pe}q$ $F_D = C_D qA$ $A = \frac{\pi}{4}d^2$ $d\sqrt{q} > 11.3$ lb$^{\frac{1}{2}}$ $C_n = 0.2$		30°	0.5	0.1	0.1	0.1
		45°	−0.1	−0.7	−0.8	−0.9
		60°	−0.7	−1.2	−1.7	−1.9
		75°	−1.1	−1.6	−2.2	−2.5
		90°	−1.2	−1.7	−2.2	−2.6
		105°	−1.0	−1.2	−1.7	−1.9
		120°	−0.6	−0.7	−0.8	−0.9
Stack working $C_{pi} = 0.1$ Stack closed $C_{pi} = -0.8$ / Closed reservoirs - / P_i = working pressure		135°	−0.2	−0.5	−0.6	−0.7
		150°	0.1	−0.4	−0.5	−0.6
		165°	0.3	−0.4	−0.5	−0.6
		180°	0.4	−0.4	−0.5	−0.6

Structure	Cross Section	Description	Value of C_D		
Upright cylinder $F_D = C_D qA$ $d\sqrt{q} > 2.3$ lb$^{\frac{1}{2}}$ $A = dh$ $h/d = $ 25 7 1		Smooth surface: metal, timber, concrete	0.45	0.5	0.55
		Rough surface; round ribs, $h = 2\% d$	0.7	0.8	0.9
		Very rough surface; sharp ribs, $h = 8\% d$	0.8	1.0	1.2
		Smooth, rough surface; sharp edges	1.0	1.2	1.4

[a]Source: *Wind Forces on Structures*, Paper No. 3269, Final Report of the Task Committee on Wind Forces of the Committee on Loads and Stresses of the Structural Division, American Society of Civil Engineers.

Example. Determine the wind loads acting on the illustrated building.

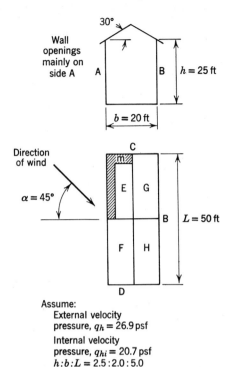

Assume:
External velocity
pressure, $q_h = 26.9$ psf
Internal velocity
pressure, $q_{hi} = 20.7$ psf
$h:b:L = 2.5:2.0:5.0$

Building Area	C_{pe}	C_{pi}	p_e[a]	p_i[b]	Net Wind Pressure $(p_e - p_i)$
Windward wall, A	+0.6	+0.5	+16.1	+10.3	+5.8 pressure
Leeward wall, B	−0.5	+0.5	−13.4	+10.3	−23.7 suction
End wall, C	+0.4	+0.5	+10.8	+10.3	+0.5 pressure
End wall, D	−0.4	+0.5	−10.8	+10.3	−21.1 suction
Windward roof, E	−0.4	+0.5	−10.8	+10.3	−21.1 suction
Windward roof, F	−0.5	+0.5	−13.4	+10.3	−23.7 suction
Leeward roof, G	−0.6	+0.5	−16.1	+10.3	−26.4 suction
Leeward roof, H	−0.7	+0.5	−18.8	+10.3	−29.1 suction
Roof portion, m	$C_{pe}^* = -1.2$				−32.3 suction

[a] $p_e = C_{pe}$ (external velocity pressure).
[b] $p_i = C_{pi}$ (internal velocity pressure).

BASIC MINIMUM ROOF LOAD COMBINATIONS

In designing, the most severe realistic distribution, concentration, and combination of roof loads and forces should be taken into consideration. Table 3.9 gives the basic minimum roof load design combinations which should be checked in all structures with these types of loads.

Each type of load should be determined individually and the effect of

TABLE 3.9

BASIC RECOMMENDED MINIMUM LOAD COMBINATIONS FOR DESIGN

Roof Load Combinations		Duration of Load	Stress Modification Factor for Duration
Windward Side	Leeward Side		
DL	DL	Permanent	0.90
DL + LL	DL + LL	7 days	1.25
DL[a]	DL + LL[a]	7 days	1.25
DL + SL	DL + SL	2 months	1.15
DL + $\frac{1}{2}$SL[b]	DL + SL[b]	2 months	1.15
DL + WL	DL + WL	Wind or earthquake	1.33

[a]Full unbalanced loading.   [b]Half unbalanced loading.

NOTES

1. See Section 2 of this *Manual* for procedure for determining the governing duration factor when loads of different durations are applied simultaneously.

2. Special configurations, locations, and occupancies of structures may require investigation of (*a*) full unbalanced SL or (*b*) combinations of WL with LL and DL, or WL with partial SL and DL.

3. Where the magnitude of DL and other permanently applied loads is great, or the structure is to be located in a zone of high seismic risk, the effect of seismic loading should be investigated.

4. It may be assumed that wind and earthquake loads will not occur simultaneously.

all possible combinations investigated. All possibilities must be investigated for unsymmetrical buildings. Special consideration should be given to structures of great span and/or height, and to trusses bearing on very long columns. In addition to analyzing the structure for the combinations of loading shown in Table 3.9, the designer should check to see that all loading combinations as required by the governing building code have been met.

Structural members or systems should be designed to resist the stresses caused by partially or fully unbalanced live or snow loads and wind loads, including uplift, in combination with dead loads on the member or system, if such loading results in reversal of stresses or stresses greater in any portion than the stresses produced on the entire roof by the load combinations. The occupancy or use of the structure, its configuration, heating considerations, local climatic conditions, or other considerations may also cause partial or full unbalanced loading on the structure.

The following symbols are employed in Table 3.9.

> DL = dead load, including weight of structure
> LL = live load
> SL = snow load, modified for roof slope
> WL = wind load, modified for shape of roof, openings, etc.

EARTHQUAKE LOADS

The lateral force provisions herein are based on the recommendations of the 1970 edition of the *Uniform Building Code* and are intended to provide minimum standards as design criteria for making buildings and other structures earthquake-resistive. These provisions apply to the structure as a unit and also to all parts thereof, including the structural frame or walls, floor and roof systems, and other structural features. The recommendations are general and, in specific cases, the governing building code regulations should be met.

In areas subject to earthquake shocks, every building or structure and every portion thereof should be so designed and constructed as to resist stresses produced by lateral forces, as provided in these recommendations. Stresses should be calculated as the effect of a force applied horizontally at each floor or roof level above the foundation. The force should be assumed to come from any horizontal direction.

Definitions

The following definitions apply to the recommendations on earthquake loads.

Box system. A structural system without a complete vertical load-carrying space frame. In this system, the required lateral forces are resisted by shear walls.

Shear wall. A wall designed to resist lateral forces parallel to the wall. Braced frames subjected primarily to axial stresses are considered shear walls for the purpose of this definition.

Space frame. A three-dimensional structural system composed of interconnected members, other than shear or bearing walls, laterally supported so as to function as a complete self-contained unit with or without the aid of horizontal diaphragms or floor bracing systems.

Space frame, moment-resisting. A vertical load-carrying space frame in which the members and joints are capable of resisting design lateral forces by bending moments.

Space frame, vertical load-carrying. A space frame designed to carry all vertical loads.

Minimum Earthquake Forces for Buildings

Total lateral force and distribution of lateral force

Every building should be designed and constructed to withstand minimum total lateral seismic forces assumed to act nonconcurrently in the direction of each of the main axes of the building in accordance with the formula (*Note*: The following symbols apply to the recommendations on earthquake loads only):

$$V = ZKCW$$

where V = total lateral load or shear at base, lb

$$V = F_t + \sum_{i=1}^{n} F_i$$

$F_t =$ that portion of V considered concentrated at the top of the structure, at the level n. The remaining portion of the total base shear V shall be distributed over the height of the structure including level n according to the equation for F_x given on page **3-33**.

$F_i, F_n, F_x =$ lateral forces applied to level i, n, or x, respectively, lb: i designates first level above the base

$W =$ total dead load, lb, except in storage and warehouse occupancies, where $W =$ total dead load plus 25% of floor live load

$K =$ numerical coefficient as given in Table 3.10

$Z =$ numerical coefficient dependent on the zone as determined from Figure 3.8

$C =$ numerical coefficient for base shear

$C = 0.10$ for all one- and two-story buildings

$C = \dfrac{0.05}{\sqrt[3]{T}}$ for all other buildings

where $T =$ fundamental period of vibration of the building or structure in the direction under consideration, seconds

Properly substantiated technical data for establishing the period T for the contemplated structure may be used. In the absence of such data, the value of T should be determined by the formulas

$T = 0.10N$ in all buildings in which the lateral resisting system consists of a moment-resisting space frame which resists 100% of the required lateral forces and whose frame is not enclosed by or adjoined by more rigid elements which would tend to prevent the frame from resisting lateral forces; or

$T = \dfrac{0.05H}{\sqrt{D}}$ in all other buildings

where $N =$ total number of stories above exterior grade

$H =$ height of the main portion of the building above the base, ft

$D =$ dimension of the building in a direction parallel to the applied forces, ft

The lateral force, V, should be distributed over the height of the structure in the following manner:

(a) $F_t = 0.004V \left(\dfrac{H}{D_s}\right)^2$

where $D_s =$ the plan dimensions of the vertical lateral force-resisting system, ft

F_t need not exceed $0.15V$ and may be considered as 0 for values $(H/D_s) \leqslant 3$

TABLE 3.10

HORIZONTAL FORCE FACTOR, *K*, FOR BUILDINGS OR OTHER
STRUCTURES[a]

Type or Arrangement of Resisting Elements	Value[b] of *K*
All building framing systems except as classified below	1.00
Buildings with a box system as defined in definitions	1.33
Buildings with a dual bracing system consisting of a ductile moment resisting space frame and shear walls using the following design criteria: (1) The frames and shear walls should resist the total lateral force in accordance with their relative rigidities considering the interaction of the shear walls and frames (2) The shear walls acting independently of the ductile moment resisting portions of the space frame should resist the total required lateral forces (3) The ductile moment resisting space frame should have the capacity to resist not less than 25% of the required lateral force	0.80
Buildings with a ductile moment resisting space frame designed in accordance with the following criteria: The ductile moment resisting space frame shall have the capacity to resist the total required lateral force	0.67
Elevated tanks plus full contents, on four or more cross-braced legs and not supported by a building[c, d]	3.00[e]
Structures other than buildings and other than those set forth in Table 3.11	2.00

[a]Where wind load would produce higher stresses, it should be used instead of the loads resulting from earthquake forces.
[b]See Figure 3.8 for seismic probability zones and values for *Z*.
[c]The minimum value of *KC* should be 0.12 and the maximum value of *KC* need not exceed 0.25.
[d]For overturning, the factor *J* shall be 1.00.
[e]The tower should be designed for an accidental torsion of 5% as determined under *Horizontal Torsional Moments* on page 3–36.

$$(b) \quad F_x = \frac{(V - F_t)W_x h_x}{\sum\limits_{i=1}^{n} W_i h_i}$$

where W_i, W_x = that portion of W which is located at or is assigned to level i
or x, respectively
h_i, h_x = height above the base to level i or x, respectively, ft

At each level designated as x, the force F_x should be applied over the area of the building in accordance with the mass distribution on that level.

(c) One- and two-story buildings should have uniform distribution.

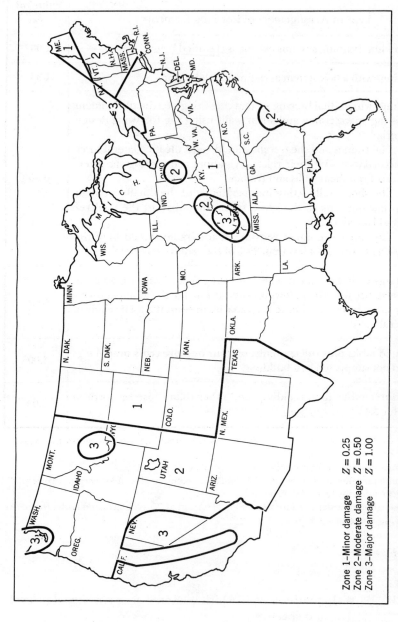

Figure 3.8.   ZONES OF APPROXIMATELY EQUAL SEISMIC PROBABILITY. Based on earthquake data compiled by the Environmental Science Services Administration.

Zone 1–Minor damage   Z = 0.25
Zone 2–Moderate damage   Z = 0.50
Zone 3–Major damage   Z = 1.00

Lateral force on parts or portions of buildings or other structures

Parts or portions of buildings or structures and their anchorage should be designed for lateral forces in accordance with the formula

$$F_p = ZC_pW_p$$

with the additional notation

W_p = weight of a part or portion of the structure, lb
C_p = numerical coefficient as defined and tabulated in Table 3.11

TABLE 3.11

HORIZONTAL FORCE FACTOR, C_p, FOR PARTS OR PORTIONS
OF BUILDINGS OR OTHER STRUCTURES

Part or Portion of Buildings	Direction of Force	Value of C_p
Exterior bearing and nonbearing walls, interior bearing walls and partitions, interior non-bearing walls and partitions over 10 ft in height, masonry or concrete fences over 6 ft in height	Normal to flat surface	0.20
Cantilever parapet and other cantilever walls, except retaining walls	Normal to flat surface	1.00
Exterior and interior ornamentations and appendages	Any direction	1.00
When connected to or a part of a building: towers, tanks, towers and tanks plus contents, chimneys, smokestacks, and penthouses	Any direction	0.20[a]
When resting on the ground, tank plus effective mass of its contents	Any direction	0.10
Floors and roofs acting as diaphragms[b]	Any direction	0.10
Connections for exterior panels	Any direction	2.00
Connections for prefabricated structural elements other than walls, with force applied at center of gravity of assembly[c]	Any horizontal direction	0.30

[a]When H/D of any building is equal to or greater than 5 to 1, value must be increased 50%.
[b]Floors and roofs acting as diaphragms should be designed for a minimum value of C_p of 10% applied to loads tributary from that story, unless a greater value of C_p is required by the basic seismic formula, $V = ZKCW$.
[c]W_p should be equal to the total dead load plus 25% of the floor live load in storage and warehouse occupancies.

Pile foundations

Individual pile or caisson footings of every building or structure should be interconnected by ties each of which can carry by tension and compression a horizontal force equal to 10% of the larger pile cap loading, unless it can be demonstrated that equivalent restraint can be provided by other approved methods.

Distribution of Horizontal Shear

Total shear in any horizontal plane should be distributed to the various resisting elements in proportion to their rigidities, the rigidity of the horizontal bracing system or diaphragm as well as the rigidities of the vertical resisting elements being taken into consideration.

Rigid elements that are assumed not to be part of the lateral force resisting system may be incorporated into buildings provided that their effect on the action of the system is considered and provided for in the design.

Drift

Lateral deflections or drift of a story relative to its adjacent stories should be considered in accordance with accepted engineering practice.

Horizontal Torsional Moments

Provisions should be made for the increase in shear resulting from the horizontal torsion due to an eccentricity between the center of mass and the center of rigidity. Negative torsional shears should be neglected. Where the vertical resisting elements depend on diaphragm action for shear distribution at any level, the shear resisting elements should be capable of resisting a torsional moment assumed to be equivalent to the story shear acting with an eccentricity of not less than 5% of the maximum building dimension at that level.

Overturning

Every building or structure should be designed to resist the overturning effects caused by wind forces or by earthquake forces as specified in these recommendations on earthquake loads, whichever govern; with the exception that the axial loads from earthquake forces on vertical elements and footings in every building or structure may be modified in accordance with the following provisions.

1. The overturning moment, M, at the base of the building or structure should be determined in accordance with the formula

$$M = J\left(F_t H + \sum_{i=1}^{n} F_i h_i\right)$$

where $J = 0.6/\sqrt[3]{T^2}$.

The value of J need not be more than 1.00. For structures other than buildings, the value of J shall be not less than 0.45.

2. The overturning moment, M_x, at any level designated x should be determined in accordance with the formula

$$M_x = J_x \left[F_t(H - h_x) + \sum_{i=x}^{n} F_i(h_i - h_x) \right]$$

where $J_x = J + (1 - J)(h_x/H)^3$

At any level, the overturning moments should be distributed to the various resisting elements in the same proportion as the distribution of the shears in the resisting system. Where other vertical members, which are capable of partially resisting the overturning moments, are provided, a redistribution may be made to these members if framing systems of sufficient strength and stiffness to transmit the required loads are provided.

When a vertical resisting element is discontinuous, the overturning moment carried by the lowest story of that element should be carried down as loads to the foundation.

Design Requirements

Building separations

All portions of structures should be designed and constructed to act as an integral unit in resisting horizontal forces unless separated structurally by a distance sufficient to avoid contact under deflection from seismic action or wind forces.

Minor alterations

Minor structural alterations may be made in existing buildings and other structures, but the resistance to lateral forces should be not less than that before such alterations were made, unless the building as altered meets the requirements of the governing building code.

Combined vertical and horizontal forces

In computing the effect of seismic force in combination with vertical loads, gravity load stresses induced in members by dead load plus design live load, except roof live load, should be considered.

MOVING LOADS

General

When the maximum vertical shear due to a single moving concentrated load or to one moving concentrated load that is considerably larger than any of the others is being calculated, the load is placed at a distance from one support equal to the depth of the member, others being kept in their normal relationship to each other. With two or more moving loads of about equal weight, and in proximity, the loads are placed in the position that produces the greatest vertical shear; any load within a distance from the support equal to the depth of the member is neglected.

For simple beams, the maximum bending moment produced by moving concentrated loads occurs under one of the loads when that load is as far from one support as the center of gravity of all the moving loads on the beam is from the other support. In Figure 3.9, the maximum bending moment, M, occurs under load P_1 when $x = z$. This condition also occurs when the centerline of the span is midway between the center of gravity of loads and the nearest concentrated load.

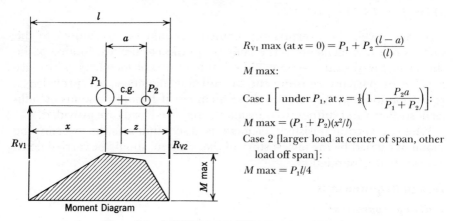

$$R_{V1} \text{ max (at } x = 0) = P_1 + P_2 \frac{(l-a)}{(l)}$$

M max:

Case 1 $\left[\text{under } P_1, \text{ at } x = \tfrac{1}{2}\left(1 - \frac{P_2 a}{P_1 + P_2}\right) \right]$:

M max $= (P_1 + P_2)(x^2/l)$

Case 2 [larger load at center of span, other load off span]:

M max $= P_1 l/4$

Moment Diagram

Figure 3.9.   MOVING CONCENTRATED LOADS.

Highway Loading

As indicated by the excellent performance of timber highway bridges over the years, wood bridges meet all the general bridge design requirements for modern highway traffic loads. In addition, wood offers the important advantage of being able to absorb impact stresses to the degree that impact loads may be neglected in the design of wood highway structures; however, they must be considered in the metal-to-metal connections. Highway design loads and their application should be in accordance with *Standard Specifications for Highway Bridges,* adopted by the American Association of State Highway Officials (AASHO). Normal duration of loading should be used for design.

Railway Loading

Timber railway bridges and trestles have proved very economical and have been long and extensively used in this country. With the advent of pressure treatments, service lives as long as 50 years are commonplace. In the design of timber bridges and trestles, the recommendations of the American Railway Engineering Association (AREA) are ordinarily applied. Recognizing the increased strength of wood under quickly applied loading, the AREA specifications permit omission of impact loads in determining stresses in the wood. Impact must be considered, however, in metal-to-metal connections. It should be pointed out that AREA specifications assume that all railway bridges and trestles are under "long-time" loading.

Crane Beam Loading

Timber is often used for crane beams and girders because of its ability to absorb impact forces. In designing crane beams, wheel loads recommended by crane manufacturers should be used if available.

The American National Standards Institute recommends that for the design of all crane runways, the design loads should be increased for impact as follows:

(*a*) a vertical force equal to 25% of the maximum wheel load;

(*b*) a lateral force equal to 20% of the weight of trolley and lifted load only, applied one-half at the top of each rail; and

(*c*) a longitudinal force of 10% of the maximum wheel loads of the crane applied at the top of the rail.

Some crane manufacturers specify wheel loads that include a percentage for impact. In designing, this factor should be taken into account, because it is unnecessary to add impact to wheel loads for timber designs unless there is a steel connection through which the load must pass or unless impact exceeds 100% of other normal loads. Impact must be considered for metal-to-metal connections. Normal duration of loading should be used for design.

Crane runway rails should be designed to prevent undue vertical and lateral deflection in accordance with crane manufacturers' recommendations.

Cyclic Loading

Tests to date indicate that wood is less sensitive to repeated loads than are crystalline structural materials such as metals. In general, the fatigue strength of wood is higher in proportion to the ultimate strength values than are the endurance limits for most structural metals. In present design practice, no factor is applied for fatigue in deriving working stress values for wood, nor is it considered necessary to do so. For these reasons, normal duration of load is used for cyclic loading design.

Where estimation of repetitions of design or near design loads are indicated to approximate one million or more cycles, the designer should investigate the possibility of fatigue failures when major stresses are in shear. When shear governs design and fatigue is a distinct possibility, shear stresses should be reduced 10%, or changes should be made on the basis of · a detailed analysis as indicated by examination of U.S. Forest Products Laboratory Report No. 2236, *Fatigue Resistance of Quarter-Scale Bridge Stringers in Flexure and Shear*, and/or of ASCE Paper No. 2470, *Design Considerations for Fatigue in Timber Structures*, both by Wayne C. Lewis. Analyses made on the research available indicate that failure due to fatigue in bending is not critical and need not be considered. The stresses for which fatigue need be considered are those at a given section, not those which occur throughout the member.

SPECIAL LOADS

Vibration

Vibration is closely related to impact and cyclic loading. The effects of vibration can usually be neglected in timber structures, except in those portions made of materials for which impact or vibration forces may be critical. Vibration may cause loosening of threaded connections used in timber structures. If the possibility of fatigue failure due to vibration may occur, it should be considered, and care should be taken to avoid notches, eccentric connections, and similar design conditions which might cause cross-grain tension.

Blast Loads

Data on the design of structures resistant to blast loading such as may be caused by nuclear weapon explosions is beyond the scope of this *Manual*. Such data may be found in the American Society of Civil Engineers Manual No. 42, *Design of Structures To Resist Nuclear Weapons Effects* and in TR-20 (Volume 4), *Protective Construction*, Office of Civil Defense.

SECTION 4
DESIGN

DESIGN

INTRODUCTION

This section is concerned with the basic types of structural members as well as several of the more common wood structural systems. Under the headings herein are contained general information on the design features of the member or system, tabular data, a typical design procedure, and, in most cases, a design example.

The procedures presented have been found to be the methods most suited to the particular member or system in question; however, other methods may be used if substantiated by tests or by sound engineering principles.

The examples are illustrative only. In actual designs, all the conditions which might be expected to have a bearing on the ability of the member or structure to support all anticipated loads safely should be considered.

COLUMNS

The column design charts, Figures 4.2 through 4.4, may be used to determine allowable unit loads for simple solid and spaced columns under normal duration of loading. Simple solid columns consist of a single piece of solid sawn or glued laminated timber. Spaced columns consist of two or more individual members with their longitudinal axes parallel, separated at their ends and midpoints by blocking, and joined at the ends by connectors capable of developing the required shear resistance.

The l/d ratio for simple solid columns may not exceed 50. For individual members of a spaced column, l/d may not exceed 80, nor may l_2/d exceed 40 (see Figure 4.1). To obtain spaced column action, end blocks are required when the l/d ratio for the individual members exceeds $\sqrt{0.30E/F_c}$. When l/d ratios for the individual members of spaced columns do not exceed this value, the individual members are designed as simple solid columns. A multiplying factor is introduced in the spaced column design formulas which depends on fixity conditions of the column (see Figure 4.1).

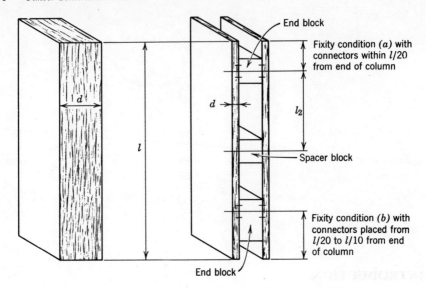

End block

Fixity condition *(a)* with connectors within *l*/20 from end of column

Spacer block

Fixity condition *(b)* with connectors placed from *l*/20 to *l*/10 from end of column

End block

Simple Solid Column	Spaced Column
d = dimension of least side of column, in.	*d* = dimension of least side of individual member, in.
l = overall unsupported length of column, in.	*l* = overall unsupported length from center to center of lateral supports of continuous column, or from end to end of simple columns, in.
	l_2 = distance from center of connector in end block to center of spacer block, in.

Figure 4.1.   COLUMNS.

Simple Solid Rectangular Columns

The column design chart as represented by Figure 4.2 is based on the following formula and limitations:

$$F_c' = \frac{0.30E}{(l/d)^2}$$

where F_c' = allowable unit stress in compression parallel to grain, psi, adjusted for l/d ratio

E = modulus of elasticity, psi

l and d are illustrated in Fig. 4.1

The formula is based on pin end conditions, but it is also applied to square end conditions.

The allowable stress values as determined from the formula may not exceed the values for compression parallel to grain, F_c, for the species, adjusted for service conditions and duration of loading. The allowable unit stress values as determined from the formula are subject to the duration of loading adjustments given in Figure 2.3 or Table 2.12 of this *Manual*.

Example. Using the column design charts, determine the load which can be

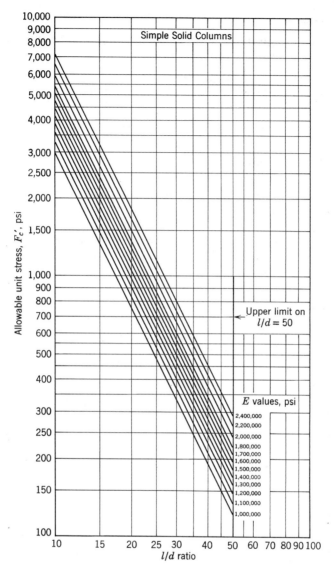

Figure 4.2. ALLOWABLE COLUMN LOADS.

carried by an 8×10 column which meets the following requirements:

Normal duration of loading (factor $= 1.00$)

$L = 10\,\text{ft}$ $\qquad E = 1,700,000\,\text{psi}$

$F_c = 1,400\,\text{psi}$

$l/d = \dfrac{(10)(12)}{7.5} = 16 < 50 \qquad \text{O.K.}$

By entering Figure 4.2 with $l/d = 16$ and $E = 1,700,000$, the allowable unit stress, F_c', is determined to be $2,000 > F_c = 1,400\,\text{psi}$. Use $F_c' = 1,400\,\text{psi}$. $P = AF_c' = (1,400)(7.5)(9.5) = 99,750\,\text{lb}$.

Spaced Columns

The column design charts as represented by Figures 4.3 and 4.4 are based on the following formulas and limitations:

$$F_c' = \frac{0.75E}{(l/d)^2} \qquad \text{fixity condition } (a)$$

$$F_c' = \frac{0.90E}{(l/d)^2} \qquad \text{fixity condition } (b)$$

where terms are as defined above.

The individual members in a spaced column are considered to act together to carry the total column load. Each member is designed separately on the basis of its l/d ratio. Because of the end fixity developed in spaced columns, a greater l/d ratio than that allowed for simple solid columns is permitted. This fixity is effective only in the thickness direction; the l/d in the width direction is subject to the provisions for simple solid columns.

Connectors are not required for a single spacer block located in the middle tenth of the column length, l. Connectors are required for multiple spacer blocks, and the distance between two adjacent blocks may not exceed one-half the distance between centers of connectors in the end blocks. When spaced columns are used as truss compression members, panel points which are stayed laterally are considered as the ends of the spaced column. The portion of the web members between the individual pieces of which the spaced column is comprised may be considered as the end blocks. In the case of multiple connectors in a contact face, the center of gravity of the connector group is used in measuring the distance from connectors to the end of the column. (See Figure 4.1.)

The total load capacity determined by using the spaced column formulas should be checked against the sum of the load capacities of the individual members taken as simple solid columns without regard to fixity; their greater d and the l between lateral supports which provide restraint in a direction parallel to the greater d should be used.

The values for F_c' determined by either of the formulas may not exceed the values for compression parallel to grain, F_c, for the species, adjusted for service conditions and duration of loading.

The values for F_c' computed by using the formulas are subject to duration of loading adjustments as given in Figure 2.3 and Table 2.12 of this *Manual*.

Spacer and end block thickness may not be less than that of the individual members of the spaced column, nor shall thickness, width, and length of spacer and end block be less than required for connectors of a size and number capable of carrying the computed load.

To obtain spaced column action, the connectors in mutually contacting surfaces of end blocks and individual members at each end of a spaced column must be of a size and number to provide a load capacity equal to the required cross-sectional area of one of the individual members times the appropriate constant from Table 4.1. For spaced columns that are part of a truss system, the connectors required by joint design should be checked against the values obtained by using the constants from Table 4.1.

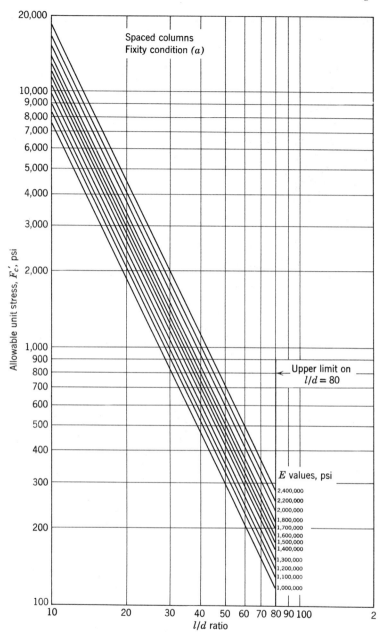

Figure 4.3. ALLOWABLE COLUMN LOADS.

Example. Using the column design charts, select a two-member spaced column of Group A species to meet the following requirements:

7-day duration of loading (factor = 1.25)

$P = 40,000\,\text{lb}$ $\quad E = 1,700,000\,\text{psi}$
$L = 12\,\text{ft}$ $\qquad F_c = (1,200)(1.25) = 1,500\,\text{psi}$

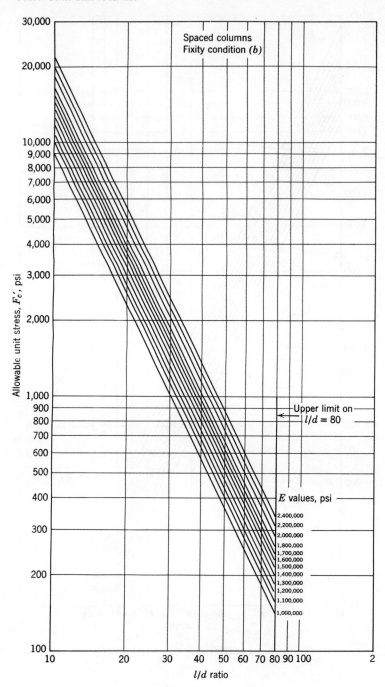

Figure 4.4.   ALLOWABLE COLUMN LOADS.

TABLE 4.1

END BLOCK CONSTANT FOR CONNECTOR
JOINED SPACED COLUMNS

l/d Ratio of Individual Member of Spaced Column[a]	End Spacer Block Constant for Connector Load Groups[b]			
	Group A[c]	Group B[c]	Group C[c]	Group D[c]
0 to 11	0	0	0	0
15	38	33	27	21
20	86	73	61	48
25	134	114	94	75
30	181	155	128	101
35	229	195	162	128
40	277	236	195	154
45	325	277	229	181
50	372	318	263	208
55	420	358	296	234
60 to 80	468	399	330	261

[a]Constants for intermediate l/d ratios may be obtained by straight-line interpolation.
[b]Constants are based on areas in square inches and load in pounds.
[c]See Table 5.1 for species in each group.

Distance from end of column to center of 4 in. split rings in end blocks $= x = 1$ ft:

$$L/20 = \frac{12}{20} = 0.6 \text{ ft} \qquad L/10 = \frac{12}{10} = 1.2 \text{ ft}$$

Column is under fixity condition (b), since $L/20 < x < L/10$.
Try two 3×6 members, $A = 27.50$ in.²:

$$l/d = \frac{(12)(12)}{2.50} = 57.6$$

Entering Figure 4.4 with $l/d = 57.6$ and $E = 1,700,000$, the allowable stress, F_c', is determined to be 460 psi. Adjusting for duration of loading, $F_c' = (460)(1.25) = 575$ psi $< 1,500$. Use $F_c' = 575$ psi.

$$\text{Required } A = \frac{P}{F_c'} = \frac{40,000}{575} = 69.6 \text{ in.}^2 > 27.50 \qquad \text{N.G.}$$

Try two 4×8 members, $A = 50.75$ in.²:

$$l/d = \frac{(12)(12)}{3.50} = 41.1$$

From Figure 4.4, $F_c' = 920$ psi. Adjusting for duration of load,
$F_c' = (920)(1.25) = 1,150$ psi $< 1,500$

Use $F_c' = 1{,}150$ psi.

$$\text{Required } A = \frac{P}{F_c'} = \frac{40{,}000}{1{,}150} = 34.8 \text{ in.}^2 < 50.75 \qquad \text{O.K.}$$

Check as a solid column using the greater d:

$$l/d = \frac{(12)(12)}{7.25} = 19.9$$

From Figure 4.2, $F_c' = 1{,}275$ psi. Adjusting for duration of load, $F_c' = (1{,}275)(1.25) = 1{,}594$ psi; use $F_c' = 1{,}500$ psi. Allowable $P = AF_c' = (50.75)(1{,}500) = 76{,}125$ lb $> 40{,}000$ O.K.

Check the connectors for spaced column action. From Table 4.1, the end block constant for $l/d = 41.1$ in Group A species is 288.
Total connector load $= (288)(25.37) = 7{,}307$ lb.
Allowable load per 4 in. split ring (from page 5-22) $= (6{,}140)(1.25) = 7{,}680$ lb $> 7{,}307$. Therefore, one 4 in. split ring is required in each face.

Round Columns

The allowable stress for a round column may not exceed that for a square column of the same cross-sectional area or that determined by the formula

$$F_c' = \frac{3.619E}{(l/r)^2}$$

where $r =$ least radius of gyration of section, in., and other terms are as defined above.

The values for F_c' determined by the formula may not exceed the values for compression parallel to grain, F_c, for the species, adjusted for service conditions and duration of loading.

The allowable unit stress values as determined from the formula are subject to the duration of loading adjustments given in Figure 2.3 and Table 2.12 of this *Manual*.

Tapered Columns

In determining d for tapered columns, the diameter of a round column or the least dimension of a rectangular column, tapered at one or both ends, is taken as the sum of the minimum diameter or least dimension and one-third the difference between the minimum and maximum diameters or lesser and greater dimensions.

Combined Loading in Columns

End loads, side loads, and eccentricity

The following formulas may be used for pin-end columns of rectangular cross section subjected to both axial compression and moment (from eccentricity or side loads).

l/d Ratio	Concentric End and Side Loads	Eccentric Load Only	Combined End Loads, Side Loads, and Eccentricity
End load / Side load	Eccentric load	Eccentric load / End load / Side load	
$\sqrt{\dfrac{0.30E}{F_c}}$ or less	$\dfrac{M/S}{F_b} + \dfrac{P/A}{F_c'} = 1$	$\dfrac{(P/A)(6e/d)}{F_b} + \dfrac{P/A}{F_c'} = 1$	$\dfrac{M/S + (P/A)(6e/d)}{F_b} + \dfrac{P/A}{F_c'} = 1$
Greater than $\sqrt{\dfrac{0.30E}{F_c}}$	$\dfrac{M/S}{F_b - P/A} + \dfrac{P/A}{F_c'} = 1$	$\dfrac{(P/A)(15e/2d)}{F_b - P/A} + \dfrac{P/A}{F_c'} = 1$	$\dfrac{M/S + (P/A)(15e/2d)}{F_b - P/A} + \dfrac{P/A}{F_c'} = 1$

where E = modulus of elasticity, psi

$\quad F_b$ = allowable unit stress in extreme fiber in bending, psi, permitted if flexural stress only existed

$\quad F_c$ = allowable unit stress in compression parallel to grain, psi, permitted if axial compressive stress only existed

$\quad F_c'$ = allowable unit stress in compression parallel to grain adjusted for l/d ratio, psi

$\quad M/S$ = flexural stress induced by side loads, psi

$\quad P/A$ = direct compressive stress induced by axial loads, psi

$\quad e$ = eccentricity, in.

$\quad d$ = dimension of side of rectangular column, in. (measured in the direction of side loads)

$\quad l$ = length of column, in.

In the combined stress formulas, the size factor, C_F, is applied to the allowable unit bending stresses in accordance with Section 2 of this *Manual*.

Columns with bracket loads

The formulas given for combined loading in columns assume that the eccentric load is applied at the end of the columns as shown. If the eccentric load is applied through a bracket at some point below the upper end, the following procedure may be applied.

Assume that a bracket load, P, at a distance, a, from the center of the column is replaced by the same load, P, centrally applied at the top of the column, plus a side load, P', applied at midheight. This condition is shown in Figure 4.5. The load P' is determined from the following formula:

$$P' = \frac{3al'P}{l^2}$$

where P' = assumed horizontal side load, placed at mid-height of the column, lb

$\quad P$ = actual load on bracket, lb

$\quad a$ = horizontal distance from bracket load to center of column, in.

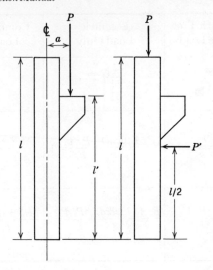

Figure 4.5.   COLUMNS WITH LOADS APPLIED AT SIDE BRACKETS.

l = length of column, in.
l' = distance from point of application of load on bracket to farther end of column, in.

The assumed centrally applied load, P, should be added to other concentric column loads, and the calculated side load P', should be used to determine the flexural stress, M/S, for use in the formula for concentric end and side loading.

Example. Determine the adequacy of an 8×8 pinned end column subjected to the following loading conditions:

Normal duration of loading (factor = 1.00)
Bracket load, $P = 10,000$ lb
$a = 12$ in.
$L = 10$ ft
$F_b = 1,400$ psi; $F_c = 1,200$ psi; $E = 1,700,000$ psi

Note: Top of bracket at point of load application is located 2 ft below top of column

$$P' = \frac{(3)(12)(96)}{(120)^2} 10,000 = 2,400 \text{ lb}$$

Analyze for combined stresses due to concentric load, P, and side load, P'.

$$l/d = \frac{(10)(12)}{7.5} = 16$$

$$F_c' = \frac{(0.30)(1,700,000)}{(16)^2} = 1,992 \text{ psi.}$$

$$\sqrt{\frac{(0.30)(1,700,000)}{1,200}} = 20.6$$

$$\therefore l/d < \sqrt{\frac{0.30E}{F_c}}$$

$$M = (1{,}200)(5)(12) = 72{,}000 \text{ in.-lb}$$

$$\frac{72{,}000/70.3}{1{,}400} + \frac{10{,}000/56.25}{1{,}200} \leqslant 1$$

$$0.73 + 0.15 = 0.88 < 1 \qquad \text{O.K.}$$

BEAMS

Straight Beams

Simple span beams

The beam design charts as given in Figures 4.6, 4.7, and 4.8 may be used for the design or analysis of simple span timber beams with uniformly distributed loads.

The charts are based on the following formulas:

Bending: $\qquad M = \frac{wl^2}{8}$ and $S = \frac{M}{F_b}$

Horizontal shear: $R_V = \frac{wl}{2}$ and $F_v = \frac{3R_V}{2bd}$

Deflection: $\qquad \Delta_A = \frac{5wl^4}{384EI}$

Each chart includes directions for its use.

After a beam has been selected on the basis of one design criterion, the size selected should be checked for the other criteria. For example, if a beam is designed for bending, it should be checked for shear and deflection.

Lateral stability considerations for beams as given on pages 4-173 through 4-176 should be appropriately applied.

Size factor must be considered for beams deeper than 12 in. See Section 2 of this *Manual* for size factor considerations.

Design procedure.

1. Determine size of beam required in bending. Use the bending chart, Figure 4.6. Place a straightedge to intersect the unit stress (F_b) scale at the known allowable unit stress value for the species and grade adjusted for duration of loading and any other appropriate adjustment factors, and the span (L) scale at the known value for span length, in feet. Pivot the straightedge about its point of intersection with the pivot line (P) until it intersects the load (w) scale at the known value for total uniform load, in pounds per lineal foot. Read the required section modulus value at the intersection of the straightedge with the section modulus (S) scale.

For glued laminated beams, the selection of the size may be based on Table 2.16 and the industry standard depths and widths as given on page 2-86. For solid sawn beams, the size corresponding to the required section modulus may be determined using Table 2.17 for common sizes or the complete table of sizes in Section 6 of this *Manual*. If the required size is deeper than 12 in., determine the size factor, C_F, for the depth, d, from Figure 2.4 or from the formula

$$C_F = (12/d)^{1/9}$$

(See pages **2**-35 to **2**-38 for a detailed discussion of size factor.)

If a size factor is determined, check the section modulus value to make certain that it still is adequate. Several repetitions may be required. The size finally determined in this manner is the required size if it meets shear and deflection requirements.

2. Check adequacy of the section based on the lateral stability provisions on pages **4**-173 through **4**-176.

3. Determine size of beam required in shear. Use the shear chart, Figure 4.7. If the allowable unit horizontal shear stress, F_v, adjusted for duration of loading and any other appropriate adjustment factors is other than 165 psi or 200 psi, an adjusted load value must be determined before the chart is used. The adjusted load value equals the total uniform load, in pounds per lineal foot, times either ratio, $165/F_v$ or $200/F_v$. To use the shear chart, the effective span must be computed. Effective span is equal to the clear span, in feet, less twice the beam depth, in feet. For preliminary design purposes. It may be necessary to assume a beam depth. Place the straightedge to intersect the load (w) scale for the proper horizontal shear value, and the effective span (L) scale at the computed value for effective span, in feet. Read the required area value at the intersection of the straightedge with the area (A) scale.

The size corresponding to the required area may be determined by using Table 2.16 for glued laminated beams or Table 2.17 for solid sawn beams.

If shear governs, the size so determined is the required size if it meets deflection requirements.

4. Determine size of beam required for deflection. Use the deflection chart, Figure 4.8. If the modulus of elasticity, E, for the species and grade is other than 1,800,000 psi, an adjusted load value must be determined before using the chart. The adjusted load value equals the uniform load, in pounds per lineal foot, times the ratio $1,800,000/E$. Place the straightedge to intersect the appropriate load (w) scale at the adjusted value for uniform load, in pounds per lineal foot, and the span (L) scale at the known value for span length, in feet. Read the required moment of inertia value at the intersection of the straightedge with the moment of inertia (I) scale.

For deflection limit of $l/180$, use one-half of the load value for the $l/360$ limit. For a deflection limit of $l/120$, use one-half of the load value for the $l/240$ limit.

The size corresponding to the required moment of inertia may be determined by using Table 2.16 for glued laminated beams or Table 2.17 for solid sawn beams.

If deflection governs, the size so determined is the required size.

5. Determine actual deflection and required camber for a beam. Use the beam deflection chart, Figure 4.9. Place the straightedge to intersect the moment of inertia (I) scale at the known value for moment of inertia and

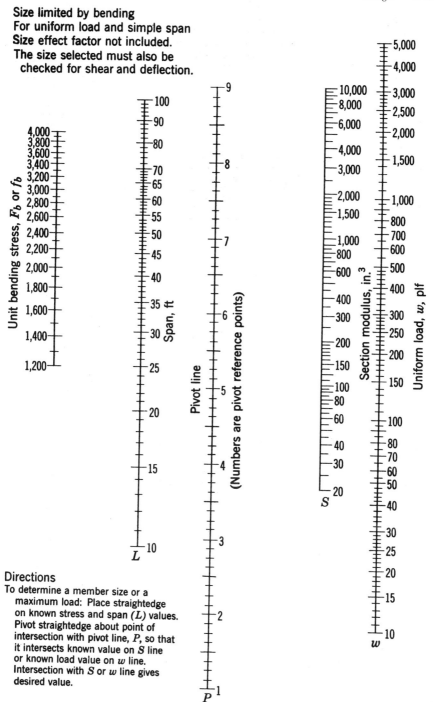

Size limited by bending
For uniform load and simple span
Size effect factor not included.
The size selected must also be
checked for shear and deflection.

Unit bending stress, F_b or f_b

4,000
3,800
3,600
3,400
3,200
3,000
2,800
2,600
2,400
2,200
2,000
1,800
1,600
1,400
1,200

Span, ft

100
90
80
70
65
60
55
50
45
40
35
30
25
20
15
10

L

Pivot line

(Numbers are pivot reference points)

9
8
7
6
5
4
3
2
1

P

Section modulus, in.^{3}

10,000
8,000
6,000
4,000
3,000
2,000
1,500
1,000
800
600
400
300
200
150
100
80
60
40
30
20

S

Uniform load, w, plf

5,000
4,000
3,000
2,500
2,000
1,500
1,000
800
700
600
500
400
300
250
200
150
100
80
70
60
50
40
30
25
20
15
10

w

Directions
To determine a member size or a
maximum load: Place straightedge
on known stress and span (*L*) values.
Pivot straightedge about point of
intersection with pivot line, *P*, so that
it intersects known value on *S* line
or known load value on *w* line.
Intersection with *S* or *w* line gives
desired value.

Figure 4.6.   BEAM DESIGN CHART – BENDING.

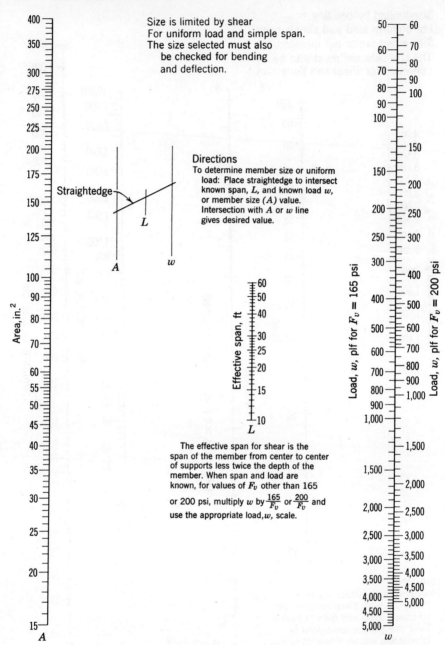

Figure 4.7.   **BEAM DESIGN CHART – SHEAR.**

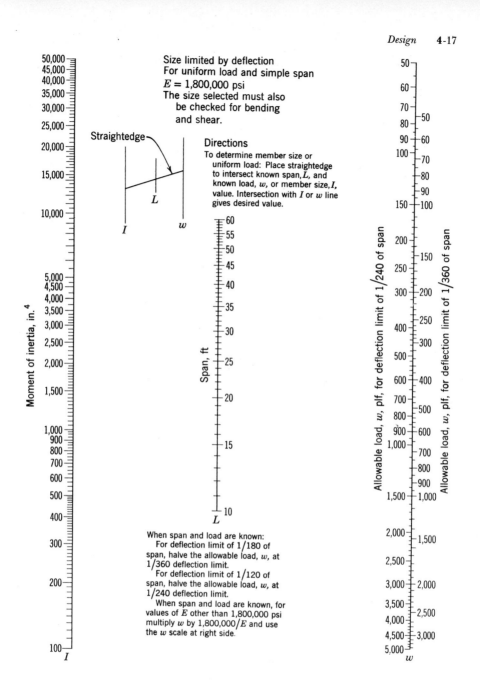

Figure 4.8.   BEAM DESIGN CHART – DEFLECTION.

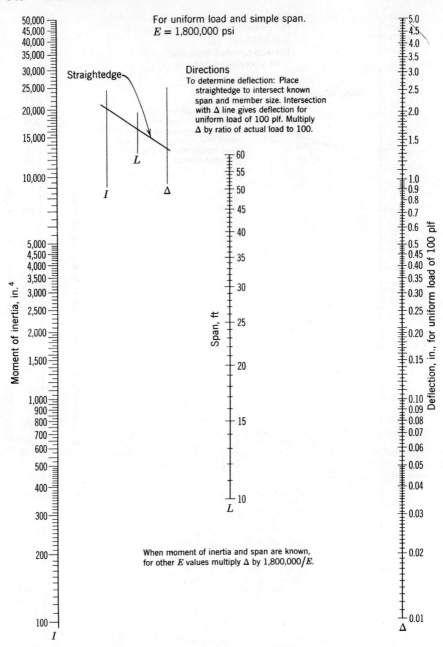

For uniform load and simple span.
$E = 1,800,000$ psi

Directions

To determine deflection: Place straightedge to intersect known span and member size. Intersection with Δ line gives deflection for uniform load of 100 plf. Multiply Δ by ratio of actual load to 100.

When moment of inertia and span are known, for other E values multiply Δ by $1,800,000/E$.

Figure 4.9.   BEAM DEFLECTION CHART.

the span (*L*) scale at the known value for span length, in feet. Read the deflection value for a uniform load of 100 plf at the intersection of the straightedge with the deflection (Δ_a) scale. Multiply this deflection value by the ratio of the actual uniform load to 100 to determine the actual deflection corresponding to the actual load.

Camber for glued laminated beams is usually specified as some multiple of the dead load deflection for appearance purposes and/or to provide drainage. The camber for the actual dead load may be computed by multiplying the actual dead load deflection by the appropriate camber constant. See Table 4.25 for camber recommendations.

If the value of the modulus of elasticity, *E*, for the species and grade is other than 1,800,000 psi, an adjusted deflection value must be determined. The adjusted deflection value equals the deflection, in inches, times the ratio 1,800,000/*E*.

6. Determine the actual bending stress in a beam. Use the bending chart, Figure 4.6. Place a straightedge to intersect the load (*w*) scale at the known value for the total uniform load, in pounds per lineal foot, and the section modulus (*S*) scale at the known value for section modulus, in cubic inches. Pivot the straightedge about its point of intersection with the pivot line, *P*, until it intersects the span (*L*) scale at the known value for the span length, in feet. Read the actual stress value at the intersection of the straightedge with the unit stress (f_b) scale.

7. Determine the actual horizontal shear stress in a beam. Use the shear chart, Figure 4.7. Place the straightedge to intersect the area (*A*) scale at the known value for area, in square inches, and the effective span (*L*) scale at the computed value for effective span, in feet (see step 3 for determination of effective span). At the intersection of the straightedge with the load (*w*) scale for either the 165 psi or the 200 psi horizontal shear value, read the uniform load value.

The actual horizontal shear stress is determined by multiplying either 165 psi or 200 psi, depending on which load (*w*) scale was used, by the ratio of the actual uniform load to the uniform load determined as above.

Glued Laminated Beam Example. Design a glued laminated roof beam to meet the following requirements (two months duration of loading, factor = 1.15).

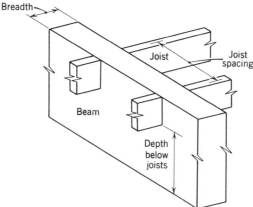

Joist loaded (2 × 12 joists on 20 in. centers)
$L = 40$ ft   Deflection limits:
Spacing = 20 ft $\Delta_{SL} = l/240$
SL = 30 psf $\Delta_{TL} = l/180$
DL = 10 psf   Camber required $1\frac{1}{2}\Delta_{DL}$
$F_b = (2{,}400)(1.15) = 2{,}760$ psi
$F_v = (165)(1.15) = 190$ psi
$E = 1{,}800{,}000$ psi

1. Determine size of beam required in bending.

$w_{DL} = $ (spacing)(DL) $= (20)(10) = 200$ plf
$w_{SL} = $ (spacing)(SL) $= (20)(30) = \underline{600 \text{ plf}}$
$w_{TL} = w_{DL} + w_{SL} \qquad = \qquad 800$ plf

Assume $C_F = 0.90$; then, $F_b = (2{,}760)(0.90) = 2{,}484$ psi
From the beam design chart – bending, Figure 4.6, S required = 730 in.[3]
From Table 2.16; Try a $5\frac{1}{8} \times 30$ section based on the use of $1\frac{1}{2}$ in. multiples of lamination thickness. $S = 768.8$; $C_F = 0.90$
$l/d = (40)(12)/30 = 16$; therefore adjusted $C_F = (0.90)(1.016) = 0.91$ (see pages 2-35 to 2-38). Adjusted allowable unit bending stress $F_b = (2{,}760)(0.91) = 2{,}512$ psi.

Check S required, using actual C_F:

$$S = \frac{M}{F_b C_F} = (730)\,\frac{0.90}{0.91} = 722 \text{ in.}^3 < 768.8 \qquad \text{O.K.}$$

Note: A $5\frac{1}{8} \times 29\frac{1}{4}$ section having a section modulus of 730.8 would be adequate. However this would require the use of a $\frac{3}{4}$ in. lamination and would not be a standard size based on the use of multiples of $1\frac{1}{2}$ in. laminations.

2. Check allowable unit stress in bending based on lateral support provisions on pages 4-173 through 4-176.

The beam is laterally braced by joists spaced 20 in. on centers.

(a) When the joists are firmly attached to the top flange of the beam in hangers, the joists carry a properly nailed sheathing, and torsional rotation is prevented at the beam ends, a diaphragm has been created which causes the unsupported length of the beam to be zero, and the full allowable stress in bending may be used.

(b) Consider the beam braced laterally only every 20 in., with the only mode of lateral buckling possibly taking place being between the joists. In this case, which is similar to equal end moments (between the joists), the effective length, l_e, would be $(1.84)(20) = 36.8$ in. (from Table 4.27).

$$C_S = \sqrt{\frac{l_e d}{b^2}} = \sqrt{\frac{(36.8)(30.0)}{(5.125)^2}} = \sqrt{42.0} = 6.48$$

Thus since $C_S < 10$, there is no reduction in bending stress because of slenderness.

(c) If the joists are not properly fastened, or if the diaphragm action is not provided by the joists and the sheathing to the compression flange, then the beam could buckle over the unsupported distance of 40 ft. Then:

$$l_e = (1.92)(12)(40) = 921.6 \text{ in.}$$

$$C_S = \sqrt{\frac{(921.6)(30.0)}{(5.125)^2}} = \sqrt{1,053} = 32.4$$

$$C_K = \sqrt{\frac{3E}{5F_b}} = \sqrt{\frac{(0.6)(1,800,000)}{2,400}} = \sqrt{450} = 21.2$$

Since $50 > C_S > C_K$, the beam is a long beam and the allowable unit stress is:

$$F_b' = \frac{0.40E}{C_S^2} = \frac{(0.40)(1,800,000)}{1,050} = 686 \text{ psi}$$

Note: This value of F_b' could also have been determined from Figure 4.37. Adjusting for duration of load, $F_b' = (686)(1.15) = 789 \text{ psi} < 2,512 \text{ psi}$. Therefore, the cross section determined in step 1 would be overstressed. The obvious and easy answer is to provide the adequate resistance to torsional rotation at the end support points and full lateral bracing between these end supports so that the unsupported length becomes zero and the full allowable bending stress may be used.

3. Check size of beam required in shear.
   Determine adjusted load, w', for actual shear stress value:

$$w' = w_{TL} \frac{200}{F_v} = 800 \frac{200}{190} = 843 \text{ plf}$$

Determine effective span, L_e,

$$L_e = L - 2d = 40 - \frac{(2)(30.0)}{12} = 35.0 \text{ ft}$$

From the beam design chart – shear, Figure 4.7, required $A = 110 \text{ in.}^2$.
From Table 2.16, for $5\frac{1}{8} \times 30$ section, $A = 153.8 \text{ in.}^2$.
In this example, therefore, shear does not govern.

4. Check size of beam required for deflection. Use deflection criteria given in Table 4.21 for roof beam.

From the beam design chart – deflection, Figure 4.8:
(a) Using $w_{SL} = 600$ plf on $l/240$ scale,
Required $I = 10,000 \text{ in.}^4 < 11,531$ O.K.
(b) Using $\frac{1}{2}w_{TL} = 400$ plf on $l/360$ scale,
Required $I = 10,000 \text{ in.}^4 < 11,531$ O.K.
In this example, therefore, deflection does not govern.

5. Determine required camber for the beam.

From deflection chart, Figure 4.9, $\Delta_{100} = 0.28$,

Required camber $= 1.5\Delta_{DL} = (1.5)(0.28)\dfrac{200}{100} = 0.84$ in.

Solid Sawn Beam Example. Analyze a 4×12 solid sawn timber roof beam under the following conditions. The roof deck is applied directly to beams, and

$L = 18$ ft $F_b = (1{,}550)(1.15) = 1{,}782$ psi
Spacing $= 10$ ft $F_v = (85)(1.15) = 98$ psi
$SL = 20$ psf $E = 1{,}700{,}000$ psi
$DL = 10$ psf $\Delta_{SL} = l/240$
              $\Delta_{TL} = l/180$

1. Determine actual bending stress, f_b:

$w_{DL} = (\text{spacing})(DL) = (10)(10) = 100$ plf
$w_{SL} = (\text{spacing})(SL) = (10)(20) = 200$ plf

$w_{TL} = w_{DL} + w_{SL} \qquad = \qquad 300$ plf
For a 4×12 section, $A = 39.38$ in.², $S = 73.83$ in.³, and $I = 415.28$ in.⁴ (from Table 2.17).
From the beam design chart—bending, Figure 4.6,
$f_b = 1{,}600$ psi $< F_b = 1{,}782$ psi   O.K.

2. Determine area required based on horizontal shear:
Effective span $(L_e) = L - 2d = 18 - \dfrac{(2)(11.25)}{12} = 16.12$ ft

From the beam design chart—shear, Figure 4.7,
$w' = 612$ plf on the 200 psi scale
Area required $= 37$ in.² < 39.38 in.²   O.K.

3. Determine the actual deflection of the beam. From the beam deflection chart, Figure 4.9,

$\Delta_{100} = 0.31$ in. for $E = 1{,}800{,}000$ psi

$\Delta'_{100} = 0.31\left(\dfrac{1{,}800{,}000}{1{,}700{,}000}\right) = 0.33$ in.

$\Delta_{SL} = \Delta'_{100}\dfrac{w_{SL}}{100} = 0.33\dfrac{200}{100} = 0.66$ in. $< l/240 = 0.90$ O.K.

$\Delta_{TL} = \Delta'_{100}\dfrac{w_{TL}}{100} = 0.33\dfrac{300}{100} = 0.99$ in. $< l/180 = 1.20$ O.K.

Cantilever beams

Cantilever beam systems may be comprised of any of the various types and combinations of beams illustrated in Figure 4.10. Cantilever systems

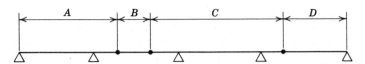

Figure 4.10.   CANTILEVERED BEAM SYSTEMS. *A* is a single cantilever, *B* is a suspended beam, *C* has a double cantilever, and *D* is a beam with one end suspended.

permit longer spans or larger loads for a given size member than do simple span systems, provided member size is not controlled by compression perpendicular to grain at the supports or by horizontal shear. In general, a uniform section should be used throughout the length of a cantilever system. Increasing the depth of section at supports to meet shear requirements causes areas of stress concentration at the point of change, and it should be avoided. For economy, the negative bending moment at the supports of a cantilevered beam should be equal in magnitude to the positive moment.

Consideration must be given to deflection and camber in cantilevered multiple spans. When possible, roofs should be sufficiently sloped to eliminate water pockets or provisions should be made to ensure that accumulation of water does not produce greater deflection and live loads than anticipated. Unbalanced loading conditions should be investigated for maximum bending moment, deflection, and stability. The lateral support rules given in Tables 4.27 and 4.28 should be applied to cantilevered beams.

Typical connection details for suspended and cantilevered beams may be found in *Typical Construction Details*, AITC 104, in Part II of this *Manual*. The cantilevered beam diagrams in Section 6 give moment, shear, reaction, and deflection coefficients.

Continuous beams

Continuous span beams are commonly used in both building and bridge construction to reduce maximum moments, thus reducing the section size required. To aid the designer, the beam diagrams and formulas and fixed end moment diagrams and formulas given in Section 6 of this *Manual* may be used in determining shear and moment values.

Crane beams

Timber has a natural advantage for use as crane runway beams because of its ability to absorb impact forces. In design, impact may be disregarded up to 100% of the static effect of the live load producing the impact, unless there is a steel connection through which the load must pass.

The crane manufacturer's recommended wheel loads should be used. For design purposes, the wheel placement producing the greatest moment should be used. The wheel placement which produces the maximum vertical reaction should also be employed, any loads within a distance from the supports equal to the depth of the member being neglected. See page **3**-38 for determination of maximum moment and vertical reaction for simple beams with two unequal wheel loads.

The lateral force on crane runways resisting the effect of the moving trolley is considered as acting in either direction normal to the runway rail. It is applied at the top of rail, one-half to each side of the runway. The American National Standards Institute recommends that this force be 20% of the sum of the lifted load and the weight of the trolley (but exclusive of other parts of the crane).

For longitudinal bracing, the design load is applied at the top of the rail and the American National Standards Institute recommends a force equalling 10% of the maximum wheel loads.

Deflection of crane runway beams should be limited in accordance with the crane manufacturer's recommendations, in order to avoid undue movement and racking of joints. Recommended deflection limits, based on total dead and applied loads at point of maximum moment, are $l/240$ for hand-operated cranes and $l/360$ for electrically operated cranes.

Some crane manufacturers specify wheel loads which include a certain percentage for impact; when they do, designers should take this factor into account. Impact must be considered for steel-to-steel connections.

Tapered Beams

Glued laminated beams are often tapered to meet architectural requirements, to provide pitched roofs, or to provide a minimum depth of beam at its bearing. The most commonly used tapered beams are simple span. Figure 4.11 illustrates various forms of these beams.

It is recommended that any sawn taper cuts be made on the compression face of tapered beams. It is also recommended that pitched or curved tension faces of beams not be sawn across the grain, but, instead, that the beam be so manufactured that the laminations are parallel to the tension face (see Figure 4.4).

Although sawn taper cuts on the tension face are not recommended, the indicated design procedures will apply to simple beams when the taper cut is on the tension face as well as on the compression face, except that the value for F_y will be the allowable stress in tension perpendicular

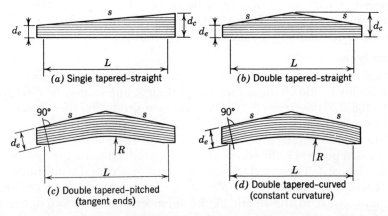

Figure 4.11. SIMPLE SPAN TAPERED BEAM FORMS. (The letter s designates sawn surface.)

to grain instead of the allowable stress in compression perpendicular to grain, $F_{c\perp}$. For Southern pine and California redwood, the allowable stress in tension perpendicular to grain shall be limited to $\frac{1}{3}$ of the allowable unit stress in horizontal shear for these species for all conditions of loading. For Douglas fir and Western larch, this criteria is also applicable when designing for wind or earthquake loadings but shall be limited to 15 psi for all other conditions of loading. These values are subject to modification for duration of load.

Camber is provided in beams which are taper cut on the compression face in a manner similar to the taper cut; that is, the minimum camber for dead load deflection (centerline camber) is built into the members so that the laminations are parallel to the tension face. Also, it is customary to saw camber into the compression face of double tapered beams. This camber should equal one-fourth of the centerline camber if the centerline camber is over 2 in. If this camber is not provided, the compression face may give an optical illusion of sagging. Provision for camber in tapered beams is the designer's responsibility. Such camber should not be provided by the fabricator unless it is shown on the shop details.

For double tapered-pitched and double tapered-curved beams, the additional provisions for curved members on pages **4-45** through **4-51** of this *Manual* must be considered. In double tapered-curved beams, when the radius of curvature is large, of the order of three times the span, as is common for this form, it is usual to treat them as double tapered-straight beams. If the curvature is sharp, double tapered-curved beams can be treated as double tapered-pitched beams.

The design of pitched and curved beams must provide for horizontal deflection at the supports. If it does not, that is, if the supports are designed to resist horizontal movement, the member must be designed as a two-hinged arch. It is usually preferable to provide for the relatively small amount of horizontal movement which occurs at the supports by detailing slotted or roller connections. (See *Typical Construction Details*, AITC 104, in Part II of this *Manual* for a typical slotted beam connection.)

Tapered beams of constant width

When the top and bottom of a beam are not parallel to each other (a variable depth along the length of the beam is created by a sawn surface), consideration must be given to the combined effects of bending, compression, tension, and shear parallel to grain and also to compression or tension perpendicular to grain. An example of the distribution of the shear stresses existing in a tapered beam is given in Figure 4.12.

This analysis involves an interaction formula when stresses f_x, f_y, and f_{xy} occur simultaneously to reduce the beam capacity below the capacity that would result from considering each stress separately.

Approximate mathematical relationships based on elementary Bernoulli-Euler theory of bending were developed for the general cases of shear and vertical stresses existing in timber bending members with varying cross section. This basic theory was then expanded to verify the applicability of an interaction formula in predicting the ultimate strength of tapered timber

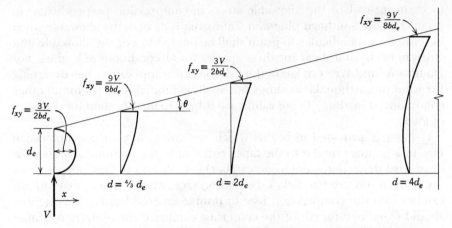

Figure 4.12. DISTRIBUTION OF SHEAR STRESSES IN A SIMPLY SUPPORTED BEAM UNDER CONCENTRATED LOADS.

bending members. Such a formula, expressing the effects of combined stresses and also used for materials other than wood, takes the form

$$\frac{f_x^2}{F_x^2}+\frac{f_y^2}{F_y^2}+\frac{f_{xy}^2}{F_{xy}^2}\leq 1$$

where F_x, F_y, and F_{xy} are maximum allowable stress values, and f_x, f_y, and f_{xy} are actual stress values encountered at the same point on the beam.

f_x = bending stress
f_y = compression or tension stress perpendicular to grain (compression if the taper cut is on the compression face, and tension if the taper cut is on the tension face)
f_{xy} = shear stress
F_x = allowable bending stress, modified for duration of load
F_y = allowable stress in compression perpendicular to grain; or tension perpendicular to grain, modified for duration of load
F_{xy} = allowable horizontal shear stress, modified for duration of load

For tapered beams, at the tapered edge the existing stresses can be expressed as a function of the bending stress, f_x, as follows:

$$f_{xy} = f_x \tan \theta$$
$$f_y \ = f_x \tan^2 \theta$$

or

$$f_y \ = f_{xy} \tan \theta$$

where $\tan \theta$ = slope of the tapered face.

By assuming an optimum design (i.e., the interaction stress equation set equal to one), it is possible to write this equation as

$$\frac{f_x^2}{F_b^2}+\frac{f_x^2}{F_v^2}\tan^2 \theta +\frac{f_x^2}{F_{c\perp}^2}\tan^4 \theta = 1$$

Solving this for f_x:

$$f_x = C_I F_b$$

where C_I = interaction stress factor

$$C_I = \sqrt{\frac{1}{1 + (F_b \tan \theta / F_v)^2 + (F_b \tan^2 \theta / F_{c\perp})^2}}$$

Therefore, to account for the interaction stresses in design, an allowable bending stress can be determined as

$$F_b' = C_I F_b$$

which is then compared to the actual calculated bending stress, f_b, to determine if the section is adequate. (F_b should be modified for duration of load.)

Since C_I is dependent only upon the slope of the tapered face and the material properties, tabular values of C_I as a function of $\tan \theta$ have been developed for commonly used species-bending combinations as given in Table 4.2.

As an alternative, a graphical solution of the interaction stress factor equation can be developed either using given stresses for a particular species

TABLE 4.2

INTERACTION STRESS FACTOR, C_I, AS A
FUNCTION OF TAN θ

$\tan \theta$	$C_I{}^a$	$C_I{}^b$	$C_I{}^c$	$C_I{}^d$
0.02	0.960	0.972	0.954	0.968
0.025	0.940	0.958	0.930	0.951
0.03	0.915	0.941	0.904	0.932
0.035	0.891	0.922	0.876	0.910
0.04	0.864	0.901	0.846	0.887
0.045	0.837	0.880	0.816	0.863
0.05	0.809	0.857	0.785	0.838
0.055	0.781	0.834	0.755	0.813
0.06	0.753	0.811	0.726	0.788
0.065	0.727	0.788	0.698	0.764
0.07	0.701	0.766	0.671	0.739
0.075	0.676	0.743	0.646	0.716
0.08	0.652	0.721	0.621	0.693
0.085	0.628	0.700	0.598	0.671
0.09	0.607	0.679	0.576	0.649
0.095	0.586	0.659	0.555	0.629
0.100	0.566	0.640	0.535	0.609
0.150	0.416	0.484	0.389	0.455
0.200	0.324	0.383	0.301	0.257

$^a F_b = 2,400$ psi; $F_v = 165$ psi; $F_{c\perp} = 385$ psi.
$^b F_b = 2,400$ psi; $F_v = 200$ psi; $F_{c\perp} = 385$ psi.
$^c F_b = 2,600$ psi; $F_v = 165$ psi; $F_{c\perp} = 385$ psi.
$^d F_b = 2,600$ psi; $F_v = 200$ psi; $F_{c\perp} = 385$ psi.

and combination, such as the ones used in developing Table 4.2, or by using fixed ratios of the strength properties involved such as illustrated in Figure 4.13.

Design procedure for tapered-straight beams (types *a* and *b* in Figure 4.11).

1. Determine minimum end depth (d_e in Figure 4.11), using the formula

$$d_e = \frac{3R_V}{2bF_v}$$

where R_V = end reaction based on effective span, lb
b = beam width (assumed), in.
F_v = allowable horizontal shear stress modified for duration of load, psi.

2. Determine depth, d_c, the greatest end depth for a simple tapered beam, or the centerline depth for a double tapered beam (see Figure 4.11). This depth may be determined by using the depth determined in step 1 and the known architectural values for span and slope of the tapered face.

3. Check maximum deflection.

(*a*) The bending deflection, Δ_B, for tapered beams with uniformly distributed loads may be determined using Figure 4.14 by entering the chart with the coefficient $C_y = (d_c - d_e)/d_e$ and then reading the ordinate value and solving for Δ_B. This maximum deflection occurs at the centerline for symmetrical double tapered beams and toward the end with the least depth, d_e, for single tapered beams. Table 4.3 gives the approximate location of the

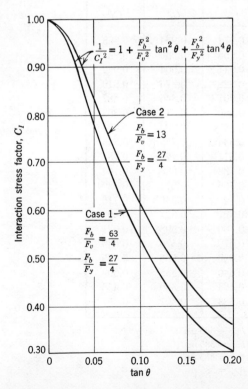

Figure 4.13. INTERACTION STRESS FACTOR FOR TAPERED BEAMS AS A FUNCTION OF TAN θ.

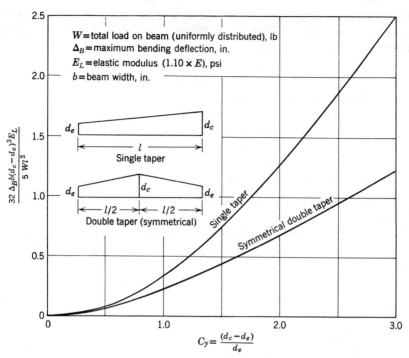

Figure 4.14. **GRAPH FOR DETERMINING TAPERED BEAM DEFLECTION UNI-FORMLY DISTRIBUTED LOAD.**

point of maximum deflection for single tapered beams as a function of the total length of the member. Other acceptable engineering methods may be used to determine deflection for beams under other than uniformly distributed loads or for unsymmetrical double tapered beams.

TABLE 4.3

APPROXIMATE LOCATION OF MAXIMUM
DEFLECTION FOR SINGLE TAPERED BEAMS

Range in C_y	Approximate Position of Maximum Deflection (distance from shallow end divided by total length)
0.1–0.6	0.46
0.7–1.1	0.45
1.2–1.4	0.44
1.5–1.7	0.43
1.8–1.9	0.42
2.0–2.2	0.41
2.3–2.5	0.40
2.6–2.8	0.39
2.9–3.0	0.38

(b) The shear deflection, Δ_S, at the centerline for symmetrical double tapered beams under uniformly distributed load may be computed with small error from the formula

$$\Delta_S = \frac{3Wl}{20Gbd_e}$$

where W = total load on beam, lb
l = span length, in.
G = shear modulus, psi (approximately equal to 0.06E, where E = modulus of elasticity)
b = beam width, in.
d_e = end depth of beam, in.

The total of $\Delta_B + \Delta_S$ should not exceed the allowable total load deflection limitation.

Note. If more refinement in design is required, see *Adjustment of Allowable Unit Stresses for Structural Glued Laminated Timber — Modulus of Elasticity,* page **2-39**.

4. Lay out the beam to scale, using the dimensions determined in steps 1 and 2 and the known architectural values.

5. Check the actual stresses at the taper cut.

(a) For a beam under uniformly distributed load, the maximum bending stress, shear stress and compression perpendicular to grain stress occur at the section where the depth, d, is given by the formula

$$d = \frac{d_e}{d_c}(2d_c - d_e)$$

(double tapered beam)

$$d = 2d_e \frac{d_e + l \tan \theta}{2d_e + l \tan \theta}$$

(single tapered beam)

At this section, the stresses are maximum at the taper cut and are given by the formulas

$$f_x = \frac{3Wl}{4bd_e(2d_c - d_e)}$$

(bending stress—double tapered)

$$f_x = \frac{3Wl}{4bd_e(d_e + l \tan \theta)}$$

(bending stress-single tapered)

$$f_{xy} = f_x \tan \theta \qquad \text{(shear stress)}$$

$$f_y = f_x \tan^2 \theta \qquad \begin{array}{l}\text{(compression perpendicular} \\ \text{to grain stress)}\end{array}$$

where $\tan \theta$ = slope of tapered face.

(b) For a beam under a concentrated load, the maximum bending stress occurs at the section where the critical depth, d, is given by the formula

$$d = 2d_e$$

or, where $d = d_c$, whichever is less.

At this section, the stresses are maximum at the taper cut and are given by the formulas

$$f_x = \frac{3R_V}{2bd_e \tan \theta} \qquad \text{(bending stress)}$$

$$f_{xy} = \frac{3R_V}{2bd_e} \qquad \text{(shear stress)}$$

$$f_y = f_x \tan^2 \theta \qquad \text{(compression perpendicular to grain stress)}$$

None of the stress values above may exceed the corresponding allowable stresses; that is,

$$f_x < F_{b_1}, \qquad f_{xy} < F_v, \qquad f_y < F_{c\perp}$$

where F_{b_1} = allowable stress in bending, psi, modified for duration of loading and size effect

F_v = allowable horizontal shear stress, psi, modified for duration of loading

$F_{c\perp}$ = allowable stress in compression perpendicular to grain, psi, modified for duration of loading

6. Check the effects of the combination of stresses occurring simultaneously by the interaction formula

$$\frac{f_x^2}{F_x^2} + \frac{f_y^2}{F_y^2} + \frac{f_{xy}^2}{F_{xy}^2} \leq 1$$

where f_x, f_y and f_{xy} are the stresses determined in step 5 and

F_x = allowable stress in bending, F_b, psi, modified for duration of loading, but not for size effect

F_y = allowable stress in compression perpendicular to grain, $F_{c\perp}$, psi, modified for duration of loading

F_{xy} = allowable horizontal shear stress, F_v, modified for duration of loading.

In lieu of using the interaction formula, the interaction stress factor, C_I, as given on page **4-27** may be applied.

7. Determine the amount of camber to be provided. Centerline camber should be in accordance with the recommendations given in Table 4.25 of this *Manual*. If centerline camber exceeds 2 in., camber equal to one-fourth of the centerline camber should be sawn into the compression face.

Design procedure for double tapered-pitched and double tapered-curved beams (types *c* and *d* in Figure 4.11).

1. Determine minimum end depth (d_e) using the equation:

$$d_e = \frac{3R_V}{2bF_v}$$

where R_V = end reaction based on effective span, lb

b = beam width, in.

F_v = allowable horizontal shear stress modified for duration of load, psi.

Note: In this step, it is necessary to assume a preliminary beam width.

2. Determine the required depth of an equivalent straight beam based on bending stress using the known span, spacing, and loading conditions. This is determined by the following relationship:

$$d' = \sqrt{\frac{6M}{bF_bC_F}}$$

where M = maximum bending moment, in.-lb
$\quad$ b = width assumed in step 1, in.
$\quad$ F_b = allowable stress in bending modified for duration of load, psi
$\quad$ C_F = size factor

Note: This requires a trial and error solution since a value for C_F must be assumed to determine an initial estimate of depth. Then a value for C_F must be computed based on the calculated depth and this procedure repeated until the values for C_F and d are compatible. It is recommended that an initial value for C_F of 0.90 be used for the first trial calculation.

3. Lay the beam out to scale using the depths determined from steps 1 and 2; the known architectural values for span and slope of the tapered face; and an assumed radius of curvature. The equivalent straight beam depth determined in step 2 should be used as the depth of the tapered curved beam at a point located 7/20 of the total span as measured from the end of the beam.

Using this scale drawing, determine the depth at the centerline of the member, d_c.

Note: The determination of the centerline depth, d_c, is based on an assumed radius of curvature and the assumption that the soffit passes through a point located $7/20l$ from the end of the member at a depth determined on the basis of an equivalent straight beam. It may be necessary to change these dimensions depending on subsequent design calculations, and these are trial dimensions only. The minimum recommended radii of curvature values that can be assumed are 9 ft 4 in. for $\frac{3}{4}$ in. laminations or 27 ft 6 in. for $1\frac{1}{2}$ in. laminations.

4. Check the trial design for radial tension stresses as determined from the formula:

$$f_r = K_r \frac{6M}{bd_c^2}$$

where K_r = radial stress factor
$\quad$ M = bending moment at the centerline, in.-lb
$\quad$ b = width of beam, in.
$\quad$ d_c = depth of beam at centerline, in.

(See pages 4-45 to 4-47 for a detailed discussion of the calculation of radial stresses.)

The radial tension stress thus determined should be checked against the allowable unit radial tension stress, F_{rt}. The allowable radial tension stress is limited to $\frac{1}{3}$ the allowable unit stress in horizontal shear for (*a*) Southern pine and California redwood (67 psi and 42 psi, respectively) for all conditions of loading and (*b*) for Douglas fir and Western larch (55 psi) for wind or earthquake loading. These stresses are limited to 15 psi for Douglas fir and Western larch (55 psi) for other conditions of loading. Duration of load modifications are applicable to each value indicated.

Note: If the actual radial tension stresses exceed the indicated allowable stresses, the trial design must be modified. Possible design changes that should be considered are: (a) increase the radius of curvature, (b) increase the depth of the member at the 7/20*l* point as determined in step 2, or (c) increase the trial width assumed in step 1. An alternative procedure is to design radial reinforcement to carry the calculated radial tension stresses as described in step 11.

5. Having satisfied preliminary radial tension design requirements, arbitrarily divide the span into equal segments of length and determine the bending moment and section modulus at the midpoint of each segment. The section modulus is based on the actual depth of the member at the midpoint locations. It is recommended that a minimum of 10 segments be evaluated for $\frac{1}{2}$ the total span, assuming a symmetric configuration.

Determine the actual bending stress, f_x, at the midpoint for each segment of length, where $f_x = M/S$. This value may not exceed the corresponding allowable unit bending stress, F_b, as modified for duration of load, size effect, and curvature (if the segment being analyzed is in a curved portion of the member).

6. Check the actual shear stress and compression perpendicular to grain stress at the taper cut at the midpoint for each segment of length using the following equations:

$$f_{xy} = f_x \tan \theta \qquad \text{(shear stress)}$$
$$f_y = f_x \tan^2 \theta \qquad \text{(compression perpendicular to grain stress)}$$

where f_x = actual bending stress determined in step 5
θ = angle between axis of bottom lamination and the tapered face, degrees

These calculated stresses may not exceed the corresponding allowable unit stresses, F_y and $F_{c\perp}$, respectively, modified for duration of loading.

7. Check the effect of the combination of stresses occuring simultaneously at the taper cut either by the use of the interaction formula

$$\frac{f_x^2}{F_x^2} + \frac{f_y^2}{F_y^2} + \frac{f_{xy}^2}{F_{xy}^2} \leq 1$$

where the terms have previously been defined or by the use of the interaction stress factor, C_I, as discussed on page **4-27**.

Note: If the interaction analysis check indicates the member is overstressed, the depth of the member should be increased. One method of accomplishing this is by increasing the radius of curvature.

8. Check maximum deflection. As an approximation, the total deflection may be estimated by using Figure 4.14, but by using E instead of E_L in the equation shown on the vertical axis and solving for Δ_B, which will then represent the total deflection rather than just deflection due to bending.

Note: The modulus of elasticity values, E, normally given in design stress tables include deflection due to shear distortion and due to bending. In designs where shear deformation is a significant consideration, more refinement in determining total deflection may be obtained by computing bending deflection and shear deflection separately as discussed on pages 4-28 to 4-30 and summing these individual deflections to obtain total deflection.

9. Determine the amount of camber to be provided. The centerline camber should be in accordance with the recommendations in Table 4.25. If the centerline camber exceeds 2 in., the camber equal to $\frac{1}{4}$ of the centerline camber should be sawn into the compression face.

10. Determine the horizontal movement at the supports, Δ_H, using the formula

$$\Delta_H = \frac{2h\Delta_c}{l}$$

where h = rise of beam, in., measured vertically from axis at end of beam to axis at centerline

l = span length, in.

Δ_c = centerline deflection as determined in step 8, in.

Note: Horizontal movement should be provided for by the use of a slotted connection or roller support.

11. Design the radial reinforcement, if required by the analysis of radial stresses in step 4, in accordance with the recommended procedures given on pages 4-47 to 4-50.

Example. Design a double tapered-straight glued laminated roof beam to meet the following requirements:

$L = 60$ ft $F_b = (2,400)(1.15) = 2,760$ psi

Spacing $= 16$ ft $F_v = (165)(1.15) = 190$ psi

Roof slope $= 1:12$ $F_{c\perp} = (385)(1.15) = 443$ psi

Camber $= 1\frac{1}{2}\Delta_{DL}$ $E = 1,800,000$ psi

SL $= 30$ psf $G = 0.06E = (0.06)(1,800,000) = 108,000$ psi

DL $= 15$ psf

$$\Delta_{TL} = l/180 = \frac{(60)(12)}{180} = 4 \text{ in.}$$

Roof decking applied directly to beams.

1. Determine minimum end depth.

Assume effective span $= L_e = 55$ ft and width $= b = 5\frac{1}{8}$ in.

$$\text{Reaction} = R_V = \frac{wL_e}{2} = \frac{(30+15)(16)(55)}{2} = 19,800 \text{ lb}$$

$$\text{End depth} = d_e = \frac{3R_V}{2bF_v} = \frac{(3)(19,800)}{(2)(5.125)(190)} = 30.50 \text{ in.; use 30 in.}$$

$$L_e = L - \frac{2d_e}{12} = 60 - \frac{(2)(30)}{12} = 55 \text{ ft} \qquad \text{O.K.}$$

2. Determine centerline depth.

Centerline depth $= d_c = d_e +$ (roof slope)(span).

$d_c = 30 + \frac{1}{12}(30)(12) = 60$ in.

3. Check maximum deflection.

(a) Bending deflection.

$$\text{Coefficient} = C_y = \frac{d_c - d_e}{d_e} = \frac{60 - 30}{30} = 1$$

Entering on the graph in Figure 4.14, $C_y = 1$, the ordinate value can be read as 0.22, and

$$0.22 = \frac{32\Delta_B b(d_c - d_e)^3 E_L}{5Wl^3}$$

$$\Delta_B = \frac{(0.22)(5)(720)(60)^4(1.728)}{(32)(5.125)(60 - 30)^3(1,980,000)} = 2.02 \text{ in.}$$

(b) Shear deflection.

$$\text{Shear deflection} = \Delta_S = \frac{3Wl}{20Gbd_e}$$

$$\Delta_S = \frac{(3)(720)(60)^2(12)}{(20)(108,000)(5.125)(30)} = 0.28 \text{ in.}$$

Total deflection $= \Delta_a = \Delta_B + \Delta_S = 2.02 + 0.28 = 2.30$ in. < 4 O.K.

4. Lay out beam to scale. (See page **4-36**.)

5. Check the actual stresses.

Depth at which maximum stresses occur $= d$.

$$d = \frac{d_e}{d_c}(2d_c - d_e) = \frac{30}{60}(120 - 30) = 45 \text{ in.}$$

Allowable bending stress, $F_b' = 2,760C_F = (2,760)(0.86) = 2,370$ psi
Actual bending stress $= f_x$.

$$f_x = \frac{9wl^2}{bd_e(2d_c - d_e)} = \frac{(9)(720)(60)^2}{(5.125)(30)(120 - 30)}$$

$f_x = 1,686$ psi $< 2,370$ O.K.

Actual shear stress $= f_{xy} = f_x \tan \theta$.

$f_{xy} = (1,686)(\frac{1}{12}) = 140$ psi < 190 O.K.

Actual compression perpendicular to grain stress $= f_y = f_x \tan^2 \theta$

$f_y = (1,686)(\frac{1}{12})^2 = 11.7$ psi < 443 O.K.

6. Check the effects of combined stresses at the point of maximum stresses ($d = 45$ in.).

Interaction formula using $F_x = F_b$; $F_y = F_{c\perp}$; and $F_{xy} = F_v$;

$$\frac{f_x^2}{F_x^2} + \frac{f_y^2}{F_y^2} + \frac{f_{xy}^2}{F_{xy}^2} \leqslant 1$$

$$\frac{(1,686)^2}{(2,760)^2} + \frac{(11.7)^2}{(443)^2} + \frac{(140)^2}{(190)^2} = 0.917 < 1 \qquad \text{O.K.}$$

Alternately, the combined stresses can be checked by using the interaction stress factor, C_I, as follows:

$\tan \theta = 0.083$

$C_I = 0.638$ (from Table 4.2).

Allowable $F_b' = (C_I)(F_b) = (0.638)(2,760)$

$F_b' = 1,761$ psi

Actual bending stress, $f_x = 1,686$ psi

$1,686 < 1,761 \qquad \text{O.K.}$

7. Determine the amount of camber.

Dead load deflection $= \Delta_{DL} = \Delta_a \dfrac{w_{DL}}{w_{TL}}$

$$\Delta_{DL} = 2.30 \frac{240}{720} = 0.77 \text{ in.}$$

Centerline camber $= 1.5 \, \Delta_{DL} = (1.5)(0.77) = 1.16$ in. Since this centerline camber is less than 2 in., no compression face camber is required.

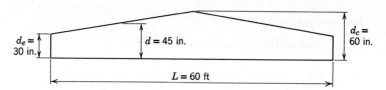

$d_e = 30$ in. $d = 45$ in. $d_c = 60$ in. $L = 60$ ft

Example. Design a double-tapered pitched curved glued laminated timber roof beam to meet the following requirements:

Species: Douglas fir-larch $F_b = (2,400)(1.15) = 2,760$ psi
$L = 60$ ft $F_v = (165)(1.15) = 190$ psi
Spacing $= 16$ ft $F_{c\perp} = (385)(1.15) = 443$ psi
Roof slope $= 3:12$ $E = 1,800,000$ psi
Camber $= 1\frac{1}{2}\Delta_{DL}$ $G = 0.06E = (0.06)(1.8 \times 10^6)$
Snow load (SL) $= 30$ psf $= 108,000$ psi
Dead load (DL) $= 15$ psf
$$\Delta_{TL} = 1/180 = \frac{(60)(12)}{180} = 4 \text{ in.}$$

Roof decking applied directly to beams.

1. Determine minimum end depth.

Assume effective span $(L_e) = 56$ ft and beam width $(b) = 6\frac{3}{4}$ in.

$$R = \frac{wL_e}{2} = \frac{(30+15)(16)(56)}{2} = 20{,}160 \text{ lb}$$

$$d_e = \frac{3R_v}{2bF_v} = \frac{(3)(20{,}160)}{(2)(6.75)(190)} = 23.58 \text{ in.; use 24 in.}$$

$$L_e = L - \frac{2d_e}{12} = 60 - \frac{(2)(24)}{12} = 56 \text{ ft}$$

2. Determine the depth of an equivalent straight beam. Assume size factor $(C_F) = 0.90$.

$$M_{\text{\c{}}} = \frac{wL^2}{8} = \frac{(45)(16)(60)^2(12)}{8} = 3.89 \times 10^6 \text{ in.-lb}$$

$$d' = \sqrt{\frac{6M}{bF_bC_F}} = \sqrt{\frac{(6)(3.89)(10^6)}{(6.75)(2{,}760)(0.90)}} = 37.3 \text{ in.; use } 37\tfrac{1}{2} \text{ in.}$$

From Table 2.12, C_F (for $d' = 37\tfrac{1}{2}$ in.) $= 0.88 \approx 0.90$

3. Draw the beam to scale.

   Minimum radius $(R_{\min}) = 27$ ft 6 in.
   Try $R = 30$ ft.

4. Check radial tension stresses

$$R_m = R + \frac{d_c}{2} = 30 + \frac{52}{(2)(12)} = 32 \text{ ft 2 in.}$$

$$\frac{d_c}{R_m} = \frac{52}{(12)(32.17)} = 0.13.$$

From Figure 4.15, $K_r = 0.07$

$$f_{rt} = K_r \frac{6M}{bd_c{}^2} = \frac{(0.07)(6)(3.89)(10^6)}{(6.75)(52)^2} = 89.5 \text{ psi}$$

$$F_{rt} = (15)(1.15) = 17.25 < 89.5 \text{ psi} \qquad \text{N.G.}$$

Increase radius to 57 ft (the radius that is tangent at the $\tfrac{7}{20}L_e$ point), and recheck radial tension stresses.

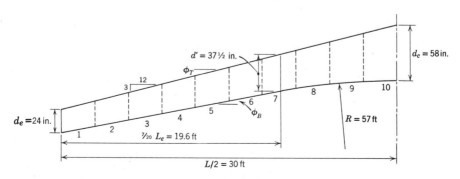

SKETCH A

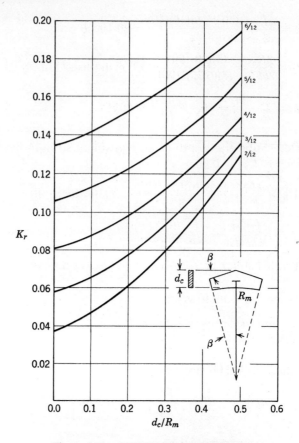

Figure 4.15.   DETERMINATION OF K_r.

$$R_m = 57 + \frac{58}{(12)(2)} = 59 \text{ ft } 5 \text{ in.}$$

$$\frac{d_c}{R_m} = \frac{4.83}{59.41} = 0.08$$

From Figure 4.15, $K_r = 0.065$.

$$f_{rt} = \frac{(0.065)(6)(3.89)(10^6)}{(6.75)(58)^2} = 66.8 \text{ psi}$$

$F_{rt} = (15)(1.15) = 17.25 \text{ psi} < 66.8 \text{ psi}.$

Therefore assume radial reinforcement will be utilized.

5. Check bending stresses at various points along the beam.

Point	Depth in.	S in.^{3}	M (in.-lb) $\times 10^6$	$f_x = M/S$ psi	$C_F{}^a$	l/d	$C_F'{}^b$	$C_c{}^c$	F_b' (allow-able)^d psi
1	25	703	0.38	539	0.92	29	0.90	1.00	2,484
2	27	820	1.08	1,316	0.91	27	0.90	1.00	2,484
3	29	946	1.70	1,798	0.90	25	0.89	1.00	2,456
4	31	1,081	2.24	2,077	0.90	23	0.89	1.00	2,456
5	34	1,300	2.71	2,086	0.89	21	0.89	1.00	2,456
6	36	1,458	3.10	2,127	0.88	20	0.89	1.00	2,456
7	38	1,624	3.41	2,121	0.88	19	0.89	0.99	2,432
8	41	1,891	3.64	1,923	0.87	18	0.88	0.99	2,404
9	46	2,380	3.80	1,597	0.86	16	0.87	0.99	2,377
10	53	3,160	3.88	1,227	0.85	14	0.87	0.99	2,377
₵	58	3,784	3.89	1,028	0.84	12	0.87	0.99	2,377

^{a}From Table 2.13.
^{b}Modified C_F for span-to-depth ratios other than 21. See page **2**-37 for table of conversions for various values of l/d.
$^c C_c = 1 - 2,000 \left(\dfrac{t}{R} \right)^2 = 1 - 2,000 \left(\dfrac{1.5}{(57)(12)} \right)^2 = 0.99.$
^{d}Allowable bending stress $(F_b') = F_b(1.15)C_F'C_c$.

6. Check actual shear stress (f_{xy}) at various points along the beam (see Sketch A for definitions of ϕ_T and ϕ_B).

Point	ϕ_T	ϕ_B	$\theta = \phi_T - \phi_B$	$\tan\theta$	$f_{xy} = f_x \tan\theta$ psi	$F_{xy} = F_v$ psi
1	14°	10.9°	3.1°	0.0542	29.2	190
2	14°	10.9°	3.1°	0.0542	71.3	190
3	14°	10.9°	3.1°	0.0542	97.4	190
4	14°	10.9°	3.1°	0.0542	112.6	190
5	14°	10.9°	3.1°	0.0542	113.1	190
6	14°	10.9°	3.1°	0.0542	115.3	190
7	14°	10.9°	3.1°	0.0542	113.9	190
8	14°	7.5°	6.5°	0.1139	219.6	190
9	14°	4.5°	9.5°	0.1673	276.2	190
10	14°	1.5°	12.5°	0.2217	272.0	190

The shear stresses in the curved portion of the beam exceed the allowable amount. Reproportion the beam to reduce the shear stresses. As an approximation, set the shear stress at the centerline of the beam approximately 25% below the allowable shear stress or, $f_{xy} = 140$ psi, to compensate for interaction stress to be checked in step 7. At the centerline, $\theta = 14°$ or $\tan\theta = 0.25$.

$$f_{xy} = f_x \tan\theta$$

$$f_x = \frac{f_{xy}}{\tan \theta} = \frac{140}{0.25} = 560 \text{ psi}$$

$$S_{\text{req'd}} = \frac{M_{\text{¢}}}{f_x} = \frac{3,890,000}{560} = 6,946 \text{ in.}^3$$

$$S = \frac{bd^2}{6} \text{ or } d_c = \sqrt{\frac{6S}{b}} = \sqrt{\frac{(6)(6,946)}{6.75}} = 78.6 \text{ in.}$$

Use $d_c = 78$ in.

Redraw the beam using $d_c = 78$ in. and maintain the 57 ft radius previously selected.

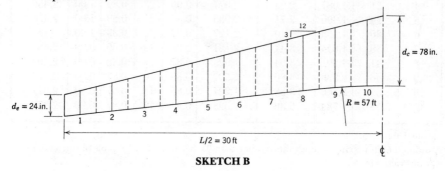

SKETCH B

4A. Recheck radial tension stress

$$R_m = 57 + \frac{78}{(2)(12)} = 60.25 \text{ ft}$$

$$\frac{d_c}{R_m} = \frac{6.5}{60.25} = 0.108$$

From Figure 4.15, $K_r = 0.069$.

$$f_{rt} = \frac{(0.069)(6)(3.89)(10^6)}{(6.75)(78)^2} = 39.22 \text{ psi} > 17.25 \text{ psi}$$

Design for radial reinforcement required.

5A. Recheck bending stresses at various points along the beam.

Point	Depth, in.	S in.^{3}	M (in.-lb) $\times 10^6$	$f_x = M/S$ psi	C_F[a]	l/d	C_F'[b]	C_c[c]	F_b' psi
1	26.4	784	0.379	483	0.92	27	0.91	1.00	2,512
2	31.4	1,109	1.079	973	0.90	23	0.90	1.00	2,484
3	36.2	1,474	1.701	1,154	0.88	20	0.88	1.00	2,429
4	41.4	1,928	2.245	1,164	0.87	17	0.88	1.00	2,429
5	46.2	2,401	2.712	1,130	0.86	16	0.87	1.00	2,401
6	51.0	2,926	3.101	1,060	0.85	14	0.87	1.00	2,401
7	57.1	2,681	3.412	927	0.84	13	0.86	1.00	2,374
8	61.2	4,214	3.645	865	0.83	12	0.86	1.00	2,374
9	66.6	4,990	3.800	762	0.83	11	0.86	0.99	2,350
10	73.4	6,061	3.878	640	0.82	10	0.86	0.99	2,350
¢	78.0	6,844	3.888	568	0.81	9	0.85	0.99	2,322

[a,b,c,d]See step 5 for footnotes.

6A. Recheck actual shear stresses (f_{xy}) at various points along the beam.

Note: If shear stresses are satisfactory, compute compression perpendicular to grain stresses, f_y, for use in interaction analysis. Compression perpendicular to grain stresses will not control design except as the result of their contribution to the interaction stresses.

Point	ϕ_T	ϕ_B	$\theta = \phi_T - \phi_B$	$\tan\theta$	$\tan^2\theta$	$f_{xy} =$ $f_x \tan\theta$ psi	$F_{xy} =$ F_v psi	$f_y =$ $f_x \tan^2\theta$ psi	$F_y =$ $F_{c\perp}$ psi
1	14°	6.5°	7.5°	0.1317	0.01734	63.6	190	8.4	443
2	14°	6.5°	7.5°	0.1317	0.01734	128.1	190	16.9	443
3	14°	6.5°	7.5°	0.1317	0.01734	152.0	190	20.0	443
4	14°	6.5°	7.5°	0.1317	0.01734	153.3	190	20.2	443
5	14°	6.5°	7.5°	0.1317	0.01734	148.8	190	19.6	443
6	14°	6.5°	7.5°	0.1317	0.01734	139.6	190	18.4	443
7	14°	6.5°	7.5°	0.1317	0.01734	122.1	190	16.1	443
8	14°	6.5°	7.5°	0.1317	0.01734	113.9	190	15.0	443
9	14°	4.5°	9.5°	0.1673	0.02799	127.5	190	20.3	443
10	14°	1.5°	12.5°	0.2217	0.04915	141.9	190	31.5	443

7. Check the effect of the interaction of stresses occurring at the taper cut at several points along the beam.

Point	f_x^2/F_x^2	f_y^2/F_y^2	f_{xy}^2/F_{xy}^2	$f_x^2/F_x^2 + f_y^2/F_y^2 + f_{xy}^2/F_{xy}^2 \leq 1$
1	0.031	≈ 0	0.112	0.143
2	0.124	≈ 0	0.455	0.579
3	0.175	≈ 0	0.640	0.815
4	0.178	≈ 0	0.651	0.829
5	0.168	≈ 0	0.613	0.781
6	0.148	≈ 0	0.540	0.688
7	0.113	≈ 0	0.413	0.526
8	0.098	≈ 0	0.359	0.457
9	0.076	≈ 0	0.450	0.526
10	0.054	≈ 0	0.558	0.612

7A. As an alternate method of computing interaction stresses, the effect of the combination of stresses can be checked by using the interaction stress factor (C_I) at the point of maximum bending stress in the noncurved portion and at all points analyzed in the curved portion as follows:

Point	tan θ	C_I [a]	F_b' [b]	f_x [c]
4	0.1317	0.462	1,275	1,164
9	0.1673	0.379	1,046	762
10	0.2217	0.295	814	640

[a] From equation for C_I on page 4-27 or from Table 4.2.
[b] $F_b' = (1.15)F_bC_I$.
[c] From step 5A.

Since $f_x < F_b'$ for all cases, interaction stresses are O.K.

8. Check maximum deflection

$$C_y = \frac{d_c - d_e}{d_e} = \frac{78 - 24}{24} = 2.25$$

From Figure 4.14

$$\frac{32\Delta_B b(d_c - d_e)^3 E_L}{5Wl^3} = 0.83$$

With $E = 1.8 \times 10^6$ substituted for E_L and Δ_c for Δ_B, the approximate centerline deflection is computed as:

$$\Delta_c = \frac{(0.83)(5)(45)(16)(60)^4(1,728)}{(32)(6.75)(78-24)^3(1.8)(10^6)} = 1.09 \text{ in.} < 4 \text{ in.} \qquad \text{O.K.}$$

9. Determine camber required

$$\Delta_{DL} = \Delta_c \frac{w_{DL}}{w_{TL}} = 1.09 \frac{15}{45} = 0.36 \text{ in.}$$

Camber $= 1.5\Delta_{DL} = (1.5)(0.36) = 0.54$ in.

10. Determine horizontal movement at supports (Δ_H)

$$\Delta_H = \frac{2h\Delta_c}{L} = \frac{(2)(63)(1.09)}{(60)(12)} = 0.19 \text{ in.}$$

11. Design radial reinforcement

$f_{rt}/\text{in.} = (39.2)(6.75) = 264.7$ lb/in.

Assume $1\frac{1}{4}$ in. diameter lag bolts because of the required length.
From Table 4.5: Allowable steel tension load $= 16,090$ lb.
Allowable wood withdrawal load per inch of thread $= 890$ lb/in.

Effective thread penetration $= \frac{78}{2} - 2 = 37$ in.

Total allowable wood withdrawal load $= (890)(37) = 32,930$ lb

Maximum allowable spacing (steel stress) $= \frac{16,090}{264.7} = 60.8$ in.

Maximum allowable spacing (wood stress) $= \dfrac{32,930}{264.7} = 124.4$ in.

Use $1\frac{1}{4}$ in. diameter lag bolts at 36 in. on center. Locate two bolts each side of the beam centerline, one at 18 in. and the other at 54 in. from the centerline.

11A. Check beam net section for bending stress at point 10.

Effective width of cross section $= 6\frac{3}{4} - 1\frac{1}{4} = 5\frac{1}{2}$ in.

Effective section modulus $= \dfrac{(5.5)(73.4)^2}{6} = 4{,}938.6$ in.^{3}

f_x (net section) $= \dfrac{M_{10}}{S_{10}} = \dfrac{3,878,000}{4,938.6} = 785.2$ psi

F_x (allowable) $= 2{,}350$ psi (from step 5A)

Bending stress O.K.

Combined Loading in Beams

Members subjected to both flexure and axial loads should be so proportioned to satisfy the following design equations:
For combined flexure and axial tension

$$\frac{P/A}{F_t} + \frac{M/S}{F_b C_F} \le 1$$

For combined flexure and axial compression when the compression portion exceeds the flexure portion

$$\frac{P/A}{F_c'} + \frac{M/S}{F_b} \le 1$$

For combined flexure and axial compression when the flexure portion exceeds the compression portion

$$\frac{P/A}{F_c'} + \frac{M/S}{F_b C_F} \le 1$$

where $P = $ total axial load, lb
$M = $ total bending moment, in.-lb
$A = $ cross-sectional area of member, in.^{2}
$S = $ section modulus of member, in.^{3}
$F_b = $ allowable unit stress in extreme fiber in bending, psi
$F_c' = $ allowable unit stress in compression parallel to g.ain adjusted for l/d of the member under consideration, psi
$F_t = $ allowable unit stress in tension parallel to grain, psi
$C_F = $ size facto1

Purlins or Joists for Sloping Roofs

Except for very high and steep roofs, wind is not a governing factor in purlin or joist design. The loads to be considered are the dead load of the roof structure and the live load or snow load. The following considerations for purlins apply also to joists.

Vertical purlin loads, W, may be resolved into components normal (W_N) and parallel (W_P) to the slope of the roof. In most curved roofs the purlins are placed with their depth normal to the roof. When sheathing is well secured to the purlins, W_P is considered transferred to sheathing, and only W_N is taken by the purlin in bending. The size required for the near-vertical purlins nearest the center of the roof is used throughout. For very steep curved roofs, as in a high parabolic arch, purlins should be designed as for pitched roofs, with reactions from blocking between purlins transmitted directly to the foundation.

On a gabled roof, if the roof sheathing or covering does not act as a rigid diaphragm or as a continuous tie from eave purlin or side wall to ridge purlin, the purlins, whether set vertical or normal to the roof slope, should be designed as individual beams in the usual manner.

On a gabled roof, both vertical purlins and those set normal to the roof slope, having roof sheathing or covering that will act as a rigid diaphragm or as a continuous tie from eave purlin or side wall to ridge purlin, may be designed by one of the following methods, depending on the type of sheathing. These methods are based on adequate fastenings at all connections.

1. When suitable diaphragm action, such as by plywood or diagonal sheathing well fastened to all supporting members, or adequate bracing is provided, component W_P is supported by the diaphragm action or the bracing and the purlin is designed for W_N in simple bending normal to the roof slope.

2. Wood sheathing laid at right angles to the purlins may be assumed to transfer part of the total parallel component from each slope to the ridge purlin, and part to the eave purlin or wall, if the fastening is strong enough. The amount of load carried by each is proportionate to the relative stiffness of each. If there is no eave purlin and the wall is inadequate, all the load must be transferred to the ridge purlin. The ridge purlin is designed for its own loading plus the vertical component of the parallel components transferred to it from both sides of the roof. The eave purlin is designed for its own loading plus the load transferred to it from the other purlins. Intermediate purlins may be designed for W_N only.

3. Sag rods, designed to transfer the parallel to roof component from the side slope purlins to the ridge purlins, may be used. The rods should be placed between the ridge purlin and intermediate purlins along the full roof slope. Each intermediate purlin is assumed to support its own W_N for its full span and W_P for the span between lines of sag rods. The moments resulting from W_N and W_P are combined for maximum bending. The eave purlin carries only its own loading. The ridge purlin carries its own loading plus the loads transmitted to it through the sag rods.

4. When none of these arrangements is satisfactory, each purlin must be designed to carry the load from its own tributary area for the full span. The side slope purlins must be designed for the combined components W_N and W_P.

CURVED MEMBERS

Minimum Bending Radii

The recommended minimum radii of curvature (R) for curved structural glued laminated timbers are 9 ft 4 in. for a lamination thickness (t) of $\frac{3}{4}$ in.; and 27 ft 6 in. for a lamination thickness of $1\frac{1}{2}$ in. If required for architectural or other design considerations, other radii of curvature may be used with these thicknesses and other radius-thickness combinations may be used provided that the ratio t/R does not exceed 1/100 for hardwoods and Southern pine, nor 1/125 for other softwoods.

Curvature Factor

Because of stresses induced in bending laminations to a required curvature, the allowable flexural stress in curved laminated members is less than in straight members. Therefore, the allowable unit stress in bending for a curved member must be modified by multiplying by the curvature factor, C_c, which is given by the formula

$$C_c = 1 - 2,000 \left(\frac{t}{R} \right)^2$$

where t = thickness of lamination, in.
       R = radius of curvature (bending radius) of the lamination, in.

The ratio t/R should not exceed 1/100 for hardwoods and for Southern pine, nor 1/125 for softwoods other than Southern pine.

This curvature factor should not be applied to stresses in straight portions of an assembly, regardless of curvature elsewhere in the assembly. See Figure 2.5 for a graphical solution of the curvature factor equation.

Radial Tension and Compression

When curved members are subjected to a bending moment, M, radial stresses are set up in a direction parallel to the radius of curvature, R, of the centerline of the member (perpendicular to grain). If the moment increases the radius of curvature (causes the member to become straighter), the stress is tension; if it decreases the radius (causes the member to become more sharply curved), the stress is compression.

The formula for computing the actual radial stress, f_r, in members of constant cross section is

$$f_r = \frac{3M}{2Rbd}$$

where M = bending moment, in.-lb
      b = width of rectangular member, in.
      d = depth of rectangular member, in.
      R = radius of curvature of centerline of member, in.

For these members, when M causes a stress in tension across the grain, this tensile stress shall be limited to $\frac{1}{3}$ the allowable unit stress in horizontal shear for Southern pine (67 psi) and California redwood (42 psi) for all load conditions and for Douglas fir and larch (55 psi) for wind and earthquake loadings. The limit shall be 15 psi for Douglas fir and larch for other conditions of loading. These values are subject to modification for duration of load.

If the calculated stress exceeds the applicable allowable unit stresses as indicated, the design should be re-evaluated by changing the geometry of the section by increasing the radius of curvature or by changing the pitch to increase the centerline depth of the member. As an alternate procedure for Douglas fir and larch, mechanical reinforcement may be designed in accordance with the recommendations given on pages 4-47 to 4-50 of this *Manual* sufficient to resist the full magnitude of the calculated radial tension stress. With radial reinforcement, the calculated radial tension stress is limited to 55 psi, subject to modification for duration of load.

When the moment is in a direction causing a stress in compression across the grain, this stress shall be limited to the allowable unit stress in compression perpendicular to the grain for the species involved.

When designing a curved bending member of variable cross section such as a double-tapered curved beam, the radial stress, f_r, is computed by the equation

$$f_r = K_r \frac{6M}{bd_c^2}$$

where K_r = radial stress factor obtained from Figure 4.15 or calculated from Table 4.4

M = bending moment in midspan, in.-lb

b = width of cross section, in.

d_c = depth of cross section at the centerline, in.

The allowable radial stresses are the same as the stresses given for members of constant cross section.

TABLE 4.4

POLYNOMIAL APPROXIMATION TO K_r

Angle of the Upper Tapered Surface, B, degrees	Constants		
	A	B	C
2.5	0.0079	0.1747	0.1284
5.0	0.0174	0.1251	0.1939
7.5	0.0279	0.0937	0.2162
10.0	0.0391	0.0754	0.2119
15.0	0.0629	0.0619	0.1722
20.0	0.0893	0.0608	0.1393
25.0	0.1214	0.0605	0.1238
30.0	0.1649	0.0603	0.1115

Example. Determine the radial tension stresses for a double-tapered curved beam based on the following design criteria:

$M = 950,000$ in.-lb

Roof pitch $= 4:12$

$R_{min} = 27$ ft 6 in.

$d_c = 34$ in.

$b = 6\frac{3}{4}$ in.

$$f_r = K_r \frac{6M}{bd_c^2}$$

$$\frac{d_c}{R_{min}} = \frac{34}{(27.5)(12)} = 0.103$$

$\therefore$ from Figure 4.15, $K_r = 0.09$

$$f_r = 0.09 \frac{(6)(950,000)}{(6.75)(34)^2} = 66 \text{ psi}$$

where $K_r = A + B\left(\dfrac{d_c}{R_m}\right) + C\left(\dfrac{d_c}{R_m}\right)^2$

R_m = radius of curvature at the centerline of the member at midspan, in.

Radial Reinforcement

If the calculated radial tension stresses, f_{rt}, exceed the allowable radial tension stresses, F_{rt}, for Douglas fir and larch, an alternate design procedure is to use radial reinforcement sufficient to resist the full magnitude of radial tension stress. This reinforcement should be designed on the basis of sound engineering principles. Any type of reinforcement such as lag bolts mechanically attached to the wood or deformed bars bonded by adhesive that will effectively transfer the radial tension stresses between the wood and the reinforcement throughout the entire depth of embedment may be used. The method of bonding or attaching the reinforcement to the wood should be of a durable quality and capable of developing the required tensile strength of the reinforcement.

One typical design is to utilize fully threaded lag bolts as radial tension reinforcement. The following comments provide general installation recommendations and design guidelines for the use of lag bolt reinforcement:

(a) The shop installed radial tension reinforcing to be used is full-length threaded lag bolts. These lag bolts should be shop installed in a prebored hole from the top edge of the member on the width centerline of the member. They should be used only in the curved or radially stressed portion of the member. The lag bolts should be installed normal to the axis of the lamination (90° to the direction of glue line) at the section where the lag bolt is located. No washer should be used under the head of the lag bolt. It is desirable, for structural reasons, not to countersink the head of the lag bolt into the top edge of the beam. If it is necessary to install the lag bolt in such a way that the top surface is smooth following installation resulting from the construction on top of the member, the head of the lag bolt can be sawed off flush with the member or can be countersunk, but the counter-sink should only be large enough to install the lag bolt head flush with the top edge of the beam.

(*b*) The diameter of the prebored hole for the lag bolt should be as fol-lows:

The lead hole for the threaded portion should have a diameter equal to 75% of the shank diameter for Group II species and 70% for Group III species (see Table 5.1 for species groupings) and a length equal to the length of the threaded portion.

The lead hole for the shank should have the same diameter as the shank, and the same depth as the length of the unthreaded shank.

Note: Although the lag bolts are specified to be threaded full length, manufacturing of the lags requires a small length of unthreaded shank.

(*c*) The length of the full thread of the lag bolt should extend from the top edge (head end of the lag bolt) of the beam to not less than 2 in. nor more than 3 in. from the soffit of the beam. Lag bolt lengths should be in multiples of 1 in.

(*d*) In general, the ⅝ in. and 1 in. diameter lag bolts have been found satisfactory to cover most reinforcing requirements. The 1 in. diameter lag bolts should be limited to a maximum length of 60 in. and the ⅝ in. diameter to a maximum length of 30 in. If greater lengths of reinforcement are required, larger diameter lag bolts should be specified.

(*e*) The full thread lag bolts should be designed to take the entire radial tension stress developed in the member with no radial tension stress carried by the wood. The lag bolts should be so spaced along the width centerline throughout the curved portion of the member as to carry the entire radial tension stress.

(*f*) The magnitude of the radial tension stress to be carried by each lag bolt should not exceed either of the following:

1. Maximum Allowable Tension in Lag Bolts on Net Area at Root of Thread.
   The maximum tension load to be carried by each lag bolt is to be limit-ed to a unit stress of 20,000 psi on the net area at the root of the thread. Table 4.5 lists the net area at the root of threads and the allowable tension at a unit stress of 20,000 psi.
2. Maximum Allowable Tension in Lag Bolts on Allowable Thread Holding in Wood (Allowable Withdrawal).
   The maximum tension to be carried by each lag bolt should not exceed the allowable withdrawal thread holding of the lag bolt threads in the wood. The effective embedded thread length to be used in this deter-mination is to be the embedded thread length from the neutral axis of the member to the point end of the lag bolt or the thread length from the neutral axis of the member to the head end of the lag bolt whichever is the lesser. The allowable unit withdrawal load for the lag bolt threads in the wood should be in accordance with the values shown in Table 4.5.

TABLE 4.5

ALLOWABLE DESIGN STRESSES FOR FULL-THREADED LAG BOLTS USED AS RADIAL REINFORCEMENT

Design Data		Lag Bolt Shank Diameter, D, in.											
Steel		1/4	5/16	3/8	7/16	1/2	9/16	5/8	3/4	7/8	1	1⅛	1¼
Net area at root of thread, in.²		0.0235	0.0405	0.0552	0.0845	0.108	0.149	0.174	0.263	0.366	0.478	0.618	0.804
Allowable tension load, lb, for a unit stress of 20,000 psi[a]		470	810	1,105	1,690	2,160	2,970	3,485	5,265	7,330	9555	12,360	16,090
Wood													
Allowable withdrawal load[b], lb/in. of threaded portion	Normal 1.00[c]	232	274	313	352	389	425	460	528	593	655	716	774
	Snow 1.15[c]	267	315	360	405	447	489	529	607	682	753	823	890
	7-Day 1.25[c]	290	342	391	440	486	531	575	660	741	819	895	967

[a]Rounded to nearest 5 lb.
[b]Based on Douglas fir-larch; specific gravity of 0.51 based on weight and volume when oven dry.
[c]Duration of load factors.

(g) The effective net section of the member in bending should be checked against the bending moment at the location under consideration. The effective net section should be determined by deducting from the cross section a hole displacement equal to the shank diameter of the lag bolt used. If a countersink is used for the lag bolt head, its effect on the net section also should be considered.

Example. Determine the required radial reinforcement (fully threaded lag bolts) for a double tapered-pitched beam satisfying the following conditions:

Douglas fir–larch	$d_c = 60$ in.
Spacing $= 15$ ft	$b = 8\frac{3}{4}$ in.
Effective span $= 60$ ft	$R_{soffit} = 60$ ft
SL $= 20$ psf	
DL $= 15$ psf	
Roof slope $= 3:12$	

1. Determine maximum radial tension stress

$$f_r = K_r \frac{6M}{bd_c^2}$$

$M =$ bending moment at the centerline $= (1.5)(560)(60)^2$

$M = (3.024)(10^6)$ in.-lb

$$R_m = 60 + \frac{d_c}{2} = 62 \text{ ft } 6 \text{ in.} = 750 \text{ in.}$$

$$\frac{d_c}{R_m} = \frac{60}{750} = 0.08$$

From Figure 4.15; $K_r = 0.065$

$$f_r = 0.065 \frac{(6)(3,204,000)}{(8.75)(60)^2} = 37.4 \text{ psi}$$

or $f_r/\text{in.} = (37.4)(8.75) = 327.2$ lb/linear in.

2. Determine size and spacing of fully threaded lag bolts required to resist calculated radial tension stresses:

Assume 1 in. diameter lag bolt.

From Table 4.5: Allowable steel tension load $= 9,555$ lb
Allowable wood withdrawal load per in. of thread $= 753$ lb/in.

Effective thread penetration $= \left(\frac{60}{2}\right) - 2 = 28$ in.

Therefore, total allowable wood withdrawal load $= (753)(28) = 21,084$ lb

Maximum allowable spacing (steel stress) $= \dfrac{9,555}{327.2} = 29$ in.

Maximum allowable spacing (wood stress) $= \dfrac{21{,}084}{327.2} = 64$ in.

Assume use of 1 in. lag bolts spaced 24 in. on center.

Note: First lag bolts will be placed at one-half of the spacing (12 in.) on either side of the centerline (see sketch).

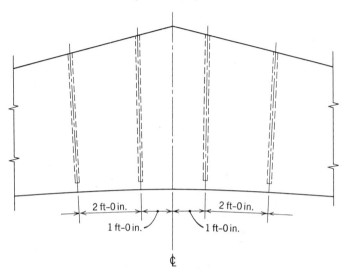

Check beam net section for bending stress.

At first lag bolt from the centerline, the depth of the section is 57 in. (from sketch)

Effective width of cross section $= 8\frac{3}{4} - 1 = 7\frac{3}{4}$ in.

Effective section modulus $= \dfrac{(7.75)(57)^2}{6} = 4{,}197$

M @ 12 in. from the centerline $= M_{\mbox{\textcent}}\left[1 - \left(\dfrac{1}{30}\right)^2\right]$

M @ 12 in. $= (3.024)(10^6)[1 - 0.001] = (3.02)(10^6)$ in.-lb

f_b (net section) $= \dfrac{(3.02)(10^6)}{4{,}197} = 720$ psi

Allowable $F_b = (2400)(1.15)C_F$

From Table 2.13, $C_F = 0.84$

$l/d = \dfrac{(60)(12)}{57} = 12.6$

Correction for $l/d = +3.2\%$ (see page **2-37**)

Therefore, corrected $C_F = (0.84)(1.032) = 0.87$

Allowable $F_b = 2{,}401$ psi > 720 O.K.

Use 1 in. lag bolts at 24 in. on centers.

ARCHES

Three-Hinged Arches

Three-hinged arches, as the name implies, are hinged at each support and at the crown or peak. They may take shapes such as radial, gothic, A-frame, tudor, three-centered, or parabolic. (See Figure 4.16.)

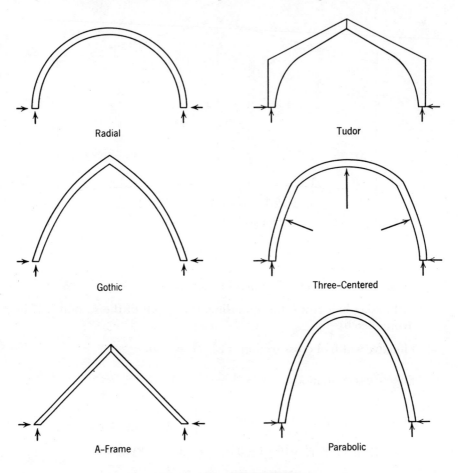

Radial

Tudor

Gothic

Three–Centered

A-Frame

Parabolic

Figure 4.16.   ARCH TYPES.

Design procedure. The following design procedure may be used to design simple three-hinged arches under usual loading conditions. This procedure is essentially a trial-and-error method, and revision of original values may be necessary. The procedure is given for a three-hinged tudor arch. The design of other three-hinged arch types will be similar.

1. Determine the application of dead, live, or snow loads and wind loads. The roof loads may be assumed to be uniform if roof decking is applied directly to the arch or may be concentrated at purlin points. See Section 3, "Loads," for dead, live, snow, and wind load recommendations.

2. Lay out to a convenient scale the arch outline indicating external

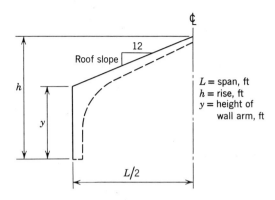

Figure 4.17.   ARCH DIMENSIONS.

architectural dimensions (see Figure 4.17). Radius of curvature is also an architectural dimension, and it should not be less than the minimums recommended for various lamination thicknesses as recommended on page 4-45. In the case of arches with concentrated loads applied at purlin points, note the locations of the loads.

3. Calculate and tabulate the approximate reactions for various combinations of loading conditions. Figure 4.18 indicates some of the more common loading conditions. Other loading conditions to be checked are given in Table 3.9.

4. Determine minimum section size at base, bd_b, by the formula

$$bd_b = \frac{3R_{\mathrm{H}}}{2F_v}$$

where R_{H} = horizontal reaction, lb, as determined in step 3
$\quad\ \ F_v$ = allowable horizontal shear stress, psi, adjusted for duration of loading

5. As a first trial in the trial-and-error process, determine approximate depths of arch at crown, d_c, and tangent points, d_t, by the formulas

$$d_c = 1.5b \quad \text{and} \quad d_t = 1.5d_b$$

where b = arch width, in. (assumed, based on section at base determined in step 4)
$\quad\ \ d_b$ = arch depth at base, in. (based on section at base determined in step 4 and assumption for b)

The section at the crown is often proportioned for architectural appearance or to meet the depth of purlins which frame into the arch at this point. In no case should the crown depth be less than the arch width. For design simplicity, the upper and lower tangent point depths are often assumed to be equal.

Note: Shipping heights for the tudor arch configuration may be a controlling factor, and the designer should check with the manufacturer to determine the applicable limitations.

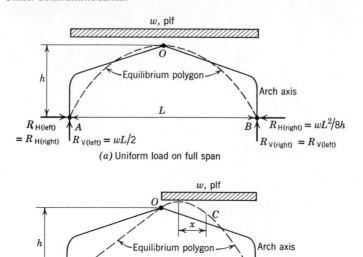

(a) Uniform load on full span

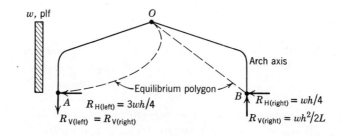

(b) Uniform load on right half span

(c) Wind load on left side

Figure 4.18   THREE-HINGED ARCH REACTIONS AND EQUILIBRIUM POLYGONS.

6. Lay out the arch to scale, using the approximate dimensions determined in steps 4 and 5 and the assumed radius of curvature, R. Locate the arch axis at the midpoint of the arch depth. Determine the effective span, L', and effective rise, h'. (See Figure 4.19.)

Design and analysis of a three-hinged arch are facilitated by using equilibrium polygons, which are moment diagrams for a specified loading drawn in such a position and to such a scale that they pass through the hinges. Equilibrium polygons for each loading condition are illustrated in Figure 4.18. For loading condition *(a)* in Figure 4.18, uniform load on full span, the equilibrium polygon is a parabola with vertex at the crown hinge, *O*. For condition *(b)*, uniform load on right half span, the equilibrium polygon is a straight line from base hinge, *A*, to *O*, and a parabola from *O* to base hinge, *B*, with its vertex $L/8$ to the right and $h/8$ above *O*. For condition *(c)*, uniform wind load on left vertical projection, the equilibrium polygon is a parabola from *A* to *O* with its vertex $L/16$ to the right and $h/4$ below *O*,

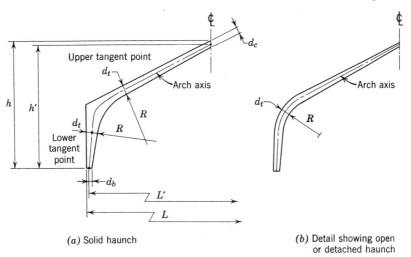

(a) Solid haunch

(b) Detail showing open
or detached haunch

Figure 4.19.   ARCH DETAILS.

and a straight line from O to B. Parabolas may easily be constructed by applying the fact that the offset from a tangent to a parabola varies directly as the square of the tangent distances. For example, the vertical offset to point C from the horizontal tangent through the vertex of the equilibrium polygon for loading condition (b) is equal to $(h/8)[x/(L/8)]^2$.

The advantages of the equilibrium polygons are that they provide a means of determining the moment at any point on the arch axis, and a means of determining by inspection the points of maximum moment and the signs of the moments; however, the maximum moment point will not be the point of maximum stress in a tapered roof arm or vertical leg. When stresses are approaching the allowable values, several points along the roof arm or vertical leg must be checked to determine this point of maximum stress.

For vertical loads, loading conditions (a) and (b) in Figure 4.18, the moment at any point may be determined by multiplying the scale length of the vertical line between the arch axis and the equilibrium polygon by the horizontal reaction, R_H, as determined in step 3. Moments are positive if the equilibrium polygon lies above the arch axis, and negative if it lies below.

For horizontal loads, loading condition (c) in Figure 4.18, the moment at any point is equal to the vertical reaction (R_V from step 3) times the scale length of the horizontal line between the arch axis and the equilibrium polygon. Moments are positive at a point on the arch axis if the point is between the equilibrium polygon and the load, and negative if the equilibrium polygon and the load are to the same side of the point. Thus for the wind from the left as illustrated in Figure 4.18, loading condition (c), moments in the left half of the arch are positive and those in the right half are negative.

7. Recalculate horizontal reactions, R_H, for vertical loads and vertical reactions, R_V, for horizontal loads, using the effective span and rise from step 6 in the appropriate formula from step 3.

8. Check arch section at several points along the arch axis for combined bending and axial compression. Points to be checked include the upper and lower tangent points and at least two points on the roof arm; and when the haunch is not glued integrally, points between the upper and lower tangent points. More points on the roof arm should be checked if the two points investigated have stresses approaching the allowable values. Point on the vertical leg should also be checked.

The combined stress formula to be applied is as follows:
If the compressive portion exceeds the bending portion

$$\frac{P'}{AF_c'} + \frac{M}{SF_b} \leq 1$$

If the bending portion exceeds the compressive portion

$$\frac{P'}{AF_c'} + \frac{M}{SF_bC_F} \leq 1$$

where P' = axial compression at the point under consideration, lb (determined by laying out loads and reactions to scale, as in Figure 4.20)

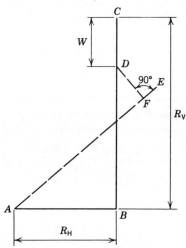

1. Lay out lines to scale:
   AB = horizontal reaction
   (steps 3 and 7)
   BC = vertical reaction
   (steps 3 and 7)
   CD = sum of vertical loads to left of point under consideration
2. Draw line AE parallel to the tangent to the arch axis at the point under consideration
3. Draw line through D perpendicular to line AE. Then AF = axial compression at point under consideration = P', and DF = shear perpendicular to arch axis at point under consideration.

Figure 4.20.   FORCE DIAGRAM.

M = bending moment at the point under consideration, in.-lb (determined by using the equilibrium polygons as explained in step 6)

A = cross-sectional area at the point under consideration, in.²

S = section modulus at the point, in.³

F_b = allowable unit stress for extreme fiber in bending, psi, adjusted for duration of loading, and curvature factor (if section is in curved portion of arch)

F_c' = allowable unit stress in compression parallel to grain adjusted for l/d (slenderness ratio) and for duration of loading, psi

$$F_c' = \frac{0.3E}{(l/d)^2}$$

where E = modulus of elasticity, psi
> l = length of arch between points of lateral bracing, in.
> d = width of arch, in.

If the combined stress formula value exceeds 1, it will be necessary to revise the original trial sections approximated in step 5, and to repeat the subsequent steps.

9. Check lateral stability considerations. When one edge of the arch is braced by decking fastened directly to the arch or braced at frequent intervals, as by girts or roof purlins, the ratio of tangent point depth, d_t, to breadth, b, of the arch, based on actual dimensions, should not exceed 6. When such lateral bracing is lacking, the ratio should not exceed 5, and the arch should be checked for column action in the lateral (width) direction.

The arch should be checked for column action in the lateral direction using the formula

$$\frac{P'}{AF_c{}'} + \frac{M}{SF_b} \leq 1$$

where terms are as previously defined.

The least dimension, d, in the slenderness ratio for lateral column action is the breadth, b, of the arch. For the roof arm of the arch, the column length, l, in the slenderness ratio is the distance between points of lateral support to the roof. For the wall arm, l is either the height of the wall arm (y in Figure 4.17) or the distance between points of lateral support to the wall.

10. Check radial stress by the formula

$$f_r = \frac{3M}{2Rbd}$$

where f_r = actual radial stress, psi, tension, f_{rt}, or compression, f_{rc}
> M = maximum bending moment, in.-lb
> R = radius of curvature at arch axis, in.
> b = arch width, in.
> d = arch depth at point of maximum moment, in.

Limitations on allowable radial stress values are given on page **4-46**.

11. Determine deflection due to bending. The deflection at any point in an arch may be determined by the formula

$$\Delta_a = \frac{s}{E} \sum \frac{Mm}{I}$$

where Δ_a = actual deflection, in.
> s = length of segments along arch axis, in. (each arch half should be divided into equal segments of length along the arch axis)
> E = modulus of elasticity, psi
> M = moment at midpoint of each segment, s, in.-lb, under the loading condition for which the deflection is desired
> m = moment at midpoint of each segment, s, in., under a unit load applied at the point where the deflection is desired and in the direction in which the magnitude of the deflection is desired

I = moment of inertia of a section perpendicular to the arch axis at midpoint of each segment, s, in.[4]

Specific deflection limitations for arches have not been generally accepted since this is a function of the intended use. Deflection limits that have been applied are $l/180$ for dead load plus live load and $l/240$ for dead load only.

Example. Design a three-hinged glued laminated tudor arch to meet the following conditions.

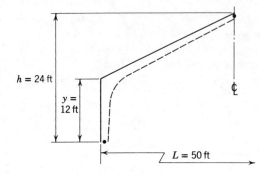

Spacing = 15 ft
Radius of curvature = R = 10.5 ft
Thickness of lamination = $t = \frac{3}{4}$ in.
Curvature factor = C_C =
$$1 - 2{,}000\,(t/R)^2$$
$$C_C = 1 - 2{,}000\left[\frac{0.75}{(10.5)(12)}\right]^2 = 0.993$$

Allowable unit stresses (1.15 = adjustment factor for snow duration of loading):

$F_b = (2{,}400)(1.15) = 2{,}760$ psi

$F_c = (1{,}500)(1.15) = 1{,}725$ psi

$F_{c\perp} = (385)(1.15) = 443$ psi

$F_v = (200)(1.15) = 230$ psi

$E = 1{,}800{,}000$ psi

Wall is laterally supported at mid-height and at top: Decking is applied directly to roof arm.

DL = 13 psf

DL converted to psf of horizontal projection = 15 psf

SL = 25 psf

WL = 20 psf

1. Application of loads.

w_{DL} = (spacing)(DL) = (15)(15) = 225 plf
w_{SL} = (spacing)(SL) = (15)(25) = 375 plf

Total vertical load   = 600 plf
w_{WL} = (spacing)(WL) = (15)(20) = 300 plf

2. Arch layout. See sketch.

3. Calculate reactions.

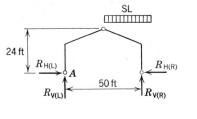

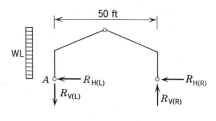

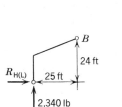

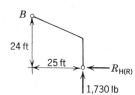

	Vertical Reactions		Horizontal Reactions	
	(Upward reactions positive)		(Reactions acting right positive)	
Load	$R_{V(left)}$	$R_{V(right)}$	$R_{H(left)}$	$R_{H(right)}$
DL	+5,620	+5,620	+2,930	−2,930
SL (full span)	+9,380	+9,380	+4,890	−4,890
DL + SL (full span)	+15,000	+15,000	+7,820	−7,820
SL (right half)	+2,340	+7,030	+2,440	−2,440
DL + SL (right half)	+7,960	+12,650	+5,370	−5,370
WL (from left)	−1,730	+1,730	−5,400	−1,800
DL + WL (from left)	+3,890	+7,350	−2,470	−4,730

4. Determine section at base.

Maximum R_H = 7,820 lb (DL + full SL)

$$bd_b = \frac{3R_H}{2F_v} = \frac{(3)(7,820)}{(2)(230)} = 51.0 \text{ in.}^2$$

Try $5\frac{1}{8} \times 10\frac{1}{2}$ section, $A = 53.8$ in.^{2}

5. Approximate crown and tangent point depths.

$d_c = 1.5b = (1.5)(5.125) = 7.7$ in.; use 7.75 in.
$d_t = 1.5d_b = (1.5)(10.5) = 15.75$ in.

6. Lay out arch to scale and determine effective dimensions. Construct equilibrium polygons. (See Drawing A, page **4-60**.)

$L' = 49.2$ ft
$h' = 23.6$ ft

7. Recalculate reactions.

	Vertical Reactions		Horizontal Reactions	
	(Upward reactions positive)		(Reactions acting right positive)	
Load	$R_{V(left)}$	$R_{V(right)}$	$R_{H(left)}$	$R_{H(right)}$
DL	+5,620	+5,620	+2,880	−2,880
SL (full span)	+9,380	+9,380	+4,800	−4,800
DL+SL (full span)	+15,000	+15,000	+7,680	−7,680
SL (right half)	+2,340	+7,030	+2,520	−2,520
DL+SL (right half)	+7,960	+12,650	+5,400	−5,400
WL (from left)	−1,700	+1,700	−5,400	−1,800
DL+WL (from left)	+3,920	+7,320	−2,520	−4,680

8. Check arch sections. Using the equilibrium polygons, determine moments at points indicated on Drawing A and also at corresponding points on right half of arch.

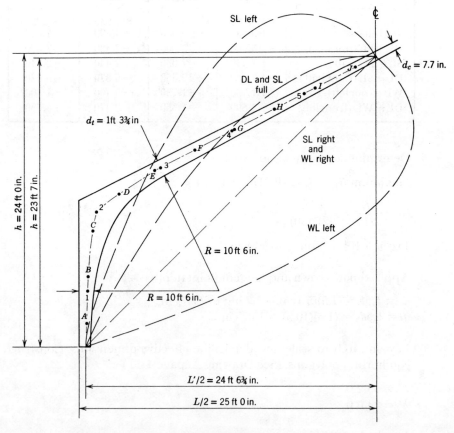

DRAWING A

(*a*) Dead load only and dead load plus snow load on full span.

Point	Vertical Distance between Arch Axis and Equilibrium Polygon		Horizontal Reaction		Moment	
			DL, lb	DL+SL, lb	DL, in.-lb	DL+SL, in.-lb
1 and 1'	4 ft 5 in.	53 in.	2,880	7,680	− 152,600	− 407,000
2 and 2'	9 ft 3 in.	111 in.	2,880	7,680	− 319,700	− 852,500
3 and 3'	3 ft 8 in.	44 in.	2,880	7,680	− 126,700	− 337,900
4 and 4'	3 in.	3 in.	2,880	7,680	+ 860	+ 23,000
5 and 5'	1 ft 7 in.	19 in.	2,880	7,680	+ 54,700	+ 145,900

(*b*) Snow load on right half span.

Point	Vertical Distance between Arch Axis and Equilibrium Polygon		Horizontal Reaction, lb	Moment	
				SL only, in.-lb	DL+SL, in.-lb
Left					
1	4 ft 6 in.	54 in.	2,520	− 136,000	− 288,600
2	10 ft 1 in.	121 in.	2,520	− 304,900	− 624,600
3	8 ft 5 in.	101 in.	2,520	− 254,500	− 381,200
4	5 ft 7 in.	67 in.	2,520	− 168,800	− 177,400
5	2 ft 9 in.	33 in.	2,520	− 83,200	− 137,900
Right					
5'	6 ft 5 in.	77 in.	2,520	+ 194,000	+ 248,700
4'	6 ft 9 in.	81 in.	2,520	+ 204,100	+ 212,700
3'	1 ft 7 in.	19 in.	2,520	+ 47,900	− 78,800
2'	7 ft 2 in.	86 in.	2,520	− 216,700	− 536,400
1'	3 ft 9 in.	45 in.	2,520	− 113,400	− 266,000

(*c*) Wind load from left.

Point	Horizontal Distance between Arch Axis and Equilibrium Polygon		Vertical Reaction, lb	Moment	
				WL only, in.-lb	DL+WL, in.-lb
Left					
1	12 ft 5 in.	149 in.	1,700	+ 253,300	+ 100,700
2	22 ft 10 in.	274 in.	1,700	+ 465,800	+ 146,100
3	20 ft 5 in.	245 in.	1,700	+ 416,500	+ 289,800
4	15 ft 2 in.	182 in.	1,700	+ 309,400	+ 318,000
5	8 ft 4 in.	100 in.	1,700	+ 170,800	+ 224,700

Point	Horizontal Distance between Arch Axis and Equilibrium Polygon		Vertical Reaction, lb	Moment	
				WL only, in.-lb	DL+WL, in.-lb
Right					
5'	2 ft 10 in.	34 in.	1,700	− 57,800	− 3,100
4'	5 ft 9 in.	69 in.	1,700	− 117,300	− 108,700
3'	8 ft 8 in.	104 in.	1,700	− 176,800	− 303,500
2'	10 ft 5 in.	125 in.	1,700	− 212,500	− 532,200
1'	4 ft 7 in.	55 in.	1,700	− 93,500	− 246,100

Tabulate maximum moments for each point along with the corresponding thrust and shear as determined from Drawings B and C, pages 4-62 and 4-63.

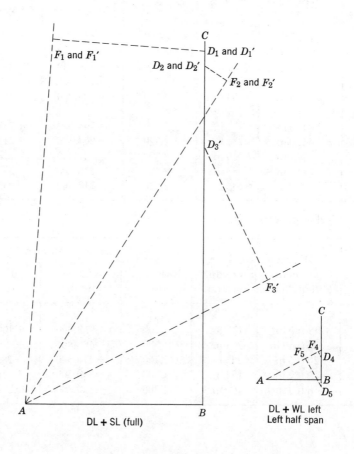

DRAWING B

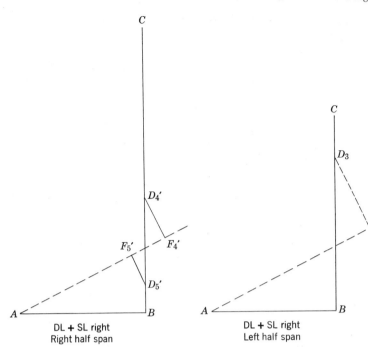

DL + SL right
Right half span

DL + SL right
Left half span

DRAWING C

Point	Loading Condition	Maximum Moment, M, in.-lb	Thrust, P', lb	Shear Perpendicular to Arch Axis, lb
Left				
1	DL + full SL	−407,000	15,240	6,480
2	DL + full SL	−852,500	16,000	1,140
3	DL + SL right	−381,200	7,640	3,240
4	DL + WL left	+318,000	2,680	220
5	DL + WL left	+224,700	2,100	1,500
Right				
5′	DL + SL right	+248,700	5,360	1,360
4′	DL + SL right	+212,700	6,960	1,860
3′	DL + full SL	−337,900	11,640	6,160
2′	DL + full SL	−852,500	16,000	1,140
1′	DL + full SL	−407,000	15,240	6,480

Properties of sections (depths scaled from Drawing A).

Point	Depth, d, in.	Area, A, in.^{2}	Section Modulus, S, in.^{3}	Size Factor, C_F (from Table 2.13)
1 and 1'	15.75	80.7	212	0.97
2 and 2'	43.0	220.4	1,579	0.87
3 and 3'	15.75	80.7	212	0.97
4 and 4'	14.0	71.8	167	0.98
5 and 5'	11.0	56.4	103	1.00

Check each point, using the formula $P'/AF_c' + M/SF_b \leq 1$ if $P'/A > M/S$ or $P'/AF_c' + M/SF_bC_F \leq 1$ if $P'/A < M/S$.

Point 1. DL + full SL. Lateral unbraced length = l = 6 ft 0 in. = 72 in.

$$l/d = \frac{72}{5.125} = 14.05$$

$$F_c' = 1.15\frac{0.3E}{(l/d)^2} = \frac{(1.15)(0.3)(1,800,000)}{(14.05)^2} = 3,145 \text{ psi} > 1,725;$$

$$F_c' = 1,725 \text{ psi}$$

$$\frac{M}{S} = \frac{407,000}{212} = 1,920 \text{ psi}, \frac{P'}{A} = \frac{15,240}{80.7} = 188.8 \text{ psi} < \frac{M}{S}; \text{ therefore, use}$$

$$\frac{P'}{AF_c'} + \frac{M}{SF_bC_FC_c} \leq 1$$

$$\frac{P'}{AF_c'} + \frac{M}{SF_bC_FC_c} = \frac{15,240}{(80.7)(1,725)} + \frac{407,000}{(212)(2,760)(0.97)(0.993)} =$$

$$0.109 + 0.722 = 0.831 < 1 \qquad \text{O.K.}$$

Point 2. Similar calculations are made for points 2, 3', 2', and 1', which are also governed by DL + full SL. These calculations are summarized in the accompanying table.

Point	Governing l/d Ratio	F_c'	$\frac{M}{S} > \frac{P'}{A}$	$\frac{P'}{AF_c'} + \frac{M}{SF_bC_FC_c}$
2	0	1,725	Yes	0.268
3'	0	1,725	Yes	0.684
2'	0	1,725	Yes	0.268
1'	14.05	1,725	Yes	0.831

Point 3. DL + SL right.
$l/d = 0 \qquad F_c' = 1,725$ psi

$$\frac{M}{S} = \frac{381,200}{212} = 1,798 \text{ psi} \qquad \frac{P'}{A} = \frac{7,640}{80.7} = 94.7 \text{ psi} < \frac{M}{S}$$

$$\frac{P'}{AF_c'} + \frac{M}{SF_b C_F C_c} = \frac{7,640}{(80.7)(1,725)} + \frac{381,200}{(212)(2,760)(0.97)(0.993)} =$$

$$0.055 + 0.676 = 0.731 < 1 \qquad \text{O.K.}$$

Point 4. DL + WL left.

$l/d = 0$; therefore, use $F_c' = (1.33)(1,500) = 1,995$ psi

$$\frac{M}{S} = \frac{318,000}{167} = 1,904 \text{ psi} \qquad \frac{P'}{A} = \frac{2,680}{71.8} = 37.3 \text{ psi} < \frac{M}{S}$$

$$\frac{P'}{AF_c'} + \frac{M}{SF_b C_F} = \frac{2,680}{(56.4)(1,995)} + \frac{224,700}{(167)(3,190)(0.98)} = 0.019 + 0.609 =$$

$$0.628 < 1 \qquad \text{O.K.}$$

Point 5. DL + WL left. l/d ratio same as for point 4.

$$\frac{P'}{AF_c'} + \frac{M}{SF_b C_F} = \frac{2,100}{(56.4)(1,995)} + \frac{224,700}{(103)(3,190)(1.0)} = 0.019 + 0.684 =$$

$$0.703 < 1 \qquad \text{O.K.}$$

Point 5'. DL + SL right.

$l/d = 0$; therefore, $F_c' = 1,725$ psi

$$\frac{P'}{AF_c'} + \frac{M}{SF_b C_F} = \frac{5,360}{(56.4)(1,725)} + \frac{248,700}{(103)(2,760)(1.0)} = 0.055 + 0.875 =$$

$$0.930 < 1 \qquad \text{O.K.}$$

Point 4'. DL + SL right. l/d same as for point 5'.

$$\frac{M}{S} = \frac{212,700}{167} = 1,274 \text{ psi} \qquad \frac{P'}{A} = \frac{6,960}{71.8} = 96.9 < \frac{M}{S}$$

$$\frac{P'}{AF_c'} + \frac{M}{SF_b C_F} = \frac{6,960}{(71.5)(1,725)} + \frac{212,700}{(167)(2,760)(0.98)} = 0.056 + 0.471 =$$

$$0.527 < 1 \qquad \text{O.K.}$$

9. Check arch for lateral stability in regard to tangent point depth to width ratio.

$$\frac{d_t}{b} = \frac{15.75}{5.125} = 3.07 < 6 \qquad \text{O.K.}$$

Check arch leg for column action in lateral direction.

$$l/d = \frac{72}{5.125} = 14.05$$

$$F_c' = 3,145 \text{ psi} > 1,725 \text{ psi}$$

Use $F_c' = 1,725$ psi

$$\frac{P'}{AF_c'}+\frac{M}{SF_b}=\frac{15,240}{(80.7)(1,725)}+\frac{407,000}{(212)(2,760)}=$$

$$0.109+0.696=0.805<1 \qquad \text{O.K.}$$

10. Check radial stress.

$$R = \text{radius of curvature}+\frac{d}{2}=(10.5)(12)+\frac{43}{2}=147.5\,\text{in.}$$

Moment is negative; therefore, radial stress is compressive.

$$F_{rc}=F_{c\perp}=443\,\text{psi}$$

$$f_r=\frac{3M}{2Rbd}=\frac{(3)(852,500)}{(2)(147.5)(5.125)(43)}=39.3\,\text{psi}<443 \qquad \text{O.K.}$$

11. Determine the outward horizontal deflection at the haunch under full snow load plus dead load. The accompanying sketch shows application of unit load for determining outward horizontal deflection at haunch and reactions due to unit load (determined by statics).

   Divide each half arch axis into ten segments, s, 45.4 in. long. The mid-points of each segment on the left half arch axis are indicated as points A through J on Drawing A, page **4-60**.

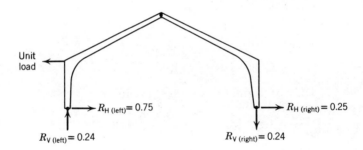

Moments at each midpoint may be determined by using the equilibrium polygon for DL + full SL for actual load moments, M, and using the equilibrium polygons for wind load right for unit load moments, m.

Point	Moment, M, in.-lb	Unit Load Moment, m, in.	Moment of Inertia, I, in.^{4}	Mm/I
Left				
A	− 176,600	− 15.8	940	+ 2,970
B	− 514,600	− 43.2	2,100	+ 10,590
C	− 783,400	− 61.2	12,700	+ 3,780
D	− 668,200	− 64.8	8,400	+ 5,150
E	− 384,000	− 58.3	1,700	+ 13,170

Point	Moment, M, in.-lb	Moment, m, in.	Moment of Intertia, I, in.^{4}	Mm/I
F	$-138,200$	-52.3	1,400	$+5,160$
G	$+\ 30,700$	-43.2	1,200	$-1,100$
H	$+130,600$	-32.6	740	$-5,750$
I	$+138,200$	-20.9	430	$-6,720$
J	$+\ 76,800$	-7.2	310	$-1,780$
Right				
J'	$+\ 76,800$	$+2.2$	310	$+540$
I'	$+138,200$	$+7.0$	430	$+2,250$
H'	$+130,600$	$+11.8$	740	$+2,080$
G'	$+30,700$	$+16.1$	1,200	$+410$
F'	$-138,200$	$+21.1$	1,400	$-2,080$
E'	$-384,000$	$+25.4$	1,700	$-5,740$
D'	$-668,200$	$+28.8$	8,400	$-2,290$
C'	$-783,400$	$+26.4$	12,700	$-1,630$
B'	$-514,600$	$+16.6$	2,100	$-4,070$
A'	$-176,600$	$+5.5$	940	$-1,030$

$$\Sigma Mm/I = +13,910$$

$$\Delta_a = \frac{s}{E} \Sigma \frac{Mm}{I}$$

$$\Delta_a = \frac{(45.4)(13,910)}{1,800,000} = 0.351 \text{ in.}$$

Summary of actual section sizes:
Base depth $= 10\frac{1}{2}$ in.
Crown depth $= 7\frac{3}{4}$ in.
Tangent depth $= 15\frac{3}{4}$ in.
Width $= 5\frac{1}{8}$ in.

Two-Hinged Arches

Two-hinged arches are hinged at each base and are statically indeterminate. They may have a profile of any shape with any combination of straight, constant, or variable section depth. The horizontal thrust at the base must be resisted by some adequate means, such as tie rods, abutments, or foundations. After the reactions, moments, shears, and axial forces have been determined, the part of the design for determining the required arch section is similar to that for the three-hinged arch.

Design procedure. This procedure may be used for arches that are symmetrical about the centerline. It neglects the effect of tie-rod elongation or differential settlement and spread of abutments.

1. Lay out one-half of the arch axis to a convenient scale, and divide it into any number of equal divisions (the more divisions used, the more

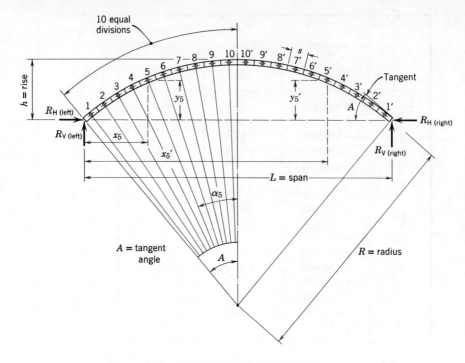

Figure 4.21.   TWO-HINGED ARCH NOTATIONS.

precise the results will be). Determine and tabulate the x and y distances for each point of division. (See Figure 4.21.) Tabulate the values for y^2 also.

2. Determine vertical reactions, R_V, for the various loading conditions by the summation of vertical forces equal to zero, or by taking moments about one hinge. For balanced loading, R_V = one-half the total live or snow and dead loads on the arch.

3. Considering the entire arch as a simple span beam, compute and tabulate the bending moment, M_s, at each division point for dead loads, balanced and unbalanced vertical loads, and horizontal loads.

4. Multiply the M_s values by the corresponding y values and tabulate.

5. Compute horizontal reactions, R_H, for the various loadings by the formula

$$R_H = \frac{\Sigma(M_s y)}{\Sigma(y^2)}$$

This formula neglects the effect of tie-rod elongation or spread in abutments, since they are usually small.

6. Determine and tabulate bending moment, M, on the arch at each division point, using the following formulas.

Dead and vertical loads:

$$M = M_s - R_H y$$

Wind load:

$$M_{(left)} = -R_{V(left)}x - \tfrac{1}{2}w_{WL}y^2 + R_{H(left)}y \qquad \text{(for left half span)}$$

$$M_{(right)} = R_{V(right)}(L-x) - R_{H(right)}y \qquad \text{(for right half span)}$$

7. Determine axial thrust, P', at each division point.

8. On the basis of the assumption of full lateral support and using the following formulas, determine the section size required at each division point.

$$A = \frac{P'}{F_c} \qquad S = \frac{M}{F_b}$$

where A = cross-sectional area, in.^{2}

       P' = axial thrust as determined in step 7, lb

       F_c = allowable unit stress in compression parallel to grain, psi, adjusted for duration of loading

       S = section modulus, in.^{3}

      M = bending moment as determined in step 6, in.-lb

      F_b = allowable unit stress for extreme fiber in bending, psi, adjusted for duration of loading, curvature factor, and size factor (assumed, for preliminary purposes, to be 0.85)

On the basis of these requirements and industry standard depths and widths (see page **2-75**), determine the required arch depths, d, and widths, b, at each division point. When one edge of the arch is braced by decking fastened directly to the arch or braced at frequent intervals, as by girts or purlins, the depth to breadth ratio, d/b, of the arch, based on actual dimensions, should not exceed 6. When such lateral bracing is lacking, the ratio should not exceed 5, and the arch should be checked for column action in the lateral (width) direction (see step 11).

9. Check the section for combined bending and axial compression as follows.

If the compressive portion exceeds the bending portion:

$$\frac{P'}{AF_c'} + \frac{M}{SF_b} \leq 1$$

or if the bending portion exceeds the compressive portion:

$$\frac{P'}{AF_c'} + \frac{M}{SF_bC_F} \leq 1$$

where F_b = allowable unit stress for extreme fiber in bending, psi, adjusted for duration of loading and curvature factor.

   C_F = size factor

   F_c' = allowable unit stress in compression parallel to grain adjusted for l/d ratio and adjusted for duration of loading, psi

$$F_c' = \frac{0.3E}{(l/d)^2}$$

where E = modulus of elasticity, psi

    l/d = slenderness ratio

Depending on the loading condition, the length, l, in the slenderness ratio may be either of the following straight-line distances, and both should be checked.

(a) Hinge to point of contraflexure on the same half of the arch; or

(b) Point of contraflexure to point of contraflexure.

In either case, d is the arch depth. If the combined stress formula exceeds 1, it will be necessary to revise the chosen section size and repeat this step.

10. Check the section for shear stress at the base and at the point of maximum shear, using the formula

$$f_v = \frac{3V}{2A}$$

where f_v = actual horizontal shear stress, psi

V = shear perpendicular to arch axis, lb

A = cross-sectional area, in.^{2}

This value may not exceed the allowable unit horizontal shear stress, F_v.

11. Lateral stability considerations. As stated in step 8, when adequate lateral bracing is not provided (in which case the depth-breadth ratio should not exceed 5), the arch should be checked for column action in the lateral (width) direction, using the formula

$$\frac{P'}{AF_c'} + \frac{M}{SF_b} \leqslant 1$$

where terms are as previously defined. The least dimension, d, in the slenderness ratio for lateral column action is the width, b, of the arch section. The column length, l, is the distance between points of lateral support to the arch.

12. Check radial stress, f_r, by the formula

$$f_r = \frac{3M}{2RA}$$

where f_r = actual radial stress, tension, f_{rt}, or compression, f_{rc}, psi, and other terms are as previously defined.

Limitations on allowable radial stress values are given on page **4-46**.

13. Determine deflection due to bending. The deflection at any point in the arch may be determined by the formula

$$\Delta_a = \frac{s}{EI} \sum Mm$$

where Δ_a = actual deflection, in.

s = length of segments along arch axis, in. (any number of equal length segments may be used; however, the greater the number of segments, the greater will be the accuracy)

E = modulus of elasticity, psi

I = moment of inertia of a section perpendicular to the arch axis, in.^{4}

M = moment at midpoint of each segment, s, in.-lb, under the loading conditions for which deflection is desired

m = moment at midpoint of each segment, s, in., under a unit load applied at the point where the deflection is desired and in the direction in which the magnitude of the deflection is desired

To facilitate deflection calculations, tabulate the values.

The following formulas will assist in the design of a two-hinged, constant-section, constant-radius arch.

Step 1.

$$x = R(\sin A - \sin \alpha_n)$$
$$y = R(\cos \alpha_n - \cos A)$$

where α_n = the central angle to the point under consideration, degrees, (see Figure 4.21), and other terms are as defined in Figure 4.21.

Step 3.

Dead load:

$$M_s = R_{V(\text{left})}x - w_{\text{DL}}Ry + w_{\text{DL}}R^2 \sin \alpha_n(A - \alpha_n) \qquad \text{(for left half span)}$$

where w_{DL} = uniform dead load along arch axis, plf
$A - \alpha_n$ = difference between tangent angle and central angle to point under consideration, radians

Balanced live or snow load:

$$M_s = R_{V(\text{left})}x - \tfrac{1}{2}w_{\text{SL}}x^2 \qquad \text{(for left half span)}$$

where w_{SL} = uniform snow load or live load along horizontal projection, plf

Unbalanced snow load on right half span:

$$M_{s(\text{left})} = R_{V(\text{left})}x \qquad \text{(simple moments in left}$$
$$\text{or unloaded half span)}$$
$$M_{s(\text{right})} = R_{V(\text{right})}(L - x) - \tfrac{1}{2}w_{\text{SL}}(L - x)^2 \qquad \text{(simple moments in right}$$
$$\text{or loaded half span)}$$

Wind load from the left:

$$M_{s(\text{left})} = -R_{V(\text{left})}x + w_{\text{WL}}y(h - \tfrac{1}{2}y) \qquad \text{(simple moments in left half span)}$$
$$M_{s(\text{right})} = R_{V(\text{right})}(L - x) \qquad \text{(simple moments in right half span)}$$

where w_{WL} = uniform wind load along vertical projection, plf, and other terms are as defined in Figure 4.21.

Step 7. At the point of maximum moment (which may be located from the tabulation in step 6) P' is determined by the formula

$$P' = R_{\text{H}} \cos \alpha_n + (R_V - \Sigma wx) \sin \alpha_n$$

where R_{H} = horizontal reaction for the loading causing maximum moment, lb (for maximum moment occurring in left half span, use $R_{\text{H(left)}}$; in right half span, use $R_{\text{H(right)}}$)
R_V = vertical reaction for the loading causing maximum moment, lb
$\Sigma \alpha_n$ = central angle to point of maximum moment, degrees

$\Sigma\,wx =$ sum of loads to left (for point on left half span) or to right (for point on right half span) of point of maximum moment, lb

Step 10.

$$V = (R_V - \Sigma wx) \cos\alpha_n - R_H \sin\alpha_n$$

Example. Design a constant-section, constant-radius glued laminated two-hinged arch to meet the following conditions.

$L = 86\ \text{ft}$ Loads:
Spacing $= B = 17\ \text{ft}$ $DL = 10\ \text{psf}$
$A = \text{tangent angle} = 42°$ $SL = 20\ \text{psf}$
$R = 64\ \text{ft}$ $WL = 15\ \text{psf}$
Lamination thickness $= t = 1\frac{1}{2}\ \text{in.}$
Curvature factor $= C_c = 1 - 2{,}000(t/R)^2 = 0.992$

Allowable unit stresses:

$F_b = (2{,}400)(1.15)(0.992) = 2{,}740\ \text{psi}$
$F_c = (1{,}500)(1.15) = 1{,}725\ \text{psi}$
$F_{c\perp} = (385)(1.15) = 443\ \text{psi}$
$F_v = (165)(1.15) = 190\ \text{psi}$
$E = 1{,}800{,}000\ \text{psi}$

Lateral support provided by 3×12 purlins spaced at 7ft 2 in. intervals measured along the span.

1. Lay out arch to scale.

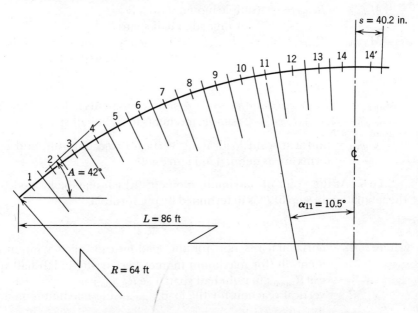

Point	α_n degrees	α_n radians	$\sin \alpha_n$	$\cos \alpha_n$	x, ft	y, ft	y^2, ft²
Left							
1	40.5	0.70686	0.64945	0.76041	1.260	1.105	1.221
2	37.5	0.65450	0.60876	0.79335	3.86	3.21	10.30
3	34.5	0.60214	0.56641	0.82413	6.57	5.18	26.8
4	31.5	0.54978	0.52250	0.85264	9.38	7.01	49.1
5	28.5	0.49742	0.47716	0.87882	12.29	8.68	75.3
6	25.5	0.44506	0.43051	0.90259	15.27	10.20	104.0
7	22.5	0.39270	0.38268	0.92388	18.33	11.57	133.9
8	19.5	0.34034	0.33381	0.94264	21.5	12.77	163.1
9	16.5	0.28798	0.28402	0.95882	24.6	13.80	190.4
10	13.5	0.23562	0.23345	0.97237	27.9	14.67	215
11	10.5	0.18326	0.18224	0.98325	31.2	15.37	236
12	7.5	0.13090	0.13053	0.99144	34.5	15.89	252
13	4.5	0.07854	0.07846	0.99692	37.8	16.24	264
14	1.5	0.02618	0.02618	0.99966	41.1	16.42	270
Right							
14′					44.9	16.42	270
13′					48.2	16.24	264
12′					51.5	15.89	252
11′		$A = 42° = 0.73304$ radian			54.8	15.37	236
10′		$\sin A = 0.66913$			58.1	14.67	215
9′		$\cos A = 0.74314$			61.4	13.80	190.4
8′					64.5	12.77	163.1
7′					67.67	11.57	133.9
6′					70.73	10.20	104.0
5′					73.71	8.68	75.3
4′					76.62	7.01	49.1
3′					79.43	5.18	26.8
2′					82.14	3.21	10.30
1′					84.74	1.105	1.221

$$\Sigma y^2 = 3{,}982.2 \text{ ft}^2$$

2. Determine vertical reactions.

    Dead Load:

$$R_{V(left)} = R_{V(right)} = \frac{(DL)(B)(\text{length of arch axis})}{2}$$

$$= \frac{(10)(17)(93.8)}{2} = 7{,}980 \text{ lb}$$

    Balanced snow load:

$$R_{V(left)} = R_{V(right)} = \frac{(SL)(B)(L)}{2} = \frac{(20)(17)(86)}{2} = 14{,}620 \text{ lb}$$

Unbalanced snow load (full snow load on right half span, no snow load on left half span):

By the sum of the moments about left hinge = 0:

$$R_{V(right)} = \frac{3(SL)(B)(L)}{8} = \frac{(3)(20)(17)(86)}{8} = 10{,}960 \text{ lb}$$

$$R_{V(left)} = \frac{(SL)(B)(L)}{2} - R_{V(right)} = \frac{(20)(17)(86)}{2} - 10{,}960$$

$$R_{V(left)} = 3{,}660 \text{ lb}$$

Wind load acting from the left:

$$\text{Arch rise} = h = \frac{L}{2} \tan \frac{A}{2} = 43 \tan 21° = 16.51 \text{ ft}$$

By the sum of the moments about left hinge = 0:

$$R_{V(right)} = \frac{(WL)(B)(h)^2}{2L} = \frac{(15)(17)(16.51)^2}{(2)(86)} = 404 \text{ lb}$$

$$R_{V(left)} = -R_{V(right)} = -404 \text{ lb} \quad \text{(acts downward)}$$

Steps 3 and 4. Tabulation of M_s and $M_s y$ values.

Point	Dead Load		Balanced SL		Unbalanced SL		Wind Load	
	M_s	$M_s y$	M_s	$M_s y$	M_s	$M_s y$	M_s	$M_s y$
Left								
1	9,860	10,900	18,150	20,100	4,610	5,090	3,985	4,400
2	29,200	93,700	53,870	172,900	14,130	45,400	10,638	34,100
3	47,600	247,000	88,760	460,000	24,000	124,300	15,730	81,500
4	65,300	458,000	122,140	856,000	34,300	240,000	19,450	136,300
5	81,900	711,000	154,000	1,337,000	45,000	391,000	21,930	190,400
6	97,300	992,000	183,400	1,871,000	55,900	570,000	23,470	239,000
7	110,900	1,283,000	210,900	2,440,000	67,100	776,000	24,220	280,000
8	123,800	1,581,000	235,400	3,010,000	78,700	1,005,000	24,310	310,000
9	134,200	1,852,000	257,100	3,550,000	90,000	1,242,000	23,860	329,000
10	144,300	2,120,000	275,700	4,040,000	102,100	1,498,000	23,130	339,000
11	151,600	2,330,000	290,500	4,460,000	114,200	1,755,000	22,000	338,000
12	156,800	2,490,000	302,000	4,800,000	126,300	2,010,000	20,860	331,000
13	161,000	2,610,000	310,000	5,030,000	138,300	2,250,000	19,430	316,000
14	162,290	2,660,000	314,000	5,160,000	150,400	2,470,000	18,000	297,000
Right								
14'					163,000	2,680,000	16,600	273,000
13'					171,000	2,780,000	15,270	248,000
12'					176,000	2,800,000	13,940	222,000
11'					176,500	2,710,000	12,600	193,700
10'					173,700	2,550,000	11,270	165,300
9'					167,100	2,310,000	9,940	137,200
8'					157,400	2,010,000	8,690	110,000
7'					143,900	1,665,000	7,410	85,700

Simple Beam Moments, ft-lb

	Simple Beam Moments, ft-lb							
	Dead Load		Balanced SL		Unbalanced SL		Wind Load	
Point	M_s	$M_s y$	M_s	$M_s y$	M_s	$M_s y$	M_s	$M_s y$
6'					127,800	1,304,000	6,170	62,900
5'					109,000	946,000	4,970	43,100
4'					87,840	616,000	3,790	26,600
3'					64,660	335,000	2,650	13,730
2'					39,770	127,700	1,559	5,000
1'					13,540	14,960	509	562
$\Sigma M_s y =$		38,877,200		74,414,000		37,230,450		4,812,492

5. Compute horizontal reactions. $R_H = \dfrac{\Sigma M_s y}{\Sigma y^2}$

$$R_{HDL} = \frac{38,877,200}{3,982.242} = 9,760 \text{ lb}$$

$$R_{HSL} = \frac{74,414,000}{3,982.242} = 18,690 \text{ lb}$$

$$R_{HUL} = \frac{37,230,450}{3,982.242} = 9,350 \text{ lb}$$

$$R_{HWL(right)} = \frac{4,812,492}{3,982.242} = 1,208 \text{ lb} \qquad \text{(acting to left)}$$

$$R_{HWL(left)} = w_{WL}h - R_{HWL(right)} = (15)(17)(16.51) - 1,208 = 3,002 \text{ lb}$$
(acting to left)

6. Tabulation of actual moment values.

	Actual Moments, ft-lb						
Point	DL	SL	$\tfrac{1}{2}$SL	WL	DL+SL	DL+$\tfrac{1}{2}$SL	DL+WL
Left							
1	−920	−2,550	−5,720	2,655	−3,470	−6,640	1,735
2	−2,100	−6,130	−16,240	6,768	−8,230	−18,340	4,668
3	−3,000	−8,040	−24,400	9,480	−11,040	−27,400	6,480
4	−3,100	−8,860	−31,200	10,950	−11,960	−34,360	7,850
5	−2,800	−8,200	−36,200	11,530	−11,000	−39,000	8,730
6	−2,300	−7,200	−39,500	11,170	−9,500	−41,800	8,870
7	−2,000	−5,100	−41,100	10,220	−7,100	−43,100	8,220
8	−800	−3,600	−40,700	8,810	−4,400	−41,500	8,010
9	−500	−900	−39,000	7,160	−1,400	−39,500	6,660
10	1,100	1,700	−35,100	5,330	2,800	−34,000	6,430
11	1,600	3,500	−29,500	3,400	5,100	−27,900	5,000
12	1,700	5,000	−22,300	1,660	6,700	−20,600	3,360
13	2,500	6,000	−13,500	−170	8,500	−11,000	2,330
14	1,990	7,000	−3,100	−1,700	8,990	−1,110	290

Point	\multicolumn{7}{c}{Actual Moments, ft-lb}

Point	DL	SL	$\frac{1}{2}$SL	WL	DL+SL	DL+$\frac{1}{2}$SL	DL+WL
Right							
14′	1,990	7,000	9,500	−3,240	8,990	11,490	−1,250
13′	2,500	6,000	19,200	−4,350	8,500	21,700	−1,850
12′	1,700	5,000	27,400	−5,260	6,700	29,100	−3,560
11′	1,600	3,500	32,800	−5,970	5,100	34,400	−4,370
10′	1,100	1,700	36,500	−6,450	2,800	37,600	−5,350
9′	−500	−900	38,100	−6,730	−1,400	37,600	−7,230
8′	−800	−3,600	38,000	−6,740	−4,400	37,200	−7,540
7′	−2,000	−5,100	35,700	−6,570	−7,100	33,700	−8,570
6′	−2,300	−7,200	32,400	−6,150	−9,500	30,100	−8,450
5′	−2,800	−8,200	27,800	−5,520	−11,000	25,000	−8,320
4′	−3,100	−8,860	22,340	−4,680	−11,960	19,240	−7,780
3′	−3,000	−8,040	16,260	−3,610	−11,040	13,260	−6,610
2′	−2,100	−6,130	9,770	−2,321	−8,230	7,670	−4,421
1′	−920	−2,550	3,210	−826	−3,470	2,290	−1,746

7. **Determine axial thrust.**

   From step 6, the point of maximum moment occurs at point 7 under dead load on full span and full snow load on the right half span (unbalanced snow load). At point 7:

   $$P' = (R_{\text{HDL(left)}} + R_{\text{HUL(left)}}) \cos 22.5° + (R_{\text{VDL(left)}} + R_{\text{VUL(left)}} - \Sigma wx) \sin 22.5°$$

   $$\Sigma wx = Rw_{\text{DL}}(A - \alpha_n) = (64)(10)(17)(0.73304 - 0.39270) = 3,700 \text{ lb}$$

   $$P' = (9,760 + 9,350)(0.92388) + (7,980 + 3,600 - 3,700)(0.38268) = 20,700 \text{ lb}$$

8. **Determine section size.**

   $$A = \frac{P'}{F_c} = \frac{20,700}{1,725} = 12.0 \text{ in.}^2$$

   $$S = \frac{M}{F_b} = \frac{(43,100)(12)}{(2,740)(0.85)} = 222 \text{ in.}^3$$

   Try a $5\frac{1}{8} \times 16\frac{1}{2}$ section, $A = 84.6$ in.^{2}, $S = 232.5$ in.^{3}, $C_F = 0.97$ (from Figure 2.13).

9. **Check for combined stresses.**

   $$R/d = \frac{(64)(12) + 16.5/2}{16.5} = 47.0$$

   From step 6, point of contraflexure for this loading condition occurs at the centerline of the arch.
   Straight-line distance to this point $= l = 46.1$ ft $= 553$ in.

   $$l/d = \frac{553}{16.5} = 33.5$$

$$F_c' = 1.15\frac{0.3E}{(l/d)^2} = \frac{(1.15)(0.3)(1,800,000)}{(33.5)^2} = 553 \text{ psi} < 1,725; \text{ use}$$

$$F_c' = 553 \text{ psi}$$

$$\frac{M}{S} = \frac{(43,100)(12)}{232} = 2,230 \text{ psi} \qquad \frac{P'}{A} = \frac{20,700}{84.6} = 245 \text{ psi} < \frac{M}{S};$$

therefore, use $\dfrac{P'}{AF_c'} + \dfrac{M}{SF_bC_F} \leq 1$

$$\frac{P'}{AF_c'} + \frac{M}{SF_bC_F} = \frac{20,700}{(84.6)(553)} + \frac{(43,100)(12)}{(232)(2,740)(0.97)} =$$

$$0.442 + 0.839 = 1.281 > 1 \quad \text{overstressed}$$

Repeating the same procedure, using a $5\frac{1}{8} \times 19\frac{1}{2}$ section;

$A = 99.9 \text{ in.}^2, S = 324.8 \text{ in.}^3, C_F = 0.95$
F_c' is determined to be 770 psi

$$\frac{P'}{AF_c'} + \frac{M}{SF_bC_F} = \frac{20,700}{(99.9)(770)} + \frac{(43,100)(12)}{(325)(2,740)(0.95)} =$$

$$0.269 + 0.611 = 0.880 < 1 \quad \text{O.K.}$$

10. Check for shear.

    Maximum horizontal and vertical reactions occur under dead load plus full snow load; therefore, check shear at base for this condition.

    $$V = (R_{VDL} + R_{VSL}) \cos 42° - (R_{HDL} + R_{HSL}) \sin 42°$$
    $$= (7,980 + 14,620)(0.74314) - (9,760 + 18,690)(0.66913)$$
    $$= 2,250 \text{ lb}$$
    $$f_v = \frac{3V}{2A} = \frac{(3)(2,250)}{(2)(99.9)} = 33.8 \text{ psi} < 190 \quad \text{O.K.}$$

    The point of maximum shear occurs at the crown of the arch under dead load plus unbalanced snow load.

    $$V = (R_{VDL} + R_{VUL(left)} - \Sigma wx) \cos \alpha_n - (R_{HDL} + R_{HUL(left)}) \sin \alpha_n$$

    $\alpha_n = 0$; therefore,

    $$V = R_{VDL} + R_{VUL(left)} - \Sigma wx \qquad \text{(snow load on right)}$$
    $$V = 7,980 + 3,660 - 7,980 = 3,660 \text{ lb}$$
    $$f_v = \frac{3V}{2A} = \frac{(3)(3,660)}{(2)(99.9)} = 55.0 \text{ psi} < 220 \quad \text{O.K.}$$

11. Check the arch for lateral stability.

    For $5\frac{1}{8} \times 19\frac{1}{2}$ section braced by 3×12 purlins,

    $$\frac{d}{b} = \frac{19.5 - 11.25}{5.125} = 1.61 < 5 \quad \text{O.K.}$$

Spacing of purlins is 7 ft 2 in. measured along the span. The straight-line distance between the hinge and the first point of support $= l = 9.06$ ft $= 108.7$ in.

$d = b = 5.125$ in.

$$l/d = \frac{108.7}{5.125} = 21.2$$

$$F_c' = 1.15 \frac{0.3E}{(l/d)^2} = \frac{(1.15)(0.3)(1,800,000)}{(21.2)^2} = 1,382 \text{ psi} < 1,725;$$

therefore, use $F_c' = 1,382$ psi

$$\frac{P'}{AF_c'} + \frac{M}{SF_bC_F} = \frac{20,700}{(99.9)(1,382)} + \frac{(43,100)(12)}{(325)(2,740)(0.95)} =$$

$$0.150 + 0.611 = 0.761 < 1 \qquad \text{O.K.}$$

12. Check radial stress.

$$R = \text{radius of curvature} + \frac{d}{2} = (64)(12) + \frac{19.5}{2} = 777.75 \text{ in.}$$

Maximum moment is negative; therefore, radial stress is compressive.

$$F_{rc} = F_{c\perp} = 443 \text{ psi}$$

$$f_{rc} = \frac{3M}{2RA} = \frac{(3)(43,100)(12)}{(2)(777.75)(99.9)} = 9.98 \text{ psi} < 443 \qquad \text{O.K.}$$

13. Determine vertical deflection at the centerline under unbalanced snow load. Using the layout from step 1 of this example, $s = 40.2$ in. Moments due to unbalanced snow loads were determined in step 6 and are retabulated below. Moments due to the unit load are calculated in the same manner. They are also tabulated below.

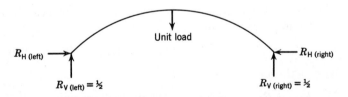

Point	Unit Load			Moments DL$+\frac{1}{2}$SL, ft-lb	Mm, (ft-lb)^2
	M_s	$M_s y$	m		
Left					
1	0.630	0.696	0.085	− 6,640	− 564
2	1.93	6.20	0.347	− 18,340	− 636
3	3.285	17.02	0.735	− 27,400	− 20,100
4	4.69	32.9	1.23	− 34,360	− 42,300
5	6.145	53.3	1.865	− 39,000	− 72,700

Point	Unit Load			Moments DL+½SL, ft-lb	Mm, (ft-lb)²
	M_s	$M_s y$	m		
6	7.635	77.9	2.605	−41,800	−108,900
7	9.165	106.0	3.465	−43,100	−149,300
8	10.75	137.3	4.45	−41,500	−184,700
9	12.3	169.7	5.50	−39,500	−217,000
10	13.95	205	6.72	−34,000	−228,000
11	15.6	240	8.02	−27,900	−224,000
12	17.25	274	9.42	−20,600	−194,100
13	18.9	307	10.89	−11,000	−119,800
14	20.55	337	12.45	−1,110	−13,820
Right					
14'	$\Sigma M_s y = 1{,}964{,}016$		12.45	11,490	143,100
13'			10.89	21,700	236,000
12'	$R_H = \dfrac{\Sigma M_s y}{\Sigma y^2} = \dfrac{1{,}964{,}016}{3{,}982{,}242}$		9.42	29,100	274,000
11'			8.02	34,400	276,000
10'	$R_H = 0.493$		6.72	37,600	253,000
9'			5.50	37,600	207,000
8'			4.45	37,200	165,500
7'			3.465	33,700	116,800
6'			2.605	30,100	78,400
5'			1.865	25,000	46,600
4'			1.23	19,240	23,700
3'			0.735	13,260	9,750
2'			0.347	7,640	2,660
1'			0.085	2,290	195

$$\Sigma Mm = +256{,}785$$

$$\Delta_a = \frac{s}{EI}\Sigma Mm = \frac{(40.2)(256{,}785)(144)}{(1{,}800{,}000)(3{,}167)}$$

$$\Delta_a = 0.26 \text{ in.}$$

Dome Structures

Timber dome structures are commonly spherical in shape, with a low rise-to-span ratio. They may consist of a series of three-hinged or two-hinged arches having a common connection at the top, or crown, of the dome and with the bases arranged in a circle, or may be true domes made up of interconnecting members forming various patterns. One type of true dome is the radial rib type illustrated in Figure 4.22.

The design procedures for three-hinged and two-hinged arches can be followed for the design of domes consisting of arches joined at the crown. It should be pointed out, however, that the plane projection of the tributary area of load for each half of the arch is wedge-shaped, the apex being at the crown. Lateral support may be provided by purlins or joists spanning between adjacent arches, their span decreasing from supports to crown.

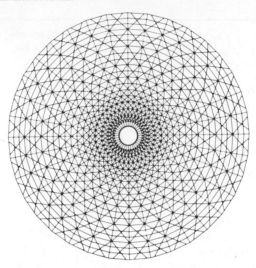

Figure 4.22.   RADIAL RIB-TYPE DOME.

The radial rib-type dome is commonly comprised of glued laminated timber ribs, which are continuous but not necessarily one piece from base to crown; rings, which are made up of straight members spanning between the ribs; a tension ring, which resists outward thrust at the base; and diagonals which are usually steel rods with turnbuckles for adjustment. The following principles apply to the design of radial rib domes: (1) the ribs are at maximum stress under full uniform live load plus dead load over the entire dome; (2) a ring member is in maximum tension when all of the dome above the ring is fully loaded, and in maximum compression when all of the dome below the ring, as well as the ring itself, is fully loaded; and (3) the diagonals are not stressed when the dome is polar symmetrically loaded. The diagonals in a panel are in maximum stress when the dome on one side of a vertical plane passing through the center of that panel and through the crown (meridional plane) is fully loaded and the other side unloaded.

Since timber domes have a low rise-to-span ratio, the angle between the vertical axis of rotation and the radius passing through the base (ϕ in Figure 4.23) is usually less than 50° and the ribs and rings are in compression, except for the base ring, which is in tension.

General design procedure (see Figure 4.23 for notations).

1. Determine loads at rib-ring intersections assuming full uniform loading over the entire dome. The loads W_1, W_2, etc., in Figure 4.23a are the sums of the dead and applied loads acting on the area tributary to each rib-ring intersection. For example, the sum of the loads acting on the shaded area X in Figure 4.23d is equal to load W_3.

2. Determine the required rib section. The axial compression load is greatest in that portion of the rib between rings ④ and ⑤ and may be determined from the formula

$$P' = \frac{W_1 + W_2 + W_3 + W_4}{\sin \alpha_4}$$

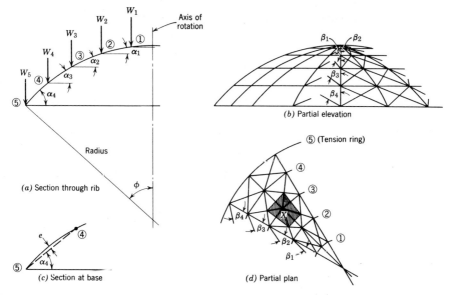

Figure 4.23.   **RADIAL RIB DOME NOTATION.**

where α_4 = angle between the horizontal and the straight line connecting rings ④ and ⑤, see Figure 4.23a, c.

The cross-sectional area, A, required to resist the compression load P' can be determined from the formula

$$A = \frac{P'}{F_c}$$

where F_c = allowable unit stress in compression parallel to grain adjusted for l/d and duration of loading, psi.

For ribs which are discontinuous at rib-ring intersections, the section modulus, S, required to resist the moment due to eccentricity between the centerline of the rib and the chord connecting adjacent joints is determined from the formula

$$S = \frac{P'e}{F_b}$$

where e = eccentricity, in.; see Figure 4.23c
   F_b = allowable unit stress in extreme fiber in bending adjusted for duration of loading, curvature factor and size effect, psi

If the rib is continuous at a joint, carry-over moments will occur at that joint. The rib section should be checked for the effect of combined compression and bending stresses in accordance with the requirements given on page **2**-38.

3. Determine the required compression ring sections. The axial compression load carried by each ring will be different, and it can be determined by the formulas

$$P_{R1} = \frac{W_1 \cot \alpha_1}{2 \sin (180°/N)} \text{ for ring ①}$$

$$P_{R2} = \frac{W_1 \cot \alpha_1 - (W_1 + W_2) \cot \alpha_2}{2 \sin (180°/N)} \text{ for ring } ②$$

$$P_{R3} = \frac{(W_1 + W_2) \cot \alpha_2 - (W_1 + W_2 + W_3) \cot \alpha_3}{2 \sin (180°/N)} \text{ for ring } ③$$

where P_{R1}, P_{R2}, P_{R3}, etc. = compression loads in rings ①, ②, ③, etc., respectively, lb

$\alpha_1, \alpha_2, \alpha_3$, etc. = angle between the horizontal and the straight lines connecting rings ① and ②, ② and ③, ③ and ④, etc., respectively; see Figure 4.23a

N = number of ribs

The cross-sectional area, A, required to resist the compression loads can be determined from the formula

$$A = \frac{P_R}{F_c}$$

Assuming each ring member spanning between ribs acts as a simply supported beam, the section must also be adequate to resist bending moment, M, as determined by the formula

$$M = \frac{wL_R{}^2}{8}$$

where w = load carried by each ring member span, plf

L_R = ring member span, ft (varies between rings ①, ②, ③, etc.)

In addition, the ring members should be checked for combined bending and axial stresses in accordance with the procedures given on page **2-38**. For appearance, it may be desirable to make all ring member sections equal.

4. Determine the required tension ring section. The tension ring should be supported directly on the foundation and may be of wood, steel or concrete. The outward thrust, T, contained by this ring, assuming the ring is segmented and consists of chords spanning between the ribs, may be determined by the formula

$$T = \frac{(W_1 + W_2 + W_3 + W_4 + W_5) \cot \alpha_4}{2 \sin (180°/N)}$$

The cross-sectional area, A, required to resist the tension load can be determined from the formula

$$A = \frac{T}{F_t}$$

where F_t = allowable unit stress in tension (parallel to grain if wood tension ring is used), psi. If the tension ring spans between supports acting as a beam, the section must also be adequate to resist the moment due to the combined weights of the dome and the ring itself

5. Determine the required diagonal rod sizes. The diagonal rods are stressed only when asymmetrical loading is applied, such as may occur dur-

ing erection. In considering such loading, it is recommended that additional loads as required to produce polar symmetry be added to simplify the analysis. The load in each diagonal can be determined by the formulas

$$P_{D1} = \frac{W_{A1}}{2 \sin \alpha_1 \cos \beta_1} \quad \text{for diagonals between rings ① and ②}$$

$$P_{D2} = \frac{W_{A1} + W_{A2}}{2 \sin \alpha_2 \cos \beta_2} \quad \text{for diagonals between rings ② and ③}$$

$$P_{D3} = \frac{W_{A1} + W_{A2} + W_{A3}}{2 \sin \alpha_3 \cos \beta_3} \quad \text{for diagonals between rings ③ and ④}$$

etc.

where P_{D1}, P_{D2}, P_{D3}, etc. = loads in diagonals, lb

W_{A1}, W_{A2}, W_{A3}, etc. = total applied load at each rib-ring intersection in rings ①, ②, ③, etc., respectively

$\beta_1, \beta_2, \beta_3$, etc. = angle between rib and diagonal between rings ① and ②, rings ② and ③, rings ③ and ④, etc., respectively; see Figure 4.23*b, d*

The cross-sectional rod area, A_s, required to resist these loads can be determined from the formula

$$A_s = \frac{P_D}{F_s}$$

where F_s = allowable unit stress in steel, psi. Cross-sectional areas of steel rods may be found in Section 6 of this *Manual*.

6. Design the rib-ring joints, considering the loads carried by each member intersecting at that joint. When possible, it is best to use the same type and size of connection at each joint in the dome. Spacing, end distance, and edge distance requirements must be met for the type and size of fastenings used. See Section 5 for design considerations for fastenings.

MOMENT SPLICES

The use of glued laminated timber has reduced the need for moment splices in beams and girders, but such splices are frequently used in arches and rigid frames where shipping requirements make the shipping of full-size structural frames impractical or uneconomical. Moment splices should be located at points of minimum moment whenever possible.

Any moment splice must be designed to resist bending moment, shear, stress reversal, uplift, and axial forces, if any, by various means such as side or edge tension or compression straps and compression plates between members. A means of holding the two sections in alignment must also be provided.

A typical moment splice is illustrated in the typical construction details in AITC 104 in Part II of this *Manual*. In this splice, compression stress is taken in end bearing between the two sections. If the unit stress for end grain in bearing parallel to grain, as determined by the loading conditions and splice location, exceeds 75% of the allowable unit stress, a snug-fitting metal bearing plate not thinner than 20 gage and not deeper than one-half the depth of the member should be installed between the abutting ends.

Tension stress is taken across the splice by means of steel straps and shear plates as illustrated, or by wood splice plates and split rings. Connector capacity must be adequate to carry the tension stress. Additional side straps and shear plates are required to keep the sides and top of the sections in position and to take the stress reversals from erection loads or wind uplift. Shear connections must be provided to transfer the maximum design shear through splice connection.

Consideration should be given to the use of separate side plates for each row of connectors in order to minimize secondary stresses due to shrinkage effects in the member. See Section 5, "Fastenings and Connections," for spacing of rows, etc.

Close fabrication tolerances are required in the fabrication of moment splices. Consideration should be given to elastic deformation in the joint. For solid-lumber sections, and for many smaller glued laminated timbers, the simplest form of moment connection can be a plywood splice plate (or pair of plates). Such plates can be glued or nailed, but are also frequently used in conjunction with bolts and shear connectors.

Example. Design a moment splice of the type illustrated in typical construction details for a two-hinged arch. At the location of the splice, maximum values are: moment $= 112,800$ in.-lb; axial compression $= 28,400$ lb, and shear $= 4,610$ lb.

$$DL = 10 \text{ psf} \qquad SL = 20 \text{ psf}$$

Allowable unit stresses:

$$F_b = (2,400)(1.15)(0.95) = 2,600 \text{ psi}$$
$$F_c = (1,500)(1.15) = 1,725 \text{ psi}$$

End grain in bearing parallel to grain (see Table 2.15) $= (2,020)(1.15) = 2,320$ psi

Section size: $5\frac{1}{8} \times 19\frac{1}{2}$

$A = 99.9$ in.^{2}

$S = 325$ in.^{3}

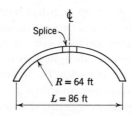

1. Determine compression requirements. Assume compression force acts in bearing on bearing plate occupying $\frac{1}{2}$ of cross section.

$$f_c = \frac{M}{S} + \frac{P}{A/2} = \frac{112,800}{325} + \frac{(28,400)(2)}{99.9} =$$

$$347 + 569 = 916 \text{ psi} < 1,725 \qquad \text{O.K.}$$

If $f_c > 0.75$ of allowable end grain bearing stress, a compression plate is needed.

$(0.75)(2,320) = 1,740 \text{ psi} > 916 \text{ psi}$; therefore, no compression plate is needed.

2. Determine the tension force. A conservative approach is to assume the compression force balancing the tension force has a triangular distribution.

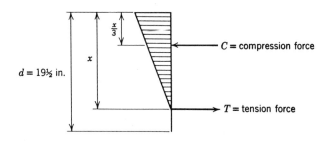

For a $2\frac{5}{8}$ in. shear plate, minimum edge distance $= 1\frac{3}{4}$ in. (see chart on page **5**-25) therefore, set $d - x = 1\frac{3}{4}$ in.

$$x = d - 1\frac{3}{4} = 19.5 - 1.75 = 17.75 \text{ in.}$$

$$T = \frac{M}{2x/3} = \frac{112,800}{(2/3)(17.75)} = 9,530 \text{ lb}$$

3. Determine tension resistance requirements.

    Angle of load to grain $= 0°$
    Value of one $2\frac{5}{8}$ in. shear plate for Group B species ($\frac{3}{4}$ in. bolt) $= 2,860$ lb (see page **5**-24).

    Adjust value for duration of load:

    $(2,860)(1.15) = 3,290 \text{ lb} > 2,900 \text{ lb}$ maximum allowable (see chart on page **5**-24); therefore, use 2,900 lb

    $$\text{Number of shear plates required} = \frac{T}{2,900} = \frac{9,530}{2,900} = 3.29$$

    Number used $= 4$ on each side of splice

    $$\text{Percentage} = \frac{3.29}{4} = 82.2\%$$

    Spacing parallel to grain $= 5\frac{1}{2}$ in. (see page **5**-25)

End distance $= 4\frac{1}{4}$ in.
Edge distance $= 1\frac{3}{4}$ in.
Use two shear plates on each face of member on each side of splice.
Use one tension strap each side of member (see sketch).

$$\text{Load resisted by one tension strap} = \frac{T}{2} = \frac{9.530}{2} = 4{,}765 \text{ lb}$$

$$\text{Area of steel required} = \frac{4{,}765}{22{,}000} = 0.217 \text{ in.}^2$$

Try a $3 \times \frac{1}{4}$ bar.
Check net section with $\frac{9}{16}$ in. hole in strap.
Net area $= (3)(\frac{1}{4}) - (\frac{13}{16})(\frac{1}{4}) = 0.55$ in.^{2}

$$\text{Stress at hole} = \frac{4{,}765}{0.55} = 8{,}660 \text{ psi} < 16{,}200 \text{ psi} \quad \text{(see AISC } \textit{Steel Con-}$$
struction Manual)
Check bearing stress on strap

$$\text{Bearing stress} = \frac{4{,}765}{(\frac{3}{4})(\frac{1}{4})} = 25{,}413 \text{ psi} < 33{,}000 \text{ psi}$$

Use one $3 \times \frac{1}{4}$ steel bar on each side of member.

The splice at the top should be of sufficient strength to resist negative moment due to handling and stress reversal.

4. Check group action of shear plates.

   Modification factor, K, for two fasteners in a row $= 1.00$ (see Table 5.3). No reduction necessary.

5. Determine shear resistance requirements.

   $V = 4{,}610$ lb   Angle of load to grain $= 90°$
   For $2\frac{5}{8}$ in. shear plate in end grain, use 60% of side grain value (see page **5-**24) adjusted for duration of loading $= (1{,}990)(1.15)(0.60) = 1{,}370$ lb $< 2{,}900$; therefore, use 1,370 lb

   Check group action of shear plates.

   For four shear plates in a row loaded perpendicular to the grain, minimum spacing for full allowable load perpendicular to grain $= 4\frac{1}{4}$ in.

   $A_1 = A_2 = (4.25)(5.125) = 21.8$ in.^{2}

   $A_1/A_2 = 1.0$

   Modification factor, $K = 0.97$ (From Table 5.2)
   $(1{,}370)(0.97) = 1{,}330$ lb (average allowable load per connector)

   $$\text{Number of shear plates required} = \frac{V}{1{,}330} = \frac{4{,}610}{1{,}330} = 3.47$$

Number used $= 4$

$$\text{Percentage} = \frac{3.47}{4} = 87\%$$

Spacing perpendicular to grain $= 4$ in. (see page **5–25**)
Use 4 in. spacing.

A check of the net section (total area less projected area of connectors and bolts) reveals that the section is adequate.

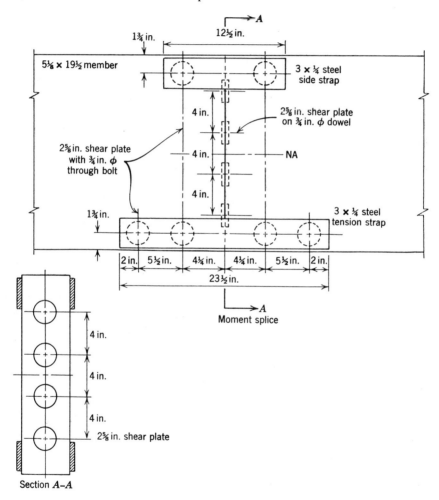

Moment splice

Section *A–A*

TRUSSES

A general discussion of truss design features and considerations and of truss types may be found in Appendix A of *Standards for the Design of Structural Timber Framing*, AITC 102, included in Part II of this *Manual*. The type of truss to be used, its overall dimensions, and spacing are generally determined by architectural and/or economic requirements. The maximum economical span for any given type of timber truss will vary with the materials available, loading conditions, ratio of labor to material cost, and fabrication methods. Table 4.6 lists aids for determining economical truss dimensions without a great deal of preliminary calculations. Table 1.1 gives, for various secondary framing systems, recommended spans that may be used in determining truss spacing.

TABLE 4.6

RECOMMENDED TIMBER TRUSS
DEPTH-TO-SPAN RATIOS

Bowstring	$\frac{1}{6}$ to $\frac{1}{8}$
Triangular or pitched	$\frac{1}{6}$ or deeper
Flat or parallel chord	$\frac{1}{8}$ to $\frac{1}{10}$

General design procedure. Given the truss type, its span, depth, spacing, and the species and grade of lumber to be used, the following general procedure may be used for all truss types. Special design features for each particular truss type should also be considered.

1. Determine dead loads acting on the truss. Dead load should include weights of roofing, sheathing, rafters, purlins, the estimated truss weight, and other permanently applied loads which will act throughout the service life of the truss.

2. Compute the stress in each member due to applicable loading conditions (dead, snow or live, wind, and special loads, if any).

3. Determine the required sizes of the truss members. Chord members may be subject to axial tension or compression, either alone or in combination with bending, and may also be subject to reversal of stresses. Web members are designed for axial stresses and, under unbalanced loading conditions, for possible reversal of stresses. In the analysis of the top chord of bowstring trusses, the moment introduced by the eccentricity due to curvature of the top chord should be distributed in the same manner as are the positive moments due to externally applied loads.

4. Design the joints, considering first the joint or joints carrying the greatest load. All joints should be concentric. Determine the size and type of fastening to be used. When possible, it is best to use fastenings of the same size and type throughout the truss. Check spacing, end distance, and edge distance requirements for each fastener. See Section 5 for design considerations for fastenings.

Truss Deflection and Camber

Deflection

The deflection, Δ_a, at any point in a truss may be determined by the method of virtual work. In this method, a unit load is applied at the point being investigated and acting in the direction of the desired component of movement, and then the stress caused in each truss member by this unit load is determined. Deflection is then determined by summing the effects in each member of the unit load and actual design loads, using the formula

$$\Delta_a = \sum \frac{Pul}{AE}$$

where P = load in a truss member caused by design loads, lb
   u = ratio of the load in a truss member caused by a unit load to the unit load itself
   l = length of truss member, in.
   A = cross-sectional area of truss member, in.^{2}
   E = modulus of elasticity, psi

The effects of truss deflection should be considered in the design of columns and walls and in the working of truss-supported doors or other building fixtures.

Camber

   Truss camber should be such that total load deflection does not produce a sag below a straight line between points of support. Camber may be determined by computation, using the deflection formula given above by adding the dead load elastic deformation (or slip) to the inelastic deformation; test data; or the following empirical formula, recommended by the Timber Engineering Company for multileaf, timber connectored trusses:

$$\text{Camber} = K_1 \frac{L^3}{h} + K_2 \frac{L^2}{h}$$

where L = span, ft; h = rise, ft; and camber is in inches.

TABLE 4.7

TRUSS CAMBER

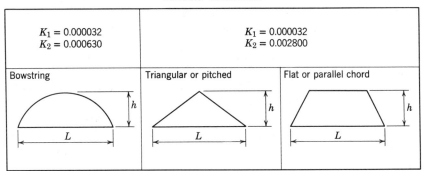

$K_1 = 0.000032$ $K_2 = 0.000630$		$K_1 = 0.000032$ $K_2 = 0.002800$	
Bowstring	Triangular or pitched	Flat or parallel chord	

   Both lower and upper chords may be cambered, but this is generally done only in flat or parallel chord trusses. When only the lower chord is cambered, as is usual for bowstring and triangular or pitched trusses, the effective depth of the truss should be reduced accordingly in stress computations.

Truss Bracing

   In structures employing trusses, a system of bracing is required to provide resistance to lateral forces and to hold the trusses true and plumb.

Both permanent bracing and temporary erection bracing should be designed according to accepted engineering principles to resist all loads which will normally act on the system. Erection bracing is that bracing which is installed during erection to hold the trusses in a safe position until sufficient permanent construction is in place to provide full stability. Permanent bracing is that bracing which forms an integral part of the completed structure. Part or all of the permanent bracing may also act as erection bracing.

Bracing must be provided in both transverse and longitudinal directions. Transverse bracing may consist of either of the following systems:

1. A structural diaphragm in the plane of the top chord. The diaphragm, acting like a plate girder, transmits forces to the end and side walls. (See "Structural Diaphragms," beginning on page 4-133 of this *Manual*.) This system is the preferred method of providing transverse truss bracing and is usually most economical.

2. Horizontal bracing between trusses and in the plane of the bottom and/or top chords. In effect, this is a horizontal truss. It is a positive method of bracing, but it is more costly and should be used only where the strength of system 1 is exceeded.

In both systems, end walls must be braced by diaphragm action, by shear walls, or by vertical sway bracing. Longitudinal bracing may consist of any of the following systems:

1. A structural diaphragm in the plane of the top chord.

2. Longitudinal struts between trusses in the plane of the bottom chords and extending the full length of the building, and vertical X-bracing between trusses in alternate bays. The rows of bracing should be spaced at intervals such that the allowable l/d for the truss chords is not exceeded.

3. Horizontal bracing in the plane of the lower chords and vertical X-bracing in alternate bays as in system 2.

In the latter two systems, side walls must be braced by diaphragm action, by shear walls, or by a system of vertical sway bracing.

To provide lateral support to the compression chord of a truss, the bracing system should be designed to withstand a horizontal force equal to 2% of the compressive force in the truss chord, if the members are in perfect alignment; or, if the members are misaligned, the calculation of the force should be based on the eccentricity of the members due to the misalignment.

Bracing is also required to brace the entire structure. This building bracing may consist of either of the following systems:

1. Buttressed or reinforced walls which will transmit forces acting on the wall as well as the roof directly into the ground.

2. Knee braces between columns and trusses which transmit forces to the ground through a rigid column-to-truss connection. Knee brace action often causes secondary stresses which can be critical. If knee braces are used, a complete analysis of their action on the truss members must be made.

Example. Design glued laminated top and bottom chords for a bowstring truss for the following conditions.

$L = R = 80$ ft

Spacing $= B = 16$ ft

Loads:

DL $= 15$ psf

SL $= 30$ psf

No ceiling loads

Allowable unit stresses:

$F_b = (2,400)(1.15) = 2,760$ psi

$F_t = (2,400)(1.15) = 2,760$ psi

$F_c = (2,000)(1.15) = 2,300$ psi

$F_{c\perp} = (410)(1.15) = 470$ psi

$E = 2,000,000$ psi

The accompanying sketch shows loads, in kips, in the chords due to balanced loads.

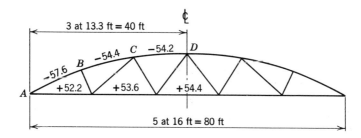

1. The top chord is spliced at the center (point D) and is made up of $1\frac{1}{2}$ in. laminations.

   Curvature factor $= C_c = 1 - 2,000(t/R)^2 = 1 - 2,000(1.56/960)^2 = 0.995$
   $F_b = (2,760)(0.995) = 2,740$ psi
   e = eccentricity with regard to a straight line between top chord panel points

   The eccentricities of the top chord can be determined by the geometrical properties of the truss to be

   $e_{A-B} = 4.42$ in. $e_{B-C} = e_{C-D} = 3.29$ in.

   Largest load is in section $A - B$:

   $P = 57,600$ lb

   Cross-sectional area required $= A = P/F_c$.

   $$A = \frac{57,600}{2,300} = 25.0 \text{ in.}^2$$

   The moment due to eccentricity, Pe, produces bending which acts opposite in direction to that produced by the dead load and snow load. This moment is distributed to the top chord in the same manner as the moment produced by the dead load and snow load.

   At point B, $M = \dfrac{wl^2}{10} - 0.8Pe$

   $$M = \frac{(45)(16)(13.3)^2(12)}{10} - (0.8)(57,600)(4.42)$$

$$M = 152,800 - 203,700 = -50,900 \text{ in.-lb}$$

Section modulus required $= S = \dfrac{M}{F_b}$

$$S = \frac{50,900}{2,740} = 18.6 \text{ in.}^3$$

A section which meets these requirements and is in accordance with industry standard depths and widths measures $3\frac{1}{8} \times 9$, $A = 28.1$ in.^{2}, $S = 42.2$ in.^{3}.

2. Check for combined stresses.

$$\frac{P}{A} = \frac{57,600}{28.1} = 2,050 \text{ psi}$$

$$\frac{M}{S} = \frac{50,900}{42.2} = 1,210 \text{ psi}$$

Since $P/A > M/S$, use

$$\frac{P}{AF_c'} + \frac{M}{SF_b} \le 1$$

$$F_c' = 1.15 \frac{(0.3)(2,000,000)}{[(13.3)(12)/9]^2} = 2,190 \text{ psi}$$

$$F_c = 2,300 \text{ psi} > 2,190 \text{ psi}$$

$\therefore$ Use $F_c' = 2,190$ psi

$$\frac{57,600}{(28.1)(2,190)} + \frac{50,900}{(42.2)(2,740)} = 0.936 + 0.440 = 1.376 > 1 \qquad \text{N.G.}$$

Try a $3\frac{1}{8} \times 12$, $A = 37.5$ in.^{2}, $S = 75.0$ in.^{3}.

$$F_c' = 1.15 \frac{(0.3)(2,000,000)}{[(13.3)(12)/12]^2} = 3,900 \text{ psi}$$

$\therefore$ Use $F_c' = 2,300$ psi

$$\frac{57,600}{(37.5)(2,300)} + \frac{50,900}{(75.0)(2,740)} = 0.668 + 0.248 = 0.916 < 1 \qquad \text{O.K.}$$

3. Check for radial stress. Moment is tending to decrease the radius, therefore, radial stress is compressive and allowable radial stress $= F_{c\perp} = 470$ psi.

$$f_{rc} = \frac{3M}{2RA} = \frac{(3)(50,900)}{(2)(80)(12)(37.5)} = 2.12 \text{ psi} < 470 \qquad \text{O.K.}$$

Use a $3\frac{1}{8} \times 12$ glued laminated top chord.

4. The bottom chord is designed for direct tension only, since there are no ceiling loads. The center panel is critical.

$$\text{Required } A = \frac{P}{F_t} = \frac{54,400}{2,760} = 19.7 \text{ in.}^2$$

A $3\frac{1}{8} \times 7\frac{1}{2}$ section would be adequate to meet this requirement. However, the section size reduced by the projected area of the fastenings at that section must meet net section requirements (see page 5-13).

If ceiling loads are present, bending is induced in the member, and the bottom chord must be designed for combined loading.

The complete design of a truss includes other factors noted in the general design procedure beginning on page 4-88.

POLE-TYPE FRAMING

Pole-type frame structures employ preservatively treated timber poles or sawn timber posts set in the ground as main structural members. Usually, the hole in which the pole or post is set furnishes both vertical and horizontal support for the pole in supporting the structure. Setting the pole in the ground tends to prevent rotation of the bottom of the pole and thereby provides some or all of the required bracing. Preservative treatment of poles should be in accordance with the *American Wood-Preservers' Association Standards* C1 and C4.

General Considerations

General considerations, which are applicable to all pole-type frame structures include the following.

1. A bracing system can be provided at the top of a pole in order to reduce bending moments at the base of the pole and to distribute loads. The design of buildings supported by poles without bracing requires good knowledge of soil conditions in order to eliminate excessive deflection or sidesway.

2. Bearing values under butt ends of poles should be checked. It is common practice to backfill holes around the pole with well-tamped native soil, sand, or gravel. Backfilling with concrete or soil-cement can develop a more effective pole diameter; consequently, it can be used as a means of reducing required depth of embedment. Concrete backfill also increases the area of the pole for skin friction and thus increases the bearing capacity. Skin friction is also effective where uplift due to wind may act on a pole through its connections to the roof framing.

3. In order to increase bearing capacity under pole butts, concrete footings may be used. If they are used, they should be designed to withstand the punching shear of the pole and bending moment due to the pole load. Thickness of concrete footings should never be less than 12 in. and may need to be greater, depending on the loads. Concrete footings should be considered even in firm soils such as dry hard clay, coarse firm sand, or gravel.

The intended use of the structure largely determines such general features as height, overall length and width, spacing of poles, height at eaves, type of roof framing, and the kind of flooring to be used, as well as any special features such as wide bays, unsymmetrical layouts, or the possible suspension of particular loads from the roof framing. These general design features having been determined, the following procedure may be used.

Design procedure.

1. Determine loads. The principal load on a pole-type frame is generally the horizontal wind load; therefore, the wind load value required by the governing building code or, in the absence of a governing code, as determined from Section 3 of this *Manual*, should be used. In addition to dead load and other loads, roofs will transmit vertical components of wind load to poles. When wind loads are involved, allowable unit stress values may be increased one-third for the duration of loading.

2. Determine soil values. If soil tests are not available, visual inspection and a careful estimate of the bearing value of samples of the soil should be made. Building codes contain allowable design values for direct bearing assigned to various soil classifications.

Normally, building codes do not give established allowable passive soil pressure values, in which case the values may be determined by using Rankine's formula

$$p = \frac{1 + \sin \phi}{1 - \sin \phi} wd$$

where p = allowable passive soil pressure, psf per ft of depth
   ϕ = angle of internal friction of soil, degrees
   w = weight of soil, pcf
   d = depth below grade, ft

Allowable soil pressure values for various classes of soil are also given in Table 4.8. For most soils suitable for foundations, a value of $p = 250$ psf is conservative.

3. Estimate the size of pole required. The American National Standards Institute (ANSI) has established certain pole classes. Table 4.9 tabulates the size requirements corresponding to ANSI Classes H-6 through 10 for Douglas fir and for Southern pine poles.

Poles of a given class and length are selected to have approximately the same load carrying capacity regardless of species. The minimum circumferences specified at 6 ft from the butt in Table 4.9 are based on the maximum fiber stress in bending that will occur at the groundline due to a given horizontal load applied 2 ft from the top of the pole. The horizontal loads used in the calculations for separating the 15 classes given in Table 4.9 are:

Class	Horizontal Load, lb
H-6	11,400
H-5	10,000
H-4	8,700
H-3	7,500
H-2	6,400
H-1	5,400
1	4,500
2	3,700
3	3,000
4	2,400
5	1,900
6	1,500
7	1,200
9	740

TABLE 4.8

ALLOWABLE LATERAL PASSIVE SOIL PRESSURE

Class of Material	Allowable Values per Foot of Depth Below Natural Grade, p, psf	Maximum Allowable S Values, psf
Good Compact, well-graded sand and gravel Hard clay Well-graded fine and coarse sand (All drained, so water will not stand)	400	8,000
Average Compact fine sand Medium clay Compact sandy loam Loose sand and gravel (All drained, so water will not stand)	200	2,500
Poor Soft clay Clay loam Poorly compacted sand Clays containing large amounts of silt (Water stands during wet season)	100	1,500

Isolated poles, such as flagpoles or signs, may be designed using lateral bearing values equal to twice these tabulated values.

Used with the copyright owner's permission.

TABLE 4.9

DIMENSIONS OF DOUGLAS FIR (BOTH[b] TYPES) AND SOUTHERN PINE POLES[a]

Class		10	9	7	6	5	4	3	2	1	H-1	H-2	H-3	H-4	H-5	H-6
Minimum Circumference at Top, in.		12	15	15	17	19	21	23	25	27	29	31	33	35	37	39
Length of Pole, ft	Groundline Distance from Butt,[c] ft	\multicolumn{15}{c}{Minimum Circumference at 6 ft from Butt, in.}

Length of Pole, ft	Groundline Distance from Butt, ft	10	9	7	6	5	4	3	2	1	H-1	H-2	H-3	H-4	H-5	H-6
20	4.0	14.0	17.5	19.5	21.0	23.0	25.0	27.0	29.0	31.0						
25	5.0	15.0	19.5	21.5	23.0	25.5	27.5	29.5	31.5	33.5						
30	5.5		20.5	23.5	25.0	27.5	29.5	32.0	34.0	36.5						
35	6.0			25.0	27.0	29.0	31.5	34.0	36.5	39.0	41.5	43.5				
40	6.0				28.5	31.0	33.5	36.0	38.5	41.0	43.5	46.0	48.5	51.0		
45	6.5				30.0	32.5	35.0	37.5	40.5	43.0	45.5	48.5	51.0	53.5	56.0	58.5
50	7.0					34.0	36.5	39.0	42.0	45.0	47.5	50.5	53.0	55.5	58.5	61.0
55	7.5						38.0	40.5	43.5	46.5	49.5	52.0	55.0	58.0	60.5	63.5
60	8.0						39.0	42.0	45.0	48.0	51.0	54.0	57.0	59.5	62.5	65.5
65	8.5						40.5	43.5	46.5	49.5	52.5	55.5	58.5	61.5	64.5	67.5
70	9.0						41.5	45.0	48.0	51.0	54.0	57.0	60.5	63.5	66.5	69.0
75	9.5							46.0	49.0	52.5	55.5	59.0	62.0	65.0	68.0	71.0
80	10.0							47.0	50.5	54.0	57.0	60.0	63.5	66.5	69.5	72.5
85	10.5							48.0	51.5	55.0	58.5	61.5	65.0	68.0	71.5	74.5
90	11.0							49.0	53.0	56.0	59.5	63.0	66.5	69.5	73.0	76.0
95	11.0								54.0	57.0	61.0	64.5	67.5	71.0	74.5	77.5
100	11.0								55.0	58.5	62.0	65.5	69.0	72.5	76.0	79.0
105	12.0								56.0	59.5	63.0	67.0	70.5	74.0	77.0	80.5
110	12.0								57.0	60.5	64.5	68.0	71.5	75.0	78.5	82.0
115	12.0								58.0	61.5	65.5	69.0	72.5	76.5	80.0	83.5
120	12.0								59.0	62.5	66.5	70.0	74.0	77.5	81.0	85.0
125	12.0								59.5	63.5	67.5	71.0	75.0	78.5	82.5	86.0

[a] Source: American National Standard Specifications and Dimensions for Wood Poles, 05.1-1972, copyright 1972 by American National Standards Institute, Inc.
[b] Includes Douglas fir, interior North and Douglas fir, coastal.
[c] The figures in this column are intended for use only when a definition of groundline is necessary in order to apply requirements relating to scars and

Safe concentric column loads for various unsupported lengths of poles of Douglas fir or Southern pine are given in Table 4.10. If Tables 4.9 and 4.10 are used, the load to be supported by the poles is known and an estimate of the size of pole required can be made.

TABLE 4.10

SAFE CONCENTRIC COLUMN LOADS ON
DOUGLAS FIR AND SOUTHERN PINE POLES

Unsupported Pole Length (above Groundline),	Safe Concentric Column Load, lb			
	Minimum Top Diameter			
	8 in.	7 in.	6 in.	5 in.
	ANSI Pole Class			
ft	2	3	5	6
0	68,500	52,500	38,500	26,000
10	68,500	51,000	28,500	14,000
12	61,500	36,500	20,500	10,000
14	46,000	27,500	15,500	8,000
16	36,000	22,000	12,500	6,500
18	29,500	17,500	10,000	5,000
20	24,500	15,000	8,500	4,500
25	16,500	10,000	6,000	
30	12,500	7,500		
35	10,000	6,000		

Circumferences at points other than those tabulated in Table 4.9 may be determined assuming an average taper of 0.25 in. circumference per foot of length of pole for Douglas fir and Southern pine.

4. Determine required embedment of pole. The following formula may be used in determining required embedment depth where no constraint (such as a rigid floor or surface pavement) is provided at the ground surface. Note that this procedure requires the assumption of an initial embedment depth.

$$d = \frac{A}{2}\left(1 + \sqrt{1 + \frac{4.36h}{A}}\right) \quad \text{(see Figure 4.24)}$$

where d = depth of embedment, ft
$A = 2.34P/S_1B$
P = applied horizontal force on pole, lb
$S_1 = pd/3$ (see Table 4.8 for p)
h = height above groundline at which force P is applied, ft
B = butt diameter of pole or diameter of concrete casing, ft

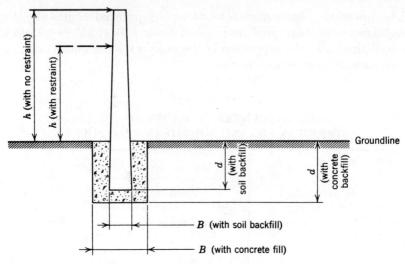

Figure 4.24.   DEPTH OF EMBEDMENT.

If the post is restrained at the groundline such as by a rigid concrete floor, the following formula is used

$$d = \sqrt{\frac{4.25Ph}{S_3 B}}$$

where $S_3 = pd$ (see Table 4.8 for p; note that S_3 values may not exceed the maximum values specified in Table 4.8)

and other terms are as previously defined.

For poles having some degree of fixity or restraint at the eave line, such as provided by knee braces, the point at which the applied horizontal force, P, acts is at the point of inflection of the pole. For round, tapered poles, the point of inflection is assumed to be at two-thirds the distance from the groundline to the point of restraint. For poles with no restraint, the height to the top of the pole is used as the value for h.

It may be desirable to repeat the procedure for determining embedment with the first determination of embedment as the basis for recalculating the parameter S_3.

5. Check pole bending stress. The actual bending stress in the pole at the point of maximum bending moment may be determined by the formula

$$f_b = \frac{32\pi^2 M}{C^3} = \frac{32M}{\pi D^3}$$

where f_b = actual bending stress, psi
C = pole circumference at point of maximum moment, in.
D = pole diameter at point of maximum moment, in.
M = maximum moment, in.-lb, which, for a round, tapered pole, is assumed to occur at one-fourth the depth of embedment below groundline; it may be determined if P and h, as previously defined, are known.

The actual bending stress cannot exceed the allowable bending stresses as tabulated in Table 4.11. These allowable bending stresses may be increased one-third for wind duration of loading.

TABLE 4.11

STRESS VALUES FOR TREATED[a] ANSI POLE SPECIES
(Normal Duration of Loading)

Species	Modulus of Rupture,[b] Extreme Fiber in Bending, psi	Extreme Fiber in Bending,[c] F_b, psi	Modulus of Elasticity,[c] E, psi	Compression Parallel to Grain[c] F_c, psi
Cedar, Northern white	4,000	1,540	600,000	740
Cedar, Western red	6,000	1,850	900,000	1,030
Douglas fir	8,000	2,700	1,500,000	1,360
Hemlock, Western	7,400	2,380	1,300,000	1,250
Larch, Western	8,400	2,940	1,500,000	1,500
Pine, jack	6,600	2,100	1,100,000	1,100
Pine, lodgepole	6,600	1,820	1,100,000	980
Pine, ponderosa	6,000	1,710	1,000,000	920
Pine, red or Norway	6,600	2,100	1,300,000	1,020
Pine, Southern	8,000	2,740	1,500,000	1,360

[a]Air-dried prior to treatment.
[b]Based on *American National Standard Specifications and Dimensions for Wood Poles*, ANSI 05.1-1972.
[c]Based on ASTM D 2899-70T, *Tentative Method for Establishing Design Stresses for Round Timber Piles*.

Above the pole's point of inflection, the bending moment reaches a maximum at the bottom of the roof bracing. The bending stress at this point should also be checked to make sure that it does not exceed the allowable bending stress.

6. Check the pole compression stress. The vertical loads on one pole include, in addition to applied live loads and/or snow loads and dead load of the supported structure, the vertical component of wind load and one-third the weight of the pole.

The allowable unit stress for a round column may be determined by the formula

$$F_c' = \frac{3.6E}{(l/r)^2} = \frac{0.225E}{(l/D)^2}$$

where F_c' = allowable unit stress in compression parallel to grain adjusted for l/d ratio, psi
E = modulus of elasticity of pole species, psi (see Table 4.11)
l = unsupported length of pole, in.
r = least radius of gyration of pole at one-third the length from the top, in. $(r^2 = D^2/16)$

D = diameter of the pole, in., taken as the sum of the minimum diameter and one-third the difference between the minimum and maximum diameters, but in no case shall it be assumed as more than $1\frac{1}{2}$ times the minimum diameter.

The ratio l/D should not exceed 44 for round columns. The unsupported length of long poles may be reduced by providing bracing in both directions at approximately the inflection point of the pole. The actual compression parallel to grain stress at the top, or small end, of the pole should be checked, and it should not exceed the allowable unit stress for a short column. Actual compressive stress, f_c, may be determined by the formula

$$f_c = \frac{P}{A}$$

where P = total vertical load on the pole, lb
A = cross-sectional area at the top of the pole, in.^{2}

7. Determine footing requirements. The pole footing requirements can be determined if the kind of soil, the vertical load on the pole, and the size of pole required are known. Soil bearing load, in pounds per square foot, can be determined by the formula

$$\text{Soil bearing load} = 144\frac{P}{A}$$

where P = total vertical load on pole, lb
A = area of butt of pole, in.^{2}

If this load exceeds the allowable bearing capacity, S_B, for the type of soil in question, a concrete footing is required.

The required area, A_c, in square feet, of a concrete footing may be determined by the formula

$$A_c = \frac{P}{S_B}$$

Concrete footings should be designed in accordance with the recommendations of the American Concrete Institute.

Example. Design the poles for the illustrated typical bent of a pole-type building to meet the stated conditions:

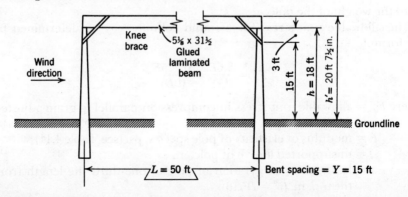

Loads:
DL = 10 psf
SL = 20 psf
WL = 15 psf

Pole stresses:
$F_b = (2,700)(1.33) = 3,590$ psi
$E = 1,500,000$ psi

1. Determine loads.

Vertical load on one pole $= V = \dfrac{YL(DL + SL)}{2}$

$V = \dfrac{(15)(50)(10 + 20)}{2} = 11,250$ lb

Wind load at top of pole $= P = \dfrac{Yh'}{2}(WL) = \dfrac{(15)(20.625)}{2}(15) = 2,320$ lb

2. Soil values.

Soil is compact, well-graded sand (good soil)
Allowable passive pressure $= p = 400$ psf (from Table 4.8)
Allowable bearing capacity $= S_B = 8,000$ psf
Concrete fill not required

3. Estimate size of pole required.

From Table 4.10, for an unsupported pole length of 15 ft carrying a
11,250 lb load, select an ANSI Class 5 pole.
Assuming a 12 ft depth of embedment, from Table 4.9 a 30 ft Class
5 pole has a minimum top circumference of 19 in. and a minimum
circumference 6 ft from the butt of 27.5 in.

4. Determine required embedment.

Distance from groundline to point of inflection $= h = \frac{2}{3}$ unsupported
pole length $= \frac{2}{3}(15) = 10$ ft

Diameter 6 ft from butt $= \dfrac{27.5}{\pi} = 8.75$ in.

Butt diameter $= B = \dfrac{27.5 + (6)(0.25)}{\pi} = 9.23$ in. $= 0.769$ ft

Soil stress $= S_1 = \dfrac{pd}{3} = \dfrac{(400)(12.0)}{3} = 1,600$ psf

$A = \dfrac{2.34P}{S_1 B} = \dfrac{(2.34)(2,320)}{(1,600)(0.769)} = 4.41$

Depth of embedment $= d$

$d = \dfrac{A}{2}\left(1 + \sqrt{1 + \dfrac{4.36h}{A}}\right)$

$d = \dfrac{4.41}{2}\left(1 + \sqrt{1 + \dfrac{(4.36)(10.0)}{4.41}}\right) = 9.48$ ft

Use a 30 ft pole; actual $d = 12$ ft, circumference 6 ft from butt = 27.5 in. (for Class 5 pole)

5. Check bending stress.

Maximum moment $= M = 12P\left(h + \dfrac{d}{4}\right)$

$M = (12)(2{,}320)\left(10.0 + \dfrac{12}{4}\right) = 362{,}000$ in.-lb

Circumference at $\frac{1}{4}$ depth of embedment

$\dfrac{3d}{4} = \dfrac{(3)(12)}{4} = 9.0$ ft (distance from butt)

$C = 27.5 - (9-6)(0.25) = 26.75$ in.

$f_b = \dfrac{32\pi^2 M}{C^3} = \dfrac{32\pi^2(362{,}000)}{(26.75)^3} = 5{,}970$ psi $> 3{,}590$ N.G.

Try a Class 2 pole — circumference 6 ft from butt = 34.0 in.
Circumference at $\frac{1}{4}$ depth of embedment

$C = 34.0 - (9-6)(0.25) = 33.25$ in.

$f_b = \dfrac{32\pi^2(362{,}000)}{(33.25)^3} = 3{,}090$ psi $< 3{,}590$ O.K.

Use a Class 2 pole
Upper maximum moment occurs at the knee brace-to-column connection, or 5 ft above the point of inflection.
Upper maximum $M = 12P(5) = (12)(2{,}320)(5)$
$M = 139{,}200$ in.-lb
Circumference at knee brace connection $= C$
Top circumference for Class 2 pole $= 25$ in.
Knee brace connection occurs 3 ft below top

$C = 25 + (3)(0.25) = 25.75$ in.

$f_b = \dfrac{32\pi^2 M}{C^3} = \dfrac{32\pi^2(139{,}200)}{(25.75)^3} = 2{,}570$ psi $< 3{,}590$ O.K.

6. Check compression stress.

Weight of 30 ft Class 2 pole $= W = 725$ lb (approx.)

Axial load $= P = V + \dfrac{W}{3} = 11{,}250 + \dfrac{725}{3}$

$P = 11{,}490$ lb

Diameter at $\frac{1}{3}$ pole length $\left(\dfrac{30}{3} = 10 \text{ ft}\right)$ from top $= D$

Diameter at top $= \dfrac{25}{\pi}$

$D = \dfrac{25 + (10)(0.25)}{\pi} = 8.75$ in.

$$l/D = \frac{(15)(12)}{8.75} = 20.6 < 44 \qquad \text{O.K.}$$

$$F_c' = \frac{0.225E}{(l/D)^2} = \frac{(0.225)(1,500,000)}{(20.6)^2} = 795 \text{ psi}$$

$$f_c = \frac{P}{A} = \frac{11,490}{(25)^2/4\pi} = 231 \text{ psi} < 795 \qquad \text{O.K.}$$

7. Determine footing requirements.

Area of pole butt $= A = \dfrac{[34.0 + (6)(0.25)]^2}{4\pi}$

$A = 100 \text{ in.}^2$

Soil bearing load $= 144\dfrac{P}{A} = 144\left(\dfrac{11,490}{100}\right) = 16,550 \text{ psf} > 8,000$; therefore, a footing is required
Required area of concrete footing $= A_c$

$$A_c = \frac{P}{S_B} = \frac{11,490}{8,000} = 1.436 \text{ ft}^2$$

TIMBER PILES

Recommendations for the use of timber piles in foundations may be found in *Pressure Treated Timber Foundation Piles for Permanent Structures*, of the American Wood Preservers Institute. The American Society for Testing and Materials publication, *Standard Specifications for Round Timber Piles*, ASTM D25–70, classifies round timber piles according to the manner in which their load carrying capacity is developed. There are two classes:

1. *Friction Piles.* Friction piles are specified when pile capacity is determined by the friction developed in contact with the surrounding soil, along with the compressive strength of the timber piles used.

2. *End-Bearing Piles.* End-bearing piles are specified when pile capacity is determined primarily by the end-bearing capacity of the soil at the pile tip, along with the compressive strength of the timber piles used.

Table 4.12 lists size requirements for piles in accordance with ASTM Specification D25-70.

FALSEWORK AND CENTERING

Framing employing either glued laminated or sawn material is often economically used as falsework to support formwork for large poured-in-place concrete structures or as centering for placing precast concrete, stone, and steel structures which are assembled in place.

Falsework is the temporary structure erected to support work in the process of construction. It may be composed of structural units such as columns, beams, trusses, arches, and bracing designed by standard engineering procedure. The type and/or combination of structural units used

TABLE 4.12

SPECIFIED BUTT DIAMETERS WITH MINIMUM TIP CIRCUMFERENCES[a]

Specified Butt Diameters, in.	7	8	9	10	11	12	13	14	15	16	18
Required Minimum Circumference 3 ft from Butt, in.	22	25	28	31	35	38	41	44	47	50	57

Length, ft	Minimum Tip Circumferences, in., and Corresponding Diameter (in Parentheses)										
20	16.0 (5.0)	16.0 (5.0)	16.0 (5.0)	18.0 (5.7)	22.0 (7.0)	25.0 (8.0)	28.0 (8.9)				
30	16.0 (5.0)	16.0 (5.0)	16.0 (5.0)	16.0 (5.0)	19.0 (6.0)	22.0 (7.0)	25.0 (8.0)	28.0 (8.9)			
40				16.0 (5.0)	17.0 (5.4)	20.0 (6.4)	23.0 (7.3)	26.0 (8.3)	29.0 (9.2)		
50					16.0 (5.0)	17.0 (5.5)	19.0 (6.0)	22.0 (7.0)	25.0 (8.0)	28.0 (8.9)	
60						16.0 (5.0)	16.0 (5.0)	18.6 (5.9)	21.6 (6.9)	24.6 (7.8)	31.6 (10.0)
70							16.0 (5.0)	16.0 (5.0)	16.2 (5.1)	19.2 (6.1)	26.2 (8.3)
80							16.0 (5.0)	16.0 (5.0)	16.0 (5.0)	16.0 (5.0)	21.8 (6.9)
90							16.0 (5.0)	16.0 (5.0)	16.0 (5.0)	16.0 (5.0)	19.5 (6.2)
100							16.0 (5.0)	16.0 (5.0)	16.0 (5.0)	16.0 (5.0)	18.0 (5.8)
110										16.0 (5.0)	16.0 (5.0)
120											16.0 (5.0)

Note: Where the taper applied to the butt circumferences calculate to a circumference at the tip of less th 16 in., the individual values have been increased to 16 in. to assure a minimum of 5 in. tip for purposes driving.

[a]Source: American Society for Testing and Materials *Specifications for Round Timber Piles*, ASTM D25-70 (und the jurisdiction of ASTM Committee D07.00 on Wood).

depends on site conditions, the type and shape of supported structure, and the sequence of operations to be followed.

Centering is specialized falsework used in the construction of arches, shells, space structures, or any continuous structure where the entire falsework must be lowered (struck or decentered) as a unit to avoid introducing injurious stresses in any part of the structure. The lowering of centering is accomplished by the use of jacks, wedges, sand jacks, or some other device which has a controlled rate of travel.

Falsework must be designed to support all vertical and lateral loads that may be applied until such time as these loads can be carried by the supported structure. Vertical loads include the weight of the concrete together with its reinforcement and attachments, the dead weight of the falsework and formwork, and the live loads imposed by workmen, equipment, and materials during construction. A concrete weight including reinforcing of 150 pcf is commonly used for design. The American Concrete Institute (ACI) recommends a minimum construction live load of 50 psf of horizontal projection. Many designers use 75 psf for construction with powered concrete buggies. Lateral forces may include the hydraulic pressure of the concrete, wind loads, and equipment loads. Concrete hydraulic pressure varies with rate of placing and temperature.

Deflections at various stages of construction and pouring and possible movement during curing are important considerations. Deflection due to dead load of the formwork, falsework, and reinforcing placed before pouring should be compensated for by cambering.

For most exterior falsework uses, the timber and its connections should be designed for wet-use conditions and normal duration of loading. Glued laminated timber bonded with dry-use adhesives may be employed if the material is protected by several coats of suitable sealer when used under prolonged moist conditions. The extra expense of wet-use adhesive may be justified under extreme service conditions or by possible salvage value.

In some structures, depending on the job conditions, falsework or centering may be reusable. If such is the case, the designer should provide for ease of reuse in designing the falsework. Reuse conditions include, among others, the amount of disassembly needed for stripping, the weight of the disassembled units in relation to the available handling equipment, the possible provision for traveling falsework (for example, rollers or track arrangements), and stresses imposed by the moving and extra handling. If reuse is not possible, demolition and salvage values should be kept in mind.

Detailed information on falsework and centering, as well as on formwork, may be found in *Formwork for Concrete*, ACI Special Publication Number 4.

SHEATHING, FLOORING, AND DECKING

Sheathing and Flooring

Lumber sheathing and flooring

Sheathing consisting of lumber up to 1 in. in nominal thickness nailed transversely or diagonally at about 45° to studs or joists is commonly used in wood frame construction. When subjected to lateral forces, such as wind or earthquakes, lumber sheathing and its supporting framework may act as diaphragms, when properly designed as such, serving to brace the building against the lateral forces and transmitting these factors to the foundations. Diaphragm design procedures for lumber sheathing 1 in. in nominal thickness are given, beginning on page **4-133**. See Table 4.21 for allowable lateral shear loads for 1 in. lumber sheathed diaphragms.

The edges of lumber sheathing may be square, shiplapped, splined, or tongued-and-grooved. Sheathing runs should always be spliced over supports unless end matched or scarfed and glued end joints or splice blocks are used. Sheathing used as subflooring in wood frame construction

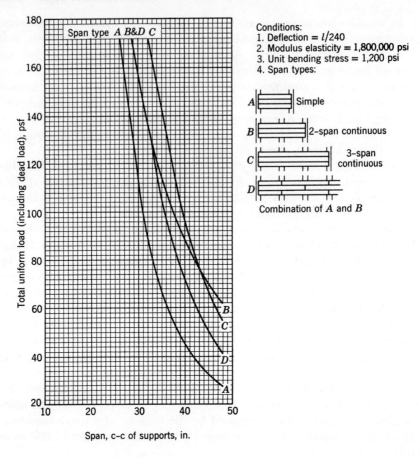

Figure 4.25.   **SPAN-LOAD CURVES.** For 1 in. nominal thickness lumber sheathing.

has the effect of a shallow beam, and, therefore, its design procedure is similar to that for beams with certain modifications. Figure 4.25 presents span-load curves for 1 in. nominal thickness lumber sheathing for various types of spans.

Plywood sheathing and flooring

Plywood. Plywood is made up of a combination of three or more layers of wood veneer, glued together with the grain of alternate plys at right angles. Plywood possesses more equal strength properties along the length and width of a panel than does solid wood. The two basic types of plywood are exterior and interior. Type depends on veneer grade and on adhesive used, whether waterproof (exterior or wet use) or water resistant (interior or dry use). Softwood plywood is manufactured from some 50 different species, which have been classified into 5 groups depending on stiffness. The strongest species such as Douglas fir, larch and Southern pine are in Group 1. The group number that appears in many plywood trademarks is based on the species used for the face and back of the panel (or the weaker species if face and back differ). For complete information about grades and plywood manufacturing, the designer should see the current

U.S. Product Standard PS 1 for softwood plywood, and *U.S. Commercial Standard CS 35* for hardwood plywood.

Table 4.13 gives recommended allowable unit stresses for grades and thicknesses of plywood listed in PS 1. These stresses are for normal duration of loading. The adjustment factors given in Table 2.12 should be applied for other durations of loading. Sanded grades of softwood plywood, referred to in Table 4.13, are generally identified by the grade of veneer used for the faces. Veneer grades range from A, the highest commonly used; through C, the lowest used in fully exterior plywood; to D, used only in inner plys and backs of interior plywood. Unsanded sheathing grades include Structural I, Structural II, and Standard. The Structural grades are intended for maximum efficiency in engineered applications. A designation called an identification index appears in the grade-trademarks of Standard sheathing, Structural I, Structural II, and C-C Exterior. It is a set of 2 numbers separated by a slash. The number on the left indicates recommended maximum spacing in inches for supports when the panel is used for roof decking with face grain across supports. The number on the right shows maximum recommended spacing in inches for supports when the panel is used for subflooring with face grain across supports.

Table 4.14 gives various properties of selected plywood constructions. Table 4.15 gives nailing recommendations for various plywood sheathing and flooring applications. Table 4.16 gives span recommendations for plywood sheathing and subflooring.

Plywood edge support. Panel edge support is required to resist concentrated loads in some cases, such as single layer floors, or where the span-thickness ratio is high in roof sheathing. Such edge supports may be furnished by solid blocking cut in between framing or by tongue and groove joints in the plywood. For roof sheathing, specially manufactured H-shaped metal clips may be used. When the panel edges are required to transmit lateral shear, as in some diaphragms, they should be attached to solid blocking or otherwise fastened to resist lateral loading.

Decking

Timber decking is commonly used for floor and roof construction in conjunction with timber joists, purlins, beams, arches, and trusses. Timber decking may also be used with other structural materials.

Three-inch and four-inch heavy timber decking

For information on species, sizes, patterns, lengths, moisture content, application, specifications, applicable allowable stresses, and allowable loads for 3 and 4 in. nominal thickness double tongue-and-groove heavy timber decking used as roof decking, see *Standard for Heavy Timber Roof Decking*, AITC 112, in Part II of this *Manual*. If 3 in. and 4 in. decking is to be used for floors or other purposes, see the recommendations given in paragraph 9.5 of AITC 112.

Two-inch timber decking

For information on species, sizes, patterns, lengths, moisture content, application, specifications, applicable allowable stresses, and allowable loads for 2 in. nominal thickness tongue-and-groove timber decking used

TABLE 4.13　ALLOWABLE UNIT STRESSES FOR PLYWOOD[a]
(To be used with section properties in Table 4.14)
Normal Duration of Loading, Dry Conditions of Use[b]

Type of Stress	Species Group	Exterior A-A, A-C, C-C[e], and Comparable Grades of Overlaid plywood. Structural I A-A, Structural I A-C, Structural I C-C, and Marine (Use Group 1 Stresses), psi	Plywood Grades	
			Exterior A-B, B-B, B-C, C-C (Plugged). Plyform Class I[c] Plyform Class II[c] and Comparable Grades of Overlaid plywood. Structural I C-D (Use Group I Stresses). Structural II C-D[e] Standard Sheathing (Exterior Glue)[c] All Interior Grades with Exterior Glue, psi	All other Grades of Interior Including Standard Sheathing[c], psi
Extreme fiber in bending, tension in plane of plys, F_b, F_t. Face grain parallel or perpendicular to span (at 45° to face grain use 1/6)	1	2,000	1,650	1,650
	2, 3	1,400	1,200	1,200
	4	1,200	1,000	1,000
Compression in plane of plys, F_c. Parallel or perpendicular to face grain (at 45° to face grain use 1/3)	1	1,650	1,550	1,550
	2, 3	1,200	1,100	1,100
	4	1,000	950	950
Shear in plane perpendicular to plys,[d] F_v. Parallel or perpendicular to face grain (at 45° increase 100%)	1	250	250	230
	2, 3	185	185	170
	4	175	175	160

Shear, rolling, in plane of plys[e], F_s. Parallel or perpendicular to face grain (at 45° increase 1/3)	All	53	53	48
Bearing (on face) perpendicular to plane of plys, $F_{c\perp}$	1 2, 3 4		340 210 160	
Modulus of Elasticity in bending, E. Face grain parallel or perpendicular to span	1 2 3 4		1,800,000 1,500,000 1,200,000 900,000	

[a] Conforming to U.S. Product Standard PS 1, *Softwood Plywood, Construction and Industrial.*

[b] Where moisture content is 16% or more, multiply the dry condition of use values by the following factors:

For all grades of exterior and interior plywood with exterior glue,

Extreme fiber in bending	75%	Modulus of Elasticity	89%
Tension	69%	Shear	84%
Compression	61%	Bearing	67%

For all other grades of interior plywood,

Extreme fiber in bending	69%	Modulus of Elasticity	80%
Tension	69%	Shear	84%
Compression	61%	Bearing	67%

[c] Exterior C-C, Structural II, and Standard Sheathing: The combination of identification index designation and panel thickness determine the minimum species group and, therefore, the stresses permitted, as follows:

5/16 in. – 20/0, 3/8 in. – 24/0, 1/2 in. – 32/16, 5/8 in. – 42/20, 3/4 in. – 48/24 – use Group 2 working stresses. All other combinations of C-C and Standard – use Group 4 working stresses. Other combinations of Structural II – use Group 3 working stresses. For Plyform Class I – use Group 3 stresses. For 2·4·1 – use Group 2 stresses. For 2·4·1 – use Group 1 stresses. For Plyform Class II – use Group 1 stresses, regardless of panel number on panel stamp.

[d] Shear through the thickness stresses are based on the most common structural applications where the plywood is attached to framing around its boundary. Where the plywood is attached to framing at only two sides – as in the heel joint of a truss – reduce the allowable shear through the thickness values by 11% where framing is parallel to the face grain and 25% where it is perpendicular.

[e] For Marine and Structural I grades use 75 psi. For Structural II use 56 psi.

TABLE 4.14 EFFECTIVE SECTION PROPERTIES FOR PLYWOOD (12 in. WIDTHS)

Part A Face plys of different species group from inner plys.
(Includes all Product Standard grades except those noted in *Part B*)

All Properties Adjusted to Account for Reduced Effectiveness of Plys with Grain Perpendicular to Applied Stress

Thickness, in.	Approx. Weight, psf	Effective Thickness for Shear, in.		Properties for Stress Applied Parallel with Face Grain				Properties for Stress Applied Perpendicular with Face Grain			
		All Grades Using Exterior Glue	All Grades Using Interior Glue	Area for Tension and Compression, in.^{2}	Moment of Inertia, I, in.^{4}	Effective Section Modulus, KS, in.^{4}	Rolling Shear Constant, I/Q, in.	Area for Tension and Compression, in.^{2}	Moment of Inertia, I, in.^{4}	Effective Section Modulus, KS, in.^{3}	Rolling Shear Constant, I/Q, in.
Unsanded panels											
$\frac{5}{16}$ U	1.0	0.286	0.270	2.400	0.026	0.147	0.216	0.600	0.001	0.024	—
$\frac{3}{8}$ U	1.1	0.323	0.323	2.400	0.047	0.215	0.286	0.750	0.002	0.031	—
$\frac{1}{2}$ U[a]	1.5	0.471	0.410	3.000	0.099	0.336	0.409	1.200	0.016	0.096	0.215
$\frac{5}{8}$ U	1.8	0.527	0.498	3.493	0.171	0.466	0.539	1.500	0.081	0.150	0.269
$\frac{3}{4}$ U	2.2	0.585	0.585	3.500	0.261	0.591	0.659	2.250	0.070	0.253	0.347
$\frac{7}{8}$ U	2.4	0.615	0.629	3.502	0.313	0.655	0.720	2.250	0.096	0.323	0.401
1 U	2.6	0.730	0.673	4.650	0.418	0.813	0.662	2.250	0.110	0.331	0.502
$1\frac{1}{8}$ U	3.0	0.788	0.760	3.876	0.531	0.903	0.800	3.320	0.204	0.521	0.585
$1\frac{1}{4}$ U	3.3	0.848	0.848	4.620	0.724	1.093	0.869	2.625	0.262	0.573	0.722

Sanded panels[b]											
¼ S	0.8	0.241	0.210	1.680	0.013	0.091	0.179	0.600	0.001	0.016	—
⅜ S	1.1	0.305	0.305	1.680	0.040	0.181	0.309	1.050	0.004	0.044	—
½ S	1.5	0.450	0.392	2.400	0.080	0.271	0.436	1.200	0.016	0.096	0.215
⅝ S	1.8	0.508	0.480	2.407	0.133	0.360	0.557	1.457	0.040	0.178	0.315
¾ S	2.2	0.567	0.567	2.778	0.201	0.456	0.687	2.200	0.088	0.305	0.393
⅞ S	2.6	0.711	0.655	2.837	0.301	0.585	0.704	2.893	0.145	0.413	0.531
1 S	3.0	0.769	0.742	3.600	0.431	0.733	0.763	3.323	0.234	0.568	0.632
1⅛ S[c]	3.3	0.825	0.825	3.829	0.566	0.855	0.849	3.307	0.334	0.702	0.748

[a]For ½ in. 3-ply use the following:

½ in. U	1.5	0.393	0.424	3.000	0.109	0.372	0.387	1.000	0.006	0.056	—

[b]Includes touch-sanded.

[c]For 2-4-1 use the following:

1⅛ 2-4-1	3.3	0.832	0.832	5.360	0.655	1.000	0.746	4.894	0.322	0.844	0.6421

4-112   *Timber Construction Manual*

TABLE 4.14 (Continued)

Part B All plys from same species group.
(Includes following grades: Structural I, Marine Exterior, all grades using Group 4 stresses)

All Properties Adjusted to Account for Reduced Effectiveness of Plys with Grain Perpendicular to Applied Stress

Thickness, in.	Approx. Weight, psf	Effective Thickness for Shear, in.		Properties for Stress Applied Parallel with Face Grain				Properties for Stress Applied Perpendicular with Face Grain			
		All Grades Using Exterior Glue	All Grades Using Interior Glue	Area for Tension and Compression, in.²	Moment of Inertia, I, in.⁴	Effective Section Modulus, KS, in.³	Rolling Shear Constant, I/Q, in.	Area for Tension and Compression, in.²	Moment of Inertia, I, in.⁴	Effective Section Modulus, KS, in.³	Rolling Shear Constant, I/Q, in.
Unsanded panels											
$\frac{5}{16}$ U	1.0	0.318	0.300	2.400	0.026	0.147	0.216	1.200	0.002	0.032	—
$\frac{3}{8}$ U	1.1	0.375	0.375	2.400	0.048	0.215	0.286	1.500	0.003	0.049	—
$\frac{1}{2}$ U[a]	1.5	0.574	0.500	3.600	0.100	0.339	0.410	2.400	0.029	0.183	0.215
$\frac{5}{8}$ U	1.8	0.662	0.625	4.586	0.175	0.477	0.546	3.000	0.056	0.286	0.269
$\frac{3}{4}$ U	2.2	0.750	0.750	4.600	0.266	0.603	0.663	4.500	0.132	0.509	0.348
$\frac{13}{16}$ U	2.4	0.794	0.813	4.605	0.319	0.668	0.722	4.500	0.182	0.628	0.403
$\frac{7}{8}$ U	2.6	0.949	0.875	6.900	0.474	0.922	0.594	4.500	0.207	0.643	0.507
1 U	3.0	1.037	1.000	5.354	0.574	0.976	0.728	6.639	0.391	1.020	0.589
$1\frac{1}{8}$ U	3.3	1.125	1.125	6.840	0.815	1.231	0.776	5.250	0.502	1.122	0.729
Sanded panels[b]											
$\frac{1}{4}$ S	0.8	0.276	0.240	1.680	0.013	0.091	0.179	1.200	0.001	0.027	—
$\frac{3}{8}$ S	1.1	0.375	0.375	1.680	0.040	0.182	0.308	2.100	0.007	0.079	—
$\frac{1}{2}$ S	1.5	0.574	0.500	3.120	0.081	0.277	0.438	2.400	0.029	0.183	0.215
$\frac{5}{8}$ S	1.8	0.662	0.625	3.135	0.135	0.367	0.557	2.914	0.076	0.345	0.316
$\frac{3}{4}$ S	2.2	0.750	0.750	3.876	0.207	0.470	0.691	4.400	0.168	0.597	0.394
$\frac{7}{8}$ S	2.6	0.949	0.875	3.994	0.329	0.639	0.637	5.786	0.279	0.811	0.535
1 S	3.0	1.037	1.000	5.520	0.498	0.846	0.673	6.646	0.454	1.119	0.636
$1\frac{1}{8}$ S	3.3	1.125	1.125	5.978	0.664	1.003	0.746	6.660	0.650	1.385	0.753

[a]For $\frac{1}{2}$ in. 3-ply use the following:

$\frac{1}{2}$ in. U	1.5	0.463	0.500	3.000	0.110	0.373	0.387	2.000	0.005	0.088	—

TABLE 4.15

RECOMMENDED MINIMUM NAILING SCHEDULES FOR PLYWOOD[a]

Plywood Use	Thickness, in.	Nail Size	Nail Type	Nail Spacing, in.	
				Panel Edges[b]	Inter-mediate
Roof sheathing[c]	$\frac{5}{16}, \frac{3}{8}, \frac{1}{2}$	6d	Common	6	12
	$\frac{5}{8}, \frac{3}{4}$	8d	Common	6	12
Wall sheathing	$\frac{5}{16}, \frac{3}{8}, \frac{1}{2}$	6d	Common	6	12
	$\frac{5}{8}$	8d	Common	6	12
Subflooring[d]	$\frac{1}{2}$	6d	Common	6	10
	$\frac{5}{8}, \frac{3}{4}$	8d	Common	6	10
	$1, 1\frac{1}{8}$	8d (or 10d com.)	Deformed shank	6	6
Diaphragms[e] and shear walls	$\frac{1}{4}$ and thicker	See Note[d]	Common	6	12
Underlay-ment[f]	$\frac{1}{4}, \frac{3}{8}, \frac{1}{2}$	3d	Ring shank	6	8 each way
	$\frac{5}{8}, \frac{3}{4}$	4d	Ring shank	6	8 each way
Interior paneling	$\frac{1}{4}$	4d	Finish or casing	6	12
	$\frac{3}{8}$	6d		6	12
Exterior and panel siding[g]	$\frac{3}{8}, \frac{1}{2}$	6d	Non-corrosive, siding, or casing	6	12
	$\frac{5}{8}$ and thicker	8d		6	12
Lap siding[h]	$\frac{3}{8}$	6d	Non-corro-sive, siding, or casing	See Note[h]	
	$\frac{1}{2}$ and thicker	8d			

[a]Recommended by the American Plywood Association. Contact APA for additional data.
[b]Minimum edge distance of $\frac{3}{8}$ in. recommended.
[c]For applications where roofing is to be guaranteed by a performance bond, recommendations may differ somewhat. Consult APA or roofing manufacturer for such recommendations.
[d]If resilient flooring is to be applied without underlayment, set nails $\frac{1}{16}$ in. and use deformed shank nails (6d for $\frac{1}{2}$ in., $\frac{5}{8}$ in., and $\frac{3}{4}$ in. plywood).
[e]Nail size and spacing determined by shear requirements; do not exceed spacing shown.
[f]Nails have 20 annular grooves per in. of shank, to within $\frac{5}{16}$ in. of head. Heads are flat countersunk.. Length is sufficient to penetrate at least $\frac{3}{4}$ in. into subfloor. For plywood $\frac{1}{2}$ in. and less, shank diameter must be at least 0.080 in., and head diameter $\frac{3}{16}$ in. For $\frac{5}{8}$ in. and $\frac{3}{4}$ in. plywood, shank diameter must be at least 0.098 in., and head diameter $\frac{1}{4}$ in.
[g]Nails on shiplap edges $\frac{3}{8}$ in. from exposed edge and slant driven toward it; do not set.
[h]One nail per stud on bottom edge. Space not more than 4 in. at vertical joints. If siding is wider than 12 in., space nails on each intermediate stud not more than 8 in. Do not set.

TABLE 4.16

SPANS FOR PLYWOOD ROOF SHEATHING AND SUBFLOORING[a]

Plywood Roof Sheathing[b] (plywood continuous over 2 or more spans; grain of face plys across supports)

| | | Allowable Roof Loads, psf[c] | | | | | | | | | | |
| | | Spacing of supports, *c–c*, in. | | | | | | | | | | |
Panel Identification Index	Thickness, in.	12	16	20	24	30	32	36	42	48	60	72
12/0	$\frac{5}{16}$	100 (130)										
16/0	$\frac{5}{16}, \frac{3}{8}$	130 (170)	55 (75)									
20/0	$\frac{5}{16}, \frac{3}{8}$		85 (110)	45 (55)								
24/0	$\frac{3}{8}, \frac{1}{2}$		150 (160)	75 (100)	45 (60)							
30/12	$\frac{5}{8}$			145 (165)	85 (110)	40 (55)						
32/16	$\frac{1}{2}, \frac{5}{8}$				90 (105)	45 (60)	40 (50)					

36/16	$\frac{3}{4}$			125 (145)	65 (85)	55 (70)	35 (50)			
42/20	$\frac{5}{8}, \frac{3}{4}, \frac{7}{8}$				80 (105)	65 (90)	45 (60)	35 (40)		
48/24	$\frac{3}{4}, \frac{7}{8}$					105 (115)	75 (90)	55 (55)	40 (40)	
2-4-1	$1\frac{1}{8}$						175 (175)	105 (105)	80 (80)	50 (50)	30 (35)
$1\frac{1}{8}$ in. Groups 1 and 2	$1\frac{1}{8}$						145 (145)	85 (85)	65 (65)	40 (40)	30 (30)
$1\frac{1}{4}$ in. Groups 3 and 4	$1\frac{1}{4}$						160 (165)	95 (95)	75 (75)	45 (45)	25 (35)

TABLE 4.16 (Continued)

Plywood Subflooring[d] (plywood continuous over 2 or more spans; grain of face plys across supports)

Panel Identification Index	Thickness, in.	Maximum Span[f], in.
30/12	$\frac{5}{8}$	12
32/16	$\frac{1}{2}, \frac{5}{8}$	16
36/16	$\frac{3}{4}$	16
42/20	$\frac{5}{8}, \frac{3}{4}, \frac{7}{8}$	20
48/24	$\frac{3}{4}, \frac{7}{8}$	24
$1\frac{1}{8}$ in., Groups 1 and 2	$1\frac{1}{8}$	48
$1\frac{1}{4}$ in., Groups 3 and 4	$1\frac{1}{4}$	48

Combined Subfloor – Underlayment[e]

Plywood Grade	Thickness, in.	Maximum Span[f], in.
Underlayment *C–C* Plugged, Group 1	$\frac{23}{32}, \frac{3}{4}$	24
	$\frac{19}{32}, \frac{5}{8}$	20
	$\frac{1}{2}$	16
Underlayment *C–C* Plugged, Groups 2 and 3	$\frac{7}{8}$	24
	$\frac{23}{32}, \frac{3}{4}$	20
	$\frac{19}{32}, \frac{5}{8}$	16

Underlayment C–C Plugged, Group 4	1 $\frac{7}{8}$ $\frac{23}{32}, \frac{3}{4}$	24 20 16
2-4-1, Groups 1, 2 and 3	$1\frac{1}{8}$	48

[a]Recommended by the American Plywood Association. Contact APA for additional data.

[b]Applies to Standard, Structural I and II, and C–C grades only.

[c]Uniform load deflection limitation: $\frac{1}{180}$ of the span under live load plus dead load, $\frac{1}{240}$ under live load only. Allowable live load shown on upper line and allowable total load shown within parentheses. The allowable live load should in no case exceed the total load less the dead load supported by the plywood.

[d]For direct application of tongue-and-groove wood strip and block flooring and lightweight concrete, or for underlayment and resilient flooring. These values apply for Structural I and II, Standard sheathing, and C–C Exterior grades only.

[e]For direct application of tile, carpeting, linoleum, or other nonstructural flooring. (Plywood continuous over 2 or more spans; grain of face plys across supports. Seasoned lumber recommended.)

[f]Edges must be tongued-and-grooved or supported with framing. Use deformed-shank nails.

as roof decking, see *Standard for Two-inch Nominal Thickness Lumber Roof Decking for Structural Applications*, AITC 118, in Part II of this *Manual*. If 2 in. decking is to be used for floors or other purposes, see the recommendations given in paragraph 9.1 of AITC 118.

For types 4 and 5, I/c is based on two-thirds of the cross section for use in the formula for stress (not for deflection formulas).

Mechanically laminated decking

Mechanically laminated decks consist of square-edged dimension lumber set on edge, wide face-to-wide face, with the pieces connected by nails or other fasteners. If side nails are used, they should be long enough to penetrate approximately $2\frac{1}{2}$ lamination thicknesses for load transfer. Where deck supports are 4 ft c–c or less, side nails should be spaced not more than 30 in. on centers and staggered one-third of the spacing in adjacent laminations. When supports are spaced more than 4 ft c–c side nails should be spaced approximately 18 in. on centers alternately near top and bottom edges, and also staggered one-third of the spacing in adjacent laminations. Two side nails should be used at each end of butt jointed pieces.

Laminations should be toe-nailed to supports, 20d or larger common nails being used. When the supports are 4 ft c–c or less, alternate laminations should be toe-nailed to alternate supports; when supports are spaced more than 4 ft c–c, alternate laminations should be toe-nailed to every support.

Span and end joint arrangements and design formulas. The five span arrangements and design formulas are also shown in *Standard for Two-inch Nominal Thickness Lumber Roof Decking for Structural Application*, AITC 118, in Part II of this *Manual* are also applicable for mechanically laminated decks.

Other decking

Other special decking products are available. They include panelized decking, glued laminated decking, and heavy plywood decking such as "2-4-1." Panelized decking is a decking component made up of splined panels, usually about 2 ft wide and of any specified length up to a maximum which may vary among manufacturers. Glued laminated decking is manufactured by laminating two or more pieces of lumber into single decking members. Common nominal lumber thicknesses of the decking are 2 in., 3 in., or 4 in., although exact finished sizes may differ between manufacturers. Special plywood panels known as "2-4-1" plywood are $1\frac{1}{8}$ in. thick, measuring 4 ft × 8 ft on the face. They are usually supplied with tongue-and-groove joints on the long edge. Manufacturers of these special decking products should be consulted for information concerning their products.

Allowable decking loads

The allowable decking loads for 3 in. and 4 in. heavy timber decking may be found in *Standard for Heavy Timber Roof Decking*, AITC 112, in Part II of this *Manual*. The allowable decking loads for 2 in. heavy timber decking may be found in *Standard for Two-inch Nominal Thickness Lumber Roof Decking for Structural Applications*, AITC 118, in Part II of this *Manual*.

Table 4.16 gives allowable loads for "2-4-1" and other plywood decking systems.

Table 4.17 gives allowable uniformly distributed loads for mechanically laminated decks for various spans as limited by bending and deflection. The table is based on the use of seasoned lumber, normal duration of loading, and loads applied normal to the decking surface. The allowable loads include dead load.

TABLE 4.17

ALLOWABLE LOADS FOR MECHANICALLY LAMINATED DECKS

For seasoned lumber, normal conditions of loading, and load applied normal to decking surface. Loads for other stress and deflection values can be determined by proportion. Load includes weight of decking which should be subtracted to determine allowable superimposed load.

Span, ft	Nominal Thickness of Deck, in.	Uniform Load, psf						
		Limited by Bending, $F_b = 1,000$ psi		Limited by Deflection, $E = 1,000,000$ psi, $\Delta_A = l/240$				
		Types 1, 2, and 3	Types 4 and 5	Type 1	Type 2	Type 3	Type 4	Type 5
4	4	1,021	851	1,488	3,587	2,114	2,036	1,939
5	4	653	544	762	1,836	1,082	1,042	993
	6	1,613	1,344	2,958	7,126	4,199	4,045	3,852
6	4	454	378	441	1,063	626	603	574
	6	1,120	934	1,712	4,124	2,430	2,341	2,229
	8	1,946	1,622	3,920	9,446	5,566	5,362	5,106
7	4	333	278	278	669	394	380	362
	6	823	686	1,078	2,597	1,530	1,474	1,404
	8	1,430	1,192	2,469	5,948	3,505	3,376	3,215
8	4	255	213	186	448	264	254	242
	6	630	525	722	1,740	1,025	988	940
	8	1,095	912	1,654	3,985	2,348	2,262	2,154
	10	1,782	1,485	3,435	8,276	4,877	4,698	4,474
9	4	201	168	131	315	186	179	170
	6	498	415	507	1,222	720	694	660
	8	865	721	1,162	2,799	1,649	1,589	1,513
	10	1,408	1,174	2,412	5,813	3,425	3,299	3,142
10	6	403	336	370	891	525	506	481
	8	701	584	847	2,040	1,202	1,158	1,103
	10	1,141	951	1,759	4,237	2,497	2,405	2,290
11	8	579	483	636	1,533	903	870	829
	10	943	786	1,321	3,184	1,876	1,807	1,721
12	8	487	406	490	1,181	696	670	638
	10	792	660	1,018	2,452	1,445	1,392	1,326

TABLE 4.17 (Continued)

Span, ft	Nominal Thickness of Deck, in.	Limited by Bending, $F_b = 1,000$ psi		Limited by Deflection, $E = 1,000,000$ psi, $\Delta_A = l/240$				
		Types 1, 2, and 3	Types 4 and 5	Type 1	Type 2	Type 3	Type 4	Type 5
13	8	415	346	385	929	547	527	502
	10	675	562	800	1,929	1,137	1,095	1,043
14	8	357	298	309	744	438	422	402
	10	582	485	641	1,544	910	877	835
15	8	311	260	251	605	356	343	327
	10	507	422	521	1,256	740	713	679
16	8	274	228	207	498	294	283	269
	10	446	371	429	1,034	610	587	559
17	8	242	202	172	415	245	236	224
	10	395	329	358	862	508	490	466
18	8	216	180	145	350	206	199	189
	10	352	293	302	727	428	412	393
19	10	316	263	256	618	364	351	334
20	10	285	238	220	530	312	301	286

For allowable bending stress, F_b, values other than 1,000 psi, tabulated values must be multiplied by $F_b/1,000$. For modulus of elasticity, E, values other than 1,00,000 psi, tabulated values must be multiplied by $E/1,000,000$. For deflection limits, Δ_A, other than $l/240$, tabulated values are to be multiplied by $240\Delta_A/l$ (i.e., for $\Delta_A = l/360$, tabulated values are multiplied by 240/360).

Cantilevered overhangs

Under uniformly distributed loads, cantilevered overhangs act to reduce the deflections in the remaining areas of a deck structure. Thus, span increases are often justified where overhangs are used. The effects of cantilevered overhangs are varied. The span arrangement and the length of overhang affect support reactions, bending stress, and span and overhang deflections. Charts which permit the determination of those factors for simple span, two-span continuous, three-span continuous, four-span continuous, and five-span continuous arrangements are given in Section 6 of this *Manual*.

The designer should also consider the effects of heating on snow loads on cantilevered overhang roofs. Unbalanced loading may be created where melting occurs over heated areas, but not over unheated overhangs.

TIMBER BRIDGES

Timber bridges consist of several basic types, including trestles, girder bridges, truss bridges, and arch bridges. In the design of any of these types, the considerations given under "Moving Loads" in Section 3 of this *Manual* should be taken into account. For highway bridges, design loads and the application should be in accordance with the recommendations of the American Association of State Highway Officials (AASHO). For railway bridges, the recommendations of the American Railway Engineering Association (AREA) should be followed.

Trestles

The trestle is probably the simplest type of timber bridge. Timber trestles consist of stringers supported by pile or frame bents. The bridge deck is applied to the stringers. Pile and frame bents are capped by timbers 12×12 or larger, adequately fastened to the tops of the piles or posts.

If pile penetration or height of bent is such that piles longer than those commercially available are required, or if pile bearing values are low and a large number of piles must be driven, posts may be used on top of the pile bents. Frame bents must rest on some type of foundation structure, such as concrete footings or piles. Sway bracing and longitudinal tower bracing, appropriate to the height of the bent, must be provided.

Spacing of bents is determined, in part, by the commercially available lengths of stringers, which are fabricated in even-foot increments. The ends of interior stringers are usually lapped and fastened at the bearing on the caps, whereas exterior stringers are butted at the ends and spliced over the bent caps. At least one end of every other exterior stringer should be adequately fastened to the bent caps.

Stringers are designed as simple span beams under the loadings recommended by AASHO or AREA. Sizes and spacing are determined by the span and loading conditions. Standard sizes of glued laminated or solid sawn timbers as given in Tables 2.16 and 2.17 should be used. Solid bridging should be provided at the ends of stringers to hold them in line and also to serve as a fire stop. Bridging should also be placed between stringers at midspan or, on long spans, at third-points. Fire curtains should be provided at intervals of about 100 ft.

Girder Bridges

Girder bridges, consisting of glued laminated or solid sawn timber girders supporting a bridge deck, may be used for spans which exceed the practical limits of timber trestles, for spans less than those economical for truss bridges, or where a truss bridge is not desirable. Substructures similar to those used for timber trestles can be used for girder bridges, the girder being fastened to the bent caps by means of a fabricated steel girder seat.

Timber girders are designed as beams in accordance with the recommendations in this section, including those for lateral support (see Tables 4.27

and 4.28). Lateral forces acting on the girder will enter into the design of the lateral bracing system.

Construction economies will usually result if the standard sizes for glued laminated or solid sawn timber as given in Tables 2.16 and 2.17 of this *Manual* are used.

Truss Bridges

Truss bridges may be of either of two types: deck-truss bridges, in which trusses support the bridge deck and roadway; or through-truss bridges, in which the roadway passes between two parallel trusses forming the bridge structure. The deck-truss type is the more economical, since substructures and lateral bracing are narrower. The use of deck trusses may be limited, however, by under-clearance. Deck trusses may be of the parallel chord type or of the bowstring type with the truss built up to the level of the floor beams. Through-trusses may be of either of these truss-types also, but the bowstring is usually more economical.

Substructures for truss bridges may be similar to those for timber trestles; however, because the vertical loads are greater and are concentrated at the ends of the trusses, the bents must be capable of carrying a greater load and a system of cribbing is required for bent caps. For longer spans and heavier loads, timber, stone, or concrete piers may be required. Lateral forces are greater on truss bridges, and a carefully designed substructure sway bracing system is necessary.

The design of trusses for bridges is similar to that for roof trusses, the length of the truss panel being determined by economical spacing of floor beams, a minimum number of joints, and commercially available lengths of timber. As in roof truss design, the joint design is an important consideration. Bridge truss joints should be designed to eliminate or minimize pockets which may tend to collect moisture.

Arch Bridges

When site conditions are such that considerable height is required between foundation and roadway or a relatively long clear span is required, an arch bridge may be most economical because of the lesser necessity for substructure framing. Arch bridges may be of the two-hinged or three-hinged type, two-hinged designs being more frequently used on short spans, and three-hinged designs on long spans.

Glued laminated timber arches may be fabricated to the desired shape, and the ends built up to the level of the roadway by means of post bents. Post bents may be connected to the arch by means of steel gusset plates which should be designed for erection loads, possible stress reversals, and lateral forces as well as for the anticipated bridge loads.

Bridge Decks

The selection of decks for timber bridges is determined by density of traffic and economics. Plank decks may be used for light traffic or for temporary bridges. Laminated decks can be used for heavier traffic conditions.

The design of plank and mechanically laminated decks can be found on pages 4-107 through 4-120. Asphaltic wearing surfaces may be applied on the decking, although this is not usually done for plank decks.

Composite timber-concrete decks are commonly used in timber bridge construction. Composite timber-concrete construction combines timber and concrete in such a manner that the wood is in tension and the concrete is in compression (except at the supports of continuous spans, where negative bending occurs and these stresses are reversed). Composite timber-concrete construction is of two basic types: T-beams and "slab" decks.

T-beams consist of timber stringers which form the stems and concrete slabs which form the flanges of a series of T-shapes. Composite beams of this type are usually simple span bridges. Slab decks use as a base for the concrete a mechanically laminated wooden deck made up of planks set on edge, with alternate planks raised 2 in. to form longitudinal grooves. This grooved surface is usually obtained by using planks of two different widths and alternating them in assembly. This composite type is commonly used for continuous span bridges and trestles.

In both types, a means of horizontal shear resistance and a means of preventing separation are needed at the joint between the two materials. In T-beams, resistance to horizontal shear is generally provided by a series of notches $\frac{1}{2}$ to $\frac{3}{4}$ in. deep cut into the top of the timber stringer, while nails and spikes partially driven into the top prevent vertical separation of the concrete and timber. Other adequate methods may be used. In slab decks, shear resistance is accomplished either by means of notches $\frac{1}{2}$ in. deep cut into the tops of all laminations, by patented triangular steel plate "shear developers" driven into precut slots in the channels formed by the raised laminations or other suitable shear connectors. When the $\frac{1}{2}$ in. notches are used, grooves are milled the full length of both faces of each raised lamination to resist uplift and separation of the wood and concrete. When the steel shear developers are used, nails or spikes are partially driven into the tops of raised laminations to resist separation.

In T-beam design, secondary shearing stresses due to temperature must be considered in designing for horizontal shear resistance. These stresses are induced by the thermal expansion or contraction of the concrete, both of which are resisted by the wood, which is assumed to be unaffected by normal temperature changes. Shear connections for temperature change are neglected in slab deck-type composite construction; however, expansion joints should be provided in the concrete slab.

The concrete slab should be reinforced for temperature stresses. In continuous spans, steel sufficient to develop negative bending stresses is necessary over interior supports.

The dead load of the composite structure is considered to be carried entirely by the timber section. The composite structure carries positive bending moment and, over interior supports in continuous spans, steel reinforcing and the wood act to resist negative bending moment.

In designing a composite structure, if it is assumed that the junction between the two materials is without inelastic deformation and has elastic characteristics in keeping with the materials, the structure can be designed by the transformed-area method, that is, by transforming the composite section into an equivalent homogeneous section. This is accomplished by multiplying the concrete width or depth by the ratio of the moduli of elasticity of the materials.

T-beam design procedure.

1. Estimate, on the basis of engineering judgement and the use of span tables, the size of timber and thickness of slab to be used.

2. Determine effective flange width of the concrete slab. The effective width of the slab as the flange of a T-beam may not exceed any of the following: (*a*) one-fourth of the T-beam span; (*b*) the distance center-to-center of T-beams; or (*c*) 12 times the least thickness of the slab.

For beams with a flange on one side of the stem only, the effective flange width may not exceed one-twelfth of the beam span, or one-half of the center-to-center distance to the adjacent beam, or 6 times the least slab thickness.

3. Compute the transformed width of the concrete flange by multiplying the effective width of the flange by the ratio of the moduli of elasticity of the two materials, E_c/E_w.

4. Determine the location of the neutral axis and the moment of inertia, I_t, of the transformed section.

5. Determine applied load and dead load bending moments for the span.

6. Check the extreme fiber stress in bending against the allowable unit stresses for the wood and concrete. The actual extreme fiber stress in bending in the concrete, f_{bc}, is calculated from the formula

$$f_{bc} = \frac{M_A}{S_t}$$

where M_A = applied load bending moment, in.-lb
   S_t = transformed area section modulus, in.[3]

The actual extreme fiber stress in bending in the wood, f_b, is determined from the formula

$$f_b = \frac{M_A}{S_t} + \frac{M_D}{S_w}$$

where M_D = dead load bending moment, in.-lb
   S_w = section modulus of the net timber section, in.[3]

Impact should be considered in the concrete but not in the wood.

7. Check the actual horizontal shear stress, f_v, at the timber-concrete junction by the formula

$$f_v = \frac{VxA}{I_t b}$$

where V = total vertical shear, lb
   A = area of the transformed section above or below the plane at which shear is being determined, in.[2]
   x = distance of center of gravity of area A from the neutral axis, in.

I_t = transformed section moment of inertia, in.[4]
b = width of timber section, in.

Since only the net area remaining after the top of the stringer has been notched is effective in shear resistance, the permissible f_v value equals the allowable unit shear stress for the species used multiplied by the ratio of the area notched to the total top surface area of the stringer. *Note:* The top of the stringer need not be notched if properly designed shear connectors are used.

8. The f_v value as determined in step 7 neglects the temperature change shear connections. The number of these connections required, N, may be determined from the formula

$$N = \frac{A_c f_c}{p}$$

where A_c = area of concrete flange considered to be involved by the restraining timber stem, in.² (this may be assumed to be one-third of the total concrete flange area)

f_c = unit stress in concrete induced by temperature change in the range selected, psi (this equals the product of coefficient of expansion of the concrete, the change in temperature from that at the time of construction, and the modulus of elasticity of the concrete, E_c)

p = the value of each shear connection, lb (this may be determined on the basis of: allowable shear and bearing values of concrete and wood for notches in the top surface of the stringer; the allowable loads for common fastenings; or tests for special devices)

In order to combine temperature shear requirements and load shear requirements, the formulas in steps 7 and 8 may be rewritten in terms of pounds per inch and combined in the form

$$f_v b = \frac{V x A}{I_t} + \frac{A_c F_c}{12L}$$

where L = span length, ft.

Example. Design a composite timber-concrete T-beam to span 30 ft carrying a 75 psf dead load and AASHO H-20 live load. Center-to-center spacing of stringers is 6 ft.

1. Material estimates.

Concrete:	Wood (wet conditions of use):
6 in. concrete slab	$6\frac{3}{4} \times 34\frac{1}{2}$ glued laminated stringers
$f_c' = 3,000$ psi	$F_b = 1,800$ psi $F_v = 145$ psi
$E_c = 3,000,000$ psi	$F_c = 1,100$ psi $E_w = 1,600,000$ psi

2. Determine effective flange width.

(a) $\frac{1}{4}L = (\frac{1}{4})(30) = 7.5$ ft

(b) c–c spacing $= 6.0$ ft

(c) (12)(slab thickness) $= (12)(\frac{1}{2}) = 6$ ft $\leftarrow$ controls

3. Compute transformed flange width.

$$\frac{E_c}{E_w} = 1 \qquad \text{(per AASHO requirements)}$$

$$b_t = b\frac{E_c}{E_w} = (6)(1) = 6 \text{ ft} = 72 \text{ in.}$$

4. Determine location of the neutral axis and the moment of inertia, I_t.
(Not to scale)

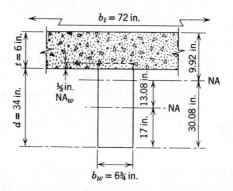

$$y = \frac{(6)(72)(37) + (6.75)(34.5)(1)}{(72)(6) + (6.75)(34.5)}$$

$$y = 30.08 \text{ in.}$$

$$I_t = \frac{(72)(6)^3}{12} + (72)(6)(6.92)^2 + \frac{(6.75)(34)^3}{12} + (6.75)(34)(13.08)^2$$

$$I_t = 65{,}600 \text{ in.}^4$$

$$S_w = \frac{(6.75)(34)^2}{6} = 1{,}300 \text{ in.}^3$$

5. Determine bending moments.

For a 30 ft span, maximum moment for one lane, H-20 loading is 246,000 ft-lb (per AASHO). Therefore, use $\frac{1}{2}$ of this moment for one stringer.

$$M_A = \frac{(246{,}000)(12)}{2} = 1{,}480{,}000 \text{ in.-lb}$$

$$M_D = \frac{(75)(6)(30)^2(12)}{8} = 607{,}500 \text{ in.-lb}$$

6. Check bending stresses.

$$f_{bc} = \frac{M_A c}{I_t} = \frac{(1{,}480{,}000)(9.92)}{65{,}600} = 223.8 \text{ psi} < 1{,}350 \qquad \text{O.K.}$$

$$f_b = \frac{M_A y}{I_t} + \frac{M_D}{S_w} = \frac{(1,480,000)(30.08)}{65,600} + \frac{607,500}{1,300} = 1,146 \text{ psi}$$

$$F_b = 1,800 C_F = (1,800)(0.89) = 1,600 \text{ psi} > 1,146 \text{ psi} \qquad \text{O.K.}$$

7. Check the horizontal shear stress.

For a 30 ft span, maximum shear for one lane, H-20 loading is 36,300 lb (per AASHO). Therefore, use $\frac{1}{2}$ of lane shear for one stringer. Ratio of notched area to total top area $= \frac{1}{2}$; therefore

$$F_v = (\tfrac{1}{2})(145) = 72.5 \text{ psi}$$

$$V_A = \frac{36,300}{2} = 18,150 \text{ lb (live load only)}$$

$$V_D = \frac{wl}{2} = \frac{(25)(30)}{2} = 1,125 \text{ lb (dead load only)}$$

$$f_c = \frac{V_A x A}{I_t b} = \frac{(18,150)(13.08)(6.75)(34)}{(65,600)(6.75)} = 123 \text{ psi} > 72.5 \qquad \text{N.G}$$

Therefore, determine number of shear connectors, N_v, required to carry additional shear stress.
Try $\frac{3}{4}$ in. $\times$ 8 in. lag screws.

$$N_v = \frac{(123 - 72.5)(6.75)(30)(12)}{935}$$

$$N_v = 131$$

8. Determine the number of temperature connections.
Load value of shear connection $= p = 935$ lb

$$f_c = (\text{concrete coefficient of expansion})(\Delta_T)(E_c)$$

$$f_c = (0.000005)(50°\text{F})(3,000,000)$$

$$f_c = 750 \text{ psi}$$

$$N = \frac{A_c f_c}{p} = \frac{(72)(6)(\tfrac{1}{3})(750)}{935} = 116$$

$$N_v + N = 131 + 116 = 247$$

Total number of shear connectors required per ft of span $= \dfrac{247}{30} = 8.2$

Use 8 per ft

Slab deck design procedure.

1. Compute the dead load of the estimated composite section and of the necessary construction loads occurring during placing of concrete and before curing.

2. Compute bending moments for dead load as for a simple span, and, in the case of continuous span-slab decks, apply the appropriate factor for wood subdeck from Table 4.18 to obtain positive and negative moments.

TABLE 4.18

MAXIMUM CONTINUOUS SPAN BENDING MOMENTS
FOR SLAB DECKS[a]

	Uniform Dead Load Moments				Applied Load Moments			
	Wood Subdeck		Composite Slab		Concentrated Load		Uniform Load	
	Pos.	Neg.	Pos.	Neg.	Pos.	Neg.	Pos.	Neg.
Span	Percentage of Simple Span Bending Moments							
Interior	50	50	55	45	75	25	75	55
End	70	60	70	60	85	30	85	65
Two-span[b]	65	70	60	75	85	30	80	75

[a]From: *Standard Specifications for Highway Bridges,* adopted by The American Association of State Highway Officials, Tenth Edition, 1969.
[b]Continuous beam with two equal spans.

3. Determine the location of the neutral axis. The distance from the neutral axis to the lower extreme fiber is critical, because applied loads add substantially to the lower extreme fiber stress. Compute moment of inertia of the wood subdeck at midspan and at interior supports of continuous spans. Assume that only two-thirds of the laminations are continuous over supports.

4. From steps 2 and 3, determine the extreme fiber stress in bending in the wood resulting from load at midspan and at interior supports in continuous spans.

5. Compute bending moments due to uniform dead load after curing and due to concentrated or uniform applied loads as for a simple span. Apply the appropriate constants from Table 4.18 to continuous spans. Concentrated loads are distributed over 5 ft for calculating moments, accounting for equal wheel loads in adjacent lanes.

6. Determine the location of the neutral axis and the distances to the extreme fibers of the wood, concrete, and reinforcing steel. Compute the moment of inertia of the composite section at midspan and over interior supports of continuous spans. Assume that only two-thirds of the laminations are continuous over supports.

7. Using the M, c, and I values from steps 5 and 6, determine the extreme fiber bending stress in the wood at midspan (tension), in the wood at interior supports of continuous spans (compression), in the concrete at midspan (compression), and in the steel at interior supports of continuous spans (tension). The concrete and steel unit stresses thus determined must be multiplied by the moduli of elasticity ratios, E_c/E_w or E_s/E_w, respectively, to determine actual unit stresses in the transformed concrete and steel areas.

These values may not exceed the allowable unit stresses for the materials. Allowance for impact must be added to static moments in determining steel and concrete stresses, but impact is neglected for wood.

The following modulus of elasticity ratios should be used:

$E_c/E_w = 1$ for slab decks in which the net concrete thickness above the wood is less than one-half the overall depth of the composite section

$E_c/E_w = 2$ for slab decks in which the net concrete thickness above the wood is equal to or greater than one-half the overall depth of the composite section (the use of a net concrete thickness equal to or greater than one-half the overall depth of the composite section has little or no advantage for most highway structures)

$E_s/E_w = 18.75$ for Douglas fir and Southern pine lumber

8. The unit stress in the wood as determined in step 7 plus that determined in step 4 is the total unit stress in the wood at midspan and at the interior supports of continuous spans. This total value may not exceed the allowable unit stress for the lumber grade and species used.

9. Compute the maximum vertical shear adjacent to supports, neglecting the shear due to the dead load of the slab and to uniform or concentrated loads within a distance of 3 times the slab depth from the supports. Concentrated moving loads are placed at 3 times the slab depth or at one-quarter the span from the support, whichever is less, and are distributed over 4 ft for calculating shear.

10. Using the vertical shear from step 9, compute the horizontal shear at mid-depth of the top channels formed by raised laminations. Use the transformed concrete-wood section for areas of positive moment and the transformed steel-wood section for areas of negative moment. This value may not exceed the allowable horizontal shear stress for the lumber grade used.

11. Compute the spacing of shear developers from step 10, or check the adequacy of notches based on the allowable shear for the concrete or the wood. For a dap length equal to $\frac{1}{2}$ the dap spacing, the concrete shear will probably control, and thus it may be desirable to make the dap length about $\frac{1}{3}$ the dap spacing to balance the allowable shear more nearly. If shear developers are employed, the required spacing at the support is generally used as far as the quarter-point of the span and is then increased uniformly to the spacing required (not to exceed 24 in.) by possible vertical shear near midspan.

Example. Design a continuous composite timber-concrete slab deck highway bridge with two 18 ft spans for an H-15 truck loading. The deck is made up of 2×6 and 2×4 mechanically laminated lumber with $4\frac{1}{2}$ in. of concrete slab. Weight of treated lumber = 50 pcf.

Wood	Concrete	Steel
$F_b = 1{,}500$ psi	$F_c' = 3{,}000$ psi	$F_s = 20{,}000$ psi
$F_v = 95$ psi		

1. Compute the dead load

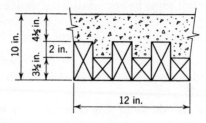

$$\text{Concrete DL} = \frac{5.5}{12}(150) = 69 \text{ psf}$$

$$\text{Wood DL} = \frac{4.5}{12}(50) = 19 \text{ psf}$$

$$\text{DL} = \overline{88 \text{ psf}}$$

2. Compute dead load bending moments.

$$\text{Simple span moment} = \frac{wl^2}{8} = (88)\frac{(18)^2(12)}{8} = 42,800 \text{ in.-lb}$$

Design moments for continuous spans:

$+(0.65)(42,800) = +27,800 \text{ in.-lb}$
$-(0.70)(42,800) = -30,000 \text{ in.-lb}$

3. Determine wood section properties (for a 1 ft section of deck).

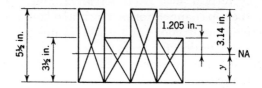

$$y = \frac{(5.5)(5.5/2) + (3.5)(3.5/2)}{(5.5) + (3.5)}$$

$$y = 2.36 \text{ in.}$$

At midspan:

$$I_w = 4\left[\frac{(1.5)(5.5)^3}{12} + (5.5)(1.5)(0.39)^2 + \frac{(1.5)(3.5)^3}{12} + (3.5)(1.5)(0.61)^2\right]$$

$$= 117.4 \text{ in.}^4$$

At interior support: $\frac{2}{3}I_w = (\frac{2}{3})(117.4) = 78.3 \text{ in.}^4$

4. Determine bending stress in wood.

$$f_b = \frac{Mc}{I_w} = \frac{(27,800)(2.36)}{117.4} = 559 \text{ psi at midspan}$$

$$f_b = \frac{Mc}{\frac{2}{3}I_w} = \frac{(30,000)(3.14)}{78.3} = 1,203 \text{ psi at interior support}$$

5. Compute slab bending moments after curing. The load on one rear wheel of an H-15 truck is 12,000 lb. This is distributed over 5 ft.

$$P = \frac{12,000}{5} = 2,400 \text{ lb per 1 ft section}$$

$$\text{Simple span moment} = \frac{Pl}{4} = \frac{(2,400)(18)(12)}{4} = 129,600 \text{ in.-lb}$$

Design moments for continuous spans:

$+ (0.85)(129,600) = + 110,200 \text{ in.-lb}$
$- (0.30)(129,600) = - 38,900 \text{ in.-lb}$

6. Determine composite section properties (for a 1 ft section of deck).

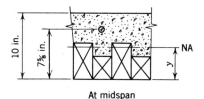

At midspan

#4's @ 9 in. o.c. cont. +
#5's @ 9 in. o.c. over
support

At support

$E_c/E_w = 1$; therefore, section is homogeneous

$$\left. \begin{array}{l} y = \dfrac{10}{2} = 5 \text{ in.} \\[2ex] I_c = \dfrac{(12)(10)^3}{12} = 1,000 \text{ in.}^4 \end{array} \right\} \text{ at midspan}$$

At interior support, assume No. 4 reinforcing bars at 9 in. centers plus No. 5 reinforcing bars at 9 in. centers.

$A_s = 0.68 \text{ in.}^2 \text{ per 1 ft of slab}$

Transformed area $= (A_s)(E_s/E_w) = (0.68)(18.75) = 12.75 \text{ in.}^2$

$$y = \frac{(2/3)(6)(5.5)(5.5/2) + (2/3)(6)(3.5)(3.5/2) + (12.75)(7.625)}{(2/3)(6)(5.5) + (2/3)(6)(3.5) + 12.75}$$

$y = 3.74 \text{ in.}$

Neglect concrete occurring above the NA

$$I_{cs} = \left(\frac{2}{3}\right)\frac{(12)(3.74)^3}{3} + \left(\frac{2}{3}\right)\frac{(6)(1.76)^3}{3} + (12.75)(3.74)^2 = 325 \text{ in.}^4$$

7. Determine bending stresses.

At midspan:

$$f_b = \frac{Mc}{I_c} = \frac{(110,200)(5)}{1,000} = 551 \text{ psi}$$

$$f_c = 1.3 \frac{Mc}{I_c} \left(\frac{E_c}{E_w}\right) = (1.3)(551)(1) = 716 \text{ psi}$$

(30% increase for impact)

At interior support:

$$f_b = \frac{Mc}{I_{cs}} = \frac{(38,900)(1.76)}{325} = 211 \text{ psi}$$

$$f_s = 1.3 \frac{Mc}{I_{cs}} \left(\frac{E_s}{E_w}\right) = (1.3) \frac{(38,900)(3.74)}{325} (18.75) = 10,910 \text{ psi}$$

(30% increase for impact)

8. Combine stresses (all values in psi).

Material		Midspan	Interior Support		
	DL	559	1,203		
Wood	LL	551	211		
	Total	1,110	1,414	< 1,500 psi	O.K.
Concrete		716		< (3,000)(0.4) = 1,200 psi	O.K.
Steel			10,910	< 20,000 psi	O.K.

9. Compute vertical shear.

Placement of load:

$3d = (3)(10) = 30 \text{ in.} \leftarrow \text{controls}$
$\frac{1}{4}l = (\frac{1}{4})(18)(12) = 54 \text{ in.}$

H-15 load is distributed over 4 ft

$$P = 1.3 \frac{12,000}{4} = 3,900 \text{ lb/ft of width}$$

(30% increase for impact)

$$V = P \frac{(L-3d)}{L} = 3,900 \frac{(18-2.5)}{18} = 3,360 \text{ lb}$$

10. Check horizontal shear.

$$f_v = \frac{3V}{2bd} = \frac{(3)(3{,}360)}{(2)(12)(10)} = 42 \text{ psi at midspan} < 95 \text{ psi} \qquad \text{O.K.}$$

$$f_v = \frac{(3)(3{,}360)}{(2)[(2/3)(6)(5.5) + (2/3)(6)(3.5) + 12.75]} = 103 \text{ psi at interior}$$

support > 95 psi.

Shear is based on pieces which are continuous over support. Allowable shear is increased up to 2 times tabulated value when checks on end are restricted (see footnote *h*, Table 2.14).

11. Determine shear developer spacing.

Number of grooves formed by laminations $= n = \frac{12}{2}(1.5) = 4$ per ft of width

Shear per ft of groove $= \dfrac{f_v}{n}$

At midspan: $\dfrac{f_v}{n} = \dfrac{(42)(144)}{4} = 1{,}512$ lb

At interior support: $\dfrac{f_v}{n} = \dfrac{(103)(144)}{4} = 3{,}710$ lb

Value of shear developer $= 1{,}750$ lb; Therefore, spacing at midspan $=$ 13.9 in., at interior support $= 5.6$ in.

Use 5.5 in. spacing from interior support to quarter-point of each span, from quarter-point increase to 14 in. at midspan. Shear developers should be staggered in adjacent laminations.

STRUCTURAL DIAPHRAGMS

Structural diaphragms are relatively thin, usually rectangular, structural elements capable of resisting shear parallel to their edges. A conventional frame roof, wall or floor will normally function as a structural diaphragm with only slight design modification. They may be used as walls in a vertical position, as roofs or floors in a horizontal position, or as roofs pitched or curved to conform with common truss shapes.

The function of the diaphragm is to brace a structure against lateral forces, such as wind or earthquake loads, and to transmit these forces to the other resisting elements of the structure. Figure 4.26 illustrates the distribution of lateral forces acting on a simple structure. The lateral loads produced act on the side walls spanning from foundation to roof. The top of the side wall thereby produces horizontal loads against the roof framing. The roof framing system, a diaphragm, acts as a large plate girder, generally with continuous chords resisting bending moment as flanges, and with the sheathing itself resisting shear forces as the web. The roof framing system

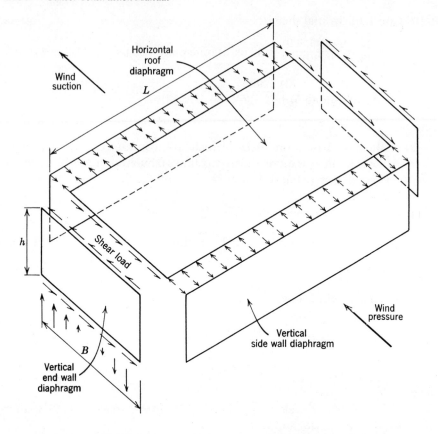

Figure 4.26.   LATERAL FORCES ON A SIMPLE STRUCTURE.

carries the side wall reactions as horizontal loads and spans to the end walls, which cantilever from the foundation to provide the necessary horizontal support.

Common Types

Common types of wood diaphragms are the following:

(*a*) *Transverse*—sheathing consisting of either 1 in. nominal boards or 2 in. nominal thickness lumber, nailed in a single layer at right angles to the direction of cross members, such as joists or studs. This type is suitable when loads are light and when deflection is not important. When used vertically as a wall diaphragm, the load capacity of transverse sheathing is quite low compared to that of other types, and it is recommended that cross bracing be used to increase the strength and stiffness.

(*b*) *Diagonal*— sheathing consisting either of 1 in. nominal thickness boards or 2 in. nominal thickness lumber, nailed at a 45° angle in a single layer to cross members. Considerably greater strength and stiffness result from this placement than when transverse sheathing is used. Tests verify that, although there may be considerable bending in the sheathing, the primary load resistance in an efficient diaphragm is due to the axial stress in the sheathing. The axial stress may be either direct tension or compression. Moment forces are resisted by the continuous chords.

(*c*) *Double diagonal*—consists of two layers of diagonal sheathing, one on top of the other, with the sheathing in one layer at a 90° angle with the sheathing in the other layer. This type is considerably stiffer and stronger than the types (*a*) and (*b*). One layer of sheathing is in axial tension and is counteracted by the other layer, which is in compression; thus, the effects counteract and cancel each other.

(*d*) *Plywood*—consists of sheets of plywood sheathing fastened to cross members usually by means of nails, although sometimes by adhesives. For additional information see *Plywood Diaphragm Construction*, American Plywood Association.

(*e*) *Heavy timber decking*—consists of 3 or 4 in. heavy timber decking covered with plywood sheathing. This type is subject to further testing and study; therefore, design methods for this type are not included herein. However, available test data on this system indicate that it can be designed as equivalent to a blocked plywood diaphragm.

Design procedure. This procedure is based on the assumption that the element has already been designed for gravity loads and, hence, that the size and spacing of framing members and sheathing thickness will have been determined. Location of supports, such as shear walls, in compliance with permissible length-width ratios (see Table 4.21) is also assumed.

1. Calculate lateral loads and shears. Lateral loads and shears may be calculated from the formulas

$$v_1 = \frac{(\text{HL})(h)}{2}$$

$$R_s = \frac{v_1 L}{2}$$

$$v_s = \frac{v_1 L}{2B}$$

where v_1 = lateral load at roof line due to reactions from side wall elements, plf, of length L

R_s = shear reaction at end walls, lb

v_s = unit shear at end walls, plf

HL = lateral load, psf

h = wall height, ft (see Figure 4.26)

L = span between end walls, ft (see Figure 4.26)

B = span between side walls, ft (see Figure 4.26)

2. Determine nailing schedule. The strength and stiffness of diaphragms are determined to a large extent by the adequacy of the nailing of the sheathing to the cross members. See Tables 4.22 and 4.23 for allowable loads on sheathed diaphragms.

(*a*) *Transverse Sheathing.* The strength of transversely sheathed diaphragms depends on the resisting moment furnished by nail couples at each joist or stud crossing (see Figure 4.27).

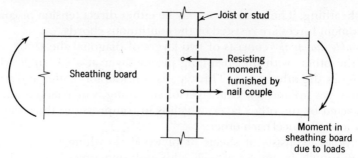

Figure 4.27.   TRANSVERSE SHEATHING.

The resisting moment, m, required to be furnished by the nail couple, may be determined from the formulas

$$m = \frac{v_s j B}{N_B} \qquad \text{for roof diaphragms}$$

$$m = \frac{v_s s h}{N_h} \qquad \text{for wall diaphragms}$$

where j = joist spacing, in.
     s = stud spacing, in.
     N_B = number of sheathing board widths per end wall span, B
     N_h = number of sheathing board widths per wall height, h and other terms are as defined above.

The resisting moment being known, the size and spacing of the nails in the couple can be determined since m equals nail spacing times the allowable lateral load for one nail (see pages **5-64** through **5-71** for data on nails). Since a couple action is required, two, or a multiple of two, nails should be used at each joist or stud crossing.

(*b*) *Diagonal Sheathing.* The axial stresses in diagonal sheathing are greatest at the perimeter of the diaphragm; therefore, nailing at the perimeters must be sufficient to transfer these stresses. Nailing requirements may be determined in the following manner:

$$V' = \frac{v_s b}{\sin 45°} \qquad \text{(for wall diaphragms, use } v_1\text{)}$$

$$t \text{ (or } c) = \frac{V_\parallel}{\sin 45°}$$

where V' = shear per board crossing, lb
     $V_\parallel$ = shear acting parallel to length of perimeter member, lb
     b = width of board, ft
     t = axial tension per board, lb
     c = axial compression per board, lb

t (or c), being known, the number of nails per board can be determined by dividing t (or c) by the allowable lateral load per nail.

(*c*) *Double Diagonal Sheathing.* The shear load along the perimeter members of a double diagonally sheathed diaphragm is divided equally between the two layers, and the shear per board crossing, V', per layer may be computed in the same manner as that for diagonally sheathed diaphragms. The nailing of the bottom layer of sheathing to the perimeter must be sufficient to transfer the sum of the shears per board crossing from both layers to the perimeter member, while the nailing of the top layer to the bottom layer at the perimeter need only be adequate to transfer the shear per board crossing of the top layer to the bottom layer. Nailing area in the perimeter members must be sufficient to accommodate the required number of nails.

(d) *Plywood Sheathing.* The nailing requirements for a horizontal plywood diaphragm are covered in Table 4.19. The requirements for vertical diaphragm nailing are covered in Table 4.20. The plywood layout can be determined from the various cases illustrated in Table 4.19.

3. Determine required sizes of perimeter members.

(a) *Transverse Sheathing.* The perimeter members in this type of diaphragm serve only as boundary pieces.

(b) *Diagonal Sheathing.* As illustrated in Figure 4.28a, the axial stresses in the diagonal sheathing boards introduce bending and axial loads in the end posts. These members must be designed for combined load, using the combined stress formula (see page 4-43).

The effect of bending introduced by the components of the sheathing forces perpendicular to the continuous chords is usually minor, because the joists or studs, with their relatively small spacing, serve to resist these

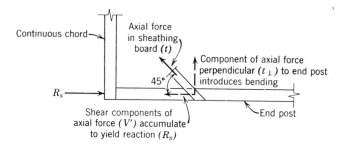

(a) Diagonal sheathing

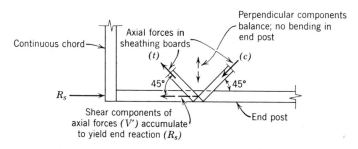

(b) Double diagonal sheathing

Figure 4.28.   DIAGONALLY SHEATHED DIAPHRAGMS.

TABLE 4.19

RECOMMENDED SHEAR IN POUNDS PER FOOT FOR HORIZONTAL PLYWOOD DIAPHRAGMS[a]
FOR WIND OR SEISMIC LOADING

(plywood and framing assumed already designed for perpendicular loads)

Plywood Grade[d]	Common Nail Size	Minimum Nail Penetration in Framing, in.	Minimum Nominal Plywood Thickness, in.	Minimum Nominal Width of Framing Member, in.	Blocked Diaphragms				Unblocked Diaphragms	
					Nail Spacing at Diaphragm Boundaries (All Cases) and Continuous Panel Edges Parallel to Load, in. (Cases 3 and 4)[b]				Nails Spaced 6 in. Max. at Supported Edges[b]	
					6	4	2½	2	Load Perpendicular to Unblocked Edges and Continuous Panel Joints (Case 1)	All Other Configurations (Cases 2, 3 and 4)
					Nail Spacing at Other Plywood Panel Edges, in.					
					6	6	4	3		
Structural I INT-DFPA or EXT-DFPA	6d	$1\frac{1}{4}$	$\frac{5}{16}$	2	185	250	375	420	165	125
				3	210	280	420	475	185	140
	8d	$1\frac{1}{2}$	$\frac{3}{8}$	2	270	360	530	600	240	180
				3	300	400	600	675	265	200
	10d	$1\frac{5}{8}$	$\frac{1}{2}$	2	320	425	640[c]	730[c]	285	215
				3	360	480	720	820	320	240

			$\frac{5}{16}$	2	170	225	335	380	150	110
				3	190	250	380	430	170	125
	6d	$1\frac{1}{4}$	$\frac{3}{8}$	2	185	250	375	420	165	125
				3	210	280	420	475	185	140
C–C EXT-DFPA Structural II INT-DFPA, Standard *C–D* INT-DFPA, sheathing and other DFPA grades except Species Group 5	8d	$1\frac{1}{2}$	$\frac{3}{8}$	2	240	320	480	545	215	160
				3	270	360	540	610	240	180
			$\frac{1}{2}$	2	270	360	530	600	240	180
				3	300	400	600	675	265	200
	10d	$1\frac{5}{8}$	$\frac{1}{2}$	2	290	385	575[c]	655[c]	255	190
				3	325	430	650	735	290	215
			$\frac{5}{8}$	2	320	425	640[c]	730[c]	285	215
				3	360	480	720	820	320	240

[a]From *Plywood Diaphragm Construction*, American Plywood Association.
[b]Space nails 12 in. on center along intermediate framing members.
[c]Reduce tabulated allowable shears 10 percent when boundary members consist of a single 2 in. lumber piece.
[d]All recommendations based on the use of DFPA grade-trademarked plywood.
Notes: Design for diaphragm stresses depends on direction of continuous panel joints with reference to load, not on direction of long dimensions of plywood sheet. Continuous framing may be in either direction for blocked diaphragms.

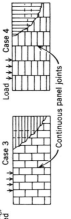

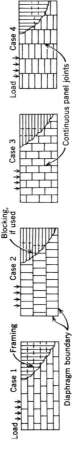

Load
Case 1
Framing
Case 2
Blocking, if used
Case 3
Load
Case 4
Diaphragm boundary
Continuous panel joints

TABLE 4.20

RECOMMENDED SHEAR IN POUNDS PER FOOT FOR PLYWOOD SHEAR WALLS[a] FOR WIND OR SEISMIC LOADING[b]

Plywood Grade	Minimum Nominal Plywood Thickness, in.	Minimum Nail Penetration, in Framing, in.	Plywood Applied Direct to Framing						Plywood Applied Over ½ in. Gypsum Sheathing					
			Nail Size (Common or Galvanized Box)	Nail Spacing at Plywood Panel Edges, in.				Nail Size (Common or Galvanized Box)	Nail Spacing at Plywood Panel Edges				
				6	4	2½	2		6	4	2½	2	
Structural I INT-DFPA or EXT-DFPA	5/16 or ¼	1¼	6d	200	300	450	510	8d	200	300	450	510	
	3/8	1½	8d	280	430	640	730	10d	280	430	640	730	
	½	1⅝	10d	340	510	770	870	—	—	—	—	—	
C-C EXT-DFPA Standard C-D INT-DFPA DFPA Panel siding and other DFPA grades[d]	5/16 or ¼[c]	1¼	6d	180	270	400	450	8d	180	270	400	450	
	3/8	1½	8d	260	380	570	640	10d	260	380	570	640	
	½	1⅝	10d	310	460	690	770	—	—	—	—	—	

DFPA plywood panel siding[d]	$\frac{5}{16}$[c]	$1\frac{1}{4}$	Nail Size (Galvanized Casing) 6d	140	210	320	360	Nail Size (Galvanized Casing) 8d	140	210	320	360
	$\frac{3}{8}$	$1\frac{1}{2}$	8d	160	240	360	410	10d	160	240	360	410

[a]From *Plywood Diaphragm Construction*, American Plywood Association.

[b]All panel edges backed with 2 in. nominal or wider framing. Plywood installed either horizontally or vertically. Space nails at 12 in. on center along intermediate framing members.

[c]$\frac{3}{8}$ in. minimum recommended when applied direct to framing as exterior siding.

[d]Except Group 5 species.

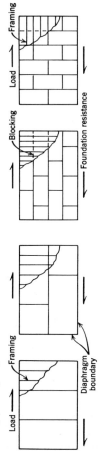

components. Tests and experience have indicated that an arbitrary but satisfactory design procedure is:

For $v_s < 300$ plf and diaphragms proportioned as noted in Table 4.21, neglect the forces acting perpendicular to the continuous chord.

TABLE 4.21

SIZE RATIOS FOR
LUMBER SHEATHED DIAPHRAGMS[a]

Type of Sheathing	Maximum Span-Width Ratios for Horizontal Diaphragms		Maximum Height-Width Ratios for Vertical Diaphragms
	Restraining Masonry or Concrete Walls	Restraining Wood or Similar Walls	
Transverse	Not recommended	Limited by acceptable deflection of walls	Limited by acceptable deflection
Diagonal	3 : 1	4 : 1	2 : 1
Double diagonal	Limited by acceptable deflection of walls		Limited by acceptable deflection

[a]Source: *Western Woods Use Book*, copyright 1973 by Western Wood Products Association.

For 300 plf $< v_s < 800$ plf, use a perpendicular force varying lineally from 150 plf for $v_s = 300$ plf to 800 plf for $v_s = 800$ plf.

For $v_s > 800$ plf, use a perpendicular force equal to the actual value of v_s. Continuous chords designed by this procedure should be designed for combined loading for shear loads over 300 plf. The normal axial loading not resulting from diaphragm loading should also be considered in the design for combined loading.

(c) *Double Diagonal Sheathing.* As illustrated in Figure 4.28b, the axial stresses in the two layers of sheathing counteract and cancel each other; thus, no bending is introduced and the perimeter members are designed for axial loads.

(d) *Plywood Sheathing.* No bending is introduced in end posts, and the continuous chords are designed for axial tension or compression load, P, caused by the maximum bending moment in the diaphragm, that is,

$$P = \frac{(v_1 \text{ or } v_s)L^2}{8B}$$

where terms are defined as above.

4. Determine diaphragm deflection. The loads on a roof cause it to deflect, thereby allowing the walls to deflect. Assuming the wall to be fixed at the base, the maximum allowable deflection, Δ_A, at the top of a masonry or concrete wall supporting a lumber sheathed diaphragm can be deter-

mined by the formula

$$\Delta_A = \frac{96h^2F}{Ed}$$

where Δ_A = deflection, in.
  h = wall height, ft
  F = allowable unit bending stress of the wall material, psi
  E = modulus of elasticity of wall material, psi
  d = wall thickness, in.

Note: For values of F and E for masonry walls, see *Building Code Requirements for Engineered Brick Masonry*, Brick Institute of America.

For plywood sheathed roof diaphragms, assuming that all panel edges are blocked, the actual deflection at the center of a diaphragm, Δ_a, in in., can be calculated from the formula

$$\Delta_a = \frac{5v_sl^3}{8EAb} + \frac{v_sL}{4Gt} + 0.094Le_n + \frac{\Delta_cX}{2b}$$

where E = modulus of elasticity of continuous chord, psi
  A = cross-sectional area of chord, in.^{2}
  G = modulus of rigidity of plywood, psi ($E/20$ for panels with exterior glue)
  t = effective plywood thickness for shear, in.
  e_n = nail deformation from Figure 4.29, in., at calculated load per nail, which is equal to the shear per foot, v_s, divided by the number of nails per foot
  Δ_cX = sum of individual chord-splice slip values each multiplied by its distance to nearest support. The constant 0.094 in the third term applies only if the nailing is uniform throughout the diaphragm, so that the load per nail varies lineally from zero at midspan of the diaphragm to the value used in Figure 4.24 at the end wall.
  b = diaphragm width, ft

and other terms are as previously defined.

The first part of this equation comes from the simple bending deflection; the second fraction represents the shear deflection; the third gives deflection due to nail slip; and the fourth yields deflection due to slip in chord splices. In rare cases end-wall deflection may be significant. It should then be added.

TABLE 4.22

ALLOWABLE SHEARS FOR
LUMBER SHEATHED DIAPHRAGMS[a]

A. Transversely Sheathed Diaphragms				
Nominal Width of Sheathing Lumber, in.	Number of 8d Common Nails per Board per Crossing of Framing Member and at Butted Ends	Allowable Shear, plf		
		Framing Member Spacing		
		12 in.	16 in.	24 in.
6	2	85	65	45
8	2	100	75	50
10	2	105	80	55

B. Diagonally Sheathed Diaphragms			
Nominal Width of Sheathing Lumber, in.	Number of 8d Common Nails per Board per Crossing		Allowable Shear, plf
	Perimeter Members and Butted Ends of Boards	Stud or Joist	
6	2	2	290
8	2	2	220
	3	2	320

C. Diagonal Sheathing — Special Perimeter Framing[b]		
Nominal Width of Sheathing Lumber, in.	Number of 8d Common Nails per Board at Perimeter Members[c]	Allowable Shear, plf
6	3	440
	4	590
	5	740
	6	880
	7	1,030
	8	1,180
8	4	430
	5	540
	6	650
	7	760
	8	870

[a]Source: *Western Woods Use Book*, copyright 1973 by Western Wood Products Association.
[b]Perimeter members designed to resist axial and bending stresses as described in design procedure.
[c]Nailing at butted ends of boards to be 75% of perimeter nailing with a minimum of 3 nails. Use minimum of 3 nails per stud or joist crossing. Preboring of nail holes may be necessary to prevent splitting.

TABLE 4.22 (Continued)

D. Double Diagonal Sheathing[d]			
Nominal Width of Sheathing Lumber, in.	Number of 8d Common Nails per Board at Perimeter Members[c]		Allowable Shear, plf
	Bottom Layer	Top Layer	
6	2	2	420
	3	3	620
	4	3	830
	5	4	1,040
	6	5	1,250
	7	5	1,460
	8	6	1,670
	9	7	1,880
8	3	3	460
	4	3	610
	5	4	760
	6	5	920
	7	5	1,070
	8	6	1,220
	9	7	1,380

[d]Perimeter members designed to resist axial stresses as described in design procedure.

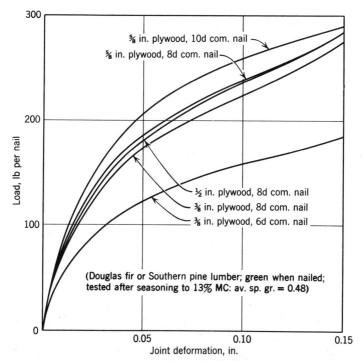

Figure 4.29. LATERAL BEARING STRENGTH OF PLYWOOD.

5. Diaphragm anchorage. The anchorage of the diaphragm along its edges must be adequate to resist shear forces. Particular attention should be paid to the anchorage of the bases of vertical (wall) diaphragms.

Splices

When it is not practical to provide a continuous perimeter member, continuity must be provided by means of splices. Splices should be located, if possible, where bending stresses in the perimeter members are low. Any fastening method may be used for splicing if it is adequate to meet joint load requirements and if end distance, edge distance, and spacing requirements are met.

Perimeter Member Connections

The corner connections between end posts and continuous chords must be adequate to prevent separation due to the loads carried by each of the members. For shear loads over 300 plf, corner connections should be reinforced by bolting steel angles or wood blocking in the corners.

Openings in Diaphragms

Openings, such as skylights or windows, decrease the sheathing area of a diaphragm and increase the shear stress in the remainder of the sheathing. Perimeter members must be provided around such openings, and nailing schedules are determined by shear loads as for other perimeter members. If necessary, these members can be doubled to accommodate stresses.

Pitched and Curved Diaphragms

The following considerations apply to roof diaphragms used on trusses or other pitched or curved structural members whereby the diaphragm is either pitched or curved.

Pitched diaphragms

Lateral forces are transferred to each "bent" by the girts. The load from the girts is then transmitted to the diaphragm through the truss (or other member) and the blocking between the truss and the sheathing. The girt load is delivered in the plane of the diaphragm. (See Figure 4.30.)

The shear load per bent, v_b, in the diaphragm on either side of the ridge may be determined by the formula

$$v_b = \frac{2v_1 L'}{B}$$

where L' = bent spacing, ft

and other terms are as previously defined.

In the case of fully active diaphragms, such as double diagonally sheathed or plywood sheathed, there are no stresses at the ridge except for the transfer of horizontal shear from the diaphragm on one side of the ridge to that on the other side. In the case of single diagonally sheathed diaphragms, boundary stresses are introduced into the ridge member by one of two possible methods. (See Figure 4.30.)

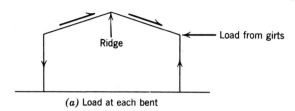

(a) Load at each bent

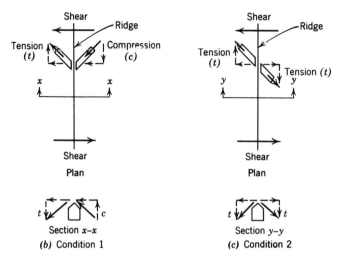

Plan

(b) Condition 1   *(c)* Condition 2

Figure 4.30. PITCHED DIAPHRAGMS.

If condition 1 of Figure 4.30 exists, the plan view shows that the components of force parallel to the ridge cancel each other, and the section view shows that the vertical components cancel each other. However, in plan it can also be seen that the horizontal components acting perpendicular to the ridge are additive and introduce a horizontal bending force in the ridge member. The ridge member must be designed for this force, which is equal to twice the bending force as indicated in Figure 4.28a, and the ends of the ridge member must be adequately fastened to the truss (or other member) to resist this force.

If condition 2 of Figure 4.30 exists, the plan view shows that forces both parallel and perpendicular to the ridge cancel each other; the section view, however, shows that the vertical components are additive, causing a vertical bending force in the ridge member which must be considered in designing that member.

A common form of pitched diaphragm is a plywood folded plate. The design of plywood folded plates has developed from diaphragm analysis; for more details, see *Plywood Folded Plate Design and Details*, American Plywood Association.

Curved diaphragms

As in pitched diaphragms, lateral loads are transferred into the curved plane of the diaphragm by the trusses (or other curved structural members). In the case of fully active diaphragms, such as double diagonally sheathed or plywood sheathed, no bending stresses are introduced into the truss (or other member) or purlins. In the case of single diagonally sheathed diaphragms, the tension or compression stress in the sheathing lumber introduces a bending force into the purlins. This force is usually quite small, however, and in most cases does not control the design of the purlins.

Preframed Panels

Preframed panels are frequently used in diaphragm construction. In such panels, plywood roof sheathing is fastened to solid sawn purlins for spans ranging from 8 to about 20 ft. These panels are then usually placed on glued laminated beams. Design of diaphragms using such panels need not differ from other diaphragm design.

STRESSED-SKIN PANELS

Plywood stressed-skin panels consist of plywood sheets glued to the top, and usually also to the bottom, of longitudinal framing members (stringers), so that the assembly will act integrally in resisting bending stresses (see Figure 4.31). These flat panels using stressed plywood skins and spaced

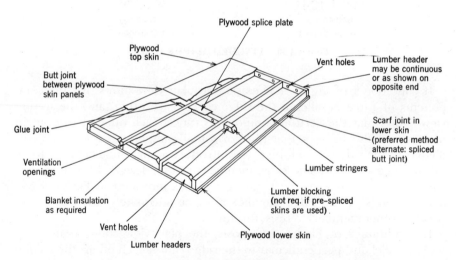

Figure 4.31.   **TYPICAL TWO-SIDED STRESSED-SKIN PANEL.**

lumber stringers act like a series of built-up I-beams, with the plywood skins taking most of the moment stresses as well as performing a sheathing function, while the lumber stringers take shear stresses. These panels are commonly used in floors, roofs, and walls.

General Concepts

Since stressed-skin panels are usually relatively shallow, any shear deformation between skins and webs would contribute materially to vertical deflection. For maximum stiffness, therefore, a rigid connection is required between the plywood and the lumber. Thus, all panels considered in this design method are assumed to be assembled with glue.

Although it is possible to use laminated or scarf-jointed members for the stringers of stressed-skin panels, such panels are usually restricted to single-lamination stringers. Their maximum length, therefore, is generally determined by the maximum length of lumber available.

Headers (at the ends of the panel) and blocking (within the panel) serve to align the stringers, back up splice plates, support skin edges, and help to distribute concentrated loads. They may be omitted in some cases, but should always be used when stressed-skin panels are applied with their stringers horizontal on a sloping roof. Without headers and blocking, panels so applied would tend to assume a parallelogram cross section.

Two-sided panels do not require bridging. Stringers in one-sided panels may be bridged as are joists of the same depth in conventional construction.

Owing to the high strength of plywood, calculations will often indicate that a thin bottom skin is structurally sufficient. There is some possibility, however, of a slight bow when $\frac{1}{4}$ in. bottom skins are used with face grain parallel to stringers on 16 in. centers. Such a bow, although of no importance structurally, may be undesirable from an appearance standpoint. For stringers so spaced, therefore, $\frac{5}{16}$-in. plywood should be a minimum if appearance is a factor.

Panels with both top and bottom skins are most common. One-sided panels are also popular, especially when special ceiling treatment is desired—or when no ceiling is required. A variation of the single-skin panel, with lumber strips on the bottom of the joists, is called a "T-flange" panel.

A number of decorative plywood surfaces are adaptable for panels where the bottom skin will serve as a ceiling for a habitable room. The design of panels using such decorative plywood must, of course, allow for the special properties of the product.

Design procedure. For stressed-skin panel with top and bottom covers. (The design of a single-cover panel is similar.)

1. Assume a trial section. Since plywood is usually manufactured in 48 in. widths, this is the common width to use in stressed-skin panel design.

2. Determine the basic spacing, B, for top and bottom covers from the following table:
The B distance represents the amount of the skin that may be considered to act in conjunction with the framing members.

3. Locate the neutral axis of the entire section for deflection by taking moments about some convenient point. If the plywood and framing members have different modulus of elasticity values, the transformed-area method should be used. Consider only plies parallel to longitudinal members. See Table 4.14 for moments of inertia of selected plywood constructions.

4. Determine the EI_g value of the entire section, where E is the modulus of elasticity, psi, and I_g is the moment of inertia, in.^{4}, considering only the material used in locating the neutral axis in step 3.

Basic Spacing, *B*, For Various Plywood Thicknesses

Plywood Thickness, in.	Basic Spacing, *B*, in.	
	Face Grain ∥ to Stringers	Face Grain ⊥ to Stringers
$\frac{1}{4}$ sanded	10.3	11.6
$\frac{5}{16}$ unsanded	11.9	16.8
$\frac{3}{8}$ unsanded (3-ply)	14.2	20.1
$\frac{3}{8}$ sanded (3-ply)	16.4	16.4
$\frac{3}{8}$ sanded (5-ply)	18.1	20.2
$\frac{1}{2}$ unsanded and sanded[a]	23.2	28.5
$\frac{5}{8}$ unsanded and sanded	29.1	35.6
$\frac{3}{4}$ unsanded and sanded (5-ply and 7-ply)	38.2	38.2
$\frac{7}{8}$ unsanded and sanded	41.6	48.1
1 unsanded	45.5	58.9
1 sanded	54.5	47.9
$1\frac{1}{8}$ 2.4.1	53.4	57.3

[a]Use only 5-ply panels

5. Determine allowable load, w_Δ (in psf), based on deflection, and using the formula

$$w_\Delta = \frac{1}{CL\left[\dfrac{7.5L^2}{EI_g} + \dfrac{0.6}{AG}\right]}$$

where w_Δ = allowable load* based on deflection, psf
$\quad C$ = factor for allowable deflection, usually 360 for floors, 240 for roofs
$\quad L$ = span length, ft
$\quad EI_g$ = stiffness factor determined in step 4 for a panel 4 ft wide, psi
$\quad A$ = actual total cross-sectional area of all stringers, in.²
$\quad G$ = modulus of rigidity of stringers, psi. *G* may be taken as 0.06 of the modulus of elasticity of the stringers.

This value must be greater than the total design load, TL, for the panel.
6. Check top skin deflection, Δ_a, using one of the following formulas

$$\Delta_a = \frac{(\text{TL})l_s^4}{384EI(12)} = \frac{(\text{TL})l_s^4}{4,608EI} \quad \text{for two-sided panels}$$

$$\Delta_a = \frac{4(\text{TL})l_s^4}{581EI(12)} = \frac{(\text{TL})l_s^4}{1,743EI} \quad \text{for one-sided panels with four stringers}$$

*If the allowable deflection factor, *C*, is based on live load only, this equation will yield allowable live load, to which dead load may be added.

where TL = total design load, psf
l_s = clear distance between stringers, in.
I = moment of inertia (in direction perpendicular to the stringers) of 1 ft width of top skin, in.[4]
E = modulus of elasticity for top skin, psi

This value may not exceed the allowable deflection limit for the application.

7. Locate the neutral axis for the bending moment, using the effective skin widths based on the basic spacing, B. (That is, for calculating neutral axis and moment of inertia, consider only the part of the skin within $B/2$ each side of each stringer.) Consider only plies parallel to longitudinal members (see Table 4.14).

8. Determine the EI_n value, using the same material as in locating the neutral axis in step 7.

9. Determine allowable stresses, in both tension and compression, for the grade of plywood used (from Table 4.13), if the clear distance between framing members is less than or equal to $B/2$. If the clear distance is greater than $B/2$, reduce the stresses in bending and in compression parallel, but not in rolling shear, proportionally from 100% at $B/2$ to 67% at B, with no further reduction up to a spacing of $2B$.

10. Determine allowable load, w_M (in psf), in bending, using the formula

$$w_M = \frac{F(EI_n)}{6nL^2E}$$

where F = allowable stress of plywood, psi (either tension or compression)
EI_n = stiffness factor for bending as computed in step 8, psi
E = modulus of elasticity for skin being considered, psi
n = distance from neutral axis to extreme fiber, in. (either tension or compression)
L = span length, ft

The load must be figured for both the top and the bottom skin, and the lower value must be greater than the total design load, TL, for the panel.

11. Determine the allowable load, w_R (in psf), based on rolling shear, using the formula

$$w_R = \frac{(EI_g) \, \Sigma \, F_s b}{2QL}$$

where EI_g = stiffness factor for a panel 4 ft wide, in.[4]
$\Sigma F_s b$ = sum of the glue-line widths over each stringer, each multiplied by its applicable allowable rolling shear stress for the plywood (see Table 4.13), pli
Q = statical moment of the parallel plies outside of the critical rolling shear plane (see below) for a panel 4 ft wide, in.[3]
L = span length, ft
E = modulus of elasticity of thicker skin, psi

This value must be greater than the total design load, TL, for the panel.

The critical rolling shear plane lies within the plywood, between the inner parallel ply and the adjacent perpendicular ply, when the plywood skin has its face grain parallel to the longitudinal framing members, as it usually does. When the face grain of the skin is perpendicular to the framing members, the critical rolling shear plane lies between the inner perpendicular ply and the framing member.

12. Determine the allowable load, w_v (in psf), based on horizontal shear, using the formula

$$w_v = \frac{(EI_g)F_v \Sigma b}{2QL\,E_{st}}$$

where F_v = allowable horizontal shear stress for the framing members, psi
  Σb = sum of stringer widths for the panel, in.
  E_{st} = modulus of elasticity of stringer, psi

and other terms are as previously defined.

This value must be greater than the total design load, TL., for the panel.

For more detailed design information related to either flat plywood stressed-skin panels, or flat plywood sandwich panels, see *Plywood Design Specifications*, Supplements No. 3 and No. 4 respectively, American Plywood Association.

HYPERBOLIC PARABOLOID SHELLS

Hyperbolic paraboloid shells may consist of glued laminated or sawn timber perimeter members with lumber or plywood sheathing placed on top or bottom, or sandwiched into the perimeter members. Design of shells with lumber sheathing is covered here; for design of plywood shells, contact the American Plywood Association. The curve of the sheathing is a convex parabola when viewed parallel to one axis drawn through opposite corners, and a concave parabola when viewed from an axis 90° to the first. Curves formed by the intersection of the surface of the shell with a horizontal plane are hyperbolic. The horizontal projection of such a shell may be square or diamond-shaped with the four sides of equal length. When a roof structure consists of a number of hyperbolic paraboloids, the horizontal projection of an individual shell may be rectangular in shape with adjacent sides of unequal length. In elevation, the opposite corners are elevated an equal distance above the other two. (See Figure 4.32.)

As a hyperbolic paraboloid shell becomes flatter, it becomes more flexible, with an increasing tendency toward buckling. For this reason, it is desirable to place a limitation on the flatness, which can be expressed as the ratio of the rise to the length of a side. A minimum ratio of rise to length of side of 1 to 5 is suggested.

The following procedure may be followed in designing simple hyperbolic paraboloid shell structures.

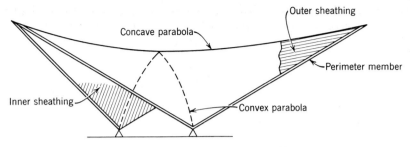

Figure 4.32.   HYPERBOLIC PARABOLOID SHELL.

Design Procedure.

1. Determine forces and loads. The principal forces to be considered in the design of a hyperbolic paraboloid shell are the reactions, the forces in the perimeter members, the shear forces at the junction of the sheathing and the perimeter members, and the direct tensile and compression forces in the sheathing. These forces are easily determined by statics, and the simplest method of computing the forces is to resolve the reactions into component forces in the surface and the perimeter members. Once the forces have been determined, the member sizes and connections are designed by standard engineering procedures. The method of analysis described here can also be applied to a series of hyperbolic paraboloid shells.

Because of curvature, the dead load is not uniform over the projected area, and the variance increases as the rise increases. However, for hyperbolic paraboloid shells built of lumber, the dead load is likely to be very small compared to the applied loads, and the nonuniform distribution of the dead load is, therefore, usually neglected.

Unsymmetrical concentrated loads or unbalanced loads could cause the structure to tip unless it is restrained by one of the following means:

(*a*) A tension tie or strut from foundation to each high point (wall framing may be designed to serve this purpose).

(*b*) A combination tension and compression member to one high point.

(*c*) Connections at the two principal points of support especially designed to resist rotation.

(*d*) Multiple hyperbolic paraboloid structures, interconnected at their adjacent high points.

Restraint of the high points that prevents normal deflection of the shell under applied loads will cause secondary stresses in the structure; however, the load and, therefore, the deflection at the high points is very small. It is suggested that these secondary stresses be neglected, since the unit stresses in the shell are normally very low.

Because wind loads, snow loads, and certain live loads are normally unbalanced as they occur on structures, the restraint against tipping must be provided even though the design assumes balanced loading. Because the dead weight of the structure is small, the structure should be well tied down during erection to resist wind forces.

For balanced loads, the vertical reactions, R_V, are equal to one-half the sum of the vertical loads. For the conditions and notations shown in Figure 4.33, horizontal thrust, R_H, is determined by the formula

$$R_H = \frac{R_V L}{2h}$$

where h = height at high point, ft
$\quad\;\; L$ = span, support-to-support, ft

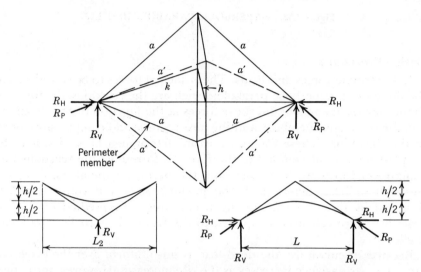

Figure 4.33. HYPERBOLIC PARABOLOID SHELL REACTIONS.

The resultant, R_P, of the vertical reaction, R_V, and of the horizontal thrust, R_H, is determined by the formula

$$R_P = \frac{R_V k}{h}$$

where k = inclined distance from support to midpoint of transverse axis, ft.

2. Determine the size of perimeter members. The perimeter members transfer all loads to the bearing points and must have a cross-sectional area sufficient to resist axial forces. When the supports are at the low points, as in Figures 4.32 and 4.33, these axial forces are compressive; when the supports are at the high points, the axial forces are tensile. For the condition in Figure 4.33 this compressive force, P, is found by the formula

$$P = \frac{R_V a}{2h}$$

where a = length of side, ft.

There is a shearing force along the length of the perimeter members at their junction with the sheathing. This boundary shear per lineal foot, v, is determined by the formula

$$v = \frac{P}{A}$$

The boundary shear is transferred from the sheathing to the perimeter members by means of the fasteners used to connect them. In this respect, the design of the perimeter connections is the same as for lumber sheathed diaphragms. Structural diaphragm design considerations may be found in this *Manual*, beginning on page 4-133. As the boundary shear forces are distributed uniformly along the length of the perimeter members, the compressive force in the perimeter members varies as a cumulative sum of the boundary shear from zero at the high point to a maximum at the supports. The perimeter members can be tapered, if desired, to meet this varying condition.

The sheathing provides lateral restraint to the perimeter members in the direction parallel to the plane of the sheathing. In the direction perpendicular to the plane of the sheathing, the perimeter members receive no lateral support, and the slenderness ratio related to this plane must be considered. As the compressive force varies uniformly from zero at the peak to a maximum at the support, the perimeter members are considered as a series of columns varying from a long column with no load to a short column with maximum load. At any point along the length, the induced stress in compression parallel to grain resulting from the accumulated load must not exceed the allowable unit stress as determined by the standard column formula for a column length equal to the distance from the support to the point being considered.

If the sheathing is placed on the top or bottom of the perimeter members, the boundary shear forces cause bending stresses in the perimeter members due to eccentricity; hence, the perimeter members are subjected to combined bending and axial compression or tension stresses (see page 4-137) and must be designed accordingly. If the sheathing is sandwiched into the perimeter members with half above and half below, there is no eccentricity and the perimeter members are subjected to axial compression or tension only.

Because a hyperbolic paraboloid shell has a doubly curved surface, the slope of the sheathing at the junction with the perimeter members is constantly and uniformly changing along the length of the perimeter members. As the surface of the perimeter members must be tangent to the sheathing where they connect, the contacting face of the perimeter members must be shaped appropriately. If the perimeter members are glued laminated members, the changing slope can be obtained by building a twist into the whole member. The total change in slope or rotation of the contact surface of the perimeter member, from one end to the other, is the total angle of twist. As the ratio of the rise to the length of the perimeter member increases, the angle of rotation also increases. The procedure for computing the angle of twist is applicable to hyperbolic paraboloids having either square or diamond-shaped horizontal projections.

Using the midpoint of the length of a perimeter member as a convenient reference and considering the twist at this point to be zero, the angle of twist from the reference point to either end of the perimeter member, as shown in Figure 4.34, can be determined from the formula

$$\theta = \arctan \frac{ha}{(a')^2 \cos(ABC)}$$

where angles *ABC* and θ are the angles shown in Figure 4.34, and $a' =$ horizontal projection of length a, ft. When the horizontal projection of the hyperbolic paraboloid is square, the angle *ABC* becomes zero. The total angle of twist from one end of the perimeter member with respect to the other is twice the angle determined from the preceding formula.

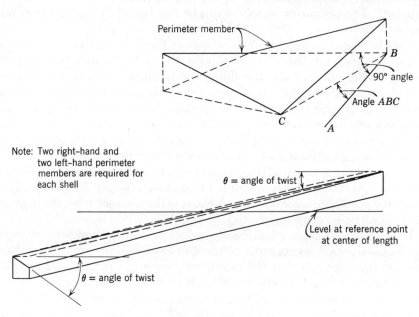

Figure 4.34.   **TWIST OF PERIMETER MEMBERS.**

3. Determine the stress in the sheathing. The sheathing resists the principal tension and compression forces parallel to the longitudinal and transverse axes. As the unit stresses in the sheathing are generally quite low, 1 in. nominal thickness lumber can be used for the sheathing material. Lumber sheathing may be applied to hyperbolic paraboloid shells in either of two ways:

(a) One layer of sheathing boards placed parallel to the transverse axis with either piece bowed to fit the curve of the convex parabola, and a second layer placed parallel to the longitudinal axis with pieces bowed to fit the concave parabola.

(b) One layer of sheathing boards placed parallel to two opposite sides of the structure, and a second layer placed parallel to the other two sides. In this system, each sheathing board twists slightly. The total amount of twist from perimeter member to perimeter member depends on their slope.

If the horizontal projection of the shell is square, the layers of roof sheathing are at right angles to each other for both systems of placement. If the horizontal projection of the structure is a diamond, the double layer of sheathing boards placed by system (a) will be at right angles to each other. When the double layer of boards is placed by system (b), the angle between layers of boards will depend on the angles between perimeter members.

Because there is a slope, but no curvature, to a series of straight lines from one edge to an opposite edge and parallel to a side of a hyperbolic paraboloid shell, falsework placed in this manner will generate the doubly curved surface and will serve as support for placement of the sheathing.

The first system of placing sheathing boards (a) is advantageous because the principal tension and compression forces in the sheathing act in a direction parallel to the grain, thus providing the most efficient use of the sheathing. For small shells, the second system (b) can be used to advantage, as the sheathing boards do not curve and have only a slight twist from end to end. This system has one disadvantage; the joints between constant width sheathing boards would leave gaps varying in width from a maximum at the ends to no gap at the midpoint. If such gaps are undesirable, the sheathing boards may be tapered to fit snugly.

Since the stresses in the sheathing result in boundary shears along the perimeters, the boundary shears can, conversely, be resolved to determine the stresses in the sheathing. The principal forces in the shell are tensile forces, t, parallel to the direction of the concave parabolas, and compressive forces, p, parallel to the direction of the convex parabolas (see Figure 4.35). When the horizontal projection is diamond-shaped, the principal tension and compression forces parallel to the longitudinal and transverse axes can be resolved by proportion by using the formulas

$$t = \frac{L_1 v}{2a'} \quad \text{and} \quad p = \frac{L_2 v}{2a'}$$

where t = principal tensile force in sheathing, lb per ft of width
L_1 = length along longitudinal axis, ft
p = principal compressive force in sheathing, lb per ft of width
L_2 = length along transverse axis, ft

When the horizontal projection of a hyperbolic paraboloid is square in shape, the principal tension and compression forces per foot of width are equal in magnitude to the boundary shear forces per foot of length, v, of perimeter members.

The unit tensile stress in the sheathing lumber is equal to the principal tension force, t, per inch of width divided by the thickness, in inches, of the sheathing which parallels the longitudinal axis. The unit compressive stress in the sheathing which acts at 90° to the tensile stress is equal to the principal compressive force, p, per inch of width divided by the thickness, in inches, of the sheathing paralleling the transverse axis.

The component of the compressive stress normal to the perimeter member exerts an outward thrust on the perimeter member, and the com-

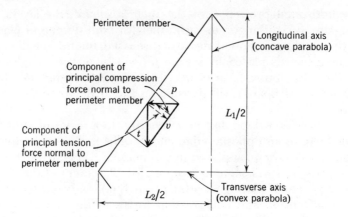

Figure 4.35.   PORTION OF HORIZONTAL PROJECTION.

ponent of the tensile stress normal to the perimeter member exerts an inward pull on the perimeter members. These components, being equal and opposite in direction, as can be seen in Figure 4.35, will cancel each other with the result that the perimeter members are subjected only to axial compression forces.

With the sheathing placed in the directions parallel to the longitudinal and transverse axes of the hyperbolic paraboloid shell, each layer acts independently, the layer parallel to the longitudinal axis transmitting the principal tensile forces to the perimeter members and the layer parallel to the transverse axis transmitting the principal compression forces to the perimeter members. Nailing or stapling the layers together, although not required for strength, is required to prevent buckling of the compression layer and imparts additional stiffness to the shell by providing interaction between the layers. Where butt joints occur in the sheathing, additional fastenings should be used to transfer the forces across the joint. If the underside of the sheathing is left exposed to serve as the finished ceiling, the nails or staples should be of a length that will not penetrate completely through the bottom layer of sheathing. They should be of a diameter large enough, however, to develop the required lateral and withdrawal resistance.

When the sheathing layers are placed with the boards parallel to the sides of the structure, each layer of boards is at an angle to the direction of the principal tension and compression forces and each layer resists a portion of the principal tension force and a portion of the principal compression force. As the joints between adjacent boards in a layer represent a discontinuity, these forces have to be transferred across the joints through the adjacent layer by means of the fastenings connecting the layers. This results in a shear between the two sheathing layers which must be resisted by the fastenings. The shear force is equal in magnitude to the boundary shear stress per unit of length, which can be converted to a shear stress per unit of surface area.

Light concentrated loads produce localized membrane stresses and tend to cause local buckling in the vicinity of the load. These effects can be ignored in design, since they dissipate rapidly a short distance away from the load. Also, the unit stresses in these shells from the usual loadings are quite low.

DESIGN CONSIDERATIONS

Deflection and Camber

The following deflection and camber recommendations apply only to beams.

Deflection

A member of given span and stiffness will deflect, on application of load, in direct proportion to the load applied and by an amount approximating that computed by standard engineering formulas. Table 4.23 may be used to simplify the calculation of the deflection of beams under more than one type of loading by combining the formulas as given in the table for the various types of loading. The following examples illustrate the use of Table 4.23. (See pages **6**-21 through **6**-61 for other deflection formulas.)

Example A. Determine maximum deflection.

$$\Delta_{P\max} = \frac{Pa^2}{6EI}(3l - a)$$

$$\Delta_{w\max} = \frac{wl^4}{8EI}$$

$$\Delta_{\max} = \Delta_{P\max} + \Delta_{w\max} = \frac{Pa^2}{6EI}(3l - a) + \frac{wl^4}{8EI} = \frac{4Pa^2(3l - a) + 3wl^4}{24EI}$$

Figure B. Determine deflection at the centerline.

$$\Delta_{P\ell} = \frac{Pb}{48EI}(3l^2 - 4b^2)$$

$$\Delta_{w\ell} = \frac{5wl^4}{384EI}$$

$$\Delta_{\ell} = \Delta_{P\ell} + \Delta_{w\ell} = \frac{Pb}{48EI}(3l^2 - 4b^2) + \frac{5wl^4}{384EI} = \frac{8Pb(3l^2 - 4b^2) + 5wl^4}{384EI}$$

Example C. Determine deflection: (1) at free end of overhang; and (2) at centerline of supported span.

Supported span   Cantilever

TABLE 4.23
BEAM DEFLECTION FORMULAS FOR VARIOUS TYPES OF LOADING

Point on Beam A ℓ B	Slope of Tangent to Elastic Curve		Deflection	
	θ_A	θ_B	Δ_x	Δ_{max} and Δ_ℓ
1	$\dfrac{Pb(l^2-b^2)}{6lEI}$	$\dfrac{Pab(2l-b)}{6lEI}$	When $x < a$: $\dfrac{Pbx}{6lEI}(l^2-x^2-b^2)$ When $x > a$: $\dfrac{Pb}{6lEI}\left[\dfrac{l}{b}(x-a)^3+(l^2-b^2)x-x^3\right]$	$\Delta_{max}\left(\text{at }x=\sqrt{\dfrac{l^2-b^2}{3}}\right)$: $\dfrac{Pb(l^2-b^2)^{3/2}}{9\sqrt{3}lEI}$ Δ_ℓ (if $a>b$): $\dfrac{Pb}{48EI}(3l^2-4b^2)$
2	$\dfrac{Pl^2}{16EI}$		When $x < l/2$: $\dfrac{Px}{48EI}(3l^2-4x^2)$	$\dfrac{Pl^3}{48EI}$
3	$\dfrac{Pa(l-a)}{2EI}$		When $x < a$: $\dfrac{Px}{6EI}(3la-3a^2-x^2)$ When $(l-a)>x>a$: $\dfrac{Pa}{6EI}(3lx-3x^2-a^2)$	$\dfrac{Pa}{24EI}(3l^2-4a^2)$

#	Diagram	Slope / end reaction	Deflection at x	Maximum deflection
4	P P P at $l/4,\ l/4,\ l/4,\ l/4$	$\dfrac{5Pl^2}{32EI}$	When $x < l/4$: $\dfrac{Px}{32EI}(5l^2 - 8x^2)$ When $l/2 > x > l/4$: $\dfrac{P}{384EI}(72l^2x - 48lx^2 - 32x^3 - l^3)$	$\dfrac{19Pl^3}{384EI}$
5	uniform load w over l	$\dfrac{wl^3}{24EI}$	$\dfrac{wx}{24EI}(l^3 - 2lx^2 + x^3)$	$\dfrac{5wl^4}{384EI}$
6	partial load w over a, remainder b	$\dfrac{wa^2(l+b)^2}{24lEI}$ $\dfrac{wa^2(2l^2 - a^2)}{24lEI}$	When $x < a$: $\dfrac{wx}{24lEI}\left[a^2(l+b)^2 - 2ax^2(l+b) + lx^3\right]$ When $x > a$: $\dfrac{wa^2(l-x)}{24lEI}(4xl - 2x^2 - a^2)$	$\Delta_{\max}\left(\text{at } x = l - \sqrt{\dfrac{2l^2 + a^2}{6}}\right)$: $\dfrac{wa^2(2l^2 - a^2)}{36lEI}\sqrt{\dfrac{2l^2 + a^2}{6}}$ Δ_{ℓ} (if $a < b$): $\dfrac{wa^2}{96EI}(3l^2 - 2a^2)$
7	loads w over a at each end, span l	$\dfrac{wa^2}{12EI}(3l - 2a)$	When $x < a$: $\dfrac{wx}{24EI}\left[2a^2(3l - 2a) + x^2(x - 4a)\right]$ When $x > a$: $\dfrac{wa^2}{24EI}(6lx - 6x^2 - a^2)$	$\dfrac{wa^2}{48EI}(3l^2 - 2a^2)$

TABLE 4.23 (Continued)

BEAM DEFLECTION FORMULAS FOR VARIOUS TYPES OF LOADING

Point on Beam	Slope of Tangent to Elastic Curve		Deflection	
A ℓ B	θ_A	θ_B	Δ_x	Δ_{max} and Δ_ℓ
8	$\dfrac{w}{24EI}\left[l^3 - 2a^2(3l-2a)\right]$		When $x < a$: $\dfrac{wx}{24EI}\left[l^3 - 2x^2(l-2a) - 2a^2(3l-2a)\right]$ When $x > a$: $\dfrac{w}{24EI}\left[a^4 + l^3x - x^3(2l-x) - 6a^2x(l-x)\right]$	$\dfrac{w}{384EI}(l^2 - 4a^2)(5l^2 - 4a^2)$
9	$\dfrac{Ml}{3EI}$	$\dfrac{Ml}{6EI}$	$\dfrac{Mx}{6lEI}(l-x)(2l-x)$	$\Delta_{max}\left(\text{at } x = l - \dfrac{l}{\sqrt{3}}\right):$ $\dfrac{Ml^2}{9\sqrt{3}EI}$ $\Delta_\ell = \dfrac{Ml^2}{16EI}$
10	$\dfrac{Ml}{6EI}$	$\dfrac{Ml}{3EI}$	$\dfrac{Mlx}{6EI}\left(1 - \dfrac{x^2}{l^2}\right)$	$\Delta_{max}\left(\text{at } x = \dfrac{l}{\sqrt{3}}\right):$ $\dfrac{Ml^2}{9\sqrt{3}EI}$ $\Delta_\ell = \dfrac{Ml^2}{16EI}$

A $\not\!\!C$ B	θ_B (at free end)	Δ_x	Δ_{max} (at free end)
11	$\dfrac{Pa^2}{2EI}$	When $x < a$: $\dfrac{Px^2}{6EI}(3a - x)$ When $x > a$: $\dfrac{Pa^2}{6EI}(3x - a)$	$\dfrac{Pa^2}{6EI}(3l - a)$
12	$\dfrac{Pl^2}{2EI}$	$\dfrac{Px^2}{6EI}(3l - x)$	$\dfrac{Pl^3}{3EI}$
13	$\dfrac{wl^3}{6EI}$	$\dfrac{wx^2}{24EI}(x^2 + 6l^2 - 4lx)$	$\dfrac{wl^4}{8EI}$
14	$\dfrac{Ml}{EI}$	$\dfrac{Mx^2}{2EI}$	$\dfrac{Ml^2}{2EI}$

1. The cantilever portion has an initial slope, θ_B, at its left end equal to the slope at the right end of the supported portion, or

$$\theta_B = \theta_M + \theta_w = \frac{Ml}{3EI} + \left(\frac{wl^3}{24EI}\right) = \frac{wa^2l}{6EI} - \frac{wl^3}{24EI}$$

$$\theta_B = \frac{wl}{24EI}(4a^2 - l^2)$$

Deflection at the free end, $\Delta_C = \Delta_w + a\theta_B$, or

$$\Delta_C = \frac{wa^4}{8EI} + \frac{wal}{24EI}(4a^2 - l^2) = \frac{wa}{24EI}(3a^3 + 4a^2l - l^3)$$

2. Deflection at centerline of supported span.

$$\Delta_{\mathbb{C}} = \Delta_w + \Delta_M = \frac{5wl^4}{384EI} - \frac{Ml^2}{16EI} = \frac{5wl^4}{384EI} - \frac{wa^2l^2}{32EI} = \frac{wl^2}{384EI}(5l^2 - 12a^2)$$

Deflection limitations

Conditions often require that a beam not exceed certain deflection limitations. Table 4.24 gives deflection limits for timber beams as recommended by AITC.

TABLE 4.24

DEFLECTION LIMITATIONS
(Recommended by AITC)

Use Classification	Applied Load Only	Dead Load + Applied Load
Roof beams		
Industrial	$l/180$	$l/120$
Commercial and institutional		
Without plaster ceiling	$l/240$	$l/180$
With plaster ceiling	$l/360$	$l/240$
Floor beams		
Ordinary usage[a]	$l/360$	$l/240$
Highway bridge stringers	$l/200$ to $l/300$	
Railway bridge stringers	$l/300$ to $l/400$	

[a]Ordinary usage classification is intended for construction in which walking comfort, minimized plaster cracking, and the elimination of objectionable springiness are of prime importance.

Member size as determined by deflection is usually limited by either applied load only or by applied load plus dead load, whichever governs, in accordance with Table 4.24. Applied load is live load, snow load, wind load, etc.

For special uses, such as beams supporting vibrating machinery or carrying moving loads, more severe limitations may be required.

Camber

Camber is built into a structural member by introducing a curvature, either circular or parabolic, opposite to the anticipated deflection movement. Camber recommendations (see Table 4.25) vary with design criteria for various conditions of use and, in addition, are dependent on: whether the member is of simple, continuous, or cantilever span; whether roof drainage is to be provided by the camber; and other factors. Reverse camber may be required in continuous and cantilever spans to permit adequate drainage. (See *Deflection and Camber of Beams*, Appendix B of AITC 102, included in Part II of this *Manual*.)

TABLE 4.25

RECOMMENDED MINIMUM CAMBER FOR GLUED
LAMINATED TIMBER BEAMS

Roof beams[a]	$1\frac{1}{2}$ times dead load deflection
Floor beams[b]	$1\frac{1}{2}$ times dead load deflection
Bridge beams[c]	
Long Span	2 times dead load deflection
Short Span	2 times dead load $+ \frac{1}{2}$ of applied load deflection

[a]Roof beams. The minimum camber of $1\frac{1}{2}$ times dead load deflection will produce a nearly level member under dead load alone after plastic deformation has occurred. Additional camber is usually provided to improve appearance and/or provide necessary roof drainage. Roof beams should have a positive slope or camber equivalent to $\frac{1}{4}$ in. per foot of horizontal distance between the level of the drain and the high point of the roof, in addition to the minimum camber, to avoid the ponding of water. In addition, on long spans, level roof beams may not be desirable because of the optical illusion that the ceiling sags. This condition may also apply to floor beams in multistory buildings.

[b]Floor beams. The minimum camber of $1\frac{1}{2}$ times dead load deflection will produce a nearly level member under dead load alone after plastic deformation has occurred. For warehouse or similar floors where live load may remain for long periods, additional camber should be provided to give a level floor under the permanently applied load.

[c]Bridge beams. Bridge members are normally cambered for dead load only on multiple spans to obtain acceptable riding qualities.

Ponding

When there is the possibility of water ponding, which may cause excessive loads and additional and progressive deflection, each component of the roof system, including decking, purlins, beams, girders, or other principal structural supports, should be designed accordingly. Continuous or cantilevered components should be designed for balanced or unbalanced load, whichever produces the most critical condition. In addition, adequate drainage capacity, provision for heavy downpours, and proper construction details should be provided.

Roof beams should have a minimum positive slope or camber equivalent to $\frac{1}{4}$ in. per foot of horizontal distance between the level of the drain and the high point of the roof, in addition to the recommended minimum camber given in Table 4.25, to avoid the ponding of water.

When flat roofs have insufficient slope for drainage (less than $\frac{1}{4}$ in. per foot), when ponding of water is intentional, or when ponding occurs because of parapet walls, high gravel stops, plugged drains, coincidence of snow loads and rain, beams of insufficient stiffness, melting of snow and ice dams, etc., deflection is initiated and continues at a progressive rate because the work energy of the ponding water is initially greater than the resistance of the beam. This deflection continues until equilibrium is reached between the added water load and the resistance of the beam, or it continues until failure occurs.

Beam deflection should not exceed the recommended limitations given in Table 4.24. When flat roofs have insufficient slope for drainage (less than $\frac{1}{4}$ in. per foot), the stiffness of supporting members should be such that a 5 psf load will cause no more than $\frac{1}{2}$ in. deflection. (See "Engineers Notebook," *Civil Engineering Magazine*, October 1962.)

The effect of ponding of water on a flat roof system supported by solid sawn beams or glued laminated beams without camber is to magnify deflections and stresses under dead load, or dead load plus uniformly distributed applied load, or concentrated applied load (whatever loading is on the roof during ponding). Uniformly distributed applied loads may consist of snow loads or depths of water created by gravel stops, parapet walls, or ice dams. This magnification can be expressed by the formula

$$C_p = \frac{1}{1 - W'l^3/\pi^4 EI}$$

where C_p = factor for multiplying stresses and deflections under existing loads to determine stresses and deflections under existing loads plus ponding

W' = total load of 1 in. depth of water on the roof area supported by the beam or deck, lb (the weight of a 1 in. depth of water is approximately 5 psf)

l = span length of beam or deck, in.

E = modulus of elasticity of beam or deck, psi

I = moment of inertia of beam or deck, in.^{4}

It is noted that as the term, $W'l^3/\pi^4 EI$, approaches unity, the magnification factor approaches infinity or deflection and bending stresses are increased indefinitely. The derivation of this magnification factor was based on approximate analysis which was verified closely by experiment (see September 1964 issue of *Forest Products Journal*). The analysis assumed elastic behavior and did not account for stresses or deflections caused by creep. The factor applies to each element of a roof system, including decking, purlins, beams, and girders. Allowable design stresses, as modified for duration of loading, size factor, and other applicable factors, and deflection limits may not be exceeded after application of the magnification factor to existing stresses and deflections.

As a further illustration of the potential effect of ponding as it relates to increasing bending stress and deflection, Figure 4.36 represents a graphic presentation of the magnification factor as a function of span length, deflection criteria, and ratio of ponding load to design load. By examining this plot, it can readily be seen that, for a given span and deflection criteria, roofs designed for a relatively low value of dead load plus applied live load (i.e., a high W'/W ratio where W' is as previously defined and W is the total design dead load plus live load) will be most susceptible to possible ponding problems.

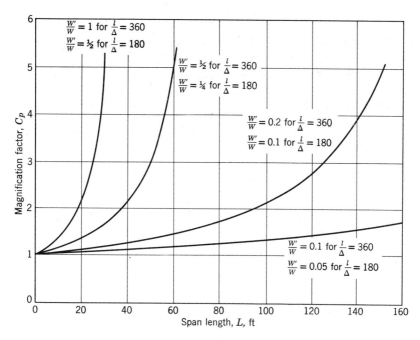

Figure 4.36. MAGNIFICATION FACTOR, C_p, RELATING DEFLECTION OR BENDING VALUES UNDER PONDING TO VALUES WITHOUT PONDING, FOR SIMPLY SUPPORTED BEAMS UNDER INITIAL UNIFORMLY DISTRIBUTED LOAD.

The magnification factor may also be used for flat roof systems with camber; however, if the effect of camber is disregarded, this method will yield conservative answers since the amount of ponding will always be less because of camber.

Examples. To illustrate the effects of ponding on flat roofs, two examples have been selected: (*a*) a beam designed for dead load plus snow load; and (*b*) a beam with a 2 in. high gravel stop designed for dead load plus live load.

(*a*) A $8\frac{3}{4} \times 34\frac{1}{2}$ glued laminated beam under the following conditions:

$L = 62$ ft $F_b = (2,400)(0.89)(1.15) = 2,460$ psi
Spacing $= 16$ ft $F_v = (165)(1.15) = 190$ psi
SL $= 25$ psf $E = 1,800,000$ psi
DL $= 23$ psf

$$A = 302 \text{ in.}^2 \qquad \Delta_{TL} = l/120 = \frac{(62)(12)}{120} = 6.20 \text{ in.}$$
$$S = 1{,}736 \text{ in.}^3$$
$$w_{SL} = (25)(16) \quad = 400 \text{ plf}$$
$$I = 29{,}900 \text{ in.}^4 \qquad w_{DL} = (23)(16) \quad = 368 \text{ plf}$$
$$C_F = 0.89 \qquad \qquad w_{TL} = w_{SL} + w_{DL} = \overline{768 \text{ plf}}$$

(from Table 2.13)

$$\text{Effective span} = L_e = L - \frac{2d}{12} = 62 - \frac{(2)(34.5)}{12}$$

$$L_e = 62 - 5.75 = 56.25 \text{ ft (for shear determination)}$$

From the shear chart, Figure 4.7, $f_v = 106 \text{ psi} < 190$ O.K.
From the bending chart, Figure 4.6, $f_b = 2{,}500 \text{ psi} < 2{,}530$ O.K.
From the deflection chart, Figure 4.9, $\Delta_{TL} = 4.53 \text{ in.} < 6.20$ O.K.

$$\Delta \text{ (for 5 psf load)} = (4.53)\frac{5}{48} = 0.472 \text{ in.} < 0.5 \qquad \text{O.K.}$$

$$\text{Magnification factor} = C_p = \frac{1}{1 - W'l^3/\pi^4 EI}$$

$$W' = (5)(62)(16) = 4{,}960 \text{ lb}$$

$$C_p = \frac{1}{1 - \dfrac{(4{,}960)(62)^3(1{,}728)}{(97.4)(1{,}800{,}000)(29{,}900)}}$$

$$C_p = \frac{1}{1 - 0.390} = 1.639$$

Multiply f_v, f_b, and Δ_{TL} by C_p to determine effects of ponding in combination with dead and snow loads.

$$f_v = (106)(1.639) = 174 \text{ psi} < 190 \qquad \text{O.K.}$$
$$f_b = (2{,}500)(1.639) = 4{,}098 \text{ psi} > 2{,}530$$
$$\Delta_{TL} = (4.53)(1.639) = 7.43 \text{ in.} > 6.20$$

In this example, it can be seen that the beam is overstressed in bending and that the deflection limit is exceeded as the result of ponding in combination with the design loads; therefore, a larger section is required. Try a $8\frac{3}{4} \times 40\frac{1}{2}$ section:

$$A = 354.4 \text{ in.}^2, \quad S = 2{,}392 \text{ in.}^3, \quad I = 48{,}439 \text{ in.}^4$$
$$C_F = 0.87, \quad F_b = (2{,}400)(0.87)(1.15) = 2{,}400 \text{ psi}$$

$$L_e = 62 - \frac{40.5}{6} = 55.25 \text{ ft}$$

$$f_v = 84.5 \text{ psi} < 190 \qquad \text{O.K.}$$

$$f_b = (2{,}500)\frac{1{,}736}{2{,}392} = 1{,}815 \text{ psi} < 2{,}400 \qquad \text{O.K.}$$

$$\Delta_{TL} = (4.53)\frac{29{,}900}{48{,}439} = 2.80 \text{ in.}$$

$$C_p = \frac{1}{1-(0.390)(29,900/48,439)} = \frac{1}{1-0.241} = 1.318$$

Effects of ponding:

$f_v = (84.5)(1.318) = 111.4$ psi<190 O.K.
$f_b = (1,815)(1.318) = 2,390$ psi$<2,400$ O.K.
$\Delta_{TL} = (2.80)(1.318) = 3.69$ in. < 6.20 O.K.

The larger section is adequate.

(b) A $6\frac{3}{4} \times 31\frac{1}{2}$ glued laminated beam with a 2 in. high gravel stop and under the following conditions:

$L = 58$ ft $\qquad$ $F_b = (2,400)(1.25)(0.90) = 2,700$ psi
Spacing $= 16$ ft $\qquad$ $F_v = (200)(1.25) = 250$ psi
LL $= 12$ psf $\qquad$ $E = 1,800,000$ psi
DL $= 15$ psf

$A = 213$ in.^{2} $\qquad$ $\Delta_{LL} = l/240 = \dfrac{(58)(12)}{240} = 2.90$ in.
$S = 1,116$ in.^{3}
$I = 17,580$ in.^{4} $\qquad$ $w_{LL} = (12)(16) = 192$ plf
$C_F = 0.90$ $\qquad$ $w_{DL} = (15)(16) = 240$ plf
(from Table 2.13) $\qquad$ $w_{TL} = w_{LL} + w_{DL} = \overline{432\ \text{plf}}$

Effective span $= L_e = L - \dfrac{2d}{12} = 58 - \dfrac{(2)(31.5)}{12}$

$$L_e = 58 - 5.25 = 52.75 \text{ ft (for shear determination)}$$

From the shear chart, Figure 4.7, $f_v = 82$ psi < 250 O.K.
From the bending chart, Figure 4.6, $f_b = 1,945$ psi $< 2,700$ O.K.
From the deflection chart, Figure 4.9, $\Delta_{LL} = 1.54$ in. < 2.90 O.K.

$$\Delta(\text{for 5 psf load}) = (1.54)\frac{5}{12} = 0.64 \text{ in.} > 0.5$$

Since the $6\frac{3}{4} \times 31\frac{1}{2}$ section has insufficient stiffness to meet the criterion that a 5 psf load will cause not more than $\frac{1}{2}$ in. deflection, a stiffer section must be selected.
Try a $6\frac{3}{4} \times 34\frac{1}{2}$ section:

$A = 233$ in.^{2}, $S = 1,339$ in.^{3}, $I = 23,098$ in.^{4}
$C_F = 0.89$, $F_b = (2,400)(1.25)(0.89) = 2,670$ psi

$$L_e = 58 - \frac{34.5}{6} = 52.25 \text{ ft}$$

$$f_v = 73.2 \text{ psi} < 188 \quad \text{O.K.}$$

$$f_b = (1,945)\frac{1,116}{1,339} = 1,620 \text{ psi} < 2,670 \quad \text{O.K.}$$

$$\Delta_{LL} = (1.54)\frac{17,580}{23,098} = 1.17 \text{ in.} < 2.90 \quad \text{O.K.}$$

$$\Delta(\text{for 5 psf load}) = (0.64)\frac{17{,}580}{23{,}098} = 0.487 \text{ in.} < 0.5 \quad \text{O.K.}$$

$$\text{Magnification factor} = C_p = \frac{1}{1 - W'l^3/\pi^4 EI}$$

$$W' = (5)(58)(16) = 4{,}640 \text{ lb}$$

$$C_p = \frac{1}{1 - \dfrac{(4{,}640)(58)^3(1{,}728)}{(97.4)(1{,}800{,}000)(23{,}098)}} = \frac{1}{1 - 0.386}$$

$$C_p = 1.629$$

In order to investigate the effects of ponding, a 2 in. depth of water created by the 2 in. high gravel stop will be assumed. It will also be assumed that the design live load (12 psf) is not acting simultaneously with the ponding load.

A 2 in. depth of water over the roof will cause a load of $(2)(5)(16) = 160$ plf. The total load on the roof beams is equal to the dead load plus the water load, or

$$w_{TL} = 240 + 160 = 400 \text{ plf}$$

$$f_v = (73.2)\frac{400}{432} = 67.8 \text{ psi}$$

$$f_b = (1{,}620)\frac{400}{432} = 1{,}500 \text{ psi}$$

$$\Delta_{LL} = (1.17)\frac{400}{432} = 1.08 \text{ in.}$$

Effects of ponding:

$$f_v = (67.8)(1.629) = 110 \text{ psi} < 250 \quad \text{O.K.}$$
$$f_b = (1{,}500)(1.629) = 2{,}444 \text{ psi} < 2{,}670 \quad \text{O.K.}$$
$$\Delta_{LL} = (1.08)(1.629) = 1.76 \text{ in.} < 2.90 \quad \text{O.K.}$$

The larger section is adequate.

Shear in Beams

Vertical shear

It is ordinarily not necessary to compute or check the strength of wood beams in cross-grain (vertical) shear.

Horizontal shear

The general formula for calculating horizontal shear stress, f_v, in a beam is

$$f_v = \frac{VQ}{It}$$

where V = vertical shear, lb

Q = statical moment of the area above or below the neutral axis about the neutral axis, in.[3]

I = moment of inertia of the section, in.[4]

t = width of beam at neutral axis, in.

For a rectangular beam, the formula becomes

$$f_v = \frac{3V}{2bd}$$

where d = depth of beam, in.

The horizontal shear stress as determined by these formulas, except in the case of checked beams, may not exceed the allowable unit horizontal shear stress, F_v, adjusted for duration of loading.

When calculating the reaction, V:

(*a*) Take into account any relief to the beam resulting from the load being distributed to adjacent parallel beams by flooring or other members.

(*b*) Neglect all loads within a distance from either support equal to the depth of the beam.

(*c*) When there is a single moving load, or one moving load that is considerably greater than the others, place that load at a distance from the support equal to the depth of the beam; place any other loads in their normal relation. When there are two or more moving loads of approximately equal weight and in proximity, place the loads in the position which produces the maximum value for V, neglecting any loads within a distance from the support equal to the depth of the beam.

Horizontal shear in checked beams

When a solid sawn wood beam is checked at or near its neutral axis, the upper and lower parts of the beam act partly as two beams and partly as a unit; thus, a part of the end reaction is resisted internally by each part of the beam acting independently and is not associated with shear stress at the neutral plane. For such a solid sawn wood beam, the vertical end shear, V, may be determined by either of the following methods.

1. Calculate the reaction, V, as stated above except that for a single moving load, or one moving load that is considerably greater than the others, place that load at a distance from the support equal to three times the depth of beam, or at the quarter-point, whichever is closer, placing any other loads in their normal relation. Loads other than moving loads should be considered in the usual manner.

2. Determine the vertical shear, using the following formulas, except that the formula for concentrated loads should be used in the case of two or more moving loads of approximately equal weight and in proximity. For concentrated loads,

$$V' = \frac{10P(l-x)(x/d)^2}{9l[2+(x/d)^2]}$$

For uniformly distributed loads,

$$V' = \frac{W}{2}\left(1-\frac{2d}{l}\right)$$

where V' = modified vertical shear, lb (for a combination of concentrated loads, $V' = V_1' + V_2' + \cdots + V_n'$, where V_1', V_2', ..., V_n' are vertical shears resulting from concentrated loads at distances x_1, x_2, ..., x_n from the support; the load combination should be placed in the position which produces the maximum value for V')

P = concentrated load, lb

W = total uniformly distributed load, lb

l = span, in.

x = distance from support to load, in.

d = depth of beam, in.

When the modified vertical shear, V', determined by either method 1 or 2, is used, the calculated horizontal shear stress, f_v, may not exceed the allowable unit horizontal shear stresses given in Table 4.26, adjusted for duration of loading.

TABLE 4.26

STRESS VALUES FOR CHECKED SOLID SAWN
TIMBER BEAMS

Species	Allowable Unit Horizontal Shear Stress Value, psi		
	Maximum Moisture Content		
	Unseasoned	19%	15%
Balsam fir	115	125	130
California redwood	150	165	170
Douglas fir – larch	170	185	195
Douglas fir – South	170	185	195
Eastern hemlock – tamarack	160	170	180
Eastern spruce	130	140	145
Eastern white pine	120	130	135
Engelmann spruce	120	130	135
Hem – fir	140	150	155
Idaho white pine	120	130	135
Lodgepole pine	130	140	145
Mountain hemlock	175	190	200
Northern pine	135	145	150
Northern white cedar	115	125	130
Ponderosa pine – sugar pine	130	140	150
Red pine	135	145	150
Sitka spruce	140	155	160
Southern pine (med. grain)	165	175	185
Spruce – pine – fir	130	140	145
Subalpine fir	115	125	130
Western white pine	120	130	140
Western cedar	130	140	150

Lateral Support

To prevent sidewise buckling in bending and compression members, and to permit the members to carry maximum loads, it may be necessary to provide lateral support at intervals; the size of the intervals will depend on the dimensions of the member.

Columns

Lateral support requirements for columns are given on pages 4-3 to 4-6 of this *Manual*.

Glued laminated beams

Economy in glued laminated timber beam design usually favors a deep and narrow section. Such a section increases the likelihood of lateral buckling of the compression flange. Many building codes have rules governing depth-breadth ratios to minimize such lateral buckling tendencies.

The limitation of depth-breadth ratio in a beam to produce lateral stability is believed to be as ineffective in preventing lateral buckling as a limitation on the same ratio in a column is in preventing Euler buckling. In stability problems of this kind, the length of compression member or compression flange is critical and should be contained in the governing parameters. A formula similar to that recommended by the AISC for the buckling of steel beams, where ld/A_f is the parameter, is necessary; therefore, a simple formula for the allowable stress in a glued laminated beam has been derived and checked. This expression is similar to that for a timber column, but the constants have been changed and l/d is replaced by ld/b^2.

Slenderness factor for a beam. The slenderness factor of a beam shall be calculated by the formula

$$C_s = \sqrt{\frac{l_e d}{b^2}}$$

where C_s = slenderness factor
  l_e = effective length of beam, in. (see Table 4.27)
  d = depth of beam, in.
  b = breadth of beam, in.

Unsupported length. When the compression edge of a beam is so supported throughout its length as to prevent its lateral displacement, and the ends at points of bearing have lateral support to prevent rotation, the unsupported length may be taken as zero.

When lateral support is provided to prevent rotation at the points of end bearing, but no other support to prevent rotation or lateral displacement is provided throughout the length of a beam, the unsupported length is the distance between such points of bearing or the length of a cantilever.

When the beams are provided with lateral support to prevent both rotational and lateral displacement at intermediate points as well as at the ends, the unsupported length may be the distance between such points of intermediate lateral support. If lateral displacement is not prevented

TABLE 4.27

EFFECTIVE LENGTH OF GLUED LAMINATED BEAMS

Type of Beam Span and Nature of Load	Value of Effective Length, l_e [a]
Single span beam, load concentrated at center	$1.61l$
Single span beam, uniformly distributed load	$1.92l$
Single span beam, equal end moments	$1.84l$
Cantilever beam, load concentrated at unsupported end	$1.69l$
Cantilever beam, uniformly distributed load	$1.06l$
Single span or cantilever beam, any load (conservative value)	$1.92l$

[a]Where l = unsupported length as defined below.

at these points of intermediate support, the unsupported length must be defined as the full distance between points of bearing with adequate provision against rotation or as the full length of the cantilever.

These lateral support provisions constitute a more rational basis for preventing lateral buckling of beams, and they are to be used in all glued laminated timber beam design.

Some of the means available for preventing rotation of a beam at its points of bearing are: to anchor the bottom of the beam to pilaster and the top of beam to parapet; to ground the roof diaphragm to the wall; and to provide a girt at the top of the wall and rod bracing for beams on wood columns with open sidewalls.

To provide continuous support of a compression flange, composite action between deck elements to create diaphragm action is essential for full lateral support. A plywood deck with edge nailing is one of the best examples of such composite action between deck elements. When plank decking is used, nailing patterns are most important so that nail couples will be created; having one nail per deck plank and no nails between planks fails to provide a system with adequate lateral support. If a wood deck is to supply such support, each piece must be securely nailed directly to the beam and to adjacent pieces to give a rigid diaphragm. If other kinds of decks are to provide such support, they must supply equivalent rigidity as a diaphragm.

If adjacent deck planks are nailed to each other so that little or no differential movement can occur between planks, then each plank will shift the same, namely zero, since planks over end supports cannot shift if torsional rotation is prevented at these end supports.

When joists have depth-breadth ratios of 8 or 9 (such joists have been in use for many years), the compression flange is continuously supported by a deck and the end bridging prevents torsional rotation. Intermediate bridging, in such cases, is provided to distribute concentrated loads to adjacent joists.

Beams with various lateral support conditions.

(a) *Without Lateral Support.* When the depth of a beam does not exceed its breadth, no lateral support is required and the allowable unit stress is determined by applying the provisions of pages **2**-32 through **2**-39.

(*b*) *With Lateral Support.* If lateral movement of the compression flange is prevented by a continuous support, there is no danger of lateral buckling and the allowable stresses require no reduction based on a slenderness ratio concept. Also, there is no need to limit the depth-breadth ratio to 5 or 6.

When the depth of a beam exceeds the breadth, bracing must be provided at the points of bearing, and it must be so arranged as to prevent rotation of the beam at those points in a plane perpendicular to its longitudinal axis; the allowable stresses are calculated by the formulas given in the following paragraphs for short, intermediate, or long beams.

Allowable unit stresses for slender beams.

(*a*) *Short Beams.* When the slenderness factor, C_s, does not exceed 10, the tabular allowable unit stress in bending, F_b, adjusted in accordance with provisions of pages **2**-32 through **2**-39, is applicable for design and is defined as F_b'.

(*b*) *Intermediate Beams.* When the slenderness factor, C_s, is greater than 10 but does not exceed C_k, an allowable unit stress in bending based on slenderness considerations, F_b', is calculated by the formula

$$F_b' = F_b \left[1 - \frac{1}{3} \left(\frac{C_s}{C_k} \right)^4 \right]$$

where F_b = tabular allowable unit stress in bending, psi
$\quad C_k = \sqrt{3E/5F_b}$
$\quad E$ = modulus of elasticity, psi

(*c*) *Long Beams.* When the slenderness factor, C_s, is greater than C_k, but less than 50, the allowable unit stress in bending is calculated by the formula

$$F_b' = \frac{0.40E}{C_s^2}$$

Note: For both intermediate and long beams, the allowable unit stress for design based on slenderness considerations is obtained by adjusting F_b' in accordance with the provisions of pages **2**-32 through **2**-39 with the exception that the size effect reduction is not applicable.

Regardless of the slenderness classification into which a beam may be put, in no case shall the allowable unit stress in bending used for design exceed the value obtained by adjusting the tabular allowable unit stress based on the provisions of pages **2**-32 through **2**-39.

Figure 4.37 graphically illustrates the relationship between C_s and F_b' for various tabular allowable bending stresses, F_b, and for a given modulus of elasticity of 1,800,000 psi. This plot can be used to readily determine the allowable unit stress in bending based on slenderness considerations, F_b', subject to further adjustments as given on pages **2**-32 through **2**-39 but excluding the size effect, for any value of C_s. Similar plots can be developed for any combination of tabular bending stress, F_b, and modulus of elasticity, E.

In no case shall C_s be greater than 50.

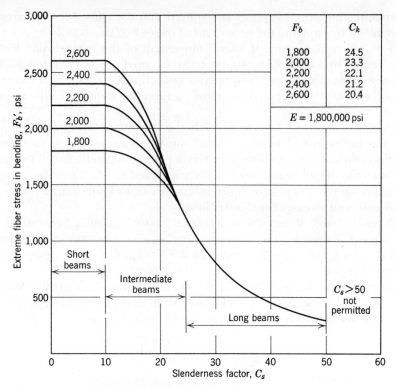

Figure 4.37.   DETERMINATION OF F_b AS A FUNCTION OF SLENDERNESS FACTOR, C_s.

Illustrative Examples. To illustrate the preceding concepts, the following three examples representing each of the possible slenderness categories have been selected. For each example, assume the design situation requires a simple-span glued laminated beam having a clear span of 40 ft. A preliminary analysis of the loads indicates that the bending moment required for this design is

$$M = 1,500,000 \text{ in.-lb}$$

For these examples it has been assumed that the wood structural system supports a translucent roofing system. In this case, the translucent roofing will provide little or no lateral support for the compression flange of the beam.

Furthermore, assume a 24F design combination has been specified with a modulus of elasticity of 1,800,000 psi.

Preliminary Design for Bending

Assume trial size of $5\frac{1}{8}$ in. $\times$ $28\frac{1}{2}$ in.; $S = 693.8$ in.^{3}

$$C_F = 0.90 \qquad \text{(from Table 2.13)}$$

Modify C_F for l/d ratio

$$l/d = \frac{(40)(12)}{28.5} = 16.8$$

Using straight line interpolation between value given on page **2-37**, percentage change is $+1.4\%$ for l/d of 16.8.

Thus, adjusted $C_F = (0.90)(1.016) = 0.91$

$$F_b = (2,400)(0.91) = 2,184 \text{ psi}$$

$$\text{Required } S = \frac{1,500,000}{2,184} = 687 \text{ in.}^3 < 693.8 \text{ in.}^3$$

Therefore, use $5\frac{1}{8} \times 28\frac{1}{2}$ in. member.

Check for slenderness assuming the following cases of lateral bracing:

(a) Assume the 40 ft main beam is laterally braced by purlins placed 24 in. on centers with the only mode of lateral buckling taking place between the purlins. For this case, which is similar to equal end moments (between the purlins), the effective length, l_e, can be determined from Table 4.27 as follows:

$$l_e = 1.84(l) = (1.84)(24) = 44.16 \text{ in.}$$

$$C_s = \sqrt{\frac{l_e d}{b^2}} = \sqrt{\frac{(44.16)(28.5)}{(5.125)^2}} = 6.92$$

Thus since $C_s < 10$ there is no reduction in bending stress resulting from slenderness, and $F_b = 2,184$ psi as previously calculated is used for design.

(b) Assume the 40 ft main beam is laterally braced by joists placed 60 in. on centers with the only mode of lateral buckling taking place between the joists.

$$l_e = (1.84)(60) = 110.4 \text{ in.}$$

$$C_s = \sqrt{\frac{l_e d}{b^2}} = \sqrt{\frac{(110.4)(28.5)}{(5.125)^2}} = 10.9 > 10$$

$$C_k = \sqrt{\frac{3E}{5F_b}} = \sqrt{\frac{(3)(1,800,000)}{(5)(2,400)}} = 21.2$$

Since $10 < C_s < C_k$, determine $F_b{}'$ from Figure 4.37 or from the following equation:

$$F_b{}' = F_b\left[1 - \frac{1}{3}\left(\frac{C_s}{C_k}\right)^4\right]$$

$$F_b{}' = 2,400\left[1 - \frac{1}{3}\left(\frac{10.9}{21.2}\right)^4\right] = (2,400)(0.977) = 2,344 \text{ psi}$$

Since F_b as determined initially based on size effect (2,184 psi) is less than $F_b{}'$ based on the slenderness analysis (2,344 psi), the allowable bending stress for design is taken as 2,184 psi, and the $5\frac{1}{8}$ in. $\times 28\frac{1}{2}$ in. section originally analyzed is satisfactory for this condition of lateral bracing.

(c) Assume the 40 ft main beam is laterally braced by a subordinate member at the center point of the span with the buckling mode taking place between the end supports and this bracing member.

$$l_e = (1.84)(240) = 441.6 \text{ in.}$$

$$C_s = \sqrt{\frac{l_e d}{b^2}} = \sqrt{\frac{(441.6)(28.5)}{(5.125)^2}} = 21.9 > C_k$$

Since $50 > C_s > C_k$, determine F_b' from Figure 4.37 or from the following equation:

$$F_b' = \frac{0.40E}{C_s^2} = \frac{(0.40)(1,800,000)}{(21.9)^2} = 1,500 \text{ psi}$$

Since F_b' based on the slenderness analysis is less than the adjusted value for F_b as initially determined based on the use of the size factor, F_b' governs and the allowable bending stress for design is taken as 1,500 psi.

$$S = \frac{1,500,000}{1,500} = 1,000 \text{ in.}^3 > 693.8 \text{ in.}^3$$

Therefore, the $5\frac{1}{8} \times 28\frac{1}{2}$ in. is inadequate because of slenderness, and either a larger member should be specified or intermediate lateral bracing should be provided to change the design from the long beam class to the intermediate beam class for which the $5\frac{1}{8} \times 28\frac{1}{2}$ in. member was previously found to be satisfactory.

Sawn beams

For solid sawn rectangular beams and joists, the approximate lateral support rules, based on nominal dimensions, listed in Table 4.28 may be applied by the designer. When adequately stabilized purlins or joists are set

TABLE 4.28

APPROXIMATE LATERAL SUPPORT RULES FOR SAWN BEAMS

Ratio of Depth to Breadth, Based on Nominal Dimensions	Rule
2 to 1 or less	No lateral support is needed
3 to 1	Ends to be held in position
4 to 1	Ends held in position and member held in line as in a well-bolted chord member in a truss
5 to 1	Ends held in position and one edge to be held in line
6 to 1	Ends held in position and one edge held in line as for 5 to 1, together with adequate bridging or solid blocking spaced at intervals not exceeding 8 ft
7 to 1	Ends held in position and both edges firmly held in line

If a beam is subject to both flexure and compression parallel to grain, the ratio may be as much as 5 to 1, if one edge is held firmly in line, for example, by rafters (or roof joists) and diagonal sheathing. If the dead load is sufficient to induce tension on the underside of the rafters, the ratio for the beam may be 6 to 1.

between sawn bending members, the depth of the member below the bottom of the purlin or joist is used as the least dimension, d, in determining depth-breadth ratio. For more exact engineering analysis of the lateral stability of solid sawn bending members, the slenderness factor considerations previously discussed for glued laminated members should be applied.

Lateral stability for bending and compression members

Where roof joists, not purlins, are set between arches or the top chords of trusses, the depth, rather than the breadth, of the arch or top chord member (compression member) may be taken as its least dimension, d, in determining l/d. The roof joists should be placed so that their upper edges are at least $\frac{1}{2}$ in. above the tops of the arch or chord, but also low enough to provide adequate lateral support.

When roof joists or planks are placed on top of an arch or top chord of a truss and are well spiked or otherwise securely fastened to the arch or top chord and to blocking placed between the joists, the depth of the arch or individual chord members may be used as the least dimension, d, in determining l/d. When joists or planks are not so fastened or blocked, the width of the arch or individual chord member should be used as the least dimension, d, in determining l/d.

When adequately stabilized roof purlins, joists, or struts are set between compression members, or securely attached to one edge, the distance between purlins, joists, or struts should be used as the effective column length, l, in determining l/d. Allowable stresses for column action should be the lesser of the two determined by calculations based on l/d ratios and by using the appropriate breadth, depth, and unsupported lengths.

For arches or trusses which have superstructures built on top of the arches or the upper chords of trusses so that the arch or upper chord is not laterally braced by roof framing, additional lateral bracing is required for the portion of the member which is not braced by roof framing to keep the l/d of the member within the prescribed limits.

Glued laminated arches

When one edge of the arch is braced by decking fastened directly to the arch or braced at frequent intervals, as by girts or roof purlins, the ratio of tangent point depth to breadth of the arch, based on actual dimensions, should not exceed 6. When such lateral bracing is lacking, the ratio should not exceed 5 and the arch should be checked for column action in the lateral (width) direction. These requirements are given in Table 4.29.

TABLE 4.29

LATERAL SUPPORT RULES FOR GLUED LAMINATED ARCHES

Ratio of Depth to Breadth Based on Actual Dimensions	Rule
5 to 1 or less	No lateral support required, should be checked for column action
6 to 1	One edge should be braced at frequent intervals

End-Notched Members

Normally beams should not be notched or tapered on the tension side. If it becomes necessary to notch a bending member at a support on the tension side, the bending load should be checked against the load computed by the equation:

$$R_v = \frac{2F_v b d_e^2}{3d}$$

where R_v = vertical reaction, lb
b = width of beam, in.
d = depth of beam, in.
d_e = depth of beam less the depth of the notch, in. (see Figure 4.38)

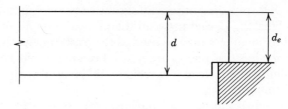

Figure 4.38.   END-NOTCHED BEAM (NOTCHED ON TENSION SIDE).

The notching of a bending member on a tension side results in a decrease in strength, the magnitude depending on the shape of the notch and the ratio of the depth of the notch to the depth of the member. The equation given above is an empirical equation developed for the condition of a square-cornered end notch, and the ratio of the depth of the notch to the depth of the beam should be limited to 1:10. The designer should also consider reducing the stress concentration that occurs when a member is notched by using a gradual tapered notch configuration in lieu of a square-cornered notch. Notching on the tension side of simple beams in the center of the span is not recommended.

When a beam is notched or beveled on its upper side at the ends, a less severe condition from the standpoint of stress concentrations is realized. If such a notch is square-cornered, as illustrated in Figure 4.39, the shear should be checked by the formula

$$R_v = \frac{2}{3} F_v b \left[d - \left(\frac{d - d_e}{d_e} \right) e \right]$$

where e = distance the notch extends inside the inner edge of the support, in.

If e exceeds d_e, the preceding formula is not used; instead, the shear strength is computed by using only the depth of beam below the notch, d_e. In no case should a notch on the upper side of a beam exceed 40% of the total depth of a beam. If the end of a beam is beveled (as shown by the dotted line in Figure 4.39), d_e is measured at the inner edge of the support,

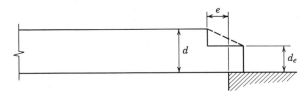

Figure 4.39.   END-NOTCHED BEAM (NOTCHED ON COMPRESSION SIDE).

and e is the distance from the inner edge of the support to the beginning of the bevel. The same formula and considerations as for beams notched on the upper side apply.

Angle of Load to Grain (Hankinson Formula)

The angle of load to grain is the angle between the direction of the resultant load acting on a member and the longitudinal axis of the member. In this *Manual*, values for allowable unit stresses in compression are given for compression parallel to grain, F_c, and compression perpendicular to grain, $F_{c\perp}$. To obtain allowable unit stresses in compression at any angle of load to grain, the Hankinson formula may be used when the loaded surface is perpendicular to the direction of load (see Figure 4.40). The Hankinson formula is

$$F_n = \frac{F_c F_{c\perp}}{F_c \sin^2 \theta + F_{c\perp} \cos^2 \theta}$$

where F_n = allowable unit stress acting perpendicular to the inclined surface, psi
F_c = allowable unit stress in compression parallel to grain, psi
$F_{c\perp}$ = allowable unit stress in compression perpendicular to grain, psi
θ = angle between the direction of load and the direction of grain, degrees

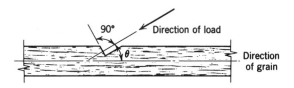

Figure 4.40.   ANGLE OF LOAD TO GRAIN.

When the resultant load is at an angle other than 90° with the surface being considered, the angle, θ, is the angle between the direction of grain and the direction of the load component which is perpendicular to the surface.

The Hankinson formula may be solved graphically through use of the nomographs in Figure 5.3.

SECTION 5
FASTENINGS AND CONNECTIONS

CONN.

FASTENINGS – GENERAL CONSIDERATIONS

The following considerations, in general, apply to all the mechanical fastenings for timber joints covered in this section. Considerations applicable to a particular mechanical fastening will be found under the appropriate headings herein. The factors that require consideration in determining allowable loads for mechanically fastened joints are (1) lumber species (density); (2) critical section; (3) angle of load to grain; (4) spacing of mechanical fastenings; (5) edge and end distances; (6) conditions of loading; and (7) eccentricity.

Lumber Species

The allowable loads for mechanical fastenings vary with the species of wood with which they are used. The species load groups in Table 5.1 apply to allowable loads for mechanical fastenings.

The recommendations herein are based on the assumption that the mechanical fastenings are used in structural glued laminated timber or material that meets the requirements for stress-graded lumber, and that proper fabrication practices have been followed.

Critical Section

The critical section of a timber in a joint is that section, taken at right angles to the direction of the load, which gives the maximum stress based on the net area. The net area at this section is equal to the full cross-sectional area of the timber less the projected area of that portion of the mechanical fastening within the member, including the projected area of associated holes not within the fastener's projected area. See specific provisions herein for determining net section when a specific type of mechanical fastening is staggered.

Angle of Load to Grain

Angle of load to grain is a factor in the determination of the allowable load on certain types of mechanical fastenings, because timber has a greater bearing value parallel to grain than perpendicular to grain. The angle of load to grain is the angle between the resultant of the load exerted by a mechanical fastening acting on a member and the longitudinal axis of the member (angle θ in Figure 5.1).

TABLE 5.1

SPECIES LOAD GROUPS FOR FASTENINGS

Species	Specific Gravity[a]	Timber Connector Load Groups	Lag Bolt and Driven Fastening[b] Load Groups
Ash, commercial white	0.62	A	I
Beech	0.68	A	I
Birch, sweet and yellow	0.66	A	I
Cedar			
Northern white	0.31	D	IV
Western	0.36	D	IV
Cottonwood, Eastern	0.41	D	IV
Cypress, Southern	0.48	C	III
Douglas fir–larch[c]	0.51	B	II
Douglas fir, South	0.48	C	III
Fir			
Balsam	0.38	D	IV
Subalpine	0.34	D	IV
Hem-fir	0.44	C	III
Hemlock			
Eastern – tamarack	0.45	C	III
Mountain	0.47	C	III
Hickory and pecan	0.75	A	I
Maple, black and sugar	0.66	A	I
Oak, red and white	0.67	A	I
Pine			
Eastern white	0.38	D	IV
Idaho white	0.42	C	III
Lodgepole	0.44	C	III
Northern	0.46	C	III
Ponderosa – sugar	0.42	C	III
Southern[c]	0.55	B	II
Poplar, yellow	0.46	C	III
Redwood, California			
Close grain	0.42	C	III
Open grain	0.37	D	IV
Spruce			
Eastern	0.43	C	III
Engelmann	0.37	D	IV
Sitka	0.43	C	III
Sweetgum and tupelo	0.54	B	II

[a]Based on weight and volume when oven-dry.
[b]Nails, spikes, wood screws, spiral dowels.
[c]When graded for density, these species qualify for group A connector loads.

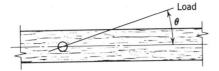

Figure 5.1. ANGLE OF LOAD TO GRAIN.

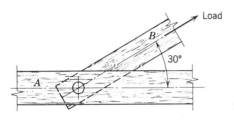

Figure 5.2. ANGLE OF LOAD TO GRAIN.

The angle of load to grain applies only to the particular member under consideration; that is, the angle of load to grain may be different for the various members being connected by the same fastening. For example, in Figure 5.2, the angle of load to grain with respect to member *A* is 30°, whereas the angle of load to grain with respect to member *B* is zero.

Angle of Load to Grain (Hankinson Formula)

When the angle of load to the grain of mechanical fastenings acts between 0° and 90° as shown in Figure 5.1, the allowable load is determined by use of the Hankinson formula

$$N = \frac{PQ}{P \sin^2\theta + Q \cos^2\theta}$$

where N = load at angle θ with direction of grain, lb
$\quad P$ = load acting parallel to grain, lb
$\quad Q$ = load acting perpendicular to grain, lb
$\quad \theta$ = angle between the direction of load and the direction of grain, degrees.

The Hankinson formula may be solved graphically through use of the nomographs in Figure 5.3. The difference between the two nomographs in the figure is in their scale. The units on the vertical scales may be applied to allowable stresses in psi, or to load values in pounds, for timber connectors, bolts, or lag screws.

Spacing of Mechanical Fastenings

The spacing of mechanical fastenings is the distance between centers of the fastenings measured on a straight line joining their centers. Spacing may also be measured parallel and perpendicular to grain. These measurements are illustrated in Figure 5.4. Spacing between fastenings in a group should be sufficient to develop the full strength of each fastening.

Edge Distance

Edge distance is the distance from the edge of a member to the center of the mechanical fastening closest to that edge of the member, measured

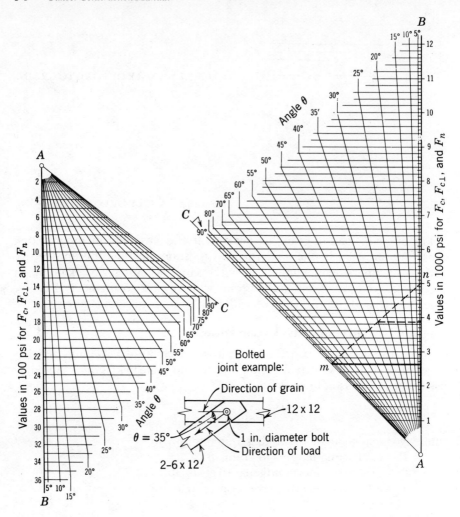

Figure 5.3. SCHOLTEN NOMOGRAPH FOR SOLUTION OF HANKINSON FORMULA. Conditions: $P = 5,030$ lb, $Q = 2,620$ lb, $\theta = 35°$. Locate 5,030 lb at n on line A-B on right-hand chart. Locate 2,620 lb at m on line A-C, opposite that value on line A-B. Where line m-n intersects the 35° radial line, project to line A-B and read allowable load $n = 3,870$ lb. Printed through courtesy of the National Forest Products Association.

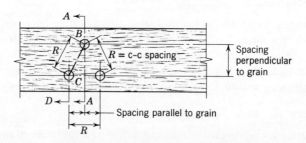

Figure 5.4. SPACING MEASUREMENTS.

perpendicular to the edge. The loaded edge is the edge toward which the load induced by the fastening acts. The unloaded edge is the edge away from which the load induced by the fastening acts. In Figure 5.5, *A* is the loaded edge distance and *B* is the unloaded edge distance. Edge distance should be sufficient to develop the required strength of fastenings.

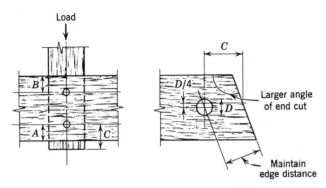

Figure 5.5.   EDGE AND END DISTANCES.

End Distance

End distance is the distance, measured parallel to grain, from the center of a mechanical fastening to the square-cut end of a member. If the end of the member is cut at an angle, the end distance is measured parallel to the length of the piece on a line that is one-fourth of the fastening diameter, *D*, from the center of the connector and on the side of the larger angle of the end cut. The dimensions *C* in Figure 5.5 are end distances. End distances should be sufficient to develop the required strength of fastenings.

Conditions of Loading

The allowable loads for mechanical fastenings given herein are for one unit installed in a seasoned timber joint under normal duration of loading and dry-use service conditions.

Duration of loadings

For other than normal durations of loading, the appropriate adjustment factor from Figure 2.3 or Table 2.12 is applied (see Section 2 of this *Manual*).

Service conditions

For other than dry-use conditions, or for timber members which season in place, the appropriate adjustment factor for the particular type of fastening as given herein is applied.

Effect of treatment

No reduction in allowable fastener loads or allowable stresses is recommended for preservatively treated wood. However, the *National Design Specification* recommends a 10% reduction in both the design stresses of lumber and the allowable loads for fasteners in lumber that has been fire retardant treated.

Eccentricity

Eccentric timber joints should be avoided wherever possible, especially in heavily stressed members. If eccentric joints are used, the effect of the induced moment should be taken into consideration when calculating fiber stresses.

Joint Shear Stress

Beams supported by timber connectors or bolts should be so designed that the joint shear stress determined by the formula below does not exceed the allowable joint shear stress, F_{vj}, for the species of lumber being used. Allowable unit stresses for shear in joint details, F_{vj}, may be increased by 50% over shear values otherwise permitted when the joint is located greater than 5 times the depth of the member from the end of the member. When fasteners are located less than 5 times the depth of the member from the end, the same reduction in end shear for notch action as given on page 4-178 for notched beams shall apply. When one large bending member supports another large bending member, such as on a girder carrying a beam, saddle type connectors are recommended rather than clip angles. The following formula may be used to determine the actual unit horizontal shear stress at the joint. The shear stress given by this formula may be increased as stated above.

$$f_v = \frac{3V}{2bd_e}$$

where V = total vertical shear, lb
$\quad b$ = breadth of member, in.
$\quad d_e$ = effective depth of member, in.

For timber connector joints, d_e = the total depth of the member less the distance from the unloaded edge to the nearest edge of the nearest connector. For bolted joints, d_e = the total depth of the member less the distance from the unloaded edge to the center of the nearest bolt.

Example. The beam supported by timber connectors as illustrated here has

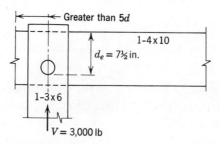

the nominal member sizes, loads, and connections indicated. The connectors are placed to realize the maximum effective depth, d_e. The allowable shear stress F_v = 95 psi. Check the connection for joint shear. (4 in. split ring timber connectors are used.)

$$F_{vj} = 1.5F_v = (1.5)(95) = 142.5 \text{ psi}$$

$$f_v = \frac{3V}{2bd_e} = \frac{(3)(3,000)}{(2)(3.5)(7.5)}$$

$$= 171.4 \,\text{psi} > 142.5$$

Therefore, the effective area, bd_e, will have to be increased either by using a thicker member (increasing b) or by using a deeper member (increasing d_e).

Group Action of Fasteners

Research has indicated that a load carried by a row of fasteners is not equally divided among the fasteners. The end fasteners tend to carry a larger portion of the load than the intermediate fasteners. The distribution of the load is determined by the relative stiffness of the main member and the side members. Tables 5.2 and 5.3 contain modification factors to be applied to allowable loads for 2 to 12 fasteners in a row. In the determination of the modification factor the following principles apply:

1. A group of fasteners consists of one or more rows of fasteners.
2. A row of fasteners consists of either two or more bolts loaded in single or multiple shear or two or more split rings, shear plates, or lag screws loaded in single shear. The row is aligned with the direction of the load.

When fasteners in adjacent rows are staggered and the distance between the rows, y, is less than $\frac{1}{4}$ the spacing between the closest fasteners in adjacent rows, x, as shown in Figure 5.6a, the fasteners in adjacent rows should be considered as one row for the purpose of determining the modification factor, K. This principle applies to groups of fasteners with either even or odd numbers of rows as shown in Fig. 5.6b.

3. The load for each row of fasteners is determined by the summation of the individual loads for each fastener in the row and then multiplying this value by the modification factor, K, in Table 5.2 or Table 5.3.
4. The allowable load for the group of the fasteners is the sum of the allowable loads on the rows in the group.
5. When a member is loaded perpendicular to grain, its equivalent cross-sectional area is the product of the thickness of the member and the overall width of the fastener group for calculating cross-sectional area ratios. When only one row of fasteners is used, the thickness is equal to the minimum spacing for full load for the type of fastening used. In general, long rows of fasteners perpendicular to grain should be avoided.

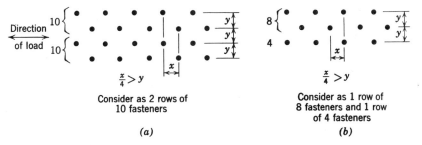

Consider as 2 rows of 10 fasteners

(a)

Consider as 1 row of 8 fasteners and 1 row of 4 fasteners

(b)

Figure 5.6.   GROUP ACTION OF FASTENERS.

TABLE 5.2

MODIFICATION FACTORS FOR CONNECTOR, BOLT AND LAG SCREW JOINTS WITH WOOD SIDE PLATES[a]

A_1/A_2	A_1, in.²[†]	Number of Fasteners in a Row										
		2	3	4	5	6	7	8	9	10	11	12
0.5 [*] [‡]	< 12	1.00	0.92	0.84	0.76	0.68	0.61	0.55	0.49	0.43	0.38	0.34
	12–19	1.00	0.95	0.88	0.82	0.75	0.68	0.62	0.57	0.52	0.48	0.43
	> 19–28	1.00	0.97	0.93	0.88	0.82	0.77	0.71	0.67	0.63	0.59	0.55
	> 28–40	1.00	0.98	0.96	0.92	0.87	0.83	0.79	0.75	0.71	0.69	0.66
	> 40–64	1.00	1.00	0.97	0.94	0.90	0.86	0.83	0.79	0.76	0.74	0.72
	> 64	1.00	1.00	0.98	0.95	0.91	0.88	0.85	0.82	0.80	0.78	0.76
1.0 [*] [‡]	< 12	1.00	0.97	0.92	0.85	0.78	0.71	0.65	0.59	0.54	0.49	0.44
	12–19	1.00	0.98	0.94	0.89	0.84	0.78	0.72	0.66	0.61	0.56	0.51
	> 19–28	1.00	1.00	0.97	0.93	0.89	0.85	0.80	0.76	0.72	0.68	0.64
	> 28–40	1.00	1.00	0.99	0.96	0.92	0.89	0.86	0.83	0.80	0.78	0.75
	> 40–64	1.00	1.00	1.00	0.97	0.94	0.91	0.88	0.85	0.84	0.82	0.80
	> 64	1.00	1.00	1.00	0.99	0.96	0.93	0.91	0.88	0.87	0.86	0.85

Notes: 1. A_1 = cross-sectional area of main member(s) before boring or grooving.
2. A_2 = sum of the cross-sectional areas of side members before boring or grooving.
[*]When A_1/A_2 exceeds 1.0, use A_2/A_1.
[†]When A_1/A_2 exceeds 1.0, use A_2 instead of A_1.
[‡]For A_1/A_2 between 0 and 1.0, interpolate or extrapolate from the tabulated values.
[a]Courtesy Canadian Standards Association.

TABLE 5.3

MODIFICATION FACTORS FOR CONNECTOR, BOLT AND LAG SCREW JOINTS WITH METAL SIDE PLATES[a]

A_1/A_2	A_1, in.^{2}	Number of Fasteners in a Row										
		2	3	4	5	6	7	8	9	10	11	12
2–12	25–39	1.00	0.94	0.87	0.80	0.73	0.67	0.61	0.56	0.51	0.46	0.42
	40–64	1.00	0.96	0.92	0.87	0.81	0.75	0.70	0.66	0.62	0.58	0.55
	65–119	1.00	0.98	0.95	0.91	0.87	0.82	0.78	0.75	0.72	0.69	0.66
	120–199	1.00	0.99	0.97	0.95	0.92	0.89	0.86	0.84	0.81	0.79	0.78
12–18	40–64	1.00	0.98	0.94	0.90	0.85	0.80	0.75	0.70	0.67	0.62	0.58
	65–119	1.00	0.99	0.96	0.93	0.90	0.86	0.82	0.79	0.75	0.72	0.69
	120–199	1.00	1.00	0.98	0.96	0.94	0.92	0.89	0.86	0.83	0.80	0.78
	> 200	1.00	1.00	1.00	0.98	0.97	0.95	0.93	0.91	0.90	0.88	0.87
18–24	40–64	1.00	1.00	0.96	0.93	0.89	0.84	0.79	0.74	0.69	0.64	0.59
	65–119	1.00	1.00	0.97	0.94	0.92	0.89	0.86	0.83	0.80	0.76	0.73
	120–199	1.00	1.00	0.99	0.98	0.96	0.94	0.92	0.90	0.88	0.86	0.85
	> 200	1.00	1.00	1.00	1.00	0.98	0.96	0.95	0.93	0.92	0.92	0.91
24–30	40–64	1.00	0.98	0.94	0.90	0.85	0.80	0.74	0.69	0.65	0.61	0.58
	65–119	1.00	0.99	0.97	0.93	0.90	0.86	0.82	0.79	0.76	0.73	0.71
	120–199	1.00	1.00	0.98	0.96	0.94	0.92	0.89	0.87	0.85	0.83	0.81
	> 200	1.00	1.00	0.99	0.98	0.97	0.95	0.93	0.92	0.90	0.89	0.89

TABLE 5.3 (Continued)

A_1/A_2	A_1, in.²	Number of Fasteners in a Row										
		2	3	4	5	6	7	8	9	10	11	12
30–35	40–64	1.00	0.96	0.92	0.86	0.80	0.74	0.68	0.64	0.60	0.57	0.55
	65–119	1.00	0.98	0.95	0.90	0.86	0.81	0.76	0.72	0.68	0.65	0.62
	120–199	1.00	0.99	0.97	0.95	0.92	0.88	0.85	0.82	0.80	0.78	0.77
	> 200	1.00	1.00	0.98	0.97	0.95	0.93	0.90	0.89	0.87	0.86	0.85
35–42	40–64	1.00	0.95	0.89	0.82	0.75	0.69	0.63	0.58	0.53	0.49	0.46
	65–119	1.00	0.97	0.93	0.88	0.82	0.77	0.71	0.67	0.63	0.59	0.56
	120–199	1.00	0.98	0.96	0.93	0.89	0.85	0.81	0.78	0.76	0.73	0.71
	> 200	1.00	0.99	0.98	0.96	0.93	0.90	0.87	0.84	0.82	0.80	0.78

Notes: 1. A_1 = cross-sectional area of main member before boring or grooving.
2. A_2 = sum of cross-sectional areas of metal side plates before drilling.
[a]Courtesy Canadian Standards Association.

TIMBER CONNECTORS

The allowable loads given here are for one timber connector unit which consists of: (*a*) one split ring with its bolt in single shear; (*b*) two shear plates used back-to-back in the contact faces of a timber-to-timber joint with their bolt in single shear; or (*c*) one shear plate with its bolt in single shear used in conjunction with a steel strap or shape in a timber-to-metal joint.

Lumber Species

The density of the wood affects the allowable loads for timber connectors. The species groupings in Table 5.1 are based on density and related factors, and they apply to connector loads.

Critical or Net Section

The critical section of a timber connector joint will probably be at the centerline of the bolt and connector. The net area at this section is equal to the full cross-sectional area of the timber less the projected area of the connectors within the member and the projected area of that portion of the bolt hole not within the connector projected area (see Table 5.5 for projected areas). When connectors are staggered, adjacent connectors with parallel to grain spacing equal to, or less than, one connector diameter are considered to occur at the same critical section. In Figure 5.4, section *A-B-C-D* is the critical section when connectors *B* and *C* have parallel to grain spacing equal to or less than one connector diameter. For greater parallel to grain spacings, section *A-A* is the critical section.

Glued laminated timber

Knots occurring at, or near, the critical section are disregarded in determining net section. The net cross-sectional area, in square inches, required at the critical section is determined by dividing the total load, in pounds, transferred through the critical section of the member by the appropriate allowable unit tensile or compressive stress for the species. In other words, for tension members divide the load by F_t and for compression members divide by F_c.

Sawn lumber

The net cross-sectional area, in square inches, required at the critical section of the member may be determined by dividing the total load in pounds transferred through the critical section by the allowable unit tensile stress, F_t, for tension members and the allowable unit compressive stress, F_c, for compression members. Values for F_t and F_c are contained in Table 2.14. Conversely the total working and load capacity, in pounds may be determined by multiplying the net area in square inches by the appropriate stress.

When the fabrication of timber connector joints is subject to supervision by the designer, the required net area may be determined by dividing total load, in pounds, transferred through the critical section by the appropriate constant in Table 5.4. This recommendation is based on the assumption that the area of knots occurring at the critical section, outside the projected area of the connector and bolt hole, will be deducted from the net section.

TABLE 5.4

REQUIRED NET SECTION CONSTANTS FOR SAWN LUMBER

Duration of Loading	Thickness of Member	Constant for Each Connector Load Group[a]			
		Group A	Group B	Group C	Group D
Normal	4 in. or less	2,350	2,000	1,650	1,300
	Over 4 in.	1,850	1,600	1,300	1,050
Long time	4 in. or less	2,100	1,800	1,500	1,200
	Over 4 in.	1,700	1,450	1,200	950
2 months	4 in. or less	2,700	2,300	1,900	1,500
(snow)	Over 4 in.	2,150	1,850	1,500	1,200
7 days	4 in. or less	2,900	2,500	2,050	1,600
	Over 4 in.	2,300	2,000	1,600	1,300
Wind or	4 in. or less	3,100	2,650	2,200	1,750
earthquake	Over 4 in.	2,500	2,150	1,750	1,400

[a]See Table 5.1 for species in each group.

Angle of Axis of Connector to Grain

The connector axis is formed by a line joining the centers of any two adjacent connectors located in the same face of a member in a joint. The angle of axis is the angle of the connector formed by the axis line and the longitudinal axis of the member. This angle is a factor in the determination of the required spacing of connectors for a given load as illustrated by angle θ in Figure 5.7.

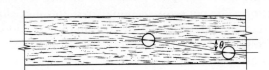

Figure 5.7.   ANGLE OF AXIS OF CONNECTOR
TO GRAIN.

Spacing of Connectors

Spacing between connectors must be considered in determining connector loads because it controls the shearing area that develops the connector load. Factors that influence spacing are angle of load to grain and angle of axis of connector to grain.

The spacing charts on pages **5**-21 to **5**-29 may be used to determine recommended spacings for full load at particular angles of load to grain. For intermediate angles of load to grain, straight-line interpolation may be used. The spacing for full load is the distance measured from the origin of the axes (lower left-hand corner of the chart) to the intersection of the proper angle of load to grain curve and radial angle of axis to grain line. The parallel to grain component of this spacing may be read at the bottom of the chart by projecting down from the point of intersection of the curve

TABLE 5.5

PROJECTED AREA OF CONNECTORS AND BOLTS
(For Use in Determining Net Sections)

Connector Type	Connector Size	Bolt Diam., in.	Placement of Connectors	Total Projected Area of Connectors and Bolts in Various Member Thicknesses, in.^{2}									
				$1\frac{1}{2}$ in.	$2\frac{1}{2}$ in.	$3\frac{1}{8}$ in.	$3\frac{1}{2}$ in.	$5\frac{1}{8}$ in.	$5\frac{1}{2}$ in.	$6\frac{3}{4}$ in.	$8\frac{3}{4}$ in	$10\frac{3}{4}$ in.	$12\frac{1}{4}$ in.
Split Rings													
1	$2\frac{1}{2}$ in.	$\frac{1}{2}$	1 face	1.73	2.29	2.65	2.86	3.77	3.98	4.69	5.81	6.94	7.78
		$\frac{1}{2}$	2 faces	2.62	3.18	3.54	3.75	4.66	4.87	5.58	6.70	7.82	8.67
2	4 in.	$\frac{3}{4}$	1 face	3.05	3.86	4.37	4.68	6.00	6.30	7.32	8.94	10.56	11.79
		$\frac{3}{4}$	2 faces	4.88	5.69	6.20	6.51	7.83	8.13	9.15	10.77	12.40	13.62
Shear Plates													
1	$2\frac{5}{8}$ in.	$\frac{3}{4}$	1 face	2.03	2.85	3.35	3.66	4.98	5.28	6.30	7.92	9.55	10.77
		$\frac{3}{4}$	2 faces	2.84	3.66	4.16	4.47	5.79	6.09	7.11	8.73	10.36	11.58
1	$2\frac{5}{8}$ in.	$\frac{3}{4}$	1 face	1.91	2.72	3.23	3.53	4.85	5.16	6.18	7.80	9.43	10.64
LG[a]		$\frac{3}{4}$	2 faces	2.60	3.41	3.92	4.22	5.54	5.85	6.87	8.49	10.11	11.33
2	4 in.	$\frac{3}{4}$	1 face	3.26	4.07	4.58	4.89	6.21	6.51	7.53	9.15	10.78	12.00
		$\frac{3}{4}$	2 faces	—	6.11	6.62	6.93	8.25	8.55	9.57	11.19	12.82	14.04
2-A	4 in.	$\frac{7}{8}$	1 face	3.37	4.30	4.89	5.24	6.77	7.12	8.29	10.16	12.04	13.45
		$\frac{7}{8}$	2 faces	—	6.26	6.85	7.20	8.73	9.08	10.25	12.12	14.00	15.41

[a]Light gage.

and the axis lines. The perpendicular to grain component may be read at the left-hand side of the chart by projecting horizontally from the point of intersection.

The quarter circle on the charts may be used to determine spacing for 50% of full load for any angle of load to grain and any angle of axis to grain; it is also the minimum spacing permissible. For loads between full load and 50% of full load, spacing is determined by interpolating radially between the 50% curve and the proper angle of load to grain curve.

When three or more connectors are used in one face of a member such as is shown in Figure 5.4, the spacing between any two connectors should be checked. In this joint the angle of load to grain is the same for all three connectors, but the angle of axis of connector to grain varies; therefore, the minimum spacing requirements are determined for each axis.

Edge Distance

The edge distance charts may be found on pages 5-21 to 5-29, the same pages as the corresponding spacing charts. The minimum edge distance is given in the lower right-hand corner of these charts. This dimension is the minimum edge distance for any condition of direction and magnitude of load. Loaded edge distance varies with angle of load to grain. Percentages of full load for various loaded edge distances and angles of load to grain are determined by projecting horizontally to either side from the point of intersection of the proper loaded edge distance line and angle of load curve.

End Distance

The end distance charts may be found on pages 5-21 to 5-29, the corresponding spacing chart pages. These charts are divided into two sections, since end distance requirements depend on whether the member is in tension or compression. If the member is in tension, the allowable percentage of full load is obtained by projecting vertically from the end distance line to the curve and then horizontally. This process can be reversed by starting with the percentage of full load required and determining the required end distance. For members in compression, the angle of load to grain must also be considered. The use of the chart is the same, except that the curve for the proper angle of load to grain should be used. Straight-line interpolation between curves should be used for intermediate angles. Some of the charts are cut off on the right-hand side. The end distance dimension at that point is the minimum permissible, and it gives the allowable percentage of load for that end distance for a 0° angle of load to grain.

Allowable Connector Loads

The connector load charts on pages 5-20 to 5-28 give the allowable load for one connector unit installed in a seasoned timber joint under normal duration of loading and dry-use conditions. For connectors, lumber is considered to be seasoned if the moisture content is no higher than approximately 15% for a depth of $\frac{3}{4}$ in. These values must be modified if end distances, edge distances, or spacing are between the minimum shown and those required for maximum load. The reductions due to reduced end distances, edge distances, and spacing are not accumulative, and the lowest value controls.

It is recommended that, wherever possible, a connector joint be designed with edge distance, end distance, and spacing for maximum load as shown on the connector load charts on pages **5-21** to **5-29**. If space is not available these dimensions can be reduced provided that the reduced allowable loads of the connectors are capable of carrying the design load. Also, a balanced design is recommended with the end distance, edge distance, and spacing proportioned so that the reduction in allowable load for each reduced dimension is approximately the same. In determining the total load capacity of a joint, however, the design load for each individual connector is calculated, and the total load that can be carried by the joint is the summation of the individual connector loads. The adjustment factors in Tables 5.2 and 5.3 apply to connectors used in a row.

The following example illustrates the design of a tension connection:

Lumber: Group B species, $F_t = 1,200$ psi, used in dry location, 4×6 main member, 2×6 side members

Connectors: $2\frac{1}{2}$ in. split rings

Design load: 15,000 lb, normal duration of load

Check net section of main and side members:

From Table 5.4, projected area, one connector and bolt is 1.73 in.^{2} in side member.

Net area $= 2(8.25 - 1.73) = 13.04$ in.^{2}

For two connectors and a bolt in the main member, projected area is 3.75 in.^{2}

Net area $= 19.25 - 3.75 = 15.50$ in.^{2}

Allowable load $= (13.04)(1,200) = 15,600$ lb $> 15,000$ lb   O.K.

Determine connector spacings for full load on each connector from charts on page **5-21**.

End distance $= 5\frac{1}{2}$ in.
Edge distance $= 2\frac{3}{4}$ in.
Spacing $= 6\frac{3}{4}$ in.

Determine number of connectors required.

From the chart on page **5-20**, full allowable load for one connector is 2,730 lb

Number of connectors required $= 15,000/2,730 = 5.4$

Try three in each side member and check for group action of connectors in a row. For this connection there are two rows of three connectors in each row.

Area of side members $A_2 = 2(8.25) = 16.50$ in.^{2}
Area of main member $A_1 = 19.25$ in.^{2}

$$\frac{A_2}{A_1} = 0.86$$

From Table 5.2, for three connectors in a row interpolate between $A_1/A_2 = 0.5$ to $A_1/A_2 = 1.0$

Modification factor $K = 0.97$
Allowable load per connector $= (0.97)(2,730) = 2,648$ lb
Allowable load $= (2)(3)(2,648) = 15,888$ lb $> 15,000$ lb   O.K.

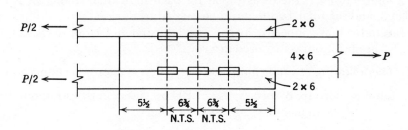

The final joint configuration would be as shown in the above sketch.

Where clearance for the connection is critical, the end distance and spacing could be reduced by the ratio of the design load to the allowable load, in this case 94%.

Adjustments of allowable connector loads for duration of load are given in Figure 2.3 or Table 2.12. Adjustment factors for various service and seasoning conditions are given on each load chart. The *National Design Specification* does not list allowable loads for connectors in end grain. Experience has shown, however, that for connectors installed in the end grain of a member, an allowable load of 60% of the allowable load at an angle of 90° to grain may be used. When the connector is installed on a sloping cut and the direction of load lies in a plane that contains the neutral axis of the member as shown in Figure 5.8a, the allowable load may be determined by application of the Hankinson formula (page **5**-5). The value for P in the Hankinson formula is the allowable load for zero angle of load to grain, and the value for Q is 60% of allowable load for a 90° angle of load to grain. When the direction of a load is perpendicular to grain on connectors installed along a sloping cut, as shown in Figure 5.8b, the allowable load may

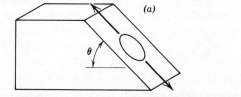

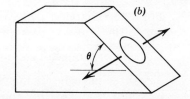

Figure 5.8.   CONNECTORS IN END GRAIN.

also be determined by the Hankinson formula using the full allowable load at 90° angle of load to grain for *P* and 60% of the allowable load at 90° angle of load to grain for *Q*. In both cases the angle θ in the formula is the angle between the sloping cut and the neutral axis of the member.

Lag bolts may be used instead of bolts in connector units, provided that: they have cut threads rather than rolled threads; they have the same diameter as the bolt specified for the connector; and they meet all other provisions for lag bolt joints as given herein. Adjustment factors for lag bolts used in place of bolts are given in Figure 5.9.

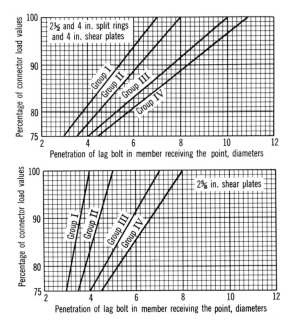

Figure 5.9.   ADJUSTMENT OF CONNECTOR LOAD VALUES WHEN LAG BOLTS ARE USED INSTEAD OF BOLTS IN CONNECTORS. (See Table 5.1 for species in each group.)

BOLTS

The allowable loads given here are for common (not high-strength) bolts.

Since a tight fit requiring forcible driving of bolts is not recommended, bolt holes should be $\frac{1}{32}$ to $\frac{1}{16}$ in. larger than the bolt, depending upon the size of the bolt. Careful centering of holes in main members and splice plates is assumed. Standard cut washers or a metal plate or strap should be inserted between the wood and the bolt head and between the wood and the nut. Nuts should be tightened snugly, but not so tightened as to cause crushing of the wood under the washer or plate.

Lumber Species

The allowable load charts on pages **5**-38 to **5**-47 apply for bolts installed in joints comprised of California redwood (close grain), Douglas fir-larch,

DESIGN AND LOAD DATA FOR CONNECTORS — $2\frac{1}{2}$ IN. SPLIT RINGS

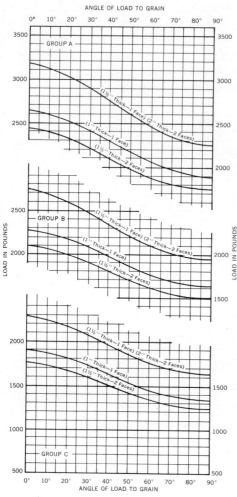

LOAD CHART
FOR NORMAL LOADING
ONE 2½″ SPLIT RING AND BOLT IN SINGLE SHEAR

Based on data from Timber Engineering Company.

$2\frac{1}{2}$ IN. SPLIT RING DATA

Split ring — dimensions, in.	
Inside diameter at center when closed	$2\frac{1}{2}$
Inside diameter at center when installed	2.54
Thickness of ring at center	0.163
Thickness of ring at edge	0.123
Depth	$\frac{3}{4}$
Lumber, minimum dimensions allowed, in.	
Width	$3\frac{1}{2}$
Thickness, rings in one face	1
Thickness, rings opposite in both faces	$1\frac{1}{2}$
Bolt, diameter, in.	$\frac{1}{2}$
Bolt hole, diameter, in.	$\frac{9}{16}$
Projected area for portion of one ring within a member, in.²	1.10
Washers, minimum	
Round, cast or malleable iron, diameter, in.	$2\frac{5}{8}$
Square plate	
Length of side, in.	2
Thickness, in.	$\frac{1}{8}$
(For trussed rafters and similar light construction standard wrought washers may be used.)	

SPLIT RING SPECIFICATIONS

Split rings shall be manufactured from hot-rolled S.A.E. 1010 carbon steel. Each ring shall form a closed true circle with the principal axis of the cross section of the ring metal parallel to the geometric axis of the ring. The ring shall fit snugly in the prepared groove. The metal section of each ring shall be beveled from the central portion towards the edges to a thickness less than that at midsection. It shall be cut through in one place in its circumference to form a tongue and slot.

ADJUSTMENTS FOR CONDITION OF LUMBER

Condition of Lumber		Percent of Load Value
When Fabricated	In Service	
Seasoned	Seasoned	100
Unseasoned	Seasoned	80
Unseasoned	Unseasoned	67

DESIGN AND LOAD DATA FOR CONNECTORS — 2½ IN. SPLIT RINGS

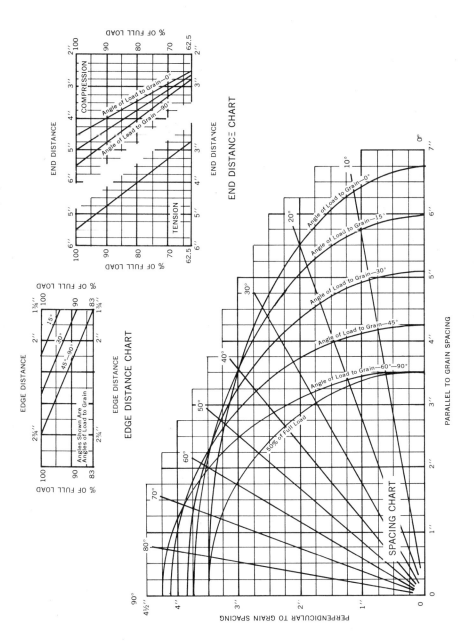

Based on data from Timber Engineering Company.

DESIGN AND LOAD DATA FOR CONNECTORS—4 IN. SPLIT RINGS

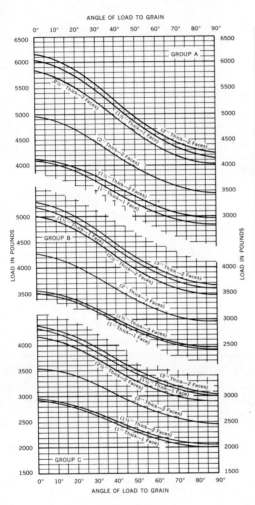

LOAD CHART
FOR NORMAL LOADING
ONE 4″ SPLIT RING AND BOLT IN SINGLE SHEAR

4 IN. SPLIT RING DATA

Split ring—dimensions, in.	
Inside diameter at center when closed	4
Inside diameter at center when installed	4.06
Thickness of ring at center	0.193
Thickness of ring at edge	0.133
Depth	1
Lumber, minimum dimensions allowed, in.	
Width	$5\frac{1}{2}$
Thickness, rings in one face	1
Thickness, rings opposite in both faces	$1\frac{1}{2}$
Bolt, diameter, in.	$\frac{3}{4}$
Bolt hole, diameter, in.	$\frac{13}{16}$
Projected area for portion of one ring within a	
member, in.²	2.24
Washers, minimum	
Round, cast or malleable iron, diameter, in.	3
Square plate	
Length of side, in.	3
Thickness, in.	$\frac{3}{16}$
(For trussed rafters and similar light construction	
standard wrought washers may be used.)	

SPLIT RING SPECIFICATIONS

Split rings shall be manufactured from hot-rolled S.A.E. 1010 carbon steel. Each ring shall form a closed true circle with the principal axis of the cross section of the ring metal parallel to the geometric axis of the ring. The ring shall fit snugly in the prepared groove. The metal section of each ring shall be beveled from the central portion toward the edges to a thickness less than that at midsection. It shall be cut through in one place in its circumference to form a tongue and slot.

ADJUSTMENTS FOR
CONDITION OF LUMBER

Condition of Lumber		Percent of Load Value
When Fabricated	In Service	
Seasoned	Seasoned	100
Unseasoned	Seasoned	80
Unseasoned	Unseasoned	67

Based on data from Timber Engineering Company.

DESIGN AND LOAD DATA FOR CONNECTORS – 4 IN. SPLIT RINGS

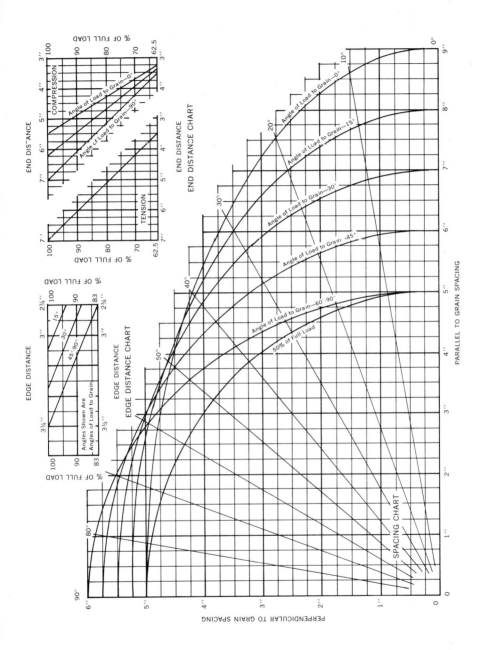

Based on data from Timber Engineering Company.

DESIGN AND LOAD DATA FOR CONNECTORS—2⅝ IN. SHEAR PLATES

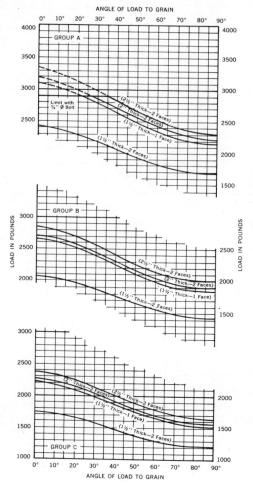

**LOAD CHART
FOR NORMAL LOADING**
ONE 2⅝″ SHEAR-PLATE UNIT AND BOLT IN SINGLE SHEAR

Based on data from Timber Engineering Company.

2⅝ IN. SHEAR PLATE DATA

Shear plates, dimensions, in. Material	Pressed Steel	
	Reg.	Lt. Ga.
Diameter of plate	2.62	2.62
Diameter of bolt hole	0.81	0.81
Depth of plate	0.42	0.35
Lumber, minimum dimensions, in.		
Face, width	3½	3½
Thickness, plates in one face only	1½	1½
Thickness, plates opposite in both faces	1½	1½
Steel shapes or straps (Thickness required when used with shear plates) Thickness of steel side plates shall be determined in accordance with AISC recommendations.		
Bolt, diameter, in.	¾	¾
Bolt hole, diameter, in.	13⁄16	13⁄16
Washers, standard, timber-to-timber connections only Round, cast or malleable iron, diameter, in.	3	3
Square plate Length of side, in.	3	3
Thickness, in.	¼	¼
(For trussed rafters and other light structures, standard wrought washers may be used.)		
Projected area, for one shear plate, in.²	1.18	1.00

SHEAR PLATE SPECIFICATIONS

Pressed steel type. Pressed steel shear plates shall be manufactured from hot-rolled S.A.E. 1010 carbon steel. Each plate shall be a true circle with a flange around the edge extending at right angles to the face of the plate and extending from one face only, the plate portion having a central bolt hole and two small perforations on opposite sides of the hole and midway from the center and circumference.

ADJUSTMENTS FOR CONDITION OF LUMBER

Condition of Lumber		Percent of Load Value
When Fabricated	In Service	
Seasoned	Seasoned	100
Unseasoned	Seasoned	80
Unseasoned	Unseasoned	67

MAXIMUM PERMISSIBLE LOADS ON SHEAR PLATES

The allowable loads for all loadings except wind shall not exceed 2,900 lb for 2⅝ in. shear plates with ¾ in. bolts. The allowable wind load shall not exceed 3,870 lb.

DESIGN AND LOAD DATA FOR CONNECTORS—2⅝ IN. SHEAR PLATES

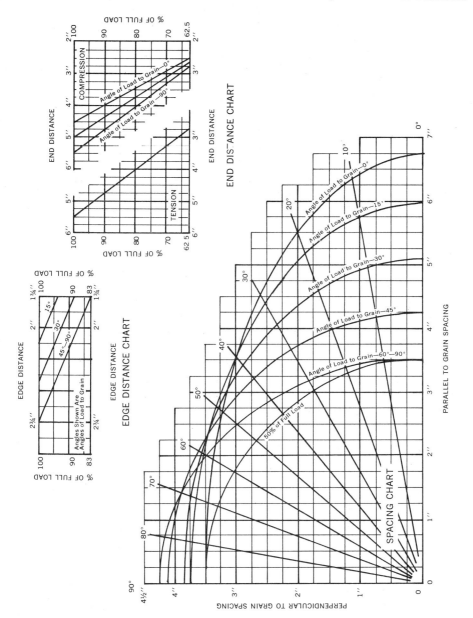

Based on data from Timber Engineering Company.

DESIGN AND LOAD DATA FOR CONNECTORS–4 IN. SHEAR PLATES (WOOD-TO-WOOD)

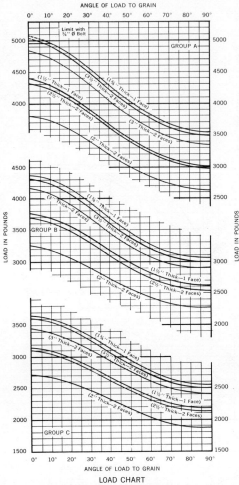

LOAD CHART
FOR NORMAL LOADING
ONE 4″ SHEAR-PLATE UNIT AND BOLT IN SINGLE SHEAR

Based on Data from Timber Engineering Company.

4 IN. SHEAR PLATE DATA

Shear plates, dimensions, in. Material	Malleable Iron	Malleable Iron
Diameter of plate	4.03	4.03
Diameter of bolt hole	0.81	0.94
Depth of plate	0.64	0.64
Lumber, minimum dimension, in.		
Face, width	$5\frac{1}{2}$	$5\frac{1}{2}$
Thickness, plates in one face only	$1\frac{1}{2}$	$1\frac{1}{2}$
Thickness, plates opposite in both faces	$1\frac{3}{4}$	$1\frac{3}{4}$
Bolt, diameter, in.	$\frac{3}{4}$	$\frac{7}{8}$
Bolt hole, diameter, in.	$\frac{13}{16}$	$\frac{15}{16}$
Washers, standard, timber-to-timber connections only Round, cast, or malleable iron, diameter, in. Square plate	3	$3\frac{1}{2}$
Length of side, in.	3	3
Thickness, in.	$\frac{1}{4}$	$\frac{1}{4}$
(For trussed rafters and other light structures, standard wrought washers may be used.)		
Projected area for one shear plate, in.²	2.58	2.58

SHEAR PLATE SPECIFICATIONS

Malleable iron types. Malleable iron shear plates shall be manufactured according to ASTM Standard Specifications A 47–68, Grade 35018, for malleable iron castings. Each casting shall consist of a perforated round plate with a flange around the edge extending at right angles to the face of the plate and projecting from one face only, the plate portion having a central bolt hole reamed to size with an integral hub concentric to the bolt hole and extending from the same face as the flange.

ADJUSTMENTS FOR CONDITION OF LUMBER

Condition of Lumber		Percent of Load Value
When Fabricated	In Service	
Seasoned	Seasoned	100
Unseasoned	Seasoned	80
Unseasoned	Unseasoned	67

MAXIMUM PERMISSIBLE LOADS ON SHEAR PLATES

The allowable loads for all loadings except wind shall not exceed 4,970 lb for 4 in. shear plates with $\frac{3}{4}$ in. bolts and 6,760 lb for 4 in. shear plates with $\frac{7}{8}$ in. bolts. The allowable wind loads shall not exceed 6,630 lb when used with a $\frac{3}{4}$ in. bolt, and 9,020 lb when used with a $\frac{7}{8}$ in. bolt.

DESIGN AND LOAD DATA FOR CONNECTOR–4 IN. SHEAR PLATES (WOOD-TO-WOOD)

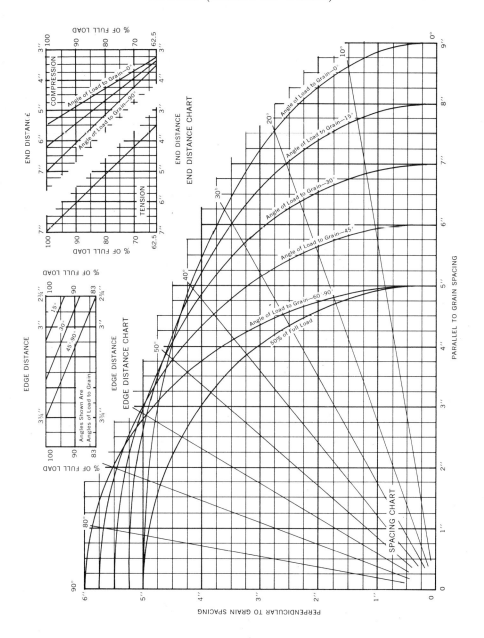

Based on data from Timber Engineering Company.

DESIGN AND LOAD DATA FOR CONNECTORS – 4 IN. SHEAR PLATES (WOOD-TO-STEEL)

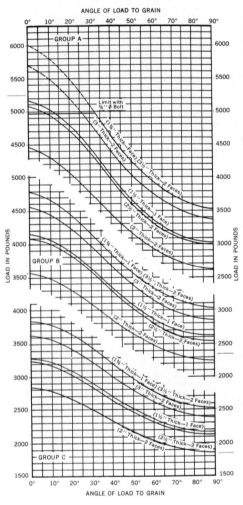

ANGLE OF LOAD TO GRAIN

LOAD CHART
FOR NORMAL LOADING
ONE 4″ SHEAR-PLATE UNIT AND BOLT IN SINGLE SHEAR

Based on data from Timber Engineering Company.

4 IN. SHEAR PLATE DATA

Shear plates, dimensions, in. Material	Malleable Iron	Malleable Iron
Diameter of plate	4.03	4.03
Diameter of bolt hole	0.81	0.94
Depth of plate	0.64	0.64
Lumber, minimum dimensions, in. Face, width	$5\frac{1}{2}$	$5\frac{1}{2}$
Thickness, plates in one face only	$1\frac{1}{2}$	$1\frac{1}{2}$
Thickness, plates opposite in both faces	$1\frac{3}{4}$	$1\frac{3}{4}$
Steel shapes or straps (Thickness required when used with shear plates) Thickness of steel side plates shall be determined in accordance with AISC recommendations.		
Bolt, diameter, in.	$\frac{3}{4}$	$\frac{7}{8}$
Bolt hole, diameter, in.	$\frac{13}{16}$	$\frac{15}{16}$
Projected area, for one shear plate, in.^{2}	2.58	2.58

SHEAR PLATE SPECIFICATIONS

Malleable iron types. Malleable iron shear plates shall be manufactured according to ASTM Standard Specifications A 47–68, Grade 35018, for malleable iron castings. Each casting shall consist of a perforated round plate with a flange around the edge extending at right angles to the face of the plate and projecting, from one face only, the plate portion having a central bolt hole reamed to size with an integral hub concentric to the bolt hole and extending from the same face as the flange.

ADJUSTMENTS FOR CONDITION OF LUMBER

Condition of Lumber		Percent of Load Value
When Fabricated	In Service	
Seasoned	Seasoned	100
Unseasoned	Seasoned	80
Unseasoned	Unseasoned	67

MAXIMUM PERMISSIBLE LOADS ON SHEAR PLATES

The allowable loads for all loadings except wind shall not exceed 4,970 lb for 4 in. shear plates with $\frac{3}{4}$ in. bolts and 6,760 lb for 4 in. shear plates with $\frac{7}{8}$ in. bolts. The allowable wind loads shall not exceed 6,630 lb when used with a $\frac{3}{4}$ in. bolt and 9,020 lb when used with a $\frac{7}{8}$ in. bolt.

For metal side plates, tabulated loads apply except that, for 4 in. shear plates, the parallel-to-grain (not perpendicular) loads for wood side plates shall be increased 18, 11, 5, and 0% for groups A, B, C, and D species, respectively, but loads shall not exceed those permitted by previous paragraph.

DESIGN AND LOAD DATA FOR CONNECTORS – 4 IN. SHEAR PLATES (WOOD-TO-STEEL)

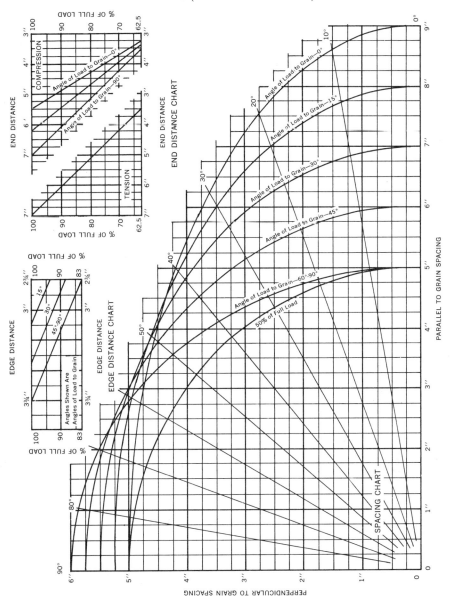

Based on data from Timber Engineering Company.

Southern pine (medium grain), or Southern cypress members. Other commonly used species, are shown in Table 5.9.

Critical or Net Section

The net area at the critical section of a bolted joint is equal to the full cross-sectional area of the timber less the projected area of bolt holes at that section. Where bolts are staggered, adjacent bolts with parallel to grain spacing less than 8 times the bolt diameter are considered to occur at the same critical section (see Figure 5.10).

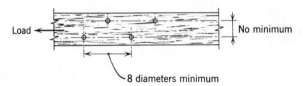

Load ←

No minimum

8 diameters minimum

Figure 5.10. STAGGERED BOLT SPACING.

The net cross-sectional area, in square inches, required at the critical section is determined by dividing the total load, in pounds, transferred through the critical section of the member by the appropriate allowable unit tensile or compressive stress for the species. In other words, for tension members, divide by F_t and for compression members divide by F_c.

Spacing of Bolts

A row of bolts is a number of bolts placed in a line parallel to the direction of load when the load is parallel or perpendicular to grain. Spacing of bolts in a row is measured from center-to-center of bolts (dimension A, Figures 5.11 and 5.12). Row spacing is measured between rows across the grain of the member (dimension B, Figures 5.11 and 5.12). Recommended bolt spacing values are given in Table 5.6.

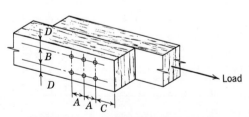

Figure 5.11. LOAD PARALLEL TO GRAIN.

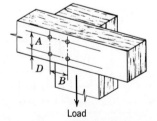

Figure 5.12. LOAD PERPENDICULAR TO GRAIN.

End and Edge Distances

End distance is the distance from the end of a member to the center of the bolt nearest the end (dimension C, Figure 5.11). Edge distance is the distance from the edge of the member to the center of the nearest bolt (dimension D, Figures 5.11 and 5.12). End and edge distance values are given in Table 5.6.

TABLE 5.6

RECOMMENDED SPACING AND DISTANCE VALUES FOR BOLTS[a]

Dimension (see Figs. 5.11 and 5.12)	Parallel to Grain Loading	Perpendicular to Grain Loading
A, c–c spacing	Minimum of 4 times bolt diameter.	4 times bolt diameter unless the design load is less than the bolt bearing capacity of side members; then spacing may be reduced proportionately.
Staggered bolts	Adjacent bolts are considered to be placed at critical section unless spaced at a minimum of 8 times the bolt diameter (see Figure 5.10).	Staggering not permitted unless design load is less than bolt bearing capacity of side members.
B, row spacing	Minimum of $1\frac{1}{2}$ times bolt diameter.	$2\frac{1}{2}$ times bolt diameter for l/d[b] ratio of 2; 5 times bolt diameter for l/d ratios of 6 or more; use straightline interpolation for l/d between 2 and 6.
	Spacing between rows paralleling a member may not exceed 5 in. unless separate splice plates are used for each row.	
C, end distance	In tension, 7 times bolt diameter for softwoods and 5 times bolt diameter for hardwoods. In compression, 4 times bolt diameter.	Minimum of 4 times bolt diameter; when members abut at a joint (not illustrated), the strength shall be evaluated also as a beam supported by fastenings (see pages **5**-8 and **5**-9).
D, edge distance	$1\frac{1}{2}$ times the bolt diameter, except that for l/d[b] ratios of more than 6, use one-half the row spacing, B.	Minimum of 4 times bolt diameter at edge toward which load acts; minimum of $1\frac{1}{2}$ times bolt diameter at opposite edge.

[a]These are minimum values for the allowable bolt loads given in the charts on pages **5**-38 to **5**-47.
[b]Ratio of length of bolt in main member, l, to diameter of bolt, d.

Allowable Bolt Loads

The charts on pages **5**-38 to **5**-47 and Table 5.9 give the allowable load for one bolt loaded in double shear in a timber joint under normal duration of loading and dry-use conditions. There is one chart for each of a number of lengths of bolts in main members. Each chart has a pair of lines, one solid and one broken, for a number of standard bolt diameters. The solid lines on the lower parts of the charts are used to determine the allowable loads for three-member joints having wood side members at least half the thickness of the main member. The broken lines on the upper parts of the charts are used to determine the allowable loads for three-member joints having steel side members which are adequate to carry the load.

Loads for more than one bolt, of either the same or miscellaneous sizes, are the sum of the loads permitted for each bolt, provided that spacings, end distances, and edge distances are sufficient to develop the full strength of each bolt in such a joint; and provided the loads are modified for group action in accordance with the recommendations given on pages **5**-9 to **5**-12.

For other than normal durations of loading, the allowable loads from the charts should be multiplied by the appropriate adjustment factor from Figure 2.3 or Table 2.12. The full allowable loads may be used for lumber that is installed at, or above, the fiber saturation point and that seasons to a maximum moisture content of 19% before full design load is applied for bolted joints with wood side members having a single bolt and loaded parallel or perpendicular to grain, or having a single row of bolts loaded parallel to grain, or having multiple rows of bolts loaded parallel to grain with separate splice plates for each row. The full allowable loads may also be used for bolted joints with steel gusset plates having a single row of bolts

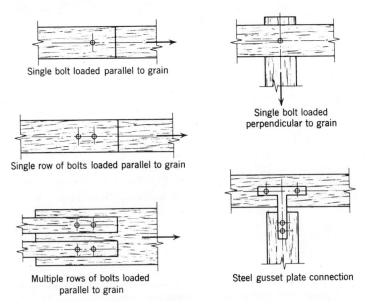

Single bolt loaded parallel to grain

Single bolt loaded
perpendicular to grain

Single row of bolts loaded parallel to grain

Multiple rows of bolts loaded
parallel to grain

Steel gusset plate connection

Figure 5.13. EXAMPLES OF BOLTED JOINTS FOR WHICH FULL ALLOWABLE LOADS MAY BE USED.

parallel to grain in each member and loaded parallel or perpendicular to grain (see Figure 5.13). For other arrangements of bolted joints, or for joints in use under other service or seasoning conditions, the allowable loads determined from the charts are multiplied by the appropriate factor from Table 5.7.

For other than three-member bolted joints, the appropriate length and load factors from Table 5.8 are applied.

TABLE 5.7

ADJUSTMENT OF BOLT LOAD VALUES FOR SERVICE AND SEASONING CONDITIONS

Condition of Lumber		Percentage Bolt Load Values
When Installed	In Service	
Seasoned[b]	Dry	100
Unseasoned (at or above fiber saturation point, MC = 30%)		
Joints as described on page **5**-32	Seasoned	100
All other joints		40
Partially seasoned	Seasoned	a
Seasoned or unseasoned	Exposed to weather	75
Seasoned or unseasoned	Always wet	67

[a]Values proportionately intermediate between 100% and 40% are used.
[b]Seasoned solid sawn lumber has a maximum moisture content of 19%. Glued laminated timber has a maximum moisture content of 16%.

TABLE 5.8

LENGTH AND LOAD FACTORS FOR BOLTED JOINTS
(For Use with Allowable Bolt Load Charts, pages **5**-38 to **5**-47 and Table 5.9)

Type of Joint	Length and Load Factors
Three-member joints Wood side members	
$b_1 = b_2 = \dfrac{b}{2}$	Use solid line for bolt length $= b$
b_1 and $b_2 > \dfrac{b}{2}$	Use solid line for bolt length $= b$
$b_1 \le b_2 < \dfrac{b}{2}$	Use solid line for bolt length $= 2b_1$
Steel side members	Use broken line for bolt length $= b$

TABLE 5.8 (Continued)

Type of Joint	Length and Load Factors
Two-member joints Wood side member $b_1 \leqslant b_2$ Steel side member	Use solid line for bolt length $= 2b_1$, and multiply the load determined by $\frac{1}{2}$. Use broken line for bolt length $=$ twice thickness of wood member, and multiply the load determined by $\frac{1}{2}$.
Multiple-member joints $b_3 < b_1, b_2$ or b_4	Use the solid line for bolt length $= 2b_3$, and multiply load determined by $\frac{1}{2}$ the number of shear planes involved. (In the illustration, number of shear planes $= 3$).
Two-member joints Load acting at angle with axis of bolt $b_1 < b_2$	To determine load component acting perpendicular to the axis of the bolt, use the solid line for bolt length $= 2b_1{}^a$, and multiply load determined by $\frac{1}{2}$. Sufficient bearing area must be provided under washers or plates to resist the component of load acting parallel to the bolt's axis. ^{a}If $b_2 < b_1$, use $2b_2$.

LAG BOLTS

The allowable loads given here are for common lag bolts (or lag screws). Lag bolts require prebored lead holes. Lead hole diameters for the shank and threaded portions of lag bolts are listed in Table 5.10. Lead holes for the shank should have a depth equal to the length of the unthreaded portion in the main member. Lag bolts should be inserted in the lead hole by turning with a wrench, not by driving with a hammer. Soap or other lubricant may be used to facilitate insertion. Standard cut washers or a metal plate or strap should be installed between the wood and the bolt head.

Lumber Species

Species load groups for lag bolt allowable loads are given in Table 5.1.

Critical or Net Section

The net section requirements for lag bolt joints are the same as for bolted joints with bolts of a diameter equal to the shank diameter of the lag bolt used. See Section 6 of this *Manual* for standard lag bolt dimensions.

TABLE 5.9
ALLOWABLE BOLT LOADS, LB[a]
ONE BOLT LOADED AT BOTH ENDS (DOUBLE SHEAR)[b,c,d]

Length of bolt in main member l	Diameter of bolt d	l/d	Projected area of bolt $A = l \times d$	Douglas Fir-Larch (Dense), Southern Pine (Dense)		California Redwood (Close grain), Douglas Fir-Larch, Southern Pine (Med. grain), Southern Cypress		Oak, Red and White		Douglas Fir, South, Southern Pine (Open grain)		Eastern Hemlock-Tamarack, California Redwood (Open grain), Hem-Fir		Spruce-Pine-Fir, Sitka Spruce, Yellow Poplar, Idaho White Pine, Eastern Spruce, Lodgepole Pine	
				Parallel to grain P	Perpendicular to grain Q	Parallel to grain P	Perpendicular to grain Q	Parallel to grain P	Perpendicular to grain Q	Parallel to grain P	Perpendicular to grain Q	Parallel to grain P	Perpendicular to grain Q	Parallel to grain P	Perpendicular to grain Q
$1\frac{1}{2}$	$\frac{1}{2}$	3.00	0.750	1,120	500	960	430	830	650	820	370	800	270	700	260
	$\frac{5}{8}$	2.40	0.937	1,410	570	1,210	490	1,050	730	1,030	420	1,000	310	870	300
	$\frac{3}{4}$	2.00	1.125	1,700	630	1,460	540	1,260	820	1,240	470	1,210	350	1,040	330
	$\frac{7}{8}$	1.71	1.312	1,990	660	1,700	590	1,470	900	1,440	520	1,410	380	1,220	370
	1	1.50	1.500	2,270	760	1,940	650	1,680	980	1,650	570	1,610	420	1,390	400
2	$\frac{1}{2}$	4.00	1.000	1,400	670	1,200	570	1,040	870	1,020	500	990	370	900	350
	$\frac{5}{8}$	3.20	1.250	1,860	760	1,590	650	1,380	980	1,350	560	1,320	410	1,160	400
	$\frac{3}{4}$	2.67	1.500	2,260	840	1,930	720	1,680	1,090	1,640	630	1,600	460	1,390	440
	$\frac{7}{8}$	2.29	1.750	2,650	930	2,270	790	1,970	1,200	1,920	690	1,880	510	1,620	490
	1	2.00	2.000	3,030	1,010	2,590	870	2,250	1,310	2,200	760	2,150	550	1,860	530
$2\frac{1}{2}$	$\frac{1}{2}$	5.00	1.250	1,510	840	1,290	720	1,130	1,080	1,100	620	1,030	460	1,020	440
	$\frac{5}{8}$	4.00	1.562	2,190	950	1,870	810	1,620	1,220	1,590	710	1,550	520	1,410	500
	$\frac{3}{4}$	3.33	1.875	2,780	1,050	2,370	900	2,060	1,360	2,020	790	1,970	580	1,730	560
	$\frac{7}{8}$	2.86	2.187	3,290	1,160	2,810	990	2,440	1,500	2,390	860	2,330	630	2,030	610
	1	2.50	2.500	3,770	1,270	3,220	1,080	2,800	1,640	2,740	940	2,630	690	2,320	670

TABLE 5.9 (Continued)

Length of bolt in main member *l*	Diameter of bolt *d*	*l/d*	Projected area of bolt *A* = *l* × *d*	Douglas Fir-Larch (Dense), Southern Pine (Dense)		California Redwood (Close grain), Douglas Fir-Larch, Southern Pine (Med. grain), Southern Cypress		Oak, Red and White		Douglas Fir, South, Southern Pine (Open grain)		Eastern Hemlock-Tamarack, California Redwood (Open grain), Hem-Fir		Spruce-Pine-Fir, Sitka Spruce, Yellow Poplar, Idaho White Pine, Eastern Spruce, Lodgepole Pine	
				Parallel to grain *P*	Perpendicular to grain *Q*	Parallel to grain *P*	Perpendicular to grain *Q*	Parallel to grain *P*	Perpendicular to grain *Q*	Parallel to grain *P*	Perpendicular to grain *Q*	Parallel to grain *P*	Perpendicular to grain *Q*	Parallel to grain *P*	Perpendicular to grain *Q*
3	1/2	6.00	1.500	1,530	970	1,300	860	1,130	1,130	1,110	750	1,080	550	1,050	530
	5/8	4.80	1.875	2,340	1,140	2,000	970	1,740	1,470	1,700	850	1,670	620	1,590	600
	3/4	4.00	2.250	3,150	1,270	2,690	1,080	2,340	1,630	2,290	940	2,240	690	2,030	670
	7/8	3.43	2.625	3,870	1,390	3,310	1,190	2,870	1,800	2,810	1,040	2,750	760	2,420	730
	1	3.00	3.000	4,500	1,520	3,840	1,300	3,340	1,960	3,270	1,130	3,190	830	2,780	800
3½	1/2	7.00	1.750	1,530	1,020	1,300	970	1,130	1,130	1,110	870	1,080	640	1,060	620
	5/8	5.60	2.187	2,400	1,300	2,050	1,130	1,780	1,680	1,740	990	1,700	720	1,630	700
	3/4	4.67	2.625	3,350	1,480	2,860	1,260	2,480	1,910	2,430	1,100	2,380	810	2,260	780
	7/8	4.00	3.062	4,290	1,620	3,670	1,390	3,180	2,100	3,120	1,210	3,040	890	2,770	860
	1	3.50	3.500	5,140	1,770	4,390	1,520	3,810	2,290	3,730	1,320	3,650	970	3,220	930
4	1/2	8.00	2.000	1,530	1,010	1,300	1,010	1,130	1,130	1,110	960	1,080	700	1,060	680
	5/8	6.40	2.500	2,400	1,410	2,050	1,290	1,780	1,780	1,740	1,130	1,700	830	1,650	800
	3/4	5.33	3.000	3,440	1,670	2,940	1,440	2,550	2,160	2,500	1,260	2,440	920	2,330	890
	7/8	4.57	3.500	4,520	1,860	3,860	1,590	3,350	2,400	3,280	1,380	3,210	1,010	3,050	980
	1	4.00	4.000	5,600	2,030	4,790	1,730	4,160	2,620	4,070	1,510	3,980	1,110	3,620	1,070
4½	5/8	7.20	2.812	2,400	1,430	2,050	1,400	1,780	1,780	1,740	1,220	1,700	890	1,650	860
	3/4	6.00	3.375	3,440	1,830	2,940	1,620	2,550	2,360	2,500	1,410	2,440	1,040	2,370	1,000
	7/8	5.14	3.937	4,670	2,080	3,990	1,790	3,460	2,690	3,390	1,560	3,310	1,140	3,160	1,100
	1	4.50	4.500	5,860	2,280	5,010	1,950	4,350	2,940	4,260	1,700	4,160	1,250	3,940	1,200
	1¼	3.60	5.625	8,190	2,670	7,000	2,280	6,080	3,450	5,950	1,990	5,820	1,460	5,160	1,410

5½	⅝	8.80	3.437	2,400	1,390	2,050	1,400	1,780	1,780	1,740	1,360	1,700	1,000	1,650	960
	¾	7.33	4.125	3,440	1,920	2,940	1,880	2,550	2,480	2,500	1,710	2,440	1,260	2,370	1,210
	⅞	6.29	4.812	4,670	2,410	3,990	2,170	3,460	3,100	3,390	1,900	3,310	1,400	3,220	1,340
	1	5.50	5.500	6,140	2,750	5,250	2,380	4,560	3,550	4,460	2,070	4,360	1,520	4,170	1,470
	1¼	4.40	6.875	9,080	3,260	7,770	2,790	6,740	4,210	6,600	2,430	6,450	1,780	6,070	1,720
7½	⅝	12.00	4.687	2,400	1,210	2,050	1,260	1,780	1,560	1,740	1,290	1,700	950	1,650	910
	¾	10.00	5.625	3,440	1,760	2,940	1,810	2,550	2,270	2,500	1,790	2,440	1,320	2,370	1,270
	⅞	8.57	6.562	4,670	2,390	3,990	2,420	3,460	3,090	3,390	2,360	3,310	1,730	3,220	1,670
	1	7.50	7.500	6,140	3,060	5,250	3,040	4,560	3,950	4,460	2,790	4,360	2,050	4,230	1,980
	1¼	6.00	9.375	9,540	4,280	8,150	3,800	7,080	5,530	6,930	3,110	6,770	2,430	6,590	2,340
9½	¾	12.67	7.125	3,440	1,570	2,940	1,640	2,550	2,030	2,500	1,700	2,440	1,250	2,370	1,200
	⅞	10.86	8.312	4,670	2,180	3,990	2,270	3,460	2,810	3,390	2,250	3,310	1,650	3,220	1,590
	1	9.50	9.500	6,140	2,870	5,250	2,950	4,560	3,710	4,460	2,900	4,360	2,130	4,230	2,050
	1¼	7.60	11.875	9,540	4,490	8,150	4,470	7,080	5,790	6,930	4,120	6,770	3,030	6,610	2,910
	1½	6.33	14.250	13,760	6,080	11,770	5,510	10,210	7,850	10,000	4,820	9,780	3,540	9,510	3,410
11½	⅞	13.14	10.062	4,670	1,980	3,990	2,060	3,460	2,550	3,390	2,170	3,310	1,590	3,220	1,530
	1	11.50	11.500	6,140	2,650	5,250	2,760	4,560	3,420	4,460	2,780	4,360	2,040	4,230	1,970
	1¼	9.20	14.375	9,540	4,250	8,150	4,360	7,080	5,490	6,930	4,260	6,770	3,130	6,610	3,010
	1½	7.67	17.250	13,760	6,170	11,770	6,160	10,210	7,970	10,000	5,720	9,780	4,200	9,510	4,050
13½	1	13.50	13.500	6,140	2,410	5,250	2,530	4,560	3,120	4,460	2,680	4,360	1,970	4,230	1,900
	1¼	10.80	16.875	9,540	3,990	8,150	4,160	7,080	5,150	6,920	4,120	6,770	3,020	6,610	2,910
	1½	9.00	20.250	13,760	5,940	11,770	6,030	10,210	7,670	10,000	5,900	9,780	4,330	9,510	4,170

a From *National Design Specification.*
b Three (3) member joint.
c Normal loading conditions.
d When metal plates are used for side members the tabulated loads for parallel to grain loading may be increased 25%, but no increase should be made for perpendicular to grain loads.

ALLOWABLE BOLT LOADS FOR LENGTH OF BOLT
IN MAIN MEMBER = 1½ IN.

For one bolt in shear installed in California redwood (close grain), Douglas fir-larch, Southern pine (medium grain), or Southern cypress lumber under normal duration of loading. See Table 5.7 for adjustments for service and seasoning conditions. See Table 5.8 for joint and side member thickness considerations. Project from the intersection of the appropriate bolt diameter and angle of load to grain lines to the appropriate load scale. For wood side members, project vertically down from the intersection; for steel side members, project horizontally to the left from the intersection.

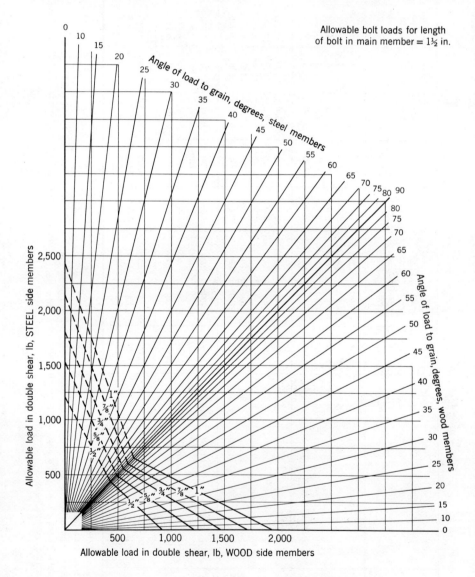

ALLOWABLE BOLT LOADS FOR LENGTH OF BOLT
IN MAIN MEMBER = $2\frac{1}{2}$ IN.

For one bolt in shear installed in California redwood (close grain), Douglas fir-larch, Southern pine (medium grain), or Southern cypress lumber under normal duration of loading. See Table 5.7 for adjustments for service and seasoning conditions. See Table 5.8 for joint and side member thickness considerations. Project from the intersection of the appropriate bolt diameter and angle of load to grain lines to the appropriate load scale. For wood side members, project vertically down from the intersection; for steel side members, project horizontally to the left from the intersection.

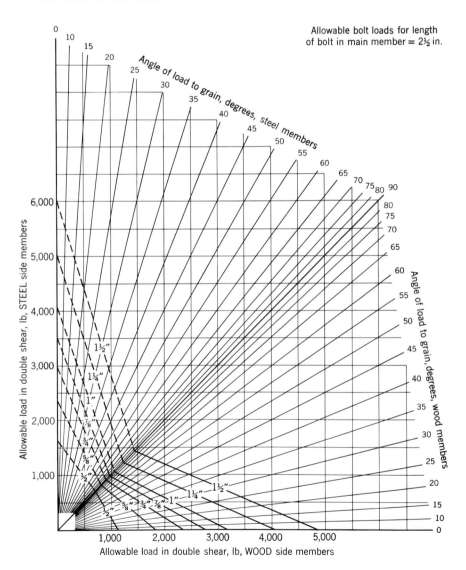

ALLOWABLE BOLT LOADS FOR LENGTH OF BOLT
IN MAIN MEMBER = 3⅛ IN.

For one bolt in shear installed in California redwood (close grain), Douglas fir-larch, Southern pine (medium grain), or Southern cypress lumber under normal duration of loading. See Table 5.7 for adjustments for service and seasoning conditions. See Table 5.8 for joint and side member thickness considerations. Project from the intersection of the appropriate bolt diameter and angle of load to grain lines to the appropriate load scale. For wood side members, project vertically down from the intersection; for steel side members, project horizontally to the left from the intersection.

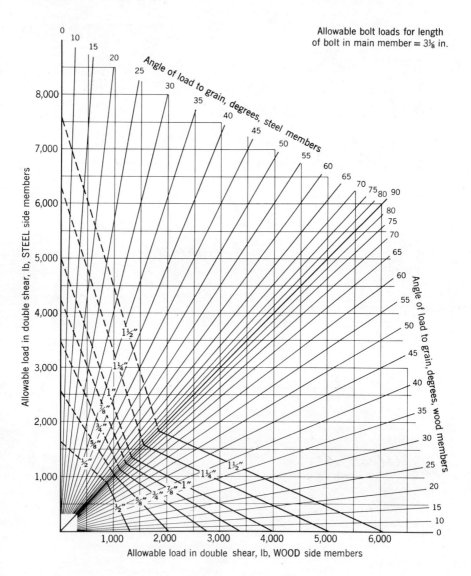

ALLOWABLE BOLT LOADS FOR LENGTH OF BOLT
IN MAIN MEMBER = $3\frac{1}{2}$ IN.

For one bolt in shear installed in California redwood (close grain), Douglas fir-larch, Southern pine (medium grain), or Southern cypress lumber under normal duration of loading. See Table 5.7 for adjustments for service and seasoning conditions. See Table 5.8 for joint and side member thickness considerations. Project from the intersection of the appropriate bolt diameter and angle of load to grain lines to the appropriate load scale. For wood side members, project vertically down from the intersection; for steel side members, project horizontally to the left from the intersection.

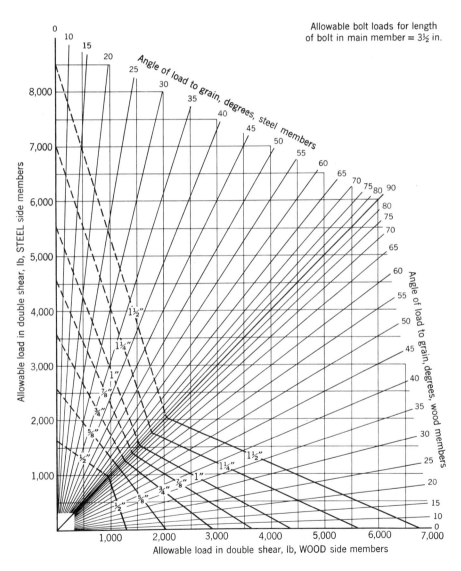

ALLOWABLE BOLT LOADS FOR LENGTH OF BOLT
IN MAIN MEMBER = 5⅛ IN.

For one bolt in shear installed in California redwood (close grain), Douglas fir-larch, Southern pine (medium grain), or Southern cypress lumber under normal duration of loading. See Table 5.7 for adjustments for service and seasoning conditions. See Table 5.8 for joint and side member thickness considerations. Project from the intersection of the appropriate bolt diameter and angle of load to grain lines to the appropriate load scale. For wood side members, project vertically down from the intersection; for steel side members, project horizontally to the left from the intersection.

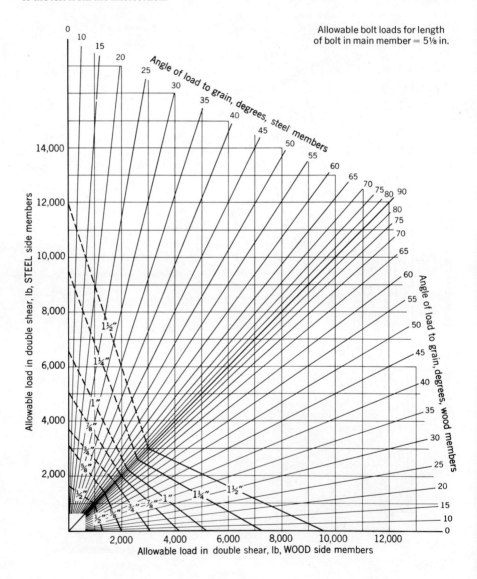

ALLOWABLE BOLT LOADS FOR LENGTH OF BOLT IN MAIN MEMBER = $5\frac{1}{2}$ IN.

For one bolt in shear installed in California redwood (close grain), Douglas fir-larch, Southern pine (medium grain), or Southern cypress lumber under normal duration of loading. See Table 5.7 for adjustments for service and seasoning conditions. See Table 5.8 for joint and side member thickness considerations. Project from the intersection of the appropriate bolt diameter and angle of load to grain lines to the appropriate load scale. For wood side members, project vertically down from the intersection; for steel side members, project horizontally to the left from the intersection.

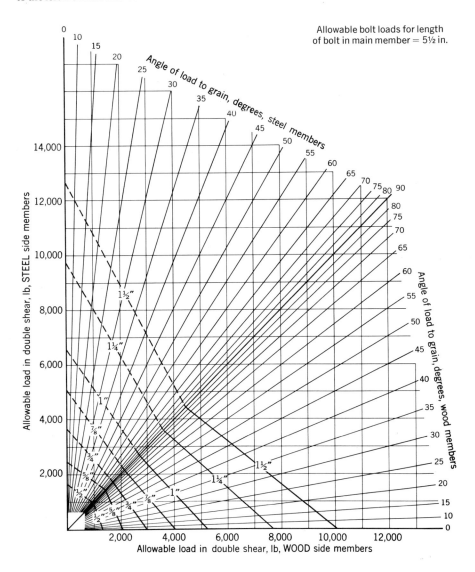

Allowable bolt loads for length of bolt in main member = $5\frac{1}{2}$ in.

ALLOWABLE BOLT LOADS FOR LENGTH OF BOLT
IN MAIN MEMBER = $6\frac{3}{4}$ IN.

For one bolt in shear installed in California redwood (close grain), Douglas fir-larch, Southern pine (medium grain), or Southern cypress lumber under normal duration of loading. See Table 5.7 for adjustments for service and seasoning conditions. See Table 5.8 for joint and side member thickness considerations. Project from the intersection of the appropriate bolt diameter and angle of load to grain lines to the appropriate load scale. For wood side members, project vertically down from the intersection; for steel side members, project horizontally to the left from the intersection.

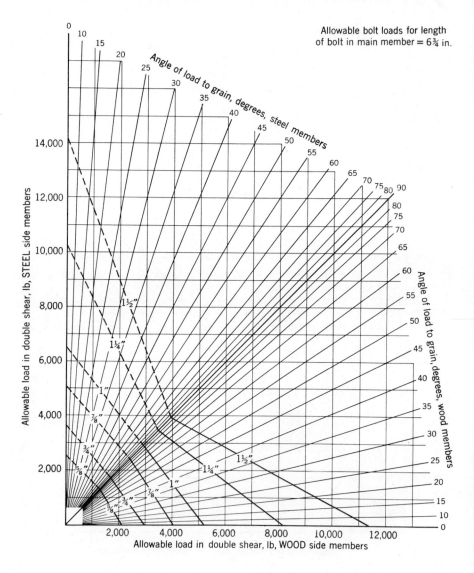

ALLOWABLE BOLT LOADS FOR LENGTH OF BOLT
IN MAIN MEMBER = 8¾ IN.

For one bolt in shear installed in California redwood (close grain), Douglas fir-larch, Southern pine (medium grain), or Southern cypress lumber under normal duration of loading. See Table 5.7 for adjustments for service and seasoning conditions. See Table 5.8 for joint and side member thickness considerations. Project from the intersection of the appropriate bolt diameter and angle of load to grain lines to the appropriate load scale. For wood side members, project vertically down from the intersection; for steel side members, project horizontally to the left from the intersection.

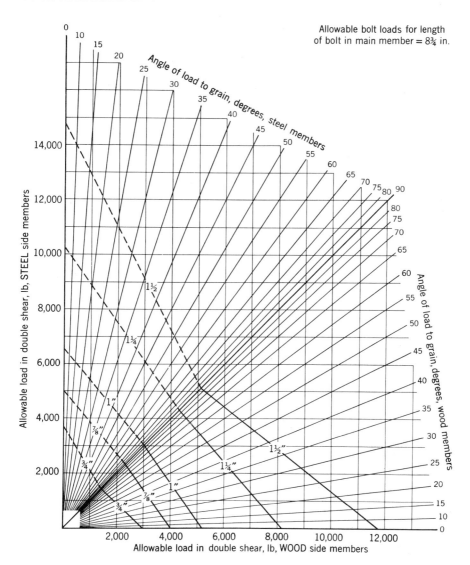

Allowable bolt loads for length of bolt in main member = 8¾ in.

ALLOWABLE BOLT LOADS FOR LENGTH OF BOLT
IN MAIN MEMBER = 10¾ IN.

For one bolt in shear installed in California redwood (close grain), Douglas fir-larch, Southern pine (medium grain), or Southern cypress lumber under normal duration of loading. See Table 5.7 for adjustments for service and seasoning conditions. See Table 5.8 for joint and side member thickness considerations. Project from the intersection of the appropriate bolt diameter and angle of load to grain lines to the appropriate load scale. For wood side members, project vertically down from the intersection; for steel side members, project horizontally to the left from the intersection.

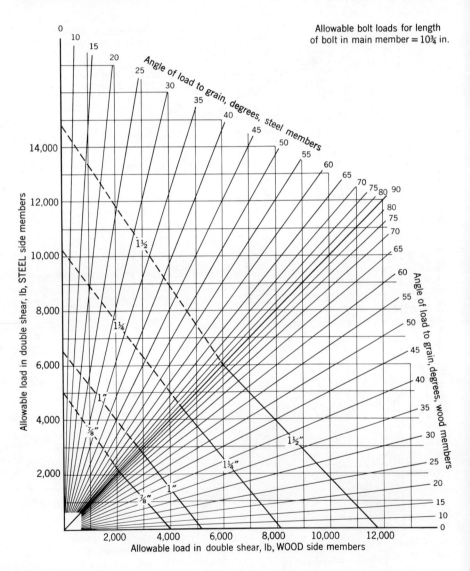

ALLOWABLE BOLT LOADS FOR LENGTH OF BOLT
IN MAIN MEMBER = 12¼ IN.

For one bolt in shear installed in California redwood (close grain), Douglas fir-larch, Southern pine (medium grain), or Southern cypress lumber under normal duration of loading. See Table 5.7 for adjustments for service and seasoning conditions. See Table 5.8 for joint and side member thickness considerations. Project from the intersection of the appropriate bolt diameter and angle of load to grain lines to the appropriate load scale. For wood side members, project vertically down from the intersection; for steel side members, project horizontally to the left from the intersection.

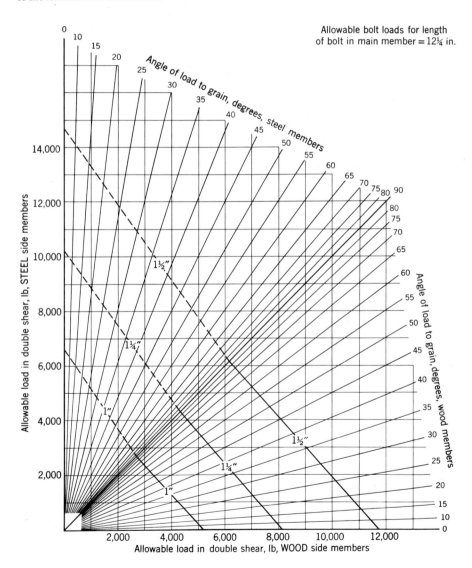

Spacing, End Distance, and Edge Distance

Spacing, end distance, and edge distance requirements for lag bolts are the same as those for bolts of a diameter equal to the shank diameter of the lag bolt used.

Allowable Lag Bolt Loads

The allowable loads apply for one lag bolt in a two-member joint under normal duration of loading and dry-use conditions. The total allowable load for more than one lag bolt is the sum of the loads for each lag bolt, provided that spacings, end distances, and edge distances are sufficient to develop the full strength of each lag bolt and provided the loads are modified for group action in accordance with the recommendations given on pages **5**-9 to **5**-12. For other than normal durations of loading, the allowable loads should be multiplied by the appropriate adjustment factor from Figure 2.3 or Table 2.12.

The full allowable loads may be used for lumber that is installed unseasoned and which seasons to a maximum moisture content of 19% before full design load is applied for lag bolt joints having a single lag bolt loaded parallel or perpendicular to grain, or a single row of lag bolts loaded parallel to grain, or multiple rows of lag bolts loaded parallel to grain with separate splice plates for each row. For other types of lag bolt joints, the full allowable lag bolt load is multiplied by 0.40. For joints in use under other service or seasoning conditions, the loads determined are multiplied by the appropriate factor from Table 5.7 for bolted joints.

Withdrawal loads

The chart on page **5**-56 may be used to determine the allowable withdrawal load for lag bolts installed in the side grain of a member. If possible, lag bolts should not be loaded in withdrawal from end grain. When this condition is unavoidable, the allowable load as determined from the chart is multiplied by 0.75.

The withdrawal load may not exceed the allowable tensile strength of the lag bolt at its net (root) section. A depth of engagement of the lag bolt thread in its lead hole of 7 diameters for Group I species, 8 diameters for Group II, 10 diameters for Group III, and 11 diameters for Group IV species (see Table 5.1 for species in each group) will develop approximately the ultimate tensile strength of the lag bolt in axial withdrawal.

Lateral loads

Tables 5.11 and 5.12 may be used to determine the allowable lateral load for one lag bolt installed in the side grain of a two-member joint comprised of seasoned Group II or Group III (see Table 5.1) species with load applied either parallel or perpendicular to grain. Member thickness and shank and thread penetration in the main member have been taken into account in preparing Tables 5.11 and 5.12. To determine allowable lateral loads for any other angle of load to grain, the Hankinson formula or nomographs given

TABLE 5.10

LEAD HOLE DIAMETER FOR LAG BOLTS

Nominal Diameter of Lag Bolt, in.	Shank (Unthreaded) Portion, in.	Diameter of Lead Hole, in.		
		Threaded Portion		
		Group I Species[a]	Group II Species[a]	Groups III and IV Species[a]
$\frac{1}{4}$	$\frac{1}{4}$	$\frac{3}{16}$	$\frac{5}{32}$	$\frac{3}{32}$
$\frac{5}{16}$	$\frac{5}{16}$	$\frac{13}{64}$	$\frac{3}{16}$	$\frac{9}{64}$
$\frac{3}{8}$	$\frac{3}{8}$	$\frac{1}{4}$	$\frac{15}{64}$	$\frac{11}{64}$
$\frac{7}{16}$	$\frac{7}{16}$	$\frac{19}{64}$	$\frac{9}{32}$	$\frac{13}{64}$
$\frac{1}{2}$	$\frac{1}{2}$	$\frac{11}{32}$	$\frac{5}{16}$	$\frac{15}{64}$
$\frac{9}{16}$	$\frac{9}{16}$	$\frac{13}{32}$	$\frac{23}{64}$	$\frac{9}{32}$
$\frac{5}{8}$	$\frac{5}{8}$	$\frac{29}{64}$	$\frac{13}{32}$	$\frac{5}{16}$
$\frac{3}{4}$	$\frac{3}{4}$	$\frac{9}{16}$	$\frac{1}{2}$	$\frac{13}{32}$
$\frac{7}{8}$	$\frac{7}{8}$	$\frac{43}{64}$	$\frac{39}{64}$	$\frac{33}{64}$
1	1	$\frac{51}{64}$	$\frac{23}{32}$	$\frac{5}{8}$
$1\frac{1}{8}$	$1\frac{1}{8}$	$\frac{59}{64}$	$\frac{53}{64}$	$\frac{3}{4}$
$1\frac{1}{4}$	$1\frac{1}{4}$	$1\frac{1}{16}$	$\frac{15}{16}$	$\frac{7}{8}$

[a]See Table 5.1 for species in each group.

in Figure 5.3 are used. Allowable loads for lateral resistance, when the load acts perpendicular to grain and the lag bolt is inserted parallel to the fibers (i.e., in the end grain of the member), may be taken as two-thirds of those for lateral resistance when the load acts perpendicular to the grain and the lag bolt is inserted perpendicular to the grain (i.e., in the side grain of the member).

For allowable loads for lateral resistance, when lag bolts are installed with metal side members, see Table 5.13. If metal side members greater than $\frac{1}{2}$ in. thick are used, the loads for lag bolts should be reduced in proportion to the lesser penetration of the lag bolt. The allowable stresses for the metal in the side member should not be exceeded.

TABLE 5.11

ALLOWABLE LATERAL LOADS FOR LAG BOLTS IN GROUP II SPECIES[a,b] WOOD SIDE MEMBERS

Lag Bolt Diameter	Thickness of Side Member															
	1½ in.				2½ in.				3½ in.				5½ in.			
Length, in.	4	5	6	7	6	7	8	9	8	9	10	11	11	12	13	14
Diameter, in.	Load Acting Parallel to Grain, lb															
1/4	170	200	230	240												
5/16	210	280	330	350												
3/8	240	370	420	450	370	430	480	520	390	430						
7/16	270	400	510	560	430	570	630	680	530	570						
1/2	290	440	600	660	470	650	770	840	640	740	830	920	690	740		
5/8	360	530	710	790	550	750	970	1,130	770	1,000	1,240	1,360	980	1,140	1,210	1,290
3/4					620	840	1,080	1,340	890	1,140	1,430	1,740	1,150	1,420	1,700	1,810
7/8					710	950	1,200	1,450	980	1,260	1,570	1,910	1,320	1,630	1,950	2,290
1					790	1,070	1,360	1,640	1,070	1,370	1,710	2,070	1,490	1,830	2,190	2,560
1⅛									1,180	1,510	1,840	2,220	1,620	2,000	2,390	2,790
1¼									1,270	1,630	1,990	2,340	1,720	2,120	2,540	2,970

	Load Acting Perpendicular to Grain, lb															
$\frac{1}{4}$	170	190	220	230	280	330	360	390	300	330	550	600	450	480	730	770
$\frac{5}{16}$	180	240	280	300	310	410	440	480	370	410	740	820	590	680	930	990
$\frac{3}{8}$	180	280	320	340	310	420	500	540	420	480	790	960	640	780	1,010	1,190
$\frac{7}{16}$	190	290	360	400	330	450	580	680	470	600	820	990	680	840	1,090	1,280
$\frac{1}{2}$	190	290	390	430	340	460	600	740	490	650	850	1,030	740	910	1,190	1,400
$\frac{5}{8}$	210	320	430	470	370	500	630	760	510	650	920	1,110	810	1,000	1,270	1,480
$\frac{3}{4}$					390	540	680	820	530	680	990	1,170	860	1,060		
$\frac{7}{8}$									590	750						
1									640	810						
$1\frac{1}{8}$																
$1\frac{1}{4}$																

aSee Table 5.1 for species in this group.
bSee *National Design Specification for Stress-Grade Lumber and Its Fastenings* for Group I and IV species.

TABLE 5.12

ALLOWABLE LATERAL LOADS FOR LAG BOLTS IN GROUP III SPECIES[a,b]
WOOD SIDE MEMBERS

Load Acting Parallel to Grain, lb

Lag Bolt Diameter / Length, in.	Thickness of Side Member															
	1½ in.				2½ in.				3½ in.				5½ in.			
Diameter, in.	4	5	6	7	6	7	8	9	8	9	10	11	11	12	13	14
$\frac{1}{4}$	130	180	200	210												
$\frac{5}{16}$	150	220	290	310												
$\frac{3}{8}$	170	260	360	410	270	370	430	460	350	380						
$\frac{7}{16}$	190	290	400	500	310	420	550	610	410	520						
$\frac{1}{2}$	210	310	430	560	340	460	600	750	460	590	750	830	620	670		
$\frac{5}{8}$	260	380	510	640	400	540	700	860	560	720	900	1,110	700	870	1,040	1,160
$\frac{3}{4}$					440	600	780	960	640	820	1,030	1,250	830	1,020	1,220	1,440
$\frac{7}{8}$					500	680	860	1,040	700	910	1,130	1,370	950	1,170	1,400	1,640
1					560	770	970	1,180	770	990	1,230	1,490	1,070	1,320	1,580	1,840
$1\frac{1}{8}$									850	1,080	1,320	1,600	1,170	1,440	1,720	2,010
$1\frac{1}{4}$									910	1,170	1,430	1,690	1,230	1,530	1,830	2,140

	Load Acting Perpendicular to Grain. lb															
$\frac{1}{4}$	120	170	200	210	200	280	330	350	260	290						
$\frac{5}{16}$	130	190	250	270	220	300	390	430	290	370						
$\frac{3}{8}$	130	200	280	310	220	300	390	490	300	380						
$\frac{7}{16}$	140	210	280	350	240	320	420	520	330	430						
$\frac{1}{2}$	140	210	280	360	240	330	430	530	350	450	480	540	400	430		
$\frac{5}{8}$	150	230	310	380	260	360	450	540	360	470	540	660	420	520	620	690
$\frac{3}{4}$					280	380	490	590	380	490	560	680	450	560	670	790
$\frac{7}{8}$									420	540	580	710	490	610	730	850
1									450	580	610	740	530	660	790	920
$1\frac{1}{8}$											660	800	580	720	860	1,000
$1\frac{1}{4}$											710	840	610	760	910	1,070

[a]See Table 5.1 for species in this group.
[b]See *National Design Specification for Stress-Grade Lumber and Its Fastenings* for Group I and IV species.

TABLE 5.13

ALLOWABLE LATERAL LOADS FOR LAG BOLTS IN GROUP II AND III SPECIES[a,b,c] $\frac{1}{2}$ IN. METAL SIDE MEMBERS

Length of Lag Bolt, in.	Diameter of Lag Bolt Shank, in.	GROUP II		GROUP III	
		Total Lateral Load per Lag Bolt in Single Shear, lb		Total Lateral Load per Lag Bolt in Single Shear, lb	
		Parallel to Grain	Perpendicular to Grain	Parallel to Grain	Perpendicular to Grain
3	$\frac{1}{4}$	210	160	155	120
	$\frac{5}{16}$	265	180	190	130
	$\frac{3}{8}$	320	195	230	140
	$\frac{7}{16}$	370	210	265	150
	$\frac{1}{2}$	415	215	295	155
	$\frac{5}{8}$	490	235	350	170
4	$\frac{1}{4}$d	235	185	210	165
	$\frac{5}{16}$	355	240	290	200
	$\frac{3}{8}$	480	290	345	210
	$\frac{7}{16}$	575	320	405	230
	$\frac{1}{2}$	625	325	450	235
	$\frac{5}{8}$	740	355	530	255
5	$\frac{5}{16}$	375	255	335	230
	$\frac{3}{8}$	535	325	470	295
	$\frac{7}{16}$	710	405	535	350
	$\frac{1}{2}$	850	440	610	315
	$\frac{5}{8}$	1,005	480	720	345
	$\frac{3}{4}$	1,190	525	855	375
6	$\frac{5}{16}$d	400	270	345	235
	$\frac{3}{8}$	545	330	490	300
	$\frac{7}{16}$	735	415	660	375
	$\frac{1}{2}$	945	490	770	400
	$\frac{5}{8}$	1,250	600	900	430
	$\frac{3}{4}$	1,480	650	1,060	460
7	$\frac{3}{8}$d	555	340	500	305
	$\frac{7}{16}$	750	425	670	380
	$\frac{1}{2}$	970	505	865	450
	$\frac{5}{8}$	1,460	700	1,020	490
	$\frac{3}{4}$	2,030	890	1,290	570
8	$\frac{7}{16}$d	760	430	680	385
	$\frac{1}{2}$	985	510	880	455
	$\frac{5}{8}$	1,500	720	1,325	635
	$\frac{3}{4}$	2,130	935	1,550	680
	$\frac{7}{8}$	2,720	1,130	1,950	810

TABLE 5.13 (Continued)

Length of Lag Bolt, in.	Diameter of Lag Bolt Shank, in.	GROUP II		GROUP III	
		Total Lateral Load per Lag Bolt in Single Shear, lb		Total Lateral Load per Lag Bolt in Single Shear, lb	
		Parallel to Grain	Perpendicular to Grain	Parallel to Grain	Perpendicular to Grain
9	$\frac{1}{2}$d	990	515	885	460
	$\frac{5}{8}$	1,510	725	1,360	650
	$\frac{3}{4}$	2,160	950	1,780	785
	$\frac{7}{8}$	2,880	1,200	2,060	855
10	$\frac{5}{8}$d	1,540	740	1,380	660
	$\frac{3}{4}$	2,190	965	1,970	865
	$\frac{7}{8}$	2,960	1,230	2,340	970
	1	3,710	1,485	2,660	1,065
11	$\frac{3}{4}$d	2,220	970	2,000	880
	$\frac{7}{8}$	2,990	1,240	2,600	1,080
	1	3,880	1,550	2,970	1,190
12	$\frac{7}{8}$	3,000	1,250	2,690	1,120
	1	3,900	1,560	3,290	1,320
	$1\frac{1}{8}$	4,900	1,960	3,570	1,430
13	$\frac{7}{8}$d	3,030	1,260	2,710	1,130
	1	3,930	1,570	3,520	1,410
	$1\frac{1}{8}$	4,920	1,970	3,920	1,570
14	1	3,950	1,570	3,530	1,410
	$1\frac{1}{8}$	4,950	1,980	4,380	1,750
	$1\frac{1}{4}$	6,060	2,420	4,830	1,930
15	1	3,960	1,580	3,550	1,420
	$1\frac{1}{8}$	4,980	1,990	4,460	1,790
	$1\frac{1}{4}$	6,110	2,450	5,250	2,100
16	1 d	3,960	1,580	3,550	1,420
	$1\frac{1}{8}$d	5,000	2,000	4,470	1,790
	$1\frac{1}{4}$d	6,150	2,460	5,500	2,200

[a]See Table 5.1 for species in groups II and III.
[b]From *National Design Specification*.
[c]Metal side plates less than $\frac{1}{2}$ in. thick may be used provided the allowable stress in the plate and the bearing of the lag bolt on the plate does not exceed the allowable stresses for the metal used.
[d]Greater lengths do not provide higher loads.

ALLOWABLE WITHDRAWAL LOADS FOR LAG BOLTS

For one lag bolt installed in side grain of seasoned wood under normal duration of loading in pounds per inch of penetration of threaded portion of lag bolt into main member. Based on the formula: $P = 1800\,G^{3/2}D^{3/4}$.

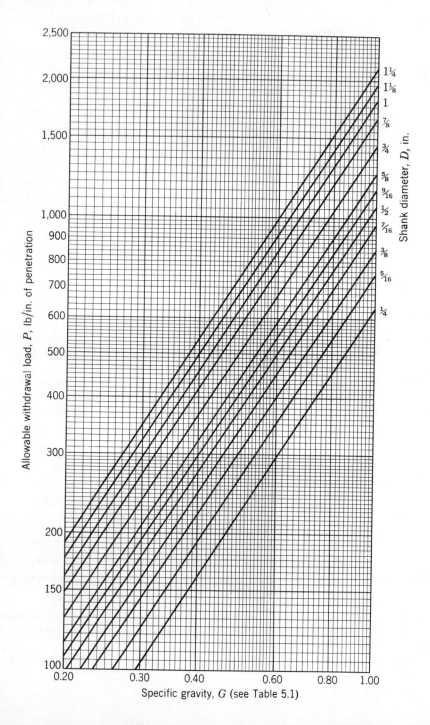

WOOD SCREWS

The allowable loads given here are for any wood screw of sufficient strength to cause failure in the wood rather than in the metal. Wood screws require prebored lead holes to prevent splitting of the wood. Lead hole diameters for the shank and threaded portions of wood screws are given in Table 5.14. Wood screws should be inserted by turning with a screwdriver and not by driving with a hammer. Soap or other lubricant may be used to aid insertion.

Lumber Species

Species load groups for wood screw allowable loads are given in Table 5.1.

Spacing, End Distance, and Edge Distance

Spacing, end distance, and edge distance should be sufficient to prevent splitting of the wood.

Allowable Wood Screw Loads

The allowable loads apply for one wood screw in a two-member joint under normal duration of loading and dry-use conditions. The total allowable load for more than one wood screw is the sum of the loads for each wood screw, provided that spacings, end distances, and edge distances are sufficient to develop the full strength of each wood screw.

For other than normal durations of loading, the allowable loads should be multiplied by the appropriate adjustment factor from Figure 2.3 or Table 2.12. For wood screw joints under other service or seasoning conditions, the load determined is multiplied by the appropriate factor from Table 5.15.

Withdrawal loads

If possible, structural designs should be such that wood screws are not loaded in withdrawal. When it is unavoidable that they are, the tensile strength of the wood screw at its net (root) section may not be exceeded. Loading in withdrawal from end grain is not permitted.

The chart on page **5-58** may be used to determine allowable withdrawal loads for one wood screw inserted in side grain of the member holding the screw point of a two-member joint. The effective depth of penetration used to determine allowable load is the length of the threaded portion of the screw in the member receiving the point. Approximately two-thirds of the length of a wood screw is threaded.

Lateral loads

The chart on page **5-59** may be used to determine the allowable lateral load for one wood screw loaded in single shear at any angle of load to grain when the screw is inserted in the side grain and embedded approximately 7 diameters into the member receiving the point. For wood screws penetrating less than 7 diameters, the allowable load must be reduced in proportion to the actual depth of penetration (see Figure 5.14).

ALLOWABLE WITHDRAWAL LOADS FOR WOOD SCREWS

For one wood screw installed in side grain of seasoned wood under normal duration of loading, in pounds per inch of penetration of threaded portion of wood screw into main member. Based on the formula: $P = 2,850G^2D$ (D = shank diameter).

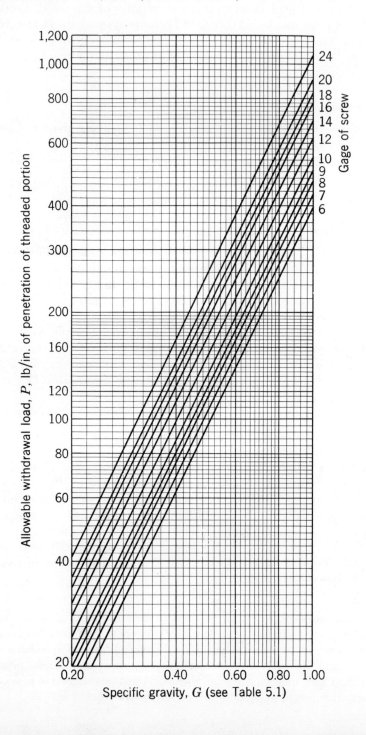

ALLOWABLE LATERAL LOADS FOR WOOD SCREWS

For one wood screw under normal duration of loading installed in side grain of seasoned wood and embedded approximately $7D$ in the member receiving the point. See Table 5.1 for species in each group.

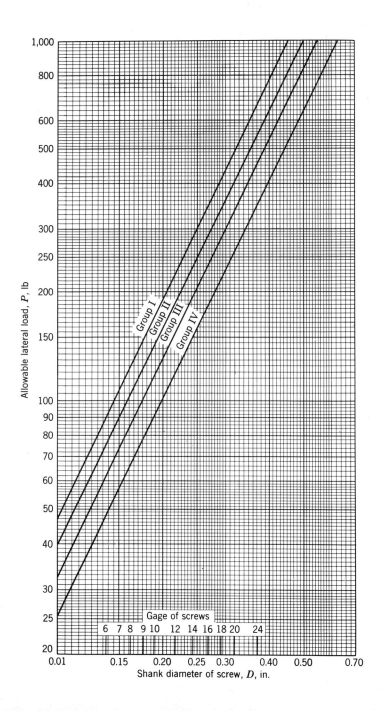

TABLE 5.14

LEAD HOLE DIAMETERS FOR WOOD SCREWS

Gage of Screw	Shank Diameter of Screw, in.	Diameter of Lead Hole, in.					
		Withdrawal Loads		Lateral Loads			
		Group I Species[a]	Groups II, III and IV Species[a]	Group I Species[a]		Groups II, III, and IV Species[a]	
				Shank Portion	Threaded Portion	Shank Portion	Threaded Portion
6	0.138	$\frac{5}{64}$	$\frac{1}{16}$	$\frac{9}{64}$	$\frac{3}{32}$	$\frac{1}{8}$	$\frac{5}{64}$
7	0.151	$\frac{3}{32}$	$\frac{5}{64}$	$\frac{5}{32}$	$\frac{7}{64}$	$\frac{1}{8}$	$\frac{3}{32}$
8	0.164	$\frac{7}{64}$	$\frac{5}{64}$	$\frac{5}{32}$	$\frac{7}{64}$	$\frac{9}{64}$	$\frac{3}{32}$
9	0.177	$\frac{7}{64}$	$\frac{5}{64}$	$\frac{11}{64}$	$\frac{1}{8}$	$\frac{5}{32}$	$\frac{7}{64}$
10	0.190	$\frac{7}{64}$	$\frac{3}{32}$	$\frac{3}{16}$	$\frac{1}{8}$	$\frac{11}{64}$	$\frac{7}{64}$
12	0.216	$\frac{9}{64}$	$\frac{7}{64}$	$\frac{7}{32}$	$\frac{9}{64}$	$\frac{3}{16}$	$\frac{1}{8}$
14	0.242	$\frac{5}{32}$	$\frac{7}{64}$	$\frac{1}{4}$	$\frac{5}{32}$	$\frac{7}{32}$	$\frac{9}{64}$
16	0.268	$\frac{11}{64}$	$\frac{1}{8}$	$\frac{17}{64}$	$\frac{3}{16}$	$\frac{15}{64}$	$\frac{5}{32}$
18	0.294	$\frac{3}{16}$	$\frac{9}{64}$	$\frac{19}{64}$	$\frac{13}{64}$	$\frac{1}{4}$	$\frac{11}{64}$
20	0.320	$\frac{13}{64}$	$\frac{5}{32}$	$\frac{5}{16}$	$\frac{7}{32}$	$\frac{9}{32}$	$\frac{3}{16}$
24	0.372	$\frac{15}{64}$	$\frac{3}{16}$	$\frac{3}{8}$	$\frac{1}{4}$	$\frac{21}{64}$	$\frac{15}{64}$

[a]See Table 5.1 for species in each group.

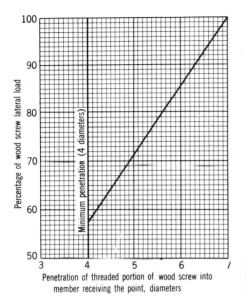

Penetration of threaded portion of wood screw into member receiving the point, diameters

Figure 5.14. ADJUSTMENT OF WOOD SCREW LATERAL LOAD VALUES FOR REDUCED PENETRATIONS.

TABLE 5.15

ADJUSTMENT OF WOOD SCREW LOAD VALUES FOR SERVICE, SEASONING, AND USE CONDITIONS

Lumber Condition	Percentage of Wood Screw Load Values	
	Withdrawal Loads	Lateral Loads
Service condition in use		
Seasoned and always dry	100	100
Exposed to weather	75	75
Always wet	67	67
Use condition		
Wood screw in end grain	Not recommended	67
Metal side member	100	125

Lateral load adjustment factors for wood screws inserted in end grain and for metal side members are given in Table 5.15.

SPIRAL DOWELS

A spiral dowel is a twisted steel rod with spirally grooved ridges in its entire length, the lead of the spiral thread being sufficient to permit driving by any suitable means. The allowable loads given under this heading are for any spiral dowel of sufficient strength to cause failure in the wood rather than in the metal. Ranges of diameters and lengths of stock sizes of spiral dowels are listed in Table 5.16. Spiral dowels require pre-bored lead holes of the diameters given in Table 5.16. The detail illustrated in Figure 5.15 is recommended for driving long dowels.

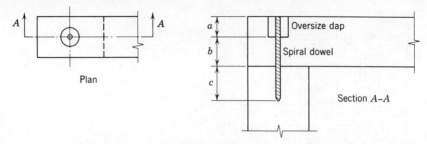

Figure 5.15. DRIVING OF LONG SPIRAL DOWELS. a = overall length of dowel less maximum driving length; $b = c = \frac{1}{2}$ maximum driving length (see Table 5.16).

TABLE 5.16

DIMENSIONS AND LEAD HOLE DIAMETERS FOR STOCK
SIZES OF SPIRAL DOWELS

Outside Diameter of Dowel, in.	Minimum Length,[a] in.	Maximum Length,[a] in.	Maximum Driving Length,[b,c] in.	Diameter of Lead Hole,[b] in.
$\frac{1}{4}$	$2\frac{1}{2}$	6		$\frac{3}{16}$
$\frac{5}{16}$	3	$6\frac{1}{2}$		$\frac{1}{4}$
$\frac{3}{8}$	$3\frac{1}{2}$	10		$\frac{9}{32}$
$\frac{7}{16}$	$3\frac{1}{2}$	12	12	$\frac{11}{32}$
$\frac{1}{2}$	4	18	12	$\frac{3}{8}$
$\frac{5}{8}$	4	24	12	$\frac{15}{32}$
$\frac{3}{4}$	Lengths in these three sizes must be specially ordered		12	$\frac{9}{16}$
$\frac{7}{8}$			13	$\frac{21}{32}$
1			14	$\frac{3}{4}$

[a]Increments of length of $\frac{1}{2}$ in. up to length of 8 in., and 1 in. for lengths over 8 in.
[b]For Group II species see Table 5.1.
[c]See Figure 5.15.

Lumber Species

The allowable loads for spiral dowels are for Douglas fir-larch and Southern pine (Group II species) joints.

Spacing, End Distance, and Edge Distance

Spacing, end distances, and edge distances should be sufficient to prevent splitting of the wood.

Allowable Spiral Dowel Loads

The allowable loads in Table 5.18 apply for one spiral dowel in a two-member joint under normal duration of loading and dry-use conditions. The total allowable load for more than one spiral dowel is the sum of the

TABLE 5.17

ADJUSTMENT OF SPIRAL DOWEL LOAD VALUES FOR
SERVICE, SEASONING, AND USE CONDITIONS

Condition of Lumber		Percentage of Withdrawal Load Value	Percentage of Lateral Load Value
When Installed	In Service		
Seasoned[a]	Seasoned	100	100
Unseasoned (MC 30%)	Seasoned	25	100
Seasoned or unseasoned	Exposed to weather	25	70
Use condition	Always wet	100	70
Use condition: Spiral dowel in end grain		See Table 5.18	60

[a]Seasoned solid sawn lumber has a maximum moisture content of 19%. Glued laminated timber has a maximum moisture content of 16%.

TABLE 5.18

ALLOWABLE LOADS FOR SPIRAL DOWELS[a, b]

Outside Diameter of Dowel, in.	Allowable Lateral Load, lb	Allowable Withdrawal Load, lb/in. of penetration	
		Side Grain	End Grain
$\frac{1}{4}$	111	103	59
$\frac{5}{16}$	174	123	70
$\frac{3}{8}$	249	141	81
$\frac{7}{16}$	340	158	90
$\frac{1}{2}$	444	174	99
$\frac{5}{8}$	692	206	117
$\frac{3}{4}$	998	236	135
$\frac{7}{8}$	1,360	266	151
1	1,775	293	168

[a]All applicable provisions under the heading "Allowable Spiral Dowel Loads" must be met to develop these loads.
[b]Values are for Group II Species (see Table 5.1).

loads for each spiral dowel, provided that spacings, end distances, and edge distances are sufficient to develop the full strength of each spiral dowel.

For other than normal durations of loading, the allowable loads should be multiplied by the appropriate adjustment factor from Figure 2.3 or Table 2.12. For spiral dowel joints under other service or seasoning conditions, the load determined is multiplied by the appropriate factor from Table 5.17.

Withdrawal loads

Allowable withdrawal loads for one spiral dowel installed in side or end grain are given in Table 5.18.

Lateral loads

Allowable lateral loads for one spiral dowel installed in side grain of a two-member joint, when the thickness of the side member is at least 5 times the diameter of the spiral dowel and the dowel penetrates at least 7 diameters into the member receiving the point, are given in Table 5.18.

Lateral strength in end grain is 60% of the allowable side grain lateral strength, and a penetration of 12 diameters into the end grain is required to develop that strength.

NAILS AND SPIKES

The allowable loads given under this heading are for common wire nails and spikes and for hardened deformed-shank nails and spikes of the sizes listed in Table 5.19. Hardened deformed-shank nails and spikes as covered herein are made of high-carbon steel wire, headed, pointed, annularly or helically threaded, and heat-treated and tempered to provide greater strength than is developed by common wire nails and spikes of corresponding sizes.

When it is necessary to avoid splitting of the wood, a prebored hole of a diameter specified in Table 5.19 may be used. The allowable loads apply for nails and spikes used in prebored holes of the specified sizes, or for a fastener of the same size used without a prebored hole.

Lumber Species

Species load groups for allowable loads for nails and spikes are given in Table 5.1.

Spacing, End Distance, and Edge Distance

Spacing, end distances, and edge distances should be sufficient to avoid unusual splitting of the wood.

Allowable Nail and Spike Loads

The charts on pages **5-67**, **5-68** and **5-69** are for one nail or spike in a two-member joint under normal duration of loading and dry-use conditions. Hardened deformed-shank nails may be used with the same loads as given for common wire nails of the corresponding pennyweight, except as provided in Table 5.20. The total allowable load for more than one nail or spike is the sum of the loads for each nail or spike.

For joints in use under other service or seasoning conditions, the loads determined from the charts are multiplied by the appropriate factor from Table 5.20.

Withdrawal loads

If possible, structural designs should be such that nails or spikes are not loaded in withdrawal. When it is unavoidable that they are, the allowable

TABLE 5.19

MINIMUM SIZES AND HOLE DIAMETERS FOR NAILS AND SPIKES

Pennyweight	Length, in.	Wire Diameter, in.	Prebored Hole Diameter, in.	
			Group I Species[a]	Group II, III, and IV Species[a]
Common Wire Nails				
6d	2	0.113	$\frac{3}{32}$	$\frac{5}{64}$
8d	$2\frac{1}{2}$	0.131	$\frac{7}{64}$	$\frac{3}{32}$
10d	3	0.148	$\frac{1}{8}$	$\frac{7}{64}$
12d	$3\frac{1}{4}$	0.148	$\frac{1}{8}$	$\frac{7}{64}$
16d	$3\frac{1}{2}$	0.162	$\frac{9}{64}$	$\frac{7}{64}$
20d	4	0.192	$\frac{11}{64}$	$\frac{9}{64}$
30d	$4\frac{1}{2}$	0.207	$\frac{11}{04}$	$\frac{9}{64}$
40d	5	0.225	$\frac{3}{16}$	$\frac{5}{32}$
50d	$5\frac{1}{2}$	0.244	$\frac{7}{32}$	$\frac{11}{64}$
60d	6	0.263	$\frac{15}{64}$	$\frac{3}{16}$
Common Spikes				
10d	3	0.192	$\frac{11}{64}$	$\frac{9}{64}$
12d	$3\frac{1}{4}$	0.192	$\frac{11}{64}$	$\frac{9}{64}$
16d	$3\frac{1}{2}$	0.207	$\frac{11}{64}$	$\frac{9}{64}$
20d	4	0.225	$\frac{3}{16}$	$\frac{5}{32}$
30d	$4\frac{1}{2}$	0.244	$\frac{7}{32}$	$\frac{11}{64}$
40d	5	0.263	$\frac{15}{64}$	$\frac{3}{16}$
50d	$5\frac{1}{2}$	0.283	$\frac{1}{4}$	$\frac{13}{64}$
60d	6	0.283	$\frac{1}{4}$	$\frac{13}{64}$
$\frac{5}{16}$ in.	7	0.312	$\frac{9}{32}$	$\frac{15}{64}$
$\frac{3}{8}$ in.	$8\frac{1}{2}$	0.375	$\frac{21}{64}$	$\frac{9}{32}$
Hardened Deformed-Shank Nails and Spikes				
6d	2	0.120	$\frac{3}{32}$	$\frac{5}{64}$
8d	$2\frac{1}{2}$	0.120	$\frac{3}{32}$	$\frac{5}{64}$
10d	3	0.135	$\frac{7}{64}$	$\frac{3}{32}$
12d	$3\frac{1}{4}$	0.135	$\frac{7}{64}$	$\frac{3}{32}$
16d	$3\frac{1}{2}$	0.148	$\frac{1}{8}$	$\frac{7}{64}$
20d	4	0.177	$\frac{5}{32}$	$\frac{1}{8}$
30d	$4\frac{1}{2}$	0.177	$\frac{5}{32}$	$\frac{1}{8}$
40d	5	0.177	$\frac{5}{32}$	$\frac{1}{8}$
50d	$5\frac{1}{2}$	0.177	$\frac{5}{32}$	$\frac{1}{8}$
60d	6	0.177	$\frac{5}{32}$	$\frac{1}{8}$
70d	7	0.207	$\frac{11}{64}$	$\frac{9}{64}$
80d	8	0,207	$\frac{11}{64}$	$\frac{9}{64}$
90d	9	0.207	$\frac{11}{64}$	$\frac{9}{64}$

[a]See Table 5.1 for species in each group.

TABLE 5.20

ADJUSTMENT OF NAIL AND SPIKE LOAD VALUES FOR SERVICE AND SEASONING CONDITIONS

	Percentage of Nail or Spike Load Values	
Condition of Lumber	Withdrawal from Side Grain	Lateral
Seasoned	100	100
Unseasoned, always wet	100	75[a]
Seasoned in place	25[a]	75[a]

[a]For hardened deformed-shank nails, full load value (percentage = 100) is used.

withdrawal loads per inch of penetration for nails or spikes driven in side grain (perpendicular to grain) as determined from the chart on page **5-67** apply. Loading of nails or spikes in withdrawal from end grain is not recommended.

The allowable withdrawal loads for toe-nailed joints, for all conditions of seasoning, are 0.67 times those determined from the chart on page **5-67**. It is recommended that toe-nails be driven at an angle of approximately 30° to the piece and be started at approximately one-third the nail length from the end of the piece.

The withdrawal resistance of clinched common wire nails is considerably higher than that of unclinched fasteners. The ratio between loads for clinched and unclinched nails varies with the moisture content of the wood when the nail is driven and when the withdrawal load is applied, the species of wood, the size of nail, and the direction of clinch with respect to grain. In dry or green wood, a clinched nail provides from 45% to 170% more withdrawal resistance than does an unclinched nail withdrawn soon after driving. Nails clinched across the grain have approximately 20% more resistance to withdrawal than do nails clinched along the grain.

Lateral loads

The charts on pages **5-68** and **5-69** may be used to determine the allowable lateral load, applied in any lateral direction, for one nail or spike driven in the side grain of Group II or III species main member to any depth of penetration of the point in the member receiving the point down to the minimum permissible penetration. The minimum permissible penetration is one-third the depth of penetration required for full allowable load. These loads apply when side and main members have approximately the same density. When side and main members have different densities, the lighter density member controls.

For nails or spikes which are driven in three-member joints, and which fully penetrate all three members, the appropriate factor from Table 5.21 is used. Lateral load adjustment factors for nails or spikes driven in end grain and for metal side members are also given in the table.

For three-member joints with wood side plates at least ⅜ in. thick; and

ALLOWABLE WITHDRAWAL LOADS FOR NAILS AND SPIKES

For one nail or spike installed in side grain under normal duration of loading, in pounds per inch of penetration into the member receiving the point. Based on the formula: $P = 1,380G^{5/2}D$. (D = diameter of nail or spike.)

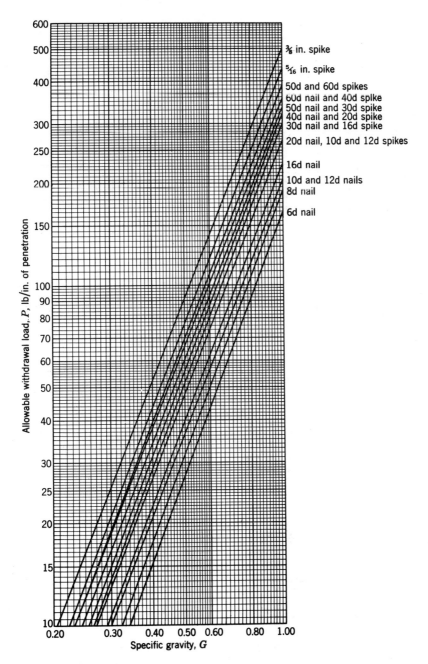

ALLOWABLE LATERAL LOADS FOR NAILS AND SPIKES
(GROUP II SPECIES)

For one nail or spike driven in a two-member joint of seasoned Douglas fir-larch or Southern pine under normal duration of load.

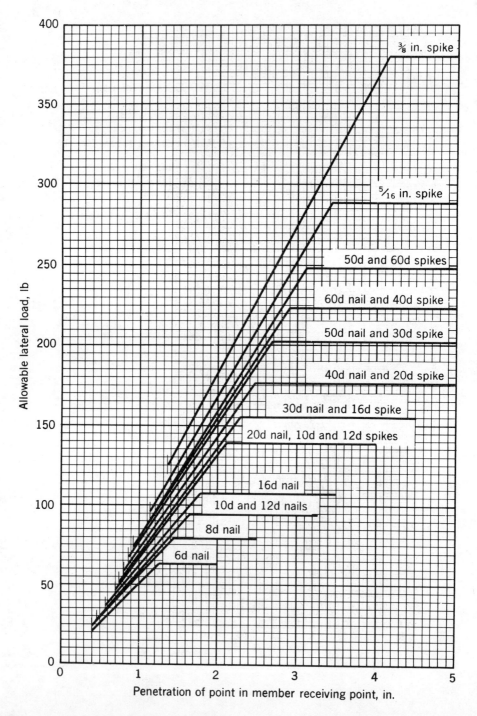

ALLOWABLE LATERAL LOADS FOR NAILS AND SPIKES
(GROUP III SPECIES)

For one nail or spike driven in a two-member joint of seasoned Group III species (see Table 5.1 for species in this group) under normal duration of load.

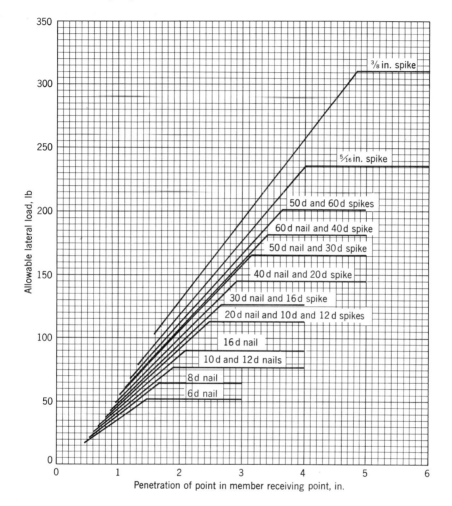

TABLE 5.21

ADJUSTMENT OF NAIL AND SPIKE LOAD VALUES FOR VARIOUS
USE CONDITIONS

Use Condition	Percentage of Nail or Spike Load Values	
	Withdrawal	Lateral
Three-member joints (nail or spike in double shear), where ratio of thickness of each side member to thickness of center members is		
One-third	Not applicable	133[a]
One	Not applicable	167[a]
Three-member joints with side members, at least $\frac{3}{8}$ in. thick and clinched nails not exceeding 12d in size. Clinched nails require 3 nail diameters beyond side member[c]	Not applicable	200
Nail or spike driven in end grain	Not recommended	67
Metal side plates	100	125
Toe-nailed joints[b]	67	83
Slant-nailed joints[b]	100	100

[a]For intermediate thickness ratios, straight-line interpolation is used.
[b]See Figure 5.16.
[c]Hardened steel nails need not be clinched.

with nails not exceeding 12d in size, extending at least 3 diameters beyond the side member, and clinched, lateral load values may be doubled.

The allowable lateral loads for toe-nailed joints are five-sixths of those determined from the charts on pages **5-68** or **5-69**. It is recommended that toe-nails be driven at an angle of approximately 30° to the piece and be started at approximately one-third the nail length from the end of the piece.

Allowable loads for nails and spikes may be increased 30% for use in diaphragm construction (see Table 5.21). Since diaphragms are subject to wind or seismic loading, the allowable diaphragm loads may be further increased by 33% for wind or earthquake duration of loading. Diaphragm lateral loads are also subject to the penetration requirements stated above and shown on the charts on pages **5-68** or **5-69**.

Special deformed-shank nails for use with strap-type purlin hangers, tie straps on pipe-type hangers, and other metal ties and straps have been developed. Specifications for such nails are: length = 2 in., diameter = 0.203 in., annular fetter ring full length of shank, diamond point, galvanized, and flat head. The allowable lateral load for one nail meeting these specifications and driven in Group II species under normal duration of loading and used with a metal strap is 250 lb.

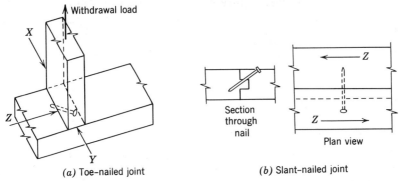

(*a*) Toe-nailed joint   (*b*) Slant-nailed joint

Figure 5.16.   TOE-NAILED AND SLANT-NAILED JOINTS. When load is applied in direction *X* or *Y*, the toe-nailed joint lateral load value applies. When load is applied in direction *Z*, the slant-nailed joint lateral load value applies.

Staples

Because staples and nails are similar in nature, the loads for staples may be determined in a manner similar to that for nails. The allowable load for one staple of a given diameter equals twice the allowable load for a nail of equal diameter, provided that the staple leg spacing (or crown width) is adequate, and that the penetration of both legs of the staple into the member receiving the points is approximately two-thirds of their length. In

TABLE 5.22

SIZES AND APPLICATIONS OF POWER-DRIVEN
GALVANIZED WIRE STAPLES[a]

Minimum Crown, in.	Minimum Length, in.	Application
$\frac{3}{8}$	$1\frac{1}{8}$	Plywood sheathing
	$1\frac{1}{2}$	Plywood subflooring
$\frac{7}{16}$	$1\frac{1}{8}$	Fiberboard sheathing
	$1\frac{5}{8}$	Plywood sheathing
$\frac{3}{8}$	$1\frac{1}{8}$	Plywood sheathing; plywood, hardboard, or particle board underlayment
	$1\frac{1}{2}$	Plywood subflooring
$\frac{7}{16}$	$\frac{7}{8}$	Gypsum lath; tin caps for built-up roofing
	1	Gypsum drywall (interior finish)
	$1\frac{1}{8}$	Fiberboard sheathing
	$1\frac{5}{8}$	Plywood sheathing
	$\frac{3}{4}$	Asphalt roofing shingles
$\frac{3}{16}$	$\frac{7}{8}$	Plywood, hardboard, or particleboard underlayment

[a]Recommended by the Federal Housing Administration.

general, nail penetration requirements and other provisions regarding seasoning of members, service conditions, etc., apply equally to staples. Table 5.22 gives minimum size requirements for various applications of power-driven galvanized wire staples as recommended by the Federal Housing Administration.

LIGHT METAL FRAMING DEVICES

Framing Anchors

Framing anchors are metal fittings used to provide a more positive connection between wood members than does toe-nailing. The several types of manufactured framing anchors are right-angled pieces formed from light gage galvanized sheet steel. (See Figure 5.17.) These may be bent to

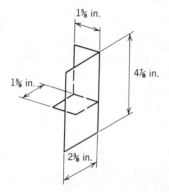

Figure 5.17.   **TYPICAL FRAMING ANCHOR DIMENSIONS.** Metal thickness = 18 gage.

TABLE 5.23

ALLOWABLE LOADS FOR ONE TYPE OF FRAMING ANCHOR[a]

Type of Connection	Top of Header	Side of Header	Top of Joist	Side of Joist	Direction of Load	Normal Duration of Load, lb
	Number of 0.120 in. Diameter Nails					
	2	4	0	4	A	300
					C	290
					E	300
	4	2	1	4	A	300
					B	530
					C	290
					D	200
	0	5	0	6	F	450

[a]Used with Douglas fir-larch or Southern pine members.
[b]For other durations of load the adjustments in Figure 2.3 or Table 2.12 apply.

conform with special conditions of use. The outstanding legs may be of rectangular, triangular, or other shape, and they are predrilled or prepunched to receive special nails. Nails appropriate to the particular framing anchor should be used in all holes provided in the anchor to develop its full load-carrying capacity. Framing anchors are manufactured with right- and left-hand bends and are commonly used in pairs to avoid eccentricity.

Allowable load values for framing anchors are generally determined by test, but an estimate may be based on the lateral resistance of the nails used. Allowable loads for framing anchors are generally given for normal duration of load but may be adjusted for other duration of load as given in Figure 2.3 or Table 2.12. Before making adjustments for duration of load, the manufacturer's literature should be checked to ascertain the duration of load basis on which the recommended values were based and also to make sure that the stresses in the anchors or nails are not exceeded by increases for duration of load. Table 5.23 gives the allowable loads based on tests and established nail loads and the required number of nails for one type of framing anchor used with Douglas fir-larch or Southern pine members. The manufacturer's data for the particular type of framing anchor being used should be followed.

JOIST AND PURLIN HANGERS

Joist and purlin hangers are usually standard items fabricated by several manufacturers. The allowable loads shown in manufacturer's literature are usually determined by tests. Two types of hangers are shown in Table 5.24. The manufacturer's data for the particular type of hanger being used should be followed.

See Table 5.24 for typical allowable loads and dimensions. See manufacturer's literature for other joist or purlin sizes or for other hanger configurations.

TABLE 5.24

DIMENSIONS AND LOADS FOR TYPICAL JOIST AND PURLIN HANGERS

Type A

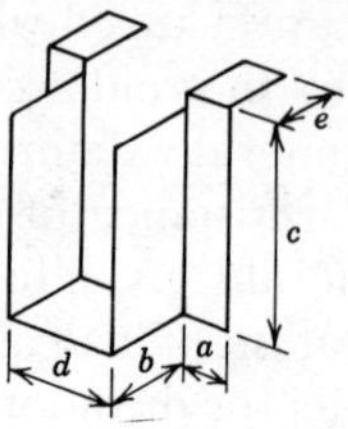

Nail Sizes: 10d nails are 9 gage × $1\frac{1}{2}$ in.; 16d nails are 8 gage × $2\frac{1}{2}$ in.; 20d nails are 0.192 × $1\frac{3}{4}$ in., annular ringed

Size of Joist or Purlin, in.	Hanger Dimensions, in.					Metal Thickness	Number and Size of Nails		Allowable Load,[a] lb
	a	*b*	*c*	*d*	*e*		Header	Joist	
Nominal									
2 × 8	$1\frac{1}{4}$	2	$7\frac{1}{4}$	$1\frac{9}{16}$	$2\frac{1}{2}$	12 gage	10–16d	4–10d	1,670
10		2	$9\frac{1}{4}$				12–16d	4–10d	1,670
12		2	$11\frac{1}{8}$				14–16d	6–10d	1,870
14		$2\frac{1}{2}$	$13\frac{1}{8}$				16–16d	6–10d	1,870
16		$2\frac{1}{2}$	$15\frac{1}{8}$				18–16d	8–10d	2,070
3 × 8	$1\frac{1}{4}$	2	$7\frac{1}{4}$	$2\frac{9}{16}$	$2\frac{1}{2}$	12 gage	12–16d	4–10d	2,450
10		2	$9\frac{1}{4}$				14–16d	6–10d	2,650
12		$2\frac{1}{2}$	$11\frac{1}{8}$				16–16d	6–10d	2,650
14		$2\frac{1}{2}$	$13\frac{1}{8}$				18–16d	8–10d	3,360
16		$2\frac{1}{2}$	$15\frac{1}{8}$				20–16d	8–10d	3,360
4 × 8	$1\frac{1}{4}$	2	$7\frac{1}{4}$	$3\frac{9}{16}$	$2\frac{1}{2}$	12 gage	12–16d	4–10d	3,210
8		2	$7\frac{1}{4}$				12–20d	4–20d	3,523
10		2	$9\frac{1}{4}$				14–16d	6–10d	3,428
10		2	$9\frac{1}{4}$				14–20d	6–20d	3,871
12		$2\frac{1}{2}$	$11\frac{1}{8}$				16–16d	6–10d	4,140
12		$2\frac{1}{2}$	$11\frac{1}{8}$				16–20d	6–20d	4,578
14		$2\frac{1}{2}$	$13\frac{1}{8}$				18–16d	8–10d	4,340
14		$2\frac{1}{2}$	$13\frac{1}{8}$				18–20d	8–20d	4,925
16		$2\frac{1}{2}$	$15\frac{1}{8}$				20–16d	8–10d	4,340
16		$2\frac{1}{2}$	$15\frac{1}{8}$				20–20d	8–20d	4,925
Actual									
$3\frac{1}{8}$	$1\frac{1}{4}$	$2\frac{1}{2}$	$11\frac{1}{8}$	$3\frac{1}{4}$	$2\frac{1}{2}$	12 gage	16–20d	6–20d	4,699
$3\frac{1}{8}$			$15\frac{1}{8}$	$3\frac{1}{4}$			20–20d	8–20d	5,046
$5\frac{1}{8}$			$11\frac{1}{8}$	$5\frac{1}{4}$			16–20d	6–20d	5,767
$5\frac{1}{8}$			$15\frac{1}{8}$	$5\frac{1}{4}$			20–20d	8–20d	6,700

TABLE 5.24 (Continued)

Type B

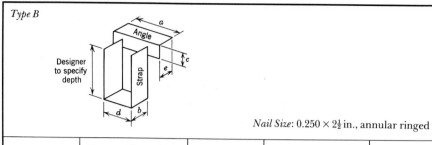

Nail Size: 0.250 × 2½ in., annular ringed

Actual Width of Purlin, in.	Hanger Dimensions, in.					Metal Thickness, in.	Number of Nails		Allowable Load, lb
	a	b	c	d	e		Header	Purlin	
$3\frac{1}{8}$	10	5	$3\frac{1}{8}$	$3\frac{1}{4}$	$2\frac{1}{2}$	Angle $-\frac{1}{4}$ Strap $-\frac{3}{16}$	10	6	7,000
$5\frac{1}{8}$	10	5	$3\frac{1}{8}$	$5\frac{1}{4}$	$2\frac{1}{2}$	Angle $-\frac{1}{4}$ Strap $-\frac{3}{16}$	10	6	7,000
$6\frac{3}{4}$	12	5	$3\frac{1}{8}$	$6\frac{7}{8}$	$2\frac{1}{2}$	Angle $-\frac{1}{4}$ Strap $-\frac{3}{16}$	10	6	7,000

[a] Normal duration of load. For other duration of load, the adjustments in Figure 2.3 or Table 2.12 apply.

SECTION 6
REFERENCE DATA

REF.

SOFTWOOD LUMBER AND TIMBER SIZES

Nominal Size, in. $b \times d$	Actual Size (s4s), in. $b \times d$	Area, A, in.²	Moment of Inertia, I, in.⁴	Section Modulus, S, in.³	Board Measure, per lineal ft	Weight of Piece, plf — Weight of Wood					
						25 pcf	30 pcf	35 pcf	40 pcf	45 pcf	50 pcf
1 × 3	¾ × 2½	1.875	0.977	0.781	¼	0.326	0.391	0.456	0.521	0.586	0.651
1 × 4	¾ × 3½	2.625	2.680	1.531	⅓	0.456	0.547	0.638	0.729	0.820	0.911
1 × 6	¾ × 5½	4.125	10.398	3.781	½	0.716	0.859	1.003	1.146	1.289	1.432
1 × 8	¾ × 7¼	5.438	23.817	6.570	⅔	0.944	1.133	1.322	1.510	1.699	1.888
1 × 10	¾ × 9¼	6.938	49.466	10.695	⅚	1.204	1.445	1.686	1.927	2.168	2.409
1 × 12	¾ × 11¼	8.438	88.989	15.820	1	1.465	1.758	2.051	2.344	2.637	2.930
2 × 3	1½ × 2½	3.750	1.953	1.563	½	0.651	0.781	0.911	1.042	1.172	1.302
2 × 4	1½ × 3½	5.250	5.359	3.063	⅔	0.911	1.094	1.276	1.458	1.641	1.823
2 × 6	1½ × 5½	8.250	20.797	7.563	1	1.432	1.719	2.005	2.292	2.578	2.865
2 × 8	1½ × 7¼	10.875	47.635	13.141	1⅓	1.888	2.266	2.643	3.021	3.398	3.776
2 × 10	1½ × 9¼	13.875	98.932	21.391	1¼	2.409	2.891	3.372	3.854	4.336	4.818
2 × 12	1½ × 11¼	16.875	177.979	31.641	2	2.930	3.516	4.102	4.638	5.273	5.859
2 × 14	1½ × 13¼	19.875	290.775	43.891	2⅓	3.451	4.141	4.831	5.521	6.211	6.901
3 × 1	2½ × ¾	1.875	0.088	0.234	¼	0.326	0.391	0.456	0.521	0.586	0.651
3 × 2	2½ × 1½	3.750	0.703	0.938	½	0.651	0.781	0.911	1.042	1.172	1.302
3 × 4	2½ × 3½	8.750	8.932	5.104	1	1.319	1.823	2.127	2.431	2.734	3.038
3 × 6	2½ × 5½	13.750	34.661	12.604	1½	2.387	2.865	3.342	3.819	4.297	4.774
3 × 8	2½ × 7¼	18.125	79.391	21.901	2	3.147	3.776	4.405	5.035	5.664	6.293
3 × 10	2½ × 9¼	23.125	164.886	35.651	2½	4.015	4.818	5.621	6.424	7.227	8.030
3 × 12	2½ × 11¼	28.125	296.631	52.734	3	4.883	5.859	6.836	7.813	8.789	9.766
3 × 14	2½ × 13¼	33.125	484.625	73.151	3½	5.751	6.901	8.051	9.201	10.352	11.502
3 × 16	2½ × 15¼	38.125	738.870	96.901	4	6.619	7.943	9.266	10.590	11.914	13.238

SOFTWOOD LUMBER AND TIMBER SIZES (Continued)

Nominal Size, in. $b \times d$	Actual Size (s4s), in. $b \times d$	Area, A, in.^{2}	Moment of Inertia, I, in.^{4}	Section Modulus, S, in.^{3}	Board Measure, per lineal ft	Weight of Piece, plf — Weight of Wood 25 pcf	30 pcf	35 pcf	40 pcf	45 pcf	50 pcf
4×1	$3\frac{1}{2} \times \frac{3}{4}$	2.625	0.123	0.328	$\frac{1}{3}$	0.456	0.547	0.638	0.729	0.820	0.911
4×2	$3\frac{1}{2} \times 1\frac{1}{2}$	5.250	0.984	1.313	$\frac{2}{3}$	0.911	1.094	1.276	1.458	1.641	1.823
4×3	$3\frac{1}{2} \times 2\frac{1}{2}$	8.750	4.557	3.646	1	1.519	1.823	2.127	2.431	2.734	3.038
4×4	$3\frac{1}{2} \times 3\frac{1}{2}$	12.250	12.505	7.146	$1\frac{1}{3}$	2.127	2.552	2.977	3.403	3.828	4.253
4×6	$3\frac{1}{2} \times 5\frac{1}{2}$	19.250	48.526	17.646	2	3.342	4.010	4.679	5.347	6.016	6.684
4×8	$3\frac{1}{2} \times 7\frac{1}{4}$	25.375	111.148	30.661	$2\frac{2}{3}$	4.405	5.286	6.168	7.049	7.930	8.811
4×10	$3\frac{1}{2} \times 9\frac{1}{4}$	32.375	230.840	49.911	$3\frac{1}{3}$	5.621	6.745	7.869	8.933	10.117	11.241
4×12	$3\frac{1}{2} \times 11\frac{1}{4}$	39.375	415.283	73.828	4	6.836	8.203	9.570	10.938	12.305	13.672
4×14	$3\frac{1}{2} \times 13\frac{1}{2}$	47.250	717.609	106.313	$4\frac{2}{3}$	8.203	9.844	11.484	13.125	14.766	16.406
4×16	$3\frac{1}{2} \times 15\frac{1}{2}$	54.250	1,086.130	140.146	$5\frac{1}{3}$	9.418	11.302	13.186	15.069	16.953	18.837
6×1	$5\frac{1}{2} \times \frac{3}{4}$	4.125	0.193	0.516	$\frac{1}{2}$	0.716	0.859	1.003	1.146	1.289	1.432
6×2	$5\frac{1}{2} \times 1\frac{1}{2}$	8.250	1.547	2.063	1	1.432	1.719	2.005	2.292	2.578	2.865
6×3	$5\frac{1}{2} \times 2\frac{1}{2}$	13.750	7.161	5.729	$1\frac{1}{2}$	2.387	2.865	3.342	3.819	4.297	4.774
6×4	$5\frac{1}{2} \times 3\frac{1}{2}$	19.250	19.651	11.229	2	3.342	4.010	4.679	5.347	6.016	6.684
6×6	$5\frac{1}{2} \times 5\frac{1}{2}$	30.250	76.255	27.729	3	5.252	6.302	7.352	8.403	9.453	10.503
6×8	$5\frac{1}{2} \times 7\frac{1}{2}$	41.250	193.359	51.563	4	7.161	8.594	10.026	11.458	12.891	14.323
6×10	$5\frac{1}{2} \times 9\frac{1}{2}$	52.250	392.963	82.729	5	9.071	10.885	12.700	14.514	16.328	18.142
6×12	$5\frac{1}{2} \times 11\frac{1}{2}$	63.250	697.068	121.229	6	10.981	13.177	15.373	17.569	19.766	21.962
6×14	$5\frac{1}{2} \times 13\frac{1}{2}$	74.250	1,127.672	167.063	7	12.891	15.469	18.047	20.625	23.203	25.781
6×16	$5\frac{1}{2} \times 15\frac{1}{2}$	85.250	1,706.776	220.229	8	14.800	17.760	20.720	23.681	26.641	29.601
6×18	$5\frac{1}{2} \times 17\frac{1}{2}$	96.250	2,456.380	280.729	9	16.710	20.052	23.394	26.736	30.078	33.420
6×20	$5\frac{1}{2} \times 19\frac{1}{2}$	107.250	3,398.484	348.563	10	18.620	22.344	26.068	29.792	33.516	37.240
6×22	$5\frac{1}{2} \times 21\frac{1}{2}$	118.250	4,555.086	423.729	11	20.530	24.635	28.741	32.847	36.953	41.059
6×24	$5\frac{1}{2} \times 23\frac{1}{2}$	129.250	5,948.191	506.229	12	22.439	26.927	31.415	35.903	40.391	44.878

8 × 1	7¼ × ¾	5.438	0.255	0.680	⅔	0.944	1.133	1.322	1.510	1.699	1.888
8 × 2	7¼ × 1½	10.875	2.039	2.719	1⅓	1.888	2.266	2.643	3.021	3.398	3.776
8 × 3	7¼ × 2½	18.125	9.440	7.552	2	3.147	3.776	4.405	5.035	5.664	6.293
8 × 4	7¼ × 3½	25.375	25.904	14.802	2⅔	4.405	5.286	6.168	7.049	7.930	8.811
8 × 6	7½ × 5½	41.250	103.984	37.813	4	7.161	8.594	10.026	11.458	12.891	14.323
8 × 8	7½ × 7½	56.250	263.672	70.313	5⅓	9.766	11.719	13.672	15.625	17.578	19.531
8 × 10	7½ × 9½	71.250	535.859	112.813	6⅔	12.370	14.844	17.318	19.792	22.266	24.740
8 × 12	7½ × 11½	86.250	950.547	165.313	8	14.974	17.969	20.964	23.958	26.953	29.948
8 × 14	7½ × 13½	101.250	1,537.734	227.813	9⅓	17.578	21.094	24.609	28.125	31.641	35.156
8 × 16	7½ × 15½	116.250	2,327.422	300.313	10⅔	20.182	24.219	28.255	32.292	36.328	40.365
8 × 18	7½ × 17½	131.250	3,349.609	382.813	12	22.786	27.344	31.901	36.458	41.016	45.573
8 × 20	7½ × 19½	146.250	4,634.297	475.313	13⅓	25.391	30.469	35.547	40.625	45.703	50.781
8 × 22	7½ × 21½	161.250	6,211.484	577.813	14⅔	27.995	33.594	39.193	44.792	50.391	55.990
8 × 24	7½ × 23½	176.250	8,111.172	690.313	16	30.599	36.719	42.839	48.958	55.078	61.198
10 × 1	9¼ × ¾	6.938	0.325	0.867	⅚	1.204	1.445	1.686	1.927	2.168	2.409
10 × 2	9¼ × 1½	13.875	2.602	3.469	1⅔	2.409	2.891	3.372	3.854	4.336	4.818
10 × 3	9¼ × 2½	23.125	12.044	9.635	2½	4.015	4.818	5.621	6.424	7.227	8.030
10 × 4	9¼ × 3½	32.375	33.049	18.885	3⅓	5.621	6.745	7.869	8.993	10.117	11.241
10 × 6	9½ × 5½	52.250	131.714	47.896	5	9.071	10.885	12.700	14.514	16.328	18.142
10 × 8	9½ × 7½	71.250	333.984	89.063	6⅔	12.370	14.844	17.318	19.792	22.266	24.740
10 × 10	9½ × 9½	90.250	678.755	142.896	8⅓	15.668	18.802	21.936	25.069	28.203	31.337
10 × 12	9½ × 11½	109.250	1,204.026	209.396	10⅓	18.967	22.760	26.554	30.347	34.141	37.934
10 × 14	9½ × 13½	128.250	1,947.797	288.563	11⅔	22.266	26.719	31.172	35.625	40.078	44.531
10 × 16	9½ × 15½	147.250	2,948.068	380.396	13⅓	25.564	30.677	35.790	40.903	46.016	51.128
10 × 18	9½ × 17½	166.250	4,242.836	484.896	15	28.863	34.635	40.408	46.181	51.953	57.726
10 × 20	9½ × 19½	185.250	5,870.109	602.063	16⅔	32.161	38.594	45.026	51.458	57.891	64.323
10 × 22	9½ × 21½	204.250	7,867.879	731.896	18⅓	35.460	42.552	49.644	56.736	63.828	70.920
10 × 24	9½ × 23½	223.250	10,274.148	874.396	20	38.759	46.510	54.262	62.014	69.776	77.517
12 × 1	11¼ × ¾	8.438	0.396	1.055	1	1.465	1.758	2.051	2.344	2.637	2.930
12 × 2	11¼ × 1½	16.875	3.164	4.219	2	2.930	3.516	4.102	4.688	5.273	5.859
12 × 3	11¼ × 2½	28.125	14.648	11.719	3	4.883	5.859	6.836	7.313	8.789	9.766
12 × 4	11¼ × 3½	39.375	40.195	22.969	4	6.836	8.203	9.570	10.938	12.305	13.672

SOFTWOOD LUMBER AND TIMBER SIZES (Continued)

Nominal Size, in. $b \times d$	Actual Size (s4s), in. $b \times d$	Area, A, in.^{2}	Moment of Inertia, I, in.^{4}	Section Modulus, S, in.^{3}	Board Measure, per lineal ft	Weight of Piece, plf — Weight of Wood					
						25 pcf	30 pcf	35 pcf	40 pcf	45 pcf	50 pcf
12 × 6	11½ × 5½	63.250	159.443	57.979	6	10.981	13.177	15.373	17.569	19.766	21.962
12 × 8	11½ × 7½	86.250	404.297	107.813	8	14.974	17.969	20.964	23.958	26.953	29.948
12 × 10	11½ × 9½	109.250	821.651	172.979	10	18.967	22.760	26.554	30.347	34.141	37.934
12 × 12	11½ × 11½	132.250	1,457.505	253.479	12	22.960	27.552	32.144	36.736	41.328	45.920
12 × 14	11½ × 13½	155.250	2,357.859	349.313	14	26.953	32.344	37.734	43.125	48.516	53.906
12 × 16	11½ × 15½	178.250	3,568.713	460.479	16	30.946	37.135	43.325	49.514	55.703	61.892
12 × 18	11½ × 17½	201.250	5,136.066	586.979	18	34.939	41.927	48.915	55.903	62.891	69.878
12 × 20	11½ × 19½	224.250	7,105.922	728.813	20	38.932	46.719	54.505	62.292	70.078	77.865
12 × 22	11½ × 21½	247.250	9,524.273	885.979	22	42.925	51.510	60.095	68.681	77.266	85.851
12 × 24	11½ × 23½	270.250	12,437.129	1,058.479	24	46.918	56.302	65.686	75.069	84.453	93.837
14 × 2	13¼ × 1½	19.875	3.727	4.969	2⅓	3.451	4.141	4.831	5.521	6.211	6.901
14 × 3	13¼ × 2½	33.125	17.253	13.802	3½	5.751	6.901	8.051	9.201	10.352	11.502
14 × 4	13½ × 3½	47.250	48.234	27.563	4⅔	8.203	9.844	11.484	13.125	14.766	16.406
14 × 6	13½ × 5½	74.250	187.172	68.063	7	12.891	15.469	18.047	20.625	23.203	25.781
14 × 8	13½ × 7½	101.250	474.609	126.563	9⅓	17.578	21.094	24.609	28.125	31.641	35.156
14 × 10	13½ × 9½	128.250	964.547	203.063	11⅔	22.266	26.719	31.172	35.625	40.078	44.531
14 × 12	13½ × 11½	155.250	1,710.984	297.563	14	26.953	32.344	37.734	43.125	48.516	53.906
14 × 16	13½ × 15½	209.250	4,189.359	540.563	18⅔	36.328	43.594	50.859	58.125	65.391	72.656
14 × 18	13½ × 17½	236.250	6,029.297	689.063	21	41.016	49.219	57.422	65.625	73.828	82.031
14 × 20	13½ × 19½	263.250	8,341.734	855.563	23⅓	45.703	54.844	63.984	73.125	82.266	91.406
14 × 22	13½ × 21½	290.250	11,180.672	1,040.063	25⅔	50.391	60.469	70.547	80.625	90.703	100.781
14 × 24	13½ × 23½	317.250	14,600.109	1,242.563	28	55.078	66.094	77.109	88.125	99.141	110.156

Size	Actual											
16 × 3	15½ × 2½	38.750	20.182	16.146	4	6.727	8.073	9.418	10.764	12.109	13.455
16 × 4	15½ × 3½	54.250	55.380	31.646	5⅓	9.418	11.302	13.186	15.069	16.953	18.837
16 × 6	15½ × 5½	85.250	214.901	78.146	8	14.800	17.760	20.720	23.681	26.641	29.601
16 × 8	15½ × 7½	116.250	544.922	145.313	10⅔	20.182	24.219	28.255	32.292	36.328	40.365
16 × 10	15½ × 9½	147.250	1,107.443	233.146	13⅓	25.564	30.677	35.790	40.903	46.016	51.128
16 × 12	15½ × 11½	178.250	1,964.463	341.646	16	30.946	37.135	43.325	49.514	55.703	61.892
16 × 14	15½ × 13½	209.250	3,177.984	470.813	18⅔	36.328	43.594	50.859	58.125	65.391	72.656
16 × 16	15½ × 15½	240.250	4,810.004	620.646	21⅓	41.710	50.052	58.394	66.736	75.078	83.420
16 × 18	15½ × 17½	271.250	6,922.523	791.146	24	47.092	56.510	65.929	75.347	84.766	94.184
16 × 20	15½ × 19½	302.250	9,577.547	982.313	26⅔	52.474	62.969	73.464	83.958	94.453	104.948
16 × 22	15½ × 21½	333.250	12,837.066	1,194.146	29⅓	57.856	69.427	80.998	92.569	104.141	115.712
16 × 24	15½ × 23½	364.250	16,763.086	1,426.646	32	63.238	75.885	88.533	101.181	113.828	126.476
18 × 6	17½ × 5½	96.250	242.630	88.229	9	16.710	20.052	23.394	26.736	30.078	33.420
18 × 8	17½ × 7½	131.250	615.234	164.063	12	22.786	27.344	31.901	36.458	41.016	45.573
18 × 10	17½ × 9½	166.250	1,250.338	263.229	15	28.863	34.635	40.408	46.181	51.953	57.726
18 × 12	17½ × 11½	201.250	2,217.943	385.729	18	34.939	41.927	48.915	55.903	62.891	69.878
18 × 14	17½ × 13½	236.250	3,588.047	531.563	21	41.016	49.219	57.422	65.625	73.828	82.031
18 × 16	17½ × 15½	271.250	5,430.648	700.729	24	47.092	56.510	65.929	75.347	84.766	94.184
18 × 18	17½ × 17½	306.250	7,815.754	893.229	27	53.168	63.802	74.436	85.069	95.703	106.337
18 × 20	17½ × 19½	341.250	10,813.359	1,109.063	30	59.245	71.094	82.943	94.792	106.641	118.490
18 × 22	17½ × 21½	376.250	14,493.461	1,348.229	33	65.321	78.385	91.450	104.514	117.578	130.642
18 × 24	17½ × 23½	411.250	18,926.066	1,610.729	36	71.398	85.677	99.957	114.236	128.516	142.795
20 × 6	19½ × 5½	107.250	270.359	98.313	10	18.620	22.344	26.068	29.792	33.516	37.240
20 × 8	19½ × 7½	146.250	685.547	182.813	13⅓	25.391	30.469	35.547	40.625	45.703	50.781
20 × 10	19½ × 9½	185.250	1,393.234	293.313	16⅔	32.161	38.594	45.026	51.458	57.891	64.323
20 × 12	19½ × 11½	224.250	2,471.422	429.813	20	38.932	46.719	54.505	62.292	70.078	77.865
20 × 14	19½ × 13½	263.250	3,998.109	592.313	23⅓	45.703	54.844	63.984	73.125	82.266	91.406
20 × 16	19½ × 15½	302.250	6,051.297	780.813	26⅔	52.474	62.969	73.464	83.958	94.453	104.948
20 × 18	19½ × 17½	341.250	8,708.984	995.313	30	59.245	71.094	82.943	94.792	106.641	118.490
20 × 20	19½ × 19½	380.250	12,049.172	1,235.813	33⅓	66.016	79.219	92.422	105.625	118.828	132.031
20 × 22	19½ × 21½	419.250	16,149.859	1,502.313	36⅔	72.786	87.344	101.901	116.458	131.016	145.573
20 × 24	19½ × 23½	458.250	21,089.047	1,794.813	40	79.557	95.469	111.380	127.292	243.203	159.115

SOFTWOOD LUMBER AND TIMBER SIZES (Continued)

Nominal Size, in. $b \times d$	Actual Size (s4s), in. $b \times d$	Area, A, in.²	Moment of Inertia, I, in.⁴	Section Modulus, S, in.³	Board Measure, per lineal ft	Weight of Piece, plf — Weight of Wood					
						25 pcf	30 pcf	35 pcf	40 pcf	45 pcf	50 pcf
22 × 6	21½ × 5½	118.250	298.088	108.396	11	20.530	24.635	28.741	32.847	36.953	41.059
22 × 8	21½ × 7½	161.250	755.859	201.563	14⅔	27.995	33.594	39.193	44.792	50.391	55.990
22 × 10	21½ × 9½	204.250	1,536.130	323.396	18⅓	35.460	42.552	49.644	56.736	63.828	70.920
22 × 12	21½ × 11½	247.250	2,724.901	473.896	22	42.925	51.510	60.095	68.681	77.266	85.851
22 × 14	21½ × 13½	290.250	4,408.172	653.063	25⅔	50.391	60.469	70.547	80.625	90.703	100.781
22 × 16	21½ × 15½	333.250	6,671.941	860.896	29⅓	57.856	69.427	80.998	92.569	104.141	115.712
22 × 18	21½ × 17½	376.250	9,602.211	1,097.396	33	65.321	78.385	91.450	104.514	117.578	130.642
22 × 20	21½ × 19½	419.250	13,284.984	1,362.563	36⅔	72.786	87.344	101.901	116.458	131.016	145.573
22 × 22	21½ × 21½	462.250	17,806.254	1,656.396	40⅓	80.252	96.302	112.352	128.403	144.453	160.503
22 × 24	21½ × 23½	505.250	23,252.023	1,978.896	44	87.717	105.260	122.804	140.347	157.891	175.434
24 × 6	23½ × 5½	129.250	325.818	118.479	12	22.439	26.927	31.415	35.903	40.391	44.878
24 × 8	23½ × 7½	176.250	826.172	220.313	16	30.599	36.719	42.839	48.958	55.078	61.198
24 × 10	23½ × 9½	223.250	1,679.026	353.479	20	38.759	46.510	54.262	62.014	69.766	77.517
24 × 12	23½ × 11½	270.250	2,978.380	517.979	24	46.918	56.302	65.686	75.069	84.453	93.837
24 × 14	23½ × 13½	317.250	4,818.234	713.813	28	55.078	66.094	77.109	88.125	99.141	110.156
24 × 16	23½ × 15½	364.250	7,292.586	940.979	32	63.238	75.885	88.533	101.181	113.828	126.476
24 × 18	23½ × 17½	411.250	10,495.441	1,199.479	36	71.398	85.677	99.957	114.236	128.516	142.795
24 × 20	23½ × 19½	458.250	14,520.797	1,489.313	40	79.557	95.469	111.380	127.292	143.203	159.115
24 × 22	23½ × 21½	505.250	19,462.648	1,810.479	44	87.717	105.260	122.804	140.347	157.891	175.434
24 × 24	23½ × 23½	552.250	25,415.004	2,162.979	48	95.877	115.052	134.227	153.403	172.578	191.753

HARDWOOD LUMBER SIZES[a]

Grades

A finish and B finish.
No. 1, No. 2, and No. 3 construction boards and utility boards.
No. 1 and No. 2 dimension, rough or dressed, as specified.

Nominal and Dressed Sizes			
Thicknesses			
Nominal Rough Thickness, in.	Dressed Thickness, S1S or S2S, in.		
1	$\frac{25}{32}$		
$1\frac{1}{4}$	$1\frac{1}{16}$		
$1\frac{1}{2}$	$1\frac{5}{16}$		
2	$1\frac{5}{8}$		
$2\frac{1}{2}$	$2\frac{1}{8}$		
3	$2\frac{5}{8}$		
Widths			
Nominal Width,	Dressed Width, S1E or S2E		
	Finish,	Construction and Utility Boards,	Dimension,
in.	in.	in.	in.
3	$2\frac{5}{8}$	$2\frac{5}{8}$	
4	$3\frac{5}{8}$	$3\frac{5}{8}$	$3\frac{5}{8}$
5	$4\frac{5}{8}$	$4\frac{5}{8}$	
6	$5\frac{5}{8}$	$5\frac{5}{8}$	$5\frac{5}{8}$
7	$6\frac{5}{8}$	$6\frac{5}{8}$	
8	$7\frac{1}{2}$	$7\frac{1}{2}$	$7\frac{1}{2}$
9	$8\frac{1}{2}$	$8\frac{1}{2}$	
10	$9\frac{1}{2}$	$9\frac{1}{2}$	$9\frac{1}{2}$
11	$10\frac{1}{2}$	$10\frac{1}{2}$	
12	$11\frac{1}{2}$	$11\frac{1}{2}$	$11\frac{1}{2}$
Over 12	$\frac{5}{8}$ off	$\frac{5}{8}$ off	$\frac{5}{8}$ off

[a]Source: National Hardwood Lumber Association.

TRIGONOMETRIC FORMULAS

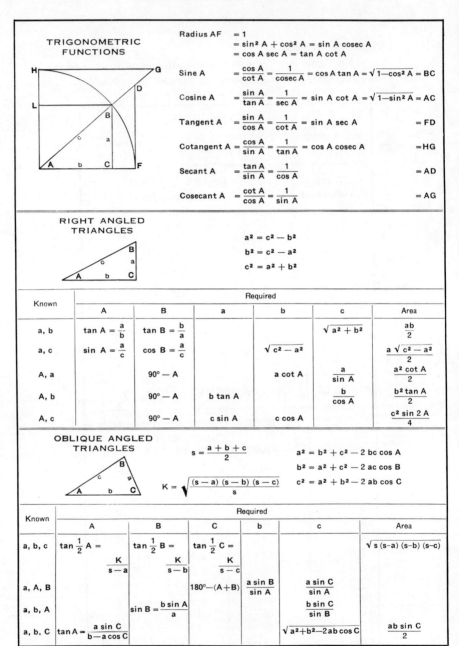

TRIGONOMETRIC FUNCTIONS

Radius AF $= 1$
$= \sin^2 A + \cos^2 A = \sin A \operatorname{cosec} A$
$= \cos A \sec A = \tan A \cot A$

Sine A $= \dfrac{\cos A}{\cot A} = \dfrac{1}{\operatorname{cosec} A} = \cos A \tan A = \sqrt{1-\cos^2 A} = BC$

Cosine A $= \dfrac{\sin A}{\tan A} = \dfrac{1}{\sec A} = \sin A \cot A = \sqrt{1-\sin^2 A} = AC$

Tangent A $= \dfrac{\sin A}{\cos A} = \dfrac{1}{\cot A} = \sin A \sec A \qquad = FD$

Cotangent A $= \dfrac{\cos A}{\sin A} = \dfrac{1}{\tan A} = \cos A \operatorname{cosec} A \qquad = HG$

Secant A $= \dfrac{\tan A}{\sin A} = \dfrac{1}{\cos A} \qquad = AD$

Cosecant A $= \dfrac{\cot A}{\cos A} = \dfrac{1}{\sin A} \qquad = AG$

RIGHT ANGLED TRIANGLES

$a^2 = c^2 - b^2$
$b^2 = c^2 - a^2$
$c^2 = a^2 + b^2$

Known	Required					
	A	B	a	b	c	Area
a, b	$\tan A = \dfrac{a}{b}$	$\tan B = \dfrac{b}{a}$			$\sqrt{a^2 + b^2}$	$\dfrac{ab}{2}$
a, c	$\sin A = \dfrac{a}{c}$	$\cos B = \dfrac{a}{c}$		$\sqrt{c^2 - a^2}$		$\dfrac{a\sqrt{c^2 - a^2}}{2}$
A, a		$90° - A$		$a \cot A$	$\dfrac{a}{\sin A}$	$\dfrac{a^2 \cot A}{2}$
A, b		$90° - A$	$b \tan A$		$\dfrac{b}{\cos A}$	$\dfrac{b^2 \tan A}{2}$
A, c		$90° - A$	$c \sin A$	$c \cos A$		$\dfrac{c^2 \sin 2A}{4}$

OBLIQUE ANGLED TRIANGLES

$s = \dfrac{a+b+c}{2}$

$K = \sqrt{\dfrac{(s-a)(s-b)(s-c)}{s}}$

$a^2 = b^2 + c^2 - 2bc \cos A$
$b^2 = a^2 + c^2 - 2ac \cos B$
$c^2 = a^2 + b^2 - 2ab \cos C$

Known	Required					
	A	B	C	b	c	Area
a, b, c	$\tan \frac{1}{2} A = \dfrac{K}{s-a}$	$\tan \frac{1}{2} B = \dfrac{K}{s-b}$	$\tan \frac{1}{2} C = \dfrac{K}{s-c}$			$\sqrt{s(s-a)(s-b)(s-c)}$
a, A, B			$180° - (A+B)$	$\dfrac{a \sin B}{\sin A}$	$\dfrac{a \sin C}{\sin A}$	
a, b, A		$\sin B = \dfrac{b \sin A}{a}$			$\dfrac{b \sin C}{\sin B}$	
a, b, C	$\tan A = \dfrac{a \sin C}{b - a \cos C}$				$\sqrt{a^2 + b^2 - 2ab \cos C}$	$\dfrac{ab \sin C}{2}$

Data reproduced by courtesy of AISC, Inc.

LENGTH OF CIRCULAR ARCS FOR UNIT RADIUS

Using this table, the length of any arc may be determined if the length of the radius and the angle of the segment are known.

Example: Determine the length of arc of a 41° 26′ 32″ segment with a radius of 9 ft 4 in.

$$\text{For unit radius: } 41° = 0.7155850$$
$$26′ = 0.0075631$$
$$32″ = \underline{0.0001551}$$
$$0.7233032$$

$$(0.7233032)(9.33) = 6.75 \text{ ft}$$

DEGREES						MINUTES		SECONDS	
1	.017 4533	61	1.064 6508	121	2.111 8484	1	.000 2909	1	.000 0048
2	.034 9066	62	1.082 1041	122	2.129 3017	2	.000 5818	2	.000 0097
3	.052 3599	63	1.099 5574	123	2.146 7550	3	.000 8727	3	.000 0145
4	.069 8132	64	1.117 0107	124	2.164 2083	4	.001 1636	4	.000 0194
5	.087 2665	65	1.134 4640	125	2.181 6616	5	.001 4544	5	.000 0242
6	.104 7198	66	1.151 9173	126	2.199 1149	6	.001 7453	6	.000 0291
7	.122 1730	67	1.169 3706	127	2.216 5682	7	.002 0362	7	.000 0339
8	.139 6263	68	1.186 8239	128	2.234 0214	8	.002 3271	8	.000 0388
9	.157 0796	69	1.204 2772	129	2.251 4747	9	.002 6180	9	.000 0436
10	.174 5329	70	1 221 7305	130	2.268 9280	10	.002 9089	10	.000 0485
11	.191 9862	71	1.239 1838	131	2.286 3813	11	.003 1998	11	.000 0533
12	.209 4395	72	1.256 6371	132	2.303 8346	12	.003 4907	12	.000 0582
13	.226 8928	73	1.274 0904	133	2.321 2879	13	.003 7815	13	.000 0630
14	.244 3461	74	1.291 5436	134	2.338 7412	14	.004 0724	14	.000 0679
15	.261 7994	75	1.308 9969	135	2.356 1945	15	.004 3633	15	.000 0727
16	.279 2527	76	1.326 4502	136	2.373 6478	16	.004 6542	16	.000 0776
17	.296 7060	77	1.343 9035	137	2.391 1011	17	.004 9451	17	.000 0824
18	.314 1593	78	1.361 3568	138	2.408 5544	18	.005 2360	18	.000 0873
19	.331 6126	79	1.378 8101	139	2.426 0077	19	.005 5269	19	.000 0921
20	.349 0659	80	1.396 2634	140	2.443 4610	20	.005 8178	20	.000 0970
21	.366 5191	81	1.413 7167	141	2.460 9142	21	.006 1087	21	.000 1018
22	.383 9724	82	1.431 1700	142	2.478 3675	22	.006 3995	22	.000 1067
23	.401 4257	83	1.448 6233	143	2.495 8208	23	.006 6904	23	.000 1115
24	.418 8790	84	1.466 0766	144	2.513 2741	24	.006 9813	24	.000 1164
25	.436 3323	85	1.483 5299	145	2.530 7274	25	.007 2722	25	.000 1212
26	.453 7856	86	1.500 9832	146	2.548 1807	26	.007 5631	26	.000 1261
27	.471 2389	87	1.518 4364	147	2.565 6340	27	.007 8540	27	.000 1309
28	.488 6922	88	1.535 8897	148	2.583 0873	28	.008 1449	28	.000 1357
29	.506 1455	89	1.553 3430	149	2.600 5406	29	.008 4358	29	.000 1406
30	.523 5988	90	1.570 7963	150	2.617 9939	30	.008 7266	30	.000 1454
31	·541 0521	91	1.588 2496	151	2.635 4472	31	.009 0175	31	.000 1503
32	.558 5054	92	1.605 7029	152	2.652 9005	32	.009 3084	32	.000 1551
33	.575 9587	93	1.623 1562	153	2.670 3538	33	.009 5993	33	.000 1600
34	.593 4119	94	1.640 6095	154	2.687 8070	34	.009 8902	34	.000 1648
35	.610 8652	95	1.658 0628	155	2.705 2603	35	.010 1811	35	.000 1697
36	.628 3185	96	1.675 5161	156	2.722 7136	36	.010 4720	36	.000 1745
37	.645 7718	97	1.692 9694	157	2.740 1669	37	.010 7629	37	.000 1794
38	.663 2251	98	1.710 4227	158	2.757 6202	38	.011 0538	38	.000 1842
39	.680 6784	99	1.727 8760	159	2.775 0735	39	.011 3446	39	.000 1391
40	.698 1317	100	1.745 3293	160	2.792 5268	40	.011 6355	40	.000 1939
41	.715 5850	101	1.762 7825	161	2.809 9801	41	.011 9264	41	.000 1988
42	.733 0383	102	1.780 2358	162	2.827 4334	42	.012 2173	42	.000 2036
43	.750 4916	103	1.797 6891	163	2.844 8867	43	.012 5082	43	.000 2085
44	.767 9449	104	1.815 1424	164	2.862 3400	44	.012 7991	44	.000 2133
45	.785 3982	105	1.832 5957	165	2.879 7933	45	.013 0900	45	.000 2182
46	.802 8515	106	1.850 0490	166	2.897 2466	46	.013 3809	46	.000 2230
47	.820 3047	107	1.867 5023	167	2.914 6999	47	.013 6717	47	.000 2279
48	.837 7580	108	1.884 9556	168	2.932 1531	48	.013 9626	48	.000 2327
49	.855 2113	109	1.902 4089	169	2.949 6064	49	.014 2535	49	.000 2376
50	.872 6646	110	1.919 8622	170	2.967 0597	50	.014 5444	50	.000 2424
51	.890 1179	111	1.937 3155	171	2.984 5130	51	.014 8353	51	.000 2473
52	.907 5712	112	1.954 7688	172	3.001 9663	52	.015 1262	52	.000 2521
53	.925 0245	113	1.972 2221	173	3.019 4196	53	.015 4171	53	.090 2570
54	.942 4778	114	1.989 6753	174	3.036 8729	54	.015 7080	54	.000 2618
55	.959 9311	115	2.007 1286	175	3.054 3262	55	.015 9989	55	.000 2666
56	.977 3844	116	2.024 5819	176	3.071 7795	56	.016 2897	56	.000 2715
57	.994 8377	117	2.042 0352	177	3.089 2328	57	.016 5806	57	.000 2763
58	1.012 2910	118	2.059 4885	178	3.106 6861	58	.016 8715	58	.000 2812
59	1.029 7443	119	2.076 9418	179	3.124 1394	59	.017 1624	59	.000 2860
60	1.047 1976	120	2.094 3951	180	3.141 5927	60	.017 4533	60	.000 2909

Data reproduced by courtesy of AISC, Inc.

PROPERTIES OF THE CIRCLE

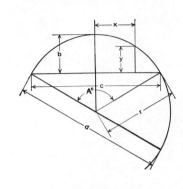

Circumference = 6.28318 r = 3.14159 d
Diameter   = 0.31831 circumference
Area   = 3.14159 r²

Arc   a $= \dfrac{\pi r A^\circ}{180^\circ} = 0.017453\ r\ A^\circ$

Angle   A° $= \dfrac{180^\circ a}{\pi r} = 57.29578\ \dfrac{a}{r}$

Radius r $= \dfrac{4 b^2 + c^2}{8 b}$

Chord   c $= 2 \sqrt{2 br - b^2} = 2 r \sin \dfrac{A}{2}$

Rise   b $= r - \frac{1}{2} \sqrt{4 r^2 - c^2} = \dfrac{c}{2} \tan \dfrac{A}{4}$

           $= 2 r \sin^2 \dfrac{A}{4} = r + y - \sqrt{r^2 - x^2}$

        y $= b - r + \sqrt{r^2 - x^2}$

        x $= \sqrt{r^2 - (r + y - b)^2}$

Diameter of circle of equal periphery as square = 1.27324 side of square
Side of square of equal periphery as circle   = 0.78540 diameter of circle
Diameter of circle circumscribed about square   = 1.41421 side of square
Side of square inscribed in circle   = 0.70711 diameter of circle

---

CIRCULAR SECTOR

r = radius of circle   y = angle ncp in degrees

Area of Sector ncpo = ½ (length of arc nop × r)

$= $ Area of Circle $\times \dfrac{y}{360}$

$= 0.0087266 \times r^2 \times y$

CIRCULAR SEGMENT

r = radius of circle   x = chord   b = rise

Area of Segment nop = Area of Sector ncpo — Area of triangle ncp

$= \dfrac{(\text{Length of arc nop} \times r) - x\ (r - b)}{2}$

Area of Segment nsp = Area of Circle — Area of Segment nop

VALUES FOR FUNCTIONS OF π

$\pi = 3.14159265359$,   log = 0.4971499

$\pi^2 = 9.8696044$, log = 0.9942997 $\dfrac{1}{\pi} = 0.3183099$, log = $\overline{1}.5028501$ $\sqrt{\dfrac{1}{\pi}} = 0.5641896$, log = $\overline{1}.7514251$

$\pi^3 = 31.0062767$, log = 1.4914496 $\dfrac{1}{\pi^2} = 0.1013212$, log = $\overline{1}.0057003$ $\dfrac{\pi}{180} = 0.0174533$, log = $\overline{2}.2418774$

$\sqrt{\pi} = 1.7724539$, log = 0.2485749 $\dfrac{1}{\pi^3} = 0.0322515$, log = $\overline{2}.5085500$ $\dfrac{180}{\pi} = 57.2957795$, log = 1.7581226

Note: Logs of fractions such as $\overline{1}.5028501$ and $\overline{2}.5085500$ may also be written 9.5028501 — 10 and 8.5085500 — 10 respectively.

Data reproduced by courtesy of AISC, Inc.

PROPERTIES OF GEOMETRIC SECTIONS

SQUARE

Axis of moments through center

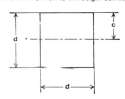

$A = d^2$

$c = \dfrac{d}{2}$

$I = \dfrac{d^4}{12}$

$S = \dfrac{d^3}{6}$

$r = \dfrac{d}{\sqrt{12}} = .288675\,d$

SQUARE

Axis of moments on base

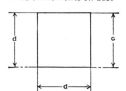

$A = d^2$

$c = d$

$I = \dfrac{d^4}{3}$

$S = \dfrac{d^3}{3}$

$r = \dfrac{d}{\sqrt{3}} = .577350\,d$

SQUARE

Axis of moments on diagonal

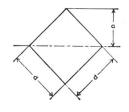

$A = d^2$

$c = \dfrac{d}{\sqrt{2}} = .707107\,d$

$I = \dfrac{d^4}{12}$

$S = \dfrac{d^3}{6\sqrt{2}} = .117851\,d^3$

$r = \dfrac{d}{\sqrt{12}} = .288675\,d$

RECTANGLE

Axis of moments through center

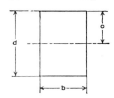

$A = bd$

$c = \dfrac{d}{2}$

$I = \dfrac{bd^3}{12}$

$S = \dfrac{bd^2}{6}$

$r = \dfrac{d}{\sqrt{12}} = .288675\,d$

Data reproduced by courtesy of AISC, Inc.

PROPERTIES OF GEOMETRIC SECTIONS

RECTANGLE

Axis of moments on base

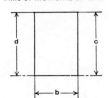

$$A = bd$$

$$c = d$$

$$I = \frac{bd^3}{3}$$

$$S = \frac{bd^2}{3}$$

$$r = \frac{d}{\sqrt{3}} = .577350\,d$$

RECTANGLE

Axis of moments on diagonal

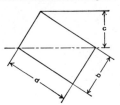

$$A = bd$$

$$c = \frac{bd}{\sqrt{b^2 + d^2}}$$

$$I = \frac{b^3 d^3}{6\,(b^2 + d^2)}$$

$$S = \frac{b^2 d^2}{6\sqrt{b^2 + d^2}}$$

$$r = \frac{bd}{\sqrt{6\,(b^2 + d^2)}}$$

RECTANGLE

Axis of moments any line
through center of gravity

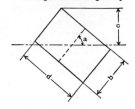

$$A = bd$$

$$c = \frac{b \sin a + d \cos a}{2}$$

$$I = \frac{bd\,(b^2 \sin^2 a + d^2 \cos^2 a)}{12}$$

$$S = \frac{bd\,(b^2 \sin^2 a + d^2 \cos^2 a)}{6\,(b \sin a + d \cos a)}$$

$$r = \sqrt{\frac{b^2 \sin^2 a + d^2 \cos^2 a}{12}}$$

HOLLOW RECTANGLE

Axis of moments through center

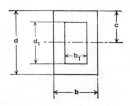

$$A = bd - b_1 d_1$$

$$c = \frac{d}{2}$$

$$I = \frac{bd^3 - b_1 d_1^3}{12}$$

$$S = \frac{bd^3 - b_1 d_1^3}{6d}$$

$$r = \sqrt{\frac{bd^3 - b_1 d_1^3}{12\,A}}$$

PROPERTIES OF GEOMETRIC SECTIONS

EQUAL RECTANGLES

Axis of moments through center of gravity

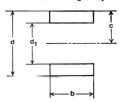

$A = b(d - d_1)$

$c = \dfrac{d}{2}$

$I = \dfrac{b(d^3 - d_1^3)}{12}$

$S = \dfrac{b(d^3 - d_1^3)}{6d}$

$r = \sqrt{\dfrac{d^3 - d_1^3}{12(d - d_1)}}$

UNEQUAL RECTANGLES

Axis of moments through center of gravity

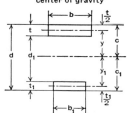

$A = bt + b_1 t_1$

$c = \dfrac{\frac{1}{2} bt^2 + b_1 t_1 (d - \frac{1}{2} t_1)}{A}$

$I = \dfrac{bt^3}{12} + bty^2 + \dfrac{b_1 t_1^3}{12} + b_1 t_1 y_1^2$

$S = \dfrac{I}{c} \qquad S_1 = \dfrac{I}{c_1}$

$= \sqrt{\dfrac{I}{A}}$

TRIANGLE

Axis of moments through center of gravity

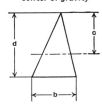

$A = \dfrac{bd}{2}$

$c = \dfrac{2d}{3}$

$I = \dfrac{bd^3}{36}$

$S = \dfrac{bd^2}{24}$

$r = \dfrac{d}{\sqrt{18}} = .235702\, d$

TRIANGLE

Axis of moments on base

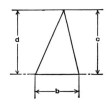

$A = \dfrac{bd}{2}$

$c = d$

$I = \dfrac{bd^3}{12}$

$S = \dfrac{bd^2}{12}$

$r = \dfrac{d}{\sqrt{6}} = .408248\, d$

Data reproduced by courtesy of AISC, Inc.

PROPERTIES OF GEOMETRIC SECTIONS

TRAPEZOID
Axis of moments through center of gravity

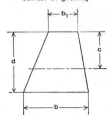

$$A = \frac{d(b + b_1)}{2}$$

$$c = \frac{d(2b + b_1)}{3(b + b_1)}$$

$$I = \frac{d^3 (b^2 + 4 bb_1 + b_1{}^2)}{36 (b + b_1)}$$

$$S = \frac{d^2 (b^2 + 4 bb_1 + b_1{}^2)}{12 (2b + b_1)}$$

$$r = \frac{d}{6(b + b_1)} \sqrt{2 (b^2 + 4 bb_1 + b_1{}^2)}$$

CIRCLE

Axis of moments through center

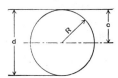

$$A = \frac{\pi d^2}{4} = \pi R^2 = .785398\ d^2 = 3.141593\ R^2$$

$$c = \frac{d}{2} = R$$

$$I = \frac{\pi d^4}{64} = \frac{\pi R^4}{4} = .049087\ d^4 = .785398\ R^4$$

$$S = \frac{\pi d^3}{32} = \frac{\pi R^3}{4} = .098175\ d^3 = .735398\ R^3$$

$$r = \frac{d}{4} = \frac{R}{2}$$

HOLLOW CIRCLE

Axis of moments through center

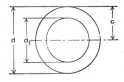

$$A = \frac{\pi (d^2 - d_1{}^2)}{4} = .785398\ (d^2 - d_1{}^2)$$

$$c = \frac{d}{2}$$

$$I = \frac{\pi (d^4 - d_1{}^4)}{64} = .049087\ (d^4 - d_1{}^4)$$

$$S = \frac{\pi (d^4 - d_1{}^4)}{32d} = .098175\ \frac{d^4 - d_1{}^4}{d}$$

$$r = \frac{\sqrt{d^2 + d_1{}^2}}{4}$$

HALF CIRCLE

Axis of moments through center of gravity

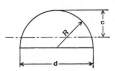

$$A = \frac{\pi R^2}{2} = 1.570796\ R^2$$

$$c = R \left(1 - \frac{4}{3\pi}\right) = .575587\ R$$

$$I = R^4 \left(\frac{\pi}{8} - \frac{8}{9\pi}\right) = .109757\ R^4$$

$$S = \frac{R^3}{24} \frac{(9\pi^2 - 64)}{(3\pi - 4)} = .190687\ R^3$$

$$r = R \frac{\sqrt{9\pi^2 - 64}}{6\pi} = .264336\ R$$

Data reproduced by courtesy of AISC, Inc.

PROPERTIES OF GEOMETRIC SECTIONS

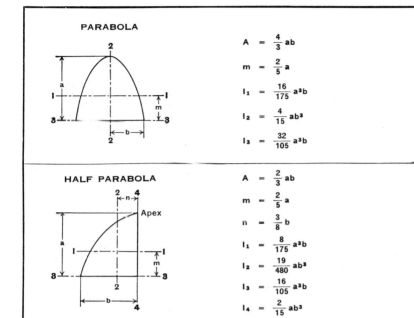

PARABOLA

$$A = \frac{4}{3}\,ab$$

$$m = \frac{2}{5}\,a$$

$$I_1 = \frac{16}{175}\,a^3b$$

$$I_2 = \frac{4}{15}\,ab^3$$

$$I_3 = \frac{32}{105}\,a^3b$$

HALF PARABOLA

$$A = \frac{2}{3}\,ab$$

$$m = \frac{2}{5}\,a$$

$$n = \frac{3}{8}\,b$$

$$I_1 = \frac{8}{175}\,a^3b$$

$$I_2 = \frac{19}{480}\,ab^3$$

$$I_3 = \frac{16}{105}\,a^3b$$

$$I_4 = \frac{2}{15}\,ab^3$$

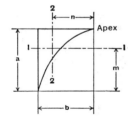

COMPLEMENT OF HALF PARABOLA

$$A = \frac{1}{3}\,ab$$

$$m = \frac{7}{10}\,a$$

$$n = \frac{3}{4}\,b$$

$$I_1 = \frac{37}{2100}\,a^3b$$

$$I_2 = \frac{1}{80}\,ab^3$$

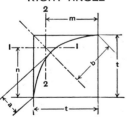

PARABOLIC FILLET IN RIGHT ANGLE

$$a = \frac{t}{2\sqrt{2}}$$

$$b = \frac{t}{\sqrt{2}}$$

$$A = \frac{1}{6}\,t^2$$

$$m = n = \frac{4}{5}\,t$$

$$I_1 = I_2 = \frac{11}{2100}\,t^4$$

Data reproduced by courtesy of AISC, Inc.

PROPERTIES OF GEOMETRIC SECTIONS

* HALF ELLIPSE

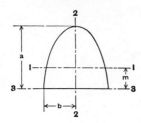

$$A = \frac{1}{2}\pi ab$$

$$m = \frac{4a}{3\pi}$$

$$I_1 = a^3 b \left(\frac{\pi}{8} - \frac{8}{9\pi} \right)$$

$$I_2 = \frac{1}{8}\pi ab^3$$

$$I_3 = \frac{1}{8}\pi a^3 b$$

* QUARTER ELLIPSE

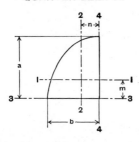

$$A = \frac{1}{4}\pi ab$$

$$m = \frac{4a}{3\pi}$$

$$n = \frac{4b}{3\pi}$$

$$I_1 = a^3 b \left(\frac{\pi}{16} - \frac{4}{9\pi} \right)$$

$$I_2 = ab^3 \left(\frac{\pi}{16} - \frac{4}{9\pi} \right)$$

$$I_3 = \frac{1}{16}\pi a^3 b$$

$$I_4 = \frac{1}{16}\pi ab^3$$

* ELLIPTIC COMPLEMENT

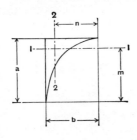

$$A = ab \left(1 - \frac{\pi}{4} \right)$$

$$m = \frac{a}{6\left(1 - \frac{\pi}{4} \right)}$$

$$n = \frac{b}{6\left(1 - \frac{\pi}{4} \right)}$$

$$I_1 = a^3 b \left(\frac{1}{3} - \frac{\pi}{16} - \frac{1}{36\left(1 - \frac{\pi}{4} \right)} \right)$$

$$I_2 = ab^3 \left(\frac{1}{3} - \frac{\pi}{16} - \frac{1}{36\left(1 - \frac{\pi}{4} \right)} \right)$$

* To obtain properties of half circle, quarter circle and circular complement substitute a = b = R.

PROPERTIES OF GEOMETRIC SECTIONS

REGULAR POLYGON

Axis of moments
through center

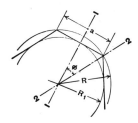

n = Number of sides

ϕ = $\dfrac{180°}{n}$

a = $2\sqrt{R^2 - R_1^2}$

R = $\dfrac{a}{2 \sin \phi}$

R_1 = $\dfrac{a}{2 \tan \phi}$

A = $\dfrac{1}{4} n a^2 \cot \phi - \dfrac{1}{2} n R^2 \sin 2\phi = n R_1^2 \tan \phi$

$I_1 = I_2$ = $\dfrac{A(6R^2 - a^2)}{24}$ = $\dfrac{A(12R_1^2 + a^2)}{48}$

$r_1 = r_2$ = $\sqrt{\dfrac{6R^2 - a^2}{24}}$ = $\sqrt{\dfrac{12R_1^2 + a^2}{48}}$

ANGLE

Axis of moments through
center of gravity

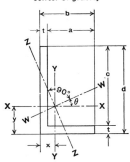

Z-Z is axis of minimum I

$\tan 2\theta$ = $\dfrac{2K}{I_Y - I_X}$

A = $t(b + c)$ $x = \dfrac{b^2 + ct}{2(b + c)}$ $y = \dfrac{d^2 + at}{2(b + c)}$

K = Product of Inertia about X-X & Y-Y

= $\dfrac{abcdt}{\mp 4(b + c)}$

I_X = $\dfrac{1}{3} \left(t(d - y)^3 + by^3 - a(y - t)^3 \right)$

I_Y = $\dfrac{1}{3} \left(t(b - x)^3 + dx^3 - c(x - t)^3 \right)$

I_z = $I_X \sin^2\theta + I_Y \cos^2\theta + K \sin2\theta$

I_w = $I_X \cos^2\theta + I_Y \sin^2\theta - K \sin2\theta$

K is negative when heel of angle, with respect
to c. g., is in 1st or 3rd quadrant, positive
when in 2nd or 4th quadrant.

BEAMS AND CHANNELS

Transverse force oblique
through center of gravity

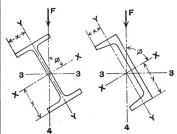

I_3 = $I_X \sin^2\phi + I_Y \cos^2\phi$

I_4 = $I_X \cos^2\phi + I_Y \sin^2\phi$

= $M \left(\dfrac{y}{I_X} \sin\phi + \dfrac{x}{I_Y} \cos\phi \right)$

where M is bending moment due to force F.

PROPERTIES OF STRUCTURAL SHAPES

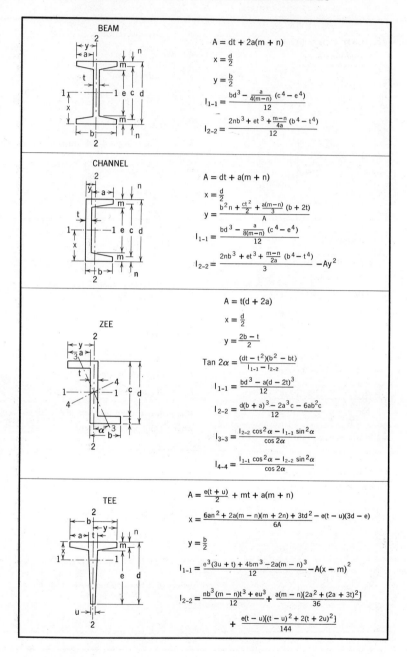

BEAM

$$A = dt + 2a(m + n)$$

$$x = \frac{d}{2}$$

$$y = \frac{b}{2}$$

$$I_{1-1} = \frac{bd^3 - \frac{a}{4(m-n)}\ (c^4 - e^4)}{12}$$

$$I_{2-2} = \frac{2nb^3 + et^3 + \frac{m-n}{4a}\ (b^4 - t^4)}{12}$$

CHANNEL

$$A = dt + a(m + n)$$

$$x = \frac{d}{2}$$

$$y = \frac{b^2 n + \frac{ct^2}{2} + \frac{a(m-n)}{3}\ (b + 2t)}{A}$$

$$I_{1-1} = \frac{bd^3 - \frac{a}{8(m-n)}\ (c^4 - e^4)}{12}$$

$$I_{2-2} = \frac{2nb^3 + et^3 + \frac{m-n}{2a}\ (b^4 - t^4)}{3} - Ay^2$$

ZEE

$$A = t(d + 2a)$$

$$x = \frac{d}{2}$$

$$y = \frac{2b - t}{2}$$

$$Tan\ 2\alpha = \frac{(dt - t^2)(b^2 - bt)}{I_{1-1} - I_{2-2}}$$

$$I_{1-1} = \frac{bd^3 - a(d - 2t)^3}{12}$$

$$I_{2-2} = \frac{d(b + a)^3 - 2a^3c - 6ab^2c}{12}$$

$$I_{3-3} = \frac{I_{2-2}\cos^2\alpha - I_{1-1}\sin^2\alpha}{\cos 2\alpha}$$

$$I_{4-4} = \frac{I_{1-1}\cos^2\alpha - I_{2-2}\sin^2\alpha}{\cos 2\alpha}$$

TEE

$$A = \frac{e(t + u)}{2} + mt + a(m + n)$$

$$x = \frac{6an^2 + 2a(m - n)(m + 2n) + 3td^2 - e(t - u)(3d - e)}{6A}$$

$$y = \frac{b}{2}$$

$$I_{1-1} = \frac{e^3(3u + t) + 4bm^3 - 2a(m - n)^3}{12} - A(x - m)^2$$

$$I_{2-2} = \frac{nb^3(m - n)t^3 + eu^3}{12} + \frac{a(m - n)[2a^2 + (2a + 3t)^2]}{36}$$

$$+ \frac{e(t - u)[(t - u)^2 + 2(t + 2u)^2]}{144}$$

Data reproduced by courtesy of AISC, Inc.

BEAM DIAGRAMS AND FORMULAS
For meaning of symbols see *General Nomenclature*

1. SIMPLE BEAM—UNIFORMLY DISTRIBUTED LOAD

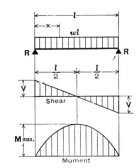

$$R = V \quad \ldots \quad \ldots \quad = \frac{wl}{2}$$

$$V_x \quad \ldots \quad \ldots \quad = w\left(\frac{l}{2} - x\right)$$

$$M \text{ max } \left(\text{ at center }\right) \quad \ldots \quad = \frac{wl^2}{8}$$

$$M_x \quad \ldots \quad \ldots \quad = \frac{wx}{2}(l-x)$$

$$\Delta\text{max.} \left(\text{ at center }\right) \quad \ldots \quad = \frac{5\,wl^4}{384\,EI}$$

$$\Delta_x \quad \ldots \quad \ldots \quad = \frac{wx}{24EI}(l^3 - 2lx^2 + x^3)$$

2. SIMPLE BEAM—LOAD INCREASING UNIFORMLY TO ONE END

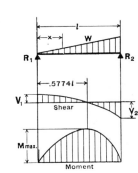

$$R_1 = V_1 \quad \ldots \quad \ldots \quad = \frac{W}{3}$$

$$R_2 = V_2 \text{ max.} \quad \ldots \quad \ldots \quad = \frac{2W}{3}$$

$$V_x \quad \ldots \quad \ldots \quad = \frac{W}{3} - \frac{Wx^2}{l^2}$$

$$M \text{ max. }\left(\text{at } x = \frac{l}{\sqrt{3}} = .5774l\right) \quad \ldots \quad = \frac{2Wl}{9\sqrt{3}} = .1283\,Wl$$

$$M_x \quad \ldots \quad \ldots \quad = \frac{Wx}{3l^2}(l^2 - x^2)$$

$$\Delta\text{max.} \left(\text{at } x = l\sqrt{1 - \sqrt{\frac{8}{15}}} = .5193l\right) = .01304\frac{Wl^3}{EI}$$

$$\Delta_x \quad \ldots \quad = \frac{Wx}{180EI\,l^2}(3x^4 - 10l^2x^2 + 7l^4)$$

3. SIMPLE BEAM—LOAD INCREASING UNIFORMLY TO CENTER

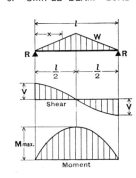

$$R = V \quad \ldots \quad \ldots \quad = \frac{W}{2}$$

$$V_x \left(\text{when } x < \frac{l}{2}\right) \quad \ldots \quad = \frac{W}{2l^2}(l^2 - 4x^2)$$

$$M \text{ max. } \left(\text{ at center }\right) \quad \ldots \quad = \frac{Wl}{6}$$

$$M_x \left(\text{when } x < \frac{l}{2}\right) \quad \ldots \quad = Wx\left(\frac{1}{2} - \frac{2x^2}{3l^2}\right)$$

$$\Delta\text{max.} \left(\text{ at center }\right) \quad \ldots \quad = \frac{Wl^3}{60EI}$$

$$\Delta_x \quad \ldots \quad \ldots \quad = \frac{Wx}{480\,EI\,l^2}(5l^2 - 4x^2)^2$$

BEAM DIAGRAMS AND FORMULAS
For meaning of symbols see *General Nomenclature*

---

4. SIMPLE BEAM—UNIFORM LOAD PARTIALLY DISTRIBUTED

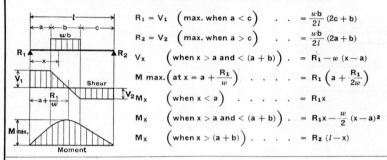

$R_1 = V_1$ $\left(\text{max. when } a < c\right)$ . . $= \dfrac{wb}{2l}(2c+b)$

$R_2 = V_2$ $\left(\text{max. when } a > c\right)$ . . $= \dfrac{wb}{2l}(2a+b)$

V_x $\left(\text{when } x > a \text{ and} < (a+b)\right)$. $= R_1 - w(x-a)$

M max. $\left(\text{at } x = a + \dfrac{R_1}{w}\right)$ . . . . $= R_1\left(a + \dfrac{R_1}{2w}\right)$

M_x $\left(\text{when } x < a\right)$ . . . . . $= R_1 x$

M_x $\left(\text{when } x > a \text{ and} < (a+b)\right)$. $= R_1 x - \dfrac{w}{2}(x-a)^2$

M_x $\left(\text{when } x > (a+b)\right)$ . . . . $= R_2(l-x)$

---

5. SIMPLE BEAM—UNIFORM LOAD PARTIALLY DISTRIBUTED AT ONE END

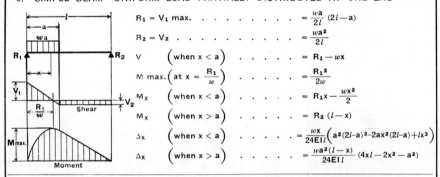

$R_1 = V_1$ max. . . . . $= \dfrac{wa}{2l}(2l-a)$

$R_2 = V_2$ . . . . $= \dfrac{wa^2}{2l}$

V $\left(\text{when } x < a\right)$ . . . . $= R_1 - wx$

M max. $\left(\text{at } x = \dfrac{R_1}{w}\right)$ . . . . $= \dfrac{R_1{}^2}{2w}$

M_x $\left(\text{when } x < a\right)$ . . . . $= R_1 x - \dfrac{wx^2}{2}$

M_x $\left(\text{when } x > a\right)$ . . . . $= R_2(l-x)$

Δ_x $\left(\text{when } x < a\right)$ . . . . $= \dfrac{wx}{24EIl}\left(a^2(2l-a)^2 - 2ax^2(2l-a) + lx^3\right)$

Δ_x $\left(\text{when } x > a\right)$ . . . . $= \dfrac{wa^2(l-x)}{24EIl}(4xl - 2x^2 - a^2)$

---

6. SIMPLE BEAM—UNIFORM LOAD PARTIALLY DISTRIBUTED AT EACH END

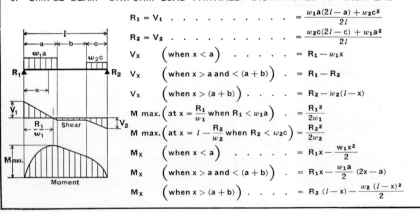

$R_1 = V_1$ . . . . $= \dfrac{w_1 a(2l-a) + w_2 c^2}{2l}$

$R_2 = V_2$ . . . . $= \dfrac{w_2 c(2l-c) + w_1 a^2}{2l}$

V_x $\left(\text{when } x < a\right)$ . . . . . $= R_1 - w_1 x$

V_x $\left(\text{when } x > a \text{ and} < (a+b)\right)$. $= R_1 - R_2$

V_x $\left(\text{when } x > (a+b)\right)$ . . . . $= R_2 - w_2(l-x)$

M max. $\left(\text{at } x = \dfrac{R_1}{w_1} \text{ when } R_1 < w_1 a\right)$. $= \dfrac{R_1{}^2}{2w_1}$

M max. $\left(\text{at } x = l - \dfrac{R_2}{w_2} \text{ when } R_2 < w_2 c\right)$ $= \dfrac{R_2{}^2}{2w_2}$

M_x $\left(\text{when } x < a\right)$ . . . . . $= R_1 x - \dfrac{w_1 x^2}{2}$

M_x $\left(\text{when } x > a \text{ and} < (a+b)\right)$. $= R_1 x - \dfrac{w_1 a}{2}(2x-a)$

M_x $\left(\text{when } x > (a+b)\right)$ . . . . $= R_2(l-x) - \dfrac{w_2(l-x)^2}{2}$

Data reproduced by courtesy of AISC, Inc.

BEAM DIAGRAMS AND FORMULAS
For meaning of symbols see *General Nomenclature*

---

7. SIMPLE BEAM—CONCENTRATED LOAD AT CENTER

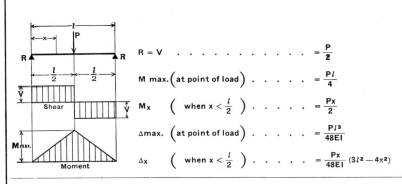

$R = V$ . . . . $= \dfrac{P}{2}$

M max. $\left(\text{at point of load}\right)$ . . . . . $= \dfrac{Pl}{4}$

M_x $\left(\text{when } x < \dfrac{l}{2}\right)$ . . . . . $= \dfrac{Px}{2}$

Δmax. $\left(\text{at point of load}\right)$ . . . . . $= \dfrac{Pl^3}{48EI}$

Δ_x $\left(\text{when } x < \dfrac{l}{2}\right)$ . . . . . $= \dfrac{Px}{48EI}(3l^2 - 4x^2)$

---

8. SIMPLE BEAM—CONCENTRATED LOAD AT ANY POINT

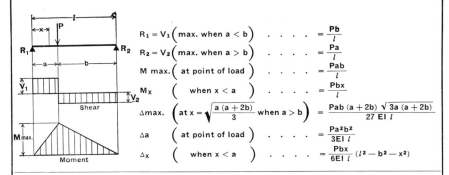

$R_1 = V_1\left(\text{max. when } a < b\right)$ . . . . $= \dfrac{Pb}{l}$

$R_2 = V_2\left(\text{max. when } a > b\right)$ . . . . $= \dfrac{Pa}{l}$

M max. $\left(\text{at point of load}\right)$ . . . . $= \dfrac{Pab}{l}$

M_x $\left(\text{when } x < a\right)$ . . . . $= \dfrac{Pbx}{l}$

Δmax. $\left(\text{at } x = \sqrt{\dfrac{a(a+2b)}{3}} \text{ when } a > b\right)$ $= \dfrac{Pab(a+2b)\sqrt{3a(a+2b)}}{27\,EI\,l}$

Δa $\left(\text{at point of load}\right)$ . . . . $= \dfrac{Pa^2b^2}{3EI\,l}$

Δ_x $\left(\text{when } x < a\right)$ . . . . $= \dfrac{Pbx}{6EI\,l}(l^2 - b^2 - x^2)$

---

9. SIMPLE BEAM—TWO EQUAL CONCENTRATED LOADS SYMMETRICALLY PLACED

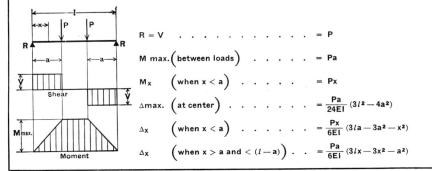

$R = V$ . . . . $= P$

M max. $\left(\text{between loads}\right)$ . . . . . $= Pa$

M_x $\left(\text{when } x < a\right)$ . . . . . $= Px$

Δmax. $\left(\text{at center}\right)$ . . . . . . $= \dfrac{Pa}{24EI}(3l^2 - 4a^2)$

Δ_x $\left(\text{when } x < a\right)$ . . . . . $= \dfrac{Px}{6EI}(3la - 3a^2 - x^2)$

Δ_x $\left(\text{when } x > a \text{ and } < (l-a)\right)$ . . $= \dfrac{Pa}{6EI}(3lx - 3x^2 - a^2)$

Data reproduced by courtesy of AISC, Inc.

BEAM DIAGRAMS AND FORMULAS
For meaning of symbols see *General Nomenclature*

10. SIMPLE BEAM—TWO EQUAL CONCENTRATED LOADS UNSYMMETRICALLY PLACED

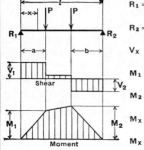

$$R_1 = V_1 \left(\text{max. when a} < \text{b} \right) \quad \ldots \ldots = \frac{P}{l} (l - a + b)$$

$$R_2 = V_2 \left(\text{max. when a} > \text{b} \right) \quad \ldots \ldots = \frac{P}{l} (l - b + a)$$

$$V_x \quad \left(\text{when x} > \text{a and} < (l - b) \right) \ldots = \frac{P}{l} (b - a)$$

$$M_1 \quad \left(\text{max. when a} > \text{b} \right) \quad \ldots \ldots = R_1 a$$

$$M_2 \quad \left(\text{max. when a} < \text{b} \right) \quad \ldots \ldots = R_2 b$$

$$M_x \quad \left(\text{when x} < \text{a} \right) \quad \ldots \ldots \ldots = R_1 x$$

$$M_x \quad \left(\text{when x} > \text{a and} < (l - b) \right) \ldots = R_1 x - P(x - a)$$

11. SIMPLE BEAM—TWO UNEQUAL CONCENTRATED LOADS UNSYMMETRICALLY PLACED

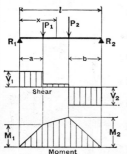

$$R_1 = V_1 \quad \ldots \ldots \ldots \ldots \ldots = \frac{P_1 (l - a) + P_2 b}{l}$$

$$R_2 = V_2 \quad \ldots \ldots \ldots \ldots \ldots = \frac{P_1 a + P_2 (l - b)}{l}$$

$$V_x \quad \left(\text{when x} > \text{a and} < (l - b) \right) \ldots = R_1 - P_1$$

$$M_1 \quad \left(\text{max. when } R_1 < P_1 \right) \quad \ldots \ldots = R_1 a$$

$$M_2 \quad \left(\text{max. when } R_2 < P_2 \right) \quad \ldots \ldots = R_2 b$$

$$M_x \quad \left(\text{when x} < \text{a} \right) \quad \ldots \ldots \ldots = R_1 x$$

$$M_x \quad \left(\text{when x} > \text{a and} < (l - b) \right) \ldots = R_1 x - P_1 (x - a)$$

12. BEAM FIXED AT ONE END, SUPPORTED AT OTHER— UNIFORMLY DISTRIBUTED LOAD

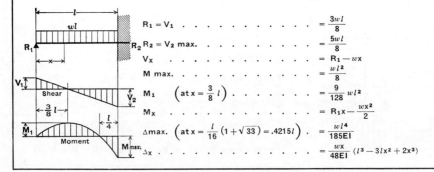

$$R_1 = V_1 \quad \ldots \ldots \ldots \ldots \ldots = \frac{3wl}{8}$$

$$R_2 = V_2 \text{ max.} \quad \ldots \ldots \ldots \ldots = \frac{5wl}{8}$$

$$V_x \quad \ldots \ldots \ldots \ldots \ldots \ldots = R_1 - wx$$

$$M \text{ max.} \quad \ldots \ldots \ldots \ldots \ldots = \frac{wl^2}{8}$$

$$M_1 \quad \left(\text{at x} = \frac{3}{8} l \right) \quad \ldots \ldots \ldots = \frac{9}{128} wl^2$$

$$M_x \quad \ldots \ldots \ldots \ldots \ldots \ldots = R_1 x - \frac{wx^2}{2}$$

$$\Delta \text{max.} \quad \left(\text{at x} = \frac{l}{16} (1 + \sqrt{33}) = .4215 l \right) = \frac{wl^4}{185EI}$$

$$\Delta_x \quad \ldots \ldots \ldots \ldots \ldots \ldots = \frac{wx}{48EI} (l^3 - 3lx^2 + 2x^3)$$

BEAM DIAGRAMS AND FORMULAS
For meaning of symbols see *General Nomenclature*

---

13. BEAM FIXED AT ONE END, SUPPORTED AT OTHER— CONCENTRATED LOAD AT CENTER

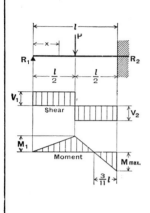

$R_1 = V_1$ . . . . $= \dfrac{5P}{16}$

$R_2 = V_2$ max. . . . . $= \dfrac{11P}{16}$

M max. $\left(\text{at fixed end}\right)$ . . . . . $= \dfrac{3Pl}{16}$

M_1 $\left(\text{at point of load}\right)$ . . . . $= \dfrac{5Pl}{32}$

M_x $\left(\text{when } x < \dfrac{l}{2}\right)$ . . . . . $= \dfrac{5Px}{16}$

M_x $\left(\text{when } x > \dfrac{l}{2}\right)$ . . . . . $= P\left(\dfrac{l}{2} - \dfrac{11x}{16}\right)$

Δmax. $\left(\text{at } x = l\sqrt{\dfrac{1}{5}} = .4472l\right)$ . . $= \dfrac{Pl^3}{48EI\sqrt{5}} = .009317\dfrac{Pl^3}{EI}$

Δ_x $\left(\text{at point of load}\right)$ . . . . $= \dfrac{7Pl^3}{768EI}$

Δ_x $\left(\text{when } x < \dfrac{l}{2}\right)$ . . . . . $= \dfrac{Px}{96EI}(3l^2 - 5x^2)$

Δ_x $\left(\text{when } x > \dfrac{l}{2}\right)$ . . . . . $= \dfrac{P}{96EI}(x - l)^2(11x - 2l)$

---

14. BEAM FIXED AT ONE END, SUPPORTED AT OTHER— CONCENTRATED LOAD AT ANY POINT

$R_1 = V_1$ . . . . $= \dfrac{Pb^2}{2l^3}(a + 2l)$

$R_2 = V_2$ . . . . $= \dfrac{Pa}{2l^3}(3l^2 - a^2)$

M_1 $\left(\text{at point of load}\right)$ . . . . $= R_1 a$

M_2 $\left(\text{at fixed end}\right)$ . . . . . $= \dfrac{Pab}{2l^2}(a + l)$

M_x $\left(\text{when } x < a\right)$ . . . . . $= R_1 x$

M_x $\left(\text{when } x > a\right)$ . . . . . $= R_1 x - P(x - a)$

Δmax. $\left(\text{when } a < .414l \text{ at } x = l\dfrac{l^2 + a^2}{3l^2 - a^2}\right) = \dfrac{Pa}{3EI}\dfrac{(l^2 - a^2)^3}{(3l^2 - a^2)^2}$

Δmax. $\left(\text{when } a > .414l \text{ at } x = l\sqrt{\dfrac{a}{2l + a}}\right) = \dfrac{Pab^2}{6EI}\sqrt{\dfrac{a}{2l + a}}$

Δa $\left(\text{at point of load}\right)$ . . . . $= \dfrac{Pa^2 b^3}{12EIl^3}(3l + a)$

Δ_x $\left(\text{when } x < a\right)$ . . . . . $= \dfrac{Pb^2 x}{12EIl^3}(3al^2 - 2lx^2 - ax^2)$

Δ_x $\left(\text{when } x > a\right)$ . . . . . $= \dfrac{Pa}{12EIl^3}(l-x)^2(3l^2 x - a^2 x - 2a^2 l)$

BEAM DIAGRAMS AND FORMULAS
For meaning of symbols see *General Nomenclature*

---

15.   BEAM FIXED AT BOTH ENDS—UNIFORMLY DISTRIBUTED LOADS

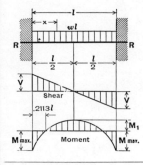

$R = V$ . . . . $= \dfrac{wl}{2}$

V_x . . . . $= w\left(\dfrac{l}{2} - x\right)$

M max. $\left(\text{at ends}\right)$ . . . . . $= \dfrac{wl^2}{12}$

M_1 $\left(\text{at center}\right)$ . . . . . $= \dfrac{wl^2}{24}$

M_x . . . . $= \dfrac{w}{12}(6lx - l^2 - 6x^2)$

Δmax. $\left(\text{at center}\right)$ . . . . . $= \dfrac{wl^4}{384EI}$

Δ_x . . . . $= \dfrac{wx^2}{24EI}(l - x)^2$

---

16   BEAM FIXED AT BOTH ENDS—CONCENTRATED LOAD AT CENTER

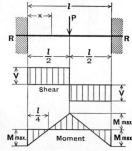

$R = V$ . . . . $= \dfrac{P}{2}$

M max. $\left(\text{at center and ends}\right)$ . . . $= \dfrac{Pl}{8}$

M_x $\left(\text{when } x < \dfrac{l}{2}\right)$ . . . . . $= \dfrac{P}{8}(4x - l)$

Δmax. $\left(\text{at center}\right)$ . . . . . . $= \dfrac{Pl^3}{192EI}$

Δ_x . . . . $= \dfrac{Px^2}{48EI}(3l - 4x)$

---

17.   BEAM FIXED AT BOTH ENDS—CONCENTRATED LOAD AT ANY POINT

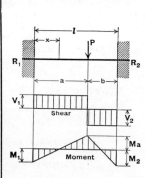

$R_1 = V_1\left(\text{max. when } a < b\right)$ . . . $= \dfrac{Pb^2}{l^3}(3a + b)$

$R_2 = V_2\left(\text{max. when } a > b\right)$ . . . $= \dfrac{Pa^2}{l^3}(a + 3b)$

M_1 $\left(\text{max. when } a < b\right)$ . . . $= \dfrac{Pab^2}{l^2}$

M_2 $\left(\text{max. when } a > b\right)$ . . . $= \dfrac{Pa^2b}{l^2}$

Ma $\left(\text{at point of load}\right)$ . . . $= \dfrac{2Pa^2b^2}{l^3}$

M_x $\left(\text{when } x < a\right)$ . . . . . $= R_1x - \dfrac{Pab^2}{l^2}$

Δmax. $\left(\text{when } a > b \text{ at } x = \dfrac{2al}{3a + b}\right)$. $= \dfrac{2Pa^3b^2}{3EI(3a + b)^2}$

Δa $\left(\text{at point of load}\right)$ . . . $= \dfrac{Pa^3b^3}{3EIl^3}$

Δ_x $\left(\text{when } x < a\right)$ . . . . $= \dfrac{Pb^2x^2}{6EIl^3}(3al - 3ax - bx)$

BEAM DIAGRAMS AND FORMULAS
For meaning of symbols see *General Nomenclature*

18. CANTILEVER BEAM—LOAD INCREASING UNIFORMLY TO FIXED END

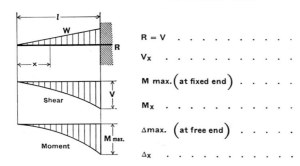

$$R = V \quad\ldots\ldots\ldots\ldots\ldots = W$$

$$V_x \quad\ldots\ldots\ldots\ldots\ldots = W \frac{x^2}{l^2}$$

$$M \text{ max.} \left(\text{at fixed end}\right) \ldots\ldots = \frac{Wl}{3}$$

$$M_x \quad\ldots\ldots\ldots\ldots\ldots = \frac{Wx^3}{3l^2}$$

$$\Delta \text{max.} \left(\text{at free end}\right) \ldots\ldots = \frac{Wl^3}{15EI}$$

$$\Delta_x \quad\ldots\ldots\ldots\ldots\ldots = \frac{W}{60EIl^2}(x^5 - 5l^4x + 4l^5)$$

19. CANTILEVER BEAM—UNIFORMLY DISTRIBUTED LOAD

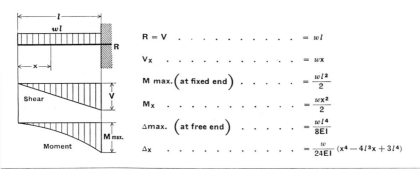

$$R = V \quad\ldots\ldots\ldots\ldots\ldots = wl$$

$$V_x \quad\ldots\ldots\ldots\ldots\ldots = wx$$

$$M \text{ max.} \left(\text{at fixed end}\right) \ldots\ldots = \frac{wl^2}{2}$$

$$M_x \quad\ldots\ldots\ldots\ldots\ldots = \frac{wx^2}{2}$$

$$\Delta \text{max.} \left(\text{at free end}\right) \ldots\ldots = \frac{wl^4}{8EI}$$

$$\Delta_x \quad\ldots\ldots\ldots\ldots\ldots = \frac{w}{24EI}(x^4 - 4l^3x + 3l^4)$$

20. BEAM FIXED AT ONE END, FREE TO DEFLECT VERTICALLY BUT NOT ROTATE AT OTHER—UNIFORMLY DISTRIBUTED LOAD

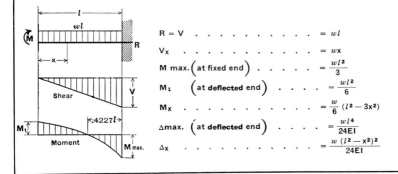

$$R = V \quad\ldots\ldots\ldots\ldots\ldots = wl$$

$$V_x \quad\ldots\ldots\ldots\ldots\ldots = wx$$

$$M \text{ max.} \left(\text{at fixed end}\right) \ldots\ldots = \frac{wl^2}{3}$$

$$M_1 \left(\text{at deflected end}\right) \ldots\ldots = \frac{wl^2}{6}$$

$$M_x \quad\ldots\ldots\ldots\ldots\ldots = \frac{w}{6}(l^2 - 3x^2)$$

$$\Delta \text{max.} \left(\text{at deflected end}\right) \ldots\ldots = \frac{wl^4}{24EI}$$

$$\Delta_x \quad\ldots\ldots\ldots\ldots\ldots = \frac{w(l^2 - x^2)^2}{24EI}$$

Data reproduced by courtesy of AISC, Inc.

BEAM DIAGRAMS AND FORMULAS
For meaning of symbols see *General Nomenclature*

21.   CANTILEVER BEAM—CONCENTRATED LOAD AT ANY POINT

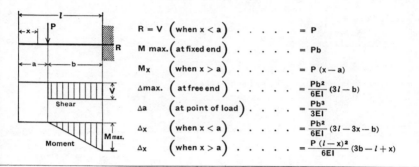

$R = V \left(\text{when } x < a\right)$ . . . . . $= P$

$M \text{ max.} \left(\text{at fixed end}\right)$ . . . . . $= Pb$

$M_x \left(\text{when } x > a\right)$ . . . . . $= P(x-a)$

$\Delta\text{max.} \left(\text{at free end}\right)$ . . . . . $= \dfrac{Pb^2}{6EI}(3l - b)$

$\Delta a \left(\text{at point of load}\right)$ . . . . $= \dfrac{Pb^3}{3EI}$

$\Delta x \left(\text{when } x < a\right)$ . . . . . $= \dfrac{Pb^2}{6EI}(3l - 3x - b)$

$\Delta x \left(\text{when } x > a\right)$ . . . . . $= \dfrac{P(l-x)^2}{6EI}(3b - l + x)$

22.   CANTILEVER BEAM—CONCENTRATED LOAD AT FREE END

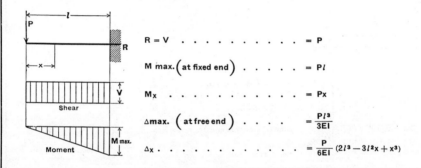

$R = V$ . . . . $= P$

$M \text{ max.} \left(\text{at fixed end}\right)$ . . . . . $= Pl$

M_x . . . . $= Px$

$\Delta\text{max.} \left(\text{at free end}\right)$ . . . . $= \dfrac{Pl^3}{3EI}$

Δx . . . . $= \dfrac{P}{6EI}(2l^3 - 3l^2x + x^3)$

23.   BEAM FIXED AT ONE END, FREE TO DEFLECT VERTICALLY BUT NOT ROTATE AT OTHER—CONCENTRATED LOAD AT DEFLECTED END

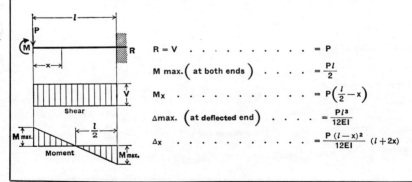

$R = V$ . . . . $= P$

$M \text{ max.} \left(\text{at both ends}\right)$ . . . . $= \dfrac{Pl}{2}$

M_x . . . . $= P\left(\dfrac{l}{2} - x\right)$

$\Delta\text{max.} \left(\text{at deflected end}\right)$ . . . . $= \dfrac{Pl^3}{12EI}$

Δx . . . . $= \dfrac{P(l-x)^2}{12EI}(l + 2x)$

BEAM DIAGRAMS AND FORMULAS
For meaning of symbols see *General Nomenclature*

---

24. BEAM OVERHANGING ONE SUPPORT—UNIFORMLY DISTRIBUTED LOAD

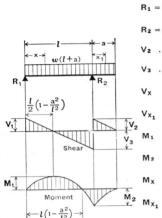

$R_1 = V_1$ . . . . $= \dfrac{w}{2l}(l^2 - a^2)$

$R_2 = V_2 + V_3$ . . . . $= \dfrac{w}{2l}(l + a)^2$

V_2 . . . . $= wa$

V_3 . . . . $= \dfrac{w}{2l}(l^2 + a^2)$

V_x $\left(\text{between supports}\right)$ . . $= R_1 - wx$

V_{x_1} $\left(\text{for overhang}\right)$ . . . . $= w(a - x_1)$

M_1 $\left(\text{at } x = \dfrac{l}{2}\left[1 - \dfrac{a^2}{l^2}\right]\right)$ . . $= \dfrac{w}{8l^2}(l + a)^2(l - a)^2$

M_2 $\left(\text{at } R_2\right)$ . . . . . . $= \dfrac{wa^2}{2}$

M_x $\left(\text{between supports}\right)$ . . $= \dfrac{wx}{2l}(l^2 - a^2 - xl)$

M_{x_1} $\left(\text{for overhang}\right)$ . . . . $= \dfrac{w}{2}(a - x_1)^2$

Δ_x $\left(\text{between supports}\right)$ . . $= \dfrac{wx}{24EIl}(l^4 - 2l^2x^2 + lx^3 - 2a^2l^2 + 2a^2x^2)$

Δ_{x_1} $\left(\text{for overhang}\right)$ . . . . $= \dfrac{wx_1}{24EI}(4a^2l - l^3 + 6a^2x_1 - 4ax_1^2 + x_1^3)$

---

25. BEAM OVERHANGING ONE SUPPORT—UNIFORMLY DISTRIBUTED LOAD ON OVERHANG

$R_1 = V_1$ . . . . $= \dfrac{wa^2}{2l}$

$R_2 = V_1 + V_2$ . . . . $= \dfrac{wa}{2l}(2l + a)$

V_2 . . . . $= wa$

V_{x_1} $\left(\text{for overhang}\right)$ . . . . $= w(a - x_1)$

$M \text{ max.}\left(\text{at } R_2\right)$ . . . . . . $= \dfrac{wa^2}{2}$

M_x $\left(\text{between supports}\right)$ . . $= \dfrac{wa^2x}{2l}$

M_{x_1} $\left(\text{for overhang}\right)$ . . . . $= \dfrac{w}{2}(a - x_1)^2$

$\Delta \text{ max.}$ $\left(\text{between supports at } x = \dfrac{l}{\sqrt{3}}\right) = \dfrac{wa^2l^2}{18\sqrt{3}EI} = .03208\,\dfrac{wa^2l^2}{EI}$

$\Delta \text{ max.}$ $\left(\text{for overhang at } x_1 = a\right)$. $= \dfrac{wa^3}{24EI}(4l + 3a)$

Δ_x $\left(\text{between supports}\right)$ . . $= \dfrac{wa^2x}{12EIl}(l^2 - x^2)$

Δ_{x_1} $\left(\text{for overhang}\right)$ . . . . $= \dfrac{wx_1}{24EI}(4a^2l + 6a^2x_1 - 4ax_1^2 + x_1^3)$

Data reproduced by courtesy of AISC, Inc.

BEAM DIAGRAMS AND FORMULAS
For meaning of symbols see *General Nomenclature*

---

26. BEAM OVERHANGING ONE SUPPORT—CONCENTRATED LOAD AT END OF OVERHANG

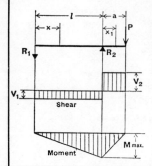

$R_1 = V_1$ . . . . $= \dfrac{Pa}{l}$

$R_2 = V_1 + V_2$ . . . . $= \dfrac{P}{l}(l + a)$

V_2 . . . . $= P$

$M \text{ max.} \left(\text{at } R_2\right)$ . . . . . $= Pa$

$M_x \left(\text{between supports}\right)$ . . $= \dfrac{Pax}{l}$

$M_{x_1} \left(\text{for overhang}\right)$ . . . . $= P(a - x_1)$

$\Delta \text{max.} \left(\text{between supports at } x = \dfrac{l}{\sqrt 3}\right) = \dfrac{Pal^2}{9\sqrt 3 EI} = .06415 \dfrac{Pal^2}{EI}$

$\Delta \text{max.} \left(\text{for overhang at } x_1 = a\right)$. $= \dfrac{Pa^2}{3EI}(l + a)$

$\Delta_x \left(\text{between supports}\right)$ . . . $= \dfrac{Pax}{6EIl}(l^2 - x^2)$

$\Delta_{x_1} \left(\text{for overhang}\right)$ . . . . $= \dfrac{Px_1}{6EI}(2al + 3ax_1 - x_1^2)$

---

27. BEAM OVERHANGING ONE SUPPORT—UNIFORMLY DISTRIBUTED LOAD BETWEEN SUPPORTS

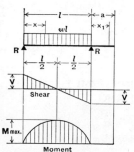

Equivalent Tabular Load . . . $= wl$

$R = V$ . . . . $= \dfrac{wl}{2}$

V_x . . . . $= w\left(\dfrac{l}{2} - x\right)$

$M \text{ max.} \left(\text{at center}\right)$ . . . . . $= \dfrac{wl^2}{8}$

M_x . . . . $= \dfrac{wx}{2}(l - x)$

$\Delta \text{max.} \left(\text{at center}\right)$ . . . . $= \dfrac{5wl^4}{384EI}$

Δ_x . . . . $= \dfrac{wx}{24EI}(l^3 - 2lx^2 + x^3)$

Δ_{x_1} . . . . $= \dfrac{wl^3 x_1}{24EI}$

---

28. BEAM OVERHANGING ONE SUPPORT—CONCENTRATED LOAD AT ANY POINT BETWEEN SUPPORTS

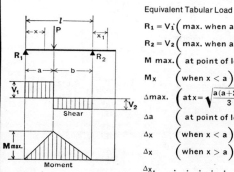

Equivalent Tabular Load . . . $= \dfrac{8Pab}{l^2}$

$R_1 = V_1 \left(\text{max. when } a < b\right)$ . . . $= \dfrac{Pb}{l}$

$R_2 = V_2 \left(\text{max. when } a > b\right)$ . . . $= \dfrac{Pa}{l}$

$M \text{ max.} \left(\text{at point of load}\right)$ . . . $= \dfrac{Pab}{l}$

$M_x \left(\text{when } x < a\right)$ . . . . . $= \dfrac{Pbx}{l}$

$\Delta \text{max.} \left(\text{at } x = \sqrt{\dfrac{a(a+2b)}{3}} \text{ when } a > b\right) = \dfrac{Pab(a+2b)\sqrt{3a(a+2b)}}{27EIl}$

$\Delta a \left(\text{at point of load}\right)$ . . . $= \dfrac{Pa^2b^2}{3EIl}$

$\Delta_x \left(\text{when } x < a\right)$ . . . . $= \dfrac{Pbx}{6EIl}(l^2 - b^2 - x^2)$

$\Delta_x \left(\text{when } x > a\right)$ . . . . $= \dfrac{Pa(l-x)}{6EIl}(2lx - x^2 - a^2)$

Δ_{x_1} . . . . $= \dfrac{Pabx_1}{6EIl}(l + a)$

BEAM DIAGRAMS AND FORMULAS
For meaning of symbols see *General Nomenclature*

---

29. CONTINUOUS BEAM – TWO EQUAL SPANS – UNIFORM LOAD ON BOTH SPANS

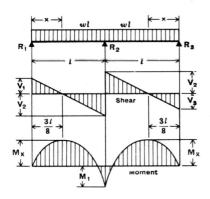

$$R_1 = V_1 = R_3 = V_3 \quad . \quad . \quad = \quad \frac{3}{8}\,wl$$

$$R_2 = 2V_2 \quad . \quad . \quad . \quad . \quad . \quad = \quad \frac{10}{8}\,wl$$

$$V_2 \quad . \quad . \quad . \quad . \quad . \quad . \quad . \quad - \quad \frac{5}{8}\,wl$$

$$M_x \quad . \quad . \quad . \quad . \quad . \quad . \quad = \quad R_1 x - \frac{wx^2}{2}$$

$$M_x \left(\text{at } x = \frac{3l}{8}\right) \quad . \quad . \quad . \quad = \quad \frac{9}{128}\,wl^2$$

$$M_1 \text{ (at support } R_2) . \quad . \quad = -\frac{wl^2}{8}$$

Δ Max. $(0.4215l$ from R_1 or $R_3) = wl^4/185EI$

$$\Delta_x = \frac{wx}{48EI}\,(l^3 - 3lx^2 + 2x^3)$$

---

30. CONTINUOUS BEAM – TWO EQUAL SPANS – UNIFORM LOAD ON ONE SPAN

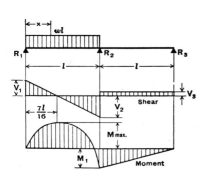

$$R_1 = V_1 . \quad . \quad . \quad . \quad . \quad = \quad \frac{7}{16}\,wl$$

$$R_2 = V_2 + V_3 \quad . \quad . \quad . \quad . \quad = \quad \frac{5}{8}\,wl$$

$$R_3 = V_3 . \quad . \quad . \quad . \quad . \quad = -\frac{1}{16}\,wl$$

$$V_2 \quad . \quad . \quad . \quad . \quad . \quad . \quad = \quad \frac{9}{16}\,wl$$

$$\text{M Max.}\left(\text{at } x = \frac{7}{16}l\right) . \quad = \quad \frac{49}{512}\,wl^2$$

$$M_1 \text{ (at support } R_2) . \quad . \quad = \quad \frac{1}{16}\,wl^2$$

$$M_x \text{ (when } x < l) \quad . \quad . \quad = \quad \frac{wx}{16}\,(7l - 8x)$$

Δ Max. $(0.472l$ from $R_1) = wl^4/109EI$

BEAM DIAGRAMS AND FORMULAS
For meaning of symbols see *General Nomenclature*

31. CONTINUOUS BEAM—TWO EQUAL SPANS—CONCENTRATED LOAD AT CENTER OF ONE SPAN

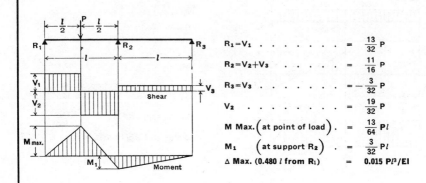

$R_1 = V_1 \quad \ldots \ldots \ldots = \dfrac{13}{32} P$

$R_2 = V_2 + V_3 \quad \ldots \ldots = \dfrac{11}{16} P$

$R_3 = V_3 \quad \ldots \ldots \ldots = -\dfrac{3}{32} P$

$V_2 \quad \ldots \ldots \ldots \ldots = \dfrac{19}{32} P$

M Max. $\left(\text{at point of load}\right) = \dfrac{13}{64} Pl$

$M_1 \quad \left(\text{at support } R_2\right) \quad = \dfrac{3}{32} Pl$

Δ Max. (0.480 l from R_1) $= 0.015\ Pl^3/EI$

32. CONTINUOUS BEAM—TWO EQUAL SPANS—CONCENTRATED LOAD AT ANY POINT

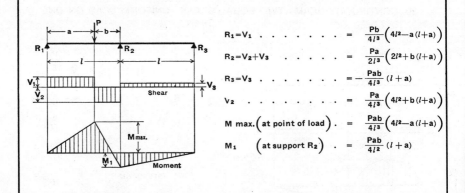

$R_1 = V_1 \quad \ldots \ldots \ldots = \dfrac{Pb}{4l^3}\left(4l^2 - a(l+a)\right)$

$R_2 = V_2 + V_3 \quad \ldots \ldots = \dfrac{Pa}{2l^3}\left(2l^2 + b(l+a)\right)$

$R_3 = V_3 \quad \ldots \ldots \ldots = -\dfrac{Pab}{4l^3}(l+a)$

$V_2 \quad \ldots \ldots \ldots \ldots = \dfrac{Pa}{4l^3}\left(4l^2 + b(l+a)\right)$

M max. $\left(\text{at point of load}\right) = \dfrac{Pab}{4l^3}\left(4l^2 - a(l+a)\right)$

$M_1 \quad \left(\text{at support } R_2\right) \quad = \dfrac{Pab}{4l^2}(l+a)$

BEAM DIAGRAMS AND FORMULAS
For meaning of symbols see *General Nomenclature*

---

33.   BEAM—UNIFORMLY DISTRIBUTED LOAD AND VARIABLE END MOMENTS

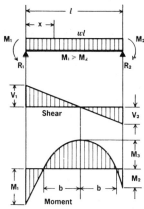

$$R_1 = V_1 = \frac{wl}{2} + \frac{M_1 - M_2}{l}$$

$$R_2 = V_2 = \frac{wl}{2} - \frac{M_1 - M_2}{l}$$

$$V_x = w\left(\frac{l}{2} - x\right) + \frac{M_1 - M_2}{l}$$

$$M_3 \left(\text{at } x = \frac{l}{2} + \frac{M_1 - M_2}{wl}\right)$$

$$= \frac{wl^2}{8} - \frac{M_1 + M_2}{2} + \frac{(M_1 - M_2)^2}{2wl^2}$$

$$M_x = \frac{wx}{2}(l - x) + \left(\frac{M_1 - M_2}{l}\right)x - M_1$$

$$b\left(\begin{matrix}\text{To locate}\\\text{inflection points}\end{matrix}\right) = \sqrt{\frac{l^2}{4} - \left(\frac{M_1 + M_2}{w}\right) + \left(\frac{M_1 - M_2}{wl}\right)^2}$$

$$\Delta_x = \frac{wx}{24EI}\left[x^3 - \left(2l + \frac{4M_1}{wl} - \frac{4M_2}{wl}\right)x^2 + \frac{12M_1}{w}x + l^3 - \frac{8M_1 l}{w} - \frac{4M_2 l}{w}\right]$$

---

34.   BEAM—CONCENTRATED LOAD AT CENTER AND VARIABLE END MOMENTS

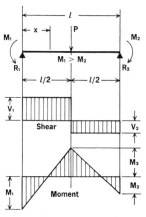

$$R_1 = V_1 = \frac{P}{2} + \frac{M_1 - M_2}{l}$$

$$R_2 = V_2 = \frac{P}{2} - \frac{M_1 - M_2}{l}$$

$$M_3 \text{ (At center)} = \frac{Pl}{4} - \frac{M_1 + M_2}{2}$$

$$M_x \left(\text{When } x < \frac{l}{2}\right) = \left(\frac{P}{2} + \frac{M_1 - M_2}{l}\right)x - M_1$$

$$M_x \left(\text{When } x > \frac{l}{2}\right) = \frac{P}{2}(l - x) + \frac{(M_1 - M_2)x}{l} - M_1$$

$$\Delta_x \left(\text{When } x < \frac{l}{2}\right) = \frac{Px}{48EI}\left(3l^2 - 4x^2 - \frac{8(l - x)}{Pl}[M_1(2l - x) + M_2(l + x)]\right)$$

BEAM DIAGRAMS AND FORMULAS
For meaning of symbols see *General Nomenclature*

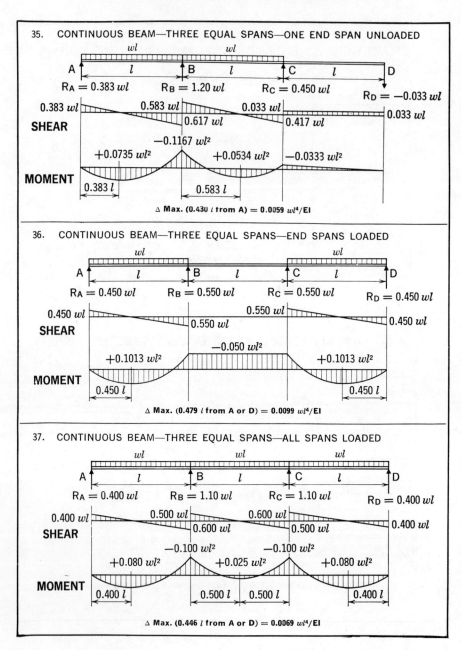

35.   CONTINUOUS BEAM—THREE EQUAL SPANS—ONE END SPAN UNLOADED

$R_A = 0.383 \, wl$ $R_B = 1.20 \, wl$ $R_C = 0.450 \, wl$ $R_D = -0.033 \, wl$

SHEAR $0.383 \, wl$ $0.583 \, wl$ $0.033 \, wl$ $0.033 \, wl$ $0.617 \, wl$ $0.417 \, wl$

$-0.1167 \, wl^2$

MOMENT $+0.0735 \, wl^2$ $+0.0534 \, wl^2$ $-0.0333 \, wl^2$ $0.383 \, l$ $0.583 \, l$

$\triangle$ Max. (0.430 *l* from A) = 0.0059 wl^4/EI

36.   CONTINUOUS BEAM—THREE EQUAL SPANS—END SPANS LOADED

$R_A = 0.450 \, wl$ $R_B = 0.550 \, wl$ $R_C = 0.550 \, wl$ $R_D = 0.450 \, wl$

SHEAR $0.450 \, wl$ $0.550 \, wl$ $0.550 \, wl$ $0.450 \, wl$

$-0.050 \, wl^2$

MOMENT $+0.1013 \, wl^2$ $+0.1013 \, wl^2$ $0.450 \, l$ $0.450 \, l$

$\triangle$ Max. (0.479 *l* from A or D) = 0.0099 wl^4/EI

37.   CONTINUOUS BEAM—THREE EQUAL SPANS—ALL SPANS LOADED

$R_A = 0.400 \, wl$ $R_B = 1.10 \, wl$ $R_C = 1.10 \, wl$ $R_D = 0.400 \, wl$

SHEAR $0.400 \, wl$ $0.500 \, wl$ $0.600 \, wl$ $0.400 \, wl$ $0.600 \, wl$ $0.500 \, wl$

$-0.100 \, wl^2$ $-0.100 \, wl^2$

MOMENT $+0.080 \, wl^2$ $+0.025 \, wl^2$ $+0.080 \, wl^2$ $0.400 \, l$ $0.500 \, l$ $0.500 \, l$ $0.400 \, l$

$\triangle$ Max. (0.446 *l* from A or D) = 0.0069 wl^4/EI

BEAM DIAGRAMS AND FORMULAS
For meaning of symbols see *General Nomenclature*

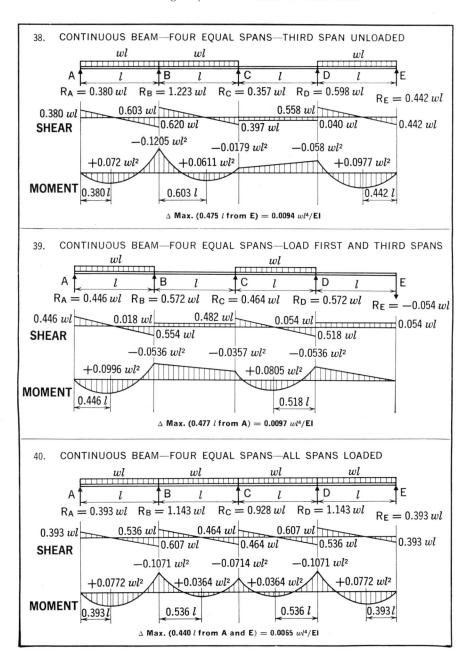

38. CONTINUOUS BEAM—FOUR EQUAL SPANS—THIRD SPAN UNLOADED

$R_A = 0.380\,wl$ $R_B = 1.223\,wl$ $R_C = 0.357\,wl$ $R_D = 0.598\,wl$ $R_E = 0.442\,wl$

SHEAR
0.380 wl 0.603 wl 0.620 wl 0.397 wl 0.558 wl 0.040 wl 0.442 wl

−0.1205 wl² −0.0179 wl² −0.058 wl²
+0.072 wl² +0.0611 wl² +0.0977 wl²

MOMENT 0.380 l 0.603 l 0.442 l

△ Max. (0.475 *l* from E) = 0.0094 *wl⁴*/El

39. CONTINUOUS BEAM—FOUR EQUAL SPANS—LOAD FIRST AND THIRD SPANS

$R_A = 0.446\,wl$ $R_B = 0.572\,wl$ $R_C = 0.464\,wl$ $R_D = 0.572\,wl$ $R_E = -0.054\,wl$

SHEAR
0.446 wl 0.018 wl 0.482 wl 0.054 wl 0.054 wl
0.554 wl 0.518 wl

−0.0536 wl² −0.0357 wl² −0.0536 wl²
+0.0996 wl² +0.0805 wl²

MOMENT 0.446 l 0.518 l

△ Max. (0.477 *l* from A) = 0.0097 *wl⁴*/El

40. CONTINUOUS BEAM—FOUR EQUAL SPANS—ALL SPANS LOADED

$R_A = 0.393\,wl$ $R_B = 1.143\,wl$ $R_C = 0.928\,wl$ $R_D = 1.143\,wl$ $R_E = 0.393\,wl$

SHEAR
0.393 wl 0.536 wl 0.464 wl 0.607 wl 0.393 wl
0.607 wl 0.464 wl 0.536 wl

−0.1071 wl² −0.0714 wl² −0.1071 wl²
+0.0772 wl² +0.0364 wl² +0.0364 wl² +0.0772 wl²

MOMENT 0.393 l 0.536 l 0.536 l 0.393 l

△ Max. (0.440 *l* from A and E) = 0.0065 *wl⁴*/El

Data reproduced by courtesy of AISC, Inc.

BEAM DIAGRAMS AND FORMULAS
For meaning of symbols see *General Nomenclature*

---

41.   SIMPLE BEAM—ONE CONCENTRATED MOVING LOAD

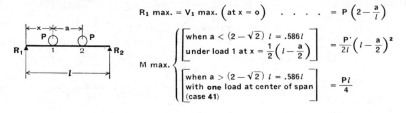

R_1 max. $= V_1$ max. $\left(\text{at } x = 0\right)$ . . . . $= P$

M max. $\left(\text{at point of load, when } x = \dfrac{l}{2}\right)$. $= \dfrac{Pl}{4}$

---

42.   SIMPLE BEAM—TWO EQUAL CONCENTRATED MOVING LOADS

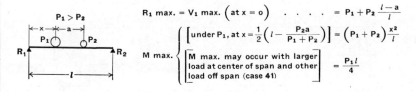

R_1 max. $= V_1$ max. $\left(\text{at } x = 0\right)$ . . . . $= P\left(2 - \dfrac{a}{l}\right)$

M max.
$\begin{cases} \left[\begin{array}{l}\text{when } a < (2 - \sqrt{2})\, l = .586l \\ \text{under load 1 at } x = \dfrac{1}{2}\left(l - \dfrac{a}{2}\right)\end{array}\right] = \dfrac{P}{2l}\left(l - \dfrac{a}{2}\right)^2 \\[2em] \left[\begin{array}{l}\text{when } a > (2 - \sqrt{2})\, l = .586l \\ \text{with \textbf{one} load at center of span} \\ \text{(case 41)}\end{array}\right] = \dfrac{Pl}{4} \end{cases}$

---

43.   SIMPLE BEAM—TWO UNEQUAL CONCENTRATED MOVING LOADS

$P_1 > P_2$

R_1 max. $= V_1$ max. $\left(\text{at } x = 0\right)$ . . . . $= P_1 + P_2\,\dfrac{l - a}{l}$

M max.
$\begin{cases} \left[\text{under } P_1, \text{ at } x = \dfrac{1}{2}\left(l - \dfrac{P_2 a}{P_1 + P_2}\right)\right] = \left(P_1 + P_2\right)\dfrac{x^2}{l} \\[2em] \left[\begin{array}{l}\text{M max. may occur with larger} \\ \text{load at center of span and other} \\ \text{load off span (case 41)}\end{array}\right] = \dfrac{P_1 l}{4} \end{cases}$

Data reproduced by courtesy of AISC, Inc.

FIXED END MOMENTS
FOR BEAMS OF CONSTANT MOMENT OF INERTIA

Beam fixed at both ends	Left end fixed, Right end hinged	Left end hinged, Right end fixed
$M_A = \dfrac{Pa^2b}{l^2}$ $M_B = \dfrac{Pb^2a}{l^2}$	$M_A = \dfrac{P}{l^2}\left(a^2b + \dfrac{b^2a}{2}\right)$	$M_B = \dfrac{P}{l^2}\left(b^2a + \dfrac{a^2b}{2}\right)$
$M_A = \dfrac{wl^2}{12}$ $M_B = M_A$	$M_A = \dfrac{wl^2}{8}$	$M_B = \dfrac{wl^2}{8}$
$M_A = \dfrac{11}{192}\,wl^2$ $M_B = \dfrac{5}{192}\,wl^2$	$M_A = \dfrac{9}{128}\,wl^2$	$M_B = \dfrac{7}{128}\,wl^2$
$M_A = \dfrac{wl^2}{12}\,k^2(6-8k+3k^2)$ $M_B = \dfrac{wl^2}{12}\,k^3(4-3k)$	$M_A = \dfrac{wl^2k^2}{8}(4-4k+k^2)$	$M_B = \dfrac{wl^2k^2}{8}(2-k^2)$
$M_A = \dfrac{wl^2}{6}k^2(3-2k)$ $M_B = M_A$	$M_A = \dfrac{wl^2}{4}k^2(3-2k)$	$M_B = \dfrac{wl^2}{4}k^2(3-2k)$

FIXED END MOMENTS
FOR BEAMS OF CONSTANT MOMENT OF INERTIA

Beam fixed at both ends	Left end fixed, Right end hinged	Left end hinged, Right end fixed
$M_A = M_B = \dfrac{wl^2}{12}(1 - 6k^2 + 4k^3)$	$M_A = \dfrac{wl^2}{8}(1 - 6k^2 - 4k^3)$	$M_B = \dfrac{wl^2}{8}(1 - 6k^2 - 4k^3)$
$M_A = M_A\,(\text{for } k_1 l) - M_A\,(\text{for } k_2 l)$ $M_B = M_B\,(\text{for } k_1 l) - M_B\,(\text{for } k_2 l)$	$M_A = M_A\,(\text{for } k_1 l) - M_A\,(\text{for } k_2 l)$	$M_B = M_B\,(\text{for } k_1 l) - M_B\,(\text{for } k_2 l)$
$M_A = \dfrac{wl^2}{20}$ $M_B = \dfrac{wl^2}{30}$	$M_A = \dfrac{wl^2}{15}$	$M_B = \dfrac{7wl^2}{120}$
$M_A = \dfrac{w_1 l^2}{12} + \dfrac{w_2 l^2}{20}$ $M_B = \dfrac{w_1 l^2}{12} + \dfrac{w_2 l^2}{30}$	$M_A = \dfrac{w_1 l^2}{8} + \dfrac{w_2 l^2}{15}$	$M_B = \dfrac{w_1 l^2}{8} + \dfrac{7w_2 l^2}{120}$
$M_A = M_B = \dfrac{5wl^2}{96}$	$M_A = \dfrac{5wl^2}{64}$	$M_B = \dfrac{5wl^2}{64}$

FIXED END MOMENTS
FOR BEAMS OF CONSTANT MOMENT OF INERTIA

Beam fixed at both ends	Left end fixed, Right end hinged	Left end hinged, Right end fixed

Row 1

$M_A = \dfrac{wl^2}{30}$ $M_B = \dfrac{3wl^2}{160}$

$M_A = \dfrac{41wl^2}{960}$

$M_B = \dfrac{17wl^2}{480}$

Row 2

$M_A = \dfrac{wl^2}{30} k^2(10 - 15k + 6k^2)$
$M_B = \dfrac{wl^2}{20} k^3(5 - 4k)$

$M_A = \dfrac{wl^2 k^2}{120} (40 - 45k + 12k^2)$

$M_B = \dfrac{wl^2 k^2}{30} (5 - 3k^2)$

Row 3

$M_A = \dfrac{23wl^2}{960}$ $M_B = \dfrac{7wl^2}{960}$

$M_A = \dfrac{53wl^2}{1,920}$

$M_B = \dfrac{37wl^2}{1,920}$

Row 4

$M_A = \dfrac{wl^2}{60} k^2(10 - 10k + 3k^2)$
$M_B = \dfrac{wl^2}{60} k^3(5 - 3k)$

$M_A = \dfrac{wl^2}{120} k^2(20 - 15k + 3k^2)$

$M_B = \dfrac{wl^2}{120} k^2(10 - 3k^2)$

Row 5

$M_A = M_B = \dfrac{wl^2}{32}$

$M_A = \dfrac{3wl^2}{64}$

$M_B = \dfrac{3wl^2}{64}$

FIXED END MOMENTS
FOR BEAMS OF CONSTANT MOMENT OF INERTIA

Beam fixed at both ends	Left end fixed, Right end hinged	Left end hinged, Right end fixed
$M_A = M_B = \frac{wl^2}{15}$	$M_A = \frac{wl^2}{10}$	$M_B = \frac{wl^2}{10}$
$M_A = M_B = \frac{Pl}{8}$	$M_A = \frac{3Pl}{16}$	$M_B = \frac{3Pl}{16}$
$M_A = M_B = \frac{2Pl}{9}$	$M_A = \frac{Pl}{3}$	$M_B = \frac{Pl}{3}$
$M_A = M_B = \frac{15Pl}{48}$	$M_A = \frac{45Pl}{96}$	$M_B = \frac{45Pl}{96}$
$M_A = -M_1 k_1 (1 - 3k_2)$ $M_B = +M_1 k_2 (1 - 3k_1)$	$M_A = -\frac{M_1}{2}(3k_1^2 - 1)$	$M_B = +\frac{M_1}{2}(3k_2^2 - 1)$

EFFECT OF OVERHANG ON MAXIMUM DEFLECTION
FOR A SIMPLE SPAN SYSTEM

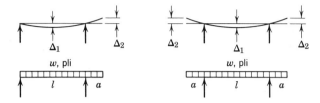

Without overhang $\Delta = \dfrac{5wl^4}{384EI}$

$\Delta_1 = C_1\Delta$, deflection between supports with overhang, in.

$\Delta_2 = C_2\Delta$, deflection of overhanging end, in.

$w =$ uniformly distributed load, pli
$l =$ span, in.
$a =$ overhang, in.
$\Delta =$ deflection, in.
$E =$ modulus of elasticity, psi
$I =$ moment of inertia, in.⁴

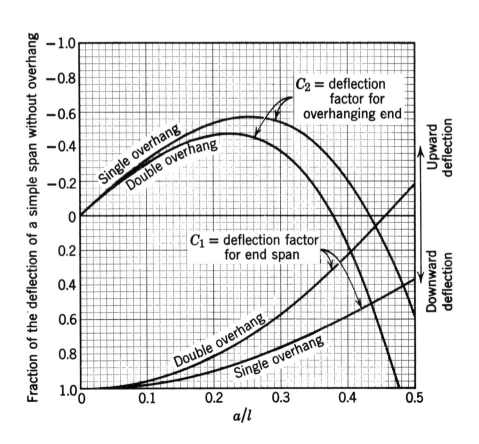

EFFECT OF OVERHANG ON MAXIMUM BENDING STRESS FOR A SIMPLE SPAN SYSTEM

Maximum bending stress without overhangs: $f_b = \dfrac{wl^2c}{8I}$

Maximum bending stress with overhangs: $f_b\max = C_1 f_b$ for $0 < a/l < 0.408$

$f_b\max = C_2 f_b$ for $0.408 < a/l$

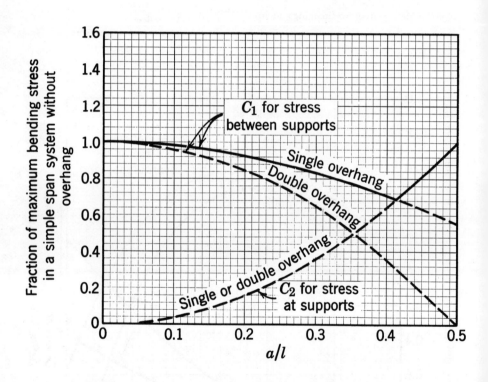

EFFECT OF OVERHANG ON REACTIONS
FOR A SIMPLE SPAN SYSTEM

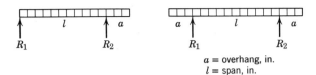

a = overhang, in.
l = span, in.

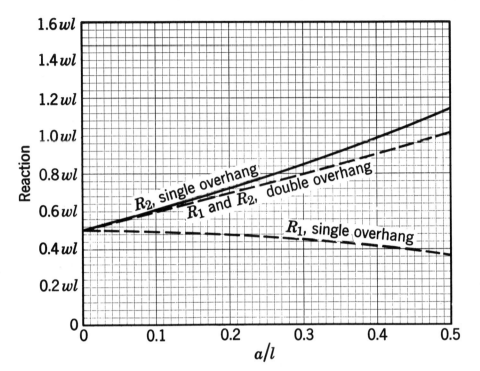

EFFECT OF OVERHANG ON MAXIMUM VERTICAL SHEAR
FOR A SIMPLE SPAN SYSTEM

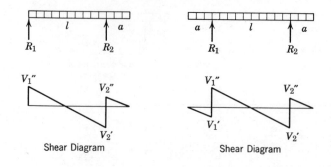

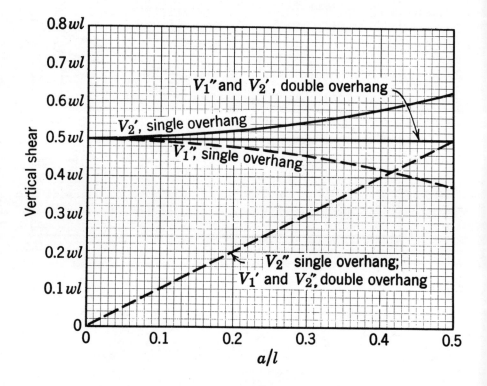

EFFECT OF OVERHANG ON MAXIMUM DEFLECTION
FOR A TWO SPAN CONTINUOUS SYSTEM

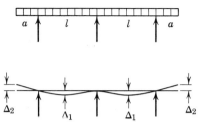

Δ = deflection of end span of two span continuous deck, without overhangs, calculated using the appropriate formula for end joint pattern to be used, in.

$\Delta_1 = C_1\Delta$ = deflection of end span with overhang, in.
$\Delta_2 = C_2\Delta$ = deflection of overhanging end, in.

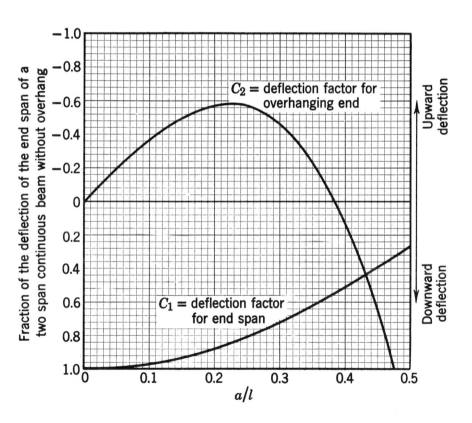

EFFECT OF OVERHANG ON MAXIMUM BENDING STRESS
FOR A TWO SPAN CONTINUOUS SYSTEM

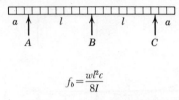

$$f_b = \frac{wl^2c}{8I}$$

I/c is the section modulus for the end joint pattern under consideration. With no overhang, the maximum bending moment occurs at support B. With overhang, the bending moment at B decreases, and the bending moments at A and C increase. The bending moment at B is larger than at A and C for values of a/l less than 0.408. At a/l greater than 0.408, the bending moments at A and C exceed that at B. In the following graph, the maximum imposed stress is expressed as a fraction of the bending stress over support B when $a = 0$.

$$f_b \max = C_1 f_b \text{ for } 0 < a/l < 0.408$$
$$f_b \max = C_2 f_b \text{ for } 0.408 < a/l$$

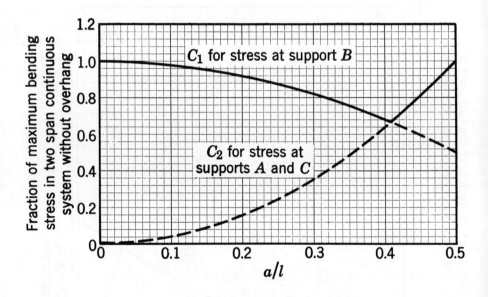

EFFECT OF OVERHANG ON REACTIONS
FOR A TWO SPAN CONTINUOUS SYSTEM

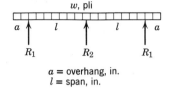

a = overhang, in.
l = span, in.

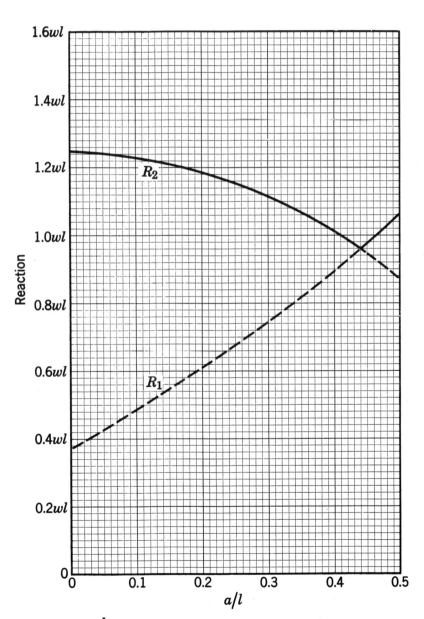

EFFECT OF OVERHANG ON MAXIMUM VERTICAL SHEAR
FOR A TWO SPAN CONTINUOUS SYSTEM

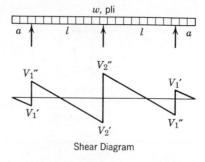

Shear Diagram

Note: Maximum shear occurs at support 2 for values of a/l less than 0.408. At higher values of a/l, maximum shear is at support 1.

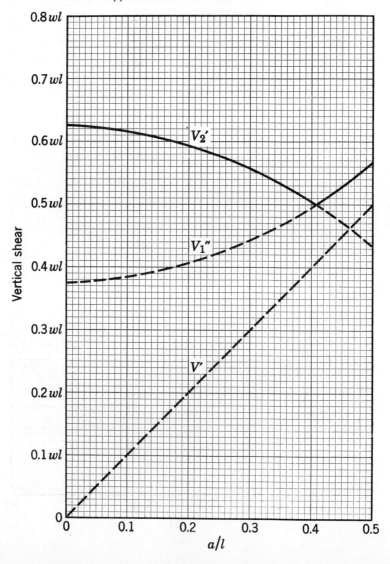

EFFECT OF OVERHANG ON MAXIMUM DEFLECTION
FOR A THREE SPAN CONTINUOUS SYSTEM

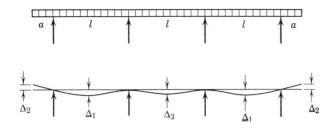

Δ = deflection of end span of three span continuous deck, without overhangs, calculated using the appropriate formula for end joint pattern to be used, in.

$\Delta_1 = C_1\Delta$ = deflection of end span with overhang, in.

$\Delta_2 = C_2\Delta$ = deflection of overhanging end, in.

$\Delta_1 > \Delta_3$

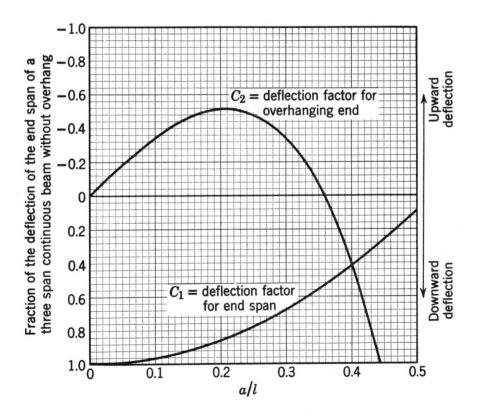

EFFECT OF OVERHANG ON MAXIMUM BENDING STRESS FOR A THREE SPAN CONTINUOUS SYSTEM

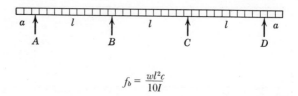

$$f_b = \frac{wl^2c}{10I}$$

I/c is the section modulus for the end joint pattern under consideration. With no overhang, the maximum bending moment occurs at supports B and C. With overhang, the bending moments at B and C decrease, and the bending moments at A and D increase. The bending moments at B and C are larger than at A and D for values of a/l less then 0.408. At a/l greater than 0.408, the bending moments at A and D exceed those at B and C. In the following graph, the maximum imposed stress is expressed as a fraction of the bending stress over supports B and C when $a = 0$.

$$f_b \max = C_1 f_b \text{ for } \quad 0 < a/l < 0.408$$
$$f_b \max = C_2 f_b \text{ for } \quad 0.408 < a/l$$

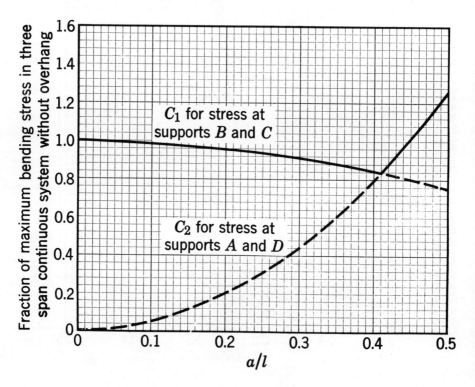

EFFECT OF OVERHANG ON REACTIONS
FOR A THREE SPAN CONTINUOUS SYSTEM

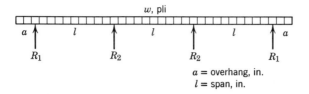

a = overhang, in.
l = span, in.

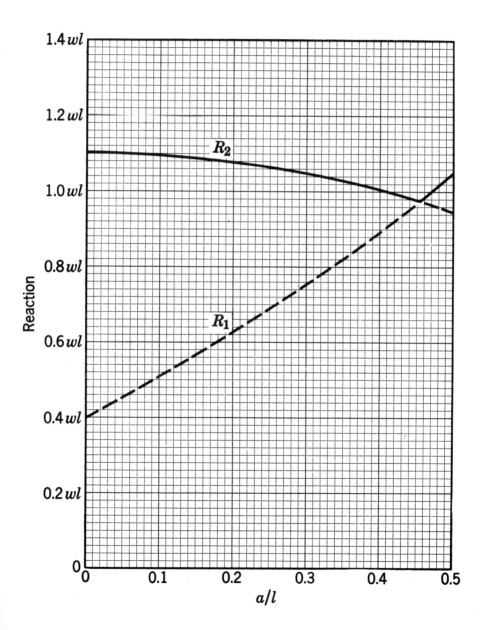

EFFECT OF OVERHANG ON MAXIMUM VERTICAL SHEAR
FOR A THREE SPAN CONTINUOUS SYSTEM

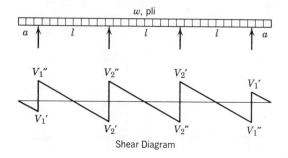

Shear Diagram

Note: Maximum shear occurs at support 2 for values of a/l less than 0.408. At higher values of a/l, maximum shear is at support 1.

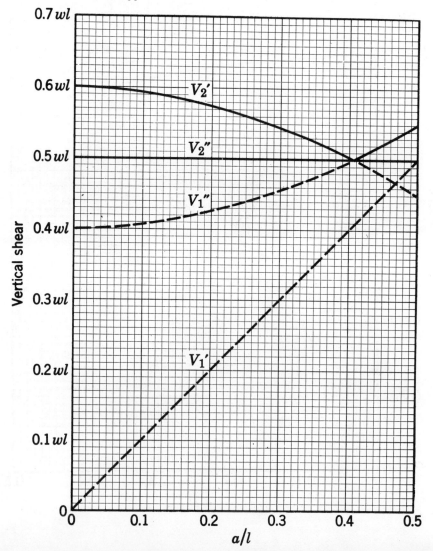

EFFECT OF OVERHANG ON MAXIMUM DEFLECTION
FOR A FOUR SPAN CONTINUOUS SYSTEM

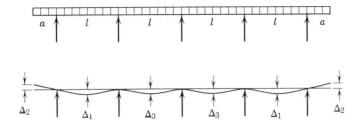

Δ = deflection of end span of four span continuous deck, without overhangs, calculated using the appropriate formula for end joint pattern to be used, in.

$\Delta_1 = C_1\Delta$ = deflection of end span with overhang, in.

$\Delta_2 = C_2\Delta$ = deflection of overhanging end, in.

$\Delta_1 > \Delta_3$

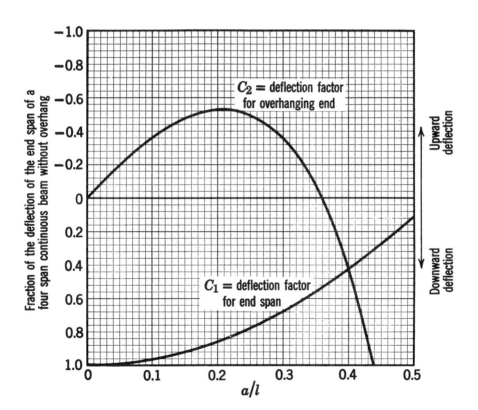

EFFECT OF OVERHANG ON MAXIMUM BENDING STRESS FOR A FOUR SPAN CONTINUOUS SYSTEM

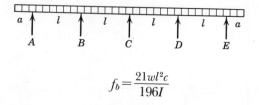

$$f_b = \frac{21wl^2c}{196I}$$

I/c is the section modulus for the end joint pattern under consideration. With no overhang, the maximum bending moment occurs at supports B and D. With overhang, the bending moments at B and D decrease, and the bending moments at A and E increase. The bending moments at B and D are larger than at A and E for values of a/l less than 0.408. At a/l greater than 0.408, the bending moments at A and E exceed those at B and D. In the following graph, the maximum imposed stress is expressed as a fraction of the bending stress over supports B and D when $a = 0$.

$$f_b \max = C_1 f_b \quad \text{for} \quad 0 < a/l < 0.408$$

$$f_b \max = C_2 f_b \quad \text{for} \quad 0.408 < a/l$$

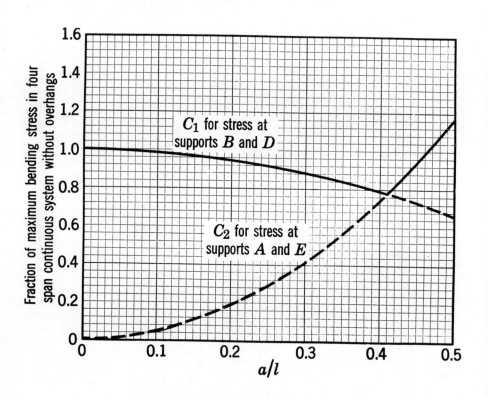

EFFECT OF OVERHANG ON REACTIONS
FOR A FOUR SPAN CONTINUOUS SYSTEM

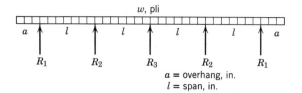

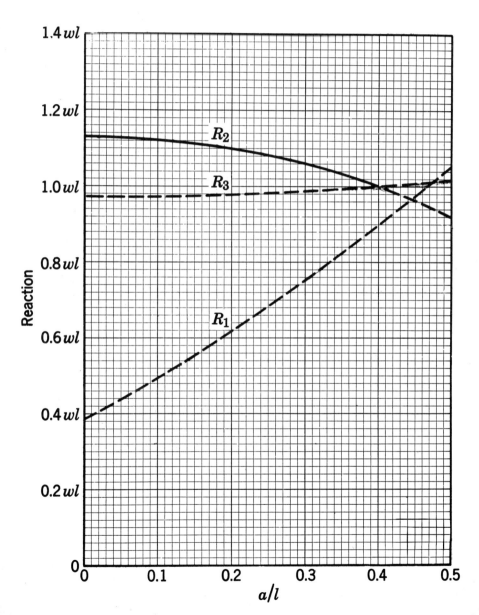

EFFECT OF OVERHANG ON MAXIMUM VERTICAL SHEAR FOR A FOUR SPAN CONTINUOUS SYSTEM

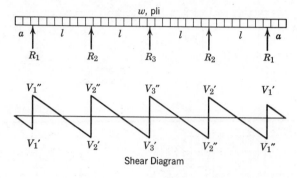

Note: Maximum shear occurs at support 2 for values of a/l less than 0.408. At higher values of a/l, maximum shear is at support 1.

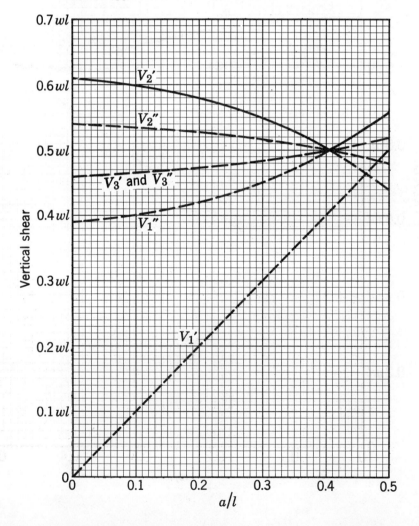

EFFECT OF OVERHANG ON MAXIMUM DEFLECTION FOR A FIVE SPAN CONTINUOUS SYSTEM

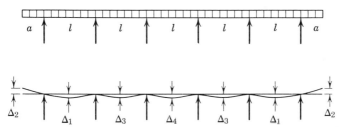

Δ = deflection of end span of five span continuous deck, without overhangs, calculated using the appropriate formula for end joint pattern to be used, in.

$\Delta_1 = C_1\Delta$ = deflection of end span with overhang, in.

$\Delta_2 = C_2\Delta$ = deflection of overhanging end, in.

$\Delta_1 > \Delta_3$

$\Delta_1 > \Delta_4$

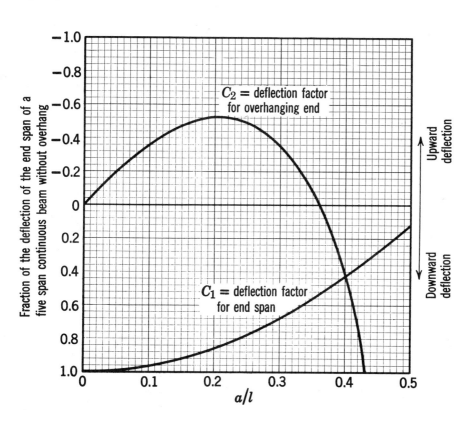

EFFECT OF OVERHANG ON MAXIMUM BENDING STRESS FOR A FIVE SPAN CONTINUOUS SYSTEM

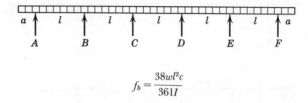

$$f_b = \frac{38wl^2c}{361I}$$

I/c is the section modulus for the end joint pattern under consideration. With no overhang, the maximum bending moment occurs at supports B and E. With overhang, the bending moments at B and E decrease, and the bending moments at A and F increase. The bending moments at B and E are larger than at A and F for values of a/l less than 0.408. At a/l greater than 0.408, the bending moments at A and F exceed those at B and E. In the following graph, the maximum imposed stress is expressed as a fraction of the bending stress over supports B and E when $a = 0$.

$$f_b \max = C_1 f_b \quad \text{for} \quad 0 < a/l < 0.408$$

$$f_b \max = C_2 f_b \quad \text{for} \quad 0.408 < a/l$$

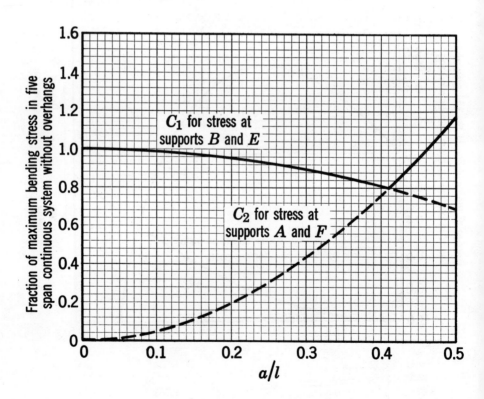

EFFECT OF OVERHANG ON REACTIONS FOR
FIVE SPAN CONTINUOUS SYSTEM

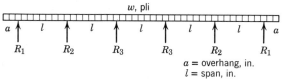

a = overhang, in.
l = span, in.

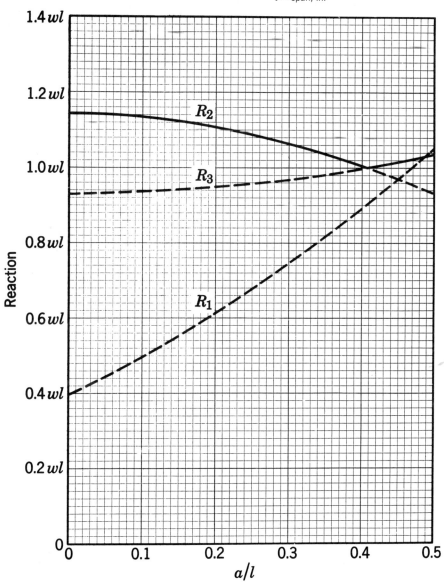

EFFECT OF OVERHANG ON MAXIMUM VERTICAL SHEAR
FOR A FIVE SPAN CONTINUOUS SYSTEM

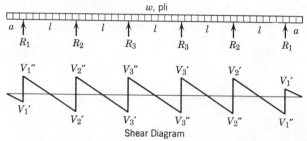

Note. Maximum shear occurs at support 2 for values of a/l less than 0.408. At higher values of a/l, maximum shear is at support 1.

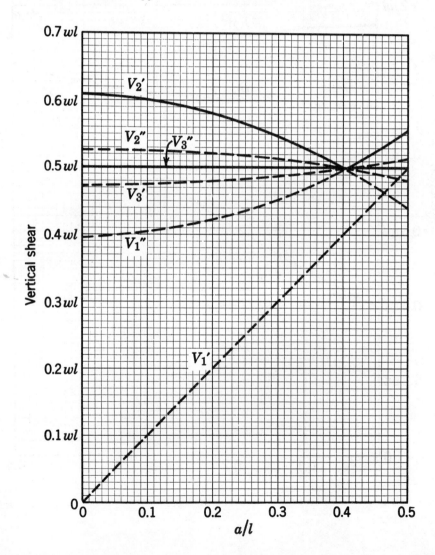

CANTILEVER BEAM COEFFICIENTS
All spans equal, uniformly distributed load.

$$\text{Moment} = M = CwL^2 \qquad \text{Reaction} = R = CwL$$

$$\text{Shear} = V = CwL \qquad \text{Deflection} = \Delta = \frac{CwL^4}{48EI}$$

$$w = \text{load, plf} \qquad L = \text{span, ft}$$

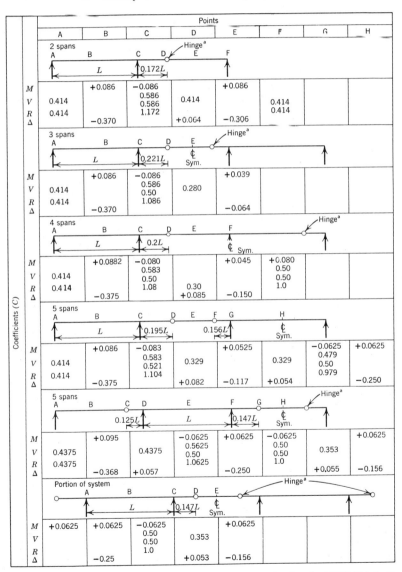

NATURAL TRIGONOMETRIC FUNCTIONS FOR DECIMAL FRACTIONS OF A DEGREE

0°–14.9°

Degs.	Function	0.0°	0.1°	0.2°	0.3°	0.4°	0.5°	0.6°	0.7°	0.8°	0.9°
0	sin	0.0000	0.0017	0.0035	0.0052	0.0070	0.0087	0.0105	0.0122	0.0140	0.0157
	cos	1.0000	1.0000	1.0000	1.0000	1.0000	1.0000	0.9999	0.9999	0.9999	0.9999
	tan	0.0000	0.0017	0.0035	0.0052	0.0070	0.0087	0.0105	0.0122	0.0140	0.0157
1	sin	0.0175	0.0192	0.0209	0.0227	0.0244	0.0262	0.0279	0.0297	0.0314	0.0332
	cos	0.9998	0.9998	0.9998	0.9997	0.9997	0.9997	0.9996	0.9996	0.9995	0.9995
	tan	0.0175	0.0192	0.0209	0.0227	0.0244	0.0262	0.0279	0.0297	0.0314	0.0332
2	sin	0.0349	0.0366	0.0384	0.0401	0.0419	0.0436	0.0454	0.0471	0.0488	0.0506
	cos	0.9994	0.9993	0.9993	0.9992	0.9991	0.9990	0.9990	0.9989	0.9988	0.9987
	tan	0.0349	0.0367	0.0384	0.0402	0.0419	0.0437	0.0454	0.0472	0.0489	0.0507
3	sin	0.0523	0.0541	0.0558	0.0576	0.0593	0.0610	0.0628	0.0645	0.0663	0.0680
	cos	0.9986	0.9985	0.9984	0.9983	0.9982	0.9981	0.9980	0.9979	0.9978	0.9977
	tan	0.0524	0.0542	0.0559	0.0577	0.0594	0.0612	0.0629	0.0647	0.0664	0.0682
4	sin	0.0698	0.0715	0.0732	0.0750	0.0767	0.0785	0.0802	0.0819	0.0837	0.0854
	cos	0.9976	0.9974	0.9973	0.9972	0.9971	0.9969	0.9968	0.9966	0.9965	0.9963
	tan	0.0699	0.0717	0.0734	0.0752	0.0769	0.0787	0.0805	0.0822	0.0840	0.0857
5	sin	0.0872	0.0889	0.0906	0.0924	0.0941	0.0958	0.0976	0.0993	0.1011	0.1028
	cos	0.9962	0.9960	0.9959	0.9957	0.9956	0.9954	0.9952	0.9951	0.9949	0.9947
	tan	0.0875	0.0892	0.0910	0.0928	0.0945	0.0963	0.0981	0.0998	0.1016	0.1033
6	sin	0.1045	0.1063	0.1080	0.1097	0.1115	0.1132	0.1149	0.1167	0.1184	0.1201
	cos	0.9945	0.9943	0.9942	0.9940	0.9938	0.9936	0.9934	0.9932	0.9930	0.9928
	tan	0.1051	0.1069	0.1086	0.1104	0.1122	0.1139	0.1157	0.1175	0.1192	0.1210
7	sin	0.1219	0.1236	0.1253	0.1271	0.1288	0.1305	0.1323	0.1340	0.1357	0.1374
	cos	0.9925	0.9923	0.9921	0.9919	0.9917	0.9914	0.9912	0.9910	0.9907	0.9905
	tan	0.1228	0.1246	0.1263	0.1281	0.1299	0.1317	0.1334	0.1352	0.1370	0.1388
8	sin	0.1392	0.1409	0.1426	0.1444	0.1461	0.1478	0.1495	0.1513	0.1530	0.1547
	cos	0.9903	0.9900	0.9898	0.9895	0.9893	0.9890	0.9888	0.9885	0.9882	0.9880
	tan	0.1405	0.1423	0.1441	0.1459	0.1477	0.1495	0.1512	0.1530	0.1548	0.1566
9	sin	0.1564	0.1582	0.1599	0.1616	0.1633	0.1650	0.1668	0.1685	0.1702	0.1719
	cos	0.9877	0.9874	0.9871	0.9869	0.9866	0.9863	0.9860	0.9857	0.9854	0.9851
	tan	0.1584	0.1602	0.1620	0.1638	0.1655	0.1673	0.1691	0.1709	0.1727	0.1745
10	sin	0.1736	0.1754	0.1771	0.1788	0.1805	0.1822	0.1840	0.1857	0.1874	0.1891
	cos	0.9848	0.9845	0.9842	0.9839	0.9836	0.9833	0.9829	0.9826	0.9823	0.9820
	tan	0.1763	0.1781	0.1799	0.1817	0.1835	0.1853	0.1871	0.1890	0.1908	0.1926
11	sin	0.1908	0.1925	0.1942	0.1959	0.1977	0.1994	0.2011	0.2028	0.2045	0.2062
	cos	0.9816	0.9813	0.9810	0.9806	0.9803	0.9799	0.9796	0.9792	0.9789	0.9785
	tan	0.1944	0.1962	0.1980	0.1998	0.2016	0.2035	0.2053	0.2071	0.2089	0.2107
12	sin	0.2079	0.2096	0.2113	0.2130	0.2147	0.2164	0.2181	0.2198	0.2215	0.2232
	cos	0.9781	0.9778	0.9774	0.9770	0.9767	0.9763	0.9759	0.9755	0.9751	0.9748
	tan	0.2126	0.2144	0.2162	0.2180	0.2199	0.2217	0.2235	0.2254	0.2272	0.2290
13	sin	0.2250	0.2267	0.2284	0.2300	0.2318	0.2334	0.2351	0.2368	0.2385	0.2402
	cos	0.9744	0.9740	0.9736	0.9732	0.9728	0.9724	0.9720	0.9715	0.9711	0.9707
	tan	0.2309	0.2327	0.2345	0.2364	0.2382	0.2401	0.2419	0.2438	0.2456	0.2475
14	sin	0.2419	0.2436	0.2453	0.2470	0.2487	0.2504	0.2521	0.2538	0.2554	0.2571
	cos	0.9703	0.9699	0.9694	0.9690	0.9686	0.9681	0.9677	0.9673	0.9668	0.9664
	tan	0.2493	0.2512	0.2530	0.2549	0.2568	0.2586	0.2605	0.2623	0.2642	0.2661
Degs.	Function	0'	6'	12'	18'	24'	30'	36'	42'	48'	54'

Reproduced courtesy of John Wiley & Sons, Inc., from *The Engineers' Manual* by Ralph G. Hudson, 2nd edition, 1939.

NATURAL TRIGONOMETRIC FUNCTIONS FOR DECIMAL FRACTIONS OF A DEGREE

15°–29.9°

Degs.	Function	0.0°	0.1°	0.2°	0.3°	0.4°	0.5°	0.6°	0.7°	0.8°	0.9°
15	sin	0.2588	0.2605	0.2622	0.2639	0.2656	0.2672	0.2689	0.2706	0.2723	0.2740
	cos	0.9659	0.9655	0.9650	0.9646	0.9641	0.9636	0.9632	0.9627	0.9622	0.9617
	tan	0.2679	0.2698	0.2717	0.2736	0.2754	0.2773	0.2792	0.2811	0.2830	0.2849
16	sin	0.2756	0.2773	0.2790	0.2807	0.2823	0.2840	0.2857	0.2874	0.2890	0.2907
	cos	0.9613	0.9608	0.9603	0.9598	0.9593	0.9588	0.9583	0.9578	0.9572	0.9568
	tan	0.2867	0.2886	0.2905	0.2924	0.2943	0.2962	0.2981	0.3000	0.3019	0.3038
17	sin	0.2924	0.2940	0.2957	0.2974	0.2990	0.3007	0.3024	0.3040	0.3057	0.3074
	cos	0.9563	0.9558	0.9553	0.9548	0.9542	0.9537	0.9532	0.9527	0.9521	0.9516
	tan	0.3057	0.3076	0.3096	0.3115	0.3134	0.3153	0.3172	0.3191	0.3211	0.3230
18	sin	0.3090	0.3107	0.3123	0.3140	0.3156	0.3173	0.3190	0.3206	0.3223	0.3239
	cos	0.9511	0.9505	0.9500	0.9494	0.9489	0.9483	0.9478	0.9472	0.9466	0.9461
	tan	0.3249	0.3269	0.3288	0.3307	0.3327	0.3346	0.3365	0.3385	0.3404	0.3424
19	sin	0.3256	0.3272	0.3289	0.3305	0.3322	0.3338	0.3355	0.3371	0.3387	0.3404
	cos	0.9455	0.9449	0.9444	0.9438	0.9432	0.9426	0.9421	0.9415	0.9409	0.9403
	tan	0.3443	0.3463	0.3482	0.3502	0.3522	0.3541	0.3561	0.3581	0.3600	0.3620
20	sin	0.3420	0.3437	0.3453	0.3469	0.3486	0.3502	0.3518	0.3535	0.3551	0.3567
	cos	0.9397	0.9391	0.9385	0.9379	0.9373	0.9367	0.9361	0.9354	0.9348	0.9342
	tan	0.3640	0.3659	0.3679	0.3699	0.3719	0.3739	0.3759	0.3779	0.3799	0.3819
21	sin	0.3584	0.3600	0.3616	0.3633	0.3649	0.3665	0.3681	0.3697	0.3714	0.3730
	cos	0.9336	0.9330	0.9323	0.9317	0.9311	0.9304	0.9298	0.9291	0.9285	0.9278
	tan	0.3839	0.3859	0.3879	0.3899	0.3919	0.3939	0.3959	0.3979	0.4000	0.4020
22	sin	0.3746	0.3762	0.3778	0.3795	0.3811	0.3827	0.3843	0.3859	0.3875	0.3891
	cos	0.9272	0.9265	0.9259	0.9252	0.9245	0.9239	0.9232	0.9225	0.9219	0.9212
	tan	0.4040	0.4061	0.4081	0.4101	0.4122	0.4142	0.4163	0.4183	0.4204	0.4224
23	sin	0.3907	0.3923	0.3939	0.3955	0.3971	0.3987	0.4003	0.4019	0.4035	0.4051
	cos	0.9205	0.9198	0.9191	0.9184	0.9178	0.9171	0.9164	0.9157	0.9150	0.9143
	tan	0.4245	0.4265	0.4286	0.4307	0.4327	0.4348	0.4369	0.4390	0.4411	0.4431
24	sin	0.4067	0.4083	0.4099	0.4115	0.4131	0.4147	0.4163	0.4179	0.4195	0.4210
	cos	0.9135	0.9128	0.9121	0.9114	0.9107	0.9100	0.9092	0.9085	0.9078	0.9070
	tan	0.4452	0.4473	0.4494	0.4515	0.4536	0.4557	0.4578	0.4599	0.4621	0.4642
25	sin	0.4226	0.4242	0.4258	0.4274	0.4289	0.4305	0.4321	0.4337	0.4352	0.4368
	cos	0.9063	0.9056	0.9048	0.9041	0.9033	0.9026	0.9018	0.9011	0.9003	0.8996
	tan	0.4663	0.4684	0.4706	0.4727	0.4748	0.4770	0.4791	0.4813	0.4834	0.4856
26	sin	0.4384	0.4399	0.4415	0.4431	0.4446	0.4462	0.4478	0.4493	0.4509	0.4524
	cos	0.8988	0.8980	0.8973	0.8965	0.8957	0.8949	0.8942	0.8934	0.8926	0.8918
	tan	0.4877	0.4899	0.4921	0.4942	0.4964	0.4986	0.5008	0.5029	0.5051	0.5073
27	sin	0.4540	0.4555	0.4571	0.4586	0.4602	0.4617	0.4633	0.4648	0.4664	0.4679
	cos	0.8910	0.8902	0.8894	0.8886	0.8878	0.8870	0.8862	0.8854	0.8846	0.8838
	tan	0.5095	0.5117	0.5139	0.5161	0.5184	0.5206	0.5228	0.5250	0.5272	0.5295
28	sin	0.4695	0.4710	0.4726	0.4741	0.4756	0.4772	0.4787	0.4802	0.4818	0.4833
	cos	0.8829	0.8821	0.8813	0.8805	0.8796	0.8788	0.8780	0.8771	0.8763	0.8755
	tan	0.5317	0.5340	0.5362	0.5384	0.5407	0.5430	0.5452	0.5475	0.5498	0.5520
29	sin	0.4848	0.4863	0.4879	0.4894	0.4909	0.4924	0.4939	0.4955	0.4970	0.4985
	cos	0.8746	0.8738	0.8729	0.8721	0.8712	0.8704	0.8695	0.8686	0.8678	0.8669
	tan	0.5543	0.5566	0.5589	0.5612	0.5635	0.5658	0.5681	0.5704	0.5727	0.5750
Degs.	Function	0′	6′	12′	18′	24′	30′	36′	42′	48′	54′

Reproduced courtesy of John Wiley & Sons, Inc., from *The Engineers' Manual* by Ralph G. Hudson, 2nd edition, 1939.

NATURAL TRIGONOMETRIC FUNCTIONS FOR DECIMAL FRACTIONS OF A DEGREE

30°–44.9°

Degs.	Function	0.0°	0.1°	0.2°	0.3°	0.4°	0.5°	0.6°	0.7°	0.8°	0.9°
30	sin	0.5000	0.5015	0.5030	0.5045	0.5060	0.5075	0.5090	0.5105	0.5120	0.5135
	cos	0.8660	0.8652	0.8643	0.8634	0.8625	0.8616	0.8607	0.8599	0.8590	0.8581
	tan	0.5774	0.5797	0.5820	0.5844	0.5867	0.5890	0.5914	0.5938	0.5961	0.5985
31	sin	0.5150	0.5165	0.5180	0.5195	0.5210	0.5225	0.5240	0.5255	0.5270	0.5284
	cos	0.8572	0.8563	0.8554	0.8545	0.8536	0.8526	0.8517	0.8508	0.8499	0.8490
	tan	0.6009	0.6032	0.6056	0.6080	0.6104	0.6128	0.6152	0.6176	0.6200	0.6224
32	sin	0.5299	0.5314	0.5329	0.5344	0.5358	0.5373	0.5388	0.5402	0.5417	0.5432
	cos	0.8480	0.8471	0.8462	0.8453	0.8443	0.8434	0.8425	0.8415	0.8406	0.8396
	tan	0.6249	0.6273	0.6297	0.6322	0.6346	0.6371	0.6395	0.6420	0.6445	0.6469
33	sin	0.5446	0.5461	0.5476	0.5490	0.5505	0.5519	0.5534	0.5548	0.5563	0.5577
	cos	0.8387	0.8377	0.8368	0.8358	0.8348	0.8339	0.8329	0.8320	0.8310	0.8300
	tan	0.6494	0.6519	0.6544	0.6569	0.6594	0.6619	0.6644	0.6669	0.6694	0.6720
34	sin	0.5592	0.5606	0.5621	0.5635	0.5650	0.5664	0.5678	0.5693	0.5707	0.5721
	cos	0.8290	0.8281	0.8271	0.8261	0.8251	0.8241	0.8231	0.8221	0.8211	0.8202
	tan	0.6745	0.6771	0.6796	0.6822	0.6847	0.6873	0.6899	0.6924	0.6950	0.6976
35	sin	0.5736	0.5750	0.5764	0.5779	0.5793	0.5807	0.5821	0.5835	0.5850	0.5864
	cos	0.8192	0.8181	0.8171	0.8161	0.8151	0.8141	0.8131	0.8121	0.8111	0.8100
	tan	0.7002	0.7028	0.7054	0.7080	0.7107	0.7133	0.7159	0.7186	0.7212	0.7239
36	sin	0.5878	0.5892	0.5906	0.5920	0.5934	0.5948	0.5962	0.5976	0.5990	0.6004
	cos	0.8090	0.8080	0.8070	0.8059	0.8049	0.8039	0.8028	0.8018	0.8007	0.7997
	tan	0.7265	0.7292	0.7319	0.7346	0.7373	0.7400	0.7427	0.7454	0.7481	0.7508
37	sin	0.6018	0.6032	0.6046	0.6060	0.6074	0.6088	0.6101	0.6115	0.6129	0.6143
	cos	0.7986	0.7976	0.7965	0.7955	0.7944	0.7934	0.7923	0.7912	0.7902	0.7891
	tan	0.7536	0.7563	0.7590	0.7618	0.7646	0.7673	0.7701	0.7729	0.7757	0.7785
38	sin	0.6157	0.6170	0.6184	0.6198	0.6211	0.6225	0.6239	0.6252	0.6266	0.6280
	cos	0.7880	0.7869	0.7859	0.7848	0.7837	0.7826	0.7815	0.7804	0.7793	0.7782
	tan	0.7813	0.7841	0.7869	0.7898	0.7926	0.7954	0.7983	0.8012	0.8040	0.8069
39	sin	0.6293	0.6307	0.6320	0.6334	0.6347	0.6361	0.6374	0.6388	0.6401	0.6414
	cos	0.7771	0.7760	0.7749	0.7738	0.7727	0.7716	0.7705	0.7694	0.7683	0.7672
	tan	0.8098	0.8127	0.8156	0.8185	0.8214	0.8243	0.8273	0.8302	0.8332	0.8361
40	sin	0.6428	0.6441	0.6455	0.6468	0.6481	0.6494	0.6508	0.6521	0.6534	0.6547
	cos	0.7660	0.7649	0.7638	0.7627	0.7615	0.7604	0.7593	0.7581	0.7570	0.7559
	tan	0.8391	0.8421	0.8451	0.8481	0.8511	0.8541	0.8571	0.8601	0.8632	0.8662
41	sin	0.6561	0.6574	0.6587	0.6600	0.6613	0.6626	0.6639	0.6652	0.6665	0.6678
	cos	0.7547	0.7536	0.7524	0.7513	0.7501	0.7490	0.7478	0.7466	0.7455	0.7443
	tan	0.8693	0.8724	0.8754	0.8785	0.8816	0.8847	0.8878	0.8910	0.8941	0.8972
42	sin	0.6691	0.6704	0.6717	0.6730	0.6743	0.6756	0.6769	0.6782	0.6794	0.6807
	cos	0.7431	0.7420	0.7408	0.7396	0.7385	0.7373	0.7361	0.7349	0.7337	0.7325
	tan	0.9004	0.9036	0.9067	0.9099	0.9131	0.9163	0.9195	0.9228	0.9260	0.9293
43	sin	0.6820	0.6833	0.6845	0.6858	0.6871	0.6884	0.6896	0.6909	0.6921	0.6934
	cos	0.7314	0.7302	0.7290	0.7278	0.7266	0.7254	0.7242	0.7230	0.7218	0.7206
	tan	0.9325	0.9358	0.9391	0.9424	0.9457	0.9490	0.9523	0.9556	0.9590	0.9623
44	sin	0.6947	0.6959	0.6972	0.6984	0.6997	0.7009	0.7022	0.7034	0.7046	0.7059
	cos	0.7193	0.7181	0.7169	0.7157	0.7145	0.7133	0.7120	0.7108	0.7096	0.7083
	tan	0.9657	0.9691	0.9725	0.9759	0.9793	0.9827	0.9861	0.9896	0.9930	0.9965
Degs.	Function	0′	6′	12′	18′	24′	30′	36′	42′	48′	54′

Reproduced courtesy of John Wiley & Sons, Inc., from *The Engineers' Manual* by Ralph G. Hudson, 2nd edition, 1939.

NATURAL TRIGONOMETRIC FUNCTIONS FOR
DECIMAL FRACTIONS OF A DEGREE

45°–59.9°

Degs.	Function	0.0°	0.1°	0.2°	0.3°	0.4°	0.5°	0.6°	0.7°	0.8°	0.9°
45	sin	0.7071	0.7083	0.7096	0.7108	0.7120	0.7133	0.7145	0.7157	0.7169	0.7181
	cos	0.7071	0.7059	0.7046	0.7034	0.7022	0.7009	0.6997	0.6984	0.6972	0.6959
	tan	1.0000	1.0035	1.0070	1.0105	1.0141	1.0176	1.0212	1.0247	1.0283	1.0319
46	sin	0.7193	0.7206	0.7218	0.7230	0.7242	0.7254	0.7266	0.7278	0.7290	0.7302
	cos	0.6947	0.6934	0.6921	0.6909	0.6896	0.6884	0.6871	0.6858	0.6845	0.6833
	tan	1.0355	1.0392	1.0428	1.0464	1.0501	1.0538	1.0575	1.0612	1.0649	1.0686
47	sin	0.7314	0.7325	0.7337	0.7349	0.7361	0.7373	0.7385	0.7396	0.7408	0.7420
	cos	0.6820	0.6807	0.6794	0.6782	0.6769	0.6756	0.6743	0.6730	0.6717	0.6704
	tan	1.0724	1.0761	1.0799	1.0837	1.0875	1.0913	1.0951	1.0990	1.1028	1.1067
48	sin	0.7431	0.7443	0.7455	0.7466	0.7478	0.7490	0.7501	0.7513	0.7524	0.7536
	cos	0.6691	0.6678	0.6665	0.6652	0.6639	0.6626	0.6613	0.6600	0.6587	0.6574
	tan	1.1106	1.1145	1.1184	1.1224	1.1263	1.1303	1.1343	1.1383	1.1423	1.1463
49	sin	0.7547	0.7559	0.7570	0.7581	0.7593	0.7604	0.7615	0.7627	0.7638	0.7649
	cos	0.6561	0.6547	0.6534	0.6521	0.6508	0.6494	0.6481	0.6468	0.6455	0.6441
	tan	1.1504	1.1544	1.1585	1.1626	1.1667	1.1708	1.1750	1.1792	1.1833	1.1875
50	sin	0.7660	0.7672	0.7683	0.7694	0.7705	0.7716	0.7727	0.7738	0.7749	0.7760
	cos	0.6428	0.6414	0.6401	0.6388	0.6374	0.6361	0.6347	0.6334	0.6320	0.6307
	tan	1.1918	1.1960	1.2002	1.2045	1.2088	1.2131	1.2174	1.2218	1.2261	1.2305
51	sin	0.7771	0.7782	0.7793	0.7804	0.7815	0.7826	0.7837	0.7848	0.7859	0.7869
	cos	0.6293	0.6280	0.6266	0.6252	0.6239	0.6225	0.6211	0.6198	0.6184	0.6170
	tan	1.2349	1.2393	1.2437	1.2482	1.2527	1.2572	1.2617	1.2662	1.2708	1.2753
52	sin	0.7880	0.7891	0.7902	0.7912	0.7923	0.7934	0.7944	0.7955	0.7965	0.7976
	cos	0.6157	0.6143	0.6129	0.6115	0.6101	0.6088	0.6074	0.6060	0.6046	0.6032
	tan	1.2799	1.2846	1.2892	1.2938	1.2985	1.3032	1.3079	1.3127	1.3175	1.3222
53	sin	0.7986	0.7997	0.8007	0.8018	0.8028	0.8039	0.8049	0.8059	0.8070	0.8080
	cos	0.6018	0.6004	0.5990	0.5976	0.5962	0.5948	0.5934	0.5920	0.5906	0.5892
	tan	1.3270	1.3319	1.3367	1.3416	1.3465	1.3514	1.3564	1.3613	1.3663	1.3713
54	sin	0.8090	0.8100	0.8111	0.8121	0.8131	0.8141	0.8151	0.8161	0.8171	0.8181
	cos	0.5878	0.5864	0.5850	0.5835	0.5821	0.5807	0.5793	0.5779	0.5764	0.5750
	tan	1.3764	1.3814	1.3865	1.3916	1.3968	1.4019	1.4071	1.4124	1.4176	1.4229
55	sin	0.8192	0.8202	0.8211	0.8221	0.8231	0.8241	0.8251	0.8261	0.8271	0.8281
	cos	0.5736	0.5721	0.5707	0.5693	0.5678	0.5664	0.5650	0.5635	0.5621	0.5606
	tan	1.4281	1.4335	1.4388	1.4442	1.4496	1.4550	1.4605	1.4659	1.4715	1.4770
56	sin	0.8290	0.8300	0.8310	0.8320	0.8329	0.8339	0.8348	0.8358	0.8368	0.8377
	cos	0.5592	0.5577	0.5563	0.5548	0.5534	0.5519	0.5505	0.5490	0.5476	0.5461
	tan	1.4826	1.4882	1.4938	1.4994	1.5051	1.5108	1.5166	1.5224	1.5282	1.5340
57	sin	0.8387	0.8396	0.8406	0.8415	0.8425	0.8434	0.8443	0.8453	0.8462	0.8471
	cos	0.5446	0.5432	0.5417	0.5402	0.5388	0.5373	0.5358	0.5344	0.5329	0.5314
	tan	1.5399	1.5458	1.5517	1.5577	1.5637	1.5697	1.5757	1.5818	1.5880	1.5941
58	sin	0.8480	0.8490	0.8499	0.8508	0.8517	0.8526	0.8536	0.8545	0.8554	0.8563
	cos	0.5299	0.5284	0.5270	0.5255	0.5240	0.5225	0.5210	0.5195	0.5180	0.5165
	tan	1.6003	1.6066	1.6128	1.6191	1.6255	1.6319	1.6383	1.6447	1.6512	1.6577
59	sin	0.8572	0.8581	0.8590	0.8599	0.8607	0.8616	0.8625	0.8634	0.8643	0.8652
	cos	0.5150	0.5135	0.5120	0.5105	0.5090	0.5075	0.5060	0.5045	0.5030	0.5015
	tan	1.6643	1.6709	1.6775	1.6842	1.6909	1.6977	1.7045	1.7113	1.7182	1.7251
Degs.	Function	0′	6′	12′	18′	24′	30′	36′	42′	48′	54′

Reproduced courtesy of John Wiley & Sons, Inc., from *The Engineers' Manual* by Ralph G. Hudson, 2nd edition, 1939.

NATURAL TRIGONOMETRIC FUNCTIONS FOR DECIMAL FRACTIONS OF A DEGREE

60°–74.9°

Degs.	Function	0.0°	0.1°	0.2°	0.3°	0.4°	0.5°	0.6°	0.7°	0.8°	0.9°
60	sin	0.8660	0.8669	0.8678	0.8686	0.8695	0.8704	0.8712	0.8721	0.8729	0.8738
	cos	0.5000	0.4985	0.4970	0.4955	0.4939	0.4924	0.4909	0.4894	0.4879	0.4863
	tan	1.7321	1.7391	1.7461	1.7532	1.7603	1.7675	1.7747	1.7820	1.7893	1.7966
61	sin	0.8746	0.8755	0.8763	0.8771	0.8780	0.8788	0.8796	0.8805	0.8813	0.8821
	cos	0.4848	0.4833	0.4818	0.4802	0.4787	0.4772	0.4756	0.4741	0.4726	0.4710
	tan	1.8040	1.8115	1.8190	1.8265	1.8341	1.8418	1.8495	1.8572	1.8650	1.8728
62	sin	0.8829	0.8838	0.8846	0.8854	0.8862	0.8870	0.8878	0.8886	0.8894	0.8902
	cos	0.4695	0.4679	0.4664	0.4648	0.4633	0.4617	0.4602	0.4586	0.4571	0.4555
	tan	1.8807	1.8887	1.8967	1.9047	1.9128	1.9210	1.9292	1.9375	1.9458	1.9542
63	sin	0.8910	0.8918	0.8926	0.8934	0.8942	0.8949	0.8957	0.8965	0.8973	0.8980
	cos	0.4540	0.4524	0.4509	0.4493	0.4478	0.4462	0.4446	0.4431	0.4415	0.4399
	tan	1.9626	1.9711	1.9797	1.9883	1.9970	2.0057	2.0145	2.0233	2.0323	2.0413
64	sin	0.8988	0.8996	0.9003	0.9011	0.9018	0.9026	0.9033	0.9041	0.9048	0.9056
	cos	0.4384	0.4368	0.4352	0.4337	0.4321	0.4305	0.4289	0.4274	0.4258	0.4242
	tan	2.0503	2.0594	2.0686	2.0778	2.0872	2.0965	2.1060	2.1155	2.1251	2.1348
65	sin	0.9063	0.9070	0.9078	0.9085	0.9092	0.9100	0.9107	0.9114	0.9121	0.9128
	cos	0.4226	0.4210	0.4195	0.4179	0.4163	0.4147	0.4131	0.4115	0.4099	0.4083
	tan	2.1445	2.1543	2.1642	2.1742	2.1842	2.1943	2.2045	2.2148	2.2251	2.2355
66	sin	0.9135	0.9143	0.9150	0.9157	0.9164	0.9171	0.9178	0.9184	0.9191	0.9198
	cos	0.4067	0.4051	0.4035	0.4019	0.4003	0.3987	0.3971	0.3955	0.3939	0.3923
	tan	2.2460	2.2566	2.2673	2.2781	2.2889	2.2998	2.3109	2.3220	2.3332	2.3445
67	sin	0.9205	0.9212	0.9219	0.9225	0.9232	0.9239	0.9245	0.9252	0.9259	0.9265
	cos	0.3907	0.3891	0.3875	0.3859	0.3843	0.3827	0.3811	0.3795	0.3778	0.3762
	tan	2.3559	2.3673	2.3789	2.3906	2.4023	2.4142	2.4262	2.4383	2.4504	2.4627
68	sin	0.9272	0.9278	0.9285	0.9291	0.9298	0.9304	0.9311	0.9317	0.9323	0.9330
	cos	0.3746	0.3730	0.3714	0.3697	0.3681	0.3665	0.3649	0.3633	0.3616	0.3600
	tan	2.4751	2.4876	2.5002	2.5129	2.5257	2.5386	2.5517	2.5649	2.5782	2.5916
69	sin	0.9336	0.9342	0.9348	0.9354	0.9361	0.9367	0.9373	0.9379	0.9385	0.9391
	cos	0.3584	0.3567	0.3551	0.3535	0.3518	0.3502	0.3486	0.3469	0.3453	0.3437
	tan	2.6051	2.6187	2.6325	2.6464	2.6605	2.6746	2.6889	2.7034	2.7179	2.7326
70	sin	0.9397	0.9403	0.9409	0.9415	0.9421	0.9426	0.9432	0.9438	0.9444	0.9449
	cos	0.3420	0.3404	0.3387	0.3371	0.3355	0.3338	0.3322	0.3305	0.3289	0.3272
	tan	2.7475	2.7625	2.7776	2.7929	2.8083	2.8239	2.8397	2.8556	2.8716	2.8878
71	sin	0.9455	0.9461	0.9466	0.9472	0.9478	0.9483	0.9489	0.9494	0.9500	0.9505
	cos	0.3256	0.3239	0.3223	0.3206	0.3190	0.3173	0.3155	0.3140	0.3123	0.3107
	tan	2.9042	2.9208	2.9375	2.9544	2.9714	2.9887	3.0061	3.0237	3.0415	3.0595
72	sin	0.9511	0.9516	0.9521	0.9527	0.9532	0.9537	0.9542	0.9548	0.9553	0.9558
	cos	0.3090	0.3074	0.3057	0.3040	0.3024	0.3007	0.2990	0.2974	0.2957	0.2940
	tan	3.0777	3.0961	3.1146	3.1334	3.1524	3.1716	3.1910	3.2106	3.2305	3.2506
73	sin	0.9563	0.9568	0.9573	0.9578	0.9583	0.9588	0.9593	0.9598	0.9603	0.9608
	cos	0.2924	0.2907	0.2890	0.2874	0.2857	0.2840	0.2823	0.2807	0.2790	0.2773
	tan	3.2709	3.2914	3.3122	3.3332	3.3544	3.3759	3.3977	3.4197	3.4420	3.4646
74	sin	0.9613	0.9617	0.9622	0.9627	0.9632	0.9636	0.9641	0.9646	0.9650	0.9655
	cos	0.2756	0.2740	0.2723	0.2706	0.2689	0.2672	0.2656	0.2639	0.2622	0.2605
	tan	3.4874	3.5105	3.5339	3.5576	3.5816	3.6059	3.6305	3.6554	3.6806	3.7062
Degs.	Function	0'	6'	12'	18'	24'	30'	36'	42'	48'	54'

Reproduced courtesy of John Wiley & Sons, Inc., from *The Engineers' Manual* by Ralph G. Hudson, 2nd edition, 1939

NATURAL TRIGONOMETRIC FUNCTIONS FOR DECIMAL FRACTIONS OF A DEGREE

75°–89.9°

Degs.	Function	0.0°	0.1°	0.2°	0.3°	0.4°	0.5°	0.6°	0.7°	0.8°	0.9°
75	sin	0.9659	0.9664	0.9668	0.9673	0.9677	0.9681	0.9686	0.9690	0.9694	0.9699
	cos	0.2588	0.2571	0.2554	0.2538	0.2521	0.2504	0.2487	0.2470	0.2453	0.2436
	tan	3.7321	3.7583	3.7848	3.8118	3.8391	3.8667	3.8947	3.9232	3.9520	3.9812
76	sin	0.9703	0.9707	0.9711	0.9715	0.9720	0.9724	0.9728	0.9732	0.9736	0.9740
	cos	0.2419	0.2402	0.2385	0.2368	0.2351	0.2334	0.2317	0.2300	0.2284	0.2267
	tan	4.0108	4.0408	4.0713	4.1022	4.1335	4.1653	4.1976	4.2303	4.2635	4.2972
77	sin	0.9744	0.9748	0.9751	0.9755	0.9759	0.9763	0.9767	0.9770	0.9774	0.9778
	cos	0.2250	0.2232	0.2215	0.2198	0.2181	0.2164	0.2147	0.2130	0.2113	0.2096
	tan	4.3315	4.3662	4.4015	4.4374	4.4737	4.5107	4.5483	4.5864	4.6252	4.6646
78	sin	0.9781	0.9785	0.9789	0.9792	0.9796	0.9799	0.9803	0.9806	0.9810	0.9813
	cos	0.2079	0.2062	0.2045	0.2028	0.2011	0.1994	0.1977	0.1959	0.1942	0.1925
	tan	4.7046	4.7453	4.7867	4.8288	4.8716	4.9152	4.9594	5.0045	5.0504	5.0970
79	sin	0.9816	0.9820	0.9823	0.9826	0.9829	0.9833	0.9836	0.9839	0.9842	0.9845
	cos	0.1908	0.1891	0.1874	0.1857	0.1840	0.1822	0.1805	0.1788	0.1771	0.1754
	tan	5.1446	5.1929	5.2422	5.2924	5.3435	5.3955	5.4486	5.5026	5.5578	5.6140
80	sin	0.9848	0.9851	0.9854	0.9857	0.9860	0.9863	0.9866	0.9869	0.9871	0.9874
	cos	0.1736	0.1719	0.1702	0.1685	0.1668	0.1650	0.1633	0.1616	0.1599	0.1582
	tan	5.6713	5.7297	5.7894	5.8502	5.9124	5.9758	6.0405	6.1066	6.1742	6.2432
81	sin	0.9877	0.9880	0.9882	0.9885	0.9888	0.9890	0.9893	0.9895	0.9898	0.9900
	cos	0.1564	0.1547	0.1530	0.1513	0.1495	0.1478	0.1461	0.1444	0.1426	0.1409
	tan	6.3138	6.3859	6.4596	6.5350	6.6122	6.6912	6.7720	6.8548	6.9395	7.0264
82	sin	0.9903	0.9905	0.9907	0.9910	0.9912	0.9914	0.9917	0.9919	0.9921	0.9923
	cos	0.1392	0.1374	0.1357	0.1340	0.1323	0.1305	0.1288	0.1271	0.1253	0.1236
	tan	7.1154	7.2066	7.3002	7.3962	7.4947	7.5958	7.6996	7.8062	7.9158	8.0285
83	sin	0.9925	0.9928	0.9930	0.9932	0.9934	0.9936	0.9938	0.9940	0.9942	0.9943
	cos	0.1219	0.1201	0.1184	0.1167	0.1149	0.1132	0.1115	0.1097	0.1080	0.1063
	tan	8.1443	8.2636	8.3863	8.5126	8.6427	8.7769	8.9152	9.0579	9.2052	9.3572
84	sin	0.9945	0.9947	0.9949	0.9951	0.9952	0.9954	0.9956	0.9957	0.9959	0.9960
	cos	0.1045	0.1028	0.1011	0.0993	0.0976	0.0958	0.0941	0.0924	0.0906	0.0889
	tan	9.5144	9.6768	9.8448	10.02	10.20	10.39	10.58	10.78	10.99	11.20
85	sin	0.9962	0.9963	0.9965	0.9966	0.9968	0.9969	0.9971	0.9972	0.9973	0.9974
	cos	0.0872	0.0854	0.0837	0.0819	0.0802	0.0785	0.0767	0.0750	0.0732	0.0715
	tan	11.43	11.66	11.91	12.16	12.43	12.71	13.00	13.30	13.62	13.95
86	sin	0.9976	0.9977	0.9978	0.9979	0.9980	0.9981	0.9982	0.9983	0.9984	0.9985
	cos	0.0698	0.0680	0.0663	0.0645	0.0628	0.0610	0.0593	0.0576	0.0558	0.0541
	tan	14.30	14.67	15.06	15.46	15.89	16.35	16.83	17.34	17.89	18.46
87	sin	0.9986	0.9987	0.9988	0.9989	0.9990	0.9990	0.9991	0.9992	0.9993	0.9993
	cos	0.0523	0.0506	0.0488	0.0471	0.0454	0.0436	0.0419	0.0401	0.0384	0.0366
	tan	19.08	19.74	20.45	21.20	22.02	22.90	23.86	24.90	26.03	27.27
88	sin	0.9994	0.9995	0.9995	0.9996	0.9996	0.9997	0.9997	0.9997	0.9998	0.9998
	cos	0.0349	0.0332	0.0314	0.0297	0.0279	0.0262	0.0244	0.0227	0.0209	0.0192
	tan	28.64	30.14	31.82	33.69	35.80	38.19	40.92	44.07	47.74	52.08
89	sin	0.9998	0.9999	0.9999	0.9999	0.9999	1.000	1.000	1.000	1.000	1.000
	cos	0.0175	0.0157	0.0140	0.0122	0.0105	0.0087	0.0070	0.0052	0.0035	0.0017
	tan	57.29	63.66	71.62	81.85	95.49	114.6	143.2	191.0	286.5	573.0
Degs.	Function	0′	6′	12′	18′	24′	30′	36′	42′	48′	54′

Reproduced courtesy of John Wiley & Sons, Inc., from *The Engineers' Manual* by Ralph G. Hudson, 2nd edition, 1939.

WEIGHTS AND MEASURES

UNITED STATES SYSTEM

Linear Measure

Inches	Feet	Yards	Rods	Furlongs	Miles
1.0 =	0.08333 =	0.02778 =	0.0050505 =	0.00012626 =	0.00001578
12.0 =	1.0 =	0.33333 =	0.0606061 =	0.00151515 =	0.00018939
36.0 =	3.0 =	1.0 =	0.1818182 =	0.00454545 =	0.00056818
198.0 =	16.5 =	5.5 =	1.0	= 0.025	= 0.003125
7,920.0 =	660.0 =	220.0 =	40.0	= 1.0	= 0.125
63,360.0 =	5,280.0 =	1,760.0 =	320.0	= 8.0	= 1.0

Square and Land Measure

Sq. Inches	Sq. Feet	Sq. Yards	Sq. Rods	Acres	Sq. Miles
1.0 =	0.006944 =	0.000772			
144.0 =	1.0 =	0.111111			
1,296.0 =	9.0 =	1.0 =	0.03306 =	0.000207	
39,204.0 =	272.25 =	30.25 =	1.0 =	0.00625	= 0.0000098
	43,560.0 =	4,840.0 =	160.0 =	1.0	= 0.0015625
		3,097,600.0 =	102,400.0 =	640.0	= 1.0

Avoirdupois Weights

Grains	Drams	Ounces	Pounds	Tons
1.0 =	0.03657 =	0.002286 =	0.000143 =	0.0000000714
27.34375 =	1.0 =	0.0625 =	0.003906 =	0.00000195
437.5 =	16.0 =	1.0 =	0.0625 =	0.00003125
7,000.0 =	256.0 =	16.0 =	1.0 =	0.0005
14,000,000.0 =	512,000.0 =	32,000.0 =	2,000.0 =	1.0

Dry Measure

Pints	Quarts	Pecks	Cubic Feet	Bushels
1.0 =	0.5 =	0.0625 =	0.01945 =	0.01563
2.0 =	1.0 =	0.125 =	0.03891 =	0.03125
16.0 =	8.0 =	1.0 =	0.31112 =	0.25
51.42627 =	25.71314 =	3.21414 =	1.0 =	0.80354
64.0 =	32.0 =	4.0 =	1.2445 =	1.0

Liquid Measure

Gills	Pints	Quarts	U.S. Gallons	Cubic Feet
1.0	= 0.25	= 0.125	= 0.03125	= 0.00418
4.0	= 1.0	= 0.5	= 0.125	= 0.01671
8.0	= 2.0	= 1.0	= 0.250	= 0.03342
32.0	= 8.0	= 4.0	= 1.0	= 0.1337
			7.48052	= 1.0

Data reproduced by courtesy of AISC, Inc.

METRIC SYSTEM
Units

Length — Meters : Mass — Grams : Capacity — Liters
for pure water at 4°C (39.2°F)

1 cubic decimeter or 1 liter = 1 kilogram

$$1,000 \text{ Milli} \begin{cases} meters \text{ (mm)} \\ grams \text{ (mg)} \\ liters \text{ (ml)} \end{cases} = 100 \text{ Centi} \begin{cases} meters \text{ (cm)} \\ grams \text{ (cg)} \\ liters \text{ (cl)} \end{cases} = 10 \text{ Deci} \begin{cases} meters \text{ (dm)} \\ grams \text{ (dg)} \\ liters \text{ (dl)} \end{cases} = 1 \begin{cases} meter \\ gram \\ liter \end{cases}$$

$$1,000 \begin{cases} meters \\ grams \\ liters \end{cases} = 100 \text{ Deka} \begin{cases} meters \text{ (dkm)} \\ grams \text{ (dkg)} \\ liters \text{ (dkl)} \end{cases} = 10 \text{ Hecto} \begin{cases} meters \text{ (hm)} \\ grams \text{ (hg)} \\ liters \text{ (hl)} \end{cases} - 1 \text{ Kilo} \begin{cases} meter \text{ (km)} \\ gram \text{ (kg)} \\ liter \text{ (kl)} \end{cases}$$

1 metric ton	= 1000 kilograms
100 square meters	= 1 are
100 ares	= 1 hectare
100 hectares	= 1 square kilometer

Data reproduced by courtesy of AISC, Inc.

ENGINEERING CONVERSION FACTORS

Multiply	by	to obtain
acres	.404687	hectares
"	4.04687×10^{-3}	square kilometers
ares	1076.39	square feet
board feet	144 sq. in. $\times$ 1 in.	cubic inches
" "	.0833	cubic feet
centimeters	3.28083×10^{-2}	feet
"	.3937	inches
cubic centimeters	3.53145×10^{-5}	cubic feet
" "	6.102×10^{-2}	cubic inches
cubic feet	2.8317×10^{4}	cubic centimeters
" "	2.8317×10^{-2}	cubic meters
" "	6.22905	gallons, British Imperial
" "	28.3170	liters
" "	2.38095×10^{-2}	tons, British Shipping
" "	.025	tons, U. S. Shipping
cubic inches	16.38716	cubic centimeters
cubic meters	35.3145	cubic feet
" "	1.30794	cubic yards
cubic yards	.764559	cubic meters
degrees, angular	.0174533	radians
degrees, Fahrenheit (less 32 F.)	.5556	degrees, Centigrade
" Centigrade	1.8	degrees, Fahrenheit (less 32 F.)
foot pounds	.13826	kilogram meters
feet	30.4801	centimeters
"	.304801	meters
"	304.801	millimeters
"	1.64468×10^{-4}	miles, nautical
gallons, British Imperial	.160538	cubic feet
" " "	1.20091	gallons, U. S.
" " "	4.54596	liters
gallons, U. S.	.832702	gallons, British Imperial
" "	.13368	cubic feet
" "	231.	cubic inches
" "	3.78543	liters
grams, metric	2.20462×10^{-3}	pounds, avoirdupois
hectares	2.47104	acres
"	1.076387×10^{5}	square feet
"	3.86101×10^{-3}	square miles
horse-power, metric	.98632	horse-power, U. S.
horse-power, U. S.	1.01387	horse-power, metric
inches	2.54001	centimeters
"	2.54001×10^{-2}	meters
"	25.4001	millimeters
kilograms	2.20462	pounds
"	9.84206×10^{-4}	long tons
"	1.10231×10^{-3}	short tons
kilogram meters	7.233	foot pounds
kilograms per meter	.671972	pounds per foot
kilograms per square centimeter	14.2234	pounds per square inch
kilograms per square meter	.204817	pounds per square foot
" " " "	9.14362×10^{-5}	long tons per square foot
kilograms per square millimeter	1422.34	pounds per square inch
" " " "	.634973	long tons per square inch
kilograms per cubic meter	6.24283×10^{-2}	pounds per cubic foot
kilometers	.62137	miles, statute
"	.53959	miles, nautical

ENGINEERING CONVERSION FACTORS

Multiply	by	to obtain
liters	.219975	gallons, British Imperial
"	.26417	gallons, U. S.
"	3.53145×10^{-2}	cubic feet
meters	3.28083	feet
"	39.37	inches
"	1.09361	yards
miles, statute	1.60935	kilometers
" "	.8684	miles, nautical
miles, nautical	6080.204	feet
" "	1.85325	kilometers
" "	1.1516	miles, statute
millimeters	3.28083×10^{-3}	feet
"	3.937×10^{-2}	inches
pounds, avoirdupois	453.592	grams, metric
" "	.453592	kilograms
" "	4.464×10^{-4}	tons, long
" "	4.53592×10^{-4}	tons, metric
pounds per foot	1.48816	kilograms per meter
pounds per square foot	4.88241	kilograms per square meter
pounds per square inch	7.031×10^{-2}	kilograms per square centimeter
" " " "	7.031×10^{-4}	kilograms per square millimeter
pounds per cubic foot	16.0184	kilograms per cubic meter
radians	57.29578	degrees, angular
square centimeters	.1550	square inches
square feet	9.29034×10^{-4}	ares
" "	9.29034×10^{-6}	hectares
" "	.0929034	square meters
square inches	6.45163	square centimeters
" "	645.163	square millimeters
square kilometers	247.104	acres
" "	.3861	square miles
square meters	10.7639	square feet
" "	1.19599	square yards
square miles	259.0	hectares
" "	2.590	square kilometers
square millimeters	1.550×10^{-3}	square inches
square yards	.83613	square meters
tons, long	1016.05	kilograms
" "	2240.	pounds
" "	1.01605	tons, metric
" "	1.120	tons, short
tons, long, per square foot	1.09366×10^{4}	kilograms per square meter
tons, long, per square inch	1.57494	kilograms per square millimeter
tons, metric	2204.62	pounds
" "	.98421	tons, long
" "	1.10231	tons, short
tons, short	907.185	kilograms
" "	.892857	tons, long
" "	.907185	tons, metric
tons, British Shipping	42.00	cubic feet
" " "	.952381	tons, U. S. Shipping
tons, U. S. Shipping	40.00	cubic feet
" " "	1.050	tons, British Shipping
yards	.914402	meters

Data reproduced by courtesy of AISC, Inc.

DECIMALS OF A FOOT
For each 32nd of an inch

Inch	0	1	2	3	4	5
0	0	.0833	.1667	.2500	.3333	.4167
1/32	.0026	.0859	.1693	.2526	.3359	.4193
1/16	.0052	.0885	.1719	.2552	.3385	.4219
3/32	.0078	.0911	.1745	.2578	.3411	.4245
1/8	.0104	.0938	.1771	.2604	.3438	.4271
5/32	.0130	.0964	.1797	.2630	.3464	.4297
3/16	.0156	.0990	.1823	.2656	.3490	.4323
7/32	.0182	.1016	.1849	.2682	.3516	.4349
1/4	.0208	.1042	.1875	.2708	.3542	.4375
9/32	.0234	.1068	.1901	.2734	.3568	.4401
5/16	.0260	.1094	.1927	.2760	.3594	.4427
11/32	.0286	.1120	.1953	.2786	.3620	.4453
3/8	.0313	.1146	.1979	.2812	.3646	.4479
13/32	.0339	.1172	.2005	.2839	.3672	.4505
7/16	.0365	.1198	.2031	.2865	.3698	.4531
15/32	.0391	.1224	.2057	.2891	.3724	.4557
1/2	.0417	.1250	.2083	.2917	.3750	.4583
17/32	.0443	.1276	.2109	.2943	.3776	.4609
9/16	.0469	.1302	.2135	.2969	.3802	.4635
19/32	.0495	.1328	.2161	.2995	.3828	.4661
5/8	.0521	.1354	.2188	.3021	.3854	.4688
21/32	.0547	.1380	.2214	.3047	.3880	.4714
11/16	.0573	.1406	.2240	.3073	.3906	.4740
23/32	.0599	.1432	.2266	.3099	.3932	.4766
3/4	.0625	.1458	.2292	.3125	.3958	.4792
25/32	.0651	.1484	.2318	.3151	.3984	.4818
13/16	.0677	.1510	.2344	.3177	.4010	.4844
27/32	.0703	.1536	.2370	.3203	.4036	.4870
7/8	.0729	.1563	.2396	.3229	.4063	.4896
29/32	.0755	.1589	.2422	.3255	.4089	.4922
15/16	.0781	.1615	.2448	.3281	.4115	.4948
31/32	.0807	.1641	.2474	.3307	.4141	.4974

Data reproduced by courtesy of AISC, Inc.

DECIMALS OF A FOOT
For each 32nd of an inch

Inch	6	7	8	9	10	11
0	.5000	.5833	.6667	.7500	.8333	.9167
1/32	.5026	.5859	.6693	.7526	.8359	.9193
1/16	.5052	.5885	.6719	.7552	.8385	.9219
3/32	.5078	.5911	.6745	.7578	.8411	.9245
1/8	.5104	.5938	.6771	.7604	.8438	.9271
5/32	.5130	.5964	.6797	.7630	.8464	.9297
3/16	.5156	.5990	.6823	.7656	.8490	.9323
7/32	.5182	.6016	.6849	.7682	.8516	.9349
1/4	.5208	.6042	.6875	.7708	.8542	.9375
9/32	.5234	.6068	.6901	.7734	.8568	.9401
5/16	.5260	.6094	.6927	.7760	.8594	.9427
11/32	.5286	.6120	.6953	.7786	.8620	.9453
3/8	.5313	.6146	.6979	.7813	.8646	.9479
13/32	.5339	.6172	.7005	.7839	.8672	.9505
7/16	.5365	.6198	.7031	.7865	.8698	.9531
15/32	.5391	.6224	.7057	.7891	.8724	.9557
1/2	.5417	.6250	.7083	.7917	.8750	9583
17/32	.5443	.6276	.7109	.7943	.8776	.9609
9/16	.5469	.6302	.7135	.7969	.8802	.9635
19/32	.5495	.6328	.7161	.7995	.8828	.9661
5/8	.5521	.6354	.7188	.8021	.8854	.9688
21/32	.5547	.6380	.7214	.8047	.8880	.9714
11/16	.5573	.6406	.7240	.8073	.8906	.9740
23/32	.5599	.6432	.7266	.8099	.8932	.9766
3/4	.5625	.6458	.7292	.8125	.8958	.9792
25/32	.5651	.6484	.7318	.8151	.8984	.9818
13/16	.5677	.6510	.7344	.8177	.9010	.9844
27/32	.5703	.6536	.7370	.8203	.9036	.9870
7/8	.5729	.6563	.7396	.8229	.9063	.9896
29/32	.5755	.6589	.7422	.8255	.9089	.9922
15/16	.5781	.6615	.7448	.8281	.9115	.9948
31/32	.5807	.6641	.7474	.8307	.9141	.9974

Data reproduced by courtesy of AISC, Inc.

DECIMALS OF AN INCH
For each 64th of an inch
with millimeter equivalents

Fraction	1/64ths	Decimal	Millimeters (Approx.)	Fraction	1/64ths	Decimal	Millimeters (Approx.)
...	1	.015625	0.397	...	33	.515625	13.097
1/32	2	.03125	0.794	17/32	34	.53125	13.494
...	3	.046875	1.191	...	35	.546875	13.891
1/16	4	.0625	1.588	9/16	36	.5625	14.288
...	5	.078125	1.984	...	37	.578125	14.684
3/32	6	.09375	2.381	19/32	38	.59375	15.081
...	7	.109375	2.778	...	39	.609375	15.478
1/8	8	.125	3.175	5/8	40	.625	15.875
...	9	.140625	3.572	...	41	.640625	16.272
5/32	10	.15625	3.969	21/32	42	.65625	16.669
...	11	.171875	4.366	...	43	.671875	17.066
3/16	12	.1875	4.763	11/16	44	.6875	17.463
...	13	.203125	5.159	...	45	.703125	17.859
7/32	14	.21875	5.556	23/32	46	.71875	18.256
...	15	.234375	5.953	...	47	.734375	18.653
1/4	16	.250	6.350	3/4	48	.750	19.050
...	17	.265625	6.747	...	49	.765625	19.447
9/32	18	.28125	7.144	25/32	50	.78125	19.844
...	19	.296875	7.541	...	51	.796875	20.241
5/16	20	.3125	7.938	13/16	52	.8125	20.638
...	21	.328125	8.334	...	53	.828125	21.034
11/32	22	.34375	8.731	27/32	54	.84375	21.431
...	23	.359375	9.128	...	55	.859375	21.828
3/8	24	.375	9.525	7/8	56	.875	22.225
...	25	.390625	9.922	...	57	.890625	22.622
13/32	26	.40625	10.319	29/32	58	.90625	23.019
...	27	.421875	10.716	...	59	.921875	23.416
7/16	28	.4375	11.113	15/16	60	.9375	23.813
...	29	.453125	11.509	...	61	.953125	24.209
15/32	30	.46875	11.906	31/32	62	.96875	24.606
...	31	.484375	12.303	...	63	.984375	25.003
1/2	32	.500	12.700	1	64	1.000	25.400

Data reproduced by courtesy of AISC, Inc.

SQUARE AND ROUND STEEL BARS
WEIGHT AND AREA

Size Inches	Weight Lb. per Foot ■	Weight Lb. per Foot ●	Area Square Inches ▨	Area Square Inches ◎	Size Inches	Weight Lb. per Foot ■	Weight Lb. per Foot ●	Area Square Inches ▨	Area Square Inches ◎
0					3	30.60	24.03	9.000	7.069
1/16	.013	.010	.0039	.0031	1/16	31.89	25.05	9.379	7.366
1/8	.053	.042	.0156	.0123	1/8	33.20	26.08	9.766	7.670
3/16	.120	.094	.0352	.0276	3/16	34.54	27.13	10.160	7.980
1/4	.213	.167	.0625	.0491	1/4	35.91	28.21	10.563	8.296
5/16	.332	.261	.0977	.0767	5/16	37.31	29.30	10.973	8.618
3/8	.478	.376	.1406	.1105	3/8	38.73	30.42	11.391	8.946
7/16	.651	.511	.1914	.1503	7/16	40.18	31.55	11.816	9.281
1/2	.850	.668	.2500	.1963	1/2	41.65	32.71	12.250	9.621
9/16	1.076	.845	.3164	.2485	9/16	43.15	33.89	12.691	9.968
5/8	1.328	1.043	.3906	.3068	5/8	44.68	35.09	13.141	10.321
11/16	1.607	1.262	.4727	.3712	11/16	46.23	36.31	13.598	10.680
3/4	1.913	1.502	.5625	.4418	3/4	47.81	37.55	14.063	11.045
13/16	2.245	1.763	.6602	.5185	13/16	49.42	38.81	14.535	11.416
7/8	2.603	2.044	.7656	.6013	7/8	51.05	40.10	15.016	11.793
15/16	2.988	2.347	.8789	.6903	15/16	52.71	41.40	15.504	12.177
1	3.400	2.670	1.0000	.7854	4	54.40	42.73	16.000	12.566
1/16	3.838	3.015	1.1289	.8866	1/16	56.11	44.07	16.504	12.962
1/8	4.303	3.380	1.2656	.9940	1/8	57.85	45.44	17.016	13.364
3/16	4.795	3.766	1.4102	1.1075	3/16	59.62	46.83	17.535	13.772
1/4	5.313	4.172	1.5625	1.2272	1/4	61.41	48.23	18.063	14.186
5/16	5.857	4.600	1.7227	1.3530	5/16	63.23	49.66	18.598	14.607
3/8	6.428	5.049	1.8906	1.4849	3/8	65.08	51.11	19.141	15.033
7/16	7.026	5.518	2.0664	1.6230	7/16	66.95	52.58	19.691	15.466
1/2	7.650	6.008	2.2500	1.7671	1/2	68.85	54.07	20.250	15.904
9/16	8.301	6.519	2.4414	1.9175	9/16	70.78	55.59	20.816	16.349
5/8	8.978	7.051	2.6406	2.0739	5/8	72.73	57.12	21.391	16.800
11/16	9.682	7.604	2.8477	2.2365	11/16	74.71	58.67	21.973	17.257
3/4	10.413	8.178	3.0625	2.4053	3/4	76.71	60.25	22.563	17.721
13/16	11.170	8.773	3.2852	2.5802	13/16	78.74	61.85	23.160	18.190
7/8	11.953	9.388	3.5156	2.7612	7/8	80.80	63.46	23.766	18.665
15/16	12.763	10.024	3.7539	2.9483	15/16	82.89	65.10	24.379	19.147
2	13.600	10.681	4.0000	3.1416	5	85.00	66.76	25.000	19.635
1/16	14.463	11.359	4.2539	3.3410	1/16	87.14	68.44	25.629	20.129
1/8	15.353	12.058	4.5156	3.5466	1/8	89.30	70.14	26.266	20.629
3/16	16.270	12.778	4.7852	3.7583	3/16	91.49	71.86	26.910	21.135
1/4	17.213	13.519	5.0625	3.9761	1/4	93.71	73.60	27.563	21.648
5/16	18.182	14.280	5.3477	4.2000	5/16	95.96	75.36	28.223	22.166
3/8	19.178	15.062	5.6406	4.4301	3/8	98.23	77.15	28.891	22.691
7/16	20.201	15.866	5.9414	4.6664	7/16	100.53	78.95	29.566	23.221
1/2	21.250	16.690	6.2500	4.9087	1/2	102.85	80.78	30.250	23.758
9/16	22.326	17.534	6.5664	5.1572	9/16	105.20	82.62	30.941	24.301
5/8	23.428	18.400	6.8906	5.4119	5/8	107.58	84.49	31.641	24.850
11/16	24.557	19.287	7.2227	5.6727	11/16	109.98	86.38	32.348	25.406
3/4	25.713	20.195	7.5625	5.9396	3/4	112.41	88.29	33.063	25.967
13/16	26.895	21.123	7.9102	6.2126	13/16	114.87	90.22	33.785	26.535
7/8	28.103	22.072	8.2656	6.4918	7/8	117.35	92.17	34.516	27.109
15/16	29.338	23.042	8.6289	6.7771	15/16	119.86	94.14	35.254	27.688
3	30.600	24.033	9.0000	7.0686	6	122.40	96.13	36.000	28.274

Data reproduced by courtesy of AISC, Inc.

SQUARE AND ROUND STEEL BARS
WEIGHT AND AREA

Size Inches	Weight Lb. per Foot ■	Weight Lb. per Foot ●	Area Square Inches ▨	Area Square Inches ◎	Size Inches	Weight Lb. per Foot ■	Weight Lb. per Foot ●	Area Square Inches ▨	Area Square Inches ◎
6	122.40	96.13	36.000	28.274	9	275.40	216.30	81.000	63.617
1/16	124.96	98.15	36.754	28.866	1/16	279.24	219.31	82.129	64.504
1/8	127.55	100.18	37.516	29.465	1/8	283.10	222.35	83.266	65.397
3/16	130.17	102.23	38.285	30.069	3/16	286.99	225.41	84.410	66.296
1/4	132.81	104.31	39.063	30.680	1/4	290.91	228.48	85.563	67.201
5/16	135.48	106.41	39.848	31.296	5/16	294.86	231.58	86.723	68.112
3/8	138.18	108.53	40.641	31.919	3/8	298.83	234.70	87.891	69.029
7/16	140.90	110.66	41.441	32.548	7/16	302.83	237.84	89.066	69.953
1/2	143.65	112.82	42.250	33.183	1/2	306.85	241.00	90.250	70.882
9/16	146.43	115.00	43.066	33.824	9/16	310.90	244.18	91.441	71.818
5/8	149.23	117.20	43.891	34.472	5/8	314.98	247.38	92.641	72.760
11/16	152.06	119.43	44.723	35.125	11/16	319.08	250.61	93.848	73.708
3/4	154.91	121.67	45.563	35.785	3/4	323.21	253.85	95.063	74.662
13/16	157.79	123.93	46.410	36.450	13/16	327.37	257.12	96.285	75.622
7/8	160.70	126.22	47.266	37.122	7/8	331.55	260.40	97.516	76.589
15/16	163.64	128.52	48.129	37.800	15/16	335.76	263.71	98.754	77.561
7	166.60	130.85	49.000	38.485	10	340.00	267.04	100.000	78.540
1/16	169.59	133.19	49.879	39.175	1/16	344.26	270.38	101.254	79.525
1/8	172.60	135.56	50.766	39.871	1/8	348.55	273.75	102.516	80.516
3/16	175.64	137.95	51.660	40.574	3/16	352.87	277.14	103.785	81.513
1/4	178.71	140.36	52.563	41.282	1/4	357.21	280.55	105.063	82.516
5/16	181.81	142.79	53.473	41.997	5/16	361.58	283.99	106.348	83.525
3/8	184.93	145.24	54.391	42.718	3/8	365.98	287.44	107.641	84.541
7/16	188.07	147.71	55.316	43.445	7/16	370.40	290.91	108.941	85.563
1/2	191.25	150.21	56.250	44.179	1/2	374.85	294.41	110.250	86.590
9/16	194.45	152.72	57.191	44.918	9/16	379.33	297.92	111.566	87.624
5/8	197.68	155.26	58.141	45.664	5/8	383.83	301.46	112.891	88.664
11/16	200.93	157.81	59.098	46.415	11/16	388.36	305.02	114.223	89.710
3/4	204.21	160.39	60.063	47.173	3/4	392.91	308.59	115.563	90.763
13/16	207.52	162.99	61.035	47.937	13/16	397.49	312.19	116.910	91.821
7/8	210.85	165.60	62.016	48.707	7/8	402.10	315.81	118.266	92.886
15/16	214.21	168.24	63.004	49.483	15/16	406.74	319.45	119.629	93.957
8	217.60	170.90	64.000	50.265	11	411.40	323.11	121.000	95.033
1/16	221.01	173.58	65.004	51.054	1/16	416.09	326.80	122.379	96.116
1/8	224.45	176.29	66.016	51.849	1/8	420.80	330.50	123.766	97.205
3/16	227.92	179.01	67.035	52.649	3/16	425.54	334.22	125.160	98.301
1/4	231.41	181.75	68.063	53.456	1/4	430.31	337.97	126.563	99.402
5/16	234.93	184.52	69.098	54.269	5/16	435.11	341.73	127.973	100.510
3/8	238.48	187.30	70.141	55.088	3/8	439.93	345.52	129.391	101.623
7/16	242.05	190.11	71.191	55.914	7/16	444.78	349.33	130.816	102.743
1/2	245.65	192.93	72.250	56.745	1/2	449.65	353.16	132.250	103.869
9/16	249.28	195.78	73.316	57.583	9/16	454.55	357.00	133.691	105.001
5/8	252.93	198.65	74.391	58.426	5/8	459.48	360.87	135.141	106.139
11/16	256.61	201.54	75.473	59.276	11/16	464.43	364.76	136.598	107.284
3/4	260.31	204.45	76.563	60.132	3/4	469.41	368.68	138.063	108.434
13/16	264.04	207.38	77.660	60.994	13/16	474.42	372.61	139.535	109.591
7/8	267.80	210.33	78.766	61.863	7/8	479.45	376.56	141.016	110.754
15/16	271.59	213.31	79.879	62.737	15/16	484.51	380.54	142.504	111.923
9	275.40	216.30	81.000	63.617	12	489.60	384.53	144.000	113.098

Data reproduced by courtesy of AISC, Inc.

WEIGHT OF RECTANGULAR STEEL SECTIONS
POUNDS PER LINEAR FOOT

Width In.	Thickness, Inches													
	$3/16$	$1/4$	$5/16$	$3/8$	$7/16$	$1/2$	$9/16$	$5/8$	$11/16$	$3/4$	$13/16$	$7/8$	$15/16$	1
$1/4$	.16	.21	.27	.32	.37	.43	.48	.53	.58	.64	.69	.74	.80	.85
$1/2$	.32	.43	.53	.64	.74	.85	.96	1.06	1.17	1.28	1.38	1.49	1.59	1.70
$3/4$	.48	.64	.80	.96	1.12	1.28	1.43	1.59	1.75	1.91	2.07	2.23	2.39	2.55
1	.64	.85	1.06	1.28	1.49	1.70	1.91	2.13	2.34	2.55	2.76	2.98	3.19	3.40
$1\,1/4$	.80	1.06	1.33	1.59	1.86	2.13	2.39	2.66	2.92	3.19	3.45	3.72	3.98	4.25
$1\,1/2$	.96	1.28	1.59	1.91	2.23	2.55	2.87	3.19	3.51	3.83	4.14	4.46	4.78	5.10
$1\,3/4$	1.12	1.49	1.86	2.23	2.60	2.98	3.35	3.72	4.09	4.46	4.83	5.21	5.58	5.95
2	1.28	1.70	2.13	2.55	2.98	3.40	3.83	4.25	4.68	5.10	5.53	5.95	6.38	6.80
$2\,1/4$	1.43	1.91	2.39	2.87	3.35	3.83	4.30	4.78	5.26	5.74	6.22	6.69	7.17	7.65
$2\,1/2$	1.59	2.13	2.66	3.19	3.72	4.25	4.78	5.31	5.84	6.38	6.91	7.44	7.97	8.50
$2\,3/4$	1.75	2.34	2.92	3.51	4.09	4.68	5.26	5.84	6.43	7.01	7.60	8.18	8.77	9.35
3	1.91	2.55	3.19	3.83	4.46	5.10	5.74	6.38	7.01	7.65	8.29	8.93	9.56	10.2
$3\,1/4$	2.07	2.76	3.45	4.14	4.83	5.53	6.22	6.91	7.60	8.29	8.98	9.67	10.4	11.1
$3\,1/2$	2.23	2.98	3.72	4.46	5.21	5.95	6.69	7.44	8.18	8.93	9.67	10.4	11.2	11.9
$3\,3/4$	2.39	3.19	3.98	4.78	5.58	6.38	7.17	7.97	8.77	9.56	10.4	11.2	12.0	12.8
4	2.55	3.40	4.25	5.10	5.95	6.80	7.65	8.50	9.35	10.2	11.1	11.9	12.8	13.6
$4\,1/4$	2.71	3.61	4.52	5.42	6.32	7.23	8.13	9.03	9.93	10.8	11.7	12.6	13.6	14.5
$4\,1/2$	2.87	3.83	4.78	5.74	6.69	7.65	8.61	9.56	10.5	11.5	12.4	13.4	14.3	15.3
$4\,3/4$	3.03	4.04	5.05	6.06	7.07	8.08	9.08	10.1	11.1	12.1	13.1	14.1	15.1	16.2
5	3.19	4.25	5.31	6.38	7.44	8.50	9.56	10.6	11.7	12.8	13.8	14.9	15.9	17.0
$5\,1/4$	3.35	4.46	5.58	6.69	7.81	8.93	10.0	11.2	12.3	13.4	14.5	15.6	16.7	17.9
$5\,1/2$	3.51	4.68	5.84	7.01	8.18	9.35	10.5	11.7	12.9	14.0	15.2	16.4	17.5	18.7
$5\,3/4$	3.67	4.89	6.11	7.33	8.55	9.78	11.0	12.2	13.4	14.7	15.9	17.1	18.3	19.6
6	3.83	5.10	6.38	7.65	8.93	10.2	11.5	12.8	14.0	15.3	16.6	17.9	19.1	20.4
$6\,1/4$	3.98	5.31	6.64	7.97	9.30	10.6	12.0	13.3	14.6	15.9	17.3	18.6	19.9	21.3
$6\,1/2$	4.14	5.53	6.91	8.29	9.67	11.1	12.4	13.8	15.2	16.6	18.0	19.3	20.7	22.1
$6\,3/4$	4.30	5.74	7.17	8.61	10.0	11.5	12.9	14.3	15.8	17.2	18.7	20.1	21.5	23.0
7	4.46	5.95	7.44	8.93	10.4	11.9	13.4	14.9	16.4	17.9	19.3	20.8	22.3	23.8
$7\,1/4$	4.62	6.16	7.70	9.24	10.8	12.3	13.9	15.4	17.0	18.5	20.0	21.6	23.1	24.7
$7\,1/2$	4.78	6.38	7.97	9.56	11.2	12.8	14.3	15.9	17.5	19.1	20.7	22.3	23.9	25.5
$7\,3/4$	4.94	6.59	8.23	9.88	11.5	13.2	14.8	16.5	18.1	19.8	21.4	23.1	24.7	26.4
8	5.10	6.80	8.50	10.2	11.9	13.6	15.3	17.0	18.7	20.4	22.1	23.8	25.5	27.2
$8\,1/4$	5.26	7.01	8.77	10.5	12.3	14.0	15.8	17.5	19.3	21.0	22.8	24.5	26.3	28.1
$8\,1/2$	5.42	7.23	9.03	10.8	12.6	14.5	16.3	18.1	19.9	21.7	23.5	25.3	27.1	28.9
$8\,3/4$	5.58	7.44	9.30	11.2	13.0	14.9	16.7	18.6	20.5	22.3	24.2	26.0	27.9	29.8
9	5.74	7.65	9.56	11.5	13.4	15.3	17.2	19.1	21.0	23.0	24.9	26.8	28.7	30.6
$9\,1/4$	5.90	7.86	9.83	11.8	13.8	15.7	17.7	19.7	21.6	23.6	25.6	27.5	29.5	31.5
$9\,1/2$	6.06	8.08	10.1	12.1	14.1	16.2	18.2	20.2	22.2	24.2	26.2	28.3	30.3	32.3
$9\,3/4$	6.22	8.29	10.4	12.4	14.5	16.6	18.7	20.7	22.8	24.9	26.9	29.0	31.1	33.2
10	6.38	8.50	10.6	12.8	14.9	17.0	19.1	21.3	23.4	25.5	27.6	29.8	31.9	34.0

Data reproduced by courtesy of AISC, Inc.

WEIGHT OF RECTANGULAR STEEL SECTIONS
POUNDS PER LINEAR FOOT

Width In.	Thickness, Inches													
	3/16	1/4	5/16	3/8	7/16	1/2	9/16	5/8	11/16	3/4	13/16	7/8	15/16	1
10¼	6.53	8.71	10.9	13.1	15.3	17.4	19.6	21.8	24.0	26.1	28.3	30.5	32.7	34.9
10½	6.69	8.93	11.2	13.4	15.6	17.9	20.1	22.3	24.5	26.8	29.0	31.2	33.5	35.7
10¾	6.85	9.14	11.4	13.7	16.0	18.3	20.6	22.8	25.1	27.4	29.7	32.0	34.3	36.6
11	7.01	9.35	11.7	14.0	16.4	18.7	21.0	23.4	25.7	28.1	30.4	32.7	35.1	37.4
11¼	7.17	9.56	12.0	14.3	16.7	19.1	21.5	23.9	26.3	28.7	31.1	33.5	35.9	38.3
11½	7.33	9.78	12.2	14.7	17.1	19.6	22.0	24.4	26.9	29.3	31.8	34.2	36.7	39.1
11¾	7.49	9.99	12.5	15.0	17.5	20.0	22.5	25.0	27.5	30.0	32.5	35.0	37.5	40.0
12	7.65	10.2	12.8	15.3	17.9	20.4	23.0	25.5	28.1	30.6	33.2	35.7	38.3	40.8
12½	7.97	10.6	13.3	15.9	18.6	21.3	23.9	26.6	29.2	31.9	34.5	37.2	39.8	42.5
13	8.29	11.1	13.8	16.6	19.3	22.1	24.9	27.6	30.4	33.2	35.9	38.7	41.4	44.2
13½	8.61	11.5	14.3	17.2	20.1	23.0	25.8	28.7	31.6	34.4	37.3	40.2	43.0	45.9
14	8.93	11.9	14.9	17.9	20.8	23.8	26.8	29.8	32.7	35.7	38.7	41.7	44.6	47.6
14½	9.24	12.3	15.4	18.5	21.6	24.7	27.7	30.8	33.9	37.0	40.1	43.1	46.2	49.3
15	9.56	12.8	15.9	19.1	22.3	25.5	28.7	31.9	35.1	38.3	41.4	44.6	47.8	51.0
15½	9.88	13.2	16.5	19.8	23.1	26.4	29.6	32.9	36.2	39.5	42.8	46.1	49.4	52.7
16	10.2	13.6	17.0	20.4	23.8	27.2	30.6	34.0	37.4	40.8	44.2	47.6	51.0	54.4
16½	10.5	14.0	17.5	21.0	24.5	28.1	31.6	35.1	38.6	42.1	45.6	49.1	52.6	56 1
17	10.8	14.5	18.1	21.7	25.3	28.9	32.5	36.1	39.7	43.4	47.0	50.6	54.2	57.8
17½	11.2	14.9	18.6	22.3	26.0	29.8	33.5	37.2	40.9	44.6	48.3	52.1	55.8	59.5
18	11.5	15.3	19.1	23.0	26.8	30.6	34.4	38.3	42.1	45.9	49.7	53.6	57.4	61.2
18½	11.8	15.7	19.7	23.6	27.5	31.5	35.4	39.3	43.2	47.2	51.1	55.0	59.0	62.9
19	12.1	16.2	20.2	24.2	28.3	32.3	36.3	40.4	44.4	48.5	52.5	56.5	60.6	64.6
19½	12.4	16.6	20.7	24.9	29.0	33.2	37.3	41.4	45.6	49.7	53.9	58.0	62.2	66.3
20	12.8	17.0	21.3	25.5	29.8	34.0	38.3	42.5	46.8	51.0	55.3	59.5	63.8	68.0
20½	13.1	17.4	21.8	26.1	30.5	34.9	39.2	43.6	47.9	52.3	56.6	61.0	65.3	69.7
21	13.4	17.9	22.3	26.8	31.2	35.7	40.2	44.6	49.1	53.6	58.0	62.5	66.9	71.4
21½	13.7	18.3	22.8	27.4	32.0	36.6	41.1	45.7	50.3	54.8	59.4	64.0	68.5	73.1
22	14.0	18.7	23.4	28.1	32.7	37.4	42.1	46.8	51.4	56.1	60.8	65.5	70.1	74.8
22½	14.3	19.1	23.9	28.7	33.5	38.3	43.0	47.8	52.6	57.4	62.2	66.9	71.7	76.5
23	14.7	19.6	24.4	29.3	34.2	39.1	44.0	48.9	53.8	58.7	63.5	68.4	73.3	78.2
23½	15.0	20.0	25.0	30.0	35.0	40.0	44.9	49.9	54.9	59.9	64.9	69.9	74.9	79.9
24	15.3	20.4	25.5	30.6	35.7	40.8	45.9	51.0	56.1	61.2	66.3	71.4	76.5	81.6
25	15.9	21.3	26.6	31.9	37.2	42.5	47.8	53.1	58.4	63.8	69.1	74.4	79.7	85.0
26	16.6	22.1	27.6	33.2	38.7	44.2	49.7	55.3	60.8	66.3	71.8	77.4	82.9	88.4
27	17.2	23.0	28.7	34.4	40.2	45.9	51.6	57.4	63.1	68.9	74.6	80.3	86.1	91.8
28	17.9	23.8	29.8	35.7	41.7	47.6	53.6	59.5	65.5	71.4	77.4	83.3	89.3	95.2
29	18.5	24.7	30.8	37.0	43.1	49.3	55.5	61.6	67.8	74.0	80.1	86.3	92.4	98.6
30	19.1	25.5	31.9	38.3	44.6	51.0	57.4	63.8	70.1	76.5	82.9	89.3	95.6	102
31	19.8	26.4	32.9	39.5	46.1	52.7	59.3	65.9	72.5	79.1	85.6	92.2	98.8	105
32	20.4	27.2	34.0	40.8	47.6	54.4	61.2	68.0	74.8	81.6	88.4	95.2	102	109

Data reproduced by courtesy of AISC, Inc.

WEIGHT OF RECTANGULAR STEEL SECTIONS
POUNDS PER LINEAR FOOT

Width In.	Thickness, Inches													
	³⁄₁₆	¼	⁵⁄₁₆	⅜	⁷⁄₁₆	½	⁹⁄₁₆	⅝	¹¹⁄₁₆	¾	¹³⁄₁₆	⅞	¹⁵⁄₁₆	1
33	21.0	28.1	35.1	42.1	49.1	56.1	63.1	70.1	77.1	84.2	91.2	98.2	105	112
34	21.7	28.9	36.1	43.4	50.6	57.8	65.0	72.3	79.5	86.7	93.9	101.	108	116
35	22.3	29.8	37.2	44.6	52.1	59.5	66.9	74.4	81.8	89.3	96.1	104.	112	119
36	23.0	30.6	38.3	45.9	53.6	61.2	68.9	76.5	84.2	91.8	99.5	107.	115	122
37	23.6	31.5	39.3	47.2	55.0	62.9	70.8	78.6	86.5	94.4	102	110	118	126
38	24.2	32.3	40.4	48.5	56.5	64.6	72.7	80.8	88.8	96.9	105	113	121	129
39	24.9	33.2	41.4	49.7	58.0	66.3	74.6	82.9	91.2	99.5	108	116	124	133
40	25.5	34.0	42.5	51.0	59.5	68.0	76.5	85.0	93.5	102.	111	119	128	136
41	26.1	34.9	43.6	52.3	61.0	69.7	78.4	87.1	95.8	105	113	122	131	139
42	26.8	35.7	44.6	53.6	62.5	71.4	80.3	89.3	98.2	107	116	125	134	143
43	27.4	36.6	45.7	54.8	64.0	73.1	82.2	91.4	101.	110	119	128	137	146
44	28.1	37.4	46.8	56.1	65.5	74.8	84.2	93.5	103.	112	122	131	140	150
45	28.7	38.3	47.8	57.4	66.9	76.5	86.1	95.6	105	115	124	134	143	153
46	29.3	39.1	48.9	58.7	68.4	78.2	88.0	97.8	108	117	127	137	147	156
47	30.0	40.0	49.9	59.9	69.9	79.9	89.9	99.9	110	120	130	140	150	160
48	30.6	40.8	51.0	61.2	71.4	81.6	91.8	102.	112	122	133	143	153	163

Data reproduced by courtesy of AISC, Inc.

WIRE AND SHEET METAL GAGES
In decimals of an inch

Name of Gage	*United States Standard Gage		The United States Steel Wire Gage	American or Brown & Sharpe Wire Gage	New Birmingham Standard Sheet & Hoop Gage	British Imperial or English Legal Standard Wire Gage	Birmingham or Stubs Iron Wire Gage	Name of Gage
Principal Use	Uncoated Steel Sheets and Light Plates		Steel Wire except Music Wire	Non-Ferrous Sheets and Wire	Iron and Steel Sheets and Hoops	Wire	Strips, Bands, Hoops and Wire	Principal Use
Gage No.	Weight Oz. per Sq. Ft.	Approx. Thickness Inches	Thickness, Inches					Gage No.
7/0's			.4900		.6666	.500		7/0's
6/0's			.4615	.5800	.625	.464		6/0's
5/0's			.4305	.5165	.5883	.432	.500	5/0's
4/0's			.3938	.4600	.5416	.400	.454	4/0's
3/0's			.3625	.4096	.500	.372	.425	3/0's
2/0's			.3310	.3648	.4452	.348	.380	2/0's
1/0			.3065	.3249	.3964	.324	.340	1/0
1			.2830	.2893	.3532	.300	.300	1
2			.2625	.2576	.3147	.276	.284	2
3	160	.2391	.2437	.2294	.2804	.252	.259	3
4	150	.2242	.2253	.2043	.250	.232	.238	4
5	140	.2092	.2070	.1819	.2225	.212	.220	5
6	130	.1943	.1920	.1620	.1981	.192	.203	6
7	120	.1793	.1770	.1443	.1764	.176	.180	7
8	110	.1644	.1620	.1285	.1570	.160	.165	8
9	100	.1495	.1483	.1144	.1398	.144	.148	9
10	90	.1345	.1350	.1019	.1250	.128	.134	10
11	80	.1196	.1205	.0907	.1113	.116	.120	11
12	70	.1046	.1055	.0808	.0991	.104	.109	12
13	60	.0897	.0915	.0720	.0882	.092	.095	13
14	50	.0747	.0800	.0641	.0785	.080	.083	14
15	45	.0673	.0720	.0571	.0699	.072	.072	15
16	40	.0598	.0625	.0508	.0625	.064	.065	16
17	36	.0538	.0540	.0453	.0556	.056	.058	17
18	32	.0478	.0475	.0403	.0495	.048	.049	18
19	28	.0418	.0410	.0359	.0440	.040	.042	19
20	24	.0359	.0348	.0320	.0392	.036	.035	20
21	22	.0329	.0317	.0285	.0349	.032	.032	21
22	20	.0299	.0286	.0253	.0313	.028	.028	22
23	18	.0269	.0258	.0226	.0278	.024	.025	23
24	16	.0239	.0230	.0201	.0248	.022	.022	24
25	14	.0209	.0204	.0179	.0220	.020	.020	25
26	12	.0179	.0181	.0159	.0196	.018	.018	26
27	11	.0164	.0173	.0142	.0175	.0164	.016	27
28	10	.0149	.0162	.0126	.0156	.0148	.014	28
29	9	.0135	.0150	.0113	.0139	.0136	.013	29
30	8	.0120	.0140	.0100	.0123	.0124	.012	30
31	7	.0105	.0132	.0089	.0110	.0116	.010	31
32	6.5	.0097	.0128	.0080	.0098	.0108	.009	32
33	6	.0090	.0118	.0071	.0087	.0100	.008	33
34	5.5	.0082	.0104	.0063	.0077	.0092	.007	34
35	5	.0075	.0095	.0056	.0069	.0084	.005	35
36	4.5	.0067	.0090	.0050	.0061	.0076	.004	36
37	4.25	.0064	.0085	.0045	.0054	.0068		37
38	4	.0060	.0080	.0040	.0048	.0060		38
39			.0075	.0035	.0043	.0052		39
40			.0070	.0031	.0039	.0048		40

* U. S. Standard Gage is officially a weight gage, in oz. per sq. ft. as tabulated.   The Approx. Thickness shown is the "Manufacturers' Standard" of the American Iron and Steel Institute, based on steel as weighing 501.81 lb. per cu. ft. (489.6 true weight plus 2.5 per cent for average over-run in area and thickness).   The AISI standard nomenclature for flat rolled carbon steel is as follows:

Thickness (Inches)	Width (Inches)					
	To 3½ incl.	Over 3½ To 6	Over 6 To 8	Over 8 To 12	Over 12 To 48	Over 48
0.2300 & thicker	Bar	Bar	Bar	Plate	Plate	Plate
0.2299 to 0.2031	Bar	Bar	Strip	Strip	Sheet	Plate
0.2030 to 0.1800	Strip	Strip	Strip	Strip	Sheet	Plate
0.1799 to 0.0449	Strip	Strip	Strip	Strip	Sheet	Sheet
0.0448 to 0.0344	Strip	Strip				
0.0343 to 0.0255	Strip		Hot rolled sheet and strip not generally produced in these widths and thicknesses			
0.0254 & thinner						

Data reproduced by courtesy of AISC, Inc.

ROUND AND SQUARE UPSET RODS

UNC and 4UN Class 2A Thread

Diameter, d, or Side, s, in.	Round Bars			Square Bars		
	Strength,[a] lb	Upset		Strength,[a] lb	Upsct	
		Diam. D, in.	Length, L, in.		Diam. D, in.	Length, L, in.
$\frac{3}{4}$	9,720	1	4	12,400	$1\frac{1}{8}$	4
$\frac{7}{8}$	13,200	$1\frac{1}{8}$	4	16,800	$1\frac{1}{4}$	4
1	17,300	$1\frac{3}{8}$	4	22,000	$1\frac{1}{2}$	4
$1\frac{1}{8}$	21,900	$1\frac{1}{2}$	4	27,800	$1\frac{3}{4}$	4
$1\frac{1}{4}$	27,000	$1\frac{3}{4}$	4	34,400	2	$4\frac{1}{2}$
$1\frac{3}{8}$	32,700	$1\frac{3}{4}$	4	41,600	2	$4\frac{1}{2}$
$1\frac{1}{2}$	38,900	2	$4\frac{1}{2}$	49,500	$2\frac{1}{4}$	5
$1\frac{5}{8}$	45,600	$2\frac{1}{4}$	5	58,100	$2\frac{1}{2}$	$5\frac{1}{2}$
$1\frac{3}{4}$	52,900	$2\frac{1}{4}$	5	67,400	$2\frac{1}{2}$	$5\frac{1}{2}$
$1\frac{7}{8}$	60,700	$2\frac{3}{8}$	$5\frac{1}{2}$	77,300	$2\frac{3}{4}$	$5\frac{1}{2}$
2	69,100	$2\frac{1}{2}$	$5\frac{1}{2}$	88,000	$2\frac{3}{4}$	$5\frac{1}{2}$
$2\frac{1}{8}$	78,000	$2\frac{3}{4}$	$5\frac{1}{2}$	99,300	3	6
$2\frac{1}{4}$	87,500	$2\frac{3}{4}$	$5\frac{1}{2}$	111,400	$3\frac{1}{4}$	$6\frac{1}{2}$
$2\frac{3}{8}$	97,500	3	6	124,100	$3\frac{1}{4}$	$6\frac{1}{2}$
$2\frac{1}{2}$	108,000	$3\frac{1}{4}$	$6\frac{1}{2}$	137,500	$3\frac{1}{2}$	7
$2\frac{5}{8}$	119,100	$3\frac{1}{4}$	$6\frac{1}{2}$	151,600	$3\frac{3}{4}$	7

[a]Based on ASTM A36 steel.

CLEVISES

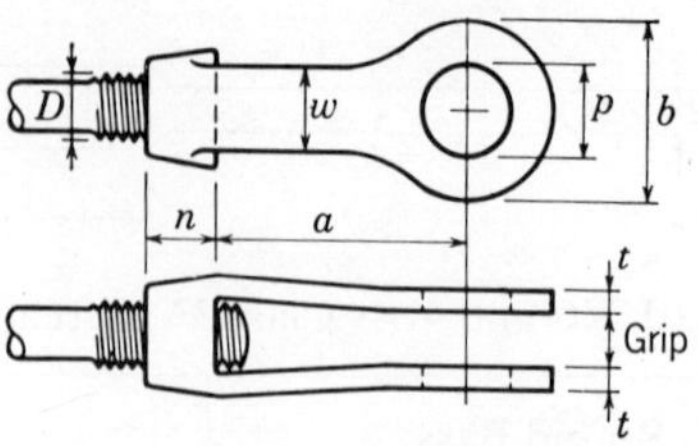

Thread: UNC Class 2B

Grip = thickness plate + 1/4″

Clevis Number	Dimensions, in.							Weight, lb.	Safe Working Load, kips[a]
	Max. *D*	Max. *p*	*b*	*n*	*a*	*w*	*t*		
2	5/8	3/4	1 7/16	5/8	3 7/8	1 1/16	5/16 (+1/32 −0)	1.0	7.0
2 1/2	7/8	1 1/2	2 1/2	1 1/8	4	1 1/4	5/16 (+1/32 −0)	2.0	7.5
3	1 3/8	1 3/4	3	1 5/16	5	1 1/2	1/2 (+1/32 −0)	4.0	15
3 1/2	1 1/2	2	3 1/2	1 5/8	6	1 3/4	1/2 (+1/32 −0)	6.0	18
4	1 3/4	2 1/4	4	1 3/4	6	2	1/2 (+1/32 −0)	8.0	21
5	2	2 1/2	5	2 1/4	7	2 1/2	5/8 (+1/16 −0)	16.0	37.5
6	2 1/2	3	6	2 3/4	8	3	3/4 (+3/32 −0)	26.0	54
7	3	3 3/4	7	3	9	3 1/2	7/8 (+1/8 −0)	36.0	68.5
8	4	4	8	4	10	4	1 1/2 (+1/8 −0)	80.0	135

[a]Safe working load based on 5:1 safety factor using maximum pin diameter.

Clevis Numbers for Various Rods and Pins

Diameter of Tap, in.	Diameter of Pin, in.															
	5/8	3/4	7/8	1	1 1/4	1 1/2	1 3/4	2	2 1/4	2 1/2	2 3/4	3	3 1/4	3 1/2	3 3/4	4
5/8	2	2	2 1/2	2 1/2	2 1/2	2 1/2										
3/4		2 1/2	2 1/2	2 1/2	2 1/2	2 1/2										
7/8			2 1/2	2 1/2	2 1/2	2 1/2										
1				3	3	3	3									
1 1/4				3	3	3	3	3 1/2								
1 3/8				3	3	3	3 1/2	3 1/2	4							
1 1/2				3 1/2	3 1/2	3 1/2	4	4	5							
1 3/4					4	4	5	5	5	5						
2						5	5	5	5	5	6	6				
2 1/4								6	6	6	6	6	7	7		
2 1/2								6	6	6	7	7	7	7	7	
2 3/4										7	7	7	7	8	8	
3										7	8	8	8	8	8	8
3 1/4											8	8	8	8	8	8
3 1/2											8	8	8	8	8	8
3 3/4											8	8	8	8	8	8
4											8	8	8	8	8	8

Above table of clevis sizes is based on the net area of clevis through pin hole being equal to or greater than 125% of net area of rod. Table applies to round rods without upset ends. Pins are sufficient for shear but must be investigated for bending. For other combinations of pin and rod or net area ratios, required clevis size can be calculated by reference to the tabulated dimensions.

Weights and dimensions of clevises are Cleveland City Forge Company Standard. Similar products of other manufacturers are essentially the same.

Data reproduced by courtesy of AISC, Inc.

TURNBUCKLES

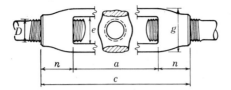

Thread: UNC and 4 UN Class 2B

Diam. D in.	Standard Turnbuckles Dimensions, in.					Weight of Turnbuckles, lb — Length, a, in.						Turnbuckle Safe Working Load, kips[a]
	a	n	c	e	g	6	9	12	18	24	36	
$\frac{3}{8}$	6	$\frac{9}{16}$	$7\frac{1}{8}$	$\frac{9}{16}$	$1\frac{1}{32}$	0.41						1.2
$\frac{1}{2}$	6	$\frac{3}{4}$	$7\frac{1}{2}$	$\frac{11}{16}$	$1\frac{5}{16}$	0.75	0.80	1.00				2.2
$\frac{5}{8}$	6	$\frac{29}{32}$	$7\frac{13}{16}$	$\frac{13}{16}$	$1\frac{1}{2}$	1.00	1.38	1.50	2.43			3.5
$\frac{3}{4}$	6	$1\frac{1}{16}$	$8\frac{5}{8}$	$\frac{15}{16}$	$1\frac{23}{32}$	1.45	1.63	2.13	3.06	4.25		5.2
$\frac{7}{8}$	6	$1\frac{7}{32}$	$8\frac{7}{16}$	$1\frac{3}{32}$	$1\frac{7}{8}$	1.85		2.83	4.20	5.43		7.2
1	6	$1\frac{3}{8}$	$8\frac{3}{4}$	$1\frac{9}{32}$	$2\frac{1}{16}$	2.60		3.20	4.40	6.85	10.0	9.3
$1\frac{1}{8}$	6	$1\frac{9}{16}$	$9\frac{1}{8}$	$1\frac{13}{32}$	$2\frac{9}{32}$	2.72		4.70	6.10			11.6
$1\frac{1}{4}$	6	$1\frac{3}{4}$	$9\frac{1}{2}$	$1\frac{9}{16}$	$2\frac{17}{32}$	3.58		4.70	7.13	11.30	13.1	15.2
$1\frac{3}{8}$	6	$1\frac{15}{16}$	$9\frac{7}{8}$	$1\frac{11}{16}$	$2\frac{3}{4}$	4.50						17.4
$1\frac{1}{2}$	6	$2\frac{1}{8}$	$10\frac{1}{4}$	$1\frac{27}{32}$	$3\frac{1}{32}$	5.50		8.00	9.13	16.80	19.4	21.0
$1\frac{5}{8}$	6	$2\frac{1}{4}$	$10\frac{1}{2}$	$1\frac{31}{32}$	$3\frac{3}{32}$	7.50						24.5
$1\frac{3}{4}$	6	$2\frac{1}{2}$	11	$2\frac{1}{8}$	$3\frac{9}{16}$	9.50		15.25	16.00	19.50		28.3
$1\frac{7}{8}$	6	$2\frac{3}{4}$	$11\frac{1}{2}$	$2\frac{3}{8}$	4	11.50						37.2
2	6	$2\frac{3}{4}$	$11\frac{1}{2}$	$2\frac{3}{8}$	4	11.50		15.25		27.50		37.2
$2\frac{1}{4}$	6	$3\frac{3}{8}$	$12\frac{3}{4}$	$2\frac{11}{16}$	$4\frac{5}{8}$	18.00		35.25		43.50		48.0
$2\frac{1}{2}$	6	$3\frac{3}{4}$	$13\frac{1}{2}$	3	5	23.25		33.60		42.38		60.0
$2\frac{3}{4}$	6	$4\frac{1}{8}$	$14\frac{1}{4}$	$3\frac{1}{4}$	$5\frac{5}{8}$	31.50				54.00		75.0
3	6	$4\frac{1}{2}$	15	$3\frac{5}{8}$	$6\frac{1}{4}$	39.50						96.7
$3\frac{1}{4}$	6	$5\frac{1}{4}$	$16\frac{1}{2}$	$3\frac{7}{8}$	$6\frac{3}{4}$	60.50						122.2
$3\frac{1}{2}$	6	$5\frac{1}{4}$	$16\frac{1}{2}$	$3\frac{7}{8}$	$6\frac{3}{4}$	60.50						122.2
$3\frac{3}{4}$	6	6	18	$4\frac{5}{8}$	$8\frac{1}{4}$	95.00						167.8
4	6	6	18	$4\frac{5}{8}$	$8\frac{1}{2}$	95.00						167.8
$4\frac{1}{4}$	9	$6\frac{3}{4}$	$22\frac{1}{2}$	$5\frac{1}{4}$	$9\frac{3}{4}$		152.0					233.8
$4\frac{1}{2}$	9	$6\frac{3}{4}$	$22\frac{1}{2}$	$5\frac{1}{4}$	$9\frac{3}{4}$		152.0					233.8
$4\frac{3}{4}$	9	$6\frac{3}{4}$	$22\frac{1}{2}$	$5\frac{1}{4}$	$9\frac{3}{4}$		152.0					233.8
5	9	$7\frac{1}{2}$	24	6	10		200.0					294.7

[a] Safe working load based on 5:1 safety factor.
Weights and dimensions of turnbuckles are Cleveland City Forge Company Standard. Similar products of other companies are essentially the same.

Data reproduced by courtesy of AISC, Inc.

SLEEVE NUTS

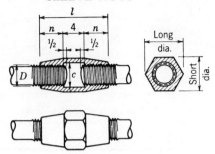

Thread: UNC and 4 UN Class 2B

Diameter of Screw, D, in.	Dimensions, in.					
	Short Diameter	Long Diameter	Length l	Nut n	Clear c	Weight, lb
$\frac{3}{8}$	$\frac{11}{16}$	$\frac{25}{32}$	4			0.27
$\frac{7}{16}$	$\frac{25}{32}$	$\frac{7}{8}$	4			0.34
$\frac{1}{2}$	$\frac{7}{8}$	1	4			0.43
$\frac{9}{16}$	$\frac{15}{16}$	$1\frac{1}{16}$	5			0.64
$\frac{5}{8}$	$1\frac{1}{16}$	$1\frac{3}{32}$	5			0.93
$\frac{3}{4}$	$1\frac{1}{4}$	$1\frac{7}{16}$	5			1.12
$\frac{7}{8}$	$1\frac{7}{16}$	$1\frac{5}{8}$	7	$1\frac{7}{16}$	1	1.75
1	$1\frac{5}{8}$	$1\frac{13}{16}$	7	$1\frac{7}{16}$	$1\frac{1}{8}$	2.46
$1\frac{1}{8}$	$1\frac{13}{16}$	$2\frac{1}{16}$	$7\frac{1}{2}$	$1\frac{5}{8}$	$1\frac{1}{4}$	3.10
$1\frac{1}{4}$	2	$2\frac{1}{4}$	$7\frac{1}{2}$	$1\frac{5}{8}$	$1\frac{3}{8}$	4.04
$1\frac{3}{8}$	$2\frac{3}{16}$	$2\frac{1}{2}$	8	$1\frac{7}{8}$	$1\frac{1}{2}$	4.97
$1\frac{1}{2}$	$2\frac{3}{8}$	$2\frac{11}{16}$	8	$1\frac{7}{8}$	$1\frac{5}{8}$	6.16
$1\frac{5}{8}$	$2\frac{9}{16}$	$2\frac{15}{16}$	$8\frac{1}{2}$	$2\frac{1}{16}$	$1\frac{3}{4}$	7.36
$1\frac{3}{4}$	$2\frac{3}{4}$	$3\frac{1}{8}$	$8\frac{1}{2}$	$2\frac{1}{16}$	$1\frac{7}{8}$	8.87
$1\frac{7}{8}$	$2\frac{15}{16}$	$3\frac{5}{16}$	9	$2\frac{5}{16}$	2	10.42
2	$3\frac{1}{8}$	$3\frac{1}{2}$	9	$2\frac{5}{16}$	$2\frac{1}{8}$	12.24
$2\frac{1}{4}$	$3\frac{1}{2}$	$3\frac{15}{16}$	$9\frac{1}{2}$	$2\frac{1}{2}$	$2\frac{3}{8}$	16.23
$2\frac{1}{2}$	$3\frac{7}{8}$	$4\frac{3}{8}$	10	$2\frac{3}{4}$	$2\frac{5}{8}$	21.12
$2\frac{3}{4}$	$4\frac{1}{4}$	$4\frac{13}{16}$	$10\frac{1}{2}$	$2\frac{13}{16}$	$2\frac{7}{8}$	26.71
3	$4\frac{5}{8}$	$5\frac{1}{4}$	11	$3\frac{3}{16}$	$3\frac{1}{8}$	33.22
$3\frac{1}{4}$	5	$5\frac{5}{8}$	$11\frac{1}{2}$	$3\frac{3}{8}$	$3\frac{3}{8}$	40.62
$3\frac{1}{2}$	$5\frac{3}{8}$	6	12	$3\frac{5}{8}$	$3\frac{5}{8}$	49.07
$3\frac{3}{4}$	$5\frac{3}{4}$	$6\frac{3}{8}$	$12\frac{1}{2}$	$3\frac{13}{16}$	$3\frac{7}{8}$	58.57
4	$6\frac{1}{8}$	$6\frac{7}{8}$	13	$4\frac{1}{16}$	$4\frac{1}{8}$	69.22
$4\frac{1}{4}$	$6\frac{1}{2}$	$7\frac{1}{2}$	$13\frac{1}{2}$	$4\frac{3}{4}$	$4\frac{3}{8}$	75.00
$4\frac{1}{2}$	$6\frac{7}{8}$	$7\frac{15}{16}$	14	5	$4\frac{3}{4}$	90.00
$4\frac{3}{4}$	$7\frac{1}{4}$	$8\frac{3}{8}$	$14\frac{1}{2}$	$5\frac{1}{4}$	5	98.00
5	$7\frac{7}{8}$	$8\frac{7}{8}$	15	$5\frac{1}{2}$	$5\frac{1}{4}$	110.0
$5\frac{1}{4}$	8	$9\frac{1}{4}$	$15\frac{1}{2}$	$5\frac{3}{4}$	$5\frac{1}{2}$	122.0
$5\frac{1}{2}$	$8\frac{3}{8}$	$9\frac{3}{4}$	16	6	$5\frac{3}{4}$	142.0
$5\frac{3}{4}$	$8\frac{3}{4}$	$10\frac{1}{8}$	$16\frac{1}{2}$	$6\frac{1}{4}$	6	157.0
6	$9\frac{1}{8}$	$10\frac{5}{8}$	17	$6\frac{1}{2}$	$6\frac{1}{4}$	176.0

Strengths are greater than the corresponding connecting rod when same material is used

Weights and dimensions are standard as furnished by Cleveland City Forge Company. Similar products of other manufacturers are essentially the same.

Data reproduced by courtesy of AISC, Inc.

RECESSED PIN NUTS AND COTTER PINS

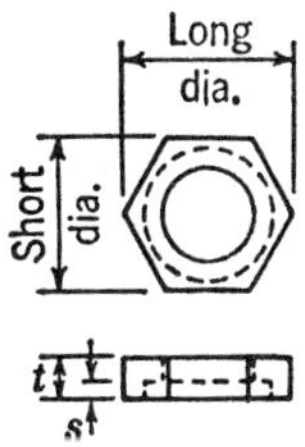

Material: Steel

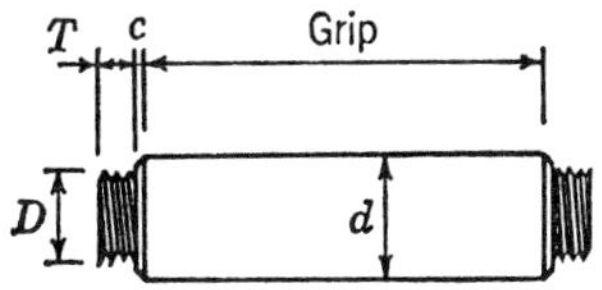

Thread: 6 UN Class 2A/2B

Diameter of Pin d			Pin: Thread D	Pin: Thread T	Pin: c	Nut (Suggested Dimensions): Thickness t	Diameter: Short Diam.	Diameter: Long Diam.	Recess: Rough Diam.	Recess: s	Weight, lb
	2	$2\frac{1}{4}$	$1\frac{1}{2}$	1	$\frac{1}{8}$	$\frac{7}{8}$	3	$3\frac{3}{8}$	$2\frac{5}{8}$	$\frac{1}{4}$	1
	$2\frac{1}{2}$	$2\frac{3}{4}$	2	$1\frac{1}{8}$	$\frac{1}{8}$	1	$3\frac{5}{8}$	$4\frac{1}{8}$	$3\frac{1}{8}$	$\frac{1}{4}$	2
3	$3\frac{1}{4}$	$3\frac{1}{2}$	$2\frac{1}{2}$	$1\frac{1}{4}$	$\frac{1}{8}$	$1\frac{1}{8}$	$4\frac{3}{8}$	5	$3\frac{7}{8}$	$\frac{3}{8}$	3
	$3\frac{3}{4}$	4	3	$1\frac{3}{8}$	$\frac{1}{4}$	$1\frac{1}{4}$	$4\frac{7}{8}$	$5\frac{5}{8}$	$4\frac{3}{8}$	$\frac{3}{8}$	4
$4\frac{1}{4}$	$4\frac{1}{2}$	$4\frac{3}{4}$	$3\frac{1}{2}$	$1\frac{1}{2}$	$\frac{1}{4}$	$1\frac{3}{8}$	$5\frac{3}{4}$	$6\frac{5}{8}$	$5\frac{1}{4}$	$\frac{1}{2}$	5
	5	$5\frac{1}{4}$	4	$1\frac{5}{8}$	$\frac{1}{4}$	$1\frac{1}{2}$	$6\frac{1}{4}$	$7\frac{1}{4}$	$5\frac{3}{4}$	$\frac{1}{2}$	6
$5\frac{1}{2}$	$5\frac{3}{4}$	6	$4\frac{1}{2}$	$1\frac{3}{4}$	$\frac{1}{4}$	$1\frac{5}{8}$	7	$8\frac{1}{8}$	$6\frac{1}{2}$	$\frac{5}{8}$	8
	$6\frac{1}{4}$	$6\frac{1}{2}$	5	$1\frac{7}{8}$	$\frac{3}{8}$	$1\frac{3}{4}$	$7\frac{5}{8}$	$8\frac{7}{8}$	7	$\frac{5}{8}$	10
	$6\frac{3}{4}$	7	$5\frac{1}{2}$	2	$\frac{3}{8}$	$1\frac{7}{8}$	$8\frac{1}{8}$	$9\frac{3}{8}$	$7\frac{1}{2}$	$\frac{3}{4}$	12
	$7\frac{1}{4}$	$7\frac{1}{2}$	$5\frac{1}{2}$	2	$\frac{3}{8}$	$1\frac{7}{8}$	$8\frac{5}{8}$	10	8	$\frac{3}{4}$	14
$7\frac{3}{4}$	8	$8\frac{1}{4}$	6	$2\frac{1}{4}$	$\frac{3}{8}$	$2\frac{1}{8}$	$9\frac{3}{8}$	$10\frac{7}{8}$	$8\frac{3}{4}$	$\frac{3}{4}$	19
$8\frac{1}{2}$	$8\frac{3}{4}$	9	6	$2\frac{1}{4}$	$\frac{3}{8}$	$2\frac{1}{8}$	$10\frac{1}{4}$	$11\frac{7}{8}$	$9\frac{5}{8}$	$\frac{3}{4}$	24
	$9\frac{1}{4}$	$9\frac{1}{2}$	6	$2\frac{3}{8}$	$\frac{3}{8}$	$2\frac{1}{4}$	$11\frac{1}{4}$	13	$10\frac{5}{8}$	$\frac{3}{4}$	32
	$9\frac{3}{4}$	10	6	$2\frac{3}{8}$	$\frac{3}{8}$	$2\frac{1}{4}$	$11\frac{1}{4}$	13	$10\frac{5}{8}$	$\frac{3}{4}$	32

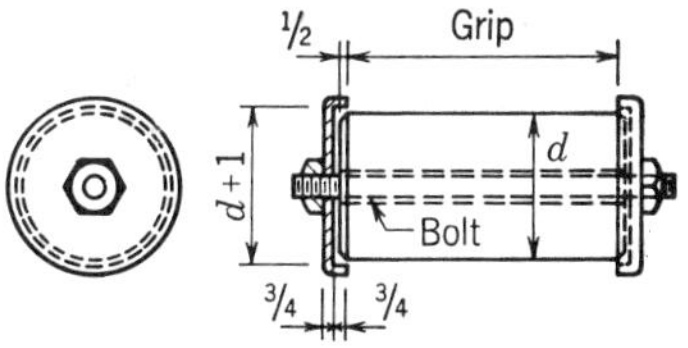

Typical Pin Cap Detail for Pins over 10 in. in Diameter
Dimensions shown are approximate

Although nuts may be used on all sizes of pins as shown above, for pins over 10 in. in diameter the preferred practice is a detail similar to that shown at the left, in which the pin is held in place by a recessed cap at each end and secured by a bolt passing completely through the caps and pin. Suitable provision must be made for attaching pilots and driving nuts.

RECESSED PIN NUTS AND COTTER PINS (Continued)

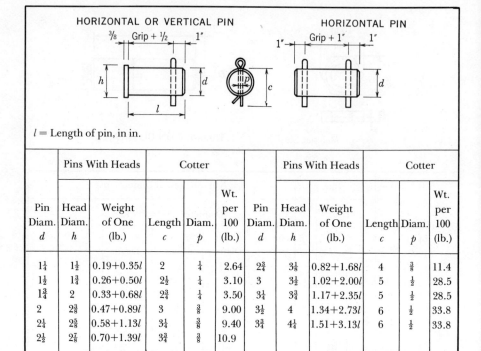

l = Length of pin, in in.

Pin Diam. d	Head Diam. h	Weight of One (lb.)	Length c	Diam. p	Wt. per 100 (lb.)	Pin Diam. d	Head Diam. h	Weight of One (lb.)	Length c	Diam. p	Wt. per 100 (lb.)
$1\frac{1}{4}$	$1\frac{1}{2}$	$0.19+0.35l$	2	$\frac{1}{4}$	2.64	$2\frac{3}{4}$	$3\frac{1}{8}$	$0.82+1.68l$	4	$\frac{3}{8}$	11.4
$1\frac{1}{2}$	$1\frac{3}{4}$	$0.26+0.50l$	$2\frac{1}{2}$	$\frac{1}{4}$	3.10	3	$3\frac{1}{2}$	$1.02+2.00l$	5	$\frac{1}{2}$	28.5
$1\frac{3}{4}$	2	$0.33+0.68l$	$2\frac{3}{4}$	$\frac{1}{4}$	3.50	$3\frac{1}{4}$	$3\frac{3}{4}$	$1.17+2.35l$	5	$\frac{1}{2}$	28.5
2	$2\frac{3}{8}$	$0.47+0.89l$	3	$\frac{3}{8}$	9.00	$3\frac{1}{2}$	4	$1.34+2.73l$	6	$\frac{1}{2}$	33.8
$2\frac{1}{4}$	$2\frac{5}{8}$	$0.58+1.13l$	$3\frac{1}{4}$	$\frac{3}{8}$	9.40	$3\frac{3}{4}$	$4\frac{1}{4}$	$1.51+3.13l$	6	$\frac{1}{2}$	33.8
$2\frac{1}{2}$	$2\frac{7}{8}$	$0.70+1.39l$	$3\frac{3}{4}$	$\frac{3}{8}$	10.9						

Data reproduced by courtesy of AISC, Inc.

PIPE
Dimensions and Properties

Dimension				Weight per Foot lb. Plain Ends	Properties			
Nominal Diameter in.	Outside Diameter in.	Inside Diameter in.	Wall Thickness in.		A in.^{2}	I in.^{4}	S in.^{3}	r in.
Standard Weight								
$\frac{1}{2}$	0.840	0.622	0.109	0.85	0.250	0.017	0.041	0.261
$\frac{3}{4}$	1.050	0.824	0.113	1.13	0.333	0.037	0.071	0.334
1	1.315	1.049	0.133	1.68	0.494	0.087	0.133	0.421
$1\frac{1}{4}$	1.660	1.380	0.140	2.27	0.669	0.195	0.235	0.540
$1\frac{1}{2}$	1.900	1.610	0.145	2.72	0.799	0.310	0.326	0.623
2	2.375	2.067	0.154	3.65	1.07	0.666	0.561	0.787
$2\frac{1}{2}$	2.875	2.469	0.203	5.79	1.70	1.53	1.06	0.947
3	3.500	3.068	0.216	7.58	2.23	3.02	1.72	1.16
$3\frac{1}{2}$	4.000	3.548	0.226	9.11	2.68	4.79	2.39	1.34
4	4.500	4.026	0.237	10.79	3.17	7.23	3.21	1.51
5	5.563	5.047	0.258	14.62	4.30	15.2	5.45	1.88
6	6.625	6.065	0.280	18.97	5.58	28.1	8.50	2.25
8	8.625	7.981	0.322	28.55	8.40	72.5	16.8	2.94
10	10.750	10.020	0.365	40.48	11.9	161	29.9	3.67
12	12.750	12.000	0.375	49.56	14.6	279	43.8	4.38
Extra Strong								
$\frac{1}{2}$	0.840	0.546	0.147	1.09	0.320	0.020	0.048	0.250
$\frac{3}{4}$	1.050	0.742	0.154	1.47	0.433	0.045	0.085	0.321
1	1.315	0.957	0.179	2.17	0.639	0.106	0.161	0.407
$1\frac{1}{4}$	1.660	1.278	0.191	3.00	0.881	0.242	0.291	0.524
$1\frac{1}{2}$	1.900	1.500	0.200	3.63	1.07	0.391	0.412	0.605
2	2.375	1.939	0.218	5.02	1.48	0.868	0.731	0.766
$2\frac{1}{2}$	2.875	2.323	0.276	7.66	2.25	1.92	1.34	0.924
3	3.500	2.900	0.300	10.25	3.02	3.89	2.23	1.14
$3\frac{1}{2}$	4.000	3.364	0.318	12.50	3.68	6.28	3.14	1.31
4	4.500	3.826	0.337	14.98	4.41	9.61	4.27	1.48
5	5.563	4.813	0.375	20.78	6.11	20.7	7.43	1.84
6	6.625	5.761	0.432	28.57	8.40	40.5	12.2	2.19
8	8.625	7.625	0.500	43.39	12.8	106	24.5	2.88
10	10.750	9.750	0.500	54.74	16.1	212	39.4	3.63
12	12.750	11.750	0.500	65.42	19.2	362	56.7	4.33
Double-Extra Strong								
2	2.375	1.503	0.436	9.03	2.66	1.31	1.10	0.703
$2\frac{1}{2}$	2.875	1.771	0.552	13.69	4.03	2.87	2.00	0.844
3	3.500	2.300	0.600	18.58	5.47	5.99	3.42	1.05
4	4.500	3.152	0.674	27.54	8.10	15.3	6.79	1.37
5	5.563	4.063	0.750	38.55	11.3	33.6	12.1	1.72
6	6.625	4.897	0.864	53.16	15.6	66.3	20.0	2.06
8	8.625	6.875	0.875	72.42	21.3	162	37.6	2.76

The listed sections are available in conformance with ASTM Specification A53 Grade B or A501. Other sections are made to these specifications. Consult with pipe manufacturers or distributors for availability.

$F_y = 36$ ksi

COLUMNS

Standard steel pipe
Allowable concentric loads, in kips

Nominal Diameter	12	10	8	6	5	4	$3\frac{1}{2}$	3
Wall Thickness	0.375	0.365	0.322	0.280	0.258	0.237	0.226	0.216
Weight per Foot	49.56	40.48	28.55	18.97	14.62	10.79	9.11	7.58

Effective length in feet KL with respect to radius of gyration	12	10	8	6	5	4	$3\frac{1}{2}$	3
6	303	246	171	110	83	59	48	38
7	301	243	168	108	81	57	46	36
8	299	241	166	106	78	54	44	34
9	296	238	163	103	76	52	41	31
10	293	235	161	101	73	49	38	28
11	291	232	158	98	71	46	35	25
12	288	229	155	95	68	43	32	22
13	285	226	152	92	65	40	29	19
14	282	223	149	89	61	36	25	16
15	278	220	145	86	58	33	22	14
16	275	216	142	82	55	29	19	12
17	272	213	138	79	51	26	17	11
18	268	209	135	75	47	23	15	10
19	265	205	131	71	43	21	14	9
20	261	201	127	67	39	19	12	
22	254	193	119	59	32	15	10	
24	246	185	111	51	27	13		
26	238	176	102	43	23			
28	229	167	93	37	20			
30	220	158	83	32	17			
32	211	148	73	29				
34	201	137	65	25				
36	192	127	58	23				
38	181	115	52					
40	171	104	47					

Properties

	12	10	8	6	5	4	$3\frac{1}{2}$	3
Area A (in.^{2})	14.6	11.9	8.40	5.58	4.30	3.17	2.68	2.23
I (in.^{4})	279.0	161.0	72.5	28.1	15.2	7.23	4.79	3.02
r (in.)	4.38	3.67	2.94	2.25	1.88	1.51	1.34	1.16
B (Bending factor)	0.333	0.398	0.500	0.657	0.789	0.987	1.12	1.29
a (Multiply values by 10^6)	41.7	23.9	10.8	4.21	2.26	1.08	0.717	0.447

Heavy line indicates $Kl/r = 120$. Values omitted for $Kl/r > 200$.

Data reproduced by courtesy of AISC, Inc.

$F_y = 36$ ksi

COLUMNS

Extra Strong Steel Pipe
Allowable concentric loads, in kips

Nominal Diameter		12	10	8	6	5	4	$3\frac{1}{2}$	3
Wall Thickness		0.500	0.500	0.500	0.432	0.375	0.337	0.318	0.300
Weight per Foot		65.42	54.74	43.39	28.57	20.78	14.98	12.50	10.25
Effective length in feet KL with respect to radius of gyration	6	400	332	259	166	118	81	66	52
	7	397	328	255	162	114	78	63	48
	8	394	325	251	159	111	75	59	45
	9	390	321	247	155	107	71	55	41
	10	387	318	243	151	103	67	51	37
	11	383	314	239	146	99	63	47	33
	12	379	309	234	142	95	59	43	28
	13	375	305	229	137	91	54	38	24
	14	371	301	224	132	86	49	33	21
	15	367	296	219	127	81	44	29	18
	16	363	291	214	122	76	39	25	16
	17	358	286	209	116	71	34	23	14
	18	353	281	203	111	65	31	20	12
	19	349	276	197	105	59	28	18	11
	20	344	271	191	99	54	25	16	
	22	334	260	179	86	44	21		
	24	323	248	166	73	37	17		
	26	312	236	152	62	32			
	28	301	224	137	54	27			
	30	289	211	122	47	24			
	32	277	197	107	41				
	34	264	183	95	36				
	36	251	168	85	32				
	38	237	152	76					
	40	223	137	69					
Properties									
Area A (in.^{2})		19.2	16.1	12.8	8.40	6.11	4.41	3.68	3.02
I (in.^{4})		362.0	212.0	106.0	40.5	20.7	9.61	6.28	3.89
r (in.)		4.33	3.63	2.88	2.19	1.84	1.48	1.31	1.14
B (Bending factor)		0.339	0.408	0.521	0.688	0.822	1.03	1.17	1.36
a (Multiply values by 10^6)		53.6	31.6	15.8	6.00	3.08	1.44	0.941	0.585

Heavy line indicates $Kl/r = 120$. Values omitted for $Kl/r > 200$.

Data reproduced by courtesy of AISC, Inc.

$F_y = 36$ ksi

COLUMNS
Double-Extra Strong Steel Pipe
Allowable concentric loads, in kips

Nominal Diameter		8	6	5	4	3
Wall Thickness		0.875	0.864	0.750	0.674	0.600
Weight per Foot		72.42	53.16	38.55	27.54	18.58
	6	431	306	216	147	91
	7	424	299	209	140	84
	8	417	292	202	133	77
	9	410	284	195	126	69
	10	403	275	187	118	60
	11	395	266	178	109	51
	12	387	257	170	100	43
	13	378	247	160	91	37
	14	369	237	151	81	32
	15	360	227	141	70	28
	16	351	216	130	62	24
	17	341	205	119	55	22
	18	331	193	108	49	
	19	321	181	97	44	
	20	310	168	87	40	
	22	288	142	72	33	
	24	264	119	61		
	26	240	102	52		
	28	213	88	44		
	30	187	76			
	32	164	67			
	34	145	60			
	36	130				
	38	116				
	40	105				

Effective length in feet KL with respect to radius of gyration

Properties

		8	6	5	4	3
Area A (in.^{2})		21.3	15.6	11.3	8.10	5.47
I (in.^{4})		162.	66.3	33.6	15.3	5.99
r (in.)		2.76	2.06	1.72	1.37	1.05
B (Bending factor)		0.567	0.781	0.938	1.19	1.60
a (Multiply values by 10^6)		24.2	9.86	4.98	2.27	0.899

Heavy line indicates $Kl/r = 120$. Values omitted for $Kl/r > 200$.

Data reproduced by courtesy of AISC, Inc.

CONCRETE FILLED STEEL PIPE COLUMN LOADS[a]
Concentric loading in kips

Outside Diameter of Column, in.	Weight, lb/ft	Area of Steel, in.²	Area of Concrete, in.²	Unbraced Length of Column, ft											
				6	8	10	12	14	16	18	20	25	30	35	40
Standard Heavyweight Columns															
3½	15	2.23	7.39	45	40	33	26								
4	20	2.68	9.89	58	53	47	39	30							
4½	24	3.17	12.73	72	67	61	54	45	35						
5	29	3.69	15.96	87	82	76	69	61	51	41					
5½	36	4.30	20.01	105	101	95	88	80	71	60	50				
6⅝	49	5.58	28.89	144	140	134	128	120	110	100	88	60			
8⅝	81	8.40	50.03	232	228	223	217	209	200	191	180	148	111	82	
10¾	123	11.91	78.86	347	343	338	332	325	316	307	297	266	228	183	144
12¾	169	14.58	113.10	457	452	448	443	436	427	419	409	379	343	300	250
Extra Heavyweight Columns															
3½	17	3.02	6.61	56	50	42	33	24	18						
4	21	3.68	8.89	72	65	57	48	37	29						
4½	27	4.41	11.50	89	83	76	66	55	44	35					
5½	39	6.11	18.19	131	126	119	110	100	88	75	62				
6⅝	56	8.41	26.07	185	180	173	165	155	143	130	116	79			
8⅝	91	12.76	45.66	297	292	285	277	268	258	245	232	192	145	108	
10¾	133	16.10	74.66	409	404	398	391	383	374	363	350	315	272	220	173
12¾	178	19.24	108.44	527	523	517	511	503	495	484	474	440	400	352	297
Double-Extra Heavyweight Columns															
3½	23	5.47	4.15	89	79	69	52	39							
4	29	6.72	5.86	112	101	88	71	55							
4½	35	8.10	7.80	142	130	117	102	83	67	51					
5½	52	11.34	12.90	205	196	185	170	154	134	112	93				
6⅝	72	15.64	18.86	290	281	270	257	240	220	199	175	118			
8⅝	110	21.30	37.12	423	416	406	395	381	366	349	329	270	204		

[a]Source: Lally Column Co. Based on minimum steel yield point of 35,000 psi and concrete compressive strength of 4,200 psi.

DIMENSIONS OF STANDARD LAG BOLTS OR SCREWS FOR WOOD — CUT THREAD, GIMLET, AND CONE POINT

(All dimensions in inches)

D = nominal diameter
$D_S = D$ = diameter of shank
D_R = diameter at root of thread
W = width of bolt head across flats

H = height of bolt head
L = nominal length of bolt
S = length of shank
T = length of thread

E = length of tapered tip
N = number of threads per inch

Nominal Length of Bolt, l^a	Item	Dimensions of Lag Bolt with Nominal Diameter D of											
		$1/4$	$5/16$	$3/8$	$7/16$	$1/2$	$9/16$	$5/8$	$3/4$	$7/8$	1	$1 1/8$	$1 1/4$
All lengths	$D_S = D$	0.250	0.3125	0.375	0.4375	0.500	0.5625	0.625	0.750	0.875	1.000	1.125	1.250
	D_R	0.173	0.227	0.265	0.328	0.371	0.435	0.471	0.579	0.683	0.780	0.887	1.012
	E	$3/16$	$1/4$	$1/4$	$9/32$	$5/16$	$3/8$	$3/8$	$7/16$	$1/2$	$9/16$	$5/8$	$3/4$
	H	$11/64$	$13/64$	$1/4$	$19/64$	$21/64$	$3/8$	$3/8$	$27/64$	$1/2$	$19/32$	$3/4$	$27/32$
	W	$3/8$	$1/2$	$9/16$	$5/8$	$3/4$	$7/8$	$15/16$	$1 1/8$	$1 5/16$	$1 1/2$	$1 11/16$	$1 7/8$
	N	10	9	7	7	6	6	5	$4 1/2$	4	$3 1/2$	$3 1/4$	$3 1/4$
	D^2	0.0625	0.0977	0.1406	0.1914	0.2500	0.3164	0.3906	0.5625	0.7656	1.0000	1.2656	1.5625
	$D^{3/4}$	0.354	0.418	0.479	0.538	0.595	0.649	0.703	0.806	0.905	1.000	1.0924	1.1822
1	S	$1/4$	$1/4$	$1/4$	$1/4$	$1/4$							
	T	$3/4$	$3/4$	$3/4$	$3/4$	$3/4$							
	$T-E$	$9/16$	$1/2$	$1/2$	$15/32$	$7/16$							
$1 1/2$	S	$3/8$	$3/8$	$3/8$	$3/8$	$3/8$							
	T	$1 1/8$	$1 1/8$	$1 1/8$	$1 1/8$	$1 1/8$							
	$T-E$	$15/16$	$7/8$	$7/8$	$27/32$	$13/16$							
2	S	$1/2$	$1/2$	$1/2$	$1/2$	$1/2$	$1/2$	$1/2$					
	T	$1 1/2$	$1 1/2$	$1 1/2$	$1 1/2$	$1 1/2$	$1 1/2$	$1 1/2$					
	$T-E$	$1 5/16$	$1 1/4$	$1 1/4$	$1 17/32$	$1 3/16$	$1 1/8$	$1 1/8$					
$2 1/2$	S	1	$7/8$	$7/8$	$3/4$	$3/4$	$3/4$	$3/4$					
	T	$1 1/2$	$1 5/8$	$1 5/8$	$1 3/4$	$1 3/4$	$1 3/4$	$1 3/4$					
	$T-E$	$1 5/16$	$1 3/8$	$1 3/8$	$1 15/32$	$1 7/16$	$1 3/8$	$1 3/8$					
3	S	1	1	1	1	1	1	1	1	1	1		
	T	2	2	2	2	2	2	2	2	2	2		
	$T-E$	$1 13/16$	$1 3/4$	$1 3/4$	$1 23/32$	$1 11/16$	$1 5/8$	$1 5/8$	$1 9/16$	$1 1/2$	$1 7/16$		
4	S	$1 1/2$	$1 1/2$	$1 1/2$	$1 1/2$	$1 1/2$	$1 1/2$	$1 1/2$	$1 1/2$	$1 1/2$	$1 1/2$	$1 1/2$	$1 1/2$
	T	$2 1/2$	$2 1/2$	$2 1/2$	$2 1/2$	$2 1/2$	$2 1/2$	$2 1/2$	$2 1/2$	$2 1/2$	$2 1/2$	$2 1/2$	$2 1/2$
	$T-E$	$2 5/16$	$2 1/4$	$2 1/4$	$2 7/32$	$2 3/16$	$2 1/8$	$2 1/8$	$2 1/8$	$2 1/16$	2	$1 15/16$	$1 3/4$
5	S	2	2	2	2	2	2	2	2	2	2	2	2
	T	3	3	3	3	3	3	3	3	3	3	3	3
	$T-E$	$2 13/16$	$2 3/4$	$2 3/4$	$2 23/32$	$2 11/16$	$2 5/8$	$2 5/8$	$2 9/16$	$2 1/2$	$2 7/16$	$2 3/8$	$2 1/4$
6	S	$2 1/2$	$2 1/2$	$2 1/2$	$2 1/2$	$2 1/2$	$2 1/2$	$2 1/2$	$2 1/2$	$2 1/2$	$2 1/2$	$2 1/2$	$2 1/2$
	T	$3 1/2$	$3 1/2$	$3 1/2$	$3 1/2$	$3 1/2$	$3 1/2$	$3 1/2$	$3 1/2$	$3 1/2$	$3 1/2$	$3 1/2$	$3 1/2$
	$T-E$	$3 5/16$	$3 1/4$	$3 1/4$	$3 7/32$	$3 3/16$	$3 1/8$	$3 1/8$	$3 1/16$	3	$2 15/16$	$2 7/8$	$2 3/4$
7	S	3	3	3	3	3	3	3	3	3	3	3	3
	T	4	4	4	4	4	4	4	4	4	4	4	4
	$T-E$	$3 13/16$	$3 3/4$	$3 3/4$	$3 23/32$	$3 11/16$	$3 5/8$	$3 5/8$	$3 9/16$	$3 1/2$	$3 7/16$	$3 3/8$	$3 1/4$

^{a}Length of thread T on intervening bolt lengths is the same as that of the next shorter bolt length listed. The length of thread, T, on standard bolt lengths, L, in excess of 12 in. is equal to $1/2$ the bolt length, $L/2$.

DIMENSIONS OF STANDARD LAG BOLTS OR SCREWS FOR WOOD — CUT THREAD, GIMLET, AND CONE POINT

(All dimensions in inches)

D = nominal diameter
D_S = D = diameter of shank
D_R = diameter at root of thread
W = width of bolt head across flats

H = height of bolt head
L = nominal length of bolt
S = length of shank
T = length of thread

E = length of tapered tip
N = number of threads per inch

Nominal Length of Bolt, l[a]	Item	Dimensions of Lag Bolt with Nominal Diameter D of											
		$\frac{1}{4}$	$\frac{5}{16}$	$\frac{3}{8}$	$\frac{7}{16}$	$\frac{1}{2}$	$\frac{9}{16}$	$\frac{5}{8}$	$\frac{3}{4}$	$\frac{7}{8}$	1	$1\frac{1}{8}$	$1\frac{1}{4}$
All lengths	D_S=D	0.250	0.3125	0.375	0.4375	0.500	0.5625	0.625	0.750	0.875	1.000	1.125	1.250
	D_R	0.173	0.227	0.265	0.328	0.371	0.435	0.471	0.579	0.683	0.780	0.887	1.012
	E	$\frac{3}{16}$	$\frac{1}{4}$	$\frac{1}{4}$	$\frac{9}{32}$	$\frac{5}{16}$	$\frac{3}{8}$	$\frac{3}{8}$	$\frac{7}{16}$	$\frac{1}{2}$	$\frac{9}{16}$	$\frac{5}{8}$	$\frac{3}{4}$
	H	$\frac{11}{64}$	$\frac{13}{64}$	$\frac{1}{4}$	$\frac{19}{64}$	$\frac{21}{64}$	$\frac{3}{8}$	$\frac{27}{64}$	$\frac{1}{2}$	$\frac{19}{32}$	$\frac{21}{32}$	$\frac{3}{4}$	$\frac{27}{32}$
	W	$\frac{3}{8}$	$\frac{1}{2}$	$\frac{9}{16}$	$\frac{5}{8}$	$\frac{3}{4}$	$\frac{7}{8}$	$\frac{15}{16}$	$1\frac{1}{8}$	$1\frac{5}{16}$	$1\frac{1}{2}$	$1\frac{11}{16}$	$1\frac{7}{8}$
	N	10	9	7	7	6	6	5	$4\frac{1}{2}$	4	$3\frac{1}{2}$	$3\frac{1}{4}$	$3\frac{1}{4}$
	D'	0.0625	0.0977	0.1406	0.1914	0.2500	0.3164	0.3906	0.5625	0.7656	1.0000	1.2656	1.5625
	$D^{3/4}$	0.354	0.418	0.479	0.538	0.595	0.649	0.703	0.806	0.905	1.000	1.0924	1.1822
1	S	$\frac{1}{4}$	$\frac{1}{4}$	$\frac{1}{4}$	$\frac{1}{4}$	$\frac{1}{4}$							
	T	$\frac{3}{4}$	$\frac{3}{4}$	$\frac{3}{4}$	$\frac{3}{4}$	$\frac{3}{4}$							
	$T-E$	$\frac{9}{16}$	$\frac{1}{2}$	$\frac{1}{2}$	$\frac{15}{32}$	$\frac{7}{16}$							
8	S	$3\frac{1}{2}$	$3\frac{1}{2}$	$3\frac{1}{2}$	$3\frac{1}{2}$	$3\frac{1}{2}$	$3\frac{1}{2}$	$3\frac{1}{2}$	$3\frac{1}{2}$	$3\frac{1}{2}$	$3\frac{1}{2}$	$3\frac{1}{2}$	$3\frac{1}{2}$
	T	$4\frac{1}{2}$	$4\frac{1}{2}$	$4\frac{1}{2}$	$4\frac{1}{2}$	$4\frac{1}{2}$	$4\frac{1}{2}$	$4\frac{1}{2}$	$4\frac{1}{2}$	$4\frac{1}{2}$	$4\frac{1}{2}$	$4\frac{1}{2}$	$4\frac{1}{2}$
	$T-E$	$4\frac{5}{16}$	$4\frac{1}{4}$	$4\frac{1}{4}$	$4\frac{7}{32}$	$4\frac{3}{16}$	$4\frac{1}{8}$	$4\frac{1}{8}$	$4\frac{1}{16}$	4	$3\frac{15}{16}$	$3\frac{7}{8}$	$3\frac{3}{4}$
9	S	4	4	4	4	4	4	4	4	4	4	4	4
	T	5	5	5	5	5	5	5	5	5	5	5	5
	$T-E$	$4\frac{13}{16}$	$4\frac{3}{4}$	$4\frac{3}{4}$	$4\frac{23}{32}$	$4\frac{11}{16}$	$4\frac{5}{8}$	$4\frac{5}{8}$	$4\frac{9}{16}$	$4\frac{1}{2}$	$4\frac{7}{16}$	$4\frac{3}{8}$	$4\frac{1}{4}$
10	S	$4\frac{3}{4}$	$4\frac{3}{4}$	$4\frac{3}{4}$	$4\frac{3}{4}$	$4\frac{3}{4}$	$4\frac{3}{4}$	$4\frac{3}{4}$	$4\frac{3}{4}$	$4\frac{3}{4}$	$4\frac{3}{4}$	$4\frac{3}{4}$	$4\frac{3}{4}$
	T	$5\frac{1}{4}$	$5\frac{1}{4}$	$5\frac{1}{4}$	$5\frac{1}{4}$	$5\frac{1}{4}$	$5\frac{1}{4}$	$5\frac{1}{4}$	$5\frac{1}{4}$	$5\frac{1}{4}$	$5\frac{1}{4}$	$5\frac{1}{4}$	$5\frac{1}{4}$
	$T-E$	$5\frac{1}{16}$	5	5	$4\frac{31}{32}$	$4\frac{15}{16}$	$4\frac{7}{8}$	$4\frac{7}{8}$	$4\frac{13}{16}$	$4\frac{3}{4}$	$4\frac{11}{16}$	$4\frac{5}{8}$	$4\frac{1}{2}$
11	S	$5\frac{1}{2}$	$5\frac{1}{2}$	$5\frac{1}{2}$	$5\frac{1}{2}$	$5\frac{1}{2}$	$5\frac{1}{2}$	$5\frac{1}{2}$	$5\frac{1}{2}$	$5\frac{1}{2}$	$5\frac{1}{2}$	$5\frac{1}{2}$	$5\frac{1}{2}$
	T	$5\frac{1}{2}$	$5\frac{1}{2}$	$5\frac{1}{2}$	$5\frac{1}{2}$	$5\frac{1}{2}$	$5\frac{1}{2}$	$5\frac{1}{2}$	$5\frac{1}{2}$	$5\frac{1}{2}$	$5\frac{1}{2}$	$5\frac{1}{2}$	$5\frac{1}{2}$
	$T-E$	$5\frac{9}{32}$	$5\frac{1}{4}$	$5\frac{1}{4}$	$5\frac{7}{32}$	$5\frac{3}{16}$	$5\frac{1}{8}$	$5\frac{1}{8}$	$5\frac{1}{16}$	5	$4\frac{15}{16}$	$4\frac{7}{8}$	$4\frac{3}{4}$
12	S	6	6	6	6	6	6	6	6	6	6	6	6
	T	6	6	6	6	6	6	6	6	6	6	6	6
	$T-E$	$5\frac{13}{16}$	$5\frac{3}{4}$	$5\frac{3}{4}$	$5\frac{23}{32}$	$5\frac{11}{16}$	$5\frac{5}{8}$	$5\frac{5}{8}$	$5\frac{9}{16}$	$5\frac{1}{2}$	$5\frac{7}{16}$	$5\frac{3}{8}$	$5\frac{1}{4}$

[a]Length of thread T on intervening bolt lengths is the same as that of the next shorter bolt length listed. The length of thread, T, on standard bolt lengths, L, in excess of 12 in. is equal to $\frac{1}{2}$ the bolt length, $L/2$.

Printed through courtesy of the National Forest Products Association.

1-1

RIVETS AND THREADED FASTENERS
Bearing
Allowable loads in kips
All rivets and bolts in bearing type connections

Diam., in.	7/8								1							
F_y, ksi	36	42	45	50	55	60	65	100	36	42	45	50	55	60	65	100
Bearing F_p, ksi	48.6	58.7	60.8	67.5	74.3	81.0	87.8	135	48.6	56.7	60.8	67.5	74.3	81.0	87.8	135
Material Thickness																
1/8	5.32	6.20	6.65	7.38	8.13	8.86	9.60	14.8	6.08	7.09	7.60	8.44	9.29	10.1	11.0	16.9
3/16	7.97	9.30	9.98	11.1	12.2	13.3	14.4	22.1	9.11	10.6	11.4	12.7	13.9	15.2	16.5	25.3
1/4	10.6	12.4	13.3	14.8	16.3	17.7	19.2	29.5	12.2	14.2	15.2	16.9	18.6	20.3	22.0	33.8
5/16	13.3	15.5	16.6	18.5	20.3	22.1	24.0	36.9	15.2	17.7	19.0	21.1	23.2	25.3	27.4	42.2
3/8	15.9	18.6	20.0	22.1	24.4	26.6	28.8	44.3	18.2	21.3	22.8	25.3	27.9	30.4	32.9	50.6
7/16	18.6	21.7	23.3	25.8	28.4	31.0	33.6	51.7	21.3	24.8	26.6	29.5	32.5	35.4	38.4	59.1
1/2	21.3	24.8	26.6	29.5	32.5	35.4	38.4	59.1	24.3	28.4	30.4	33.8	37.2	40.5	43.9	67.5
9/16	23.9	27.9	29.9	33.2	36.6	39.9	43.2	66.4	27.3	31.9	34.2	38.0	41.8	45.6	49.4	75.9
5/8	26.6	31.0	33.3	36.9	40.6			73.8	30.4	35.4	38.0	42.2	46.4	50.6	54.9	84.4
11/16	29.2	34.1	36.6	40.6				81.2	33.4	39.0	41.8	46.4	51.1			92.8
3/4	31.9	37.2	39.9					88.6	36.5	42.5	45.6	50.6				101
13/16	34.6	40.3						96.0	39.5	46.1	49.4					110
7/8	37.2							103	42.5	49.6	53.2					118
15/16	39.9							111	45.6	53.2						127
1	42.5	49.6	53.2	59.1	65.0	70.9	76.8	118	48.6	56.7	60.8	67.5	74.3	81.0	87.8	135
1-1/16	49.6							126	51.6							143

This table not applicable to fasteners in friction type connections.

F_y is the yield stress of the connected material; see *AISC Specification*, Sect. 1.5.2.2.

F_p, the unit bearing stress, applies equally to conditions of single shear and enclosed bearing.

Values for thicknesses not listed may be obtained by multiplying the unlisted thickness by the value given for a 1 in. thickness in the appropriate F_y column.

Values for F_y's not listed may be obtained by multiplying the value given for $F_y = 100$ ksi by the unlisted F_y and dividing by 100.

Data reproduced by courtesy of AISC, Inc.

RIVETS AND THREADED FASTENERS
Shear, Allowable loads in kips

$\frac{5}{8}-\frac{3}{4}$

Power-Driven Shop and Field Rivets				
Diameter — Area	$\frac{5}{8}$ in.–0.3068 in.^{2}		$\frac{3}{4}$ in.–0.4418 in.^{2}	
ASTM Designation	A502-1	A502-2	A502-1	A502-2
Shear F_v, ksi	15.0	20.0	15.0	20.0
Single Shear, kips Double Shear, kips	4.60 9.20	6.14 12.27	6.63 13.25	8.84 17.67

Unfinished Bolts, ASTM A307, and Threaded Parts, $F_y = 36$ ksi[a]				
Diameter — Area	$\frac{5}{8}$ in.–0.3068 in.^{2}		$\frac{3}{4}$ in.–0.4418 in.^{2}	
ASTM Designation or Yield Stress, ksi	A307	$F_y = 36$	A307	$F_y = 36$
Shear F_v, ksi	10.0	10.8[a]	10.0	10.8[a]
Single Shear, kips Double Shear, kips	3.07 6.14	3.31 6.63	4.42 8.84	4.77 9.54

High Strength Bolts in Friction Type Connections and in Bearing Type Connections with Threads in Shear Planes						
Diameter — Area	$\frac{5}{8}$ in.–0.3068 in.^{2}			$\frac{3}{4}$ in.–0.4418 in.^{2}		
[b]ASTM Designation	A325-F A325-N	A490-F	A490-N	A325-F A325-N	A490-F	A490-N
Shear F_v, ksi	15.0	20.0	22.5	15.0	20.0	22.5
Single Shear, kips Double Shear, kips	4.60 9.20	6.14 12.27	6.90 13.81	6.63 13.25	8.84 17.67	9.94 19.88

High Strength Bolts in Bearing Type Connections with Threads Excluded from Shear Planes				
Diameter — Area	$\frac{5}{8}$ in.–0.3068 in.^{2}		$\frac{3}{4}$ in.–0.4418 in.^{2}	
[b]ASTM Designation	A325-X	A490-X	A325-X	A490-X
Shear F_v, ksi	22.0	32.0	22.0	32.0
Single Shear, kips Double Shear, kips	6.75 13.50	9.82 19.64	9.72 19.44	14.14 28.28

[a]For threaded parts of material other than $F_y = 36$ ksi steel, use $F_v = 0.30 F_y$.
[b]The letter suffixes following the ASTM Designations A325 and A490 represent the following:
 F: Friction type connection
 N: Bearing type connection with threads included in shear plane
 X: Bearing type connection with threads excluded from shear plane

Data reproduced by courtesy of AISC, Inc.

$\frac{7}{8}$-1   RIVETS AND THREADED FASTENERS
Shear, Allowable loads in kips

Power-Driven Shop and Field Rivets

Diameter — Area	$\frac{7}{8}$ in.–0.6013 in.^{2}		1 in.–0.7854 in.^{2}	
ASTM Designation	A502-1	A502-2	A502-1	A502-2
Shear F_v, ksi	15.0	20.0	15.0	20.0
Single Shear, kips	9.02	12.03	11.78	15.71
Double Shear, kips	18.04	24.05	23.56	31.42

Unfinished Bolts, ASTM A307, and Threaded Parts, $F_y = 36$ ksi[a]

Diameter — Area	$\frac{7}{8}$ in.–0.6013 in.^{2}		1 in.–0.7854 in.^{2}	
ASTM Designation or Yield Stress, ksi	A307	$F_y = 36$	A307	$F_y = 36$
Shear F_v, ksi	10.0	10.8[a]	10.0	10.8[a]
Single Shear, kips	6.01	6.49	7.85	8.48
Double Shear, kips	12.03	12.99	15.71	16.96

High Strength Bolts in Friction Type Connections and in Bearing Type Connections with Threads in Shear Planes

Diameter — Area	$\frac{7}{8}$ in.–0.6013 in.^{2}			1 in.–0.7854 in.^{2}		
[b]ASTM Designation	A325-F A325-N	A490-F	A490-N	A325-F A325-N	A490-F	A490-N
Shear F_v, ksi	15.0	20.0	22.5	15.0	20.0	22.5
Single Shear, kips	9.02	12.03	13.53	11.78	15.71	17.67
Double Shear, kips	18.04	24.05	27.06	23.56	31.42	35.34

High Strength Bolts in Bearing Type Connections with Threads Excluded from Shear Planes

Diameter — Area	$\frac{7}{8}$ in. — 0.6013 in.^{2}		1 in. — 0.7854 in.^{2}	
[b]ASTM Designation	A325-X	A490-X	A325-X	A490-X
Shear F_v, ksi	22.0	32.0	22.0	32.0
Single Shear, kips	13.23	19.24	17.28	25.13
Double Shear, kips	26.46	38.48	34.56	50.27

[a]For threaded parts of material other than $F_y = 36$ ksi steel, use $F_v = 0.30\, F_y$.
[b]The letter suffixes following the ASTM Designations A325 and A490 represent the following:
  F: Friction type connection
  N: Bearing type connection with threads included in shear plane
  X: Bearing type connection with threads excluded from shear plane

RIVETS AND THREADED FASTENERS
Bearing
Allowable loads in kips
All rivets and bolts in bearing type connections

Diam. = 5/8 in.

Material Thickness	36	42	45	50	55	60	65	100
F_y, ksi → Bearing F_p, ksi	48.6	56.7	60.8	67.5	74.3	81.0	87.8	135
1/8	3.80	4.43	4.75	5.27	5.80	6.33	6.86	10.5
3/16	5.70	6.64	7.13	7.91	8.71	9.49	10.3	15.8
1/4	7.59	8.86	9.50	10.6	11.6	12.7	13.7	21.1
5/16	9.49	11.1	11.9	13.2	14.5	15.8	17.1	26.4
3/8	11.4	13.3	14.3	15.8	17.4	19.0	20.6	31.6
7/16	13.3	15.5	16.6	18.5	20.3	22.1		36.9
1/2	15.2	17.7	19.0	21.1				42.2
9/16	17.1	19.9	21.4					47.5
5/8	19.0							52.7
11/16	20.9							58.0
3/4								63.3
13/16								68.6
7/8								73.8
15/16								79.1
1	30.4	35.4	38.0	42.2	46.4	50.6	54.9	84.4

Diam. = 3/4 in.

Material Thickness	36	42	45	50	55	60	65	100
F_y, ksi → Bearing F_p, ksi	48.6	56.7	60.8	67.5	74.3	81.0	87.8	135
1/8	4.56	5.31	5.70	6.33	6.97	7.59	8.23	12.7
3/16	6.83	7.97	8.55	9.49	10.4	11.4	12.3	19.0
1/4	9.11	10.6	11.4	12.7	13.9	15.2	16.5	25.3
5/16	11.4	13.3	14.3	15.8	17.4	19.0	20.6	31.6
3/8	13.7	15.9	17.1	19.0	20.9	22.8	24.7	38.0
7/16	15.9	18.6	19.9	22.1	24.4	26.6	28.8	44.3
1/2	18.2	21.3	22.8	25.3	27.9	30.4		50.6
9/16	20.5	23.9	25.7	28.5	31.3			57.0
5/8	22.8	26.5	28.5					63.3
11/16	25.1	29.2						69.6
3/4	27.3							75.9
13/16	29.6							82.3
7/8								88.6
15/16								94.9
1	36.5	42.5	45.6	50.6	55.7	60.8	65.9	101

This table not applicable to fasteners in friction type connections.

F_y is the yield stress of the connected material; see AISC Specification, Sect. 1.5.2.2.

F_p, the unit bearing stress, applies equally to conditions of single shear and enclosed bearing.

Values for thicknesses not listed may be obtained by multiplying the unlisted thickness by the value given for a 1 in. thickness in the appropriate F_p column.

Values for F_y's not listed may be obtained by multiplying the value given for $F_y = 100$ ksi by the unlisted F_y and dividing by 100.

Data reproduced by courtesy of AISC, Inc.

RIVETS AND THREADED FASTENERS

Bearing

Allowable loads in kips
All rivets and bolts in bearing type connections

Material Thickness = ⅞

Diam., in.	F_y, ksi 36	42	45	50	55	60	65	100
Bearing F_p, ksi	48.6	56.7	60.8	67.5	74.3	81.0	87.8	135
⅛	5.32	6.20	6.65	7.38	8.13	8.86	9.60	14.8
3/16	7.97	9.30	9.98	11.1	12.2	13.3	14.4	22.1
¼	10.6	12.4	13.3	14.8	16.3	17.7	19.2	29.5
5/16	13.3	15.5	16.6	18.5	20.3	22.1	24.0	36.9
⅜	15.9	18.6	20.0	22.1	24.4	26.6	28.8	44.3
7/16	18.6	21.7	23.3	25.8	28.4	31.0	33.6	51.7
½	21.3	24.8	26.6	29.5	32.5	35.4	38.4	59.1
9/16	23.9	27.9	29.9	33.2	36.6	39.9	43.2	66.4
⅝	26.6	31.0	33.3	36.9	40.6			73.8
11/16	29.2	34.1	36.6	40.6				81.2
¾	31.9	37.2	39.9					88.6
13/16	34.6	40.3						96.0
⅞	37.2							103
15/16	39.9							111
1	42.5	49.6	53.2	59.1	65.0	70.9	76.8	118
1 1/16								126

Material Thickness = 1

Diam., in.	F_y, ksi 36	42	45	50	55	60	65	100
Bearing F_p, ksi	48.6	56.7	60.8	67.5	74.3	81.0	87.8	135
⅛	6.08	7.09	7.60	8.44	9.29	10.1	11.0	16.9
3/16	9.11	10.6	11.4	12.7	13.9	15.2	16.5	25.3
¼	12.2	14.2	15.2	16.9	18.6	20.3	22.0	33.8
5/16	15.2	17.7	19.0	21.1	23.2	25.3	27.4	42.2
⅜	18.2	21.3	22.8	25.3	27.9	30.4	32.9	50.6
7/16	21.3	24.8	26.6	29.5	32.5	35.4	38.4	59.1
½	24.3	28.4	30.4	33.8	37.2	40.5	43.9	67.5
9/16	27.3	31.9	34.2	38.0	41.8	45.6	49.4	75.9
⅝	30.4	35.4	38.0	42.2	46.4	50.6	54.9	84.4
11/16	33.4	39.0	41.8	46.4	51.1			92.8
¾	36.5	42.5	45.6	50.6				101
13/16	39.5	46.1	49.4					110
⅞	42.5	49.6	53.2					118
15/16	45.6	53.2						127
1	48.6	56.7	60.8	67.5	74.3	81.0	87.8	135
1 1/16	51.6							143

This table not applicable to fasteners in friction type connections.

F_y is the yield stress of the connected material; see AISC Specification, Sect. 1.5.2.2.

F_p, the unit bearing stress, applies equally to conditions of single shear and enclosed bearing.

Values for thicknesses not listed may be obtained by multiplying the unlisted thickness by the value given for a 1 in. thickness in the appropriate F_p column.

Values for F_p's not listed may be obtained by multiplying the value given for F_y = 100 ksi by the unlisted F_y and dividing by 100.

ANCHOR BOLT LOAD VALUES
FOR STEEL BASE SHOES[a]

Bolt Diameter, in.	Allowable Shear Load,[b] lb	Embedment in Concrete, in.
$\frac{1}{2}$	1,500	4
$\frac{5}{8}$	2,200	4
$\frac{3}{4}$	3,000	5
$\frac{7}{8}$	3,500	6
1	4,000	8
$1\frac{1}{4}$	5,000	8
$1\frac{1}{2}$	7,000	9
$1\frac{3}{4}$	9,000	9
2	11,000	10
$2\frac{1}{4}$	13,500	10
$2\frac{1}{2}$	16,000	12
$2\frac{3}{4}$	19,000	12
3	22,000	14

[a]Source: American Concrete Institute.
[b]Based on concrete strength of 3,000 psi and bolt yield stress of 50,000 psi.

Part II

DESIGN SPECIFICATIONS

AMERICAN INSTITUTE
333 West Hampden Avenue

TIMBER CONSTRUCTION
Englewood, Colorado 80110

AITC 101-72
STANDARD DEFINITIONS,
ABBREVIATIONS, AND REFERENCES

Adopted as Recommendations March 17, 1969
Copyright 1972 by American Institute of Timber Construction

CONTENTS

1. DEFINITIONS

(As used in AITC documents and industry practice.)

Adhesive. A substance capable of holding materials together by bonding of contact surfaces.

Adhesives, Dry-Use. Adhesives that perform satisfactorily when the moisture content of the wood does not exceed 16% for repeated or prolonged periods of service.

Adhesives, Wet-Use. Adhesives that perform satisfactorily for all conditions of service including exposure to weather, dry use, marine use, and pressure treatment.

Ambient. Surrounding or encompassing.

Assembly. The process of fastening together, by means of hand or portable tools, fabricated components of structural timber framing with nails, bolts, connectors, and/or other fastening devices to form larger components or subassemblies of a structural frame. Assembly in a fabricating plant (shop assembly) or at the job site (field assembly) is included. In the manufacture of structural glued laminated timber the term *assembly* refers to that part of the manufacturing procedure in which individual laminations, after being spread with adhesive, are collected together in the clamping jig, form, or press where pressure is applied.

Assembly Time. The time interval between the spreading of the adhesive on

1

the laminations and the application of final pressure or heat or both to the entire assembly. Assembly time is composed of two parts, open and closed.

1. *Open Assembly Time.* The time elapsed between spreading the adhesive and assembling the spread surfaces into close contact with one another.
2. *Closed Assembly Time.* The time elapsed from the assembly of the first laminations of the package into intimate contact until final application of pressure or heat or both to the entire package.

Batch. A term generally used by adhesive manufacturers to identify a "lot" or a "blending" or "cook" of adhesive. (Generally speaking, the weight may vary from 2,500 to 10,000 lb for casein adhesives and from 500 to 2,000 lb for resin adhesives; these figures are representative only, and variations may be wide.)

Block Shear (test). A method of testing wood or glue lines for shear strength.

Board. Lumber less than 2 in. thick and 1 or more inches wide. (Boards less than 6 in. wide may be classified as strips.)

Bonding. Joining materials together with adhesive.

Bracing. Structural elements installed to provide restraint, support, or both to other members to enable them to function so that the complete assembly will form a stable structure. Bracing may be in lateral, longitudinal, and transverse planes and may consist of sway, cross, vertical, diagonal, horizontal, and similar elements to resist wind, earthquake, erection, and other forces. It may consist of knee braces, cables, rods, struts, ties, shores, diaphragms, rigid frames, and similar items and combinations which serve the aforementioned functions.

Bracing, Erection. Bracing installed to hold the framework in a safe condition until sufficient permanent construction is in place to provide full stability.

Bracing, Permanent. Bracing so designed and installed as to form an integral part of the final structure. Some or all of the permanent bracing may also act as erection bracing.

Break. A fracture of the wood fibers across the grain caused by external forces.

Buyer. The purchaser. (The term is used to designate the purchaser and/or owner of the structure and includes the architect, engineer, general contractor, public authority, or other designated representative of the owner.)

Calibration. The operation of determining a relationship between the actual values being measured and the values indicated by the equipment used for the measurement.

Certificate. A document which may be furnished in conjunction with identification marks to provide certification by the laminator that the work conforms with Voluntary Product Standard PS56-73, *Structural Glued Laminated Timber,* and with the job specifications, and certification by a central organization that the quality control of the plant is under its general surveillance.

Check. A separation of the wood grain due to internal stresses caused by severe moisture cycling or seasoning.

Chord. See Truss Chord.

Clamp. A device for application of uniform pressure on a laminating package.

Closed Assembly Time. See Assembly Time.

Compliance. "Compliance" or "conformance" in respect to any applicable provision of a standard shall be deemed to mean "compliance" or "conformance" therewith in all substantial respects.

Composite. A structural element consisting of wood and combinations of other materials in which all pieces are attached together to act as a single unit.

Compressometer. A device for measuring force or pressure. (In inspection work it may be used for calibrating torque wrenches.)

Curing Time. The period of time an adhesive takes to attain its full strength.

Custom Products. Products manufactured for a specific use.

Delamination. The separation of layers in an assembly because of failure of the adhesive, either in the adhesive itself or at the interface between the adhesive and the lamination. Delamination in glue joints is the result of failure either in the adhesive itself (cohesive failure) or at the wood-adhesive interface.

Depth. The dimension of the cross section that is measured parallel to the direction of the principal load on the member in bending.

Diaphragm. A relatively thin, usually rectangular element of a structure that is capable of withstanding shear in its plane. By its rigidity, it limits the deflection or deformation of other parts of the structure. Diaphragms may have a plane or curved surface.

Dielectric Heating. The process of generating heat at high frequencies in nonconducting materials by placing them in a strong alternating electric field. (This is generally accomplished by placing the material between a pair of metal plates called electrodes. The alternating electric field stresses the molecules of the material first in one direction and then in the other. This molecular stress or agitation produces heat. The higher the frequency of the R.F. voltage, the more rapid is the molecular agitation and, therefore, the heating. For this reason dielectric heating of the glue line is done at very high frequencies – millions of cycles per second.)

Dry Use. Normal use conditions where the moisture content of the wood in service does not exceed 16%, as in most covered structures. (*See also* Adhesives, Dry-Use.)

Durability. As applied to glue lines, the life expectancy of the structural qualities of the adhesive under the anticipated service conditions of the structure.

Equilibrium Moisture Content. (Any piece of wood gives off or takes in moisture from the surrounding atmosphere until the amount of moisture in the wood balances that in the atmosphere.) The moisture content of the wood at the point of balance, is expressed as a percentage of the oven-dry weight of the wood.

Erection. The hoisting and/or installing in place in the final structure of fabricated components. Cranes, hoists, and other powered equipment are generally used.

Fabricated Structural Timber. Engineered load-carrying elements of wood (including sawn lumber and/or timber, glued laminated timber, and mechanically laminated timber) that are shop-fabricated for use in frames of all kinds including but not limited to trusses, arches, beams, girders, and columns for use in schools, churches, commercial, industrial, and other buildings and for other structures such as bridges, towers, and marine installations. Components made of structural glued laminated timber should be produced in accordance with Voluntary Product Standard PS56-73, *Structural Glued Laminated Timber*.

Fabrication. Boring, cutting, sawing, trimming, dapping, routing, planing, and/or otherwise shaping and/or framing and/or furnishing wood units, sawn or laminated, including plywood, to fit them for particular places in a final structure.

Field Assembly. See Assembly.

Frame Construction. Wood framing similar to that which conforms with all requirements of *frame construction* as described in model building codes.

Glue. See Adhesive.

Glued Built-Up. Structural elements consisting of wood, plywood, or combinations of the two, in which the grain is not necessarily parallel and in which all pieces are bonded together with adhesive.

Glued Laminated. See Structural Glued Laminated Timber.

Gluing. The operation of edge, face, or end joining together of pieces or laminations with adhesives.

Heavy Timber Construction. Construction in which fire resistance is attained by placing limitations on the minimum size, thickness, or composition of all load-carrying wood members; by avoiding concealed spaces under floors and roofs; by using approved fastenings, construction details, and adhesives; and by providing the required degree of fire resistance in exterior and interior walls.

Hot Service. Normal use conditions in which the wood members may remain at temperatures of 150°F or above, continuously or for prolonged periods of time.

Identification Mark. A stamp, brand, label, or other mark that is owned and administered by a qualified central inspection organization and that is applied to a product by licensed manufacturers to evidence conformance with Voluntary Product Standard PS56-73, *Structural Glued Laminated Timber*, and with the job specifications. Such marks include identification of: PS56-73, the qualified central inspection organization, and the producing plant. In addition, the marks may identify species, allowable unit stresses, wet or dry use, and appearance grade.

In-Line Tests and/or Checking. Testing and/or checking conducted during manufacture rather than on the finished product.

Inserts. Nonstructural repairs to correct appearance defects.

Inspection. The process of measuring materials and methods for conformance with quality controls and/or standards.

Job Specifications. All agreements between buyer and seller for fabricated structural timber in a project.

Joint Area. The area of the glue line, usually expressed in square feet (i.e., 75 lb of glue spread to 1,000 ft² of joint area; this means that the quantity 75 lb of glue is contained within the 1,000 ft^2 of glue-line area bonding adjacent board surfaces which total 2,000 ft^2).

Joint, Bolted. A joint in which bolts transmit load and hold members in position. Includes wood-to-wood and wood-to-steel assemblies.

Joint, Edge. A side joint in laminations formed by the use of two or more widths of lumber to make up the full width of a lamination.

Joint, End. A joint formed by joining pieces of lumber end to end with adhesives.

Joint, Finger. An end joint made up of several meshing tongues or fingers of wood. Fingers are sloped and may be cut parallel to the wide faces or to edge faces of laminations or other single members.

Joint, Scarf. An end joint formed by joining with adhesive the ends of two pieces of lumber, that have been tapered to form sloping plane surfaces, usually to a thin edge having the same slope of the plane with respect to length in both pieces. (In some cases, a step or hook may be machined into the scarf to facilitate alignment of the two ends; then the plane is discontinuous and the joint is known as a stepped or hooked scarf joint. Wooden pegs or other scarf-positioning devices may be used.)

Joint, Shear Plate Connector. A joint in which shear plates transmit shear between bolts and wood or bolts and steel members. Bolts also hold members in position. Used in wood-to-wood and wood-to-steel assemblies.

Joint, Split Ring Connector. A joint in which split rings transmit shear and bolts hold members in position. Used in wood-to-wood assemblies only.

Lamella. A roof frame consisting of a series of intersecting skewed arches, made up of relatively short members, called lamellas, fastened together at an angle so that each is intersected by two similar adjacent members at its midpoint, forming a network of interlocking diamonds. This network of lamellas forms a structure of mutually braced and stiffened units, arching over the structure between supports; with the sheathing it forms a diaphragm for resistance to vertical and lateral loads.

Laminating. The process of bonding laminations together with adhesive. The operations to which it applies include preparation of laminations, preparation and spreading of adhesives, assembly of laminations in packages, application of pressure, and curing.

Lamination. A wood layer contained in a member composed of two or more layers bonded together with adhesive or fastened together with mechanical fastenings. It is considered to extend the full width and the full length of the member. It may be composed of one or several wood pieces in width or length but only one in depth. Wood pieces may or may not be end- or edge-glued.

Laminator. A company that performs laminating operations.

Lumber. A manufactured product derived from a log in a sawmill, or in a sawmill and planing mill, which, when rough, shall have been sawed, edged, and trimmed at least to the extent of showing saw marks in the wood on the four longitudinal surfaces of each piece for its overall length, and which has not been further manufactured than by cross cutting, ripping, resawing, joining crosswise and or endwise in a flat plane, surfacing with or without end matching, and working.

Lumber Gage. A measuring device for determining the thickness of lumber.

Mechanically Laminated. A wood structural element comprised of laminations which are not glued but are held together with mechanical fastenings such as nails or bolts and in which all laminations have the grain approximately parallel longitudinally.

Moderate Temperature Service. Normal use conditions in which the temperature of the wood members remains below 150°F.

Moisture Content. The amount of water contained in the wood, usually expressed as a percentage of the weight of the oven-dry wood. When maximum and/or minimum moisture contents specified are expressed as a percentage of the weight of the oven-dry wood, the percentage specified is the exact limiting percentage figure and not a fractional amount above or below the percentage specified.

Noncustom Products. Products manufactured for stock or general use.

Open Assembly Time. See Assembly Time.

Ordinary Construction. A construction type which conforms with all requirements of *ordinary construction* as described in model building codes.

Piece Mark. A mark placed on an individual piece of timber framing to designate its location in the assembly as indicated in the shop drawings.

Plywood. A cross-banded assembly made of layers of veneer or veneer in combination with a lumber core or plies joined with an adhesive. Two types of plywood are recognized: (1) veneer plywood, and (2) lumber core plywood. (Generally the grain of one or more plies is approximately at right angles to the other plies, and an odd number of plies almost always are used.)

Potentiometer. An instrument for measuring electromotive force. When connected to a thermocouple, the apparatus becomes a pyrometer.

Production Check Points. Locations in production where an individual production step has been completed and is checked for conformance with the requirements of Voluntary Product Standard PS56-73, *Structural Glued Laminated Timber.* (Since the quality of structural glued laminated timber cannot be fully evaluated merely by visual inspection of finished production, each production step must be checked by in-line tests and samples of finished production must be checked by physical tests.)

Production Procedures. All the manufacturing operations performed in the manufacture of structural glued laminated timber.

Psychrometer. An instrument for measuring relative humidity.

Pyrometer. An instrument for measuring temperatures by means of the change in electrical resistance, the production of thermoelectric current, the expansion of gases or solids, the specific heat of solids, or the intensity of heat or light radiated. (Pyrometers used in laminating plants are usually of the thermoelectric or expansion of metals type and are commonly employed to measure the temperature of interior glue lines.)

Quality Control. The system whereby the manufacturer assures that materials, methods, workmanship, and final product meet the requirements of a standard.

Relative Humidity. Ratio of actual pressure of existing water vapor to maximum possible pressure of water vapor in the atmosphere at the same temperature, expressed as a percentage.

Representative Sample (of glued laminated timber). A portion or a section of a glued laminated timber that represents all the conditions surrounding the manufacturing process of a specific laminated timber or a group of them and that, when it is examined and tested and the results are determined, permits it to be factually stated that the level of quality of the individual member or group of members is of comparable quality.

Rigid Frame. A frame made up of pieces in the same general plane fastened rigidly together at the joints.

Sample. A portion of a wood product to be used for examination and/or test.

Sawn. A wood structural element as grown and sawn and not laminated or built up.

Seller. The furnisher of structural timber framing who may perform one or more of the operations of design, supply, lamination, fabrication, assembly, and erection.

Shop Assembly. See Assembly.

Smoothness. The relationship of the actual surface to that of a true plane or other surface free of roughness.

Specimen. See Test Specimen.

Split. A separation of the wood fiber caused by external forces.

Spread. The quantity of adhesive per unit joint area applied to a lamination. It is preferably expressed in pounds of liquid or solid adhesive per thousand square feet of joint area.

Spread, Double. The application of adhesive to both surfaces of a joint.

Spread, Single. The application of adhesive to only one surface of a joint.

Squeezeout. The adhesive extruded from glue lines when pressure is applied. (Though only an indication, this is an excellent index of the quantity of glue spread and the amount of pressure. If glue spread is adequate and even and attains full coverage out to all edges, the pressure will force glue from between the lamination in a pattern of beads and threads. If the proper assembly period is used and spread and pressure are uniform and adequate, squeezeout will emerge in a uniform pattern along all edges. If either spread or pressure is inadequate in any location, that area will not show squeezeout. An observer can soon learn to recognize good and bad patterns.)

Starved Joints. Glue lines that do not contain enough adhesive. (They may result from low viscosity of adhesive, excessive pressure, or application of an inadequate amount of adhesive.)

Storage Life (shelf life). The period of time during which a packaged adhesive can be stored under specified temperature and humidity conditions and remain suitable for use.

Structural Glued Laminated Timber. An engineered, stress-rated product of a timber-laminating plant comprising assemblies of specially selected and prepared wood laminations securely bonded together with adhesives. The grain of all laminations is approximately parallel longitudinally. The laminations shall not exceed 2 in. net thickness. They may be comprised of pieces end-joined to form any length, of pieces placed or glued edge to edge to make wider ones, or of pieces bent to curved form during gluing.

Submerged Service. Normal use conditions in which timbers in service will be continually submerged in water.

Test Specimen. All or part of a sample that has been selected for testing.

Thermocouple. A union of two conductors, such as bars or wires of dissimilar metals joined at their extremities, for producing thermoelectric current. (Whenever two dissimilar conductors come in contact there is a difference of electric potential, and, if their other ends are joined and the two junctions are maintained at different temperatures, an electric current will be produced in the circuit thus formed. In laminating, thermocouples are used in conjunction with the determination of the temperature of the innermost glue line.)

Torque. The product of a force and a lever arm which tends to twist or rotate a body, for example, the action of a wrench turning a nut on a bolt. Torque is commonly expressed in foot-pounds, that is, the product of the applied force measured in pounds and the lever arm measured in feet. This action is also called a "moment."

Torque Wrench. A wrench with an attached dial or other indicator that registers the torque applied by the wrench.

Truss. A framework of members in the same general plane joined only at their ends. The primary stresses in the members are axial tensile or compressive stresses. Secondary stresses are generally bending stresses due to a degree of joint fixity eccentricity and/or beam action of the members under load. Trusses are generally composed of assemblages of triangles for stability.

Truss Chord. One of the principal members of a truss, usually horizontal, braced by the web members. Truss chords are classified as

1. *Monochords.* Single-leaf members with web members normally abutting the chords.
2. *Double Chords.* Two-leaf members separated by the web system.
3. *Multiple Chords.* Members of three or more leaves separated by two or more web systems.

Wet Use. Normal use conditions where the moisture content of the wood in service exceeds 16%, as it may in exterior construction. (*See also* Adhesives, Wet-Use.)

Width. The dimension of the cross section that is measured normal to the direction of the principal load on the member in bending.

Wood Failure. The rupturing of wood fibers expressed as the percentage of the total area involved that shows such failure.

Working Life (pot life). The period of time during which an adhesive, after mixing with catalyst, solvent, or other compounding ingredients, remains suitable for use.

2. ABBREVIATIONS

2.1 Technical Notations and Symbols. The following notations may be used as they are listed or with subscripts and superscripts when more specific references are needed, such as M_2 (bending moment at point 2).

A area of cross section
b breadth (width) of rectangular member

C coefficient, constant, or factor

C_c curvature factor

C_F size factor

C_f form factor

C_s slenderness factor

c distance from neutral axis to extreme fiber

D diameter

d depth of rectangular member, or least dimension of compression member

E modulus of elasticity

e eccentricity

F_b allowable unit stress for extreme fiber in bending

f_b actual unit stress for extreme fiber in bending

F_c allowable unit stress in compression parallel to grain

F_c' allowable unit stress in compression parallel to grain adjusted for l/d ratio

f_c actual unit stress in compression parallel to grain

$F_{c\perp}$ allowable unit stress in compression perpendicular to grain

$f_{c\perp}$ actual unit stress in compression perpendicular to grain

F_r allowable unit radial stress

f_r actual unit radial stress

F_{rc} allowable unit radial stress in compression

f_{rc} actual unit radial stress in compression

F_{rt} allowable unit radial stress in tension

f_{rt} actual unit radial stress in tension

F_t allowable unit stress in tension parallel to grain

f_t actual unit stress in tension parallel to grain

F_v allowable unit horizontal shear stress

f_v actual unit horizontal shear stress

h rise

I moment of inertia

L span length of beam, or unsupported length of column, ft

l span length of beam, or unsupported length of column, in.

M bending moment

m unit bending moment

P total concentrated load, or axial compression load

P/A induced axial load per unit of cross-sectional area

Q statical moment of an area about the neutral axis

R radius of curvature

R_H horizontal reaction

R_V vertical reaction

r radius of gyration

S section modulus

T total axial tension load

t thickness

V total vertical shear

W total uniform load

w uniform load per unit of length

Δ_A allowable deformation or deflection
Δ_a actual deformation or deflection
$\parallel$ parallel
$\perp$ perpendicular
π pi
$>$ greater than
$\geq$ greater than or equal to
$<$ less than
$\leq$ less than or equal to

2.2   Material Abbreviations.

bm   board measure
comb.   combination
C.B.   carriage bolt
C.W.   cut washer
EMC   equilibrium moisture content
fbm   foot board measure
fsp   fiber saturation point
lam   lamination
L.B.   lag bolt (or lag screw)
M.B.   machine bolt
MC   moisture content
M.I.   malleable iron washer
O.G.   ogee (cast) washer
P.W.   plate washer
Sh.Pl.   shear plate
S.R.   split ring
S4S   surfaced four sides
tbkl   turnbuckle
thrd.   threaded rod
W.W.   wrought washer

2.3   Organizations and Their Addresses.

AA   Aluminum Association
750 Third Avenue
New York, New York 10017

AASHO   American Association of State Highway Officials
341 National Press Building
Washington, D.C. 20004

AHMI   Appalachian Hardwood Manufacturers, Inc.
414 Walnut Street
Cincinnati, Ohio 45202

—   American Insurance Association
(formerly National Board of Fire Underwriters)
85 John Street
New York, New York 10038

AISC   American Institute of Steel Construction, Inc.
101 Park Avenue
New York, New York 10017

AITC   American Institute of Timber Construction
333 West Hampden Avenue
Englewood, Colorado 80110

ANSI   American National Standards Institute
(formerly American Standards Association)
1430 Broadway
New York, New York 10018

APA   American Plywood Association
1119 A Street
Tacoma, Washington 98401

AREA   American Railway Engineering Association
59 East Van Buren Street
Chicago, Illinois 60605

ASA   American Standards Association, Inc. (*See* ANSI)

ASTM   American Society for Testing and Materials
1916 Race Street
Philadelphia, Pennsylvania 19103

AWPA   American Wood-Preservers' Association
1012 Fourteenth Street, N.W.
Washington, D.C. 20005

AWPI   American Wood Preservers Institute
1651 Old Meadow Road
McLean, Virginia 22101

AWS   American Welding Society
United Engineering Center
345 East 47th Street
New York, New York 10017

BOCA   Building Officials and Code Administrators International
(formerly Building Officials Conference of America)
1313 East 60th Street
Chicago, Illinois 60637

DHR   Division of Housing Research
Washington, D.C. 20410

FPL   U.S. Forest Products Laboratory
Madison, Wisconsin 53705

GSA   General Services Administration
Washington, D.C. 20405

ICBO   International Conference of Building Officials
50 South Los Robles
Pasadena, California 91101

IFI   Industrial Fasteners Institute
1717 East Ninth Street
Cleveland, Ohio 44114

NBFU   National Board of Fire Underwriters (*see* American Insurance
Association)

NBS   National Bureau of Standards
U.S. Department of Commerce
Washington, D.C. 20234

NELMA Northeastern Lumber Manufacturers Association
13 South Street
Glens Falls, New York 12801

NFPA National Forest Products Association (formerly National Lumber Manufacturers Association)
1619 Massachusetts Avenue, N.W.
Washington, D.C. 20036

NHLA National Hardwood Lumber Association
59 East Van Buren Street
Chicago, Illinois 60605

NHPMA Northern Hardwood and Pine Manufacturers Association
207 Northern Building
Green Bay, Wisconsin 54301

NLMA National Lumber Manufacturers Association (*see* NFPA)

NWMA National Woodwork Manufacturers Association
400 West Madison Street
Chicago, Illinois 60606

RIS Redwood Inspection Service
617 Montgomery Street
San Francisco, California 94111

SBCC Southern Building Code Congress
3617 8th Avenue South
Birmingham, Alabama 35221

SCMA Southern Cypress Manufacturers Association
P.O. Box 5816
Jacksonville, Florida 32207

SHLMA Southern Hradwood Lumber Manufacturers Association
805 Sterrick Building
Memphis, Tennessee 38103

SOD Superintendent of Documents
U.S. Government Printing Office
Washington, D.C. 20402

SPIB Southern Pine Inspection Bureau
P.O. Box 846
Pensacola, Florida 32502

TECO Timber Engineering Company
5530 Wisconsin Avenue, N.W.
Washington, D.C. 20015

UL Underwriters' Laboratories, Inc.
207 East Ohio Street
Chicago, Illinois 60611

USDA U.S. Department of Agriculture
Washington, D.C. 20250

USDC U.S. Department of Commerce
Washington, D.C. 20230

WCLIB West Coast Lumber Inspection Bureau
P.O. Box 23145
Portland, Oregon 97223

WWPA   Western Wood Products Association
Yeon Building
Portland, Oregon 97204

2.4   Publications.

ALS   *American Softwood Lumber Standard.* NBS Voluntary Product Standard PS 20-70.

NDS   *National Design Specification for Stress-Grade Lumber and Its Fastenings.*

TCM   *Timber Construction Manual.*

3. REFERENCES

3.1   General.

Building Code Requirements for Minimum Design Loads in Buildings and other Structures (ANSI).

Design Manual for TECO Timber Connector Construction (TECO).

National Design Specification for Stress-Grade Lumber and Its Fastenings (NFPA).

Snow Load Studies (DHR). Available from SOD.

Standard Specifications for Highway Bridges (AASHO).

Wood Bridges and Trestles (AREA).

Wood Handbook, USDA Handbook No. 72 (FPL). Available from SOD.

3.2   AITC Documents.

AITC 100, *Timber Construction Standards.* (AITC 100 is the complete compilation of the following.)

AITC 101	*Standard Definitions, Abbreviations, and References*
AITC 102	*Standards for the Design of Structural Timber Framing*
AITC 103	*Standard for Structural Glued Laminated Timber*
AITC 104	*Typical Construction Details*
AITC 105	*Recommended Practice for the Erection of Structural Timber Framing*
AITC 106	*Code of Standard Practice*
AITC 107	*Guide Specifications for Structural Timber Framing*
AITC 108	*Standard for Heavy Timber Construction*
AITC 109	*Treating Standard for Structural Timber Framing*
AITC 110	*Standard Appearance Grades for Structural Glued Laminated Timber*
AITC 111	*Recommended Practice for Protection of Structural Glued Laminated Timber Framing during Transit, Storage and Erection*
AITC 112	*Standard for Heavy Timber Roof Decking*
AITC 113	*Standard for Dimensions of Glued Laminated Structural Members*
AITC 114	*Guide Specifications — Structural Glued Laminated Crossarms*
AITC 115	*Standard for Fabricated Structural Timber*
AITC 116	*Guide Specifications for Structural Glued Laminated Timber for Electric Utility Framing*
AITC 117	*Standard Specifications for Structural Glued Laminated Timber of Douglas Fir, Western Larch, Southern Pine and California Redwood*

AITC 118 *Standard for Two-Inch Nominal Thickness Lumber Roof Decking for Structural Applications*

AITC 119 *Standard Specifications for Hardwood Glued Laminated Timber*

AITC 120 *Standard Specifications for Structural Glued Laminated Timber Using "E" Rated and Visually Graded Lumber of Douglas Fir, Southern Pine, Hem-Fir and Lodgepole Pine*

AITC 200 *Inspection Manual*

AITC *Timber Construction Manual*

3.3 Adhesives.

Federal Specification MMM-A-125, Adhesive, Casein-Type, Water-and-Mold-Resistant. Available from GSA or AITC.

Military Specification MIL-A-397B, Adhesive, Room-Temperature and Inter-mediate-Temperature Setting Resin (Phenol, Resorcinol and Melamine Base). Available from AITC.

Military Specification MIL-A-5534A, Adhesive, High-Temperature Setting Resin (Phenol, Melamine and Resorcinol Base). Available from AITC.

Performance Specifications for Protein Base Adhesives for Structural Glued Laminated Wood Products for Use Under Interior (Dry Use) Exposure Conditions (ASTM).

Standard Specification for Adhesives for Structural Laminated Wood Products for Use Under Exterior (Wet Use) Exposure Conditions, ASTM D2559-70 (ASTM).

3.4 Glued Laminated Timber.

Fabrication and Design of Glued Laminated Wood Structural Members, USDA Technical Bulletin No. 1069 (FPL). Out of print.

Standard Specifications for Hardwood Glued Laminated Timber (AITC).

Standard Specifications for Structural Glued Laminated Timber of Douglas Fir, Western Larch, Southern Pine and California Redwood (AITC).

Standard Specifications for Structural Glued Laminated Timber Using "E" Rated and Visually Graded Lumber of Douglas Fir, Southern Pine, Hem-Fir and Lodgepole Pine (AITC).

Structural Glued Laminated Timber, Voluntary Product Standard PS56–73. Available from AITC or SOD.

3.5 Lumber.

American Softwood Lumber Standard, NBS Voluntary Product Standard PS20-70. Available from SOD.

Official Grading Rules for Eastern White Pine, Norway Pine, Jack Pine, Eastern Spruce, Balsam Fir, Eastern Hemlock, and Tamarack (NHPMA).

Rules for the Measurement and Inspection of Hardwood Lumber and Cypress (NHLA).

Standard Grading and Dressing Rules for Douglas Fir, West Coast Hemlock, Sitka Spruce, White Fir, and Western Red Cedar (WCLIB).

Standard Grading Rules for Northeastern Lumber (NELMA).

Standard Grading Rules for Western Lumber (WWPA).

Standard Grading Rules for Southern Pine Lumber (SPIB).

Standard Specifications for Grades of California Redwood Lumber (RIS).

Standard Specifications for Grades of Tidewater Red Cypress (SCMA).

Standard Methods for Establishing Grades for Lumber, ASTM D245-69 (ASTM).

3.6   Metal.

Aluminum Construction Manual (AA).

Bolt, Nut and Rivet Standards (IFI).

Code for Arc and Gas Welding in Building Construction (AWS).

Federal Specification FF-B-561, *Lag Bolts.* Available from GSA.

Federal Specification FF-M-101, *Nails and Spikes.* Available from GSA.

Federal Specification FF-B-571, *Bolts.* Available from GSA.

Federal Specification FF-S-111, *Wood Screws.* Available from GSA.

Specification for the Design, Fabrication, and Erection of Structural Steel for Buildings (AISC).

Steel Construction Manual (AISC).

3.7   Model Building Codes.

Basic Building Code (BOCA).

National Building Code (American Insurance Association).

Southern Standard Building Code (SBCC).

Uniform Building Code (ICBO).

3.8   Plywood.

Hardwood Plywood, U.S. Commercial Standard CS35–61. Available from SOD.

Plywood Design Specification (APA).

Softwood Plywood, Construction and Industrial, U.S. Product Standard PS1–66. Available from SOD.

3.9   Treating.

Book of Standards (AWPA).

Building Materials List, Underwriters' Laboratories, Inc.

Federal Specification TT-W-571. Available from GSA.

Federal Specification TT-W-572. Available from GSA.

LP Standards — Lumber, Timber and Plywood (AWPI).

Water Repellent Preservative Seal of Approval Program (NWMA).

AMERICAN INSTITUTE
333 West Hampden Avenue

TIMBER CONSTRUCTION
Englewood, Colorado 80110

AITC 102-72
STANDARDS FOR THE DESIGN OF STRUCTURAL TIMBER FRAMING

Adopted as Recommendations March 17, 1969
Copyright 1972 by American Institute of Timber Construction

CONTENTS

1. PREFACE

1.1 Scope. The material herein is coordinated with the AITC *Timber Construction Manual*. Provisions therein are incorporated by reference and are not repeated herein.

1.1.1 The TCM covers working stresses for sawn lumber and glued laminated timber, and design loads for fastenings. It also covers the design of basic elements such as beams and axially loaded members.

1.1.2 These standards apply to larger units and more complex members such as arches, trusses, bracing, and related items, including sawn, glued laminated, and mechanically laminated timber, and plywood. They also apply to timber construction accessories and fastenings, such as miscellaneous structural steel, hardware, adhesives, and treatments.

1

2. GENERAL

2.1 Standards. The design of structural timber framing shall conform with accepted engineering practices as described in standard AITC documents (see *References*, AITC 101). Design practices shall be consistent with good engineering and with sound construction industry practices that assure the buyer of a safe and durable structure.

2.2 Working Stresses. Each structural member and its fastenings shall be of sufficient size and strength to meet the design requirements of dead load and other loads, without exceeding the allowable unit stresses provided by the appropriate standards or governing codes or, in their absence, by the section in this standard on allowable unit stresses.

2.3 New or Alternate Materials. New or alternate materials and methods may be used, provided they have been subjected to analysis or test and their use complies with established principles of engineering practice recognizing requisite safety and durability.

3. STRUCTURAL PLANS

3.1 General. Structural plans for the complete structure shall consist in general of the two types known as (1) design plans and specifications and (2) shop details. By custom, either the architect or the structural engineer first produces design plans and specifications; shop details are then prepared by the fabricator.

3.1.1 Nominal and Net Sizes. The desired sizes shall be specified. Sizes shown on structural plans shall be nominal sizes for sawn timbers and net sizes for glued laminated, mechanically laminated, and plywood members. Where special-size sawn timbers are used, net size should be given. Appropriate descriptive words such as "nominal" or "net" should be included with sizes wherever necessary to explain meaning fully. It is recommended that, wherever practical, standard sizes be specified.

3.1.1.1 Lumber Sizes. Standard sizes for sawn lumber are those given in the *American Lumber Standards* and lumber grading rules of approved lumber grade writing organizations. (See *References*, AITC 101.)

3.1.1.2 Glued Laminated Timber Sizes. Standard sizes of glued laminated timber structural members are given in *Standard for Dimensions of Glued Laminated Structural Members*, AITC 113.

3.1.2 Length. All members shall be specified to the length required.

3.1.3 Symbols. Design plans and shop details shall employ standard symbols and abbreviations, when required.

3.2 Design Plans. Design plans and specifications shall give complete information on sizes, dimensions, sections, and arrangements of members including the total structural system and permanent bracing. Required camber shall be shown on design plans. Species and grades of lumber, loads, design stresses, finish, paint, galvanizing, service conditions, type of adhesive, treatments, and appearance grades shall be given in sufficient detail to convey the complete intent of the design.

3.2.1. Dimensions. The controlling dimensions of the structure shall be those shown on design plans. Dimensions shall be clear and definite and shall provide the fabricator with spacings, heights, or rises; and with spans and anchorage locations so that accurate shop details can be made.

3.2.2 Scale. The scale of design plans shall be large enough to show information clearly. When required, large-scale illustrative details and sections shall be provided.

3.2.3 Plan Information. Design plans shall show information in such manner and to such completeness that shop details can be made and the fabricator can determine fully the kind, quality, number, and extent of the items to be furnished and the operations to be performed under his contract.

3.3 Shop Details. Shop details, giving complete information necessary for the fabrication and assembly of the component parts of the structure, including the location, type, size, and extent of all connections, fastenings, and camber, shall be prepared in advance of the actual fabrication. Shop details may not, however, be required for timber items that have a minimun of fabrication that can be shown or described clearly in writing, such as lumber cut to length only; nor shall shop details be necessary to show fabrication or assembly where sufficient information for one or both operations, as the case may be, are adequately shown on design plans. Shop details shall conform with the latest and best modern shop practices and shall have due regard for efficiency and economy in shop and field to the best interest of the project.

4. LOADS AND FORCES

4.1 Structural timber framing shall be designed to sustain dead load, live load, snow load, wind load, impact load, earthquake load, and any other loads and forces that may reasonably affect the structure during its service life, as stipulated by the governing building code. In the absence of a governing code, the loads, forces, and combination of loads shall be in accordance with accepted engineering criteria for the area under consideration.

4.2 Extreme or unusual roof load conditions may require full unbalancing; half unbalancing will be sufficient for average or normal conditions. Full unbalancing should comprise full live or snow load plus full dead load on one half of the span and full dead load on the other half of the span. Half unbalancing should comprise full live or snow load plus full dead load on one half of the span and one half live or snow load plus full dead load on the other half of the span.

4.3 Deflection limits shall be based on the more severe of the balanced or the unbalanced loading considered in the design.

5. MATERIALS

5.1 The design of structural timber framing shall assume that materials used and specified will comply with the following standards or specifications (see *References*, AITC 101, for complete designations).

5.1.1   Sawn Lumber. The grading and dressing rules for the species.

5.1.2   Structural Glued Laminated Timber. Voluntary Product Standard PS56–73, *Structural Glued Laminated Timber*.

5.1.3   Plywood. U.S. Commercial Standard CS35-61, *Hardwood Plywood*; and U.S. Product Standard PS1-66, *Softwood Plywood, Construction and Industrial*.

5.1.4   Structural Steel. *Specification for the Design, Fabrication, and Erection of Structural Steel for Buildings*.

5.1.5   Adhesives. Voluntary Product Standard PS56-73, *Structural Glued Laminated Timber*.

5.1.6   Bolts and Lag Bolts. Federal Specification FF-B-571.

5.1.7   Timber Connectors. AITC *Timber Construction Manual*.

5.1.8   Nails and Spikes. Federal Specification FF-M-101 with Amendment 6.

5.1.9   Wood Screws. Federal Specification FF-S-111.

5.1.10   Treatments. *Treating Standard for Structural Timber Framing*, AITC 109.

6. ALLOWABLE UNIT STRESSES

6.1   Allowable Unit Stresses. Allowable unit stresses, and permissible adjustments thereto for the various service conditions for all materials and fastenings used in the design of structural timber framing, shall be in accordance with the following (see *References*, AITC 101, for complete designation).

6.1.1   Sawn Lumber. AITC *Timber Construction Manual*.

6.1.2   Structural Glued Laminated Timber. AITC *Timber Construction Manual*.

6.1.3   Plywood. *Plywood Design Specification*.

6.1.4   Structural Steel. *Specification for the Design, Fabrication, and Erection of Structural Steel for Buildings*.

6.1.5   Fastenings. AITC *Timber Construction Manual*.

6.1.6   Mechanically Laminated Members. Allowable unit stresses for individual pieces used in mechanically laminated members shall comply with those established for sawn lumber. Adhesives used in combination with nails, spikes, bolts, lag bolts, or wood screws in mechanically laminated members shall not be considered as sharing the stress with the fasteners.

6.2   Nail Pressure Gluing. Nail pressure gluing is not recognized as complying with this standard.

6.3   Field Gluing. Structural field gluing is not recognized as complying with this standard.

7. GENERAL DESIGN CRITERIA

7.1   General Design Criteria. The general design criteria for structural timber framing shall be in accordance with the AITC *Timber Construction Manual* and as further specified herein.

7.2   Rigid or Continuous Arrangements. Where rigid or continuous arrangements of framing occur, the design shall adequately provide for all conditions of continuity and take into account special conditions of fabrication and erection and the effect of secondary stresses such as those caused by eccentricity, shrinkage, and cross-grain action.

7.3   End Restraint. When full or partial end restraint is assumed due to continuous, semicontinuous, or cantilever action, the beams, girders, columns, trusses, and members to which they connect shall be designed to resist fully all stresses introduced thereby. In such cases the allowable unit working stresses shall not be exceeded except that some inelastic but self-limiting deformation of a part of the connection may be permitted when this is essential to the avoidance of overstressing of a weld or similar connection.

7.4   Lateral Stability for Compression Members. The following principles shall be used to evaluate effective dimensions for members in compression.

7.4.1   Where roof joists, not purlins, are set between arches or the top chords of trusses, the depth, rather than the breadth, of the arch or top chord member (compression member) may be taken as its least dimension, d, in determining the l/d.

7.4.2   When roof joists or planks are placed on top of an arch or top chord of a truss and are well spiked or otherwise securely fastened to the arch or top chord and to blocking placed between the joists, the depth of the arch or individual chord member may be used as the least dimension, d, in determining l/d. When joists or planks are not so fastened or blocked, the width of the arch or individual chord member shall be used as the least dimension, d, in determining l/d.

7.4.3   When adequately stabilized roof purlins, joists, or struts are set between compression members or securely attached to one edge, the distance between purlins, joists, or struts shall be used as the effective column length, l, in the determination of the lateral l/d column action. Allowable stresses for column action should be the lesser of the two as determined by calculations based on l/d ratios using the appropriate breadth, depth, and unsupported lengths.

7.4.4   For arches or trusses that have superstructures built on top of the arches or upper chords so that the arch or upper chord is not laterally braced by roof framing, additional lateral bracing shall be required for that portion of the member not braced by roof framing to keep the l/d of the member within the limits prescribed in the AITC *Timber Construction Manual*.

7.5   Deflection, Camber, and Drainage of Roof Systems. Roof systems, in addition to having adequate drainage capacity, provision for draining heavy downpours (such as overflow scuppers), and proper construction details, shall be designed to prevent the ponding of water unless such ponding is intentional. When ponding is intentional, special design considerations are necessary to assure structural adequacy. See paragraph 8.7 for trusses and paragraph 9.9 for beams.

8. TIMBER TRUSS DESIGN CRITERIA

8.1   General (see also Appendix A). Timber trusses may be bowstring, flat or parallel chord, pitched, triangular, camelback, or other special types such as scissors, sawtooth, crescent, or combinations of two types. Chords and webs may be designed as monochord, double-chord, or multiple-chord members. Web members may be connected to sides of chords or may be in the same plane and attached with straps or gusset plates. Truss members may be sawn, glued laminated, or mechanically laminated. Steel rods or other steel shapes may be used for members in timber trusses if they fulfill all conditions of design and service.

8.2   Depth-to-Span Ratios. The ratio of effective depth to span in timber trusses should be one-sixth to one-eighth for bowstring trusses, one-eighth to one-tenth for flat or parallel chord trusses, and one-sixth or deeper for triangular or pitched trusses. Normally, the relatively deeper trusses should be used; when, for special reasons, a lesser depth is used, precautions should be taken to avoid excessive deflections.

8.3   Chord Design. Chord members may be either straight or curved and may be subject to either axial tension or axial compression stresses, alone or in combination with bending stresses, and may be subject to reversal of these actions. Continuity or fixity of splice joints in chord members shall not be assumed unless moment-resisting splices are provided. Axial compression shall be assumed to be transmitted in bearing at splice joints. Net section shall be computed by deducting from the gross section the sum of the projected areas of daps, connector grooves, and rod and bolt holes as they occur in any given section. In general, both the gross and the net section of chord members shall be designed to resist the following stresses singly or in combination: axial stresses due to design load, bending stresses due to curvature eccentricity, and bending and shear stresses due to applied loading. Additional criteria depending on the construction type and use of the chord are given below.

8.3.1   Mechanically Laminated Upper Chords (horizontal laminations). Mechanically laminated upper chords are commonly laminated from lumber of 2 in. or 3 in. nominal thickness.

8.3.1.1   End Joints in Laminations. End joints in outside laminations shall be located at panel points only. End joints shall not be located closer than 24 in. in adjacent laminations; they shall not be permitted in the first panel; and end joints in a given cross section shall be separated by at least two unspliced laminations. In chords of only four laminations, only one of the outside laminations may have an end joint at a given panel point.

8.3.1.2   Lamination Bolts. One or more $\frac{1}{2}$ in. minimum diameter bolts, extending through all laminations, shall be placed at each panel point in order to distribute the stresses introduced by the web connections to all laminations. Intermediate lamination bolts between panel points should not be used.

8.3.1.3   Resisting Moment. The resisting moment of any given section shall be assumed to be the sum of the resisting moments of the individual unspliced laminations at that section.

8.3.1.4 Axial Compression. The axial compression in a mechanically laminated chord shall be assumed to be resisted by simple column action of the individual laminations, or the entire section may be assumed to act as a mechanically laminated column. In the latter case, for laminations of 2 in. nominal thickness in panels up to 5 ft, full column action may be assumed; and for panel lengths of 5 to 8 ft, a straight line reduction from full column strength to 50% of this value shall be used. Panel lengths over 8 ft shall not be used with laminations of 2 in. nominal thickness. Proportionately longer panel lengths may be used with laminations of 3 in. nominal thickness.

8.3.2 Segmental Upper Chords. Monochord segmental chords shall have splice joints at panel points, and the top surface of the segments may be straight or sawn to a curve. Multiple-leaf segmental upper chords shall have staggered splice joints at or near midpanel points, and top surfaces may be sawn to a curve. When the stress in end grain bearing exceeds 75% of the allowable unit stress in compression parallel to grain, metal bearing plates shall be used between splice joints.

8.3.3 Tension Chords. Chords subject only to axial tension shall be designed in accordance with standard engineering principles with particular attention to net section. Chords subject to axial tension and bending, whether from loading of the chord by joists or purlins, eccentric web connections, or eccentricity due to curvature, shall be designed by the following method.

8.3.3.1 The chord is designed for the combination of axial tension and bending. Bending moments due to curvature and joint eccentricity are algebraically added to moments resulting from loading of the chord by purlins or joists. Such bending is computed by considering the chord to be a continuous beam supported at the panel points and of a length equal to the unspliced length of the chord. If moment-resisting splices are provided, the length may be considered to be the span of the truss. The applicable net or gross section shall be used in these computations.

8.3.4 Glued Laminated Compression Chords. Glued laminated compression chords may be designed using criteria similar to those for the design of tension chords.

8.4 Web Member Design. Web members shall be designed for the various loads and stresses which may be applied. If built-up sections such as I- or T-sections are used, provision shall be made for the transfer of stress between the flanges and web or stem.

8.5 Design of Connections. Concentric connections shall be used whenever possible. When members are subject to reversal of stresses, both conditions shall be investigated and connections shall be provided with adequate strength, spacing, and end and edge distances to satisfy both conditions. Allowable loads, spacing, and end and edge distances shall be in accordance with the provisions for the type of connection used. Where members are composed of two or more leaves or sections, their connections shall be so arranged that the inelastic deformation of all are equal. Bolts and lag bolts used for transfer of primary forces in connections of wood trusses should be not less than $\frac{1}{2}$ in. in diameter.

8.6   Truss Bearing Design. Bearing load on timber joints shall be taken either on end grain, side grain, or inclined grain and shall not be taken in any combination on end, side, or inclined grain.

8.7   Camber. Camber shall be such that total load deflection does not produce a sag below a straight line between points of support, as determined by computation, test data, or empirical standards. Both chords may be cambered, but this is generally done only on flat or parallel chord trusses. When only the lower chord is cambered, which is usual for bowstring, camelback, and pitched trusses, the effective depth of the truss shall be reduced accordingly in stress computations. In addition to these requirements, roof systems require adequate drainage capacity, provision for draining heavy downpours, and proper construction details to prevent the ponding of water. Where it is possible for ponding to occur or when it is intentional, special design considerations are necessary to assure structural adequacy.

8.8   Minimizing Shrinkage Effects. In chord splices of unseasoned wood that use more than one row of bolts or connectors, the tendency to split the chord as the result of restraint between the rows may be minimized by spacing the rows not more than 5 in. apart. Alternatively, the splice plates may be split between rows, or a plane of weakness may be created by making a saw kerf in the surface of the splice plate between rows. Shrinkage effects may also be minimized by these means: end distances for bolts and connections may be increased above the minimum; stitch bolts may be provided; clear and straight-grained material should be used for splice plates and similar critical short members; seasoned wood may be used; precautions may be taken to protect timbers against rapid seasoning; glued laminated timber may be used.

9. TIMBER BEAM DESIGN CRITERIA

9.1   General. Timber beams may be of the simple span, continuous, or cantilevered types or combinations of them. Timber beams may be straight, pitched, curved, or trussed, with constant cross sections or variable sections in length, width, or height, or combinations of these sections. Timber beams may be of sawn lumber, glued laminated timber, mechanically laminated lumber, or composite with another material. In general, timber beams shall be designed for bending, shear, bearing, deflection and, where significant, for cross-grain tension, cross-grain compression, and combination with axial stresses. When applicable, consideration in design shall be given to curvature, size effect, form factors, and radial tension. Designs shall be in accordance with the procedures given in the AITC *Timber Construction Manual* and as specified herein.

9.2   Curved or Pitched Beams. In addition to general design provisions, the design shall provide for horizontal deflection at the supports in curved or pitched beams. If the supports are designed to resist horizontal thrust, the beam shall be designed for axial compression in combination with bending; that is, the beam shall be designed as an arch. It is usually preferable to provide for the relatively small amount of horizontal movement that occurs at the supports by making provision for slotted or roller connections. Curved glued laminated beams shall be so designed that the laminations are parallel to the curve of the beam. Horizontal end bearing surfaces of pitched or curved beams shall be so designed that the soffit edge of the beam bearing cut is on the bearing plate.

9.3   Tapered Beams. Simple beams shall not be tapered by cutting off the tension face. Straight, pitched, or curved beams may be cut to a taper on the compression face. When tapered symmetrically, the beam shall be designed to have the required depth at the critical section. In computing shear, the effective depth shall be assumed to be the same as the actual depth at the loaded side of the bearing. When glued laminated beams which use more than one grade of lamination are to be cut to a taper, the beam design shall be checked to make certain that allowable stresses for the lower-strength inner lamination are not exceeded in areas where the higher-strength outer laminations are removed by cutting. That is, the higher-strength outer laminations should be extended in such a manner as to cover all areas where the induced stress exceeds the allowable stress of the lower-strength lamination. The beam shall be checked for shear at the tapered edge and for interaction of bending, shear, and perpendicular-to-grain stresses (*see* AITC *Timber Construction Manual*).

9.4   Mechanically Laminated Beams. Mechanically laminated beams may be laminated either vertically or horizontally.

9.4.1   Beams Loaded Perpendicular to the Edges of the Laminations (wide faces of laminations parallel to the direction of the load). Mechanically laminated beams with full-length laminations all of the same grade shall be assumed to be as strong and stiff as sawn beams of the same external net dimension. Allowable stresses for members laminated of combinations of grades shall be limited to the allowable stress of the values assigned for the lowest grade used.

9.4.2   Beams Loaded Perpendicular to Wide Faces of Laminations. Mechanically laminated beams with laminations horizontal are ordinarily designed on the basis of specific placement of butt joints and test data pertaining to the particular construction with respect to butt joints, and on the basis of fastenings used to transfer shear between laminations.

9.5   Composite Beams. Beams may be designed as composite timber-steel or composite timber-concrete beams.

9.5.1   Composite timber-steel beams shall be so designed that the wood and steel carry the loads in proportion to their relative stiffness.

9.5.2   Composite timber-concrete beams may be either the T-beam type or the slab type. Either type shall be designed in accordance with the methods described in the AITC *Timber Construction Manual*. In the T-beam, the effective flange width shall be determined as follows: For composite timber-concrete T-beams having the concrete flanges on both sides of the timber beam, the effective flange width of the concrete flange shall not exceed: (1) one-fourth of the span length of the beam; (2) twelve times the least thickness of the flange; or (3) the distance center to center of beams. For beams having the flange on one side only, the effective overhanging flange width shall not exceed one-twelfth of the span length of the beam, or six times the least flange thickness, or one-half of the clear distance to the adjacent beam.

9.6   Lateral Support.

9.6.1   Sawn Beams. Maximum depth-breadth ratios for various degrees of lateral support for sawn bending members with rectangular cross sections shall be in accordance with the rules given in the AITC *Timber Construction Manual.*

9.6.1.1   When adequately stabilized purlins or joists are set between bending members, the depth of the member below the bottom of the purlin or joist shall be used as the least dimension, d, in determining depth-breadth ratio.

9.6.2   Glued Laminated Beams. The rules for lateral support given in paragraphs 9.6.2.1 through 9.6.2.3 are based on actual dimensions. Depth is always defined as the full depth of the member regardless of whether purlins are set between beams.

9.6.2.1   Beams without Lateral Support. When the depth of a beam does not exceed its breadth, no lateral support is required, and the allowable unit stress in bending may be used directly.

9.6.2.2   Beams with Lateral Support. When the depth of a beam exceeds the breadth, bracing must be provided at the points of bearing and must be so arranged as to prevent rotation of the beam at points in a plane perpendicular to its longitudinal axis; the allowable unit stress in bending is calculated using the formulas given in the AITC *Timber Construction Manual.*

9.6.2.3   Unsupported Length.

(*a*) When lateral support to prevent rotation is provided as required in paragraph 9.6.2.2, and no other support is provided to prevent rotation or lateral displacement throughout the length of the beam, the unsupported length is the distance between points of bearing or the length of a cantilever.

(*b*) When beams are provided with lateral support to prevent both rotation and lateral displacement at intermediate points as well as at the ends, the unsupported length may be the distance between such points of lateral support. If lateral displacement is not prevented at intermediate points, the unsupported length is defined as in paragraph (*a*).

(*c*) When the compression edge of a beam is supported throughout its length so as to prevent its lateral displacement, and the ends are supported as in paragraph (*a*), the unsupported length may be taken as zero.

9.7   Deflection (see also Appendix B). Deflection may govern the design of many structural systems, particularly for the longer spans. Strength calculations based on permissible working stresses alone may result in sections that have too great a deflection. Limitations on deflection increase the stiffness of the member. Deflection limits vary with conditions of use; therefore different conditions are treated separately with respect to design recommendations. Consideration should be given to all factors that permit or produce deflection, such as dead and live loads, spans, fastenings, and form. In beam design, generally only the live load is used in calculating permissible deflections. However, when the live load is less than the dead load, the dead load should be considered. For this reason, two criteria for deflection limitations are suggested for roof and floor beams for these classifications of use. Roof systems require special design considerations to ensure structural adequacy; see paragraph 9.9.

9.7.1 Recommended Deflection Limitations for Sawn and Glued Laminated Beams. See Table 1.

TABLE 1

Type of Beam	Use Classification	Live Load Only	Dead + Live Load
Roof beams	Industrial	$l/180$	$l/120$
	Commercial and institutional		
	Without plaster ceiling	$l/240$	$l/180$
	With plaster ceiling	$l/360$	$l/240$
Floor beams	Ordinary usage (construction where walking comfort, minimized plaster cracking, and elimination of objectionable springiness are of prime importance)	$l/360$	$l/240$
Bridge beams			
Highway stringers		$l/200$ to $l/300$	
Railway stringers		$l/300$ to $l/400$	

l is span length in inches for deflection in inches.

9.8 Camber (see also Appendix B). Provisions shall be made for camber in all glued laminated beams. Practical considerations usually eliminate camber in very short spans and where computed camber is very small. Roof systems require special design considerations to ensure structural adequacy; see paragraph 9.9.

9.8.1 Glued Laminated Beams. The amount of camber incorporated at the time of fabrication, and as shown on design drawings, should be at least equal to one and one-half times the calculated dead load deflection. The recommended minimum camber for beams is given in Table 2.

TABLE 2

Roof beams	$1\frac{1}{2}$ times dead load deflection
Floor beams	$1\frac{1}{2}$ times dead load deflection
Bridge beams	
Long span	2 times dead load deflection
Short span	2 times dead load deflection $+ \frac{1}{2}$ live load deflection

9.9 Roof Systems. Each component of the roof system, including decking, purlins, beams, girders, and other principal structural supports, shall be designed to avoid unintentional ponding of water. Continuous or cantilevered components shall be designed for balanced or unbalanced load, whichever produces the more critical condition.

In addition to proper construction details, adequate drainage capacity, including provision for draining heavy downpours, shall be provided. The unintentional ponding of water on roofs shall be avoided by providing a minimum roof slope or camber equivalent to $\frac{1}{4}$ in. per foot of horizontal distance between the level of the drain and the high point of the roof, in addition to providing the recommended minimum camber given in paragraph 9.8.1.

If ponding of water is intentional or if excessive ponding of water can occur as the result of parapet walls, high gravel stops, plugged drains, coincidence of snow loads and rain, beams of insufficient stiffness, melting snow and ice dams, etc., deflection is initiated and continues progressively because the work energy of the ponding water is initially greater than the resistance of the beam. Thus this deflection continues until equilibrium between the added water load equals the resistance of the beam, or it continues to failure of the beam. Where ponding can occur, roof systems shall be designed for structural adequacy under ponding in accordance with the criteria in Section 4 of the AITC *Timber Construction Manual* or other applicable engineering criteria.

10. TIMBER ARCH AND RIGID FRAME DESIGN CRITERIA

10.1 General. Timber arches or rigid frames may be of glued laminated timber, mechanically laminated lumber, or framed of sawn or glued laminated timbers.

10.1.1 Roof Systems. Roof systems shall be designed to provide adequate drainage capacity, including provision for draining heavy downpours; and proper construction details shall be used.

10.2 Analysis. Arches and rigid frames shall be analyzed in accordance with standard principles of structural analysis for all primary and secondary stresses and combinations thereof and deflections that may result from design loads.

10.3 Lateral Thrust at Support. Designs of arches, lamella roofs, and rigid frames shall include provisions for resistance of lateral thrust at the support by means of tie rods, abutments, foundations, or other adequate measures. Special consideration shall be given to horizontal loads that cause differential thrust. The arch design shall include consideration for lateral deformation and vertical settlement of supports. When the superstructure is designed separately from the foundation, the magnitude of the vertical and horizontal reactions shall be made available to the foundation designer.

10.4 Buckling. Arches and rigid frames shall be laterally supported in accordance with the provisions of paragraph 7.4. In addition, the design shall consider the slenderness ratio, l/d, in the direction normal to the roof or wall plane. The unbraced length, l, shall be the straight-line distance between hinges, hinge and point of contraflexure, or points of contraflexure, whichever is critical. The depth, *d*, for such computations shall be assumed to be the sum of the least depth of the member plus one-third the difference in depth between the points under consideration. The allowable compressive stress parallel to grain shall be limited by the column formula to the stress applicable for a column with the largest *l/d* determined as previously indicated.

10.5 Deflection. Deflection of arches and rigid frames shall be determined by the application of standard engineering principles. For arches and rigid frames having straight roof arms, as in A-frames and tudor arches, the deflection of the roof arm shall be limited as for beams (see paragraph 9.7). In such cases the length, *l*, shall be assumed to be the length of the straight portion of the arch axis in inches.

10.6 Moment Splices. Moment splices shall be located at points of minimum moment, where possible. Moment splices shall be designed to resist axial stress, shear, and bending stresses singly or in combination as required.

10.7 Complex Frames. Complex or intricate systems not readily analyzed by customary means may be subjected to engineering test, and the resulting empirical data may be used as a design basis.

11. BRACING

11.1 General. Bracing shall be so installed as to provide restraint, support, or both to members in order that they will function as designed and that the complete assembly will form a stable structure. Bracing may consist of knee braces, cable, rods, struts, ties, shores, diaphragms, rigid frames, and similar items and combinations which serve the aforementioned functions.

11.2 Permanent Bracing. The design of all timber structures shall include adequate permanent bracing so that the resulting structure will resist wind, earthquake, and other lateral forces and so that the principal structural components such as trusses, arches, beams, and girders will be held in place and thus will function as intended.

11.3 Temporary Erection Bracing. The erection operation of all timber structures shall include adequate temporary or erection bracing to resist lateral forces due to erection and construction loads, wind, earthquake, and other lateral forces during the construction period and until the permanent bracing is completely installed.

11.4 Bracing Design. The arrangement, sizes, and connections of bracing shall be designed according to accepted engineering principles.

12. MAINTENANCE

12.1 General. No structure, regardless of the materials used in its construction, is entirely and consistently maintenance-free. As for all valuable properties, some inspection and maintenance should be given to structures of timber. Whether wood members are of sawn lumber or laminated timber, and regardless of their moisture content at time of fabrication, the degree of maintenance in service is a direct function of design and selection of materials. The following discussion and recommendations, when considered along with the foregoing design standards, will assist the architect or engineer in developing a structure requiring a minimum of maintenance.

12.2   Moisture Seal. A moisture seal or moisture barrier should be placed under or around wood members which bear on or are embedded in concrete or masonry.

12.3   Air Spaces for Embedded Members. Ends of girders and trusses entering concrete or masonry should preferably have a minimum of 1 in. of air space at sides, top, and end, unless special protection is provided. (See *Typical Construction Details*, AITC 104.)

12.4   Dimensional Changes. Timber structural framing must be so designed and constructed that normal anticipated expansion and contraction can occur without structural or service injury. Dimensional changes in glued laminated members of very long span can be critical and should be checked.

12.4.1   Moisture Content Variations. Design of timber construction should include consideration of dimensional changes across grain which result from variations in moisture content. Longitudinal expansion or contraction of most wood species along the grain due to changes in moisture content is usually inappreciable for any conditions of normal service and so may generally be disregarded.

12.4.2   Temperature Changes. There is no appreciable thermal expansion or contraction of wood along the grain because of temperature changes. In composite members, thermal expansion shall be considered in all cases where expansion or differential expansion might result in high secondary stresses.

12.5   End Checks. End seals shall be applied to fresh-cut ends of timber to minimize end checking when use conditions are such that end checking is a major consideration.

12.6   Seasoning Checks. Under certain conditions, it may be desirable to minimize the effects of seasoning checks in members by one or more of the following means.

12.6.1   Minimum end distances of bolts and connections may be increased.

12.6.2   Splice plates and similar critical short members may be required to be clear and close-grained.

12.6.3   Seasoned wood may be used.

12.6.4   Precautions may be taken to protect timbers against rapid seasoning.

12.6.5   Glued laminated timber may be used.

12.7   Construction Details. Maintenance can be minimized by proper selection and design of construction details. (See *Typical Construction Details*, AITC 104.)

AMERICAN INSTITUTE TIMBER CONSTRUCTION
333 West Hampden Avenue Englewood, Colorado, 80110

AITC 102-72
APPENDIX A
TRUSSES AND BRACING

Adopted as Recommendations March 17, 1969
Copyright 1972 by American Institute of Timber Construction

CONTENTS

A1. INTRODUCTION

A1.1 This Appendix is intended to supplement and expand on Section 8 of *Standards for the Design of Structural Timber Framing*, AITC 102.

A1.2 The design of a truss, like the design of other structural units, must conform with proper design principles, sound construction practices, and good engineering. Empirical formulas developed from test programs and field experience also apply.

A1.3 Basic timber design principles for the assignment of loads and resolution of forces are like those for other materials and are as given in standard engineering works. Truss and bracing analysis may be made by graphical or analytical methods.

A2. TRUSS TYPES

A2.1 The types of timber trusses most commonly built are: (*a*) bowstring; (*b*) flat or parallel chord; (*c*) pitched, triangular, or A-type; (*d*) camelback; and (*e*) special, such as crescent and scissors. (See Figure 1.)

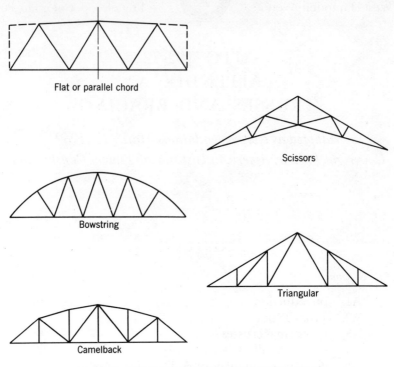

Flat or parallel chord

Scissors

Bowstring

Triangular

Camelback

Figure 1.   ILLUSTRATIVE TRUSS PATTERNS.

A2.1.1   Truss terms are general, and modifications and variations arise for different localities and for particular projects; however, the largest number of timber trusses built today fall into one of the broad classifications. For convenience, trusses may be further subdivided into the member classifications of upper chords, webs, lower chords, and bracing.

A2.2   Truss type and arrangement of members are chosen by the designer to suit shape of structure, loads, and stresses. A critical step in the design of timber structures is the design of the joints. The type of truss to be used is often governed by consideration of the joints.

A2.3   Chords and webs may be constructed as single-leaf, double-leaf, or multi-leaf members. Single-leaf chords are also known as monochords. The most common arrangements are those with double-leaf chords having a single-leaf web system located between the chord leaves, and monochord trusses with single-leaf chords and webs. Webs may be attached to sides of chords or may be in the same plane and attached thereto with straps or gussets. Truss members may be sawn, glued laminated, or mechanically laminated. The use of steel rods or other steel shapes for members in timber trusses is acceptable if they fulfill all conditions of design and service.

A2.4   Stack-type chords are constructed by using one or more stacks of laminations to form the member; laminations may be glued or mechanically fastened together, and chords may be single-leaf, two-leaf, or multi-leaf. In two-leaf or multi-leaf members, stacks are side by side and parallel to each other.

A3. BOWSTRING TRUSSES

A3.1 General.

A3.1.1 Bowstring trusses have a curved upper chord, web systems of varying patterns, and a straight or cambered lower chord. In these trusses, usually the radius of curvature of the top chord is approximately equal to the span of the truss.

A3.1.2 The chords and heel connections take the major stress; the web stresses for uniform loading conditions are negligible, and for unbalanced loading web stresses are comparatively light.

A3.1.3 Bowstring trusses, because of low web stresses, have light webs and web connections. Chord stresses are nearly equal throughout their length and, with constant cross sections, chords have full-length economy.

A3.1.4 For the convenience of description, the design and construction of bowstring trusses will be discussed under the various headings of Upper Chords, Lower Chords, and Web Systems.

A3.2 Upper Chords of Bowstring Trusses. The upper chords are usually shaped to the form of a circular arc or parabola. With the normal rise-to-span ratio used, the variation between the parabola and the circular arc is very slight and is not sufficient to change stresses materially. Circular curves are customarily used.

A3.2.1 Because of the curved shape, the upper chords must either be glued laminated, mechanically laminated, or constructed of segments whose upper surfaces conform with the desired shape. They may be constructed as single-leaf or monochord, two-leaf, or multi-leaf members.

A3.2.2 Glued laminated chord members must be fabricated in accordance with the applicable standards. Segmental chords may be made of sawn or glued laminated elements; mechanically laminated chords use sawn lumber. For a particular bowstring truss, any one of the three types may be satisfactory.

A3.2.3 Generally, continuity or fixity is not assumed in the design of end joints. Full bearing at end joints, however, is assumed. Full eccentricity is used in determining moment between panel points. Simple span beam moments are used when segments are spliced at each panel point. The effect of the omission of live load from portions of the truss must be provided for in the design, but, when simple beam moments are used, it is not necessary to consider the possibility of individual panels being unloaded.

A3.2.4 Summary of Design Principles for Upper Chords. The chord is subjected to column stresses due to axial loads and to bending moments caused by purlin or joist loads and to eccentricity.

A3.2.5 The panel point region is subjected to the shears and bending moments caused by eccentricity of web connections and axial compression produced by truss action. Sections have effective size for strength reduced by lamination joints and web bolt holes. Lamination joints are deducted for web connection shears and moments but are not deducted for column action in chords. (See Figure 2.)

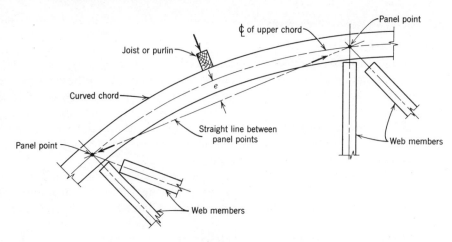

Figure 2.   ECCENTRICITY OF CURVED COMPRESSION MEMBER.

A3.3   Mechanically Laminated Upper Chords for Bowstring Trusses.
The curved upper chords of bowstring trusses may be formed of one or
more parallel stacks of laminations which are usually of 2 in. or 3 in.
nominal thickness. For two-leaf chords, one stack is placed on each side of
the web system. In the one-leaf chord arrangement, the webs may be
attached to the sides of the chords or they can be placed in the plane of the
chords and connected by steel gussets or straps.

A3.3.1   The laminations of the upper chord members are held
together in position by means of nails and bolts. Joints of outside laminations should be located at panel points only. Joints should not be located
closer than 24 in. in adjacent laminations. Joints should not be located in
the first panel. Joints at a given cross section should be separated by at least
two unspliced laminations. In four-lamination chords, only one outside
lamination should be joined at a particular panel point.

A3.3.2   Lamination bolts extending through all laminations of each
stack should be placed at each panel point. The function of the lamination
bolts at the panel points is to distribute the force introduced by the webs
into all the laminations. The size of such bolts is not a factor of the width of
the lamination or the number of laminations, but rather of the force to be
distributed. The common practice is to use $\frac{1}{2}$ in. or $\frac{5}{8}$ in. bolts for this purpose, one in each section of the chord. Where force greater than can be
taken by this bolting arrangement is present, two such bolts in each section
of the chord are used, one on either side of the web connection.

A3.3.3   Bending moment is assumed to be taken by the sum of the
resisting moments of the individual unspliced laminations at a given section. The axial stress may be assumed to be taken by the individual elements
or by the upper chord section acting as a laminated column.

A3.3.4   The action of a mechanically laminated column can be evaluated only by tests. Numerous tests have been made on column sections such
as are now used in the upper chords of bowstring trusses. These tests cover
a range of four to seven laminations of "two-by-threes," "two-by-fours,"
and "two-by-sixes" in lengths from 3 to 8 ft.

A3.3.5   The test results demonstrate that, for short panels up to 5 ft, 100% values may safely be used; and, for lengths of 5 to 8 ft, a straight-line reduction from full column strength to 50% of this value should be used. Panel lengths over 8 ft are not recommended.

A3.3.6   Chords composed of laminations of 3 in. nominal thickness may have longer panel lengths because of the proportionately lesser slenderness ratio of the individual elements.

A3.3.7   Intermediate lamination bolts between panel points are not recommended because they reduce the effective area of the chord at points of maximum bending, and tests have demonstrated that the reduction in area more than offsets any gain in column stiffness.

A3.3.8   Bolts are also used to attach webs to chords. They may be placed in the chord without regard to whether bolts fall within an individual lamination of the chord. The action of the bolt is the same whether it is within the lamination or in the joint between the laminations.

A3.3.9   Web bolts should have standard end and edge distances for full-load capacity. Where load is below capacity, distances may be reduced, but precautions should be taken by using stitch bolts and end seals. If the webs are subject to reversal of stress, both conditions must be investigated and the proper end distance must be provided for connections to satisfy both conditions.

A3.4 Segmental Upper Chords for Bowstring Trusses. Segmental upper chords for bowstring trusses are built to a curved shape using short wood segments with joints at certain intervals. They may be of the one-leaf monochord, two-leaf, or multi-leaf type. Segments are usually sawn.

A3.4.1   Single-leaf segmental chords have joints at each panel point, and top surfaces of segments may be straight or sawn to a curve. Two-leaf or multi-leaf segments usually overlap and have staggered joints at or near mid-panel. Top surfaces are sawn to a curve. Compression plates may be placed between segment ends at joints, and they are required when stress in end grain bearing exceeds 75% of allowable values. Usually two-leaf or multi-leaf chords have segment leaves separated by web systems. Segments are joined together and to web systems by bolts, connectors, and splice plates as needed.

A3.4.2   Axial compressive stress, bending moments induced by chord eccentricity and by joist or purlin loads, as well as bending moments and shears from eccentric web connections, should be determined by standard engineering procedures. The effect of stress transfer from the butted leaf end to the opposite continuous section should be considered in the design. If a cap is used, provisions should be made to transfer stresses properly into and out of the cap. (See Figure 3.)

A3.5 Glued Laminated Upper Chords for Bowstring Trusses. Glued laminated upper chords for bowstring trusses are stack type and may be one-leaf, two-leaf, or multi-leaf chords. If the chords are made of two or more leaves, they are parallel and are usually separated by the web system.

A3.5.1   Glued laminated chords shall be designed to meet the requirements of *Standards for the Design of Structural Timber Framing*, AITC 102, and *Standard for Structural Glued Laminated Timber*, AITC 103. Axial compressive stress, bending moments induced by curvature eccentricity, and joist or

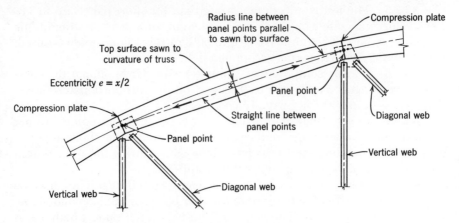

Figure 3.   ECCENTRICITY OF SEGMENTAL UPPER CHORD.

purlin loads, as well as bending moments and shears from eccentric web connections, should be determined by standard engineering procedures. Continuity conditions should be considered in selecting moment coefficients. Omission of live loads from portions of the truss should be taken into account where load arrangement so dictates.

A3.5.1.1   A conservative method uses a simple span subject to actual purlin or joist loads with full eccentricity and full truss stress all combined as a sum of adding or compensating actions.

A3.6   Lower Chords for Bowstring Trusses. Lower chords are primarily tension members, although often they are also subjected to bending either from loads applied directly to the chord or from web joint eccentricities.

A3.6.1   A conservative method is to design for a simple span beam moment of $wl^2/8$ combined with the truss direct stress. With this method, no reduction in net section due to joint connections is made for moment design. The chord should also be checked for direct tension on the actual net section at the joint combined with any bending resulting from joint eccentricity.

A3.6.2   Lower chords subjected to bending may be designed as continuous beams, and the bending stress may be combined with the direct tensile stress. When this method is used, it is necessary to make a reduction for the net section when considering the moment at joints.

A3.6.3   Deductions should be made for bolt and connector holes to determine the net section in accordance with *Standards for the Design of Structural Timber Framing*, AITC 102.

A3.6.4   Extreme care must be taken in designing, selecting, and constructing lower chords and splice plates of timber trusses. Slope of grain requirements that refer to the center portions of pieces of those grades should be applied throughout the entire length of pieces subject to longitudinal tension, in accordance with grading rule requirements for sawn lumber. For glued laminated timber, the requirements of the structural glued laminating specification for the species should be met.

A3.7   Web Systems for Bowstring Trusses. For the determination of

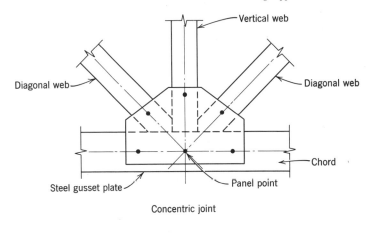

Concentric joint

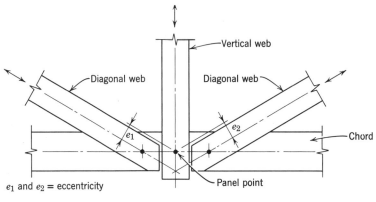

Eccentric joint

Figure 4.   WEB MEMBER CONNECTIONS.

web stresses, the webs are considered as intersecting at the center lines of the chords whether or not they actually do so. Web stresses are then found by an analytical or graphical solution of the truss. Webs are designed as compression or tension members, as the case may be. (See Figure 4.)

A3.7.1   Web members may be arranged in various patterns and may be of sawn or steel or glued laminated materials, but glued laminated webs are not common.

A3.7.2   Web connections can be made by means of bolts or bolts and timber connectors. Recommended end and edge distances for full load should be maintained. If the bolt or connector is carrying a load below its capacity, and if it is not practical to achieve such end distances, reduction in end distance is permissible, provided that precautions are taken to minimize end checking. When the webs are subject to reversal of stress, both conditions must be investigated and the proper end distance provided for connections to satisfy both conditions. In addition to wood-to-wood connections, metal strap and pin and gusset plate connections are commonly used.

A3.7.3 When bolts are used, end distance is measured from the center of the bolt parallel to the axis of the member to the cut end, whether it is square or bevel cut. When a timber connector is used, the end distance is measured parallel to the centerline of the member from any point on the center half of the connector diameter, which is perpendicular to the centerline of the member, to the cut end of the member. In no case should the perpendicular distance from the center of the connector to a sloping end cut be less than the required edge distance.

A4. FLAT OR PARALLEL CHORD TRUSSES

A4.1 One of the common forms of flat trusses is the Howe truss, in which the diagonal web compression members are of timber and the vertical tension webs are of steel. The parallel or flat chords are of timber. Many of these trusses use daps and let-in construction to transmit stress from webs to chords. With this type of construction, the points to consider are: bearing stresses, coincidence of lines of force, provisions for eccentricity, the effects of shrinkage on the larger timber elements, and the workmanship during fabrication. In computing net sections, the maximum sum of daps, rod holes, and bolt holes, as they occur in any given section, should be used. (See Figure 5.)

A4.1.1 A version of the Howe truss is built with timber connectors and multichord- and multiweb-type members; thus the high-stress web members are connected directly to the chords with concentric joints.

A4.1.2 Another variation of the Howe truss is the strap-and-pin type wherein members are connected by steel straps or gusset plates and bolts or bolts and connectors.

A4.2 The Pratt truss is also a flat or parallel chord truss, differing from the Howe truss in that the diagonal webs are in tension and the vertical webs are in compression. The tension members are fastened by bolts and steel straps or gusset plates or connectors.

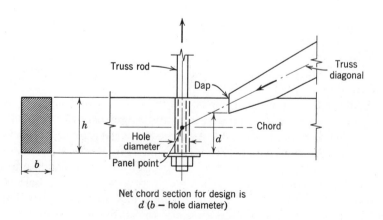

Net chord section for design is
d (b − hole diameter)

Figure 5.   ROD AND DAP DETAIL.

A4.3 Upper chords of flat or parallel chord trusses may be of the single-leaf, double-leaf, or multi-leaf varieties. Chords may be of sawn lumber or glued laminated timber. In two-leaf or multi-leaf chords, the leaves are usually separated by a web system. Truss stress at splices is usually taken in bearing.

A4.3.1 Upper chords are designed as columns using the proper l/d ratio. Moments and shears, as well as bending actions produced by purlins or joists, must be considered as they occur.

A4.4 Design of web systems and lower chords for flat or parallel chord trusses is similar to requirements for bowstring trusses, except that web stresses may be relatively larger. Webs should be joined to chords in concentric patterns. Both upper and lower chords should be cambered.

A5. PITCHED, TRIANGULAR, OR A-TYPE TRUSSES

A5.1 Pitched, triangular, or A-type trusses are best suited for short to moderate spans. Chords are usually straight, but the lower chord may be cambered or may have a low-rise curvature. Single-leaf, double-leaf, or multi-leaf chords may be used. Chords may be sawn lumber or glued laminated timber. When double-leaf or multi-leaf, chords are usually separated by the web system.

A5.1.1 Webs may be dapped into chords, fastened with connectors, connected with gusset plates, or connected with steel straps and bolts. The heel connection should receive special consideration, particularly when the slope of the upper chord is quite small.

A5.1.2 Upper chords are designed as columns using the proper l/d ratio. Moments and shears, as well as bending actions produced by purlins or joists, must be considered as they occur.

A5.2 Requirements for construction and design of web systems and lower chords for such trusses are similar to those for bowstring trusses except that web stresses are relatively large. Webs should be joined to chords in concentric patterns.

A6. CAMELBACK TRUSSES

A6.1 Camelback trusses have the same general shape as bowstrings with top chords composed of a series of straight segments. Upper chords may be single-, double-, or multi-leaf. Chords are usually of sawn material.

A6.2 A camelback truss does not use curved members for top chords but introduces flat inclined areas into the roof contour. Curvature eccentricity does not exist in the top chord. Chord joints are compression connections involving inclined-to-grain stresses, and web members resist the vertical components of chord actions and hold chord ends in position. Top chords are designed as columns subject to bending from joists or purlins.

A6.3 Requirements for construction and design of web systems and lower chords for camelback trusses are similar to those for bowstring trusses except that web stresses are relatively large.

A7. OTHER TRUSSES

A7.1   There are several other types of trusses, such as crescent, scissors, trussed rafter, sawtooth, Lank, Fink, and pony, and many combinations of arch and truss frames.

A7.2   The basic construction and design principles for other types are the same as those for the standard types given. If other types have curved chords, requirements for curved chords for bowstrings must be met; if straight chords, the trusses should be designed in accordance with the requirements for flat or parallel chord or triangular trusses. Also, the provisions indicated for single-leaf, double-leaf, or multi-leaf or for sawn, glued laminated, or mechanically laminated members will apply to similar construction in these trusses.

A8. PERMANENT TRUSS BRACING

A8.1   Permanent truss bracing is that bracing which forms an integral part of the final structure.

A8.2   Permanent truss bracing construction, as shown on design plans and for shop details exclusive of joists, purlins, rafters, or sheathing, should be installed as trusses are erected. When roof or ceiling joists, purlins, rafters and/or sheathing form part of the permanent truss bracing, these items should follow as closely as practicable the truss erection.

A8.3   When fully erected, the building should form a braced structure with trusses, truss bracing, struts, purlins, joists, and sheathing or other units that conform with the design standards that apply for resisting wind, earthquake, and other lateral forces and to hold trusses true and plumb. Permanent truss bracing should be shown on design plans and should be to the requirements of *Standards for the Design of Structural Timber Framing*, AITC 102. (See *Definitions*, AITC 101, and *Code of Standard Practice*, AITC 106, for procedures outlining responsibility in design, detailing, furnishing, and installation of bracing.)

A8.4   The arrangement, sizes, and connections of permanent bracing units, such as diagonals, laterals, and longitudinal struts, should be designed according to accepted engineering principles and sound engineering judgment to provide adequate stability against lateral forces for the particular building.

A8.5   Because buildings are so varied in size, shape, materials of construction, and site conditions, no attempt has been made to set uniform standards for bracing. There are, however, several basic methods of bracing design, and the most suitable should be used. As a guide to the designer, several common methods are given below.

A8.5.1   A diaphragm can be provided consisting of a rigid type of roof covering such as wood sheathing, which is properly fastened to the roof joists, which in turn are attached directly to the truss chords. Adequate perimeter connections of the diaphragm to the walls of the building must be provided. Horizontal struts between the lower chords of the truss and vertical sway bracing may not be required with this method.

A8.5.2 For a building with a nonrigid roof covering, a system of horizontal bracing at right angles to the truss chords may be designed for installation in the plane of the lower or upper chord. If the bracing is located in the plane of the lower chords, vertical bracing must also be installed between the trusses so that the upper chords are supported at intervals consistent with l/d requirements and so that transfer of loads to the plane of the lower chords is taken into account. This method requires that careful consideration be given to the bracing connections to the building and truss chords so that allowable stresses for the various materials are not exceeded.

A8.5.3 Use of knee braces between the trusses and columns is a method of bracing which is particularly adaptable to buildings which have a large length-to-width ratio. The stress induced in the trusses and columns by the knee braces must be considered. Lateral loads acting in the long direction of the building are usually resisted by means of diagonal bracing and struts in the end bays. The comments concerning upper chord support given in paragraph A8.5.2 apply here also.

A8.5.4 Special methods of bracing, such as cantilevered columns, buttresses, or other elements designed with sufficient rigidity to resist lateral loads, can be used. These methods require special consideration for each case.

A8.6 The lateral support at the chords of trusses is in most cases provided by the bracing system. Some building forms require that bracing in addition to that installed for lateral loads be provided to support the compression chords of a truss so that l/d requirements are met. This is especially true for trusses that have superstructures built on top of upper chords which are not supported laterally by the roof framing.

A9. ERECTION TRUSS BRACING

A9.1 Erection truss bracing is that bracing that is installed to hold trusses true and plumb and in a safe condition until permanent truss bracing and other permanent components, such as joists and sheathing contributing to the rigidity of the complete roof structure, are in place.

A9.1.1 Erection truss bracing may consist of struts, ties, cables, guys, shores, or similar items. Joists, purlins, and other permanent elements may be used as erection bracing.

A9.2 Erection bracing should be designed, furnished, and installed in accordance with *Standards for the Design of Structural Timber Framing*, AITC 102, and *Code of Standard Practice*, AITC 106, by the persons or firms charged therein with responsibility for the respective functions.

A10. TRUSS ERECTION

A10.1 Timber construction requires the same high degree of safety as does construction with other materials for the protection of life and property. It is necessary that safe erection methods be employed at all times.

A10.1.1 Trusses should be fabricated and assembled as detailed and in a workman-like manner.

A10.1.2 Trusses should be installed true and plumb by means of permanent or erection truss bracing and should be suitably anchored at column or wall connection. Erection bracing should be left in place as long as required.

A10.1.3 When trusses are being raised, they should be handled with care to prevent undue distortion and actions that might damage them. The method of erection and the erection equipment required vary with job site conditions. The selection of equipment and method of erection is the responsibility of the truss erector. Loads should not be imposed on the trusses until they are securely anchored at their heel connections and are sufficiently braced. Building materials or other loads, when placed on the trusses, should be distributed so that trusses are not overloaded.

A10.2 Erection and the responsibility for erection should be in accordance with *Recommended Practice for the Erection of Structural Timber Framing*, AITC 105.

AMERICAN INSTITUTE
333 West Hampden Avenue

TIMBER CONSTRUCTION
Englewood, Colorado 80110

AITC 102–72
APPENDIX B
DEFLECTION AND CAMBER OF BEAMS

Adopted as Recommendations March 17, 1969
Copyright 1972 by American Institute of Timber Construction

CONTENTS

B1. INTRODUCTION

B1.1 Recommended deflection limitations for beams, joists, purlins, and girders, and recommended camber limitations for glued laminated bending members are included in this appendix.

B1.2 This standard does not cover light frame construction.

B1.3 Deflection may govern the design of many structural systems, particularly for longer spans. Strength calculations based on allowable stresses alone may result in sections that have too great a deflection. Limitations on deflection increase the stiffness of a member; camber limitations for glued laminated members do not.

B1.4 Deflection is a function of stiffness, *EI*, or modulus of elasticity multiplied by the moment of inertia.

B1.5 The permissible deflection of a structural member may be determined by one of the following conditions.

(*a*) Possible damage to attached or connected materials such as plaster and roofing.

(*b*) Effect of the function of the completed structure, such as undue vibration and springiness.

(*c*) The acceptable final shape or position of the completed structure or member, such as roof pitch and pockets affecting drainage or interior appearance.

(*d*) Effect on door clearance or effect on sash and glass below the member.

B1.6 Deflection varies with classifications of use; therefore different classifications are treated separately with regard to design recommendations. Consideration should be given to all factors, such as loads, spans, fastenings, and form, which permit or produce deflection.

B1.7 Glued laminated members can be cambered in production to compensate for deflections anticipated, as well as to improve appearance. The desired amount of camber varies with the classification of use. Therefore various classifications are treated separately as to both design and camber recommendations.

B2. MODULUS OF ELASTICITY

B2.1 Two allowable *E* values apply, one for wet and one for dry use. See AITC *Timber Construction Manual* for allowable *E* values for various species of glued laminated timber and sawn lumber. No adjustment factors for duration of loading are applied to *E* values in determination of elastic deformation of beams. Except for machine-graded lumber, an average value for the modulus of elasticity for the species is used in design.

B3. DEFLECTION – GENERAL

B3.1 **Elastic Deformation.** Applying loads, forces, and end rotations to a beam causes it to bend or change shape. Upon application of load, a member of given span and stiffness will deflect, in direct proportion to the load applied, by an amount approximating that computed by usual engineering formulas. The initial deflection is elastic in nature, and the member will return to its former shape when the load is removed.

B3.2 **Plastic Deformation.** Long continuation of the applied load results in additional deflection; this is plastic or inelastic deformation. Removal of load after plastic deformation has occurred results in immediate recovery of most of the elastic part of the total deflection. Further recovery at a slower rate, which equals the remainder of the elastic deformation, occurs. None of the plastic deformation is recovered. For any load increment, the plastic deformation (sometimes known as "set") under long application may become as much as the initial deformation without endangering the safety of the member. However, tests and experience show that normally the plastic deformation under long-time loading is approximately 50% of the elastic deformation for glued laminated members and for sawn members installed seasoned. Tests and experience also show that normally the plastic deformation under long-time loading is approximately 100% of the elastic deformation for sawn members installed unseasoned.

B3.3 **Combined Deformation.** It is necessary to provide extra stiffness when deformation or deflection during long periods of loading must be limited in amount. This can be done by the following methods.

B3.3.1   For glued laminated members, either the dead and other permanently applied loads are increased by one-half or two-thirds of the recommended value of modulus of elasticity is used in computing the deformation.

B3.3.2   For sawn members, the dead and other permanently applied loads are increased by one-half for members installed seasoned, or these loads are doubled for members installed unseasoned, in computing the deformation.

B3.4   Design Loads for Deflection Limits. In beam design, only the applied load is commonly used in calculating permissible deflections. However, when the applied load is less than the dead load, the dead load should be considered. For this reason two criteria for deflection limitations are suggested for roof and floor beams for these classifications of use.

B4. DEFLECTION – ROOF BEAMS

B4.1   Member size as determined by deflection is usually limited by either applied load only or dead load plus applied load, whichever governs, in accordance with Table 1. Applied load is live load, wind load, snow load, etc., or any combination thereof.

TABLE 1

RECOMMENDED ROOF BEAM DEFLECTION LIMITATIONS

Use Classification	Applied Load Only	Dead + Applied Load
Industrial	$l/180$	$l/120$
Commercial and institutional		
Without plaster ceiling	$l/240$	$l/180$
With plaster ceiling	$l/360$	$l/240$

l is span length in inches for deflection in inches.

B4.2   For special uses, such as beams supporting vibrating machines or carrying moving loads, more severe limitations may be required.

B4.3   Industrial Classification.

B4.3.1   For glued laminated members, *industrial classification* applies to construction in which ample camber is provided to offset deflection. Within these limits, deflection is not normally visible.

B4.3.2   For sawn members, *industrial classification* applies to construction for which appearance is not of prime importance and adequate drainage is provided.

B4.4   Commercial and Institutional Classification. This classification applies to churches, schools, residences, and other buildings for which appearance, absence of visible deflection, and minimizing of plaster cracking are of prime importance.

B4.5   Tapered beams may be designed for the same criteria as constant section members. For beams tapering in one direction only, approximate deflection may be determined as for a uniformly loaded simple beam, using the moment of inertia of the section at the center of the span. For symmetrical beams tapered from the centerline, deflection may be computed, using the method given in the AITC *Timber Construction Manual.*

B5. DEFLECTION – FLOOR BEAMS

B5.1   Member size as determined by deflection may be limited by either live load only or dead load plus live load, whichever governs, in accordance with the data in Table 2.

TABLE 2

RECOMMENDED FLOOR BEAM
DEFLECTION LIMITATIONS

Use Classification	Live Load Only	Dead + Live Load
Ordinary usage	$l/360$	$l/240$

B5.2   *Ordinary Classification* applies to construction in which walking comfort, minimized plaster cracking, and elimination of objectionable springiness are of prime importance. For special uses, such as beams supporting machines or equipment with operating limitations on alignment and vibration, more severe limitations may be required. For vibrating or rotating machines, designers often double or triple the dead weight of machines for deflection computations.

B6. DEFLECTION – BRIDGE BEAMS

B6.1   Highway bridge stringers shall be designed for $l/200$ to $l/300$ deflection limitations for live load only. Railway bridge stringers shall be designed for $l/300$ to $l/400$ deflection limitations for live load only.

B7. CAMBER OF GLUED LAMINATED BEAMS – GENERAL

B7.1   Camber can be built into a structural glued laminated timber beam by introducing curvature opposite to the anticipated deflection movement.

B7.2   In addition to variations in design criteria for different classifications of use, camber recommendations also vary according to whether the member is a simple, multiple, or cantilever span, whether roof drainage is to be provided by the camber, and other factors. Camber is not provided because of any consideration of strength.

B7.2.1   Camber – Beams. Camber is provided for better appearance and for drainage purposes. The recommended minimum camber for simple and multiple noncontinuous span beams is given in Table 3. In

TABLE 3

RECOMMENDED MINIMUM CAMBER FOR
GLUED LAMINATED TIMBER BEAMS FOR ALL
USE CLASSIFICATIONS

Roof beams[a]	$1\frac{1}{2}$ times dead load deflection
Floor beams[b]	$1\frac{1}{2}$ times dead load deflection
Bridge beams[c]	
Long span	2 times dead load deflection
Short span	2 times dead load deflection
	$+\frac{1}{2}$ applied load deflection

[a]Roof beams. The minimum camber of $1\frac{1}{2}$ times dead load deflection will produce a nearly level member under dead load alone after plastic deformation has occurred. Additional camber is usually provided to improve appearance and/or provide necessary roof drainage. Roof beams shall have a positive slope or camber equivalent to $\frac{1}{4}$ in. per foot of horizontal distance between the level of the drain and the high point of the roof, in addition to the minimum camber, to avoid the ponding of water.
[b]Floor beams. The minimum camber of $1\frac{1}{2}$ times dead load deflection will produce a nearly level member under dead load alone after plastic deformation has occurred. On long spans, a level ceiling may not be desirable because of the optical illusion that the ceiling sags. For warehouse or similar floors where live load may remain for long periods, additional camber shall be provided to give a level floor under the permanently applied load.
[c]Bridge beams. Bridge members are normally cambered for dead load only on multiple spans to obtain acceptable riding qualities.

general, continuous span members require less camber than do simple span members.

    B7.2.1.1 Consideration must be given to multiple span members to provide adequate roof drainage, and also to avoid excessive humps and valleys.

    B7.2.1.2 Reverse camber may be required in continuous multispan and cantilevered beams to provide adequate drainage. It is recommended that proper slope be provided in all roof design to provide drainage.

    B7.2.2 Camber–Practices. The camber in glued laminated members may be either circular or parabolic in shape. The difference between a circular and a parabolic curve is insignificant for the average case, and the curve to be used should be chosen by the manufacturer. It is important to standardize the cambers for similar span beams in a given job insofar as this is consistent with recognized engineering and construction practices to effect economy.

    B7.2.2.1 Cambers suggested are minimum for the majority of uses, but additional camber is sometimes desirable. In manufacturing practice, standard camber radii are used when they apply. Allowable manufacturing tolerance in cambering a member is plus or minus $\frac{1}{4}$ in.

B8. SPECIAL CONDITIONS

B8.1   Beams over Walls. In many structures, beams are carried over partitions or walls. Often the design calls for a beam with a 2 to 6 ft cantilever overhang at the eaves. The need to decide whether to camber the supported beams the same as the free span beams often arises, and the answer may be affected by the sequence of construction. It is recommended that all beams be cambered the same and a soffit detail be provided to conceal the opening between the beam and the top of the interior wall. The purposes of this practice are: to have the cornice or fascia boards straight; to permit the interior walls to be removed at a future time without unpleasant results; and to eliminate the possibility of a misplacement of straight and cambered members.

B8.2   Beams over Glass. Beams over glass windows should be given individual consideration with respect to both design and camber to provide the stiffness and form required by use conditions. It is possible to provide for free movement by allowing the glass to move within a cap and mullion.

B8.3   Beams over Doors. Special consideration should be given to design, camber, and door details to assure free movement of the door.

B8.4   Combined Materials. When materials or structural systems with different stiffness characteristics are combined to perform as a unit, special consideration should be given to design and camber.

B8.5   End Connections. Because normal deflection of pitched and curved beams causes minor end movement, special anchorage may be required.

AMERICAN INSTITUTE   **AITC**   TIMBER CONSTRUCTION
333 West Hampden Avenue   Englewood, Colorado 80110

AITC 103-72
· STANDARD FOR STRUCTURAL
GLUED LAMINATED TIMBER

Adopted as Recommendations March 17, 1969
Copyright 1972 by American Institute of Timber Construction

CONTENTS

1. GENERAL

1.1 The integrity of structural glued laminated timber is of paramount importance for protection of life and property. However, since such integrity can be assured only by continuous, detailed quality control by the laminator at all levels of production, a minimum standard covering requirements for the production, testing, inspection, identification, and certification of structural glued laminated timber is essential. Voluntary Product Standard PS56-73, *Structural Glued Laminated Timber*, meets such a requirement. The AITC recommends conformance with this standard for all production. The AITC Inspection Bureau makes available to its licensees certification marks and certificates identifying material produced in conformance with the Voluntary Product Standard and AITC requirements.

1.2 The Voluntary Product Standard provides the minimum detail requirements for the production of structural glued laminated timber. Copies of the current version may be obtained from AITC.

1

AMERICAN INSTITUTE   TIMBER CONSTRUCTION
333 West Hampden Avenue   Englewood, Colorado 80110

AITC 103-72
APPENDIX A
SELECTION OF ADHESIVES

Adopted as Recommendations March 17, 1969
Copyright 1972 by American Institute of Timber Construction

CONTENTS

A1. GENERAL

A1.1 Conditions of service determine the type of adhesive required. In general, dry-use (water-resistant) adhesive should be used for interior locations and wet-use (waterproof) adhesive for exterior locations. However, under some conditions, a member glued with dry-use adhesive may be used satisfactorily on an exterior member for certain uses and architectural details.

A1.2 It is not practical to use both types of adhesives within the length of the same member. If any portion of a member's length requires wet-use adhesives, wet-use adhesives must be used throughout its length.

A1.3 It should be kept in mind that the use of a wet-use adhesive will generally increase the cost of a laminated member; therefore, it should not be specified unless actually needed.

A2. DRY-USE ADHESIVES

A2.1 Casein Adhesive. Casein adhesive with a suitable mold inhibitor is the standard dry-use adhesive of the structural glued laminated timber industry. It has proved its dependability for over two generations in Europe and North America. It is used in large quantities by other wood products manufacturers as well as this industry.

A2.1.1 Casein adhesive with mold inhibitor is satisfactory in properly designed, constructed, and maintained buildings as long as the members are not subjected to repeated wettings or high humidity over a long period of time. Although casein adhesives can withstand some wetting during erection of the members, special attention should be given to the protection of the top face of beams, rafters, or arches during shipment and erection when end or beveled end is exposed at these locations. Angular cuts are often made that pass through one or more laminations and result in feathered ends on the individual laminations. These surfaces have greater than average moisture absorption and should be properly end-sealed to prevent delamination of the feathered ends. Although such damage is not likely to be of structural concern, it may be unsightly. All end cuts should be well sealed.

A2.2   Exterior Use. Two major requirements must be met to assure proper performance of casein adhesives in exterior locations. If the requirements of paragraphs A2.2.1 and A2.2.2 cannot be met, wet-use adhesives shall be used.

A2.2.1   Complete protection from the direct effects of precipitation on members must be provided either by undercutting the ends to keep off wind-driven moisture or by the use of fascia boards or end caps to prevent water from collecting on vertical surfaces of the members. Ends of members should be coated with white lead paste or treated with water-repellent sealer or by other effective process before the cap is applied.

A2.2.2   Casein adhesives are not considered suitable for laminated members intended for exterior use where the moisture content of the wood exceeds 16% for repeated or prolonged periods of service.

A2.3   Interior Use. Only one major condition must be satisfied to ensure proper performance of casein adhesives in interior locations: the moisture content of the wood must not exceed 16% for repeated or prolonged periods of service.

A2.3.1   Examples of interior use conditions in which the moisture content of the wood in service may be found to exceed 16% are members used in or adjacent to swimming or other pools when enclosed, shower rooms, ice skating rinks, car-wash operations, dairy barns, commercial laundries, and in certain storage and processing operations, as for flax processing, certain paper and textile manufacture, vat rooms, or where highly humid conditions are induced by the processes.

A2.4   Performance Requirements. Dry-use adhesives shall comply with the requirements of Voluntary Product Standard PS56-73, *Structural Glued Laminated Timber*.

A3. WET-USE ADHESIVES

A3.1   Phenol, Resorcinol, and Melamine Base Adhesives. Phenol, resorcinol, and melamine base adhesives will withstand the most severe conditions of exposure. They are more expensive than water-resistant adhesives. Phenol-resorcinol base or resorcinol base adhesives are the most widely used wet-use adhesives in structural glued laminated members.

A3.2   Use. Although the wet-use adhesives may be employed for all conditions of use, they are generally used only when the equilibrium moisture content of the members in service exceeds 16%, such as the following.

A3.2.1　Members which must be pressure treated.

A3.2.2　Marine vessels and structures such as barges, ships, piers, wharves, docks, slips, and dredge spuds.

A3.2.3　Members used in or adjacent to swimming or other pools when enclosed, shower rooms, ice skating rinks, car-wash operations, dairy barns, commercial laundries, and in certain storage and processing operations, as for flax processing, certain paper and textile manufacture, vat rooms, or where highly humid conditions are induced by the processes.

A3.2.4　Structures and members exposed to the weather, such as bridges and bridge girders (other than for temporary construction such as falsework and centering).

A3.3　Performance Requirements. Wet-use adhesives shall comply with the requirements of Voluntary Product Standard PS56-73, *Structural Glued Laminated Timber*.

AMERICAN INSTITUTE
333 West Hampden Avenue

TIMBER CONSTRUCTION
Englewood, Colorado 80110

AITC 104-72
TYPICAL CONSTRUCTION DETAILS

Adopted as Recommendations March 16, 1969
Copyright 1972 by American Institute of Timber Construction

CONTENTS

1. INTRODUCTION

1.1 These recommended typical construction details are intended as guides and suggestions for architects and engineers to expedite their work and to give greater assurance of high quality with a minimum of maintenance for structures employing engineered timber construction. The details shown have been compiled from standard details developed and used by timber fabricators.

1.2 Because they are to be used only as guides or suggestions, dimensions have not been included and the drawings should not be scaled. The quantities and sizes of bolts, connectors, and other hardware are illustrative only. The actual quantities and sizes required will depend on the loads to be carried and the size of members used. The architect or engineer must select, modify, and design the details best suited to fit the particular requirements of the job at hand. Some environmental conditions may require special considerations for protection of timber from weathering, decay, and insect attack and for protection of metal connecting devices from corrosion. He should keep in mind ease and economy of assembly and erection.

1.3   In the preparation of these details, particular attention has been given to minimizing maintenance and increasing durability through design and construction. Consideration has been given to differential movements resulting from dimensional changes. Moisture barriers, flashing, preservative treatment, wet-use adhesives, and other features have been designated where necessary to avoid moisture or water traps. (See Section 12, *Protection Details*.) Durable structures will result when these details are incorporated with other good design and construction practices such as: providing adequate roof and site drainage, providing proper protection during construction and protecting metal from corrosion by use of corrosion-resistant metals or by resistant coatings or platings.

1.4   Other considerations are also necessary in the design of structures employing engineered timber construction. These are outlined in *Guide Specifications for Structural Timber Framing*, AITC 107, and are covered in detail in *Selection of Adhesives*, Appendix A of AITC 103, *Recommended Practice for Protection of Structural Glued Laminated Timber During Transit, Storage, and Erection*, AITC 111, and in various other AITC standards.

2. BEAM TYPES

Beam names describe the top and bottom surfaces of the beam; in Figure 1, the words before the dash describe the top surface; the word following the dash describes the bottom surface. The letter *S* designates a sawn surface. In general, "tapered" refers to a sawn surface, and "pitched" to an unsawn sloped surface. Sawn surfaces on the tension side of a beam should be avoided.

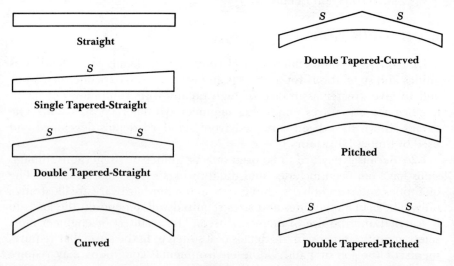

Figure 1

3. ARCH TYPES

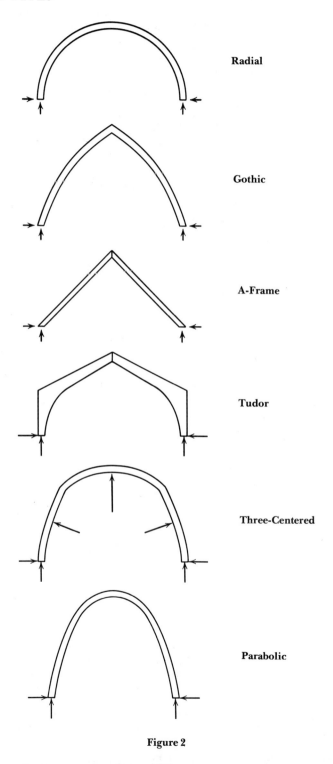

Figure 2

4. BEAM ANCHORAGES

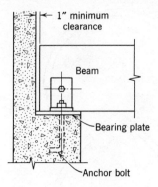

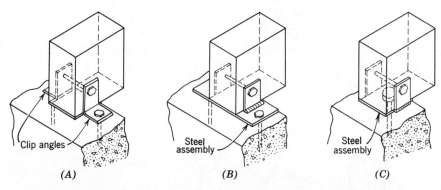

Figure 3. CLEARANCE DETAIL. For beam anchorages which resist both uplift and horital forces. May have one or more anchor bolts in masonry, and one or more bolts with or without shear plates through beam. May be separate angles with bearing plate as in (*A*), bearing plate with welded fins as in (*B*), or, when pilaster is not wide enough for outside anchor bolts, bolts may be welded to underside of bearing plate or bolts may be under beam with nuts countersunk into beam as in (*C*). One-inch minimum clearance or impervious moisture barrier on all wall contact surfaces, ends, sides, and tops (if masonry exists above beam end).

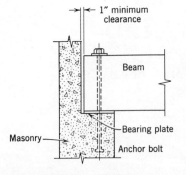

Figure 4. SIMPLE BEAM ANCHORAGE— CLEARANCE DETAIL. For beams with depths 24 in. and less. Resists uplift and small horizontal forces. Bolt holes should be field bored $\frac{3}{16}$ in. oversize. Bearing plate or moisture barrier is recommended. One-inch minimum clearance or impervious moisture barrier on all wall contact surfaces, ends, sides, and tops (if masonry exists above beam end).

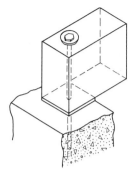

Figure 5. SIMPLE BEAM ANCHORAGE-ISOMETRIC VIEW.

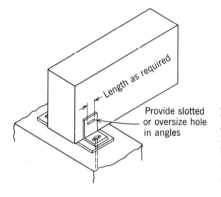

Figure 6. CURVED OR PITCHED BEAM ANCHORAGE – TYPICAL SLIP JOINT. Slotted or oversize holes at one or both ends of beam permit horizontal movement under lateral deflection or deformation. Usually, only the angle bolt holes are slotted.

5. CANTILEVER BEAM CONNECTIONS

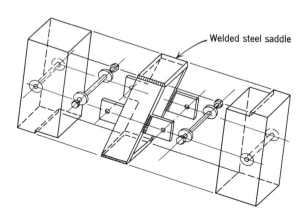

Figure 7. SADDLE TYPE WITH TENSION TIE – EXPLODED VIEW. For moderate and heavy loads. Ends of members are cut square.

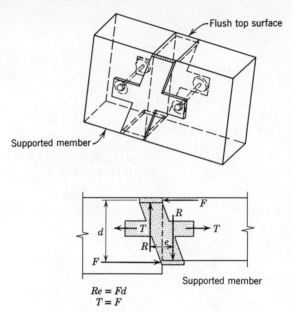

$$Re = Fd$$
$$T = F$$

Figure 8.   SADDLE TYPE WITH TENSION TIE – ASSEMBLY AND FORCE DIAGRAM.
In the saddle-type cantilever beam connection, the vertical reaction of the supported member is carried by the saddle side plates and transferred in bearing perpendicular to grain to both the supported and supporting members by the saddle bearing plates. The rotation of the saddle due to the eccentric loading is resisted by the bearing of the edge of the saddle bearing plate against the end grain of both the supported and the supporting members. To obtain this end grain bearing on the edge of the bearing plate it is necessary to let the plate into the top face of the supporting member and also into the bottom face of the supported member only when both beams are of the same depth. If the supported member is of lesser depth, this end dap on the lower face is not required to obtain the end grain bearing. The tension side plates are used to resist the separation force developed between the beams by the rotation couple of the end grain bearing on the bearing plates, and also to serve as a tension tie where an axial tension tie between the beams is required.

In deep members, the shrinkage in depth may be large enough to cause vertical end reactions to be shifted to the tension tie bolts at A and B. To prevent this from occurring, the holes in the saddle at A and B should be vertical slots. Shrinkage in depth of a laminated timber decreases the end bearing area of the plate. Where significant shrinkage is anticipated, additional bearing area can be provided by installing compression plates between ends of the members.

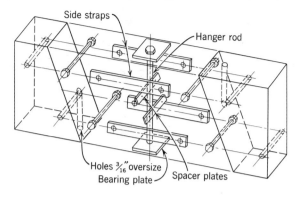

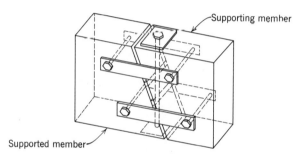

Figure 9. HANGER ROD TYPE – EXPLODED VIEW AND ASSEMBLY. For light, moderate, and heavy loads. In the hanger rod type of cantilever beam connection, the vertical reaction of the supported member is carried in tension by the hanger rod. The hanger rod must be sized to carry this load in tension. The hanger rod bearing plates must be sized to transfer the vertical reaction in bearing perpendicular to grain in both the supported and the supporting members. Spacer plates are used and located as close as possible to the neutral axis to provide clearance between the beam ends and to allow for end rotation in the members without crushing the beam ends at their top and bottom edges. These spacer plates are steel flat bars attached to the beams with nails through predrilled holes in the spacer plates. The side straps are used to hold the beam ends in alignment and to serve as tension ties where an axial tension tie between the beams is required.

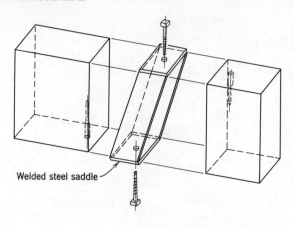

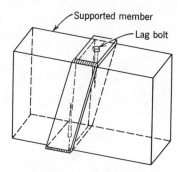

Figure 10.   SIMPLE SADDLE TYPE–EXPLODED VIEW AND ASSEMBLY. For light loads. Ends of members are cut square. The simple saddle type of cantilever beam hanger uses the same saddle-type support method as the "saddle with tie" type, but the eccentric rotation is resisted by lag bolts through the saddle bearing plate. No dapping is required. Combinations of these two types may also be used.

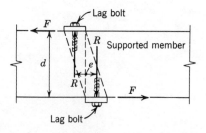

Figure 11.   SIMPLE SADDLE TYPE–FORCE DIAGRAM. The rotation due to the eccentric loading must be provided for.

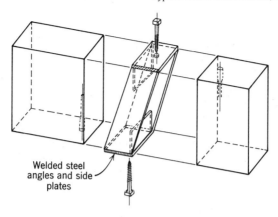

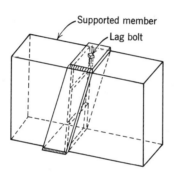

Figure 12.   WELDED ANGLE TYPE – EXPLODED VIEW AND ASSEMBLY.

6. BEAM AND PURLIN HANGERS

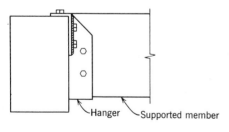

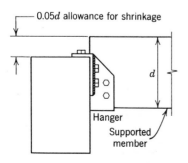

Figure 13.   SEASONED MEMBERS. When supported members are seasoned material, the top of the supported member may be set flush with the top of the hanger strap.

Figure 14.   UNSEASONED MEMBERS. When supported members are of unseasoned material, the hangers should be so dimensioned that the top edge of the supported member is raised above the top of the supporting member or the top of the hanger strap to allow for shrinkage as the members season in place. For supported members with moisture content at or above fiber saturation point when installed, the distance raised should be about 5% of the member's depth above its bearing point.

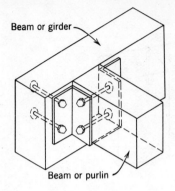

Figure 15.   SADDLE TYPE. For moderate and heavy loads. Well-suited for one-sided connections to prevent rotation of girder. The saddle may be a combination of steel shapes.

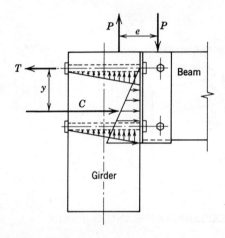

Figure 16.   SADDLE TYPE — FORCE DIA-GRAM. Eccentric moment of rotation is Pe. Direction of rotation is clockwise.

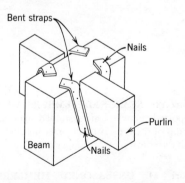

Figure 17. BENT STRAP TYPE. For light and moderate loads. Not recommended when close fit is desired for appearance. Purlins must be raised above top of beam to allow sheathing to clear straps.

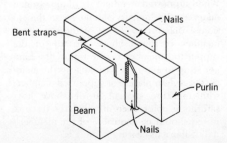

Figure 18. WELDED AND BENT STRAP TYPE. For moderate and heavy loads. Provides a uniform fit where good appearance is desired. Purlins must be raised above top of beam to allow sheathing to clear straps.

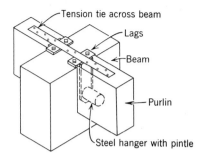

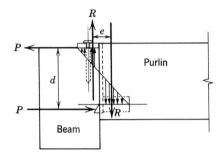

Figure 19. CONCEALED TYPE—AS-SEMBLY AND FORCE DIAGRAM. For light and moderate loads. Hardware is completely concealed. Not recommended for use with unseasoned purlins. Purlin design includes bearing area and notched beam action Fifty percent increase for shear in joint detail does not apply. Note bearing stress perpendicular to grain in force diagram. $Re = Pd$.

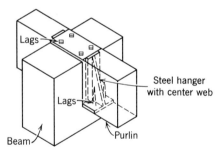

Figure 20. PARTIALLY CONCEALED TYPE. For moderate and heavy loads. Base may be let in flush with bottom of purlins.

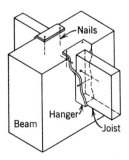

Figure 21. STAMPED BUCKET HANGER. For light loads and small joists. Stamped from light-gage metal.

7. BEAM TO COLUMN CONNECTIONS

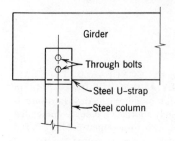

Figure 22. GIRDER TO STEEL COLUMN.
Steel U-strap passes under timber girder and is
welded to top of steel column.

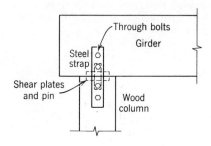

Figure 23. GIRDER TO WOOD COLUMN.
Connection provides for uplift. Metal bearing
plate may be used where column cross-sectional
area is insufficient to provide bearing for girder
in compression perpendicular to grain.

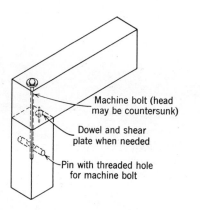

**Figure 24. CONCEALED TYPE – GIRDER
TO WOOD COLUMN.** For lighter loads, a lag
bolt and spiral dowel may be used in place of the
machine bolt and pin.

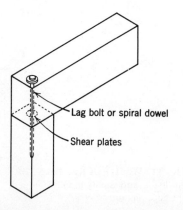

**Figure 25. CONCEALED TYPE GIRDER TO
WOOD COLUMN.**

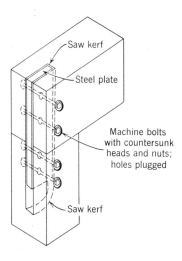

Figure 26. CONCEALED TYPE GIRDER TO WOOD COLUMN.

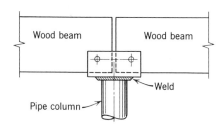

Figure 27. BEAMS TO PIPE COLUMN. Similar to the "girder to steel column" connection (see Figure 22).

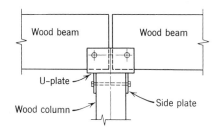

Figure 28. BEAMS TO WOOD COLUMN – U-PLATE. Steel U-plate passes under abutting wood beams and is welded to steel side plates bolted to wood column.

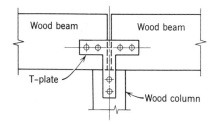

Figure 29. BEAMS TO WOOD COLUMN – T-PLATES. Steel T-plate is bolted to abutting wood beams and to wood column. Loose bearing plate may be used where column cross-sectional area is insufficient to provide bearing for beams in compression perpendicular to grain.

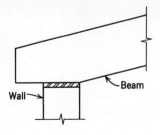

Figure 30. PITCHED BEAM END DETAIL. Soffit edge of beam bearing cut must be on bearing plate unless special consideration is given in design. (See also *Beam Anchorages*, Section 4.)

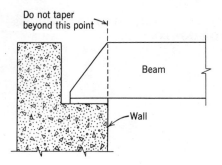

Figure 31. TAPERED END CUT. When beam end cut, or fire cut, extends beyond the inside of the wall, check the shear strength of the reduced section in accordance with the *Timber Construction Manual*. (See also *Beam Anchorages*, Section 4.)

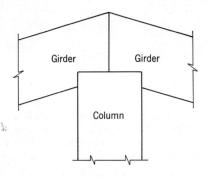

Figure 32. SHED ROOF TYPE END DETAIL. Girder is notched for connection to post or column. Girders may be pitched away from both sides, or from only one side of column. Girder must be designed for notched beam action. (See also *Beam Anchorages*, Section 4.)

8. COLUMN ANCHORAGES

Column bearing elevation should be at least 3 inches above grade or finish floor if a grade-type floor construction is used. In locations where column base anchorages are subject to damage by moving vehicles, protection of the columns from such damage should be considered.

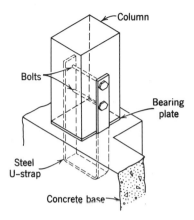

Figure 33. U-STRAP ANCHORAGE TO CONCRETE BASE. Recommended for industrial buildings and warehouses to resist both horizontal forces and uplift. Bearing plate or moisture barrier is recommended. May be used with shear plates.

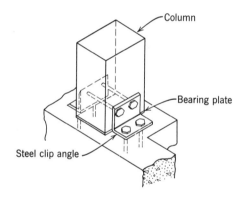

Figure 34. CLIP ANGLE ANCHORAGE TO CONCRETE BASE. Recommended for industrial buildings and warehouses to resist both horizontal forces and uplift. Bearing plate or moisture barrier is recommended.

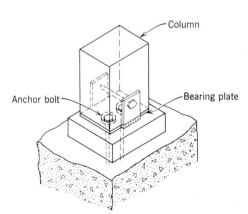

Figure 35. RAISED FOOTING COLUMN ANCHORAGE. For use where pedestal is limited in size. Resists some horizontal forces and uplift.

9. ARCH ANCHORAGES

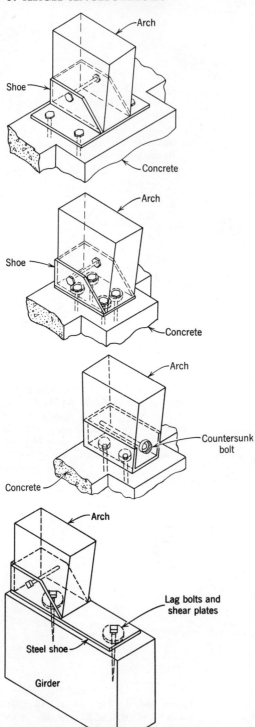

Figure 36. ARCH SHOE WITH EXPOSED ANCHOR BOLTS. Thrust is taken by the anchor bolts in shear into the concrete.

Figure 37. ARCH SHOE WITH CONCEALED ANCHOR BOLTS. Daps are provided in arch base for anchor bolt heads. Thrust is taken by the anchor bolts in shear into the concrete.

Figure 38. ARCH ANCHORAGE TO CONCRETE BASE. This anchorage provides for concealed anchor bolts as in Figure 37. Steel shoe is flush with arch surfaces, and bolt head is countersunk.

Figure 39. ARCH ANCHORAGE TO TIMBER GIRDER. Vertical load is taken directly by bearing into timber girder. Vertical uplift and thrust are taken by the lag bolts and shear plates into the girder tie.

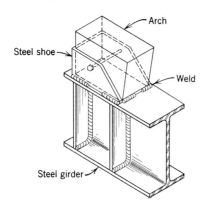

Figure 40. ARCH ANCHORAGE TO STEEL GIRDER. Vertical uplift load and thrust are taken through the weld.

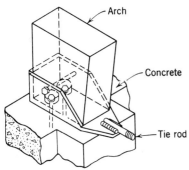

Figure 41. TIE ROD TO ARCH SHOE. Thrust due to vertical load is taken directly by the tie rod welded to the arch shoe.

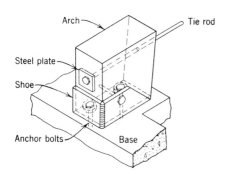

Figure 42. TIE ROD TO ARCH. Thrust due to vertical load is taken directly by the tie rod.

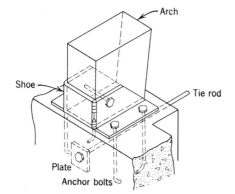

Figure 43. TIE ROD IN CONCRETE. Thrust is taken by anchor bolts in shear into the concrete foundation and tie rod.

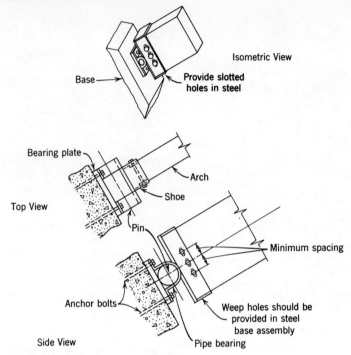

Figure 44.   TRUE HINGE ANCHORAGE FOR ARCHES. Recommended for arches where true hinge action is desired.

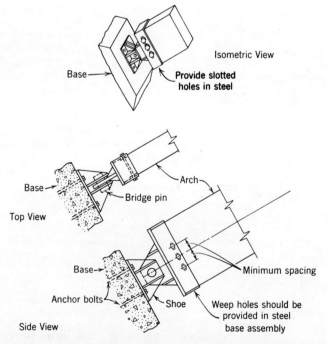

Figure 45.   TRUE HINGE ANCHORAGE FOR ARCHES. Recommended for arches where true hinge action is desired. Bridge pin is welded to arch shoe. Pipe bearings are bolted to base plate.

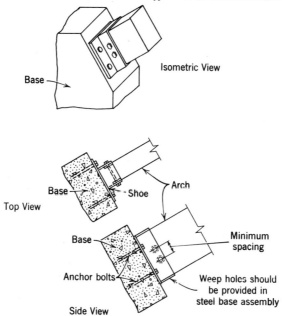

Figure 46.   ARCH ANCHORAGE WHERE TRUE HINGE IS NOT REQUIRED. Recommended for smaller foundation arches where a true hinge is not required. Base shoe is anchored directly to buttress.

10. ARCH CONNECTIONS

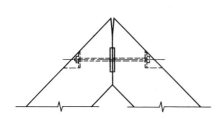

Figure 47.   ARCH PEAK. For arches with slope 4:12 and greater. This connection will transfer both vertical forces (shear) and horizontal forces (tension and compression). It consists of two shear plates back-to-back and a through bolt or threaded rod with washers counterbored into the arch. For shear value of bolts and shear plates, 60% of the value of that angle to grain in side grain is used. To avoid local crushing of the peak tips of arch due to dead load deflection, the tips are often beveled off as shown.

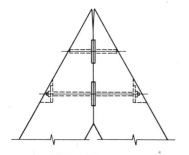

Figure 48.   ARCH PEAK. When the vertical shear is too great for one pair of shear plates, or when deep sections would require extra shear plates for alignment, additional pairs of shear plates centered on dowels or through bolts may be used.

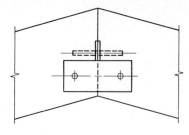

Figure 49. ARCH PEAK. For arches with slopes that would require excessively long through bolts; shear plates back-to-back centered on a dowel are used in conjunction with a tie plate and through bolts. When appearance is important, a bent plate may be dapped into the top of the arch and secured with lags.

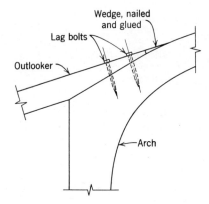

Figure 50. OUTLOOKER CONNECTION TO HAUNCHED ARCH. Lag bolts used in this connection should be of a length such that the withdrawal resistance of the threads is in the main section of the arch and so designed as to resist any cantilever action of the outlooker. Lag bolts may be counterbored when decking is applied. Arch end of outlooker must not be feathered.

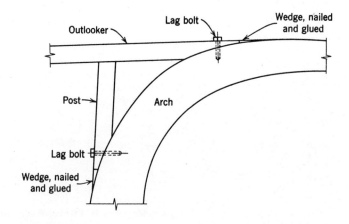

Figure 51. OUTLOOKER CONNECTION TO CURVED ARCH. Post and outlooker are let into the arch surface. Ends of post or outlooker must not be feathered.

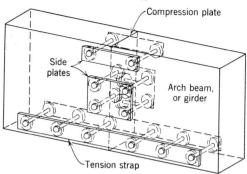

Figure 52. MOMENT SPLICE. Although moment splices are rarely used in beams or girders, they are often employed in arches and rigid frames. Drawing shows a typical moment splice. Compression stress is taken in bearing on the wood through a steel compression plate. Tension is taken across the splice by means of steel straps and shear plates. Side plates and straps are used to hold sides and tops of members in position. Shear is taken by shear plates in end grain. Bolts and shear plates are used as design and construction considerations require. All actions of compression, shear, and tension that normally pass through the splice must be properly and adequately resisted.

11. TRUSS CONNECTIONS

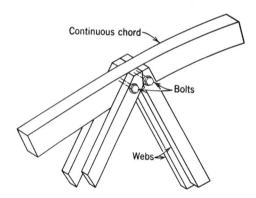

Figure 53. MONOCHORD—WEBS ON OUTSIDE. For trusses with continuous upper chord. Must be designed as an eccentric joint. When timber connectors are used, minimum end distance requirements must be met.

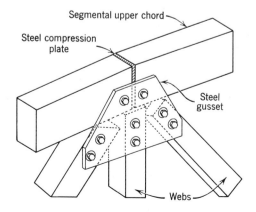

Figure 54. MONOCHORD—STEEL PLATE GUSSET. For trusses with segmental upper chord. Full bearing between upper chord members is required. Compression plate must be provided between ends of upper chord segments. When timber connectors are used, minimum end distance requirements must be met. Minimum of $\frac{1}{4}$ in. clearance between web ends and chord.

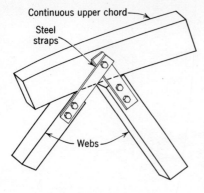

Continuous upper chord

Steel straps

Webs

Figure 55.   MONOCHORD – STEEL STRAPS. For trusses with continuous upper chord. When timber connectors are used, minimum end distance requirements must be met. Minimum of $\frac{1}{4}$ in. clearance between web ends and chord.

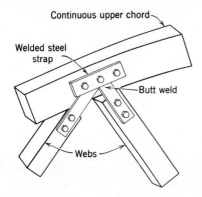

Continuous upper chord

Welded steel strap

Butt weld

Webs

Figure 56.   MONOCHORD – STEEL STRAP ASSEMBLY. Similar to connection shown in Figure 55. Steel straps are welded together. Minimum of $\frac{1}{4}$ in. clearance between web ends and chord.

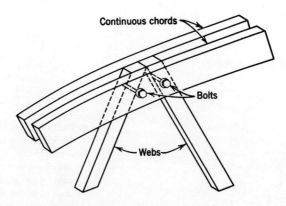

Continuous chords

Bolts

Webs

Figure 57.   TWO-LEAF CHORD – WEBS BETWEEN LEAVES. For trusses with continuous upper chord. Must be designed as an eccentric joint. When timber connectors are used, minimum end distance requirements must be met.

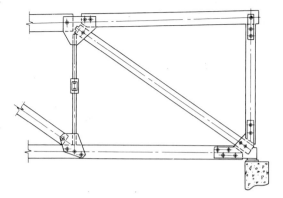

Figure 58.   TRUSS WITH TOP OR BOTTOM CHORD EXTENDING TO SUPPORT.
When top or bottom chord extends to a support, the chord should be broken and hinged at the first panel point to prevent high secondary stress in the chord due to truss deformation.

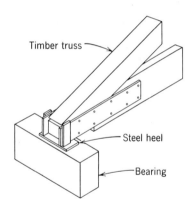

Figure 59.   TRUSS HEEL CONNECTION.
If substantial cross grain shrinkage is anticipated, double steel straps may be used in place of single strap.

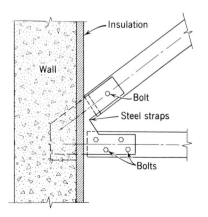

Figure 60.   TRUSS HEEL EMBEDDED IN WALL. For use in refrigerated buildings. Only steel straps extend into the wall.

12. PROTECTION DETAILS

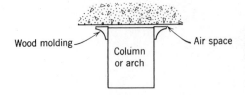

Figure 61. WOOD MEMBER AGAINST CONTINUOUS MASONRY WALL. Minimum of 1 in. air space between member and wall, or adequate moisture barrier, must be provided.

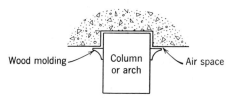

Figure 62. WOOD MEMBER SET IN MASONRY WALL POCKET. Minimum of 1 in. air space between member and wall pocket, or adequate moisture barrier, must be provided.

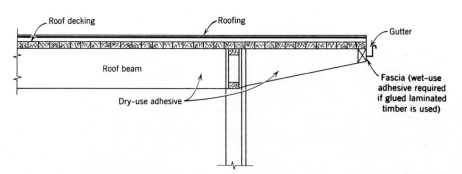

Figure 63. PROTECTION CONSIDERATIONS FOR BUILDING WITH COVERED OVERHANG. Beam is protected from direct exposure to weather by fascia. Dry-use (water-resistant) adhesives may be used. Roof should be sloped for drainage or designed to prevent ponding of water. Fascia should be preservatively treated.

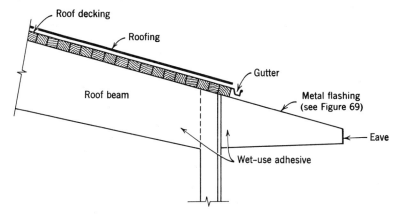

Figure 64. PROTECTION CONSIDERATIONS FOR BUILDING WITH UNCOVERED OVERHANG. Portion of beam extending outside of building to be protected by metal cap and painted regularly for protection from weathering. Wet-use (waterproof) adhesives must be used. Exposed portion of beam should be preservatively treated.

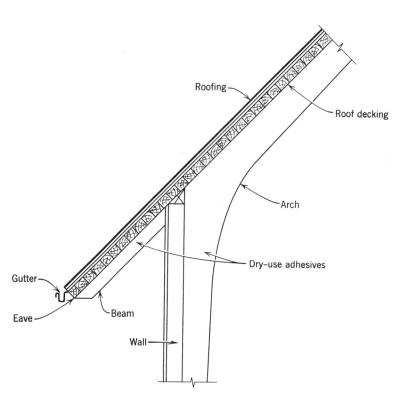

Figure 65. PROTECTION CONSIDERATIONS FOR ARCH OUTLOOKER OVERHANG. Outlooker is protected from direct exposure to weather. Dry-use (water-resistant) adhesives may be used in outlooker as well as in arch.

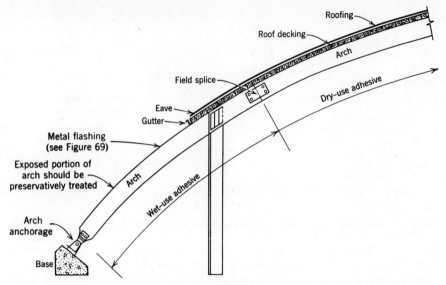

Figure 66.   PROTECTION CONSIDERATIONS FOR PARTIALLY EXPOSED ARCHES.
Portion of arch leg extending outside of building to be protected by metal flashing and
painted regularly for protection from weathering. Arch end to be set in mastic. Wet-use
(waterproof) adhesives must be used on portion of arch extending outside of building. At
least 12 in. clearance must be provided between arch base and grade. Ground must be sloped
away from building. Preservative treatment in accordance with *Treating Standard for Structural
Timber Framing*, AITC 109, should be used for exposed portion of arch.

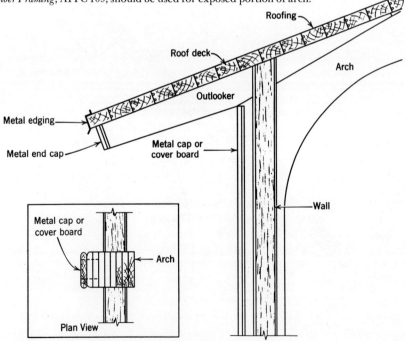

Figure 67.   ARCH LEG PROTECTION. Metal end cap or cover board on edge of exterior
portion of arch. Metal cap is as illustrated in the following details. Cover board is vertical grain
or overlaid board set in building sealant and attached with weatherproof nails or screws. All
wood with exterior exposure must be adequately protected and maintained. When the outlooker overhang is not adequate to protect the arch leg from moisture, the arch leg should be
preservatively treated.

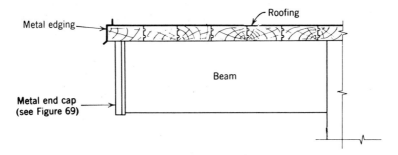

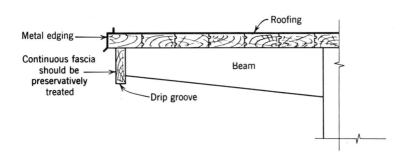

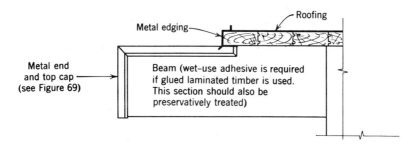

Figure 68. END AND TOP PROTECTION FOR OVERHANGS. Metal end caps of the types illustrated in the following details are used. Metal edging is an alternate for the gutters shown in the details in Figures 63 through 66.

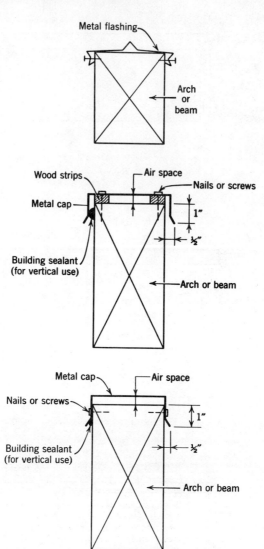

Figure 69.   PROTECTIVE METAL CAP OR FLASHING DETAILS. Caps or flashings are made of 20-gage minimum thickness weatherproof metal. Nails or screws are weatherproofed, and heads are sealed with building sealant or Neoprene washers. A minimum of $\frac{1}{2}$ in. air space must be provided between cap and top of wood section. For vertical use conditions, a continuous bead of building sealant is required.

AMERICAN INSTITUTE   TIMBER CONSTRUCTION
333 West Hampden Avenue   Englewood, Colorado 80110

AITC 105-65
RECOMMENDED PRACTICE FOR THE ERECTION OF STRUCTURAL TIMBER FRAMING

Adopted as Recommendations February 16, 1965
Copyright 1972 by American Institute of Timber Construction

CONTENTS

1. PREFACE

1.1 These erection recommendations describe acceptable practices for the assembly and erection of engineered timber construction. Usually the term erection will include assembly at the job site. (See *Definitions*, AITC 101.)

2. WORKMANSHIP

2.1 Erection of structural timber framing shall be under the direction of construction supervisors with satisfactory experience.

2.2 Construction requires a high degree of safety for the protection of life and property, and it is necessary that safe erection methods be employed at all times. Standards for erection equipment and personnel are established herein solely for these purposes.

3. ERECTION

3.1 Assembly. Job site assembly before erection shall be the responsibility of the erector. Joints shall be fastened securely without damage. End compression joints shall be brought to full bearing. Compression plates shall be installed where intended. Assemblies shall be checked for pre-

1

scribed overall dimensions, accuracy of anchorages, and prescribed camber before erection.

3.2   Bracing. All framework shall be carried up true and plumb, and temporary erection bracing shall be introduced wherever necessary to take care of all loads to which the structure may be normally subjected, including equipment and the operation of same. Such bracing shall be left in place as long as may be required for safety. See also "Bracing," Section 11 of AITC 102, and *Code of Standard Practice*, AITC 106. (See *References*, AITC 101.)

3.3   Adequacy of Temporary Connections. As erection progresses, the work shall be securely bolted up, or nailed as necessary, to take care of all dead load, erection stresses, and normal weather conditions.

3.4   Alignment. Final tightening of alignment bolts shall not be completed until the structure has been properly aligned.

3.5   Field Welding. The joining, holding, and welding of steel connections in the field shall be performed according to the requirements for shop work of such operations except such as manifestly apply to shop conditions only. Compliance shall be to the specifications of the American Institute of Steel Construction and of the American Welding Society. (See *References*, AITC 101.)

3.6   Cutting, Framing, and Boring. All end cuts shall be coated with an approved moisture seal, unless otherwise specified. All cutting, framing, and boring shall be done with due consideration for ultimate shrinkages and in accordance with the requirements of shop practice. If timber framing has been pressure-treated, cutting, framing, or boring after treatment should be avoided or at least, insofar as possible, held to a minimum; in any event, additional treatment should be applied to these areas in accordance with AWPA Standard M4.

4. MATERIALS CONTROL

4.1   All timber framing that requires moisture content control, whether sawn lumber or glued laminated timber, shall be protected against moisture pickup during erection operations. Any fabricated structural materials to be stored for an extended period of time before erection should, insofar as is practicable, be assembled into subassemblies for storage.

4.2   When erected by the buyer, all fabricated materials shall be inspected and accepted for compliance with specifications and shop drawings before being installed in assembled structures. The erector shall be responsible for any damage due to transporting, storage, or other cause beyond the control of the fabricator. Materials that do not comply with plans and specifications at the time of assembly and/or erection shall not be used.

AMERICAN INSTITUTE
333 West Hampden Avenue

TIMBER CONSTRUCTION
Englewood, Colorado 80110

AITC 106-65
CODE OF STANDARD PRACTICE

Adopted as Recommendations February 16, 1965
Copyright 1972 by American Institute of Timber Construction

CONTENTS

1. GENERAL

1.1 Scope. The rules and practices herein are adopted by the American Institute of Timber Construction as recommendations for the industry and for all conditions relating to the use of engineered timber construction, unless the contract between the buyer and the seller specifies otherwise.

1.2 Terminology. For purposes of this code, the following terminology applies.

1.2.1 Buyer. The purchaser and/or owner of the structure; the term includes the architect, engineer, general contractor, public authority, or other designated representative of the owner.

1.2.2 Seller. The furnisher of structural timber framing who may perform one or more of the operations of design, supply, lamination, fabrication, assembly, or erection.

1.3 Standards. Unless otherwise specified or required, the latest editions of the standards as listed in *References*, AITC 101, shall apply. In case of

1

conflict, the specifications recommended by the American Institute of Timber Construction shall govern.

1.4   Plans and Specifications for Bidding. The plans shall show a general design, with loads, sizes, sections, and arrangement of various members, with floor levels, column centers, roof slopes, and permanent bracing, and shall show the character and extent of the work to be performed with sufficient dimensions to permit the making of an accurate estimate of costs. Earthquake and other special bracing shall be included when required.

1.5   Responsibility for Design and Erection.

1.5.1   Responsibility for Design.

1.5.1.1   When the buyer provides any or all of the design plans and specifications, the seller is not responsible for the suitability, adequacy, or legality of the design.

1.5.1.2   When the buyer purchases a product designed to satisfy a stated set of design criteria, a stated set of conditions of use, or both, the seller's responsibility is limited by and to the representations set forth in his then current catalogs and advertising material with respect to such product and its use.

1.5.1.3   When the seller, upon instruction from the buyer, furnishes timber design service, his responsibility is limited by and to the design data furnished by the buyer and by and to the design criteria of the *Standards for the Design of Structural Timber Framing*, AITC 102, unless special conditions are made known to and accepted in writing by the seller. In all cases, the seller may rely upon the buyer's representations as to the provisions of the applicable building code or as to any other matters. (See *References*, AITC 101.)

1.5.2   Responsibility for Erection.

1.5.2.1   The seller is not responsible for erection, its practicability or its safety, if such erection is performed by others.

1.5.2.2   Excessive or improper loading of framing members or removal of any permanent or erection bracing relieves the seller from any responsibility.

1.5.2.3   The seller is not responsible for the adequacy of columns, walls, supports, and other items furnished by others.

1.5.2.4   The seller is not responsible for the structural adequacy of the structural members when they are improperly cut, drilled, or otherwise damaged by others, such as those from other trades working on the structure.

1.5.2.5   See the provisions of the following paragraphs and particularly those of paragraph 2.1, and Sections 8 and 9.

1.6   Patented Devices. The seller shall not be responsible for claims arising from the use of patented designs, devices, or parts shown on the buyer's plans or called for by the specifications furnished by the buyer, but the seller shall protect the buyer against claims arising from the use of patented designs, devices, or parts proposed by the seller.

2. CLASSIFICATION OF FURNISHED AND UNFURNISHED ITEMS

2.1 Furnished Structural Items.

2.1.1 The contract between the seller and the buyer shall specify the work to be undertaken and the structural items to be furnished by the seller in the absence of contract provisions to the contrary; the work undertaken by the seller for the complete structural framework shall include the furnishing of the items listed below. This shall not be construed to indicate that the contract is limited to these items. The structural framework so mentioned is considered to constitute a free-standing structural frame that rests upon supports furnished by others, but is generally not considered to include the light construction items, such as sheathing, studding, millwork, and like items. These light construction items and others may, however, be a part of a structural contract when so designated.

(*a*) Anchors for structural timbers.
(*b*) Steel bases for structural timbers.
(*c*) Beams and girders.
(*d*) Columns and posts.
(*e*) Purlins.
(*f*) Trusses.
(*g*) Permanent bracing.
(*h*) Struts.
(*i*) Rods.
(*j*) Fastenings such as bolts, screws, nails, spikes, and washers that interconnect structural frame.
(*k*) Bearing plates.
(*l*) Bearing shoes.
(*m*) Hangers.
(*n*) Post caps.
(*o*) Tie and sag rods.

2.1.2 Unless specifically agreed to as part of the contract, timber items and fastenings that are essentially required for the assembly or erection of materials supplied by other trades will not be furnished, even though shown on the plans as being fastened to the structural timber.

2.1.3 The size of individual pieces furnished by the seller may be limited by the permissible weight and/or clearance demands of transportation. Unless otherwise directed by the contract, the seller will provide for such field connections as will permit shipment and in his judgment require the least practicable amount of field work, and the assembly and erection of all field connections shall be a part of the erection work, whether performed by the seller or the buyer. Length and size of individual pieces shall be in accordance with the seller's details, as approved by the buyer.

2.1.4 Fabrication furnished by the seller is to include all practicable trimming, shaping, boring, framing, grooving, marking, and similar items of the various component members so that they may be readily assembled into the whole. However, occasionally there are operations that must be left for field handling, and these shall be the responsibility of the erector.

The seller should hold these operations to a practical minimum and should in general confine them to cases like or similar to those described in the following two paragraphs.

2.1.5   Exact length, end cut, or boring may not be determinable from the plans for struts, purlins, bracing, or other members in end bays between last truss or arch and end wall. Generally these are shipped with one end framed and one end not framed, and they are so shown on the shop details.

2.1.6   Unless otherwise agreed upon, when the boring of certain holes or other fabrication is limited to one or a few trusses, arches, or frames otherwise identical that, if the operation is performed in the shop, such heavy members would require individual marking and subsequent expensive sorting on the job, such operations shall be left for field work and will be so shown on the shop details.

2.1.7   Fabrication shall be considered as comprising all those operations of laminating, cutting, trimming, boring, routing, and planing as will fit the timbers for assembly without further fabrication, except for those items that, in the best interests of the work, may be left for field operations.

2.1.8   In timber work, the term *fabrication* does not include assembly, and usually all items are shipped to the job site completely knocked down unless otherwise agreed upon. Fabricator may, however, elect to shop-assemble for short-haul shipments.

2.2   Unfurnished Items.

2.2.1   Unless specifically agreed otherwise, the seller shall not furnish the following listed items and they shall not be considered part of the structural framework contract.

(*a*) Studding.
(*b*) Sheathing.
(*c*) Millwork.
(*d*) Trim.
(*e*) Joists.
(*f*) Rafters.
(*g*) Staging.
(*h*) Fastenings other than structural timber to structural timber.
(*i*) Formwork unless special.
(*j*) Roof crickets.
(*k*) Lath.
(*l*) Shingles.
(*m*) Siding.
(*n*) Flooring.
(*o*) All other items not included in the list to be furnished.

3. INVOICING

3.1   Contracts. Contracts shall be awarded on a lump sum or structural member unit basis whenever possible in order to avoid labor and confusion of pricing on unit pound or board foot basis. When it is necessary for freight or payment purposes to compute weights or board footages, the rules given in the subsequent paragraphs shall govern.

3.1.1 After acceptance of materials in accordance with paragraph 6.3 of this *Code of Standard Practice*, materials shall be paid for on a net basis with no retainages.

3.2 Ironwork. Ironwork weights shall be theoretical weights as computed according to the method described in *Code of Standard Practice* in the AISC *Steel Construction Manual*, and scale weights shall not be used. (See *References*, AITC 101.)

3.3 Aluminum. Aluminum weights shall be theoretical weights as computed according to the method described in the Aluminum Association's *Aluminum Construction Manual*, and scale weights shall not be used. (See *References*, AITC 101.)

3.4 Hardware. Hardware weights shall be unit weights as given in *Steel Construction Manual* of the American Institute of Steel Construction or in manufacturer's catalogs.

3.5 Sawn Timber. Sawn timber weights green or dry, as the case may be, shall be those given in lumber association weight tables per linear foot or per thousand board feet, and values shall be those for nominal lengths.

3.5.1 For payments, board footage of sawn timbers shall be computed, using nominal sizes and lengths in accordance with the following practice: Net finished lengths up to 8 ft shall be computed for board footage at given or next foot length, and net finished lengths 8 ft and over shall be computed at given or next even foot length; or on a lump sum or structural unit member basis. Lengths up to 8 ft will thus be in either odd or even foot lengths, and lengths over 8 ft will be in even foot lengths.

3.6 Glued Timber. Glued timber weights shall be taken as dry lumber weights per cubic foot of contents of finished assembly. For payment purposes, measure shall be per lump sum or on unit price per member basis.

3.7 Treatment. Treatment weights shall be added to the weight of sawn or glued timbers to which they are applied. When treatment is applied en route, weights for freight purposes should be figured accordingly.

4. DRAWINGS AND SPECIFICATIONS

4.1 Design. To enable the seller to enter properly upon the execution of the work, the buyer shall furnish the seller, within a period agreed to in the contract, a full design of the structure, definitely locating all openings, levels, and roof slopes, and showing all material to be furnished by the seller with such information as may be necessary for the completion of the shop drawings by the seller. All such information and drawings shall be consistent with the original drawings and specifications. Any expense caused by additions, changes, or omissions in such information and drawings, referred to above shall be at the buyer's expense.

4.2 Discrepancies. In case of discrepancies between the drawings and the specifications prepared by either the seller or the buyer, the specifications shall govern for buildings, and the drawings shall govern for bridges;

and, in case of discrepancies between the scaled dimensions on the drawings and the figures written on them, the figures shall govern.

4.2.1   Should the seller in the regular progress of his work find discrepancies in the information furnished by the buyer, he shall refer such discrepancies to the buyer and secure correct information before proceeding with work that would be affected.

4.2.2   The seller shall be reimbursed by the buyer for damage resulting from changed quantities and/or manufacturing operation caused by delays or by changes in drawings or specifications.

4.3   Shop Drawings. Shop drawings and/or erection diagrams, when required, shall be made and submitted to the buyer's representative who shall examine them and within 5 days return them approved with such corrections as he may find necessary. They shall be corrected by the seller, if necessary, and returned for the buyer's file as finally approved. The seller may proceed with shop work, but, in so doing, he shall assume responsibility for having properly made the corrections indicated by the buyer.

4.3.1   No change shall be made on any approved drawing without the written authorization of the buyer or the seller, as the case may require.

4.3.2   In addition to the set of prints of approved shop drawings for the buyer's file above referred to, the buyer may require the seller to furnish, without cost to the buyer, two additional sets of shop drawing blueprints, but any additional sets shall be paid for by the buyer. All drawings or tracings made by the seller for the execution of his work shall remain his property unless otherwise specifically agreed.

4.3.3   Shop drawings prepared by the seller and approved by a representative of the buyer shall be deemed the correct interpretation of the work to be done, but they do not relieve the seller of responsibility for the accuracy of details.

4.3.4   After the shop drawings have been "approved" or "approved as noted" by the authority designated in the contract, any changes required by said authority shall be made at the expense of the buyer.

4.3.5   When detailed shop drawings are furnished by the buyer, no responsibility for misfits due to errors in the drawings will be assumed by the seller.

5. STOCK MATERIAL

5.1   Size and Grade. Stock material used in timber construction shall be of quality, species, and grade required by plans and specifications. Sizes shall be those given in lumber grading rules for the applicable species and/or in accordance with *American Lumber Standards*. When so required by contract, grades shall be established and indicated to the buyer by mill affidavit, grade marks, or certificates of inspection by approved agencies.

5.2   Fillers. Fillers, blocking, and separators which form short sections of minor importance, or other small, unimportant wood pieces whose quality could not affect the strength of the structure, shall be exempted from grade marking or certificate of inspection requirement.

5.3 Moisture Content. For sawn timber construction, no moisture content requirement shall be met unless specifically called for in plans or specifications except that the moisture content of heavy timber decking shall be in accordance with *Standard for Heavy Timber Roof Decking*, AITC 112. In glued laminated construction, moisture content shall be in accordance with Voluntary Product Standard PS56-73, *Structural Glued Laminated Timber*. (See *References*, AITC 101.)

5.4 End Cuts. End seals shall be applied to fresh-cut ends of timbers, unless otherwise specified, in order to minimize end checking when use conditions are such that end checking is a major consideration.

5.5 Paint and Treatments. Paint and treatments on timbers, where required, shall be standard effective materials applied in accordance with standard practice or as required in plans and specifications.

5.6 Hardware. Hardware and metal items shall be regular commercial items in accordance with AISC or other pertinent standards. Galvanizing, parkerizing, or other protective coatings or painting of hardware items, when required by plans and specifications, shall be of standard commercial quality and quantity. (See *References*, AITC 101.)

5.7 Aluminum. Aluminum items shall be regular commercial items in accordance with the Aluminum Association's *Aluminum Construction Manual*. (See *References*, AITC 101.)

6. INSPECTION AND DELIVERY

6.1 Tests of Materials. The seller shall furnish tests and test reports without extra charge when so required in plans and specifications and when stipulated at time contract is made. All other tests of materials or structures shall be made in accordance with standard methods and at the buyer's expense.

6.2 Inspection. The seller's shop service includes inspection by its own quality control personnel and may include, when required by plans and specifications, identification and certification by marks and certificates of a qualified central organization to evidence conformance with an appropriate commercial standard. Mill affidavit to cover grade, lumber grade marks, or certificate of inspection by an approved agency shall be furnished without extra charge only when required by plans and specifications. Other shop or job inspections by outside agencies shall be paid for by the buyer, and the seller shall afford, without charge, reasonable facilities for the inspections of materials and workmanship at shop or job site. When conformance with a particular commercial standard is required by the plans and specifications, inspection shall be as stipulated therein. (See *References*, AITC 101.)

6.3 Acceptance of Materials

6.3.1 When material is inspected by a representative of the buyer at the shop, the acceptance of such material by the buyer's representative shall be considered the buyer's final approval and shall relieve the seller of further responsibility for the quality of such material after shipment. However, the seller shall be responsible for the accuracy of his work so that it may be assembled and erected in accordance with the plans and specifications.

6.3.2   When the assembly and/or erection is done by the buyer and he has accepted the fabricated materials, such action shall be considered as the buyer's final approval of the materials furnished by the seller.

6.3.3   When erection is done by the seller and he has completely finished his assembly and erection and left his work in a properly braced, guyed, and plumbed condition to the satisfaction of the buyer, such actions shall be considered to complete the work under the seller's contract.

6.3.4   Shipment of structural glued laminated timber shall comply with job specifications in all respects, but any complaint requiring an adjustment in the invoice or material shall be filed with the seller in writing within 15 days after receipt of unwrapped products, or within 15 days after wrapped products have been unwrapped providing they have been adequately protected since delivery, subject to the provisions of paragraphs 6.3.4.1 to 6.3.4.3, inclusive.

6.3.4.1   If a buyer requests adjustment from the seller on any material he claims to be unsatisfactory, the buyer shall hold such material intact in the same form as shipped for such reasonable time as may be necessary to permit inspection by the central inspection organization and shall protect it from damage or from conditions that would cause serious degrade or deterioration in quality.

6.3.4.2   Buyer and Seller Responsibility after Reinspection. To the extent that material deficient in quality is determined through reinspection to be a responsibility of the seller, the buyer shall be relieved of responsibility for accepting such material, but the buyer shall be obligated to accept such material as complies with the job specifications or for which he is responsible.

6.3.4.3   If it is determined through reinspection that the material under complaint was substantially up to requirements when received, the buyer shall be obligated to accept such material and pay the cost of reinspection; but, if the material was not substantially up to requirements, the seller shall be obligated for this cost.

6.3.5   The liability of the fabricator and/or erector shall at any time extend to replacement of like and kind of defective materials or services only and shall not cover direct or resultant damage which arises therefrom, nor to the replacement of items which have been furnished by other trades or suppliers.

7. ASSEMBLY

7.1   Field Assembly—by the Buyer. When assembly and/or erection is not a part of the seller's contract, the seller shall furnish only those items provided for in the contract. It shall be the responsibility of the buyer to furnish all other items necessary for assembly and erection.

7.2   Field Assembly—by the Seller. When field assembly and/or erection is performed by the seller, unless otherwise directed by the buyer, the seller shall provide for such field connections as will require the least field work; and the installation of such field connections shall be a part of the erection work. The size of assembled pieces of timber may be restricted by the permissible weight and clearance dimensions of transportation and by limitations of handling equipment in shop and field.

8. ERECTION – BY THE SELLER

8.1 Method of Erection. The seller shall base his price on the most economical method of erection that is consistent with the plans and specifications and such information as may have been furnished before the execution of the contract. Erection conditions that change between contract and erection dates and increase erection costs shall entitle the seller to an addition to the contract price to compensate for such changes.

8.2 Foundations, Piers, and Abutments. The buyer shall be responsible for the location, strength, and suitability of the supports. Foundations for arches shall properly provide for horizontal thrust loads.

8.2.1 Before the date set for starting erection, the buyer shall complete and have ready all supports, including anchors, accessible and free of obstructions.

8.3 Building Lines and Bench Marks. The building lines, lot lines, and bench marks at the site of the structure shall be accurately located by the buyer, who shall pass such information to the seller at the start of erection.

8.4 Steel Bases, Base Plates, and Anchor Bolts. The steel bases and bearing plates intended to be attached to columns, trusses, or other timber assemblies before erection shall be assembled into timber work by the seller.

8.4.1 Such loose steel bases and bearing plates as are to be furnished by the seller shall be set by the buyer and shall be positioned and leveled to take properly timber assemblies without requiring further work on such items by the seller.

8.4.2 It shall be the responsibility of the buyer to set all anchor bolts or anchor straps and to provide concrete or other bearing surfaces set to correct level and slope under all steel bases and bearing plates whether loose or attached.

8.5 Working Room. The erection crew shall be entitled to sufficient space at the site of the structure at a place convenient to them to place their derricks and other erection equipment. When conditions at the site provide working space not occupied by the structure, the erection crews shall be entitled to storage space for sufficient material to keep the working force in continuous operation.

8.5.1 The seller shall be entitled to such entrance or entrances to the site and to or into the unfinished structure as are necessary for materials and equipment.

8.6 Bracing. The temporary erection bracing, such as guys, braces, scaffolding, and falsework or cribbing, shall be the property of the seller, and if, after the timber has been plumbed and leveled, the work of completing the structure by other contractors is suspended or delayed, the seller shall receive reasonable compensation for its use. Guys and braces that must be left after the timber has been plumbed shall be removed by the buyer and returned to the seller in good condition at the expense of the buyer.

8.6.1 Unless otherwise agreed, the seller shall furnish and install such erection bracing as is needed to place the erected framework in a safe condition.

8.6.2 Unless otherwise agreed, the seller shall furnish and install the permanent truss bracing. (See *Definitions*, AITC 101.)

8.7 Completion. Immediately upon completion of the timber erector's work, the buyer shall assure himself that the timber erector's work is plumb, level, and properly guyed, and that all items attached thereto without provision for adjustment are in the proper location. If these conditions have not been complied with, the buyer should notify the erector immediately and direct him to perfect his work. After the timber erector has braced, guyed, and plumbed the work once to the satisfaction of the buyer, his responsibility ceases. Any further work in bracing, guying, or plumbing shall be performed at the buyer's expense.

8.8 Exceptions. Where some members, such as gable framing, end bay purlins or struts, and similar items, cannot be erected because of incomplete supports at time of erection of the trusses, arches, or other principal frame, the seller shall not be required to erect these members, except upon additional remuneration to be agreed upon by the buyer and the seller.

8.8.1 In general, the erection crew is entitled to conditions that will permit erection in one continuous operation.

8.9 Wall and Bearing Plates. All bearing plates for beams, columns, timbers or trusses shall be set to accurate line and grade by the buyer and shall be ready for the timber erector to place his work without interruption or unnecessary delay.

8.10 Loose Members. Loose pieces of all kinds and descriptions required by the design of a structure that can be set without a motor hoisting apparatus, and that are not attached in any way to the rest of the timber structure and cannot be placed except as the work of other trades advance, will not be erected by the timber erector unless by special agreement.

8.11 Elevator Framing for Building. The setting or erection of guides, cars, machinery, cables, sheaves, pans, and so on, for elevators or other machinery is not to be required of the timber erector.

8.12 Cutting, Drilling, and Patching. The seller shall not be required to cut, drill, or patch the work of others or his own work for the accommodation of other trades, except at the buyer's expense, unless such cutting, drilling, or patching of the timber for the accommodation of other trades as shall be specified as part of the seller's work shall be shown on the plans so that it may be done at the time of fabrication.

8.12.1 The number, size, and location of any holes for attachment of items of other trades shall be given at the time of the signing of the contract or be paid for as extra work. Cutting, drilling, and patching by other trades shall be carefully supervised to maintain structural sufficiency.

8.13   Insurance.

8.13.1   Until his work is completed and is accepted by the buyer, the seller shall maintain workmen's compensation insurance as may be required by law, as well as the standard form of public liability insurance. The public liability insurance shall be within such limits as may be agreed upon between the buyer and the seller, protecting the seller against claims for damages resulting from death of or injury to persons or destruction of property arising out of the seller's negligent acts or omissions.

8.13.2   All other forms of insurance coverage, such as fire, lightning, flood, earthquake, or windstorm, shall be provided by the buyer, protecting the seller against loss or damage to the work performed and material delivered at the site. All insurance covering such loss or damage shall be payable to the parties as their interests may appear.

8.13.3   In no event shall the seller indemnify the buyer against loss or expense other than by reason of and to the extent of the liability imposed by the law upon the seller for damages resulting from death of or injury to persons or destruction of property occasioned by the prosecution of the work.

8.14   Painting. Shop coats of paint, protective coating, or treatments are not to be considered final finishes, and the seller shall not be responsible for their condition after material has been delivered to the common carrier.

8.14.1   The field painting and the touching up of abrasions and discolorations in the shop coats shall not be performed by the seller.

8.15   Final Cleaning Up. Upon completion of erection and before final acceptance, the seller shall remove all falsework, rubbish, or temporary buildings furnished by him, unless otherwise agreed.

9. ERECTION – BY THE BUYER

9.1   The Method of Erection. The seller's parts will be furnished as individual pieces, fabricated in accordance with standard practice, but not assembled or subassembled. Any departure from this method, to meet buyer's erection procedure, shall be only upon agreement.

9.2   Steel Bases, Base Plates, and Anchor Bolts. Unless otherwise agreed upon, all steel bases, bearing plates, anchor bolts, straps, rods, and like items, which require embedment in, or setting on, the foundation, walls, piers, or other supports between the seller's work and these supports, shall be detailed by the seller, furnished by the seller or the buyer, as may be agreed upon, and set by the buyer, it being the latter's responsibility to see that they are set correctly.

9.3   Opportunity to Investigate Errors. Correction of minor misfits and a reasonable amount of reaming or cutting will be considered a legitimate part of erection. When erection is being performed by the buyer, any error in shop work which prevents the proper assembling and fitting up of parts by the moderate use of drift pins, or a moderate amount of reaming and slight cutting, shall be immediately reported to the seller and his approval of the method of correction obtained.

9.4   Bracing. The seller shall not, unless otherwise agreed upon, detail or furnish temporary erection bracing except as otherwise provided in paragraph 8.6.

10. DELAYS IN PROSECUTION OF WORK

10.1   Causes beyond the Control of the Seller. The seller shall be excused for delays in the performance, in whole or in part, of his work resulting, in whole or in part, from any cause beyond the control of the seller, including but not limited to fire, earthquake, flood, or windstorm; strikes, lockouts, or other differences with employees; or riots or embargoes; delays, losses, or damages in transportation; shortage of cars, fuel, labor, or materials. In case of the occurrence of any such cause of delay, the time of completion shall be extended accordingly.

10.2   Delays Caused by the Seller. Should the seller at any time, except as provided in the preceding paragraph, refuse or neglect to supply enough workmen of proper skill or material of proper quality, or to carry on the work with promptness and diligence, the buyer, if not in default, may give the seller 10 days' written notice, whereupon, if the seller continues to neglect the work, the buyer may provide such labor or materials and deduct a reasonable cost from any money due or to become due the seller under the contract, or may terminate the employment of the seller under the agreement and employ any other person to finish the work. In the latter case, the seller shall receive no further payment until the work is finished; then, if the unpaid balance that would be due under the contract exceeds the cost to the buyer of finishing the work, such excess shall be paid to the seller, but, if such cost exceeds the unpaid balance, the seller shall pay the excess to the buyer.

10.3   Delays Caused by the Buyer. Should the buyer fail to furnish the plans and other data described in paragraph 1.4 at the time agreed, or should he delay or obstruct the work in any way so as to cause loss or damage to the seller, the buyer shall reimburse the seller for such loss or damage.

10.3.1 Should the buyer, unless for reasons beyond his control, delay the fabrication or erection of the work, if it is to be performed by the seller, for more than thirty (30) days at any time, the seller may, upon five (5) days' written notice to the buyer, terminate the contract and tender all undelivered material, whether worked or unworked, to the buyer, who shall, upon transfer of title to such material, pay all cost or expense which the seller shall have paid or be obligated to pay, together with all loss or damage to the seller, including, but not limited to, the value of all drawings prepared, materials purchased or fabricated, or shipped, stored, delivered, erected, or in process of fabrication or erection, together with the value of the labor performed and the loss of profits suffered by the seller. Should the buyer fail to accept such material, the seller shall, at the expiration of such five (5) day period, in order to save the continuing storage and handling charges, proceed to sell all materials in his possession and control at not less than the current market value for the material and shall credit the sums received therefor against the amounts due from the buyer as set forth above.

10.3.2   The contract price and contract dates of delivery and erection shall not be binding upon the seller unless the buyer provides the information and work to be performed by him at the times and in the manner agreed.

AMERICAN INSTITUTE
333 West Hampden Avenue

TIMBER CONSTRUCTION
Englewood, Colorado 80110

AITC 107-69
GUIDE SPECIFICATIONS
FOR STRUCTURAL TIMBER FRAMING

Adopted as Recommendations March 17, 1969
Copyright 1972 by American Institute of Timber Construction

CONTENTS

1. INTRODUCTION

1.1 The following standard forms are designed for use by the specification writer as a recommended guide in writing specifications. An explanation of the several subjects included precedes the sample specification guide forms where needed. The italicized specification guide forms shown may be copied to assure compliance with best standard industry practices. Included are the items essential for a full understanding of the products to be furnished. The specification guide forms are brief but adequate. However, if desired, the latest edition of documents published by AITC and noted in the explanation may be used to supplement these forms. (See *References*, AITC 101.)

1.2 These specifications should be included in the structural timber section of the job specifications and not be included in the general carpentry or millwork section. For use in the Uniform System standard format, these specifications should be included in Division 6.

2. GUIDE FORM — STRUCTURAL GLUED LAMINATED TIMBER SPECIFICATION

Scope. All structural glued laminated timber shall be furnished as shown detailed on the plans and specified herein.

1

2.1   Shop Details.

2.1.1   See *Code of Standard Practice*, AITC 106, for explanation of standard industry practices relative to shop drawings and details.

Shop details shall be furnished by the fabricator and approval obtained from the buyer before work is commenced.

2.2   Manufacture.

2.2.1   The assurance of quality structural glued laminated timber depends on the controls in the shop of the materials and operations during the entire laminating process. Voluntary Product Standard PS56-73, *Structural Glued Laminated Timber*, requires that manufacturers have a quality control system responsible for the continuous control and inspection of the manufacturing processes and for keeping and maintenance of records on all jobs certified as conforming with the standard.

Manufacture and quality control shall be in conformance with Voluntary Product Standard PS56-73, Structural Glued Laminated Timber.

Fabrication shall be done by an experienced fabricator and shall conform with the requirements of Standard for Fabricated Structural Timber, *AITC 115*.

2.3   Lumber

2.3.1   It is preferable for the designer to specify stress values and appearance grades only and permit the laminator to select such stock as best meets structural and appearance requirements. Lumber in glued laminated members should conform with grade, manufacture, moisture content, and other requirements of the laminating standards of the species. (See *References*, AITC 101.) Service conditions should also be specified. Dry condition of service occurs when the moisture content of the member will be at or below 16% in service. Wet condition of service occurs when the moisture content of the member will be above 16% in service.

Lumber for laminating shall meet the structural requirements and laminating specifications of Voluntary Product Standard PS56-73, Structural Glued Laminated Timber, *and shall be of such stress grade as to provide glued laminated members with allowable stress values of* _____ *psi in bending,* _____ *psi in tension,* _____ *psi in compression parallel to grain for (check one):*

☐ DRY *condition of service*
☐ WET *condition of service*

2.4   Adhesives.

2.4.1   In general, the conditions of service determine the adhesive to be used in laminating; that is, water-resistant adhesives for dry use and waterproof adhesives for wet use. Casein adhesives with a suitable mold inhibitor are the standard dry-use adhesives of the structural glued laminated timber industry. They perform satisfactorily for use conditions when the moisture content of the wood does not exceed 16% for repeated or prolonged periods of service. (See Appendix A, *Selection of Adhesives*, of AITC 103.) For overhangs that are not exposed directly to rain and which have end grain and the exposed members suitably protected, dry-use adhesives may also be employed. The following are examples of interior applications for which dry-use adhesive may not be suitable:

(*a*) Swimming pools and shower rooms.

(*b*) Commercial laundries and car-washing operations.

(*c*) Certain storage and processing operations that produce highly humid conditions, such as flax processing, certain papermaking operations, and vat rooms.

Wet-use adhesives are employed when the moisture content of the wood exceeds 16% for repeated or prolonged periods of service. The following are examples of uses where wet-use adhesives are required: exposed exterior work, construction that is submerged, bridges, towers, marine work, and similar construction, and where dry-use adhesives are not satisfactory.

Adhesives shall meet the requirements for (check one):

☐ DRY *condition of service*

☐ WET *condition of service*

2.5 Appearance Grades.

2.5.1 Appearance grades apply to the surfaces of glued laminated members and include such items as growth characteristics, void filling, and surfacing operations, but not laminating procedures, stains, varnishes, or other finishes, nor sealers, wrappings, cratings, or other protective coverings. The appearance grades do not modify the design stresses, fabrication controls, grades of lumber used, and other provisions of the standards for structural glued laminated timber. (See *Standard Appearance Grades for Structural Glued Laminated Timber*, AITC 110.)

Appearance of members shall be (check one):

☐ *Industrial Appearance Grade*

☐ *Architectural Appearance Grade*

☐ *Premium Appearance Grade*

2.6 Protection.

2.6.1 Protection of glued laminated structural members includes end sealers, surface sealers, primer coats, and wrapping as may be applied for the protection of members. End sealers, surface sealers, primer coats, and wrapping offer a degree of protection but do not necessarily preclude damage resulting from negligence through factors beyond the control of the laminator during shipment, handling, storing, and placing the members. (See *Recommended Practice for Protection of Structural Glued Laminated Timber during Transit, Storage, and Erection*, AITC 111.)

Unless otherwise specified, a coat of end sealer shall be applied to the ends of all members as soon as practicable after end trimming. Surfaces of members shall be (check one):

☐ *Not sealed*

☐ *Sealed with penetrating sealer*

☐ *Sealed with sealer coat*

☐ *Other type of finish (specify)*_____

Members shall be (check one):

☐ *Not wrapped*

☐ *Bundle-wrapped*

☐ *Individually wrapped*

2.7 Quality Marks and Certificates.

2.7.1 The order between the seller and the buyer should specify the identification requirements of the job. Voluntary Product Standard PS56-73, *Structural Glued Laminated Timber* states that "structural glued laminated timber represented to comply with this Standard shall be distinctly marked with the identification of a qualified inspection and testing agency."

The AITC is a qualified inspection and testing agency and provides, through license agreements, quality marks and certificates of conformance for identifying material that conforms with the requirements of PS56-73. AITC licenses only qualified producers who demonstrate, by means of a qualification inspection, tests, and periodic unannounced inspections, their ability to produce products in accordance with the requirements of PS56-73.

(Check appropriate items):

☐ *Members shall be marked with an AITC Quality Mark indicating conformance with Voluntary Product Standard PS56-73,* Structural Glued Laminated Timber.

☐ *Members shall be marked with an AITC Quality Mark and, in addition an AITC Certificate of Conformance shall be provided to indicate conformance with Voluntary Product Standard PS56-73,* Structural Glued Laminated Timber.

3. GUIDE FORM—FABRICATED STRUCTURAL TIMBER SPECIFICATION

3.1 Scope.

3.1.1 The term *fabricated structural timber* as employed herein refers to engineered load-carrying elements of wood (including sawn lumber and/or timber, glued laminated timber, and mechanically laminated timber) that are shop-fabricated for use in frames of all kinds including but not limited to trusses, arches, beams, girders, and columns for use in schools, churches, commercial, industrial, and other buildings and for other structures such as bridges, towers, and marine installations. Components made of structural glued laminated timber should be produced in accordance with Voluntary Product Standard PS56-73, *Structural Glued Laminated Timber.*

All fabricated structural timber shall be furnished as shown on the plans and specified herein.

3.2 Shop Details.

3.2.1 See *Code of Standard Practice,* AITC 106, for explanation of standard industry practices relative to shop drawings and details.

Shop drawings, when required, shall be furnished by the fabricator and approval obtained from the buyer before fabrication.

3.3 Fabrication.

Fabrication shall be by an experienced fabricator and shall conform with the requirements of Standard for Fabricated Structural Timber, *AITC 115.*

3.4 Lumber.

Lumber shall be stress-graded in accordance with the current grading rules of the regional lumber organization for the species and shall be of the strength requirements as shown by the grades, stresses, and species noted on the plans.

3.5 Protection.

3.5.1 End seals may be applied to fresh-cut ends of timber to minimize end checking when use conditions are such that end checking is a major consideration.

Members shall be (check one):
☐ *Sealed with end sealer after trimming*
☐ *Not end sealed*

4. OPTIONAL CONSIDERATIONS

4.1 The following specifications are sometimes desired. They are covered here briefly for convenience.

4.2 Preservative Treatment.

4.2.1 When the conditions of service are such that pressure preservative treatment to prevent attack by fungi or insects is required, information such as the following should be given (refer to AITC 109,

Treating Standard for Structural Timber Framing, for complete data):
The preservative shall be_____
The retention shall be_____

4.3 Hardware.

The fabricator shall furnish connection steel and hardware for joining timber members to each other and to their supports exclusive of anchorage embedded in masonry, setting plates, and items field-welded to structural steel. Metal shapes shall have one coat of shop-applied paint containing rust inhibitor.

AMERICAN INSTITUTE
333 West Hampden Avenue

TIMBER CONSTRUCTION
Englewood, Colorado 80110

AITC 108-69
STANDARD FOR HEAVY TIMBER
CONSTRUCTION

Adopted as Recommendations March 17, 1969
Copyright 1972 by American Institute of Timber Construction

CONTENTS

1. HEAVY TIMBER CONSTRUCTION

1.1 *Heavy timber construction* is that type in which fire resistance is attained by placing limitations on the minimum size, thickness, or composition of all load-carrying wood members as given in this section; by avoiding concealed spaces under floors or roofs; by using approved fastenings, construction details, and adhesives; and by providing the required degree of fire resistance in exterior and interior walls.

2. HEAVY TIMBER FRAMING

2.1 Columns.

2.1.1 Wood columns may be sawn or glued laminated and shall be not less than 8 in., nominal, in any dimension when supporting floor loads and not less than 6 in., nominal, in width and not less than 8 in., nominal, in depth when supporting roof and ceiling loads only.

2.1.2 Columns shall be continuous or superimposed by means of reinforced concrete or metal caps with brackets, or shall be connected by properly designed steel or iron caps, with pintles and base plates, or by timber splice plates affixed to the columns by means of metal connectors housed within the contact faces, or by other approved methods.

1

2.2   Floor Framing.

2.2.1   Beams and girders of wood may be sawn or glued laminated and shall be not less than 6 in., nominal, in width and not less than 10 in., nominal, in depth.

2.2.2   Framed or glued laminated arches which spring from grade or the floor line and support floor loads shall be not less than 8 in., nominal, in any dimension.

2.2.3   Framed timber trusses supporting floor loads shall have members of not less than 8 in., nominal, in any dimension.

2.3   Roof Framing.

2.3.1   Framed or glued laminated arches for roof construction which spring from grade or the floor line and do not support floor loads shall have members not less than 6 in., nominal, in width and not less than 8 in., nominal, in depth for the lower half of the height and not less than 6 in., nominal, in depth for the upper half.

2.3.2   Framed or glued laminated arches for roof construction which spring from the top of walls or wall abutments, framed timber trusses, and other roof framing which do not support floor loads, shall have members not less than 4 in., nominal, in width and not less than 6 in., nominal, in depth. Spaced members may be composed of two or more pieces not less than 3 in., nominal, in thickness when blocked solidly throughout their intervening spaces or when such spaces are tightly closed by a continuous wood cover plate of not less than 2 in., nominal, in thickness, secured to the underside of the members. Splice plates shall be not less than 3 in., nominal, in thickness. When protected by approved automatic sprinklers under the roof deck, framing members shall be not less than 3 in., nominal, in width.

3. HEAVY TIMBER FLOORS

3.1   Floors shall be of sawn or glued laminated: (1) planks, splined or tongue-and-groove, not less than 3 in., nominal, in thickness covered with 1 in., nominal, dimension tongue-and-groove flooring, laid crosswise or diagonally to the plank or with other approved wearing surfaces, or (2) planks, not less than 4 in., nominal, in width set on edge close together and well spiked, and covered as for 3 in. thick plank. The planks shall be laid so that there is no continuous line of end joints except at points of support. Floors shall not extend closer than $\frac{1}{2}$ in. to walls to provide an expansion joint, but the joint shall be covered at top or bottom to avoid flue action.

4. HEAVY TIMBER ROOF DECKS

4.1   Roof decks shall be of sawn or glued laminated, splined or tongue-and-groove plank, not less than 2 in., nominal, in thickness, of tongue-and-groove $1\frac{1}{8}$ in. thick interior plywood (exterior glue), or of planks not less than 3 in., nominal, in width, set on edge close together and laid as required for floors. Other wood and/or wood-fiber based decking or other types of decking may be used if noncombustible.

5. WALLS

5.1 Bearing Walls. Bearing portions of exterior and interior walls shall be of approved noncombustible material and shall have a fire resistance rating of not less than 2 hours except that, where a horizontal separation of 3 ft or less is provided, bearing portions of exterior walls shall have a fire resistance rating of not less than 3 hours.

5.2 Nonbearing Walls. Nonbearing portions of exterior walls shall be of approved noncombustible materials except as otherwise noted, and:

5.2.1 Where a horizontal separation of 3 ft or less is provided, nonbearing exterior walls shall have a fire resistance rating of not less than 3 hours.

5.2.2 Where a horizontal separation of more than 3 ft but less than 20 ft is provided, nonbearing exterior walls shall have a fire resistance rating of not less than 2 hours.

5.2.3 Where a horizontal separation of 20 to 30 ft is provided, nonbearing exterior walls shall have a fire resistance rating of not less than 1 hour.

5.2.4 Where a horizontal separation of 30 ft or more is provided, no fire resistance rating is required.

5.2.5 Where a horizontal separation of 20 ft or more is provided, wood columns, arches, beams, and roof decks conforming with heavy timber sizes may be used externally.

6. CONSTRUCTION DETAILS

6.1 Wall plate boxes of self-releasing type or approved hangers shall be provided where beams and girders enter masonry. An air space of 1 in. shall be provided at the top, end, and sides of the member unless approved durable or treated wood is used.

6.2 Girders and beams shall be closely fitted around columns, and adjoining ends shall be cross-tied to each other, or intertied by caps or ties, to transfer horizontal loads across the joint. Wood bolsters may be placed on top of columns which support roof loads only.

6.3 Where intermediate beams are used to support a floor, they shall rest on top of the girders, or shall be supported by ledgers or blocks securely fastened to the sides of the girders, or they may be supported by approved metal hangers into which the ends of the beams shall be closely fitted.

6.4 Wood beams and girders supported by walls required to have a fire resistance rating of 2 hours or more shall have not less than 4 in. of solid masonry between their ends and the outside face of the wall and between adjacent beams.

6.5 Columns, beams, girders, arches, trusses, and floor slabs of material other than wood shall have a fire resistance rating of not less than 1 hour.

6.6 Floors and roof decks shall be without concealed spaces, except that building service equipment may be enclosed provided the spaces between the equipment and enclosures are fire-stopped or protected by other acceptable means.

6.7 Adequate roof anchorage shall be provided.

AMERICAN INSTITUTE
333 West Hampden Avenue

AITC

TIMBER CONSTRUCTION
Englewood, Colorado 80110

AITC 109-69
TREATING STANDARD FOR STRUCTURAL TIMBER FRAMING

Adopted as Recommendations March 17, 1969
Copyright 1972 by American Institute of Timber Construction

CONTENTS

1. PREFACE

1.1 This standard covers preservative treatments only.

1.2 Wood, properly designed and constructed, has performed in service with satisfaction for centuries. When recognized principles of design and construction are not to be applied, the wood must be preservatively treated with chemicals to resist decay fungi, insects, and marine borers.

1.3 The effectiveness of treatment is dependent upon the chemicals used and their retention and penetration. Retention and penetration must be adequate to give the required service life.

2. GENERAL

2.1 Decay. Decay of wood is caused by low forms of plant life (fungi) that develop and grow from spores just as higher forms of plants do from

1

seed. These microscopic spores are likely to be present wherever wood is used. The plant-like growth breaks down the wood substance, converting it into food required by the fungus for development. However, like all forms of plant life, these wood-destroying fungi must have air, suitable moisture, and favorable temperatures, as well as the food if they are to develop and grow. If deprived of any one of these four essentials, the spores cannot develop and the wood remains permanently sound, retaining its full strength. Wood permanently and totally submerged in water cannot decay because the necessary air is excluded. Wood will not decay when its moisture content is continuously less than 20%. Temperatures above 100°F and below 40°F will essentially stop the growth of decay fungi. Growth will begin again each time favorable climatic conditions exist. Since rainfall and temperature conditions principally influence the rate of decay, a Southern coastal region presents a greater decay hazard than a Northern inland region.

    2.1.1   Examples of installations where properly designed and constructed wood structural members are permanent without treatment include:

    2.1.1.1   Enclosed buildings for which good roof coverage, proper roof maintenance, good joint details, adequate flashings to direct rain water, ventilation, and a well-drained building site assure continuous moisture content of wood below 20%.

    2.1.1.2   Arid or semi-arid regions where climatic conditions are such that the equilibrium moisture content seldom exceeds 20% and then only for short periods.

    2.1.1.3   Any usage where wood is permantly and totally submerged in fresh water.

    2.1.2   Examples of installations where wood structural members to be permanent require treatment to definite retention and penetration include:

    2.1.2.1   Enclosed buildings housing "wet processes" where, despite ventilation, there is sufficient moisture remaining in the atmosphere to maintain equilibrium moisture content in the wood above 20%.

    2.1.2.2   Outdoor exposures where there is no protective cover for wood structural members from the weather, such as in bridges, piers and wharves, towers, and electrical utility structures.

    2.1.2.3   Direct contact with the ground or with water, as for retaining walls, or for poles or piles where the wood extends out of the water and is not permanently and totally submerged.

    2.1.3   Examples of installations where a decay hazard exists and the proper design and construction details are used to prevent the wood from exceeding 20% moisture content or a preservative treatment to a definite retention and penetration must be used to prevent decay include:

    2.1.3.1   Portions of wood structural members, such as an arch extending from outside the wall to a foundation, may be covered by a roof or be protected by adequate flashings with ventilation, or they must be preservatively treated to definite retentions and penetrations.

    2.1.3.2   Wood structural members subject to moisture condensation may be protected by proper moisture barriers (with or without insulation) and adequate ventilation, or they must be preservatively treated to definite retentions and penetrations.

2.1.3.3 Wood structural members near masonry or concrete may be protected by design details that incorporate ventilated air spaces, vapor barriers, or other moisture barrier separations preventing direct contact with masonry or concrete, or they must be preservatively treated to definite retentions and penetrations.

2.2 Insect Attack. Structural wood members that have been preservatively treated to definite retentions and penetrations are resistant to insect attack. (See American Wood-Preservers' Association *Standard C28.*) The degree of resistance offered will depend upon the type of preservative as well as the retentions and penetrations obtained.

2.3 Marine Borers. Protection for structural wood members against marine borers can be provided by the pressure treating process with recommended preservatives with retentions and penetrations as set forth in the current AWPA *Standard C2.*

3. DESIGN

3.1 The allowable stresses for preservatively treated wood, as noted in NDS, apply when treatment is in accordance with AWPA standard specifications that limit pressures and temperatures.

3.2 Pressure-treating cylinders are usually 6 to 8 ft in diameter and of lengths up to 150 ft; thus it is necessary to consider these sizes when specifying treatment and when designing the members.

4. FABRICATION

4.1 All fabrication shall be performed prior to treatment for sawn and glued laminated members treated after gluing. When laminations are treated prior to gluing and there is fabrication after treatment and laminating, additional treatment should be applied in accordance with AWPA *Standard M4.*

5. TYPES OF PRESERVATIVE TREATMENTS

5.1 All preservative treatments shall be in accordance with the current AWPA *Standards C1 and C2.*

5.1.1 Water-borne salt chemicals or oil-borne chemicals in mineral spirits or AWPA P9 volatile solvent are recommended when treating before gluing is required. Oil-borne chemicals, creosote or creosote solutions or oil-borne chemicals in mineral spirits can be used when treatment before gluing is not required. The treating of glued laminated timbers with water-borne salts after gluing is not recommended because the degree of dimensional change and the magnitude of checking that may occur in laminated timber when such treatments are employed after gluing is unpredictable.

6. RETENTION AND PENETRATION REQUIREMENTS

6.1   Each type of preservative and each method of treatment has certain distinct advantages. The preservative type should be determined by the end use of the material. The minimum recognized retentions for use under certain conditions have been established by actual service record. These

TABLE 1

SAWN AND LAMINATED TIMBERS (TREATED AFTER GLUING)
Recommended minimum retentions in pounds per cubic foot for creosote,
creosote solutions, and oil-borne chemicals

	Southern Pine		Pacific Coast Douglas Fir or Western Hemlock	
	Above Ground	Ground Contact	Above Ground	Ground Contact
Sampling for assay[a] Zone inches from edge of interior laminates	0–3	0–3	0–0.625	0–0.625
Minimum number of borings per lot	20	20	20	20
Retention by assay, pcf (min.) Creosote	6	12	6	12
Creosote–coal tar solution	6	12	6	12
Creosote petroleum	NR[b]	NR[b]	6	12
Pentachlorophenol	0.3	0.6	0.3	0.6
Determination of penetration from edge of beams, in.[c]	3.0 or 90%	3.0 or 90%	0.5	0.75

[a]More than one boring may be taken from the same piece, but not more than one from the same laminate unless there is an end-joint separation. Using an increment borer core, 0.2 in. in diameter, twenty ⅜ in. long borings will provide an adequate sample for assay of pentachlorophenol. A minimum of forty-eight ⅜ in. long borings is required for creosote and creosote solutions. A ⅜ in. plug cutter may be used to increase the size of the sample taken for analysis or to reduce the number of borings required below forty-eight.

The treated wood surface should be lightly scraped prior to taking a sample in order to remove surface deposits of preservative.

The retention requirement for pentachlorophenol is based on an assay using the lime ignition method of analysis. When the copper pyridine method of analysis is used, multiply the result by 1.1 to convert to the lime ignition basis.

[b]Not recommended.

[c]Every laminated timber shall be bored for penetration. For Southern pine, borings shall be taken from two different interior laminates in each timber. For Douglas fir and Western hemlock, one boring shall be taken from each of the two face laminations and 2 borings shall be taken from different interior laminations in each timber. If any boring taken from any timber fails to meet the penetration requirements, that timber shall be rejected. If more than 10% of the timbers in a charge treated for ground contact exposure, or more than 20% of the timbers in a charge treated for above-ground exposure fail to pass the above requirement, the charge shall be rejected.

minimums may be increased where severe climatic or exposure conditions are involved.

6.1.1 Retention recommendations given in Tables 1, 2 and 3 in pounds per cubic foot and penetration requirements are those of the AWPA *Standard C2* for sawn timbers and *Standard C28* for structural glued laminated members and laminations prior to gluing.

6.1.2 As an alternate to the use of the retentions and penetrations recommended by the AWPA, reference may be made to the American Wood Preservers Institute Quality Control Program for Preservatively Treated Lumber and Plywood and the use of the AWPI Quality Mark for preservatively treated products may be specified. Applicable AWPI *Standards* are listed in Table 5.

TABLE 2

LAMINATIONS (TREATED PRIOR TO GLUING)

Recommended minimum retentions in pounds per cubic foot for creosote, creosote solutions, and oil-borne chemicals

	Southern Pine		Pacific Coast Douglas Fir or Western Hemlock	
	Above Ground	Ground Contact	Above Ground	Ground Contact
Sampling for assay[a,b] Zone inches from edge of laminates Minimum number of borings per lot	0.5–1 20	0.5–1 20	0.5–1 20	0.5–1 20
Retention by assay, pcf (min.) Creosote Pentachlorophenol	6 0.3	12 0.6	6 0.3	12 0.6
Determination of penetration[c] Inches from edge, 18 out of 20	3.0 or 90%	3.0 or 90%	1	1.25

[a]Using an increment borer core 0.2 in. in diameter, twenty $\frac{1}{2}$ in. long borings will provide an adequate sample for assay of pentachlorophenol. Forty-eight $\frac{1}{2}$ in. long borings are required for creosote and creosote solutions. A $\frac{3}{8}$ in. plug cutter may be used to increase the size of the sample taken for analysis or to reduce the number of borings required below forty-eight.

The treated wood surface should be lightly scraped prior to taking a sample in order to remove surface deposits of preservative.

The retention requirement for pentachlorophenol is based on an assay using the lime ignition method of analysis. When the copper pyridine method of analysis is used, multiply the result by 1.1 to convert to the lime ignition basis.

[b]Laminated beams manufactured from material treated to meet the above requirements can be assayed by changing the zone samples from 0.5 to 1.0 in., as indicated above, to 0 to 0.5 in. Results of assay must meet 90% of the retention specified above.

[c]Laminated beams manufactured from material treated to meet the above requirements can be tested for penetration by taking samples from the edges of the laminated beams. The penetration required is 0.5 in. less than that required above on 18 out of 20 samples.

TABLE 3

SAWN TIMBERS AND LAMINATIONS[a]

Recommended minimum retentions in pounds per cubic foot (oxide basis)
for water-borne inorganic salts[b]

	Pacific Coast Douglas Fir, Southern Pine and Western Hemlock	
	Above Ground	Ground Contact
Sampling for assay[c,d]		
Zone inches from edge of laminates	0.5–1	0.5–1
Minimum number of borings per lot	20	20
Retention by assay, pcf (min.)		
Acid copper chromate (ACC)	0.25	NR[e]
Amoniacal copper arsenite (ACA)	0.23	0.60
Chromated copper arsenate (CCA) type A	0.23	0.60
Chromated copper arsenate (CCA) type B	0.23	0.60
Chromated copper arsenate (CCA) type C	0.23	0.60
Chromated zinc chloride (CZC)	0.46	NR[e]
Copperized chromated zinc arsenate (CuCZA)	0.27	NR[e]
Fluor chrome arsenate phenol (FCAP)	0.22	NR[e]
Determination of penetration[f]		
Inches from edge, 18 out of 20	1.00[g]	1.25[g]

[a]See paragraph 5.1.1 relative to the treating of glued laminated timbers with water-borne salts.
[b]See Table 4 for trade names of water-borne preservatives.
[c]Using an increment borer core, 0.2 in. in diameter, twenty ½ in. long borings will provide an adequate sample for assay. The method of analyses used for assaying retention of the water-borne preservatives should be based on the analytical methods of AWPA *Standard A2*.

The treated wood surface should be lightly scraped prior to taking a sample in order to remove surface deposits of preservative.
[d]Laminated beams manufactured from material treated to meet the above requirements can be assayed by changing the zone samples from 0.5 to 1.0 in., as indicated above, to 0 to 0.5 in. Results of assay must meet 90% of the retention specified above.
[e]Not recommended.
[f]Laminated beams manufactured from material treated to meet the above requirements can be tested for penetration by taking samples from the edges of the laminated beams. The penetration required is 0.5 in. less than that required above on 18 out of 20 samples.
[g]3.0 or 90% for Southern pine.

TABLE 4

TRADE NAMES OF WATER-BORNE PRESERVATIVES

Chemical Name	Trade Name
Acid copper chromate (ACC)	Celcure[a]
Ammoniacal copper arsenite (ACA)	Chemonite[a]
Chromated copper arsenate, type A (CCA-A)	Erdalith[a]
	Greensalt
Chromated copper arsenate, type B (CCA-B)	Boliden K-33
	Osmose K-33
Chromated copper arsenate, type C (CCA-C)	
Chromated zinc chloride (CZC)	
Copperized chromated zinc chloride (CuCZC)	
Fluor chrome arsenate phenol (FCAP)	Tanalith
	Wolman Salts[a]
	Osmosalts[a]
	(Osmosar[a])

[a]Registered U.S. Patent Office.

TABLE 5

AMERICAN WOOD PRESERVERS INSTITUTE STANDARDS

Type Preservative	AWPI Standard Number	
	Above Ground Use	Ground Contact Use or Structural Members Exposed to the Weather
Water-borne	LP-2	LP-22
Light petroleum solvent — penta solution	LP-3	LP-33
Volatile petroleum solvent (LPG) — penta solution	LP-4	LP-44
Creosote		LP-55
Heavy petroleum solvent — penta solution		LP-77

7. INCISING

7.1   Incising is not required for Southern pine and Western hemlock. Where the best treatment results are required for Douglas fir, assuring definite penetration and uniform distribution of preservative, incising is recommended with an approved pattern.

8. TREATING SAWN TIMBERS

8.1   The pressure treatment of sawn timbers shall be in accordance with recommended practices as specified in AWPA *Standards C1* and *C2*.

9. TREATING GLUED LAMINATED TIMBERS

9.1   Glued laminated timbers to be treated by the pressure process must be glued with waterproof adhesives conforming to Appendix A, *Selection of Adhesives*, of AITC 103. The treating of glued laminated members shall be the same as for sawn timbers, except that no retort seasoning is necessary because the members are assembled from dry lumber. Pressure when treating shall be a minimum of 50 pounds per square inch, gage (psig) and a maximum of 150 psig. Final steaming is permitted if the temperature does not exceed 240°F for a total of 3 hours.

10. TREATING INDIVIDUAL LAMINATIONS PRIOR TO GLUING
(Applicable to Douglas fir, Southern pine and Western hemlock)

10.1   All laminations to be treated prior to gluing should be blanked to a uniform thickness and width prior to treatment. Proper consideration must be given to the moisture content of wood prior to treatment.

10.2   Pressure when treating shall be a minimum of 50 psig and a maximum of 150 psig. Final steaming is permitted if the temperature does not exceed 240°F for a total of 3 hours. The full-cell process is recommended with water-borne preservatives.

10.3   Lumber treated with water-borne preservatives shall be dried after treatment to the moisture content required for gluing and the moisture content required for the glued member in service. Kiln temperatures should not exceed 180°F. Lumber to be treated with creosote, creosote solutions, and oil-borne preservatives should be dried prior to treatment to the moisture content required for gluing and the moisture content required for the glued member in service.

10.4   When surfacing laminations after treating, no more than $\frac{1}{16}$ in. of wood shall be removed from either wide face, and it shall be as small as is practical in making the surface clean, plane, and uniform in thickness for gluing. Care must be used when assembling and clamping the laminations to assure that no more than a minimum surfacing of lamination edges is required when surfacing the member to specified width.

10.5   If oil is exuded on the lamination surfaces after dressing to final thickness, it shall be removed with dry rags, or rags dampened in a solvent such as acetone, just prior to spreading the adhesive.

10.6 The time interval between surfacing and gluing should be kept as short as possible, particularly when elevated room temperatures and high retention exist. In general, the gluing of treated laminations should be completed within 8 hours of final surfacing when preservative oils are used and within 24 hours of final surfacing when water-borne salts are used.

10.7 In general, longer curing times or higher temperatures are required for treated than for untreated wood to obtain glue bonds of comparable quality. Treatment may influence the gluing surface requiring modifications in the adhesive spread and assembly times.

10.8 Certain combinations of lumber, species, treatment, and adhesive do not produce the same quality of glue bond as do other combinations even though used under the same procedures. It is, therefore, important that the use of any particular combination of species, treatment, and adhesive be supported by adequate gluing data for the individual laminator's procedures.

11. CARE AFTER TREATMENT

11.1 To assure best results, it is necessary to protect treated material from mechanical injury both in construction handling and under field service conditions. Cutting of treated material should be avoided whenever possible. When field treatments are used they should be in accordance with AWPA *Standard M4.*

12. TREATING CERTIFICATE

12.1 Treatment after gluing. For treatment after gluing, there is available a treating certificate that covers inspection at the treating plant stating that the treatment is in accordance with AWPA *Standards C1, C2,* and *C28.*

12.2 Treatment before gluing. For treatment where gluing is accomplished after treating, a certificate is available covering the stock at the time it leaves the treating plant which states that the treatment is in accordance with the AWPA *Standard C28.* A separate certificate covering the glued members utilizing this stock is available from the laminator stating that treatment is in accordance with this Standard.

Note: Fire-retardant treatments are not covered in this Standard. The self-insulating qualities of wood create a slow-burning characteristic. Good structural details, elimination of concealed spaces, and use of fire stops to interfere with the passage of flames up or across a building contribute to the excellent performance of untreated heavy timber construction in fire. Fire-retardant treatments do not increase substantially the fire resistance of heavy timber construction which, untreated, has excellent fire resistance. Building codes generally exempt heavy timber framing from interior finish flame-spread requirements. When fire-retardant treatments are used, the reduction of strength as related to amount and penetration of treatment, the compatability of treatment and adhesive, the use of special gluing procedures, and the effect on fabricating procedures should be investigated.

AMERICAN INSTITUTE
333 West Hampden Avenue

TIMBER CONSTRUCTION
Englewood, Colorado 80110

AITC 110-71
STANDARD APPEARANCE GRADES FOR STRUCTURAL GLUED LAMINATED TIMBER

Adopted as Recommendations August 26, 1971
Copyright 1972 by American Institute of Timber Construction

CONTENTS

1. INTRODUCTION

1.1 Appearance grades apply to the surfaces of glued laminated members and include such items as growth characteristics, void filling, and surfacing operations but not laminating procedures, stains, varnishes, or other finishes, nor wrappings, cratings, or other protective coverings. The appearance grades do not modify the design stresses, fabrication controls, grades of lumber used, and other provisions of the standards for structural glued laminated timber.

1.1.1 Various grades of appearance are desired for different uses, since it is evident that the same appearance is not needed for all types of use.

1.1.2 These appearance grades are for the guidance of the designer so that he may specify a product consistent with the use of the structure and provide a suitable appearance at appropriate cost. Requirements given in appearance description are intended to achieve a general and distinctive uniformity of appearance, and reasonable tolerance is permitted. Appearance grading should reflect good judgment. It should be kept in mind that often the natural growth characteristics of the wood enhance the beauty of the member and avoid an artificial appearance.

1.1.3 Measurement of knot holes and other voids is to be made in the direction of the length of the lamination and only on surfaces of the

1

member exposed in the final structure. All characteristics must be considered, however, with respect to their effect on general appearance.

1.1.4 The designer shall specify the desired appearance grade to give a clear understanding between buyer and seller.

1.1.5 Experience has shown that the following three appearance grades have a sufficient range to fulfill all normal requirements.

2. INDUSTRIAL APPEARANCE GRADE

2.1 Application. Industrial appearance grade is ordinarily suitable for construction in industrial plants, warehouses, garages, and for other uses where appearance is not of primary concern.

2.2 Specifications.

2.2.1 Laminations may possess the natural growth characteristics of the lumber grade.

2.2.2 Void filling is not required.

2.2.3 The wide face of laminations exposed to view shall be free of loose knots and open knot holes.

2.2.4 Members shall be surfaced on two sides only, an occasional miss being permitted along individual laminations.

2.2.5 Unless otherwise specified, the appearance grade for glued laminated timber truss members shall be industrial or better, except that paragraph 2.2.3 does not apply.

3. ARCHITECTURAL APPEARANCE GRADE

3.1 Application. Architectural appearance grade is ordinarily suitable for construction where appearance is an important requirement. Any small voids shall be filled by others than the fabricator if the final decorative finish so requires.

3.2 Specifications.

3.2.1 Laminations may possess the natural growth characteristics of the lumber grade.

3.2.2 In exposed surfaces, knot holes and other voids measuring over $\frac{3}{4}$ in. shall be replaced by the fabricator with clear wood inserts or a neutral colored filler. When inserts are used, they shall be selected with reasonable care for similarily of the grain and color of the wood insert to the adjacent wood.

3.2.3 The wide face of laminations exposed to view shall be free of loose knots and open knot holes. The material shall be selected with reasonable care for similarity of the grain and color of laminations at end and edge joints.

3.2.4 When an opaque finish is specified, requirements for similarity of grain and color may be disregarded.

3.2.5 Exposed faces shall be surfaced smooth. Misses are not permitted.

3.2.6 The corners on the wide face of laminations exposed to view in the final structure shall be eased.

4. PREMIUM APPEARANCE GRADE

4.1　Application. Premium appearance grade is suitable for uses which demand the finest appearance.

4.2　Specifications.

4.2.1　Laminations may possess the natural growth characteristics of the lumber grade.

4.2.2　In exposed surfaces, knot holes and other voids shall be replaced by the fabricator with clear wood inserts or a neutral colored filler. When inserts are used, they shall be selected with reasonable care for similarity of the grain and color of the wood insert to the adjacent wood.

4.2.3　The wide face of laminations exposed to view shall be selected for appearance, free of loose knots or voids, and with reasonable care for similarity of the grain and color of the laminations at end and edge joints. Knot size shall be limited in size to 20% of the net face width of the lamination. Not over two maximum size knots or their equivalent shall occur in a 6 ft length.

4.2.4　When an opaque finish is specified, requirements for similarity of grain and color may be disregarded.

4.2.5　Exposed faces shall be surfaced smooth. Misses are not permitted.

4.2.6　The corners on the wide face of laminations exposed to view in the final structure shall be eased.

AMERICAN INSTITUTE
333 West Hampden Avenue

AITC

TIMBER CONSTRUCTION
Englewood, Colorado 80110

AITC 111-65
RECOMMENDED PRACTICE FOR PROTECTION OF STRUCTURAL GLUED LAMINATED TIMBER DURING TRANSIT, STORAGE, AND ERECTION

Adopted as Recommendations February 16, 1965
Copyright 1972 by American Institute of Timber Construction

CONTENTS

1. INTRODUCTION

1.1 Protection of glued laminated structural members includes end sealers, surface sealers, primer coats, and wrappings applied for the protection of members. End sealers, surface sealers, primer coats, and wrappings offer a degree of protection, but they do not necessarily preclude damage resulting from negligence and other factors beyond the control of the laminator during shipment, handling, storing, and placing of the members.

1.2 The protection specified should be commensurate with the end use and final finish of the member. It may also vary with the method of shipment and with exposure to climatic and other conditions before construction is completed.

1.3 These recommended specifications are for the guidance of the designer so that the product may have protection consistent with the use of the member at appropriate cost. The designer shall specify the desired protection in a way that establishes a clear understanding between the buyer and the seller.

1.4 Experience has shown that the following protection methods have a sufficient range to fulfill normal requirements.

1

2. END SEALERS

2.1   End sealers retard moisture transmission and minimize end checking when use conditions are such that end checking is a major consideration. They are normally applied to the ends of all members.

2.2 Specifications.

2.2.1   A coat of sealer shall be applied to the fresh-cut ends of all members after end trimming.

2.2.2   A colorless sealer shall be used on ends exposed to view in the completed structure.

3. SURFACE SEALERS

3.1   Surface sealers increase resistance to soiling, control grain raising, minimize checking, and serve as a moisture retardant. Surface sealers fall into the two following classifications.

3.1.1   Translucent Penetrating Sealer. Translucent penetrating sealers have low solid content. They provide limited protection and are suitable for use when final finish requires staining.

3.1.1.1   Specifications. A penetrating sealer shall be applied to all surfaces before shipment.

3.1.2   Primer and Sealer Coats. Primer and sealer coats are coats of high solid content that provide maximum protection by sealing the surface of the wood. Primer and sealer coats should not be specified when final finish requires a natural or stained finish.

3.1.2.1   Specifications.

(*a*) A sealer (or primer) coat shall be applied to all surfaces before shipment.

(*b*) Sealer and primer shall have a minimum solid content of 25%.

4. WRAPPING

4.1   Wrapping the member for shipment with heavy water-resistant paper or its equivalent provides additional protection from moisture, soiling, and damage in handling. Wrapping is usually recommended when appearance is of prime importance and the additional protection is desired. Bundle wrapping may be specified in lieu of individual wrapping when further utilization of wrap after delivery is not desired. Time of removal of factory wrap is optional, but, it must be emphasized, factory-applied wrapping provides additional protection from damage in handling and in transit only. If further utilization of the wrap is desired for protection after shipment, the buyer should first inspect the members and provide additional care as necessary.

4.2 Specifications.

4.2.1   Individual Wrapping.

(*a*) Members shall be individually wrapped with heavy, water-resistant paper or its equivalent.

(*b*) Wrapping shall be secured to the member by staples, tape, or other suitable fastenings that do not damage exposed surfaces.

(*c*) Seams of wrapping shall be such that they provide for moisture resistance.

(*d*) Wrapping shall not be removed until roof covering has been applied or protection is otherwise provided.

4.2.2 Bundle Wrapping.

(*a*) Members shall be bundle-wrapped with heavy water-resistant paper or its equivalent.

(*b*) Convenience in handling, at the option of the fabricator, shall determine the size of the bundle.

(*c*) Wrapping shall be secured to the member by staples, tape, or other suitable fastenings that do not damage exposed surfaces.

(*d*) Seams of wrapping shall be such that they provide for moisture resistance.

5. UNLOADING

5.1 Recommended Specifications.

5.1.1 Material shipped f.o.b. rail cars or trucks requires unloading by the buyer. Materials shall be inspected on receipt at the delivery point, and additional care as required must be furnished until completion of construction. On materials shipped f.o.b. rail cars or trucks, this is the buyer's responsibility. Otherwise, it is the seller's responsibility until such time as he completes his portion of the work.

5.1.2 If damage or loss in transit exists, material shall not be unloaded until the delivering carrier has made an inspection. Then a written claim describing the damage or loss is filed with the carrier, and, if the material has been shipped f.o.b. rail cars or trucks, the buyer must notify the seller at time of filing claim.

5.1.3 Laminated members shall not be dragged or dropped. Care in handling is essential to prevent damage to finish surfaces. Slings or chokers used to handle laminated materials should be of the web belting type. Protection cleats or blocking shall be applied at pickup points to protect corners.

6. JOB SITE STORAGE

6.1 Specifications.

6.1.1 Laminated material stored at the job site shall be treated with the same care as the millwork. If covered storage is not available, the material shall be blocked well off the ground, and separated with stripping so that air circulates around all four sides of each member, and the top and all sides shall be covered with moisture-resistant paper. Clear polyethylene film shall not be used. Individual wrappings shall be slit or punctured on the lower side to permit drainage of water.

7. ERECTION

7.1 Specifications.

7.1.1 Padded or nonmarring slings shall be used, and corners shall be protected with wood blocking.

7.1.2 Water-resistant wrapping paper used for the in-transit protection of glued laminated members shall be left intact until the members are enclosed within the building. If wrapping has to be removed at certain connection points during the erection, it shall be replaced after the connection is made. If it is impractical to replace the wrapping, all of it shall be removed. Individual wrappings shall be slit or punctured on the lower side if there is evidence of moisture inside the wrapping.

AMERICAN INSTITUTE
333 West Hampden Avenue

TIMBER CONSTRUCTION
Englewood, Colorado 80110

AITC 112-72
STANDARD FOR
HEAVY TIMBER ROOF DECKING

Adopted as Recommendations March 13, 1972
Copyright 1972 American Institute of Timber Construction

CONTENTS

1. INTRODUCTION

1.1 This standard applies to sawn decking only and does not apply to laminated decking. It covers species, sizes, patterns, length, moisture content, application, specifications, applicable allowable unit stresses, roof load-span tables, which include weights, and slope conversion values for heavy timber roof decking in nominal 3 in. and 4 in. thicknesses, using double tongues and grooves. Select and commercial grades are shown for various species.

1.2 Heavy timber roof decking is a specialty lumber product that constitutes an important part of modern timber construction, providing an all-wood appearance and permitting long spans. It especially is well adapted for use with glued laminated arches and girders and is easily and quickly erected. To be suitable for purposes intended, it must be well manufactured to a low moisture content as described herein.

1

1.3 The lumber used in heavy decking shall be graded in accordance with the grading rules under which the species is customarily graded. The grades are listed herein.

1.4 Some species have grading and dressing rules given in both WCLIB and WWPA specifications.

1.5 The standard grading and dressing rules used for reference in this standard are:

(*a*) *1970 NELMA Standard Grading Rules for Northeastern Lumber*, Northeastern Lumber Manufacturers Association (NELMA).

(*b*) *1970 Standard Grading Rules for Southern Pine Lumber*, Southern Pine Inspection Bureau (SPIB).

(*c*) *Standard Grading Rules for West Coast Lumber, No. 16*, September 1, 1970, West Coast Lumber Inspection Bureau (WCLIB).

(*d*) *1970 Standard Grading Rules for Western Lumber*, Western Wood Products Association (WWPA).

(*e*) *Standard Grading Rules for Canadian Lumber, 1970*, National Lumber Grades Authority (NLGA).

Copies of these grading rules may be obtained from the Northeastern Lumber Manufacturers Association, 13 South Street, Glens Falls, New York 12801; Southern Pine Inspection Bureau, P.O. Box 846, Pensacola, Florida 32502; West Coast Lumber Inspection Bureau, P.O. Box 23145, Portland, Oregon 97223; Western Wood Products Association, Yeon Building, Portland, Oregon 97204; and National Lumber Grades Authority, 1055 West Hastings Street, Vancouver 1, B.C., Canada.

1.6 Moisture content requirements of the regional organization grading rules may differ from this standard. Unless this standard is followed in all requirements, the product will not conform with this standard.

1.7 Nominal 2 in. decking is not included in this standard, but it can be used for many applications that are similar to those of the nominal 3 and 4 in. decking sizes. The moisture content of 2 in. decking should be equivalent to or lower than that required for heavy decking. Specific recommendations for the use of nominal 2 in. decking are given in AITC 118-71, *Standard for Two-Inch Nominal Thickness Lumber Roof Decking for Structural Applications*.

2. SPECIES

2.1 The species usually available and currently used in this product, as well as the regional inspection bureaus under which heavy decking lumber is ordinarily graded, are given in Table 1.

3. SIZES AND PATTERNS

3.1 Standard sizes are 3×6 in. and 4×6 in., nominal, which are dressed to $2\frac{1}{2} \times 5\frac{9}{16}$ in. and $3\frac{1}{2} \times 5\frac{9}{16}$ in., respectively, at the moisture content specified herein. Finished face width overall for both thicknesses is $5\frac{1}{4}$ in. Figures 1 and 2 provide actual dimensions for 3×6 in. and 4×6 in. nominal decking, respectively, illustrating a V-joint pattern. Other thicknesses and widths may be available. Also, other patterns are available, including grooved, striated, and eased joint, and the regional grading rules agencies indicated in paragraph 1.5 should be contacted for further details concerning specific patterns and sizes.

TABLE 1

HEAVY TIMBER DECK SPECIES

Species	Grading Rules under Which Graded	Paragraph Number of Grading Rules under Which Graded[a]	
		Select Quality[b]	Commercial Quality[c]
Cedar, Western	WCLIB; WWPA	127-b; 55.11	127-c; 55.12
Douglas fir-larch	WCLIB; WWPA	127-b; 55.11	127-c; 55.12
Douglas fir, South	WWPA	55.11	55.12
Fir, balsam	NELMA	15.1	15.2
Fir, subalpine	WWPA	55.11	55.12
Hem-fir	WCLIB; WWPA	127-b; 55.11	127-c; 55.12
Hemlock, Eastern-tamarack	NELMA	15.1	15.2
Hemlock, mountain	WCLIB; WWPA	127-b; 55.11	127-c; 55.12
Hemlock, mountain-hem-fir	WWPA	55.11	55.12
Pine, Eastern white	NELMA	15.1	15.2
Pine, Idaho white	WWPA	55.11	55.12
Pine, lodgepole	WWPA	55.11	55.12
Pine, Northern	NELMA	15.1	15.2
Pine, ponderosa-sugar	WWPA	55.11	55.12
Pine, Southern[d,e]	SPIB	309	311
Spruce, Eastern	NELMA	15.1	15.2
Spruce, Engelmann	WWPA	55.11	55.12
Spruce, Sitka	WCLIB	127-b	127-c
Spruce, Western white	NLGA	127b	127c

[a]When species may be graded under WCLIB and WWPA rules, the first paragraph number given is for WCLIB and the second for WWPA rules.

[b]Select quality grades are as follows for the grading rules indicated:

WCLIB;	Select Dex	SPIB;	No. 1 Factory
WWPA;	Selected Decking	NLGA;	Select Decking
NELMA;	Selected Decking		

[c]Commercial quality grades are as follows for the grading rules indicated:

WCLIB;	Commercial Dex	SPIB;	No. 2 Factory
WWPA;	Commercial Decking	NLGA;	Commercial Decking
NELMA;	Commercial Decking		

[d]Nominal 3 and 4 in. Southern pine decking is also available in the following grades: Dense Standard Factory, paragraph 208; No. 1 Dense Factory, paragraph 310; and No. 2 Dense Factory, paragraph 312.

[e]Southern pine is limited to the botanical species of longleaf, slash, shortleaf and loblolly. Lumber cut from trees of this species is classified as "Southern pine" in the SPIB *Standard Grading Rules*.

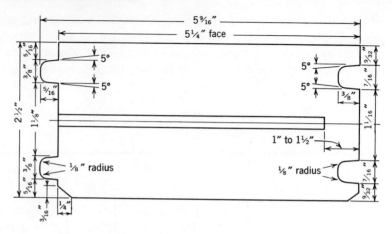

Figure 1.   3 × 6 IN., NOMINAL, V-JOINT PATTERN. *Note:* profile dimensions apply to all patterns. (See regional grading rules in paragraph 1.5 for dimensions for each species.)

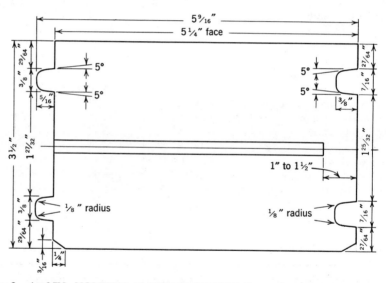

Figure 2.   4 × 6 IN., NOMINAL, V-JOINT PATTERN. (See regional grading rules listed in paragraph 1.5 for dimensions for each species.)

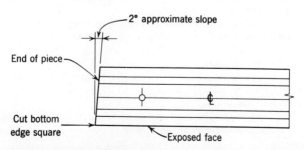

Figure 3.   BEVELED END CUT. (Beveled end cut is optional.)

3.2 Each piece shall be square end-trimmed. When random lengths are furnished, each piece must be square end-trimmed across the face so that at least 90% of the pieces will be within $\frac{3}{64}$ in. of square (for nominal 6 in. width), and the remainder within $\frac{3}{32}$ in. of square. The vertical end cut may vary from square to the bevel cut as shown in Figure 3.

4. LENGTHS

4.1 Lengths of decking pieces may be of specified lengths or may be random lengths; odd or even lengths are permitted; the minimum lengths, based on fbm percentages shall be as follows:

(*a*) 3 in. decking
  Not less than 40% to be 14 ft and longer.
  Not over 10% to be less than 10 ft.
  Not over 1% to be 4 to 5 ft.
(*b*) 4 in. decking.
  Not less than 25% to be 16 ft and longer.
  Not less than 50% to be 14 ft and longer.
  Not over 10% to be 5 to 10 ft.
  Not over 1% to be 4 to 5 ft.

5. MOISTURE CONTENT

5.1 The maximum moisture content shall be 19%. Moisture content shall be determined by such methods as will assure this limitation.

6. APPLICATION

6.1 Decking is to be installed with tongues up on sloped or pitched roofs, and outward in direction of laying on flat roofs. It is to be laid with pattern faces down and exposed on the underside. Each piece should be toenailed at each support with one 40d nail and face nailed with one 6 in. spike. Decking is most economical when laid random, but all pieces shall extend over at least one support.

6.2 There shall be a minimum distance of 4 ft between joints in adjacent courses. Joints within 6 in. of being directly in line each way shall be separated by at least two intervening courses. Courses shall be spiked to each

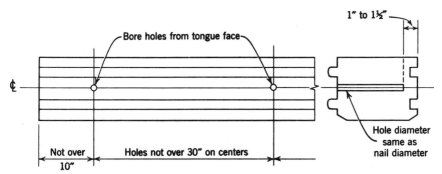

Figure 4.   BORING DETAIL. Locate end holes not over 10 in. from end of piece.

other with 8 in. spikes at intervals not to exceed 30 in. through predrilled edge holes and with one spike at a distance not exceeding 10 in. from each end of each piece. See Figure 4 for boring details.

7. SPECIFICATIONS

7.1 The specifications for heavy timber roof decking for the various species are given in Appendix A. All or nearly all of the permissible characteristics of the grade are never present in maximum size or number in any one piece.

7.2 For description of terms used in this standard and for general rules covering manufacture, the standard grading and dressing rules of the species should be consulted.

7.3 In addition to the specific provisions contained in Appendix A, heavy timber roof decking is subject to all the inspection and shipping provisions of the standard grading rules for the species under which it is graded and to such other provisions of the standard grading rules as may be applicable.

8. WEIGHTS OF INSTALLED DECKING

TABLE 2
WEIGHTS OF INSTALLED DECKING,
IN POUNDS PER SQUARE FOOT OF ROOF SURFACE[a]

Species	Nominal Thickness, in.	
	$3(2\frac{1}{2}\,net)^{b}$	$4(3\frac{1}{2}\,net)$
Cedar, Western	5.2	7.2
Douglas fir — larch	7.3	10.2
Douglas fir, South	6.8	9.5
Fir, balsam	5.3	7.4
Fir, subalpine	4.8	6.7
Hem — fir	6.1	8.6
Hemlock, Eastern — tamarack	6.5	9.1
Hemlock, mountain	6.7	9.3
Hemlock, mountain — hem — fir	6.1	8.6
Pine, Eastern white	5.5	7.6
Pine, Idaho white	5.8	8.2
Pine, lodgepole	6.1	8.6
Pine, Northern	6.7	9.3
Pine, ponderosa — sugar	6.1	8.6
Pine, Southern	7.6	10.7
Spruce, Eastern	6.0	8.4
Spruce, Engelmann	5.0	7.0
Spruce, Sitka	6.0	8.4
Spruce, Western white	5.5	7.6

[a]Weights indicated are based on an average moisture content in place of 15%.
[b]For a net thickness of $2\frac{5}{8}$ in., increase the tabulated weights by a factor of 1.05.

9. SPAN LOAD TABLES

9.1 The allowable tabulated loads for single span are on the basis of there being no end joints between supports.

9.2 The allowable tabulated loads for controlled random layup of decking, continuous over three or more spans, were obtained by multiplying the factor of 80% for bending and deflection by the allowable loads obtained from standard engineering formulas for a three-equal-span, continuous, uniformly loaded member. This percentage adjustment takes into account the differences between continuous decking without joints and the controlled random layup of decking as specified herein. This factor of 80% was selected after careful evaluation of tests and previous experience. When controlled random layup as specified herein is used for unequal spans, nonuniform loading, cantilever action, or conditions other than covered herein by the tabulated values, the same adjustment factors for deflection should be applied to the allowable loads obtained from standard engineering formulas representing the actual conditions of load and span.

9.3 Since decking is seldom used as an individual load-carrying member, the allowable unit stresses for bending as indicated in the tables represent repetitive member use values.

9.4 The allowable loads indicated in the span load tables are based on a maximum moisture content of 19%. If the maximum moisture content is limited to 15%, the allowable bending stress may be multiplied by 1.08 and the modulus of elasticity multiplied by 1.05.

9.5 For purposes of adjusting the stresses to the condition of 2 months' duration of maximum load, as for snow, the allowable unit stresses for bending indicated in the tables are 15% above the stresses for normal loading. If decking is used for floors or other purposes where other durations of load control, appropriate stress adjustments should be made to reflect the duration of loading for the condition of service. Appropriate percentage adjustments are given in the AITC *Timber Construction Manual*.

9.6 Spans of decking shall not be more than 2 ft longer than the length which 40% of the decking shipment exceeds. (Example: If 40% of shipment is 15 ft and longer, the maximum span is 17 ft irrespective of span table values.)

9.7 The span load tables are for total uniformly distributed vertical loads, including dead and live, in pounds per square foot on a horizontal roof surface. When roofs have only a moderate slope (3 in 12 or less), dead and live load may be added together without adjustment for slope of roof.

9.8 For steeper sloping roofs it is customary to adjust the loads so as to express them in terms of square feet of roof surface. For example, 10 lb dead load (6.7 lb for deck and 3.3 lb for roofing) is the vertical load on 1 ft² of sloping roof surface. Live load is usually expressed in pounds per square foor of the horizontal projection of the sloping roof surface. Therefore, the vertical live load must be converted to the vertical psf load of sloping roof surface. For example, a 60 psf live load on the horizontal projection is equivalent to a vertical load of 46 psf on a 10 in 12 sloping roof surface. This combined with 10 psf dead load results in a total vertical load of 56 psf on the 10 in 12 sloping roof surface. The 56 psf total vertical load may then be converted to two components, one perpendicular or normal to the roof surface, and one parallel to the roof surface. In the example, the vertical load of 56 psf is equivalent to a component perpendicular to the roof of 43 psf and a component parallel to the roof of 37 psf.

9.9   Where decking is laid up the slope, the component perpendicular to the roof surface will produce bending and deflection; the parallel component will produce compression. The decking must be designed for bending and axial stresses as well as deflection.

9.10   Where decking is laid horizontal, the component perpendicular to the roof surface produces bending and deflection; the parallel component, as may be induced by wind forces, is taken by diaphragm action.

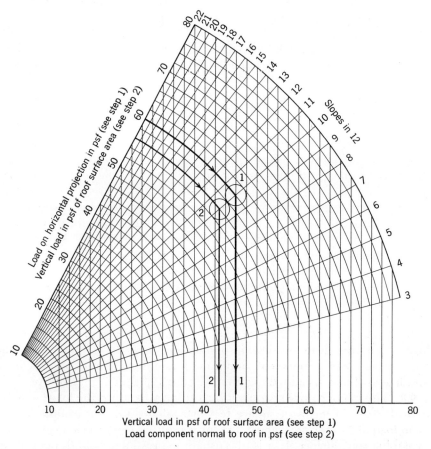

Figure 5.   LOAD CONVERSION. Example: 60 psf live load and 10 psf dead load on 10 in 12 slope. Step 1: 60 psf live load on horizontal projection = 46 psf of root surface area vertical load on 10 in 12 roof slope. Step 2: 10 psf of roof surface area dead load plus 46 psf of roof surface area live load = 56 psf of roof surface area combined load acting vertically; 56 psf of roof surface area vertical total load = 43 psf normal to roof causing bending and deflection.

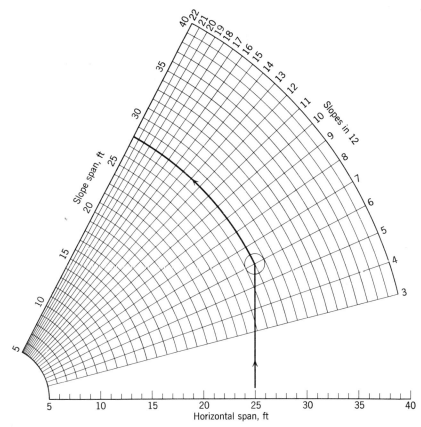

Figure 6.   SPAN CONVERSION. Example: 25 ft horizontal span = 28 ft slope span when slope is 6 in 12. Use 28 ft in determining footage.

TABLE 3

WESTERN CEDAR

Allowable Uniformly Distributed Total Roof Load in psf

Span, ft	Bending[a]		Deflection[b]							
	Select Grade	Commercial Grade	Simple Span Layup				Controlled Random Layup			
			Select Grade		Comm. Grade		Select Grade		Comm. Grade	
	1,610 psi	1,380 psi	1.10×10^6		1.00×10^6		1.10×10^6		1.00×10^6	
			$l/180$	$l/240$	$l/180$	$l/240$	$l/180$	$l/240$	$l/180$	$l/240$
3 in. ($2\frac{1}{2}$ in. net thickness)[c]										
8	210	180	99	75	90	68	150	113	136	102
9	166	142	70	52	64	48	105	79	96	72
10	134	115	51	38	46	35	77	58	70	52
11	111	95	38	29	35	26	58	43	52	39
12	93	80	29	22	27	20	44	33	40	30
13	79	68	23	17	21	16	35	26	32	24
14	68	59	19	14	17	13	28	21	25	19
15	60	51	15	11	14	10	23	17	21	16
16	52	45	12	9	11	8	19	14	17	13
17	46	40	10	8	9	7	16	12	14	11
18	41	35	9	7	8	6	13	10	12	9
19	37	32	7	6	7	5	11	8	10	8
20	34	29	6	5	6	4	10	7	9	7
4 in. ($3\frac{1}{2}$ in. net thickness)										
8	411	352	273	205	248	186	412	309	374	281
9	325	278	192	144	174	131	289	217	263	197
10	263	225	140	105	127	95	211	158	192	144
11	217	186	105	79	95	72	158	119	144	108
12	183	157	81	61	74	55	122	92	111	83
13	156	133	64	48	58	43	96	72	87	65
14	134	115	51	38	46	35	77	58	70	52
15	117	100	41	31	38	28	63	47	57	43
16	103	88	34	26	31	23	52	39	47	35
17	91	78	28	21	26	19	43	32	39	29
18	81	70	24	18	22	16	36	27	33	25
19	73	62	20	15	19	14	31	23	28	21
20	66	56	17	13	16	12	26	20	24	18

[a]These values are increased 15% over normal load values for 2 months' duration of load as for snow.

[b]For a deflection limitation of $l/360$, use $\frac{1}{2}$ the tabulated value for a deflection limit of $l/180$.

[c]To determine the allowable loads for decking having a net thickness of $2\frac{3}{8}$ in., multiply the tabulated bending values by a factor of 1.16 and the deflection values by 1.11.

TABLE 4

DOUGLAS FIR-LARCH
Allowable Uniformly Distributed Total Roof Load in psf

Span, ft	Bending[a]		Deflection[b]							
	Select Grade	Commercial Grade	Simple Span Layup				Controlled Random Layup			
			Select Grade		Comm. Grade		Select Grade		Comm. Grade	
			1.80×10^6		1.70×10^6		1.80×10^6		1.70×10^6	
	2,300 psi	1,898 psi	$l/180$	$l/240$	$l/180$	$l/240$	$l/180$	$l/240$	$l/180$	$l/240$
3 in. ($2\frac{1}{2}$ in. net thickness)[c]										
8	299	247	163	122	154	115	246	184	232	174
9	237	195	114	86	108	81	173	129	163	122
10	192	158	83	62	79	59	126	94	119	89
11	158	131	63	47	59	44	94	71	89	67
12	133	110	48	36	46	34	73	55	69	52
13	113	94	38	28	36	27	57	43	54	41
14	98	81	30	23	29	22	46	34	43	32
15	85	70	25	19	23	17	37	28	35	26
16	75	62	20	15	19	14	31	23	29	22
17	66	55	17	13	16	12	26	19	24	18
18	59	49	14	11	13	10	22	16	20	15
19	53	44	12	9	11	9	18	14	17	13
20	48	40	10	8	10	7	16	12	15	11
4 in. ($3\frac{1}{2}$ in. net thickness)										
8	587	484	446	335	422	316	674	506	636	478
9	464	383	314	235	296	222	474	355	447	335
10	376	310	229	172	216	162	345	259	326	245
11	310	256	172	129	162	122	259	195	245	184
12	261	215	132	99	125	94	200	150	189	142
13	222	183	104	78	98	74	157	118	148	111
14	192	158	83	62	79	59	126	94	119	89
15	167	138	68	51	64	48	102	77	97	72
16	147	121	56	42	53	40	84	63	80	60
17	130	107	47	35	44	33	70	53	66	50
18	116	96	39	29	37	28	59	44	56	42
19	104	86	33	25	31	24	50	38	48	36
20	94	77	29	21	27	20	43	32	41	31

[a]These values are increased 15% over normal load values for 2 months' duration of load as for snow.

[b]For a deflection limitation of $l/360$, use $\frac{1}{2}$ the tabulated value for a deflection limit of $l/180$.

[c]To determine the allowable loads for decking having a net thickness of $2\frac{5}{8}$ in., multiply the tabulated bending values by a factor of 1.16 and the deflection values by 1.11.

TABLE 5

DOUGLAS FIR, SOUTH
Allowable Uniformly Distributed Total Roof Load in psf

Span, ft	Bending[a]		Deflection[b]							
	Select Grade	Commercial Grade	Simple Span Layup				Controlled Random Layup			
			Select Grade		Comm. Grade		Select Grade		Comm. Grade	
	2,185 psi	1,840 psi	1.40×10^6 psi		1.30×10^6 psi		1.40×10^6 psi		1.30×10^6 psi	
			$l/180$	$l/240$	$l/180$	$l/240$	$l/180$	$l/240$	$l/180$	$l/240$
3 in. ($2\frac{1}{2}$ in. net thickness)[c]										
8	285	240	127	95	117	88	191	143	177	133
9	225	189	89	67	83	62	134	101	125	93
10	182	153	65	49	60	45	98	73	91	68
11	150	127	49	37	45	34	73	55	68	51
12	126	106	38	28	35	26	57	42	53	39
13	108	91	30	22	27	21	45	33	41	31
14	93	78	24	18	22	16	36	27	33	25
15	81	68	19	14	18	13	29	22	27	20
16	71	60	16	12	15	11	24	18	22	17
17	63	53	13	10	12	9	20	15	18	14
18	56	47	11	8	10	8	17	13	16	12
19	50	42	9	7	9	7	14	11	13	10
20	46	38	8	6	8	6	12	9	11	9
4 in. ($3\frac{1}{2}$ in. net thickness)										
8	558	470	347	261	322	242	524	393	487	365
9	441	371	244	183	227	170	368	276	342	256
10	357	301	178	133	165	124	269	201	249	187
11	295	248	134	100	124	93	202	151	187	140
12	248	209	103	77	96	72	155	117	144	108
13	211	178	81	61	75	56	122	92	114	85
14	182	153	65	49	60	45	98	73	91	68
15	159	134	53	40	49	37	80	60	74	55
16	139	117	43	33	40	30	66	49	61	46
17	123	104	36	27	34	25	55	41	51	38
18	110	93	30	23	28	21	46	35	43	32
19	99	83	26	19	24	18	39	29	36	27
20	89	75	22	17	21	15	34	25	31	23

[a]These values are increased 15% over normal load values for 2 months' duration of load as for snow.

[b]For a deflection limitation of $l/360$, use $\frac{1}{2}$ the tabulated value for a deflection limit of $l/180$.

[c]To determine the allowable loads for decking having a net thickness of $2\frac{5}{8}$ in., multiply the tabulated bending values by a factor of 1.16 and the deflection values by 1.11.

TABLE 6

BALSAM FIR AND ENGELMANN SPRUCE
Allowable Uniformly Distributed Total Roof Load in psf

Span, ft	Bending[a]		Deflection[b]							
	Select Grade	Commercial Grade	Simple Span Layup				Controlled Random Layup			
			Select Grade		Comm. Grade		Select Grade		Comm. Grade	
			1.20×10^6 psi		1.10×10^6 psi		1.20×10^6 psi		1.10×10^6 psi	
	1,495 psi	1,265 psi	$l/180$	$l/240$	$l/180$	$l/240$	$l/180$	$l/240$	$l/180$	$l/240$
3 in. ($2\frac{1}{2}$ in. net thickness)[c]										
8	195	165	108	81	99	75	164	123	150	113
9	154	130	76	57	70	52	115	86	105	79
10	125	105	56	42	51	38	84	63	77	58
11	103	87	42	31	38	29	63	47	58	43
12	87	73	32	24	29	22	49	36	44	33
13	74	62	25	19	23	17	38	29	35	26
14	64	54	20	15	19	14	31	23	28	21
15	55	47	16	12	15	11	25	19	23	17
16	49	41	14	10	12	9	20	15	19	14
17	43	36	11	8	10	8	17	13	16	12
18	38	33	10	7	9	7	14	11	13	10
19	35	29	8	6	7	6	12	9	11	8
20	31	26	7	5	6	5	10	8	10	7
4 in. ($3\frac{1}{2}$ in. net thickness)										
8	382	323	298	223	273	205	449	337	412	309
9	301	255	209	157	192	144	316	237	289	217
10	244	207	153	114	140	105	230	173	211	158
11	202	171	114	86	105	79	173	130	158	119
12	170	143	88	66	81	61	133	100	122	92
13	144	122	69	52	64	48	105	79	96	72
14	125	105	56	42	51	38	84	63	77	58
15	109	92	45	34	41	31	68	51	63	47
16	95	81	37	28	34	26	56	42	52	39
17	84	71	31	23	28	21	47	35	43	32
18	75	64	26	20	24	18	39	30	36	27
19	68	57	22	17	20	15	34	25	31	23
20	61	52	19	14	17	13	29	22	26	20

[a]These values are increased 15% over normal load values for 2 months' duration of load as for snow.

[b]For a deflection limitation of $l/360$, use $\frac{1}{2}$ the tabulated value for a deflection limit of $l/180$.

[c]To determine the allowable loads for decking having a net thickness of $2\frac{5}{8}$ in., multiply the tabulated bending values by a factor of 1.16 and the deflection values by 1.11.

TABLE 7

SUBALPINE FIR

Allowable Uniformly Distributed Total Roof Load in psf

Span, ft	Bending[a]		Deflection[b]							
	Select Grade	Commercial Grade	Simple Span Layup				Controlled Random Layup			
			Select Grade		Comm. Grade		Select Grade		Comm. Grade	
			0.90×10^6 psi		0.90×10^6 psi		0.90×10^6 psi		0.90×10^6 psi	
	1,380 psi	1,150 psi	$l/180$	$l/240$	$l/180$	$l/240$	$l/180$	$l/240$	$l/180$	$l/240$
3 in. (2½ in. net thickness)[c]										
8	180	150	81	61	81	61	123	92	123	92
9	142	118	57	43	57	43	86	65	86	65
10	115	96	42	31	42	31	63	47	63	47
11	95	79	31	23	31	23	47	35	47	35
12	80	67	24	18	24	18	36	27	36	27
13	68	57	19	14	19	14	29	21	29	21
14	59	49	15	11	15	11	23	17	23	17
15	51	43	12	9	12	9	19	14	19	14
16	45	37	10	8	10	8	15	12	15	12
17	40	33	8	6	8	6	13	10	13	10
18	35	30	7	5	7	5	11	8	11	8
19	32	27	6	5	6	5	9	7	9	7
20	29	24	5	4	5	4	8	6	8	6
4 in. (3½ in. net thickness)										
8	352	293	223	167	223	167	337	253	337	253
9	278	232	157	118	157	118	237	178	237	178
10	225	188	114	86	114	86	173	129	173	129
11	186	155	86	64	86	64	130	97	130	97
12	157	130	66	50	66	50	100	75	100	75
13	133	111	52	39	52	39	79	59	79	59
14	115	96	42	31	42	31	63	47	63	47
15	100	83	34	25	34	25	51	38	51	38
16	88	73	28	21	28	21	42	32	42	32
17	78	65	23	17	23	17	35	26	35	26
18	70	58	20	15	20	15	30	22	30	22
19	62	52	17	13	17	13	25	19	25	19
20	56	47	14	11	14	11	22	16	22	16

[a]These values are increased 15% over normal load values for 2 months' duration of load as for snow.

[b]For a deflection limitation of $l/360$, use ½ the tabulated value for a deflection limit of $l/180$.

[c]To determine the allowable loads for decking having a net thickness of 2⅝ in., multiply the tabulated bending values by a factor of 1.16 and the deflection values by 1.11.

TABLE 8

HEM-FIR
Allowable Uniformly Distributed Total Roof Load in psf

Span, ft	Bending[a]		Deflection[b]							
	Select Grade	Commercial Grade	Simple Span Layup				Controlled Random Layup			
			Select Grade		Comm. Grade		Select Grade		Comm. Grade	
	1,840 psi	1,495 psi	1.50×10^6 psi		1.40×10^6 psi		1.50×10^6 psi		1.40×10^6 psi	
			$l/180$	$l/240$	$l/180$	$l/240$	$l/180$	$l/240$	$l/180$	$l/240$
3 in. ($2\frac{1}{2}$ in. net thickness)[c]										
8	240	195	136	102	127	95	205	154	191	143
9	189	154	95	71	89	67	144	108	134	101
10	153	125	69	52	65	49	105	79	98	73
11	127	103	52	39	49	37	79	59	73	55
12	106	87	40	30	38	28	61	46	57	42
13	91	74	32	24	30	22	48	36	45	33
14	78	64	25	19	24	18	38	29	36	27
15	68	55	21	15	19	14	31	23	29	22
16	60	49	17	13	16	12	26	19	24	18
17	53	43	14	11	13	10	21	16	20	15
18	47	38	12	9	11	8	18	13	17	13
19	42	35	10	8	9	7	15	11	14	11
20	38	31	9	7	8	6	13	10	12	9
4 in. ($3\frac{1}{2}$ in. net thickness)										
8	470	382	372	279	347	261	562	421	524	393
9	371	301	261	196	244	183	395	296	368	276
10	301	244	191	143	178	133	288	216	269	201
11	248	202	143	107	134	100	216	162	202	151
12	209	170	110	83	103	77	166	125	155	117
13	178	144	87	65	81	61	131	98	122	92
14	153	125	69	52	65	49	105	79	98	73
15	134	109	56	42	53	40	85	64	80	60
16	117	95	47	35	43	33	70	53	66	49
17	104	84	39	29	36	27	59	44	55	41
18	93	75	33	25	30	23	49	37	46	35
19	83	68	28	21	26	19	42	31	39	29
20	75	61	24	18	22	17	36	27	34	25

[a]These values are increased 15% over normal load values for 2 months' duration of load as for snow.

[b]For a deflection limitation of $l/360$, use $\frac{1}{2}$ the tabulated value for a deflection limit of $l/180$.

[c]To determine the allowable loads for decking having a net thickness of $2\frac{5}{8}$ in., multiply the tabulated bending values by a factor of 1.16 and the deflection values by 1.11.

TABLE 9

EASTERN HEMLOCK – TAMARACK
Allowable Uniformly Distributed Total Roof Load in psf

Span, ft	Bending[a] Select Grade 1,955 psi	Bending[a] Commercial Grade 1,668 psi	Deflection[b] Simple Span Layup Select Grade 1.30×10^6 psi $l/180$	$l/240$	Comm. Grade 1.10×10^6 psi $l/180$	$l/240$	Controlled Random Layup Select Grade 1.30×10^6 psi $l/180$	$l/240$	Comm. Grade 1.10×10^6 psi $l/180$	$l/240$
\multicolumn{11}{c}{3 in. ($2\frac{1}{2}$ in. net thickness)[c]}										
8	255	217	117	88	99	75	177	133	150	113
9	201	172	83	62	70	52	125	93	105	79
10	163	139	60	45	51	38	91	68	77	58
11	135	115	45	34	38	29	68	51	58	43
12	113	96	35	26	29	22	53	39	44	33
13	96	82	27	21	23	17	41	31	35	26
14	83	71	22	16	19	14	33	25	28	21
15	72	62	18	13	15	11	27	20	23	17
16	64	54	15	11	12	9	22	17	19	14
17	56	48	12	9	10	8	18	14	16	12
18	50	43	10	8	9	7	16	12	13	10
19	45	38	9	7	7	6	13	10	11	8
20	41	35	8	6	6	5	11	9	10	7
\multicolumn{11}{c}{4 in. ($3\frac{1}{2}$ in. net thickness)}										
8	499	426	322	242	273	205	487	365	412	309
9	394	336	227	170	192	144	342	256	289	217
10	319	272	165	124	140	105	249	187	211	158
11	264	225	124	93	105	79	187	140	158	119
12	222	189	96	72	81	61	144	108	122	92
13	189	161	75	56	64	48	114	85	96	72
14	163	139	60	45	51	38	91	68	77	58
15	142	121	49	37	41	31	74	55	63	47
16	125	106	40	30	34	26	61	46	52	39
17	110	94	34	25	28	21	51	38	43	32
18	99	84	28	21	24	18	43	32	36	27
19	88	75	24	18	20	15	36	27	31	23
20	80	68	21	15	17	13	31	23	26	20

[a]These values are increased 15% over normal load values for 2 months' duration of load as for snow.

[b]For a deflection limitation of $l/360$, use $\frac{1}{2}$ the tabulated value for a deflection limit of $l/180$.

[c]To determine the allowable loads for decking having a net thickness of $2\frac{5}{8}$ in., multiply the tabulated bending values by a factor of 1.16 and the deflection values by 1.11.

TABLE 10

MOUNTAIN HEMLOCK
Allowable Uniformly Distributed Total Roof Load in psf

Span, ft	Bending[a]		Deflection[b]							
	Select Grade	Commercial Grade	Simple Span Layup				Controlled Random Layup			
			Select Grade		Comm. Grade		Select Grade		Comm. Grade	
	1,898 psi	1,610 psi	1.30×10^6 psi		1.10×10^6 psi		1.30×10^6 psi		1.10×10^6 psi	
			$l/180$	$l/240$	$l/180$	$l/240$	$l/180$	$l/240$	$l/180$	$l/240$
3 in. ($2\frac{1}{2}$ in. net thickness)[c]										
8	247	210	117	88	99	75	177	133	150	113
9	195	166	83	62	70	52	125	93	105	79
10	158	134	60	45	51	38	91	68	77	58
11	131	111	45	34	38	29	68	51	58	43
12	110	93	35	26	29	22	53	39	44	33
13	94	79	27	21	23	17	41	31	35	26
14	81	68	22	16	19	14	33	25	28	21
15	70	60	18	13	15	11	27	20	23	17
16	62	52	15	11	12	9	22	17	19	14
17	55	46	12	9	10	8	18	14	16	12
18	49	41	10	8	9	7	16	12	13	10
19	44	37	9	7	7	6	13	10	11	8
20	40	34	8	6	6	5	11	9	10	7
4 in. ($3\frac{1}{2}$ in. net thickness)										
8	484	411	322	242	273	205	487	365	412	309
9	383	325	227	170	192	144	342	256	289	217
10	310	263	165	124	140	105	249	187	211	158
11	256	217	124	93	105	79	187	140	158	119
12	215	183	96	72	81	61	144	108	122	92
13	183	156	75	56	64	48	114	85	96	72
14	158	134	60	45	51	38	91	68	77	58
15	138	117	49	37	41	31	74	55	63	47
16	121	103	40	30	34	26	61	46	52	39
17	107	91	34	25	28	21	51	38	43	32
18	96	81	28	21	24	18	43	32	36	27
19	86	73	24	18	20	15	36	27	31	23
20	77	66	21	15	17	13	31	23	26	20

[a]These values are increased 15% over normal load values for 2 months' duration of load as for snow.
[b]For a deflection limitation of $l/360$, use $\frac{1}{2}$ the tabulated value for a deflection limit of $l/180$.
[c]To determine the allowable loads for decking having a net thickness of $2\frac{5}{8}$ in., multiply the tabulated bending values by a factor of 1.16 and the deflection values by 1.11.

TABLE 11

MOUNTAIN HEMLOCK—HEM-FIR
Allowable Uniformly Distributed Total Roof Load in psf

Span, ft	Bending[a]		Deflection[b]							
	Select Grade	Commercial Grade	Simple Span Layup				Controlled Random Layup			
			Select Grade		Comm. Grade		Select Grade		Comm. Grade	
			1.30×10^6 psi		1.10×10^6 psi		1.30×10^6 psi		1.10×10^6 psi	
	1,840 psi	1,495 psi	$l/180$	$l/240$	$l/180$	$l/240$	$l/180$	$l/240$	$l/180$	$l/240$
3 in. (2½ in. net thickness)[c]										
8	240	195	117	88	99	75	177	133	150	113
9	189	154	83	62	70	52	125	93	105	79
10	153	125	60	45	51	38	91	68	77	58
11	127	103	45	34	38	29	68	51	58	43
12	106	87	35	26	29	22	53	39	44	33
13	91	74	27	21	23	17	41	31	35	26
14	78	64	22	16	19	14	33	25	28	21
15	68	55	18	13	15	11	27	20	23	17
16	60	49	15	11	12	9	22	17	19	14
17	53	43	12	9	10	8	18	14	16	12
18	47	38	10	8	9	7	16	12	13	10
19	42	35	9	7	7	6	13	10	11	8
20	38	31	8	6	6	5	11	9	10	7
4 in. (3½ in. net thickness)										
8	470	382	322	242	273	205	487	365	412	309
9	371	301	227	170	192	144	342	256	289	217
10	301	244	165	124	140	105	249	187	211	158
11	248	202	124	93	105	79	187	140	158	119
12	209	170	96	72	81	61	144	108	122	92
13	178	144	75	56	64	48	114	85	96	72
14	153	125	60	45	51	38	91	68	77	58
15	134	109	49	37	41	31	74	55	63	47
16	117	95	40	30	34	26	61	46	52	39
17	104	84	34	25	28	21	51	38	43	32
18	93	75	28	21	24	18	43	32	36	27
19	83	68	24	18	20	15	36	27	31	23
20	75	61	21	15	17	13	31	23	26	20

[a]These values are increased 15% over normal load values for 2 months' duration of load as for snow.

[b]For a deflection limitation of $l/360$, use ½ the tabulated value for a deflection limit of $l/180$.

[c]To determine the allowable loads for decking having a net thickness of 2⅝ in., multiply the tabulated bending values by a factor of 1.16 and the deflection values by 1.11.

TABLE 12

EASTERN WHITE PINE
Allowable Uniformly Distributed Total Roof Load in psf

Span, ft	Bending[a]		Deflection[b]							
	Select Grade	Commercial Grade	Simple Span Layup				Controlled Random Layup			
			Select Grade		Comm. Grade		Select Grade		Comm. Grade	
			1.20×10^6 psi		1.10×10^6 psi		1.20×10^6 psi		1.10×10^6 psi	
	1,208 psi	1,006 psi	$l/180$	$l/240$	$l/180$	$l/240$	$l/180$	$l/240$	$l/180$	$l/240$
3 in. ($2\frac{1}{2}$ in. net thickness)[c]										
8	157	131	108	81	99	75	164	123	150	113
9	124	104	76	57	70	52	115	86	105	79
10	101	84	56	42	51	38	84	63	77	58
11	83	69	42	31	38	29	63	47	58	43
12	70	58	32	24	29	22	49	36	44	33
13	60	50	25	19	23	17	38	29	35	26
14	51	43	20	15	19	14	31	23	28	21
15	45	37	16	12	15	11	25	19	23	17
16	39	33	14	10	12	9	20	15	19	14
17	35	29	11	8	10	8	17	13	16	12
18	31	26	10	7	9	7	14	11	13	10
19	28	23	8	6	7	6	12	9	11	8
20	25	21	7	5	6	5	10	8	10	7
4 in. ($3\frac{1}{2}$ in. net thickness)										
8	308	257	298	223	273	205	449	337	412	309
9	243	203	209	157	192	144	316	237	289	217
10	197	164	153	114	140	105	230	173	211	158
11	163	136	114	86	105	79	173	130	158	119
12	137	114	88	66	81	61	133	100	122	92
13	117	97	69	52	64	48	105	79	96	72
14	101	84	56	42	51	38	84	63	77	58
15	88	73	45	34	41	31	68	51	63	47
16	77	64	37	28	34	26	56	42	52	39
17	68	57	31	23	28	21	47	35	43	32
18	61	51	26	20	24	18	39	30	36	27
19	55	46	22	17	20	15	34	25	31	23
20	49	41	19	14	17	13	29	22	26	20

[a]These values are increased 15% over normal load values for 2 months' duration of load as for snow.

[b]For a deflection limitation of $l/360$, use $\frac{1}{2}$ the tabulated value for a deflection limit of $l/180$.

[c]To determine the allowable loads for decking having a net thickness of $2\frac{5}{8}$ in., multiply the tabulated bending values by a factor of 1.16 and the deflection values by 1.11.

TABLE 13

IDAHO WHITE PINE
Allowable Uniformly Distributed Total Roof Load in psf

Span, ft	Bending[a]		Deflection[b]							
	Select Grade	Commercial Grade	Simple Span Layup				Controlled Random Layup			
			Select Grade		Comm. Grade		Select Grade		Comm. Grade	
	1,610 psi	1,322 psi	1.40×10^6 psi		1.30×10^6 psi		1.40×10^6 psi		1.30×10^6 psi	
			$l/180$	$l/240$	$l/180$	$l/240$	$l/180$	$l/240$	$l/180$	$l/240$
3 in. (2½ in. net thickness)[c]										
8	210	172	127	95	117	88	191	143	177	133
9	166	136	89	67	83	62	134	101	125	93
10	134	110	65	49	60	45	98	73	91	68
11	111	91	49	37	45	34	73	55	68	51
12	93	77	38	28	35	26	57	42	53	39
13	79	65	30	22	27	21	45	33	41	31
14	68	56	24	18	22	16	36	27	33	25
15	60	49	19	14	18	13	29	22	27	20
16	52	43	16	12	15	11	24	18	22	17
17	46	38	13	10	12	9	20	15	18	14
18	41	34	11	8	10	8	17	13	16	12
19	37	31	9	7	9	7	14	11	13	10
20	34	28	8	6	8	6	12	9	11	9
4 in. (3½ in. net thickness)										
8	411	338	347	261	322	242	524	393	487	365
9	325	267	244	183	227	170	368	276	342	256
10	263	216	178	133	165	124	269	201	249	187
11	217	179	134	100	124	93	202	151	187	140
12	183	150	103	77	96	72	155	117	144	108
13	156	128	81	61	75	56	122	92	114	85
14	134	110	65	49	60	45	98	73	91	68
15	117	96	53	40	49	37	80	60	74	55
16	103	84	43	33	40	30	66	49	61	46
17	91	75	36	27	34	25	55	41	51	38
18	81	67	30	23	28	21	46	35	43	32
19	73	60	26	19	24	18	39	29	36	27
20	66	54	22	17	21	15	34	25	31	23

[a]These values are increased 15% over normal load values for 2 months' duration of load as for snow.

[b]For a deflection limitation of $l/360$, use ½ the tabulated value for a deflection limit of $l/180$.

[c]To determine the allowable loads for decking having a net thickness of 2⅝ in., multiply the tabulated bending values by a factor of 1.16 and the deflection values by 1.11.

TABLE 14

LODGEPOLE PINE

Allowable Uniformly Distributed Total Roof Load in psf

Span, ft	Bending[a]		Deflection[b]							
	Select Grade	Commercial Grade	Simple Span Layup				Controlled Random Layup			
			Select Grade		Comm. Grade		Select Grade		Comm. Grade	
			1.30×10^6 psi		1.20×10^6 psi		1.30×10^6 psi		1.20×10^6 psi	
	1,668 psi	1,380 psi	*l*/180	*l*/240	*l*/180	*l*/240	*l*/180	*l*/240	*l*/180	*l*/240
3 in. (2½ in. net thickness)[c]										
8	217	180	117	88	108	81	177	133	164	123
9	172	142	83	62	76	57	125	93	115	86
10	139	115	60	45	56	42	91	68	84	63
11	115	95	45	34	42	31	68	51	63	47
12	96	80	35	26	32	24	53	39	49	36
13	82	68	27	21	25	19	41	31	38	29
14	71	59	22	16	20	15	33	25	31	23
15	62	51	18	13	16	12	27	20	25	19
16	54	45	15	11	14	10	22	17	20	15
17	48	40	12	9	11	8	18	14	17	13
18	43	35	10	8	10	7	16	12	14	11
19	38	32	9	7	8	6	13	10	12	9
20	35	29	8	6	7	5	11	9	10	8
4 in. (3½ in. net thickness)										
8	426	352	322	242	298	223	487	365	449	337
9	336	278	227	170	209	157	342	256	316	237
10	272	225	165	124	153	114	249	187	230	173
11	225	186	124	93	114	86	187	140	173	130
12	189	157	96	72	88	66	144	108	133	100
13	161	133	75	56	69	52	114	85	105	79
14	139	115	60	45	56	42	91	68	84	63
15	121	100	49	37	45	34	74	55	68	51
16	106	88	40	30	37	28	61	46	56	42
17	94	78	34	25	31	23	51	38	47	35
18	84	70	28	21	26	20	43	32	39	30
19	75	62	24	18	22	17	36	27	34	25
20	68	56	21	15	19	14	31	23	29	22

[a]These values are increased 15% over normal load values for 2 months' duration of load as for snow.

[b]For a deflection limitation of *l*/360, use ½ the tabulated value for a deflection limit of *l*/180.

[c]To determine the allowable loads for decking having a net thickness of 2⅝ in., multiply the tabulated bending values by a factor of 1.16 and the deflection values by 1.11.

TABLE 15

NORTHERN PINE
Allowable Uniformly Distributed Total Roof Load in psf

Span, ft	Bending[a]		Deflection[b]							
	Select Grade	Commercial Grade	Simple Span Layup				Controlled Random Layup			
			Select Grade		Comm. Grade		Select Grade		Comm. Grade	
			1.40×10^6 psi		1.30×10^6 psi		1.40×10^6 psi		1.30×10^6 psi	
	1,782 psi	1,495 psi	$l/180$	$l/240$	$l/180$	$l/240$	$l/180$	$l/240$	$l/180$	$l/240$
3 in. (2½ in. net thickness)[c]										
8	232	195	127	95	117	88	191	143	177	133
9	183	154	89	67	83	62	134	101	125	93
10	149	125	65	49	60	45	98	73	91	68
11	123	103	49	37	45	34	73	55	68	51
12	103	87	38	28	35	26	57	42	53	39
13	88	74	30	22	27	21	45	33	41	31
14	76	64	24	18	22	16	36	27	33	25
15	66	55	19	14	18	13	29	22	27	20
16	58	49	16	12	15	11	24	18	22	17
17	51	43	13	10	12	9	20	15	18	14
18	46	38	11	8	10	8	17	13	16	12
19	41	35	9	7	9	7	14	11	13	10
20	37	31	8	6	8	6	12	9	11	9
4 in. (3½ in. net thickness)										
8	455	382	347	261	322	24z	524	393	487	365
9	359	301	244	183	227	170	368	276	342	256
10	291	244	178	133	165	124	269	201	249	187
11	241	202	134	100	124	93	202	151	187	140
12	202	170	103	77	96	72	155	117	144	108
13	172	144	81	61	75	56	122	92	114	85
14	149	125	65	49	60	45	98	73	91	68
15	129	109	53	40	49	37	80	60	74	55
16	114	95	43	33	40	30	66	49	61	46
17	101	84	36	27	34	25	55	41	51	38
18	90	75	30	23	28	21	46	35	43	32
19	81	68	26	19	24	18	39	29	36	27
20	73	61	22	17	21	15	34	25	31	23

[a]These values are increased 15% over normal load values for 2 months' duration of load as for snow.

[b]For a deflection limitation of $l/360$, use ½ the tabulated value for a deflection limit of $l/180$.

[c]To determine the allowable loads for decking having a net thickness of 2⅝ in., multiply the tabulated bending values by a factor of 1.16 and the deflection values by 1.11.

TABLE 16

PONDEROSA PINE — SUGAR PINE
Allowable Uniformly Distributed Total Roof Load in psf

Span, ft	Bending[a] Select Grade 1,552 psi	Bending[a] Commercial Grade 1,322 psi	Deflection[b] Simple Span Layup Select Grade 1.20×10^6 psi $l/180$	$l/240$	Comm. Grade 1.10×10^6 psi $l/180$	$l/240$	Controlled Random Layup Select Grade 1.20×10^6 psi $l/180$	$l/240$	Comm. Grade 1.10×10^6 psi $l/180$	$l/240$
\multicolumn{11}{c}{3 in ($2\frac{1}{2}$ in. net thickness)[c]}

Span, ft	Select Grade 1,552 psi	Comm. Grade 1,322 psi	SS Sel $l/180$	$l/240$	SS Comm $l/180$	$l/240$	CR Sel $l/180$	$l/240$	CR Comm $l/180$	$l/240$
\multicolumn{11}{c}{**3 in ($2\frac{1}{2}$ in. net thickness)[c]**}
8	202	172	108	81	99	75	164	123	150	113
9	160	136	76	57	70	52	115	86	105	79
10	129	110	56	42	51	38	84	63	77	58
11	107	91	42	31	38	29	63	47	58	43
12	90	77	32	24	29	22	49	36	44	33
13	77	65	25	19	23	17	38	29	35	26
14	66	56	20	15	19	14	31	23	28	21
15	58	49	16	12	15	11	25	19	23	17
16	51	43	14	10	12	9	20	15	19	14
17	45	38	11	8	10	8	17	13	16	12
18	40	34	10	7	9	7	14	11	13	10
19	36	31	8	6	7	6	12	9	11	8
20	32	28	7	5	6	5	10	8	10	7
\multicolumn{11}{c}{**4 in. ($3\frac{1}{2}$ in. net thickness)**}
8	396	338	298	223	273	205	449	337	412	309
9	313	267	209	157	192	144	316	237	289	217
10	254	216	153	114	140	105	230	173	211	158
11	210	179	114	86	105	79	173	130	158	119
12	176	150	88	66	81	61	133	100	122	92
13	150	128	69	52	64	48	105	79	96	72
14	129	110	56	42	51	38	84	63	77	58
15	113	96	45	34	41	31	68	51	63	47
16	99	84	37	28	34	26	56	42	52	39
17	88	75	31	23	28	21	47	35	43	32
18	78	67	26	20	24	18	39	30	36	27
19	70	60	22	17	20	15	34	25	31	23
20	63	54	19	14	17	13	29	22	26	20

[a]These values are increased 15% over normal load values for 2 months' duration of load as for snow.

[b]For a deflection limitation of $l/360$, use $\frac{1}{2}$ the tabulated value for a deflection limit of $l/180$.

[c]To determine the allowable loads for decking having a net thickness of $2\frac{5}{8}$ in., multiply the tabulated bending values by a factor of 1.16 and the deflection values by 1.11.

TABLE 17

SOUTHERN PINE
Allowable Uniformly Distributed Total Roof Load in psf

Span, ft	Bending[a]		Deflection[b]							
	Select Grade	Commercial Grade	Simple Span Layup				Controlled Random Layup			
			Select Grade		Comm. Grade		Select Grade		Comm. Grade	
			1.60×10^6 psi		1.60×10^6 psi		1.60×10^6 psi		1.60×10^6 psi	
	1,668 psi	1,668 psi	$l/180$	$l/240$	$l/180$	$l/240$	$l/180$	$l/240$	$l/180$	$l/240$
3 in. ($2\frac{1}{2}$ in. net thickness)[c]										
8	217	217	145	109	145	109	218	164	218	164
9	172	172	102	76	102	76	153	115	153	115
10	139	139	74	56	74	56	112	84	112	84
11	115	115	56	42	56	42	84	63	84	63
12	96	96	43	32	43	32	65	49	65	49
13	82	82	34	25	34	25	51	38	51	38
14	71	71	27	20	27	20	41	31	41	31
15	62	62	22	16	22	16	33	25	33	25
16	54	54	18	14	18	14	27	20	27	20
17	48	48	15	11	15	11	23	17	23	17
18	43	43	13	10	13	10	19	14	19	14
19	38	38	11	8	11	8	16	12	16	12
20	35	35	9	7	9	7	14	10	14	10
4 in. ($3\frac{1}{2}$ in. net thickness)										
8	426	426	397	298	397	298	599	449	599	449
9	336	336	279	209	279	209	421	316	421	316
10	272	272	203	152	203	152	307	230	307	230
11	225	225	153	115	153	115	230	173	230	173
12	189	189	118	88	118	88	178	133	178	133
13	161	161	93	69	93	69	140	105	140	105
14	139	139	74	56	74	56	112	84	112	84
15	121	121	60	45	60	45	91	68	91	68
16	106	106	50	37	50	37	75	56	75	56
17	94	94	41	31	41	31	62	47	62	47
18	84	84	35	26	35	26	53	39	53	39
19	75	75	30	22	30	22	45	34	45	34
20	68	68	25	19	25	19	38	29	38	29

[a]These values are increased 15% over normal load values for 2 months' duration of load as for snow.

[b]For a deflection limitation of $l/360$, use $\frac{1}{2}$ the tabulated value for a deflection limit of $l/180$.

[c]To determine the allowable loads for decking having a net thickness of $2\frac{5}{8}$ in., multiply the tabulated bending values by a factor of 1.16 and the deflection values by 1.11.

TABLE 18

EASTERN SPRUCE

Allowable Uniformly Distributed Total Roof Load in psf

Span, ft	Bending[a]		Deflection[b]							
	Select Grade	Commercial Grade	Simple Span Layup				Controlled Random Layup			
			Select Grade		Comm. Grade		Select Grade		Comm. Grade	
			1.40×10^6 psi		1.20×10^6 psi		1.40×10^6 psi		1.20×10^6 psi	
	1,668 psi	1,380 psi	$l/180$	$l/240$	$l/180$	$l/240$	$l/180$	$l/240$	$l/180$	$l/240$
3 in. ($2\frac{1}{2}$ in. net thickness)[c]										
8	217	180	127	95	108	81	191	143	164	123
9	172	142	89	67	76	57	134	101	115	86
10	139	115	65	49	56	42	98	73	84	63
11	115	95	49	37	42	31	73	55	63	47
12	96	80	38	28	32	24	57	42	49	36
13	82	68	30	22	25	19	45	33	38	29
14	71	59	24	18	20	15	36	27	31	23
15	62	51	19	14	16	12	29	22	25	19
16	54	45	16	12	14	10	24	18	20	15
17	48	40	13	10	11	8	20	15	17	13
18	43	35	11	8	10	7	17	13	14	11
19	38	32	9	7	8	6	14	11	12	9
20	35	29	8	6	7	5	12	9	10	8
4 in. ($3\frac{1}{2}$ in. net thickness)										
8	426	352	347	261	298	223	524	393	449	337
9	336	278	244	183	209	157	368	276	316	237
10	272	225	178	133	153	114	269	201	230	173
11	225	186	134	100	114	86	202	151	173	130
12	189	157	103	77	88	66	155	117	133	100
13	161	133	81	61	69	52	122	92	105	79
14	139	115	65	49	56	42	98	73	84	63
15	121	100	53	40	45	34	80	60	68	51
16	106	88	43	33	37	28	66	49	56	42
17	94	78	36	27	31	23	55	41	47	35
18	84	70	30	23	26	20	46	35	39	30
19	75	62	26	19	22	17	39	29	34	25
20	68	56	22	17	19	14	34	25	29	22

[a]These values are increased 15% over normal load values for 2 months' duration of load as for snow.

[b]For a deflection limitation of $l/360$, use $\frac{1}{2}$ the tabulated value for a deflection limit of $l/180$.

[c]To determine the allowable loads for decking having a net thickness of $2\frac{5}{8}$ in., multiply the tabulated bending values by a factor of 1.16 and the deflection values by 1.11.

TABLE 19

SITKA SPRUCE
Allowable Uniformly Distributed Total Roof Load in psf

Span, ft	Bending[a]		Deflection[b]							
	Select Grade	Commercial Grade	Simple Span Layup				Controlled Random Layup			
			Select Grade		Comm. Grade		Select Grade		Comm. Grade	
	1,725 psi	1,438 psi	1.50×10^6 psi		1.30×10^6 psi		1.50×10^6 psi		1.30×10^6 psi	
			$l/180$	$l/240$	$l/180$	$l/240$	$l/180$	$l/240$	$l/180$	$l/240$
3 in. (2½ in. net thickness)[c]										
8	225	187	136	102	117	88	205	154	177	133
9	177	148	95	71	83	62	144	108	125	93
10	144	120	69	52	60	45	105	79	91	68
11	119	99	52	39	45	34	79	59	68	51
12	100	83	40	30	35	26	61	46	53	39
13	85	71	32	24	27	21	48	36	41	31
14	73	61	25	19	22	16	38	29	33	25
15	64	53	21	15	18	13	31	23	27	20
16	56	47	17	13	15	11	26	19	22	17
17	50	41	14	11	12	9	21	16	18	14
18	44	37	12	9	10	8	18	13	16	12
19	40	33	10	8	9	7	15	11	13	10
20	36	30	9	7	8	6	13	10	11	9
4 in. (3½ in. net thickness)										
8	440	367	372	279	322	242	562	421	487	365
9	348	290	261	196	227	170	395	296	342	256
10	282	235	191	143	165	124	288	216	249	187
11	233	194	143	107	124	93	216	162	187	140
12	196	163	110	83	96	72	166	125	144	108
13	167	139	87	65	75	56	131	98	114	85
14	144	120	69	52	60	45	105	79	91	68
15	125	104	56	42	49	37	85	64	74	55
16	110	92	47	35	40	30	70	53	61	46
17	97	81	39	29	34	25	59	44	51	38
18	87	72	33	25	28	21	49	37	43	32
19	78	65	28	21	24	18	42	31	36	27
20	70	59	24	18	21	15	36	27	31	23

[a]These values are increased 15% over normal load values for 2 months' duration of load as for snow.

[b]For a deflection limitation of $l/360$, use ½ the tabulated value for a deflection limit of $l/180$.

[c]To determine the allowable loads for decking having a net thickness of 2⅝ in., multiply the tabulated bending values by a factor of 1.16 and the deflection values by 1.11.

TABLE 20

WESTERN WHITE SPRUCE (Spruce-Pine-Fir)
Allowable Uniformly Distributed Total Roof Load in psf

Span, ft	Bending[a]		Deflection[b]							
	Select Grade	Commercial Grade	Simple Span Layup				Controlled Random Layup			
			Select Grade		Comm. Grade		Select Grade		Comm. Grade	
	1,610 psi	1,322 psi	1.50×10^6 psi		1.30×10^6 psi		1.50×10^6 psi		1.30×10^6 psi	
			$l/180$	$l/240$	$l/180$	$l/240$	$l/180$	$l/240$	$l/180$	$l/240$
3 in. ($2\frac{1}{2}$ in. net thickness)[c]										
8	210	172	136	102	117	88	205	154	177	133
9	166	136	95	71	83	62	144	108	125	93
10	134	110	69	52	60	45	105	79	91	68
11	111	91	52	39	45	34	79	59	68	51
12	93	77	40	30	35	26	61	46	53	39
13	79	65	32	24	27	21	48	36	41	31
14	68	56	25	19	22	16	38	29	33	25
15	60	49	21	15	18	13	31	23	27	20
16	52	43	17	13	15	11	26	19	22	17
17	46	38	14	11	12	9	21	16	18	14
18	41	34	12	9	10	8	18	13	16	12
19	37	31	10	8	9	7	15	11	13	10
20	34	28	9	7	8	6	13	10	11	9
4 in. ($3\frac{1}{2}$ in. net thickness)										
8	411	338	372	279	322	242	562	421	487	365
9	325	267	261	196	227	170	395	296	342	256
10	263	216	191	143	165	124	288	216	249	187
11	217	179	143	107	124	93	216	162	187	140
12	183	150	110	83	96	72	166	125	144	108
13	156	128	87	65	75	56	131	98	114	85
14	134	110	69	.52	60	45	105	79	91	68
15	117	96	56	42	49	37	85	64	74	55
16	103	84	47	35	40	30	70	53	61	46
17	91	75	39	29	34	25	59	44	51	38
18	81	67	33	25	28	21	49	37	43	32
19	73	60	28	21	24	18	42	31	36	27
20	66	54	24	18	21	15	36	27	31	23

[a]These values are increased 15% over normal load values for 2 months' duration of load as for snow.

[b]For a deflection limitation of $l/360$, use $\frac{1}{2}$ the tabulated value for a deflection limit of $l/180$.

[c]To determine the allowable loads for decking having a net thickness of $2\frac{5}{8}$ in., multiply the tabulated bending values by a factor of 1.16 and the deflection values by 1.11.

AMERICAN INSTITUTE
333 West Hampden Avenue

TIMBER CONSTRUCTION
Englewood, Colorado 80110

AITC 112-72
APPENDIX A
APPLICABLE GRADING PROVISIONS

Adopted as Recommendations March 13, 1972
Copyright 1972 by American Institute of Timber Construction

CONTENTS

A1. SELECT GRADE PROVISIONS

A1.1 Decking of this grade is recommended and widely used where the selected face will be used to show wood at its natural best, such as in a paneled ceiling. Knots and other natural characteristics that add to the decorative character of the piece are permitted. The following specific requirements of this standard are excerpts from the grading rules unless otherwise noted.

A1.1.1 Excerpt of provisions from paragraph 127-b of the WCLIB *Grading Rules.*

Characteristics and limiting provisions on exposed faces, except as noted, are:

"Medium stained sapwood. Heart stain firm.
Occasional short splits.
Medium seasoning checks, scattered.
Holes, pin to small in size, equivalent to chipped knots.
Medium torn or raised grain.
Medium grain in Douglas fir only.
Slope of grain not to exceed 1 in 10.
Pitch, light or equivalent very small streak.
Tongue $\frac{1}{16}$ in. narrow in occasional pieces.
Medium bark pockets. Very small dry pitch pockets.
Light crook or very light twist, in occasional pieces.
Knots, sound and tight, on exposed face, except as noted below.

Knots, well spaced, are permitted in the following sizes on both wide faces:

Nominal Width, in.	Net Face Width, in.	Knot Size, in.
6	5	$2\frac{3}{8}$
6	$5\frac{1}{4}$	$2\frac{1}{2}$
8	$6\frac{3}{4}$	$3\frac{1}{4}$

In occasional pieces, firm and tight knots not exceeding $1\frac{1}{2}$ in. in diameter are permitted if not through the piece and do not exceed two in 12 ft of length, or equivalent smaller.

Spike and narrow face knots are permitted if judged to have no more effect on strength than other knots.

Knots may contain chipped or unsound spots not larger than approximately $\frac{3}{4}$ in. in diameter, if not through the piece and do not exceed two in 12 ft of length or equivalent smaller.

On back and unexposed edges, hit and miss skips, wane approximately $\frac{1}{3}$ of the face width, and other characteristics not interfering with intended use are permitted except as noted.

For cedar species the natural characteristics of pitted areas or peck is permitted on back and unexposed edges when the peck is narrow and well scattered and does not affect the strength more than other characteristics permitted in the grade."

A1.1.2 Excerpt of provisions from paragraph 55.11 of the WWPA *Grading Rules* and paragraph 15.1 of the NELMA *Grading Rules*.
Characteristics and limiting provisions on the face are:

"Light sap stain, medium heart stain.
Occasional short splits.
Medium seasoning checks, scattered.
Holes, pin to small in size, equivalent to chipped knots.
Slight torn or raised grain or a spot of medium.
Slope of grain not to exceed 1 in 10.
Tongue $\frac{1}{16}$ in. narrow in occasional pieces.
Medium bark pockets.
Very small, dry pitch pockets.
Light pitch or equivalent very small streak.
Warp, light.
Knots, sound and tight, on exposed face except as noted below.
Knots, well spaced, are limited to the following sizes on both wide faces:

Nominal Width, in.	Net Face Width, in.	Knot Size, in.
6	5*	$2\frac{3}{8}$
8	$6\frac{3}{4}$	$3\frac{1}{4}$

Note: WWPA publication *Standard Patterns* also indicates a $5\frac{1}{4}$ in. face width for a nominal width of 6 in.

In occasional pieces, unsound and fixed knots not exceeding $1\frac{1}{2}$ in. in diameter are permitted if not through the piece and not exceeding two knots or equivalent smaller in 12 ft of length.

Narrow face and spike knots are allowed when their effect is judged to be no greater than other knots allowed.

Knots may contain chipped out areas no larger than approximately $\frac{3}{4}$ in. diameter, if not through the piece and not exceeding two knots or equivalent smaller in 12 ft of length.

Characteristics and limiting provisions on the back and unexposed edges are:

Hit and miss skips.

Wane $\frac{1}{3}$ the width and other characteristics not interfering with the intended use of the grade."

A1.1.3 Excerpt of provisions from paragraphs 309 and 238 of the SPIB *Grading Rules* for No. 1 Factory flooring and decking grade.

Characteristics and limiting provisions on face are restricted to admit the following:

"Medium grain

Checks — Surface seasoning checks, not limited.

   Through checks at ends are limited as splits.

Knots — Sound, firm, encased, and pith knots, if tight and well spaced, are permitted in sizes not to exceed the following, or equivalent displacement:

Nominal Width, in.	At Edge Wide Face, in.	Centerline Wide Face, in.
6	$1\frac{1}{2}$	$2\frac{1}{4}$
8	2	$2\frac{3}{4}$

Decayed and hollow knots not permitted.

Pith knots allowed only if pith opening does not extend through piece.

Manufacture — Standard 'E'. See paragraph 722(e).

Pitch and pitch streaks — Not limited.

Pith limited to $\frac{1}{6}$ length.

Pockets — Pitch or bark — Not limited.

Shake — On ends limited to $\frac{1}{2}$ the thickness.

   Away from ends several heart shakes up to 2 in. long, none through.

Skips — Hit and miss skips in 10% of pieces. See paragraph 720(f).

Slope of grain — 1 in 10.

Splits — Equal in length to width of the piece.

Stain — Stained sapwood. Firm heart stain or firm red heart.

Wane limited to $\frac{1}{4}$ in. deep, $\frac{1}{2}$ in. wide and $\frac{1}{6}$ length of piece.

Warp — $\frac{1}{2}$ of medium. See paragraph 752.

Reverse side not lower than No. 2 Factory, but wane may not extend into tongue or groove if D & M or into $\frac{1}{2}$ thickness of lap if shiplapped, except may extend into groove or through lap or for $\frac{1}{2}$ thickness of tongue for a length of 10 in. provided wane width and length decrease in proportion to depth increase."

A1.1.4 Excerpt of provisions from paragraph 127b of the NLGA *Grading Rules:*
Characteristics and limiting provisions are:

"Bark Pockets — medium.
Checks — medium.
Crook — light, occasional piece.
Holes — equivalent to chipped knots.
Pitch — light, or equivalent, very small streak.
Pitch Pockets — very small, dry.
Rate of Growth — medium grain, Douglas Fir or Western Larch only.
Skips — very light, maximum 10% of face in occasional pieces.
Slope of Grain — 1 in 10.
Splits — short, occasional piece.
Stained Wood — medium.
Torn or Raised Grain — medium.
Twist — very light, occasional piece.
Knots — sound and tight on exposed face, well spaced. Measurements as per Paragraph 320a.

Nominal Width, in.	Knot Size (both faces), in.
6	$2\frac{3}{8}$
8	$3\frac{1}{4}$

Spike and narrow face knots — equivalent. In occasional pieces, firm and tight knots not exceeding $1\frac{1}{2}$ in. in diameter are permitted if not through the piece and limited to 2 per 12 lin. ft or equivalent smaller.
Knots may contain chipped or unsound spots approximately $\frac{3}{4}$ in. in diameter not through, 2 per 12 lin. ft or equivalent smaller.
Back and Unexposed Edges — hit and miss skips, wane approximately $\frac{1}{3}$ face and other characteristics which do not affect the intended end use.
In Cedar, peck is permitted on back and unexposed edges in narrow streaks well scattered which do not affect the strength more than other characteristics allowed."

A2. COMMERCIAL GRADE PROVISIONS

A2.1 Lumber of this grade is recommended and customarily used for the same purposes served by the higher grade when appearance is not of primary importance. The following specific requirements of this standard are excerpted from the grading rules.
A2.1.1 Excerpt of provisions from paragraph 127-c of the WCLIB *Grading Rules:*
Characteristics and limiting provisions are:

"Stained wood.

Splits approximately $\frac{1}{6}$ the length.

Seasoning checks.

Small holes.

Torn grain.

Medium grain in Douglas fir only.

Slope of grain not to exceed 1 in 8.

Pitch streaks.

Hit and miss skips.

Tongue $\frac{1}{16}$ in. narrow.

Wane approximately $\frac{1}{6}$ of the face width.

Pitch or bark pockets.

Firm white specks, narrow streak.

Unsound wood in small spots or streaks up to 1 in. wide may be accepted on any face. In Cedar species only, spots or streaks may be accepted up to $\frac{1}{3}$ the width on any face.

Shake — not serious.

Medium crook, or very light twist in occasional pieces.

Knots, well spaced, are permitted in the following sizes on both wide faces:

Nominal Width, in.	Net Face Width, in.	Knot Size, in.
6	5	$2\frac{7}{8}$
6	$5\frac{1}{4}$	3
8	$6\frac{3}{4}$	$3\frac{3}{4}$

Spike and narrow face knots are permitted if judged to have no more effect on strength than other knots.

Chipped and/or broken-out knots not larger than approximately $1\frac{1}{2}$ in. in diameter, are permitted if not through the piece.

Wane approximately $\frac{1}{3}$ of face, and other characteristics not interfering with intended use, are permitted on unexposed face and edges except as noted.

Any piece with an unusual combination of characteristics which seriously affects normal serviceability is excluded from the grade."

A2.1.2 Excerpt of provisions from paragraph 55.12 of the WWPA *Grading Rules* and paragraph 15.2 of the NELMA *Grading Rules*.

Characteristics and limiting provisions are:

"Stained Wood.

Splits approximately $\frac{1}{6}$ the length.

Seasoning checks.

Small knot holes.

Torn grain.

Slope of grain not to exceed 1 in 8.

Hit and miss skips.

Tongue $\frac{1}{16}$ in. narrow.

Wane approximately $\frac{1}{6}$ the face width.

Pitch streaks, pitch or bark pockets.

Firm white specks, narrow streak.

Unsound wood and peck in small spots or streaks up to 1 in. wide may be accepted on any face. In Cedar species only, spots or streaks may be accepted up to $\frac{1}{3}$ the width.

Shake — not serious.

Warp, $\frac{1}{4}$ in. less than medium as shown in paragraph 752.00.

Knots, well spaced, are limited to the following sizes on both wide faces:

Nominal Width, in.	Face Width, in.	Knot Size, in.
6	5*	$2\frac{7}{8}$
8	$6\frac{3}{4}$	$3\frac{7}{8}$

Note: WWPA publication *Standard Patterns* also indicates a $5\frac{1}{4}$ in. face width for a nominal width of 6 in.

Narrow face and spike knots allowed when their effect is judged to be no greater than other knots allowed.

Chipped knots and broken-out knots, not larger than approximately $1\frac{1}{2}$ in. in diameter, are permitted if not through the piece.

Characteristics and limiting provisions on the back and unexposed edges are:

Wane approximately $\frac{1}{3}$ of face and other characteristics not interfering with the intended use are permitted on unexposed back and edges, except as noted.

Any piece with an unusual combination of characteristics which seriously affects normal serviceability is excluded from this grade.''

A2.1.3   Excerpts of provisions from paragraphs 311 and 244 of the SPIB *Grading Rules* for No. 2 Factory flooring and decking grades.

Characteristics permitted and limiting provisions shall be:

"Checks — Seasoning checks not limited. Through checks at ends are limited as splits.

Knots — Well spaced knots of any quality are permitted in sizes not to exceed the following or equivalent displacement:

Nominal Width, in.	At Edge Wide Face, in.	Centerline Wide Face, in.	Holes (Any Cause), in.	
6	$1\frac{7}{8}$	$2\frac{7}{8}$	$1\frac{1}{2}$	One hole or
8	$2\frac{1}{2}$	$3\frac{1}{2}$	2	equivalent
				smaller per
				2 lin. ft.

Manufacture — Standard 'F'. See paragraph 722(f).

Pitch and pitch streaks — Not limited.

Pockets — Pitch or bark — Not limited.

Shake — On ends limited to $\frac{1}{2}$ the thickness.
  Away from ends through heart shakes up to 2 ft long, well separated. If not through, single shakes may be 3 ft long or up to $\frac{1}{4}$ the length, whichever is greater.
Skips — Hit and miss, and in addition 5% of the pieces may be hit or miss or heavy skip not longer than 2 ft. See paragraph 720(e), (f) and (g).
Slope of grain — 1 in 8.
Splits — Equal in length to $1\frac{1}{2}$ times the width of the piece.
Stain — Stained sapwood. Firm heart stain or firm red heart not limited.
Unsound wood — Not permitted in thicknesses over 2 in. but in 2 in. thickness, heart center streaks not over $\frac{1}{3}$ the width or thickness, or small spots or streaks of firm honeycomb or peck equal to $\frac{1}{6}$ the width are permitted.
Wane — $\frac{1}{3}$ the thickness, $\frac{1}{3}$ the width. Five percent of the pieces may have wane up to $\frac{2}{3}$ the thickness and $\frac{1}{2}$ the width for $\frac{1}{4}$ the length.
Warp — Light. See paragraph 752.
White speck — Firm, $\frac{1}{3}$ the face or equivalent."

A2.1.4 Excerpt of provisions from paragraph 127c of the NLGA *Grading Rules:*
Characteristics and limiting provisions are:

"Checks.
Crook — medium occasional piece.
Holes — 1 in.
Pitch — streaks.
Pockets — bark or pitch.
Rate of Growth — medium grain in Douglas Fir and Western Larch only.
Shake — not serious.
Skips — hit and miss.
Slope of Grain — 1 in 8.
Splits — $\frac{1}{6}$ length.
Torn Grain.
Twist — very light occasional piece.
Unsound Wood — in small spots or streaks up to 1 in. wide on any face.
  In Cedar spots or streaks of peck $\frac{1}{3}$ of any face.
Wane — $\frac{1}{6}$ face width.
White Specks — $\frac{1}{3}$ width or equivalent.
Knots — well spaced. Measurements as per paragraph 320a.

Nominal Width, in.	Knot Size, in.
6	$2\frac{7}{8}$ (Both faces)
8	$3\frac{3}{4}$

Spike or narrow face knots equivalent.
Chipped and/or broken out knots approximately $1\frac{1}{2}$ in. in diameter not through.
On Back and Unexposed Edges — wane approximately $\frac{1}{3}$ face and other characteristics not affecting intended end use."

AMERICAN INSTITUTE
333 West Hampden Avenue

TIMBER CONSTRUCTION
Englewood, Colorado 80110

AITC 113-71
STANDARD FOR DIMENSIONS OF GLUED LAMINATED STRUCTURAL MEMBERS

Adopted as Recommendations March 17, 1971
Copyright 1972 by American Institute of Timber Construction

CONTENTS

1. PREFACE

1.1 The most efficient and economical production of glued laminated structural members results when standard lumber sizes are used for the laminates. Industry recommended practice uses nominal 2 in. thick lumber of standard nominal width to produce straight members and curved members where the radius of curvature is within the bending radius limits for that thickness of the species. Nominal 1 in. thick boards are normally used when the bending radius is too sharp to permit use of nominal 2 in. thick laminations. These are standard practices subject to deviation to conform with specific job requirements and plant procedures. The use of nominal 1 and 2 in. thick laminations will generally be the most economical, and, therefore, conformance with this standard is recommended for all normal uses. Exceptions should be made only when the shape of the structure requires nonstandard laminates.

2. STANDARD DEPTHS OF MEMBERS

2.1 Proper gluing procedures require surfaces planed uniformly smooth to exact thickness with a maximum allowable variation of plus or minus 0.008 in. Recommended standard practice is to surface nominal 2 in. laminations to a net $1\frac{1}{2}$ in. thickness, and nominal 1 in. laminations to a net

1

$\frac{3}{4}$ in. thickness. (Previous *American Lumber Standards* specified a net thickness of $1\frac{5}{8}$ in. for nominal 2 in. thick lumber, and this net thickness may be used by some laminators, depending upon availability.) Finished depths of members are thus increments of these net thicknesses.

No. of Laminations	Net Depth of Member, in.	
	1 in. Laminations	2 in. Laminations
4	3	6
5	$3\frac{3}{4}$	$7\frac{1}{2}$
6	$4\frac{1}{2}$	9
7	$5\frac{1}{4}$	$10\frac{1}{2}$
8	6	12
Etc.	Etc.	Etc.

2.2   The use of laminations of special thicknesses because of bending radius or the mixing of thicknesses for special purposes results in net finished depths which may be nonstandard.

3. STANDARD WIDTHS OF MEMBERS

3.1   It is necessary to surface the wide faces of members to remove the glue squeezeout and provide a uniformly smooth surface. Therefore, the net finished width of the glued laminated member is less than the net finished width of industry standard boards and dimension.

3.2   Industry standard finished widths for glued laminated structural members are as follows.

Nominal width, in.	3	4	6	8	10	12	14	16
Net finished width, in.	$2\frac{1}{4}$	$3\frac{1}{8}$	$5\frac{1}{8}$	$6\frac{3}{4}$	$8\frac{3}{4}$	$10\frac{3}{4}$	$12\frac{1}{4}$	$14\frac{1}{4}$

4. STANDARD DIMENSIONS FOR HEAVY TIMBER

4.1   Excellent fire resistance is achieved with "heavy timber" construction (see *Standard for Heavy Timber Construction*, AITC 108). Minimum sawn lumber sizes have been long established and are expressed in nominal dimensions and assume surfacing to *American Lumber Standard* net sizes.

4.2   For "heavy timber" construction, the net width of glued laminated structural members shall be the standard glued laminated net width for the nominal sawn width specified, and the net depth of glued laminated structural members shall be equal to or greater than the net finished depth specified in the following table.

Minimum Nominal Size, in.			Minimum Glued Laminated Net Size, in.		
Width	×	Depth	Width	×	Depth
8	×	8	$6\frac{3}{4}$	×	9
6	×	10	$5\frac{1}{4}$	×	$10\frac{1}{2}$
6	×	8	$5\frac{1}{8}$	×	9
6	×	6	$5\frac{1}{8}$	×	6
4	×	6	$3\frac{1}{8}$	×	$7\frac{1}{2}$

5. TOLERANCE

5.1 The following tolerances shall be permitted at the time of manufacturing.

5.1.1 Width. Plus or minus $\frac{1}{16}$ in. of the specified width.

5.1.2 Depth. Plus $\frac{1}{8}$ in. per foot of specified depth. Minus $\frac{1}{16}$ in. per foot of the specified depth or $\frac{3}{32}$ in. whichever is the larger.

5.1.3 Length. Plus or minus $\frac{1}{16}$ in. up to 20 ft and plus or minus $\frac{1}{16}$ in. per 20 ft of the specified length, except where length dimensions are not specified or critical.

5.1.4 Squareness. The cross section of all glued laminated structural members shall be square within plus or minus $\frac{1}{8}$ in. per foot of specified depth of member unless a specially shaped section is specified.

AMERICAN INSTITUTE
333 West Hampden Avenue

TIMBER CONSTRUCTION
Englewood, Colorado 80110

AITC 114-71
GUIDE SPECIFICATIONS – STRUCTURAL GLUED LAMINATED CROSSARMS

Adopted as Recommendations March 17, 1971
Copyright 1972 by American Institute of Timber Construction

CONTENTS

1. PREFACE

1.1 Structural glued laminated crossarms offer these advantages: increased strength, relative freedom from checks and other seasoning effects, and virtually unlimited sizes and shapes.

1.2 The following recommended guide specification provides for the manufacture of treated or untreated structural glued laminated distribution and transmission crossarms. An explanation of the several subjects included is followed by the specification guide form, which may be copied. Included are the items essential for a full understanding of the products to be furnished and for assurance of compliance with best standard industry practices. The latest edition of referenced standards, including the AITC *Inspection Manual* and other standards, industry laminating specifications, specifications on adhesives, and adhesive manufacturer recommendations are considered a part of this specification. In order to keep this specification up to date with current recommendations and to keep it brief but complete, these standards are not repeated here, but they are cited. (See *References*, AITC 101.)

2. EXPLANATION OF GUIDE FORM

2.1 Scope. This specification is based on the crossarms being designed for known or assumed loads and for the member sizes to be in accordance with these loads and stress levels specified. Standard structural

1

laminating specifications establish stresses based on loads applied perpendicular to the glue lines and include modifications of these stresses for loads applied parallel to the glue line. The stress level specified is assumed to be for loads applied perpendicular to the glue line. When loads paralled to the glue line may limit the design, the allowable stress parallel to glue lines shall be so indicated.

2.2   Manufacture. The assurance of quality structural glued laminated timber depends on the controls in the shop of the materials and operations during the entire laminating process. Voluntary Product Standard PS56-73, *Structural Glued Laminated Timber*, requires that manufacturers have a quality control system responsible for the continuous control and inspection of the manufacturing processes and for keeping and maintenance of records on all jobs certified to conform with the standard.

2.3   Lumber. It is preferable for the design to specify stress values and thus permit the laminator to select the grades of material to meet the structural requirements in accordance with the industry laminating standards. Lumber should be to grade, manufacture, moisture content, and other requirements of the structural glued laminated standard specifications for the species, with the additional requirements of this specification on maximum knot size. Wane is not permitted.

2.4   Adhesives. Wet-use adhesives only are recommended for crossarms, whether treated or untreated. Conformance with PS56-73 as well as the adhesive manufacturers' recommendations for mixing, storage, pot life, working life, and assembly life will assure all the controls necessary for a glue bond stronger than the wood.

2.5   Standard Sizes. Standard finished sizes of structural glued laminated members vary in size from standard commercial sawn lumber sizes. Depths are normally surfaced to $\frac{3}{4}$ or $1\frac{1}{2}$ in. for the nominal 1 and 2 in. laminations used. Widths normally vary from $\frac{1}{4}$ to $\frac{1}{2}$ in. less than standard sawn lumber surfaced sizes. This is a result of manufacture, because the sides of the completed member must be surfaced after gluing.

2.6   Appearance. The appearance of crossarms is secondary to their structural quality, and no edge patching is required to meet the AITC Industrial Appearance Grade specified. Industrial Appearance Grade permits the natural growth characteristics of the lumber grade used and requires that the top and bottom laminations be free of loose knots and open knot holes. In addition, the members must be surfaced on the two sides, an occasional miss being permitted along individual laminations. Restrictions on knot sizes are included to upgrade both appearance and strength.

2.7   Protection. The application of surface sealers or end sealers before pressure treatment is not recommended, nor is it deemed necessary that crossarms be wrapped for protection. However, reasonable precautions should be taken in storage of crossarms.

2.8   Fabrication. Fabrication may be performed by the laminator or by the treater and shall be in accordance with details furnished by the buyer in accordance with *Timber Construction Standards*, AITC 100.

2.9   Quality Marks and Identification. The order between the seller and the buyer should specify the identification requirements of the job. PS56-73 states that "structural glued laminated timber represented to comply with this Standard shall be distinctly marked with the identification of a qualified inspection and testing agency."

The AITC is a qualified inspection and testing agency and provides, through license agreements, quality marks and certificates of conformance for identifying material that conforms with the requirements of PS56-73. AITC licenses only qualified producers who demonstrate, through a qualification inspection, tests, and periodic unannounced inspections, their ability to produce products in accordance with the requirements of PS56-73.

If treated, laminated crossarms should be permanently branded to show preservative, species, and year of treatment by the treater.

2.10   Treatment. Preservation treatment of crossarms should be in accordance with *Treating Standard for Structural Timber Framing*, AITC 109, and with referenced AWPA specifications when treatment is specified. Treatment after gluing is recommended unless the size and shape of the members are such that available retorts will not accommodate the members.

3. GUIDE FORM—STRUCTURAL GLUED LAMINATED CROSSARMS SPECIFICATION

3.1   Scope. All structural glued laminated crossarms shall be furnished as shown on the plans and specified herein.

3.2   Manufacture. Manufacture and quality control shall be in conformance with Voluntary Product Standard PS56-73, *Structural Glued Laminated Timber*.

3.3   Lumber. Lumber shall be California redwood, Douglas fir, Southern pine, or Western larch meeting the structural requirements and laminating specifications of the species. Other species or regional groups may be used as provided in Voluntary Product Standard PS56-73. Lumber used shall be of stress grades that provide glued laminated crossarms with normal working stress values of _____psi in bending in accordance with Table 1 of the lumber industry laminating specifications. Allowable stresses for other species shall be determined in accordance with the provisions of Voluntary Product Standard PS56-73. The maximum knot size shall be $\frac{3}{4}$ in. in outer laminations of 4 in. nominal width. The maximum knot hole or knot size shall be $1\frac{1}{2}$ in. in inner laminations of 4 in. nominal width. These allowable sizes shall vary in proportion to the width of the piece for other widths. Wane is not permitted.

3.4   Adhesives. Adhesives shall be of the wet-use type complying with PS56-73.

3.5   Standard Sizes for Structural Glued Laminated Timber. (See *Standard for Dimensions of Glued Laminated Structural Members*, AITC 113.)

   3.5.1   Depth. The finished net depth shall be a multiple of $\frac{3}{4}$ in. or $1\frac{1}{2}$ in. as required by the design and shown on the plans.

3.5.2 Width. The standard net finished width shall be one of the following as required by the design and shown on the plans.

Nominal width, in.	3	4	6	8	10
Net finished width, in.	$2\frac{1}{4}$	$3\frac{1}{8}$	$5\frac{1}{8}$	$6\frac{3}{4}$	$8\frac{3}{4}$

3.6   Appearance. The appearance of members shall meet AITC Industrial Appearance Grade. Top and bottom laminations shall be free of loose knots and open knot holes. Edges shall be eased to $\frac{3}{16}$-in. radius.

3.7   Protection. When treatment is specified, surface or end sealers shall not be applied before treating. Members shall be adequately protected in storage.

3.8   Fabrication. All drilling and dapping shall be performed before treating for members treated after gluing.

3.9   Quality Marks and Identification.

(Check appropriate items):

☐ Members shall be marked with an AITC Quality Mark indicating conformance with Voluntary Product Standard PS56-73, *Structural Glued Laminated Timber*.

☐ Members shall be marked with an AITC Quality Mark and, in addition, an AITC Certificate of Conformance shall be provided to indicate conformance with Voluntary Product Standard PS56-73, *Structural Glued Laminated Timber*.

☐ Treated members shall be permanently branded to show preservative, species, and year of treatment by the treater.

3.10   Treatment. Members shall be (check one):

☐ Untreated.

☐ Treated in accordance with the *Treating Standard for Structural Timber Framing*, AITC 109, with _____ preservative with a minimum retention of _____ pcf and minimum penetration of _____ in.

AMERICAN INSTITUTE
333 West Hampden Avenue

TIMBER CONSTRUCTION
Englewood, Colorado 80110

AITC 115-65
STANDARD FOR FABRICATED
STRUCTURAL TIMBER

Adopted as Recommendations February 16, 1965
Copyright 1972 by American Institute of Timber Construction

CONTENTS

1. PREFACE

1.1 Purpose. The increasing economic importance of structural timber in structures of all types and the need to provide satisfactory structures are matters of public concern. In view of these circumstances, the purposes of this standard are: (*a*) to provide a common basis of understanding in the trade with respect to what constitutes sound requirements for the fabrication and inspection of fabricated structural timber; (*b*) to effect economies through a wider utilization of such standards; and (*c*) to encourage production of dependable products that will be adequate for the needs of the trade.

1.2 Scope. This standard covers recommended minimum requirements for shop-fabricated structural timber, including: personnel, equipment and facilities, materials, hardware and steel accessories, fabrication, quality control, and product inspection.

1.2.1 The term "fabricated structural timber" as employed herein refers to engineered load-carrying elements of wood (including sawn lumber and/or timber, glued laminated timber, and mechanically laminated timber) which are shop-fabricated for use in frames of all kinds

1

including but not limited to trusses, arches, beams, girders, and columns; for use in schools, churches, commercial, industrial, and other buildings, and for other structures such as bridges, towers, and marine installations. Components of structural glued laminated timber should be produced in accordance with Voluntary Product Standard PS56-73, *Structural Glued Laminated Timber*.

2. GENERAL

2.1 Applicable Requirements. Fabricated structural timber, in order to be considered as complying with this standard, shall meet all applicable requirements listed below. Allowable deviations are provided for in paragraph 2.4.

Applicable Requirements for	Section No.
General items	2
Personnel	3
Equipment and facilities	4
Materials	5
Hardware and steel accessories	6
Fabrication	7
Quality control	8
Product inspection	9

2.2 Definitions. Terms used in this standard with specific meanings applicable to fabricated structural timber are defined in *Standard Definitions, Abbreviations, and References*, AITC 101. The requirements given herein are in accordance with these definitions.

2.3 References. In case of conflict between provisions of this standard and any provisions of the documents included herein by reference, this standard shall govern. It is intended that any later issues of these documents may be used, providing the requirements are applicable and consistent with the issues designated.

2.4 Although it is intended that the operation of this standard will be in the public interest and its widest possible general use is recommended, it is not intended to interfere with the right to freedom of contract between buyer and seller. When contract provisions call for exceptions or deviations from the technical provisions of this standard, the material manufactured thereunder shall be construed as conforming with this standard only when such exceptions or deviations provide a product with equal or better quality than required by this standard, and it shall be required to comply with all other applicable provisions of this standard.

2.5 The following provisions of the *Code of Standard Practice*, AITC 106, shall apply.

2.5.1 When the buyer provides any or all of the design plans and specifications, the seller is not responsible for the suitability, adequacy, or legality of the design.

2.5.2 When the buyer purchases a product designed to satisfy a stated set of design criteria, a stated set of conditions for use, or both, the seller's responsibility is limited by and to the representations set forth in writing in his then current catalogs and advertising material with respect to such product and its use.

2.5.3 When the seller, upon instruction from the buyer, furnishes timber design services, his responsibility is limited by and to the design data furnished by the buyer and by and to the design criteria of the *Standards for the Design of Structural Timber Framing*, AITC 102, unless special conditions are made known to and accepted in writing by the seller. In all cases, the seller may rely upon the buyer's representations regarding the provisions of the applicable building code or to any other matters.

2.6 Records. The following records shall be kept for at least one year.

(*a*) Job records including final approved shop drawings.

(*b*) Quality control reports.

3. PERSONNEL

3.1 General. The fabrication of structural timber in conformance with this standard requires properly trained and experienced personnel supervising the various stages of the production and the quality control system. The systems for the supervision of production and quality control by the fabricator will of necessity vary according to individual organizations, facilities, and type and amount of production. The following paragraphs set forth the minimum requirements for the qualifications and responsibilities of such personnel.

3.2 Lumber Graders. In consideration of the obligations assumed by the fabricator to use lumber graded to meet specific stress requirements, it shall be his responsibility to maintain the services of a capable lumber grader (which may include grading agencies approved by the American Lumber Standards Committee) to grade and identify lumber before fabrication in accordance with the applicable lumber quality requirements, including the grading rules for the species.

3.3 Quality Control Personnel. There shall be at least one qualified person directly responsible to management for the direction and maintenance of the quality control system. It shall be the responsibility of quality control personnel to inspect the production procedures, perform visual inspection and final inspection of the product, and maintain records in accordance with the requirements herein.

4. EQUIPMENT AND FACILITIES

4.1 General. In order to fabricate structural timber conforming with this standard, it is necessary to have proper and adequate facilities and equipment. These facilities and equipment will vary from fabricator to fabricator with the geographic location and the type and amount of work being produced. It is not the purpose of this standard to dictate the specific kind and type of facilities and equipment a fabricator should have.

This standard offers a means of determining and assuring that the minimum requirements are met for the production of a quality product in conformance with this standard.

4.2 Manufacturing Facilities. Facilities shall be such that applicable requirements of this standard can be met. This requires provision for proper storage of materials.

4.3 Manufacturing Equipment. Equipment shall be well maintained. The minimum necessary equipment to produce a quality product in conformance with this standard is as follows.

(*a*) Equipment for fabrication within the required tolerances of this standard.

(*b*) Provisions for identification and/or piece marking of individual fabricated members.

4.4 Quality Control Equipment. The following minimum quality control equipment is necessary for the manufacture of a quality product, and it should be well maintained and available in the fabricator's plant.

(*a*) Moisture meter and oven test equipment or other approved equipment for checking moisture meter, when fabrication of seasoned materials is performed.

(*b*) Identification marking equipment.

(*c*) The necessary gages and instruments to assure conformance with the fabrication tolerances of this standard.

5. MATERIALS

5.1 Materials. All materials for which the fabricator is responsible (see *Code of Standard Practice*, AITC 106) shall be of the grade, quality, and dimensions specified in the approved shop drawings and specifications or shall comply with *Standards for the Design of Structural Timber Framing*, AITC 102.

5.2 Moisture Content. When moisture content limits are specified, the lumber shall be fabricated at or below the specified moisture content. Unless moisture content limits are required by the job specifications, it shall be presumed for design purposes that sawn lumber will be fabricated unseasoned. Sawn material thicker than 3 in. is normally furnished unseasoned.

5.3 Special Selection of Lumber. If not provided for in the grading rules, in sawn tension members the slope of grain limitations applicable to the middle portion of the length of the piece shall apply throughout the length of the member. Members loaded in flexure shall be so oriented that advantage is taken of any crown.

6. HARDWARE AND STEEL ACCESSORIES

6.1 All welding for connections or accessories shall be in conformance with applicable standards of the American Welding Society.

6.2 When welding or cutting of metal by torch is required, suitable precautions shall be taken to avoid structural damage to adjacent timber.

6.3 Unfinished Bolts. Unless otherwise indicated, it shall be assumed that unfinished bolts are to be used where timber and steel are bolted.

6.4 Clearances. When not otherwise detailed, the overall side clearance between nonbearing surfaces of steel assemblies and timber members should not be less than $\frac{1}{8}$ in.

6.5 Unless shown and required on the shop details, welds should not be located where they will interfere with the assembly of the connection.

6.6 Consideration should be given to painting or coating of hardware and steel accessories to prevent staining during assembly and erection in work where appearance is a factor.

7. FABRICATION

7.1 Fabrication consists of the boring, cutting, sawing, trimming, dapping, routing, planing and/or otherwise shaping and/or framing and/or furnishing wood units, sawn or laminated, and including plywood, to fit them for particular places in a final structure.

7.2 Workmanship. The product shall exhibit a high quality of workmanship that meets all the requirements of this standard.

7.3 Patterns. Jigs, patterns, templates, stops, or other suitable means shall be used for all complicated and multiple assemblies to ensure accuracy, uniformity, and control of all dimensions.

7.4 Fabrication Controls. All tolerances in cutting, drilling, and framing shall comply with good practice in the industry and applicable specifications and controls and at the time of fabrication shall not be greater than those listed herein.

7.4.1 Location of Fastenings. Spacing and location of all fastenings within a joint shall be in accordance with the shop drawings and specifications with a maximum permissible tolerance of plus or minus $\frac{1}{16}$ in. The fabrication of members assembled at any joint shall be such that the fastenings are properly fitted.

7.4.2 Bolt Hole Sizes. Bolt holes in all fabricated structural timber, when loaded as a structural joint, shall be $\frac{1}{16}$ in. larger in diameter for bolts $\frac{1}{2}$ in. and larger in diameter, and $\frac{1}{32}$ in. larger in diameter for bolts smaller in diameter. Larger clearances may be required for other bolts, such as anchor bolts and tension rods.

7.4.3 Holes and Grooves. Holes for stress-carrying bolts, connector grooves, and connector daps shall be smooth and shall be true within $\frac{1}{16}$ in. per 12 in. of depth. The width of split ring connector grooves shall be within plus 0.02 in. and minus 0.0 in. of the thickness of the corresponding cross section of the ring. The shape of ring grooves shall conform generally with the cross-sectional shape of the ring. Departure from these requirements may be allowed when supported by test data. Drills and other cutting tools shall be set to conform with the size, shape, and depth of holes, grooves, daps, etc., specified in the *National Design Specification for Stress-Grade Lumber and Its Fastenings* by the National Forest Products Association.

7.4.4   Lengths. Plus or minus $\frac{1}{16}$ in. up to 20 ft in length, and plus or minus $\frac{1}{16}$ in. per 20 ft of specified length for members over 20 ft in length except where length dimensions are not specified or critical.

7.4.5   Square End Cuts. Unless otherwise specified, all trimmed ends shall be square within $\frac{1}{16}$ in. per foot of depth and width. End surfaces which are to be loaded in compression shall be so cut as to provide contact over substantially the entire surface.

7.4.6   Sloped End Cuts. All sloped end cuts intended to be in bearing shall be so cut as to provide an even bearing substantially over the entire section.

7.5   Piece Mark Identification. If more than one size or type of a fabricated member is to be shipped, members shall be suitably marked to reference or keyed to the assembly and/or erection diagrams.

7.6   Protection. End seals shall be applied to fresh-cut ends of timber to minimize end checking when use conditions are such that end checking is a major consideration.

7.7   Preassembly in the shop, if any, shall be done in such a manner that all component parts lie in the proper plane or planes and are properly fitted.

7.8   Abuse such as excessive forced fitting or excessive hammering with mauls, hammers, or other devices shall not be permitted.

7.9   Members which have been misfabricated may be subsequently refabricated if they are determined to be structurally adequate.

8. QUALITY CONTROL

8.1   The fabrication of structural timber for conformance with this standard shall at all times be in accordance with a suitable quality control system established and maintained by the fabricator.

8.2   The quality control system of the fabricator should be fully described in a procedures manual setting forth the production check points, and in a quality control manual.

8.3   Materials. The quality control supervisor shall determine that all materials are of the grade and quality required by the job specifications and this standard. For this purpose, grade marks, certificates or quality marks, or other identification indicating conformance with the material specifications of this standard shall be satisfactory. Records of such conformance shall be maintained by the fabricator.

.**8.3.1**   When moisture content limits are part of the job specifications, moisture content of the lumber shall be determined by moisture meter, by oven-drying, or by other standard means with sufficient frequency and on a sufficient number of pieces, before fabrication, to assure conformance.

8.4   Fabrciation Controls. The quality control supervisor shall determine that the jigs, patterns, templates, stops, or other means used to mark or hold members during fabrication are set up and maintained so that finished pieces will meet the requirements of this standard and the job specifications. He shall periodically check fabricated pieces to ascertain that the requirements of this standard are being consistently met.

9. PRODUCT INSPECTION

9.1 Production Checks. Production checks or tests shall be in accordance with the fabricator's procedures manual and quality control manual and shall be performed with sufficient frequency to assure a proper level of quality and conformance with this standard.

9.2 Visual Inspection of Finished Products. All production shall be inspected visually for conformance with the requirements of this standard and the applicable job specification as to:

(*a*) Dimensions.
  (1) Width.
  (2) Depth.
  (3) Length.

(*b*) Shape, including camber or crown when appropriate.

(*c*) Type, quality, and location of joints and their fastenings.

(*d*) Lumber species and grades.

(*e*) Moisture content when specified in the job specifications.

AMERICAN INSTITUTE
333 West Hampden Avenue

TIMBER CONSTRUCTION
Englewood, Colorado 80110

AITC 116-71
GUIDE SPECIFICATIONS FOR STRUCTURAL GLUED LAMINATED TIMBER FOR ELECTRIC UTILITY FRAMING

Adopted as Recommendations April 3, 1967
Copyright 1972 by American Institute of Timber Construction

CONTENTS

1. SCOPE

1.1 The design and manufacture of structural glued laminated timber for electric utility framing shall conform with accepted engineering practices that will assure the buyer of a safe and durable structure.

2. DRAWINGS

2.1 The fabricator shall furnish completed drawings of structural members showing all necessary details, and shall obtain the approval of the buyer prior to fabrication.

2.2 The finished dimensions shown on the drawings are actual dimensions and not nominal. (See *Standard for Dimensions of Glued Laminated Structural Members*, AITC 113.)

3. DESIGN

3.1 Each structural member shall be of sufficient size to withstand the specified loads in accordance with the engineering design principles outlined in the AITC *Timber Construction Manual*.

1

3.2   The allowable unit stresses used in design shall be adjusted as follows:

3.2.1   When a member is fully stressed by maximum design loads for many years, either continuously or cumulatively, use working stresses 90% of the allowable unit stresses.

3.2.2   For other durations of full design load, use the appropriate adjustment factors from Figure 1.

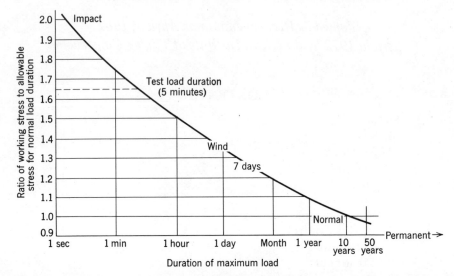

Figure 1.   DURATION OF LOAD FACTORS. Derived from Forest Products Laboratory Report No. R1916.

3.2.3   These factors do not apply to modulus of elasticity except when used to determine allowable unit loads for columns.

4. LUMBER

4.1   Lumber for laminating shall meet the species structural requirements of the standard laminating specifications which conform to Voluntary Product Standard PS56-73, *Structural Glued Laminated Timber*.

5. ADHESIVES

5.1   Adhesives for laminating shall be of a type which conforms to the wet-use requirements of Voluntary Product Standard PS56-73, *Structural Glued Laminated Timber*.

6. MANUFACTURE

6.1   The manufacture of structural glued laminated material shall be by an experienced fabricator and shall conform to Voluntary Product Standard PS56-73, *Structural Glued Laminated Timber*.

7. QUALITY CONTROL

7.1 Quality control shall be provided in accordance with Voluntary Product Standard PS56-73, *Structural Glued Laminated Timber* and the *Inspection Manual*, AITC 200.

7.2 The material shall be marked and/or certified as conforming to PS56-73 in accordance with the requirements therein.

8. APPEARANCE

8.1 Appearance of members and their protection shall be as specified by agreement between the buyer and the seller. All voids which may accumulate moisture in service shall be filled and the corners of the members shall be eased.

9. TREATMENT

9.1 Preservative treatment shall be specified by agreement between the buyer and the seller.

10. MARKING OF MEMBERS

10.1 The following marks shall be branded legibly on the face and butt or end of each member:

10.1.1 The supplier's code or trademark.

10.1.2 The plant location and the month and year of treatment.

10.1.3 Code letters denoting the material, species and preservative used and the specified amount of retention.

10.1.4 Numerals showing length of members.

AMERICAN INSTITUTE   TIMBER CONSTRUCTION
333 West Hampden Avenue   Englewood, Colorado 80110

AITC 117-71
STANDARD SPECIFICATIONS FOR STRUCTURAL GLUED LAMINATED TIMBER OF DOUGLAS FIR, WESTERN LARCH, SOUTHERN PINE AND CALIFORNIA REDWOOD

Adopted as Recommendations October 7, 1971
Copyright 1972 by American Institute of Timber Construction

CONTENTS

1. GENERAL

1.1 Structural Glued Laminated Timber.

1.1.1 The term "structural glued laminated timber" as employed herein refers to an engineered, stress-rated product of a timber laminating plant, comprising assemblies of suitably selected and prepared wood laminations bonded together with adhesives. The grain of all laminations is approximately parallel longitudinally.

1.1.2 The separate laminations shall not exceed 2 in. in net thickness. They may be comprised of pieces end joined to form any length, of pieces placed or glued edge to edge to make wider ones, or of pieces bent to curved form during gluing.

1.1.3 This specification is applicable to laminated members of four or more laminations when the load is applied perpendicular to the wide face of the laminations and to bending values for members of three or more laminations when the load is applied parallel to the wide face of the laminations.

1

1.1.4   The production of structural glued laminated timber under these specifications shall be in accordance with the current Voluntary Product Standard PS 56-73, *Structural Glued Laminated Timber*.

1.2   Lumber.

1.2.1   General.

1.2.1.1   Slope of grain shall be limited in the full length of each lamination and shall be measured over a distance sufficiently great to determine the general slope, disregarding local deviations, except as noted for tension laminations.

1.2.1.2   For that portion of the cross section that is not a structural part of the member, the strength provisions of this specification need not apply.

1.2.1.3   When a top or bottom lamination is specially selected to meet appearance requirements, the basic structural requirements of the required grade still apply.

1.2.1.4   Appearance requirements shall be in accordance with the current *Standard Appearance Grades for Structural Glued Laminated Timber*, AITC 110.

1.2.2   Douglas Fir and Larch.

1.2.2.1   Reference herein to these species shall apply only to members laminated from Douglas fir and larch grown within the states of Wyoming, Montana, Washington, Idaho, Oregon, and California, as the allowable unit stresses shown are based on a statistical analysis of the growth characteristics of the lumber from these sources.

1.2.2.2   Laminating lumber shall be of Douglas fir or larch graded in accordance with grading provisions of the West Coast Lumber Inspection Bureau or the Western Wood Products Association for laminating lumber.

1.2.2.3   There are five Douglas fir and larch laminating grades: "L1," Laminating (Dense); "L1-C," Laminating (Close Grain); "L2-D," Laminating (Dense); "L2," Laminating (Medium Grain); and "L3," Laminating (Medium Grain).

1.2.3   Southern Pine.

1.2.3.1   Laminating lumber shall be Southern pine graded by the same basic provisions as used for solid-sawn lumber as given in the current *Standard Grading Rules* of the Southern Pine Inspection Bureau, except for certain supplemental requirements as herein specified.

1.2.3.2   Laminations shall be graded either as boards or dimension, according to the finished thickness. Laminations shall be graded as boards if less than $1\frac{1}{2}$ in. in thickness and as dimension if $1\frac{1}{2}$ in. or more in thickness. Laminations of all thicknesses and grades shall be medium grain unless specified to be dense. The slope of grain for boards and dimension shall not exceed 1 in 8.

1.2.3.3   When No. 3 boards and dimension are used as laminations, wane, shake, and decay shall not exceed that allowed for No. 2 dimension. In addition, edge and centerline knots in No. 3 boards shall not exceed the allowable size of centerline knots in No. 3 dimension.

1.2.3.4   The slope of grain requirement for the individual laminations of a member stressed principally in bending shall be as shown in Table 3 for the outer 10% and the next inner 10% of the laminations on the tension face and the outer 10% of the laminations on the compression face. The slope of grain for the balance of the laminations shall be as specified for the required grades with no slope of grain steeper than 1 in 8.

1.2.3.5 There are five grades of Southern pine lumber used for laminating. These are: No. 1 Dense, No. 1, No. 2 Dense, No. 2 Medium Grain and No. 3 with medium rate of growth.

1.2.4 California Redwood.

1.2.4.1 Reference to this species herein applies only to members laminated from California redwood manufactured from timber grown within the Northern California Coastal area as defined in the *Standard Specifications for Grades of California Redwood Lumber*. The allowable unit stresses shown herein are based on a statistical analysis of the growth characteristics of the lumber from this source.

1.2.4.2 Laminating lumber shall be of California redwood graded in accordance with the *Standard Specifications for Grades of California Redwood Lumber* of the Redwood Inspection Service.

1.2.4.3 There are five grades of redwood used for laminating purposes: "L1," Clear All Heart Laminating; "L2," Clear Laminating; "L3," Select Heart Laminating; "L4," Construction Heart Laminating; and "L5," Construction Laminating.

1.2.4.4 Premium appearance grade for structural glued laminated redwood timber shall conform to *Standard Appearance Grades for Structural Glued Laminated Timber*, AITC 110, except that the wide face of laminations exposed to view shall be Clear All Heart or Clear grade.

1.3 **Adhesives**

1.3.1 Dry-use adhesives are those that perform satisfactorily when the moisture content of wood does not exceed 16% for repeated or prolonged periods of service and are to be used only when these conditions exist.

1.3.2 Wet-use adhesives will perform satisfactorily for all moisture conditions, including exposure to weather, marine use, and where approved pressure treatments are used either before or after gluing. They may be used for all moisture conditions of service, but are required when the moisture content exceeds 16% for repeated or prolonged periods of service.

1.3.3 Adhesives used shall comply with the specifications as contained in Voluntary Product Standard PS 56-73, *Structural Glued Laminated Timber*.

1.3.4 Only those adhesives meeting the requirements for wet-use adhesives as set forth in Voluntary Product Standard PS 56-73, *Structural Glued Laminated Timber* shall be used in laminating California redwood.

2. DESIGN STRESSES

2.1 **General.**

2.1.1 For the allowable unit stresses given in Tables 1 through 6 inclusive, or modifications thereof, lumber of the grades required shall be assembled in accordance with the zone requirements indicated therein.

2.1.2 The allowable unit stresses given in Tables 1 through 6 inclusive, and the modifications required for other conditions of use and loading are applicable also to structural glued laminated members that have been pressure impregnated by an approved preservative process in accordance with *Treating Standard for Structural Timber Framing*, AITC 109.

2.1.3 The allowable unit stresses given in Tables 1 through 6 inclusive, are for normal conditions of loading. Modifications for other conditions of loading are given in section 2.5.1.

2.1.4 The allowable unit bending stresses (F_b) given in Tables 1 through 6 inclusive, apply to a 12 in. deep member, uniformly loaded with a span to depth ratio of 21 to 1. Modifications for other sizes and loading conditions are given in section 2.5.4.

2.1.5 The modulus of elasticity values (E) given in Tables 1 through 6 inclusive, represent an average modulus of elasticity for the member.

2.1.6 End joints may be plane scarf joints, finger joints, or other types that qualify for the allowable unit stress in accordance with the procedure recommended in Voluntary Product Standard PS 56-73, *Structural Glued Laminated Timber*.

2.1.7 The design of glued laminated members and their fastenings shall be in accordance with the provisions of this specification and the AITC *Timber Construction Manual*.

2.2 Members Stressed in Bending.

2.2.1 Douglas Fir and Larch.

2.2.1.1 Table 1 is based on an arrangement of laminations best suited for members where the principal stress is bending when the direction of loading is perpendicular to the wide face of the laminations.

2.2.1.2 Table 2 gives allowable unit stresses for members stressed in bending when the direction of the load is either parallel to or perpendicular to the wide face of the laminations.

2.2.1.3 In addition to the grades indicated in Table 2, members loaded parallel to the wide face of the laminations may be laminated with either the structural light framing or structural joists and planks framing grades listed in the *Standard Grading Rules*. When a member consists of two laminations, the single member stress values specified in the *Standard Grading Rules* may be used. When a member consists of three or more laminations, the stress values specified for repetitive members may be used. These are 15% higher in allowable unit bending stresses (F_b) than single member values.

2.2.1.4 When a load that produces bending stress is parallel to the wide face of members of combinations of grades (Table 1 members or combinations of Table 2 grades), the allowable bending stress, modulus of elasticity, and compression perpendicular to grain value shall be the computed weighted average for the number of pieces of each grade in the member. The allowable stress in bending, modulus of elasticity and compression perpendicular to grain for each grade is shown in Table 2.

2.2.2 Southern Pine.

2.2.2.1 Table 3 is based on an arrangement of laminations best suited for members where the principal stress is bending when the direction of loading is perpendicular to the wide face of the laminations.

2.2.2.2 Table 4 gives allowable unit stresses for members stressed in bending when the direction of the load is either parallel to or perpendicular to the wide face of the laminations.

2.2.2.3 In addition to the grades indicated in Table 4, members loaded parallel to the wide face of the laminations may be laminated with either the structural light framing or structural joists and planks framing grades listed in the *Standard Grading Rules*. When a member consists of two laminations, the single member stress values specified in the *Standard Grading Rules* may be used. When a member consists of three or more laminations, the stress values specified for repetitive members may be used. These are 15% higher in allowable unit bending stresses (F_b) than single member values.

2.2.2.4 When a load that produces bending stress is parallel to the wide face of members of combinations of grades (Table 3 members or combinations of Table 4 grades), the allowable bending stress, modulus of elasticity, and compression perpendicular to grain value shall be the computed weighted average for the number of pieces of each grade in the member. The allowable bending stress, modulus of elasticity, and compression perpendicular to the grain value for each grade is shown in Table 4.

2.2.2.5 It is recommended that nominal 2 in. dimension be used for vertically laminated beams. If nominal 1 in. laminations are used, they should be graded the same as for dimension and the allowable unit stresses listed for dimension may be used.

2.2.3 California Redwood.

2.2.3.1 Table 5 is based on an arrangement of laminations best suited for members where the principal stress is bending when the direction of loading is perpendicular to the wide face of the laminations.

2.2.3.2 Table 6 gives allowable unit stresses for members stressed in bending when the direction of the load is either parallel or perpendicular to the wide face of the laminations.

2.2.3.3 In addition to the grades indicated in Table 6, members loaded parallel to the wide face of the laminations may be laminated with either the structural light framing or structural joists and planks framing grades listed in the *Standard Grading Rules*. When a member consists of two laminations, the single member stress values specified in the *Standard Grading Rules* may be used. When a member consists of three or more laminations, the stress values specified for repetitive members may be used. These are 15% higher in allowable unit bending stresses (F_b) than single member values.

2.2.3.4 When a load that produces bending stress is parallel to the wide faces of members of combinations of grades (Table 5 members or combinations of Table 6 grades), the allowable bending stress, modulus of elasticity and compression perpendicular to grain value shall be the computed weighted average for the number of pieces of each grade in the member. The allowable stress in bending, modulus of elasticity and compression perpendicular to grain value for each grade is shown in Table 6.

2.3   Members Stressed Principally in Axial Compression or Axial Tension.

   2.3.1   Douglas Fir and Larch.

   2.3.1.1   Table 2 is based on an arrangement of laminations best suited to members where the principal stress is axial and gives allowable unit stresses for such members.

   2.3.1.2   For members consisting of combinations of grades, the allowable fiber stress in bending when loaded parallel to the wide face of the laminations, tension parallel to grain and compression parallel to grain values shall be the computed weighted average for the number of laminations of each grade in the member according to the grade stress values indicated by Table 2.

   2.3.1.3   Table 1 gives values for allowable unit stress in tension parallel to grain and for compression parallel to grain. The tension parallel to the grain values may be increased by the percentages below when the slope of grain for all laminations is 1 in 14 or flatter. The compression parallel to the grain values may be increased by the noted percentages when all laminations used have a slope of grain of 1 in 12 or flatter.

	Allowable Stress Increases (%)		
	Tension Parallel To Grain		Compression Parallel to Grain
Combination Symbol	Laminations 10 or less	Laminations 11 or more	Laminations 4 or more
22F	10	25	15
24F	25	30	20
26F	20	35	20

   2.3.2   Southern Pine.

   2.3.2.1   Table 4 is based on an arrangement of laminations best suited to members where the principal stress is axial and provides allowable unit stresses for such members.

   2.3.2.2   The allowable unit stresses in Table 3 for tension parallel to grain and compression parallel to grain are based on the combinations of grades shown and their respective slope of grain limitations. The values given in Table 3 may be increased by the following tabulated percentages if the slope of grain of all laminations is equal to or flatter than the indicated slope of grain values.

Combination Symbol	Tension Parallel to Grain		Compression Parallel to Grain	
	Slope of Grain	% Increase	Slope of Grain	% Increase
18F(1)	1:14	37	1:14	26
18F(2)	1:14	37	1:12	20
20F(1)	1:16	50	1:14	26
20F(2)	1:14	37	1:14	26
22F(1) or 22F(3)	1:16	50	1:14	26
22F(2)	1:18	62	1:15	33
24F(1) or 24F(2)	1:18	62	1:15	33
24F(3)	1:16	50	1:15	33
26F(1) or 26F(2)	1:18	62	1:15	33
26F(3)	1:16	50	1:15	33

2.3.3 California Redwood.

2.3.3.1 Table 6 is based on arrangements of laminations best suited to members where the principal stress is axial and provides allowable unit stresses for such members.

2.4 Condition of Use.

2.4.1 Dry condition of use stress values shall be applicable when the moisture content in service is less than 16%, as in most covered structures.

2.4.2 Wet condition of use stress values shall be applicable when the moisture content in service is 16% or more, as may occur in members not covered or in covered locations of high relative humidity.

2.5 Modification of Stresses

2.5.1 Duration of Load.

2.5.1.1 Normal load duration contemplates fully stressing a member to the allowable unit stress by the application of the full design load for a duration of approximately 10 years (applied either continuously or cumulatively).

2.5.1.2 When a member is fully stressed by maximum design loads for long term loading conditions (greater than 10 years either continuously or cumulatively), the allowable unit stresses shall be 90% of the values tabulated.

2.5.1.3 When the duration of full design load (applied either continuously or cumulatively) does not exceed the period indicated, increase the tabulated allowable unit stresses as follows:

15% for 2 months duration, as for snow
25% for 7 days duration
33⅓% for wind or earthquake
100% for impact.

These increases are not cumulative.

2.5.1.4   The allowable unit stress for normal loading may be used without regard to impact if the stress induced by impact does not exceed the allowable unit stress for normal loading.

2.5.1.5   These adjustments do not apply to modulus of elasticity.

2.5.2   Curvature Factor.

2.5.2.1   For the curved portion of members, the allowable unit stress in bending shall be modified by multiplication by the following curvature factor:

$$C_c = 1 - 2{,}000 \left(\frac{t}{R}\right)^2$$

where t = thickness of lamination, in.

R = radius of curvature of lamination, in.

and t/R should not exceed 1/125 for Douglas fir, larch and California redwood and 1/100 for Southern pine. No curvature factor shall be applied to stress in the straight portion of an assembly, regardless of curvature elsewhere.

2.5.3   Radial Tension or Compression.

2.5.3.1   The radial stress, f_r, induced by a bending moment in a curved member of constant cross section is computed by the equation:

$$f_r = \frac{3M}{2Rbd}$$

where M = bending moment, in.-lb

R = radius of curvature at centerline of member, in.

b = width of cross section, in.

d = depth of cross section, in.

This equation can also be used to estimate the radial stresses in members of varying cross section. For further information regarding more exact procedures for calculating radial stresses in curved members of varying cross section, contact AITC.

2.5.3.2   When M is in the direction tending to decrease curvature (increase the radius), the radial stress is tension across the grain. For this condition, the tension stress across the grain shall be limited to $\frac{1}{3}$ the allowable unit stress in horizontal shear for Southern pine and California redwood for all load conditions and for Douglas fir and larch for wind or earthquake loadings. The limit shall be 15 psi for Douglas fir and larch for other types of load. These values are subject to modifications for duration of load. If these values are exceeded, mechanical reinforcing shall be used and shall be sufficient to resist all radial tension stresses.

2.5.3.3   When M is in the direction tending to increase curvature (decrease the radius), the radial stress is compression across the grain and shall be limited to the allowable unit stress in compression perpendicular to grain for all species included herein.

2.5.4   Size Factor.

2.5.4.1   When the depth of a rectangular beam exceeds 12 in., the tabulated unit stress in bending, F_b, shall be reduced by multiplying the tabulated stress by the size factor, C_F, as determined from the following relationship:

$$C_F = \left(\frac{12}{d}\right)^{1/9}$$

where C_F = size factor
 d = depth of member, in.

2.5.4.2 The size factor relationship as given under 2.5.4.1 is applicable to a bending member satisfying the following basic assumptions: (*a*) simply supported beam, (*b*) uniformly distributed load and (*c*) span to depth ratio (L/d) of 21. This factor can thus be applied with reasonable accuracy to most commonly encountered design situations. Where greater accuracy is desired for other sizes and conditions of loading, the percentage changes given in the following tables may be applied directly to the size factor calculated for the basic conditions as previously stated. Straight line interpolation may be used for other L/d ratios.

Span to Depth Ratio L/d	% Change
7	+6.3
14	+2.3
21	0
28	−1.6
35	−2.8

Loading Condition for Simply Supported Beams	% Change
Single concentrated load	+7.8
Uniform load	0
Third point load	−3.2

2.5.4.3 For a more detailed analysis of the size factor and its application to the design of bending members, contact AITC.

2.5.5 Lateral Stability.

2.5.5.1 The tabulated allowable unit bending stresses contained in this specification are applicable to members that are adequately braced. When deep, slender members not adequately braced are used, a reduction to the allowable unit bending stresses must be applied based on a computation of the slenderness factor of the member. In the check of lateral stability, the slenderness factor shall be applied in design as shown in the AITC *Timber Construction Manual*.

2.5.5.2 The reduction in bending stresses determined by applying the slenderness factor is not cumulative with a reduction in stress due to the application of size factor. In no case shall the allowable unit bending stress used in design exceed the stress as determined by applying the size factor.

3. DIMENSIONS

3.1 Standard Sizes. To the extent that other considerations will permit, the use of standard finished sizes constitutes recommended practice. These standard finished sizes are based on the widths of lumber and multiples of lamination thickness that can be used to best advantage for laminating.

3.2 Depth and Width.

3.2.1 Straight and curved members shall be furnished in accordance with the depth dimensions required by the design.

3.2.2 Recommended standard finished widths are as follows:

Nominal Width, in.	Net Finished Width, in.
3	$2\frac{1}{4}$
4	$3\frac{1}{8}$
6	$5\frac{1}{8}$
8	$6\frac{3}{4}$
10	$8\frac{3}{4}$
12	$10\frac{3}{4}$
14	$12\frac{1}{4}$
16	$14\frac{1}{4}$

Other finished widths may be used to meet the size requirements of a design or to meet other special requirements.

3.3 Radius of Curvature. The recommended minimum radii of curvature (R) for curved structural glued laminated timbers are 9 ft 4 in. for a lamination thickness (t) of $\frac{3}{4}$ in.; and 27 ft 6 in. for a lamination thickness of $1\frac{1}{2}$ in. Other radii of curvature may be used with these thicknesses and other radius-thickness combinations may be used provided the ratio t/R does not exceed 1/100 for Southern pine, nor 1/125 for other softwoods.

4. INSPECTION

4.1 Quality Control. The assurance that quality materials and workmanship are used in structural glued laminated timber members shall be vested in the laminator's quality control in day-to-day operations. Visual inspections and physical tests of samples of production are also required to assure conformance with this specification and Voluntary Product Standard PS 56-73, *Structural Glued Laminated Timber*.

5. MARKING

5.1   Straight or slightly cambered beams shall be stamped "TOP" on the top at both ends of the beam and on the wrapper of wrapped beams except that members which are fabricated in such a manner they cannot be installed upside down need not be marked. The stamp shall contain letters approximately 2 in. in height.

6. PROTECTION DURING SHIPPING AND FIELD HANDLING

6.1   Protection shall be in accordance with *Recommended Practice for Protection of Structural Glued Laminated Timber During Transit, Storage and Erection*, AITC 111.

TABLE 1

STRUCTURAL GLUED LAMINATED DOUGLAS FIR AND LARCH

Grade Requirements and Corresponding Allowable Unit Stresses (psi) For Normal Conditions of Loading, Members Stressed Principally in Bending, Loaded Perpendicular To The Wide Face of the Laminations[a,b,c]

PART A   Grade Requirements

Combination Symbol	Number of Laminations	Minimum Grade of Laminations							
		Tension Zone			Compression Zone			Inner Zone	
		Number[g]	Grade[f]	Slope of Grain	Number[g]	Grade[f]	Slope of Grain	Grade	Slope of Grain
16F	4–9	1	L2	1:12	1	L2	1:12	L3	1:8
	10 or more		L3	1:8		L3	1:8	L3	1:8
18F	4–19	1	L2	1:12	1	L2	1:12	L3	1:8
	20–39	2	L2	1:12	2	L2	1:12	L3	1:8
	40 or more	3	L2	1:12	3	L2	1:12	L3	1:8
20F	4–8	1	L2-D	1:12	1	L2-D	1:12	L3	1:8
	4–8	1	L1-C	1:12	1	L1-C	1:12	L3	1:8
	9–12	2	L2-D	1:12	2	L2-D	1:12	L3	1:8
	13 or more	10% L2		1:12	10% L2			L3	1:8
22F	4–10	1 1	L1-C L2	1:14 1:12	1 1	L1-C L2	1:14 1:12	L3	1:8
	4–10	1 1	L1 L1-C	1:14 1:14	1	L2	1:12	L3	1:8
	11–20	1 1 1	L1 L1-C L2	1:14 1:14 1:12	2	L2	1:12	L3	1:8

Combination	Laminations	No.	Grade	Slope	No.	Grade	Slope	Grade	Slope
24F	21–30	2 / 2	L1 / L2	1:14 / 1:12	3	L2	1:12	L3	1:8
	31–40	2 / 4	L1 / L2	1:14 / 1:12	4	L2	1:12	L3	1:8
	41 or more	5% L1 / 10% L2			10% L2		1:12	L3	1:8
	4–10	2	L1 / L2	1:14 / 1:12	2	L2	1:12	L3	1:8
	11–20	2 / 2	L1 / L2	1:14 / 1:12	3	L2	1:12	L3	1:8
	21–25	3 / 2	L1 / L2	1:14 / 1:12	4	L2	1:12	L3	1:8
	26–35	3 / 3	L1 / L2	1:14 / 1:12	6	L2	1:12	L3	1:8
	36–40	3 / 4	L1 / L2	1:14 / 1:12	6	L2	1:12	L3	1:8
	41 or more	10% L1 / 10% L2		1:14 / 1:12	15% L2		1:12	L3	1:8
26F	4–8	2 / 2	L1 / L2	1:14 / 1:12	1 / 1	L1-C / L2	1:12 / 1:12	L3	1:8
	9–20	2 / 2	L1 / L2	1:14 / 1:12	1 / 2	L1-C / L2	1:12 / 1:12	L3	1:8
	21–25	3 / 2	L1 / L2	1:14 / 1:12	2 / 3	L1-C / L2	1:12 / 1:12	L3	1:8
	26–30	3 / 3	L1 / L2	1:14 / 1:12	2 / 3	L1-C / L2	1:12 / 1:12	L3	1:8
	31–34	4 / 3	L1 / L2	1:14 / 1:12	2 / 4	L1-C / L2	1:12 / 1:12	L3	1:8
	35–40	4 / 4	L1 / L2	1:14 / 1:12	2 / 4	L1-C / L2	1:12 / 1:12	L3	1:8
	41 or more	10% L1 / 10% L2		1:14 / 1:12	5% L1-C / 10% L2		1:12	L3	1:8

Note: The 26F combination may not be readily available and the designer should check on availability prior to specifying.

Table 1 (Continued)

PART B Allowable Unit Stresses for Dry Condition of Use (see Part A for Grade Requirements)

Combination Symbol	Number of Laminations	Allowable Unit Stresses, psi						
		Extreme Fiber In Bending $F_b^{d,e}$	Tension Parallel To Grain F_t	Compression Parallel To Grain F_c	Compression ⊥ to Grain		Horizontal Shear F_v	Modulus of Elasticity E psi
					Tension Face $F_{c\perp}$	Compression Face $F_{c\perp}$		
16F	4–9	1,600	1,600	1,500	385	385	165	1,600,000
	10 or more	1,600	1,600	1,500	385	385	165	1,600,000
18F	4–19	1,800	1,600	1,500	385	385	165	1,700,000
	20–39	1,800	1,600	1,500	385	385	165	1,700,000
	40 or more	1,800	1,600	1,500	385	385	165	1,700,000
20F	4–8	2,000	1,600	1,500	450	450	165	1,700,000
	4–8	2,000	1,600	1,500	410	410	165	1,700,000
	9–12	2,000	1,600	1,500	450	450	165	1,700,000
	13 or more	2,000	1,600	1,500	385	385	165	1,700,000
22F	4–10	2,200	1,600	1,500	410	410	165	1,800,000
	4–10	2,200	1,600	1,500	450	385	165	1,800,000
	11–20	2,200	1,600	1,500	450	385	165	1,800,000
	21–30	2,200	1,600	1,500	450	385	165	1,800,000
	31–40	2,200	1,600	1,600	450	385	165	1,800,000
	41 or more	2,200	1,600	1,500	450	385	165	1,800,000
	4–10	2,400	1,600	1,500	450	385	165	1,800,000
	11–20	2,400	1,600	1,500	450	385	165	1,800,000

24F	21–25	2,400	1,600	1,500	450	385	165	1,800,000
	26–35	2,400	1,600	1,500	450	385	165	1,800,000
	36–40	2,400	1,600	1,500	450	385	165	1,800,000
	41 or more	2,400	1,600	1,500	450	385	165	1,800,000

Note: The 26F combination may not be readily available and the designer should check on availability prior to specifying. Other combinations are generally available from all laminators.

26F	4–8	2,600	1,600	1,500	450	410	165	1,800,000
	9–20	2,600	1,600	1,500	450	410	165	1,800,000
	21–25	2,600	1,600	1,500	450	410	165	1,800,000
	26–30	2,600	1,600	1,500	450	410	165	1,800,000
	31–34	2,600	1,600	1,500	450	410	165	1,800,000
	35–40	2,600	1,600	1,500	450	410	165	1,800,000
	41 or more	2,600	1,600	1,500	450	410	165	1,800,000

Table 1 (Continued)

PART C   Allowable Unit Stresses for Wet Conditions of Use
(see Part A for Grade Requirements)

Combination Symbol	Number of Laminations	Allowable Unit Stresses, psi						
		Extreme Fiber In Bending $F_b^{d,e}$	Tension Parallel To Grain F_t	Compression Parallel To Grain F_c	Compression ⊥ to Grain		Horizontal Shear F_v	Modulus of Elasticity E psi
					Tension Face $F_{c\perp}$	Compression Face $F_{c\perp}$		
16F	4–9	1,300	1,300	1,100	260	260	145	1,300,000
	10 or more	1,300	1,300	1,100	260	260	145	1,300,000
18F	4–19	1,400	1,300	1,100	260	260	145	1,400,000
	20–39	1,400	1,300	1,100	260	260	145	1,400,000
	40 or more	1,400	1,300	1,100	260	260	145	1,400,000
20F	4–8	1,600	1,300	1,100	305	305	145	1,400,000
	4–8	1,600	1,300	1,100	275	275	145	1,400,000
	9–12	1,600	1,300	1,100	305	305	145	1,400,000
	13 or more	1,600	1,300	1,100	260	260	145	1,400,000
22F	4–10	1,800	1,300	1,100	275	275	145	1,500,000
	4–10	1,800	1,300	1,100	305	260	145	1,500,000
	11–20	1,800	1,300	1,100	305	260	145	1,500,000
	21–30	1,800	1,300	1,100	305	260	145	1,500,000
	31–40	1,800	1,300	1,100	305	260	145	1,500,000
	41 or more	1,800	1,300	1,100	305	260	145	1,500,000
	4–10	1,900	1,300	1,100	305	260	145	1,500,000
	11–20	1,900	1,300	1,100	305	260	145	1,500,000

24F	21–25	1,900	1,300	1,100	305	260	145	1,500,000
	26–35	1,900	1,300	1,100	305	260	145	1,500,000
	36–40	1,900	1,300	1,100	305	260	145	1,500,000
	41 or more	1,900	1,300	1,100	305	260	145	1,500,000

Note: The 26F combination may not be readily available and the designer should check on availability prior to specifying. Other combinations are generally available from all laminators

26F	4–8	2,100	1,300	1,100	305	275	145	1,500,000
	9–20	2,100	1,300	1,100	305	275	145	1,500,000
	21–25	2,100	1,300	1,100	305	275	145	1,500,000
	26–30	2,100	1,300	1,100	305	275	145	1,500,000
	31–34	2,100	1,300	1,100	305	275	145	1,500,000
	35–40	2,100	1,300	1,100	305	275	145	1,500,000
	41 or more	2,100	1,300	1,100	305	275	145	1,500,000

[a]The tabulated stresses in this table are primarily applicable to members stressed in bending due to a load applied perpendicular to the wide face of the laminations. For combinations and stresses applicable to members loaded primarily axially or parallel to the wide face of the laminations, see Table 2.

[b]The tabulated bending stresses are applicable to members 12 in. or less in depth. For members greater than 12 in. in depth, the requirements of Section 2.1.4 of this specification apply.

[c]The tabulated combinations are applicable to arches, compression members, tension members and also bending members less than 16¼ in. in depth. For bending members 16¼ in. or more in depth, footnotes d and e apply.

[d]The grading restrictions as contained in AITC 301-20, 301-22, 301-24 and 301-26 tension lamination requirements shall be followed for the outermost tension laminations representing 5% of the total depth of glued laminated bending members 16¼ in. or more in depth. For all conditions of use, AITC 301-20 is applicable to combinations 16F, 18F, and 20F; AITC 301-22 is applicable to combination 22F, AITC 301-24 is applicable to combination 24F and AITC 301-26 is applicable to combination 26F. See Appendix A for details of these tension lamination requirements.

[e]In addition to other requirements, the tension laminations as described in AITC 301-20, 301-22, 301-24 and 301-26 are required to be dense.

[f]L1 is L1 dense; L1-C is L1 close grain; L2-D is L2 dense.

[g]Percent values are based on the total depth of the member.

TABLE 2

STRUCTURAL GLUED LAMINATED DOUGLAS FIR AND LARCH

Grade Requirements And Corresponding Allowable Unit Stresses (psi) For Normal Conditions Of Loading, Members Stressed Principally In Axial Tension, Axial Compression Or Loaded In Bending Parallel Or Perpendicular To The Wide Face[a]

Combination Symbol	Number of Laminations	Minimum Grade of Laminations[e]	Slope of Grain	Allowable Unit Stresses, psi							
				Tension Parallel to Grain[d] F_t	Compression Parallel to Grain[d] $F_{c\perp}$	Extreme Fiber in Bending F_b When Loaded		Compression perpendicular to Grain[d] $F_{c\perp}$	Horizontal Shear F_v When Loaded		Modulus of elasticity E psi
						Parallel to Wide Face[c]	Perpendicular to Wide Face[b,d]		Parallel to Wide Face[c]	Perpendicular to Wide Face[d]	
Dry Conditions of Use											
1	All	L3	1:8	1,200	1,500	900	1,200	385	145	165	1,600,000
2	All	L2	1:12	1,800	1,800	1,500	1,800	385	145	165	1,800,000
3	All	L2-D	1:12	2,200	2,100	1,900	2,200	450	145	165	1,900,000
4	All	L1-C	1:14	2,400	2,000	2,100	2,400	410	145	165	2,000,000
5	All	L1	1:14	2,600	2,200	2,300	2,600	450	145	165	2,100,000
Wet Conditions of Use											
1	All	L3	1:8	950	1,100	750	950	260	120	145	1,300,000
2	All	L2	1:12	1,400	1,300	1,100	1,400	260	120	145	1,500,000
3	All	L2-D	1:12	1,800	1,500	1,450	1,800	305	120	145	1,600,000
4	All	L1-C	1:14	1,900	1,450	1,500	1,900	275	120	145	1,700,000
5	All	L1	1:14	2,000	1,600	1,600	2,000	305	120	145	1,800,000

[a]The tabulated stresses in this table are primarily applicable to members loaded axially or parallel to the wide face of the laminations. For combinations and stresses applicable to members stressed principally in bending due to a load applied perpendicular to the wide face of the laminations, see Table 1. [b]It is not intended that these combinations be used for deep bending members, but if bending members 16¼ in. or deeper are used, AITC tension lamination restrictions 301-20, 301-22, 301-24, and 301-26 must be followed for combinations 2, 3, 4, and 5, respectively. [c]The tabulated stresses are applicable to members containing three (3) or more laminations. [d]The tabulated stresses are applicable to members containing four (4) or more laminations. [e]L1 is L1 dense; L1 C is L1 close grain; L2-D is L2 dense.

TABLE 3

STRUCTURAL GLUED LAMINATED SOUTHERN PINE

Grade Requirements And Corresponding Allowable Unit Stresses (psi) For Normal Conditions of Loading, Members Stressed Principally In Bending, Loaded Perpendicular To The Wide Face Of The Laminations[a,b,c]

PART A Grade Requirements

Combination Symbol		Number of Laminations	Minimum Grade of Laminations[g,h]				Slope of Grain		
			Number Each Zone			Outer 10% Tension Side	Next 10% Tension Side	Outer 10% Compression Side	Balance
			Outer Zone	Intermediate Zone	Inner Zone				
18F	1	4 or more	No. 2 MG	No. 2 MG	No. 2 MG	1:10	1:8	1:8	1:8
	2	12 or more	5% No. 2 MG	No. 3	No. 3	1:10	1:8	1:8	1:8
20F	1	10 or more	No. 2 MG	No. 2 MG	No. 2 MG	1:12	1:10	1:8	1:8
	2	8 or more	25% No. 2 MG	No. 3	No. 3	1:12	1:10	1:8	1:8
	3	7 or more[i]	10% No. 2 D	5% No. 2 MG	No. 3	1:10	1:10	1:8	1:8
22F	1	4 or more	5% No. 2 D	No. 2 MG	No. 2 MG	1:12	1:10	1:10	1:8
	2	12 or more	No. 2 MG	No. 2 MG	No. 2 MG	1:14	1:10	1:10	1:8
	3	14 or more	5% No. 1	10% No. 2 MG	No. 3	1:14	1:10	1:10	1:8
24F	1	10 or more	10% No. 1	15% No. 2 MG	No. 3	1:16	1:12	1:12	1:8
	2	4 or more	5% No. 1 D	No. 2 MG	No. 2 MG	1:14	1:12	1:12	1:8
	3	14 or more	10% No. 1 D	5% No. 2 MG	No. 3	1:12	1:12	1:12	1:8
26F	1	11 or more[j]	10% No. 1	No. 2 MG	No. 2 MG	1:18	1:12	1:14	1:8
	2	16 or more	5% No. 1 D	15% No. 2 D	No. 3	1:14	1:10	1:12	1:8
	3	11 or more	10% No. 1 D	20% No. 2 MG	No. 3	1:14	1:12	1:12	1:8

Note: The 26F combination may not be readily available and the designer should check on availability prior to specifying. Other combinations listed are generally available from all laminators.

TABLE 3 (Continued)

PART B   Allowable Unit Stresses for Dry Condition of Use
(see Part A for Grade Requirements)

Combination Symbol		Number of Laminations	Allowable Unit Stresses, psi					Modulus of Elasticity E psi
			Extreme Fiber in Bending $F_b^{d,e,f}$	Tension Parallel to Grain F_t	Compression Parallel to Grain F_c	Compression Perpendicular to Grain $F_{c\perp}$	Horizontal Shear F_v	
18F	1	4 or more	1,800	1,600	1,500	385	200	1,600,000
	2	12 or more	1,800	1,600	1,500	385	200	1,600,000
20F	1	10 or more	2,000	1,600	1,500	385	200	1,700,000
	2	8 or more	2,000	1,600	1,500	385	200	1,700,000
	3	7 or more[i]	2,000	1,600	1,500	450	200	1,700,000
22F	1	4 or more	2,200	1,600	1,500	450	200	1,700,000
	2	12 or more	2,200	1,600	1,500	385	200	1,700,000
	3	14 or more	2,200	1,600	1,500	385	200	1,700,000
24F	1	10 or more	2,400	1,600	1,500	385	200	1,800,000
	2	4 or more	2,400	1,600	1,500	450	200	1,800,000
	3	14 or more	2,400	1,600	1,500	450	200	1,800,000

Note: The 26F combination may not be readily available and the designer should check on availability prior to specifying. Other combinations listed are generally available from all laminators.

26F	1	11 or more[j]	2,600	1,600	1,500	385	200	1,800,000
	2	16 or more	2,600	1,600	1,500	450	200	1,800,000
	3	11 or more	2,600	1,600	1,500	450	200	1,800,000

[a] The tabulated stresses in this table are primarily applicable to members stressed in bending due to a load applied perpendicular to the wide face of the laminations. For combinations and stresses applicable to members loaded primarily axially or parallel to the wide face of the laminations, see Table 4.

[b] The tabulated bending stresses are applicable to members 12 in. or less in depth. For members greater than 12 in. in depth, the requirements of Section 2.1.4 of this specification apply.

[c] The tabulated combinations are applicable to arches, compression members, tension members and also bending members less than 16¼ in. in depth. For bending members 16¼ in. or more in depth, footnotes d, e and f apply.

[d] The grading restrictions as contained in AITC 301-20, 301-22, 301-24 and 301-26 tension lamination requirements shall be followed for the outermost tension laminations representing 5% of the total depth of glued laminated bending members 16¼ in. or more in depth. For all conditions of use, AITC 301-20 is applicable to combinations 18F and 20F, AITC 301-22 is applicable to combination 22F, AITC 301-24 is applicable to combination 24F and AITC 301-26 is applicable to combination 26F. See Appendix A for details of these tension lamination requirements.

TABLE 3 (Continued)

PART C   Allowable Unit Stresses for Wet Conditions of Use
(see Part A for Grade Requirements)

Combination Symbol		Number of Laminations	Allowable Unit Stresses, psi					
			Extreme Fiber in Bending $F_b^{d,e,f}$	Tension Parallel to Grain F_t	Compression Parallel to Grain F_c	Compression Perpendicular to Grain $F_{c\perp}$	Horizontal Shear F_v	Modulus of Elasticity E psi
18F	1	4 or more	1,400	1,300	1,100	260	175	1,300,000
	2	12 or more	1,400	1,300	1,100	260	175	1,300,000
20F	1	10 or more	1,600	1,300	1,100	260	175	1,400,000
	2	8 or more	1,600	1,300	1,100	260	175	1,400,000
	3	7 or more[i]	1,600	1,300	1,100	300	175	1,400,000
22F	1	4 or more	1,800	1,300	1,100	300	175	1,400,000
	2	12 or more	1,800	1,300	1,100	260	175	1,400,000
	3	14 or more	1,800	1,300	1,100	260	175	1,400,000
24F	1	10 or more	1,900	1,300	1,100	260	175	1,500,000
	2	4 or more	1,900	1,300	1,100	300	175	1,500,000
	3	14 or more	1,900	1,300	1,100	300	175	1,500,000

Note: The 26F combination may not be readily available and the designer should check on availability prior to specifying. Other combinations listed are generally available from all laminators.

26F	1	11 or more [j]	2,100	1,300	1,100	260	175	1,500,000
	2	16 or more	2,100	1,300	1,100	300	175	1,500,000
	3	11 or more	2,100	1,300	1,100	300	175	1,500,000

[e] In addition to other requirements, the tension laminations as described in AITC 301-20, 301-22, 301-24 and 301-26 are required to be dense.

[f] The next inner 5% of the outermost tension laminations are to be No. 1 Dense for the same conditions as indicated by footnote d for combinations 22F, 24F, and 26F.

[g] No. 2 MG is No. 2 medium grain dimension or No. 2 boards with medium grain rate of growth. No. 3 refers to a No. 3 grade for both boards and dimension with a medium grain rate of growth required.

[h] No. 1 D is No. 1 Dense and No. 2 D is No. 2 Dense.

[i] For fewer than seven (7) laminations, a combination with a higher allowable unit stress can be selected.

[j] For fewer than eleven (11) laminations, use three No. 1 laminations in each outer zone.

TABLE 4

STRUCTURAL GLUED LAMINATED SOUTHERN PINE

Grade Requirements And Corresponding Allowable Unit Stresses (psi) For Normal Conditions Of Loading, Members Stressed Principally In Axial Tension, Axial Compression Or Loaded In Bending Parallel Or Perpendicular To The Wide Face[a]

Combination Symbol	Number of Laminations	Minimum Grade of Laminations	Slope of Grain	Allowable Unit Stresses, psi							
				Tension Parallel to Grain[d] F_t	Compression Parallel to Grain[d] F_c	Extreme Fiber in Bending F_b When Loaded		Compression perpendicular to Grain[e] $F_{c\perp}$	Horizontal Shear F_v When Loaded		Modulus of Elasticity E psi
						Parallel to Wide Face[e]	Perpendicular to Wide Face[b,c,d]		Parallel to Wide Face[e]	Perpendicular to Wide Face[d]	
Dry Conditions of Use											
1	All	No. 3[g]	1:8	1,600	1,400	900	1,100	385	165	200	1,500,000
2	All	No. 2MG[f]	1:14	2,200	1,900	1,550	1,800	385	165	200	1,700,000
3	All	No. 2D	1:14	2,600	2,200	1,800	2,100	450	165	200	1,800,000
4	All	No. 1	1:16	2,400	2,100	1,900	2,400	385	165	200	1,900,000
5	All	No. 1D	1:14	2,600	2,200	2,200	2,600	450	165	200	2,000,000
Wet Conditions of Use											
1	All	No. 3[g]	1:8	1,300	1,000	700	850	260	145	175	1,300,000
2	All	No. 2MG[f]	1:14	1,800	1,400	1,250	1,450	260	145	175	1,400,000
3	All	No. 2D	1:14	2,100	1,600	1,450	1,700	300	145	175	1,500,000
4	All	No. 1	1:16	1,900	1,500	1,500	1,950	260	145	175	1,600,000
5	All	No. 1D	1:14	2,100	1,600	1,750	2,100	300	145	175	1,700,000

[a]The tabulated stresses in this table are primarily applicable to members loaded axially or parallel to the wide face of the laminations. For combinations and stresses applicable to members stressed principally in bending due to a load applied perpendicular to the wide face of the laminations, see Table 3. [b]It is not intended that these combinations be used for deep bending members, but if bending members 16¼ in. or deeper are used, the applicable AITC tension lamination requirements must be followed. [c]The tabulated stresses are applicable to members containing three (3) or more laminations. [d]The tabulated stresses are applicable to members containing four (4) or more laminations. [e]When members are designed for bending with the direction of load applied parallel to the wide face of the laminations, the basic slope of grain may be used for the respective grades: No. 1 and No. 1D—Slope of grain of 1:10; No. 2, 2D and No. 3—Slope of grain of 1:8. [f]No. 2MG is No. 2 medium grain dimension or No. 2 boards with medium grain rate of growth. [g]No. 3 refers to a No. 3 grade for both boards and dimension with a medium grain rate of growth required.

TABLE 5

STRUCTURAL GLUED LAMINATED CALIFORNIA REDWOOD

Grade Requirements And Corresponding Allowable Unit Stresses (psi) For Normal Conditions Of Loading, Member Stressed Principally In Bending, Loaded Perpendicular To The Wide Face Of The Laminations[a,b,c]

Combination Symbol	Minimum Grade of Laminations[f]					Allowable Unit Stresses, psi					
	Tension and Compression Zones		Inner Zone Grade	Slope of Grain		Extreme Fiber in Bending F_b^d	Tension Parallel to Grain F_t	Compression Parallel to Grain F_c	Compression Perpendicular to Grain $F_{c\perp}$	Horizontal Shear F_v	Modulus of Elasticity E psi
	Grade	Number		Outer 10% of Laminations	Balance of Laminations						
Dry Conditions of Use											
16F	L1 or L2	10%[g]	L4 or L5	1:15	1:15	1,600	1,600	1,600	325	125	1,400,000
22F[e] 1	L1 or L2	10%[g]	L4 or L5	1:20	1:15	2,200	2,000	2,000	325	125	1,400,000
2	L1 or L2	1	L3	1:20	1:15	2,200	2,000	2,000	325	125	1,400,000
3	L1 or L2		L1 or L2	1:20	1:15	2,200	2,000	2,200	325	125	1,400,000

Note: The 16F combination is generally available. The 22F combinations are generally available only in members without end joints and the designer should check with the laminator prior to specifying this stress level.

TABLE 5 (Continued)

Combination Symbol	Minimum Grade of Laminations^f					Allowable Unit Stresses, psi					
	Tension and Compression Zones		Inner Zone Grade	Slope of Grain		Extreme Fiber in Bending F_b^d	Tension Parallel to Grain F_t	Compression Parallel to Grain F_c	Compression Perpendicular to Grain $F_{c\perp}$	Horizontal Shear F_v	Modulus of Elasticity E psi
	Grade	Number		Outer 10% of Laminations	Balance of Laminations						
Wet Conditions of Use											
16F	L1 or L2	10%^g	L4 or L5	1:15	1:15	1,300	1,300	1,200	215	110	1,200,000
22F^e 1	L1 or L2	10%^g	L4 or L5	1:20	1:15	1,800	1,600	1,500	215	110	1,200,000
.2	L1 or L2	1	L3	1:20	1:15	1,800	1,600	1,500	215	110	1,200,000
	L1 or L2		L1 or L2	1:20	1:15	1,800	1,600	1,600	215	110	1,200,000

Note: The 16F combination is generally available. The 22F combinations are generally available only in members without end joints and the designer should check with the laminator prior to specifying this stress level.

[a]The tabulated stresses in this table are primarily applicable to members stressed in bending due to a load applied perpendicular to the wide face of the laminations. For combinations and stresses applicable to members loaded primarily axially or parallel to the wide face of the laminations, see Table 6.

[b]The tabulated bending stresses are applicable to members 12 in. or less in depth. For members greater than 12 in. in depth, the requirements of Section 2.1.4 of this specification apply.

[c]The tabulated combinations are applicable to arches, compression members tension members and also bending members less than 16¼ in. in depth. For bending members 16¼ in. or more in depth, footnote d applies.

[d]The grading restrictions as contained in AITC 301-20 and 301-22 tension lamination requirements shall be followed for the outermost tension laminations representing 5% of the total depth of 16F and 22F glued laminated bending members, respectively, for members 16¼ in. or more in depth for all conditions of use. See Appendix A for details of these tension lamination requirements.

[e]If slope of grain in all laminations is no steeper than 1:20, the tension parallel to grain stress can be increased to 2,200 psi for the dry condition of use and 1,800 psi for the wet condition of use.

[f]If all heartwood is required, the L1, L3 and L4 combinations may be specified.

[g]For 10 or less laminations, use two L1 or two L2 laminations in both the tension and compression zones.

TABLE 6

STRUCTURAL GLUED LAMINATED CALIFORNIA REDWOOD

Grade Requirements And Corresponding Allowable Unit Stresses (psi) For Normal Conditions of Loading, Members Stressed Principally In Axial Tension, Axial Compression Or Loaded In Bending Parallel Or Perpendicular To The Wide Face[a]

Combination Symbol[c]	Number of Laminations	Minimum Grade of Laminations[f]	Slope of Grain	Tension Parallel to Grain[e] F_t	Compression Parallel to Grain[d] F_c	Extreme Fiber in Bending F_b When Loaded		Compression Perpendicular to Grain[d] $F_{c\perp}$	Horizontal Shear F_v When Loaded		Modulus of Elasticity E psi
						Parallel to Wide Face[d]	Perpendicular to Wide Face[b,e]		Parallel to Wide Face[d]	Perpendicular to Wide Face[d]	
Dry Conditions of Use											
1	All	L4 or L5	1:15	1,800	1,800	1,000	1,400	325	115	125	1,300,000
2	All	L4	1:15	1,800	1,800	1,000	1,400	325	115	125	1,300,000
3	All	L3	1:15	2,000	2,000	1,400	2,000	325	125	125	1,400,000
4	All	L1 or L2	1:20	2,200	2,200	2,200	2,200	325	125	125	1,400,000
5	All	L1	1:20	2,200	2,200	2,200	2,200	325	125	125	1,400,000
Wet Conditions of Use											
1	All	L4 or L5	1:15	1,500	1,300	800	1,100	215	100	110	1,100,000
2	All	L4	1:15	1,500	1,300	800	1,100	215	100	110	1,100,000
3	All	L3	1:15	1,600	1,500	1,100	1,600	215	110	110	1,200,000
4	All	L1 or L2	1:20	1,800	1,600	1,800	1,800	215	110	110	1,200,000
5	All	L1	1:20	1,800	1,600	1,800	1,800	215	110	110	1,200,000

[a]The tabulated stresses in this table are primarily applicable to members loaded axially or parallel to the wide face of the laminations. For combinations and stresses applicable to members stressed principally in bending due to a load applied perpendicular to the wide face of the laminations, see Table 5.

[b]It is not intended that these combinations be used for deep bending members, but if bending members $16\frac{1}{2}$ in. or deeper are used AITC tension lamination restrictions 301-20 for combination 3 and 301-22 for combinations 4 and 5 must be followed.

[c]When used primarily as bending members loaded perpendicular to the wide face of the laminations, combinations 1 and 2 are generally available from most laminators but combinations 3, 4 and 5 are generally available only in laminated members without end joints, and the designer should check with the laminator prior to specifying combinations 3, 4 and 5.

[d]The tabulated stresses are applicable to members containing three (3) or more laminations.

[e]The tabulated stresses are applicable to members containing four (4) or more laminations.

[f]If all heartwood is required, the L1, L3 and L4 combinations may be specified.

AMERICAN INSTITUTE   TIMBER CONSTRUCTION
333 West Hampden Avenue   Englewood, Colorado 80110

AITC 117-71
APPENDIX A
GRADING REQUIREMENTS FROM
AITC 301-20, 301-22, 301-24, 301-26
TENSION LAMINATION
RECOMMENDATIONS

Adopted as Recommendations October 7, 1971
Copyright 1972 by American Institute of Timber Construction

CONTENTS

A1. AITC 301-20 TENSION LAMINATION——MEMBERS IN BENDING (1,600, 1,800 and 2,000 psi)

A1.1 Growth rate requirements (including "dense" if required) shall apply to the full length of the piece. Pieces shall have near average or above average specific gravity for the species.

A1.2 Pieces containing wide-ringed or lightweight pith associated wood over $\frac{1}{8}$ of the cross section shall be excluded. (The next inch of wood outside the area of the pith associated wood shall meet the growth rate requirements of the grade including "dense" when dense laminations are required. The line along which measurement of this inch is made shall correspond to the line used in the standard grading rules for rate of growth and percentage of summerwood. If a distance of 1 in. is not available along this line, the measurement will be made over such lesser portion as exists.)

A1.3 Any cross section shall have at least 50% clear wood with a slope of grain not steeper than 1 : 12. However, knots shall not exceed the size permitted for the outermost laminations in the tension zone as specified in the laminating combinations.

A1.4   The general slope of grain shall not exceed 1 : 12.

A1.5   Knots shall not occur within 2 knot diameters of any finger joint.

A2. AITC 301-22 TENSION LAMINATION — MEMBERS IN BENDING (2,200 psi)

A2.1   In addition to the requirements of AITC 301-20, the folllowing requirements shall apply:

A2.1.1   Knots shall not occupy more than $\frac{1}{4}$ of the cross section.

A2.1.2   The general slope of grain shall not exceed 1 : 16. Where more restrictive slope of grain requirements are required by the standard laminating specifications, these shall apply.

A2.1.3   Areas of local grain deviation steeper than 1 : 16 shall not occupy more than $\frac{1}{3}$ of the cross section.

A3. AITC 301-24 TENSION LAMINATION — MEMBERS IN BENDING (2,400 psi)

A3.1   In addition to the requirements of AITC 301-22, the following requirements shall apply:

A3.1.1   A 1 ft length of a lamination shall be considered as a cross section.

A3.1.2   Maximum size single strength-reducing characteristics when not in the same longitudinal projection of the section must be at least 2 ft apart, measured center to center.

A3.1.3   Knots shall not occupy more than $\frac{1}{5}$ of the cross section.

A3.1.4   Two-thirds of the cross section of the laminations must be free of strength-reducing characteristics and must have 1 : 16 or flatter slope of grain. (Knots plus associated localized cross grain, or knots plus associated localized cross grain plus localized cross grain not associated with knot, or localized cross grain not associated with a knot may occupy up to $\frac{1}{3}$ of the cross section.)

A4. AITC 301-26 TENSION LAMINATION — MEMBERS IN BENDING (2,600 psi)

A4.1   In addition to the requirements of AITC 301-24, the following requirements shall apply:

A4.1.1   Any cross section containing an edge knot must have 80% clear and straight-grained wood with a slope of grain not steeper than 1 : 16. (An edge knot is a knot that has any portion of itself or its associated localized cross grain at/or within $\frac{1}{2}$ in. of the edge of the piece This $\frac{1}{2}$ in. is determined based on the average of the measurements on the 2 wide faces.)

AMERICAN INSTITUTE   TIMBER CONSTRUCTION
333 West Hampden Avenue   Englewood, Colorado 80110

AITC 118-71
STANDARD FOR TWO-INCH NOMINAL THICKNESS LUMBER ROOF DECKING FOR STRUCTURAL APPLICATIONS

Adopted as Recommendations September 27, 1970
Copyright 1971 by American Institute of Timber Construction

CONTENTS

1. INTRODUCTION

1.1 This Standard applies to sawn lumber decking of 2 in. nominal thickness only and does not apply to laminated, panelized or other special decking systems. It covers species, sizes, patterns, lengths, moisture content, application, specifications, weights, roof load-span tables, and load and span conversion charts.

1.2 The lumber used in 2 in. roof decking shall be graded in accordance with standard grading rules for the individual species. Rules referenced in this Standard are:

(a) *1970 NELMA Standard Grading Rules for Northeastern Lumber*, Northeastern Lumber Manufacturers Association (NELMA).

(b) *Standard Specifications for Grades of California Redwood Lumber*, November 1970 Edition, Redwood Inspection Service (RIS).

(c) *1970 Standard Grading Rules for Southern Pine Lumber*, Southern Pine Inspection Bureau (SPIB).

1

(d) *Standard Grading Rules for West Coast Lumber, No. 16*, West Coast Lumber Inspection Bureau (WCLIB).

(e) *1970 Standard Grading Rules for Western Lumber*, Western Wood Products Association (WWPA).

Copies of these grading rules may be obtained from the Northeastern Lumber Manufacturers Association, 13 South Strees, Glens Falls, New York 12801; Southern Pine Inspection Bureau, P.O. Box 846, Pensacola, Florida 32502; Redwood Inspection Service, 617 Montgomery Street, San Francisco, California 94111; West Coast Lumber Inspection Bureau, P.O. Box 23145, Portland, Oregon 97223; and Western Wood Products Association, 1500 Yeon Building, Portland, Oregon 97204.

1.3   Regional grading rules with respect to moisture content do not always agree with the limitations set forth in this Standard. Unless this Standard is followed in all its requirements, 2 in. decking will not conform with this Standard.

2. SPECIES

2.1   The species usually available and currently used in this product, as well as the regional inspection bureaus or associations under which this decking is graded, are given in Table 1.

3. SIZES AND PATTERNS

3.1   The standard size is 2×6 in., nominal, dressed at the moisture content specified herein to the actual size and V-grooved pattern shown in Figure 1. Other thicknesses and widths are also available. See regional grading rules listed in paragraph 1.2 for dimensions for each species.

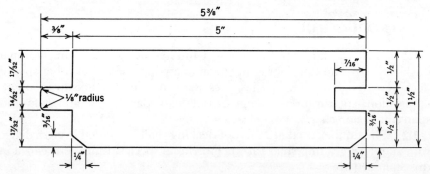

Figure 1. 2-INCH NOMINAL THICKNESS ROOF DECKING, V-JOINT PATTERN.
(See regional grading rules listed in paragraph 1.2 for dimensions for each species.)

3.2   Each piece shall be square end-trimmed. When random lengths are furnished, each piece must be square end-trimmed across the face so that at least 90% of the pieces will be within $\frac{3}{64}$ in. of square, and the remainder within $\frac{3}{32}$ in. of square. The vertical end cut may vary from square to the bevel cut shown in Figure 2.

TABLE 1

TWO-INCH ROOF DECK SPECIES

Species	Grading Rules Under Which Graded	Paragraph Number of Grading Rules Under Which Graded[a]	
		Select Quality[b]	Commercial Quality[c]
Cedar, Northern white	NELMA	15.1	15.2
Cedar, Western	WCLIB; WWPA	127-b; 55.11	127-c; 55.12
Douglas fir	WCLIB	127-b	127-c
Douglas fir — larch	WWPA	55.11	55.12
Douglas fir, South	WWPA	55.11	55.12
Fir, balsam	NELMA	15.1	15.2
Fir, subalpine	WWPA	55.11	55.12
Hem-fir	WCLIB; WWPA	127-b; 55.11	127-c; 55.12
Hemlock, Eastern-tamarack	NELMA	15.1	15.2
Hemlock, mountain	WWPA	55.11	55.12
Hemlock, mountain-hem-fir	WWPA	55.11	55.12
Pine, Eastern white	NELMA	15.1	15.2
Pine, Idaho white	WWPA	55.11	55.12
Pine, lodgepole	WWPA	55.11	55.12
Pine, Northern	NELMA	15.1	15.2
Pine, ponderosa — sugar	WWPA	55.11	55.12
Pine, Southern[d,f]	SPIB	309	311
Redwood, California[e,g]	RIS	113	115
Spruce, Eastern	NELMA	15.1	15.2
Spruce, Engelmann	WWPA	55.11	55.12
Spruce, Sitka	WCLIB	127-b	127-c

[a]When species may be graded under WCLIB and WWPA rules, the first paragraph number given is for WCLIB and the second for WWPA rules.
[b]Select quality grades are as follows for the grading rules indicated:

WCLIB;	Select Dex	SPIB;	No. 1 Factory
WWPA;	Selected Decking	RIS;	Select
NELMA;	Selected Decking		

[c]Commercial quality grades are as follows for the grading rules indicated.

WCLIB;	Commercial Dex	SPIB;	No. 2 Factory
WWPA;	Commercial Decking	RIS;	Construction Common
NELMA;	Commercial Decking		

[d]Nominal 2 in. Southern pine decking is also available in the following grades: Dense Standard Factory, para. 308; No. 1 Dense Factory, para. 310; and No. 2 Dense Factory, para. 312.
[e]Nominal 2 in. California redwood decking is available in the grade of Clear, para. 104. Heartwood grades may be specified by referring to Clear All Heart, para. 103; Select Heart, para. 112; and Construction Heart, para. 114.
[f]Southern pine is limited to the botanical species of longleaf, slash, shortleaf and loblolly. Lumber cut from trees of this species is classified as "Southern pine" in the SPIB *Standard Grading Rules.*
[g]For nominal 2 × 6 in. California redwood decking, the standard dressed thickness is 1⅜ in. and the standard dressed width is 5⅝ in.

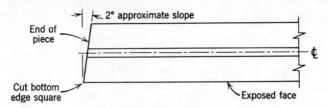

Figure 2. BEVELED END CUT. (Beveled end cut is optional.)

3.3 Exact finished patterns for striated deck are illustrated in Figure 3.

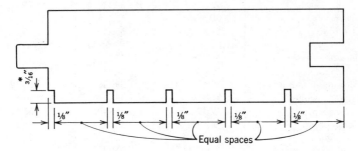

Figure 3. STRIATED PATTERN. Dimensions not shown are the same as the corresponding dimensions in Figure 1. (See regional grading rules listed in paragraph 1.2 for dimensions for each species.)

4. LENGTHS

4.1 Decking pieces may be of specified length or may be random lengths. If random lengths, odd or even lengths are permitted, and the minimum lengths based on fbm percentages shall be as follows:

> Not less than 40% to be 14 ft, and longer.
> Not over 10% to be less than 10 ft.
> Not over 1% to be 4 or 5 ft.
> Minimum length is limited to 75% of the span length (i.e., for 8 ft support spacing, 6 ft).

5. MOISTURE CONTENT

5.1 The maximum moisture content shall be 15%.

6. APPLICATION

6.1 Decking is to be installed with tongues up on sloped or pitched roofs. It is to be laid with pattern faces down, intended to be exposed on the underside. The minimum recommended nailing schedule shall be as follows: each piece toenailed through the tongue and also one face nail per piece per support, using 16d common nails.

6.2   Decking may be laid in any of the following arrangements:

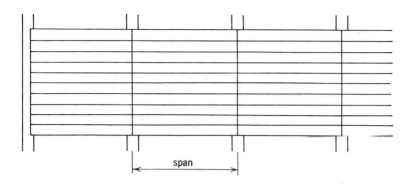

6.2.1   Simple Span. All pieces bear on 2 supports.

6.2.2   Controlled Random Layup. This arrangement is continuous for 3 or more spans. The distance between end joints in adjacent courses must be at least 2 ft. Joints in the same general line (within 6 in. of being in line each way) shall be separated by at least 2 intervening courses. Pieces must rest on at least one support, with not more than one joint between supports in each course. To provide a continuous tie for lateral restraint for the supporting member, the pieces in at least the first and second courses, and repeating at least after each group of 7 intervening courses, must bear on at least 2 supports with end joints in these 2 courses occurring in alternate spans or on alternate supports, unless some other provision, such as plywood overlayment, is made to provide continuity.

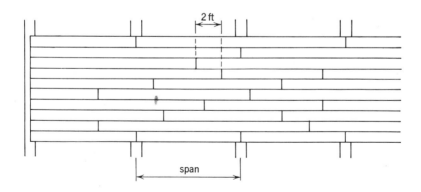

6.2.3   Cantilevered Pieces Intermixed. This arrangement is for decks continuous for 3 or more spans. Pieces in the starter course and every third course are simple span. Pieces in other courses are cantilevered over the supports with end joints at alternate quarter-points or third points of the spans, and each piece rests on at least one support. A tie between supports is provided by the simple span courses of the arrangement.

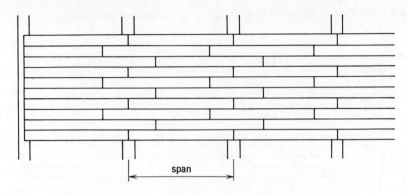

span

6.2.4 Combination Simple and Two-Span Continuous. Alternate pieces in end spans are simple spans; adjacent pieces are two-span continuous. End joints are staggered in adjacent courses and occur over supports.

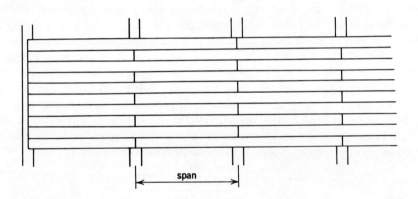

span

6.2.5 Two-Span Continuous. All pieces bear on 3 supports. All end joints occur in line on every other support.

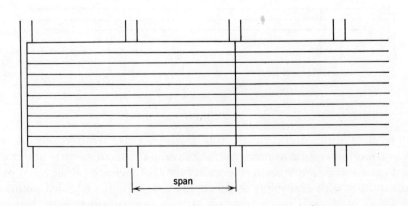

span

7. SPECIFICATIONS

7.1   The specifications for 2 in. roof decking for the various species as well as the inspection and shipping provisions shall be as specified in the standard grading rules under which the species is graded and shall be subject to such other provisions of the standard grading rules as may be applicable. (See paragraph 1.2).

7.2   Select Quality. Lumber of this quality is recommended for high-class construction for which good strength and fine appearance are desired. Knots and other natural characteristics of specified limitations are permitted.

7.3   Commercial Quality. Lumber of this quality is recommended and customarily used for the purposes served by the higher quality when appearance and strength requirements are less critical.

TABLE 2

WEIGHTS OF INSTALLED NOMINAL TWO-INCH ROOF DECKING IN POUNDS PER SQUARE FOOT OF ROOF SURFACE[a]

Species	Actual Thickness	
	$1\frac{1}{2}$ in.	$1\frac{5}{8}$ in.
Cedar, Northern white	2.8	3.0
Cedar, Western	3.2	3.5
Douglas fir	4.3	4.7
Douglas fir-larch	4.4	4.8
Douglas fir, South	4.1	4.4
Fir, balsam	3.3	3.6
Fir, subalpine	3.0	3.3
Hem-fir	3.7	4.0
Hemlock Eastern-tamarack	3.9	4.2
Hemlock, mountain	4.0	4.3
Hemlock, mountain-hem-fir	3.7	4.0
Pine, Eastern white	3.3	3.6
Pine, Idaho white	3.5	3.8
Pine, lodgepole	3.7	4.0
Pine, Northern	4.0	4.3
Pine, ponderosa-sugar	3.7	4.0
Pine, Southern	4.6	5.0
Redwood, California	3.5	3.8
Spruce, Eastern	3.6	3.9
Spruce, Engelmann	3.0	3.3
Spruce, Sitka	3.6	3.9

[a]All weights are based on volume at 15% moisture content; rounded to nearest 0.1 lb.

9. SPAN LOAD TABLES

9.1   The allowable unit stresses in bending and modulus of elasticity values recommended by the regional lumber rules-writing agencies for 2 in. decking are for normal duration of loading. If decking is used for purposes where other durations of load control, appropriate stress adjustments should be made to reflect the duration of loading for the condition of service. Appropriate percentage adjustments are given in the AITC *Timber Construction Manual.*

9.2   The allowable tabulated loads for the five decking arrangements given in Table 3 are based on the formulas given in paragraphs 9.2.1 through 9.2.5 and the span arrangements illustrated in paragraph 6.2. In calculating allowable loads limited by bending, the full moment of inertia was used for the decking arrangements in paragraphs 9.2.1, 9.2.4 and 9.2.5, and two-thirds of the moment of inertia was used for the decking arrangements in paragraphs 9.2.2 and 9.2.3. Deflection formulas are for the maximum deflections in the end spans.

9.2.1   Simple Span:

$$w = \frac{8F_b I}{l^2 c} \quad \text{and} \quad w = \frac{384 \Delta EI}{5l^4}$$

9.2.2   Controlled Random Layup:

$$w = \frac{20F_b I}{3l^2 c} \quad \text{and} \quad w = \frac{100 \Delta EI}{l^4}$$

9.2.3   Cantilevered Pieces Intermixed:

$$w = \frac{20F_b I}{3l^2 c} \quad \text{and} \quad w = \frac{105 \Delta EI}{l^4}$$

9.2.4   Combination Simple and Two-Span Continuous:

$$w = \frac{8F_b I}{l^2 c} \quad \text{and} \quad w = \frac{109 \Delta EI}{l^4}$$

9.2.5   Two-Span Continuous:

$$w = \frac{8F_b I}{l^2 c} \quad \text{and} \quad w = \frac{185 \Delta EI}{l^4}$$

9.3   Allowable bending loads for bending stress (F_b) values other than those tabulated may be determined by multiplying the tabulated values for $F_b = 1,000$ psi by $F_b/1,000$. Allowable deflection loads for modulus of elasticity (E) values other than those tabulated may be determined by multiplying the tabulated values for $E = 1,000,000$ psi by $E/1,000,000$.

9.4   The allowable loads given in Table 3 are for 2 in. nominal thickness roof decking of $1\frac{1}{2}$ in. actual thickness. To determine allowable loads for $1\frac{5}{8}$ in. actual thickness, multiply the allowable bending loads by 1.174 and the allowable deflection loads by 1.272.

9.5   When decking arrangements as specified herein are used for unequal spans, nonuniform loading, cantilever action, or conditions other than covered herein by the tabulated values, appropriate adjustment factors for deflection should be applied to the allowable loads obtained from standard engineering formulas representing the actual conditions of load and span.

9.6   The values given in Table 3 are total uniformly distributed vertical loads, including dead and live load, in pounds per square foot on a horizontal roof surface. When roofs have only a moderate slope (3 in 12 or less), dead and live load may be added together without adjustment for slope of roof.

9.7   For steeper sloping roofs it is customary to adjust the loads so as to express them in terms of square feet of roof surface. For example, 10 lb dead load (6.7 lb for deck and 3.3 lb for roofing) is the vertical load on 1 ft² of sloping roof surface. Live load is usually expressed in pounds per square

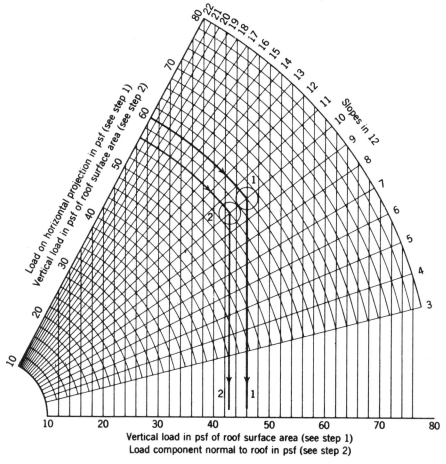

Figure 4.   LOAD CONVERSION. Example: 60 psf live load and 10 psf dead load on 10 in 12 slope. Step 1: 60 psf live load on horizontal projection = 46 psf of roof surface area vertical load on 10 in 12 roof slope. Step 2: 10 psf of roof surface area dead load plus 46 psf of roof surface area live load = 56 psf of roof surface area combined load acting vertically; 56 psf of roof surface area vertical total load = 43 psf normal to roof causing bending and deflection.

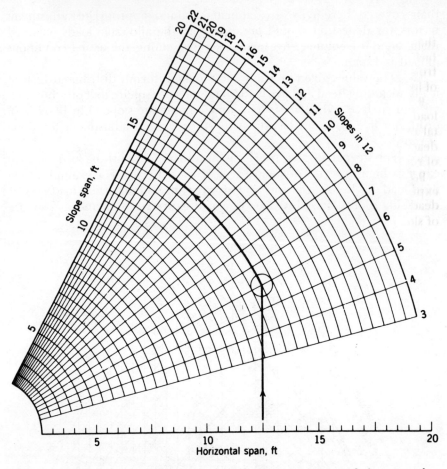

Figure 5. SPAN CONVERSION. Example: 12.5 ft horizontal span = 14 ft slope span when slope is 6 in 12. Use 28 ft in determining footage.

foot of the horizontal projection of the sloping roof surface. Therefore, the vertical live load must be converted to the vertical psf load of sloping roof surface. For example, a 60 psf live load on the horizontal projection is equivalent to a vertical load of 46 psf on a 10 in 12 sloping roof surface. This combined with 10 psf dead load results in a total vertical load of 56 psf on the 10 in 12 sloping roof surface. The 56 psf total vertical load may then be converted to two components, one perpendicular or normal to the roof surface, and one parallel to the roof surface. In the example, the vertical 43 psf and a component parallel to the roof of 37 psf.

9.8 Where decking is laid up the slope, the load component perpendicular to the roof surface will produce bending and deflection; the load component parallel to the roof surface will produce compression. The decking must be designed for bending and axial stresses as well as deflection.

TABLE 3

ALLOWABLE UNIFORMLY DISTRIBUTED TOTAL ROOF LOAD[a]

Span, ft	Limited by Bending $F_b = 1{,}000$ psi[b,d] Load, psf		Limited by Deflection $E = 1{,}000{,}000$ psi[c,d] Load, psf					
	Simple Span; Combination Simple and Two-Span; and Two-Span	Controlled Random Layup; and Cantilevered Pieces Intermixed	Deflection Ratio	Simple Span	Controlled Random Layup	Cantilevered Pieces Intermixed	Combination Simple and Two-Span	Two-Span
6	83	69	l/180	46	60	63	66	112
			l/240	35	45	47	49	84
			l/360	23	30	32	33	56
7	61	51	l/180	29	38	40	41	70
			l/240	22	28	30	31	53
			l/360	15	19	20	21	35
8	47	39	l/180	20	25	27	28	47
			l/240	15	19	20	21	35
			l/360	10	13	13	14	23
9	37	31	l/180	14	18	19	19	33
			l/240	10	13	14	15	25
			l/360	7	9	9	10	16

TABLE 3 (Continued)

| Span, ft | Limited by Bending $F_b = 1,000$ psi[b,d] Load, psf | | | Limited by Deflection $E = 1,000,000$ psi[c,d] Load, psf | | | | |
	Simple Span; Combination Simple and Two-Span and Two-Span	Controlled Random Layup; and Cantilevered Pieces Intermixed	Deflection Ratio	Simple Span	Controlled Random Layup	Cantilevered Pieces Intermixed	Combination Simple and Two-Span	Two-Span
10	30	25	$l/180$	10	13	14	14	24
			$l/240$	8	10	10	11	18
			$l/360$	5	7	7	7	12
11	25	21	$l/180$	8	10	10	11	18
			$l/240$	6	7	8	8	14
			$l/360$	4	5	5	5	9
12	21	17	$l/180$	6	8	8	8	14
			$l/240$	4	6	6	6	11
			$l/360$	3	4	4	4	7

[a]Based on 1⅜ in. actual thickness. For allowable loads for 1⅛ in. actual thickness, multiply tabulated bending loads by 1.174 and tabulated deflection loads by 1.272.

[b]For F_b values other than 1,000 psi, multiply the tabulated loads by the ratio $F_b/1,000$.

[c]For E values other than 1,000,000 psi, multiply the tabulated loads by the ratio $E/1,000,000$.

[d]Actual design values for individual species may be obtained from the regional grading rules referenced under para. 1.2 or from *National Design Specification for Stress-Grade Lumber and Its Fastenings* published by National Forest Products Association.

AMERICAN INSTITUTE
333 West Hampden Avenue

TIMBER CONSTRUCTION
Englewood, Colorado 80110

AITC 119-71
STANDARD SPECIFICATIONS FOR
HARDWOOD GLUED LAMINATED TIMBER

Adopted as Recommendations August 26, 1971
Copyright 1971 by American Institute of Timber Construction

CONTENTS

1. GENERAL

1.1 Structural Glued Laminated Timber.

1.1.1 The term "structural glued laminated timber" as employed herein refers to an engineered, stress-rated product of a timber laminating plant, comprising assemblies of suitably selected and prepared wood laminations bonded together with adhesives. The grain of all laminations is approximately parallel longitudinally.

1.1.2 The separate laminations shall not exceed 2 in. in net thickness. They may be comprised of pieces end joined to form any length, of pieces placed or glued edge to edge to make wider ones, or of pieces bent to curved form during gluing.

1.1.3 This specification is applicable to laminated members of four or more laminations when the load is applied perpendicular to the wide face of the laminations and to bending values for members of three or more laminations when the load is applied parallel to the wide face of the laminations.

1

1.1.4 The production of structural glued laminated timber under these specifications shall be in accordance with the current Voluntary Product Standard PS 56-73, *Structural Glued Laminated Timber*.

1.2 Lumber.

1.2.1 General.

1.2.1.1 Slope of grain shall be limited in the full length of each lamination and shall be measured over a distance sufficiently great to determine the general slope, disregarding local deviations, except as noted for tension laminations.

1.2.1.2 For that portion of the cross section that is not a structural part of the member, the strength provisions of this specification need not apply.

1.2.1.3 When a top or bottom lamination is specially selected to meet appearance requirements, the basic structural requirements of the required grade still apply.

1.2.1.4 Appearance requirements shall be in accordance with the current *Standard Appearance Grades for Structural Glued Laminated Timber*, AITC 110.

1.2.2 Species.   This specification is applicable to members laminated from any of the hardwood species listed in Table 1.

1.2.3 Grading.

1.2.3.1 The grading of the lumber shall be based on the knot size and slope of grain requirements given in Table 2 for a specific allowable unit stress required, and in addition, shall meet such other requirements as may be necessary for a particular use.

1.2.3.2 The slope of grain requirements for a member stressed principally in bending apply only to the laminations in the outer 10% of the depth of the member, measured from each face at any cross section of the member as finally installed. The slope of grain for the balance of the laminations shall be no steeper than 1 in 8. For tension or compression members the requirements given in Table 2 apply to all laminations.

1.2.3.3 When a member is designed such that the bending stress is produced by a load applied parallel to the wide face of the laminations, the slope of grain requirements given in Table 2 apply to all laminations.

1.2.3.4 Requirements of this standard apply to laminations ready for assembly and not to the rough lumber from which they are prepared.

1.3 Adhesives.

1.3.1 Dry-use adhesives are those that perform satisfactorily when the moisture content of wood does not exceed 16% for repeated or prolonged periods of service and are to be used only when these conditions exist.

1.3.2 Wet-use adhesives will perform satisfactorily for all moisture conditions, including exposure to weather, marine use and where approved pressure treatments are used either before or after gluing. They may be used for all moisture conditions of service, but are required when the moisture content exceeds 16% for repeated or prolonged periods of service.

1.3.3 Adhesives used shall comply with the specifications as contained in the Voluntary Product Standard PS 56-73, *Structural Glued Laminated Timber*.

2. DESIGN STRESSES

2.1 General.

2.1.1 Stress factors for the principal commercial species of hardwoods are listed in Table 1. The use of only one species in the member is assumed. Species having substantially similar strength properties are grouped together and groups are listed in order of decreasing bending strength.

2.1.2 Allowable unit stresses are computed by multiplying the stress modules given in Table 2 by the appropriate stress factor shown in Table 1 for a specified combination of species and condition of use.

2.1.3 The allowable unit stresses as determined from Tables 1 and 2 are for normal conditions of loading. Modifications for other conditions of loading are given in Section 2.5.1.

2.1.4 The allowable unit stresses as determined from Tables 1 and 2, and the modifications required for other conditions of loading are applicable also to structural glued laminated members that have been pressure impregnated by an approved preservative process in accordance with *Treating Standard for Structural Timber Framing*, AITC 109.

2.1.5 The allowable unit bending stresses (F_b) as determined from Tables 1 and 2 apply to a 12 in. deep member, uniformly loaded with a span to depth ratio of 21 to 1. Modifications for other sizes and loading conditions are given in Section 2.5.4.

2.1.6 The modulus of elasticity values (E) given in Tables 1 and 2 represent an average modulus of elasticity for the member.

2.1.7 End joints may be plane scarf joints, finger joints, or other types that qualify for the allowable unit stress in accordance with the procedure recommended in the Voluntary Product Standard PS56-73, *Structural Glued Laminated Timber*.

2.1.8 The design of glued laminated members and their fastenings shall be in accordance with the provisions of this specification and the AITC *Timber Construction Manual*.

2.2 Members Stressed in Bending.

2.2.1 Bending stress values determined from Tables 1 and 2 are based on an arrangement of laminations where the direction of loading is perpendicular to the wide face of the laminations. This arrangement is best suited when the principal stress is in bending.

2.2.2 When a member is designed such that the bending stress is produced by a load applied parallel to the wide face of the laminations, the allowable unit stresses as determined from Tables 1 and 2 are applicable provided knots at the edge of the laminations do not exceed $\frac{1}{2}$ the size of those permitted by Table 2 but may increase proportionally to a size at the center of the lamination width equivalent to that permitted by Table 2.

2.3 Members Stressed Principally in Axial Compression or Axial Tension.
Allowable unit stress values determined from Tables 1 and 2 for members stressed principally in axial compression or tension are based on all laminations having a slope of grain no steeper than the values listed in Table 2 for a specified combination.

2.4 Condition of Use.

2.4.1 Dry condition of use stress values shall be applicable when the moisture content in service is less than 16%, as in most covered structures.

2.4.2 Wet condition of use stress values shall be applicable when the moisture content in service is 16% or more, as may occur in members not covered or in covered locations of high relative humidity.

2.5 Modification of Stresses.

2.5.1 Duration of Load.

2.5.1.1 Normal load duration contemplates fully stressing a member to the allowable unit stress by the application of the full design load for a duration of approximately 10 years (either continuously or cumulatively). For the remainder of the member's life, the stress level shall be no greater than 90% of the full design stress.

2.5.1.2 When a member is fully stressed by maximum design loads for long-term loading conditions (greater than 10 years either continuously or cumulatively), the allowable unit stresses shall be 90% of the values tabulated.

2.5.1.3 When the duration of full design load (either continuously or cumulatively) does not exceed the period indicated, increase the tabulated allowable unit stresses as follows:

> 15% for 2 months duration, as for snow
> 25% for 7 days duration
> $33\frac{1}{3}\%$ for wind or earthquake
> 100% for impact

These increases are not cumulative.

2.5.1.4 The allowable unit stress for normal loading may be used without regard to impact if the stress induced by impact does not exceed the allowable unit stress for normal loading.

2.5.1.5 These adjustments do not apply to modulus of elasticity except when used to determine allowable unit loads for columns.

2.5.2 Curvature Factor.

2.5.2.1 For the curved portion of members, the allowable unit stress in bending shall be modified by multiplication by the following curvature factor:

$$C_c = 1 - 2{,}000 \left(\frac{t}{R}\right)^2$$

where t = thickness of lamination, in.
   R = radius of curvature of lamination, in.

and t/R should not exceed 1/100.

No curvature factor shall be applied to stress in the straight portion of an assembly, regardless of curvature elsewhere.

2.5.3 Radial Tension or Compression.

2.5.3.1 The radial stress, f_r, induced by a bending moment in a curved member of constant cross section is computed by the equation:

$$f_r = \frac{3M}{2Rbd}$$

where M = bending moment, in.-lb
  R = radius of curvature at centerline of member, in.
  b = width of cross section, in.
  d = depth of cross section, in.

This equation can also be used to estimate the radial stresses in members of varying cross section. For further information regarding more exact procedures for calculating radial stresses in curved members of varying cross section, contact AITC.

2.5.3.2   When M is in the direction tending to decrease curvature (increase the radius), the stress is tension across the grain. For this condition, the tension stress across the grain shall be limited to $\frac{1}{3}$ the allowable unit stress in horizontal shear.

2.5.3.3   When M is in the direction tending to increase curvature (decrease the radius), the stress is compression across the grain and shall be limited to the allowable unit stress in compression perpendicular to the grain for all species included herein.

2.5.4   Size Factor.

2.5.4.1   When the depth of a rectangular beam exceeds 12 in., the tabulated unit stress in bending, F_b, shall be reduced by multiplying the tabulated stress by the size factor, C_F, as determined from the following relationship:

$$C_F = \left(\frac{12}{d}\right)^{1/9}$$

where C_F = size factor
  d = depth of member, in.

2.5.4.2   The size factor relationship as given under 2.5.4.1 is applicable to a bending member satisfying the following basic assumptions: (a) simply supported beam; (b) uniformly distributed load, and (c) span to depth ratio (L/d) of 21. This factor can thus be applied with reasonable accuracy to most commonly encountered design situations. Where greater accuracy is desired for other sizes and conditions of loading, the percentage changes given in the following tables may be applied directly to the size factor calculated for the basic conditions as previously stated. Straight line interpolation may be used for other L/d ratios.

Span to Depth Ratio L/d	% Change
7	+6.3
14	+2.3
21	0
28	−1.6
35	−2.8

Loading Condition for Simply Supported Beams	% Change
Single concentrated load	+7.8
Uniform load	0
Third point load	−3.2

2.5.4.3   For a more detailed analysis of the size factor and its application to the design of bending members, contact AITC.

2.5.5   Lateral Stability.

2.5.5.1   The tabulated allowable unit bending stresses contained in this specification are applicable to members that are adequately braced. When deep, slender members not adequately braced are used, a reduction to the allowable unit bending stresses must be applied based on a computation of the slenderness factor of the member. In the check of lateral stability, the slenderness factor shall be applied in design as shown in the *Timber Construction Manual.*

2.5.5.2   The reduction in bending stresses determined by applying the slenderness factor is not cumulative with a reduction in stress due to the application of size factor, and in no case shall the allowable unit bending stress used in design exceed the stress as determined by applying the size factor.

3. DIMENSIONS

3.1   Standard Sizes. To the extent that other considerations will permit, the use of standard finished sizes constitutes recommended practice. These standard finished sizes are based on the widths of lumber and multiples of lamination thickness that can be used to best advantage for laminating.

3.2   Depth and Width.

3.2.1   Straight and curved members shall be furnished in accordance with the depth dimensions required by the design.

3.2.2   Recommended standard finished widths are as follows:

Nominal Width, in.	Net Finished Width, in.
3	$2\frac{1}{4}$
4	$3\frac{1}{8}$
6	$5\frac{1}{8}$
8	$6\frac{3}{4}$
10	$8\frac{3}{4}$
12	$10\frac{3}{4}$
14	$12\frac{1}{4}$
16	$14\frac{1}{4}$

Other finished widths may be used to meet the size requirements of a design or to meet other special requirements.

3.3 Radius of Curvature. The recommended minimum radii of curvature for curved structural glued laminated hardwood timbers are 6 ft 3 in. for a lamination thickness of $\frac{3}{4}$ in.; and 12 ft 6 in. for a lamination thickness of $1\frac{1}{2}$ in. Other radii of curvature may be used with these thicknesses and other radius-thickness combinations may be used provided the t/R ratio does not exceed 1/100.

4. INSPECTION

4.1 Quality Control. The assurance that quality materials and workmanship are used in structural glued laminated timber members shall be vested in the laminator's quality control in day-to-day operations. Visual inspections and physical tests of samples of production are also required to assure conforman e with this specification and the Voluntary Product Standard PS56-73, *Structural Glued Laminated Timber*.

5. MARKING

5.1 Straight or slightly cambered beams shall be stamped "TOP" on the top at both ends of the beam and on the wrapper of wrapped beams except that members which are fabricated in such a manner that they cannot be installed upside down, need not be marked. The stamp shall contain letters approximately 2 in. in height.

6. PROTECTION DURING SHIPPING AND FIELD HANDLING

6.1 Protection shall be in accordance with *Recommended Practice for Protection of Structural Glued Laminated Timber During Transit, Storage and Erection*, AITC 111.

TABLE 1

STRESS FACTORS FOR USE IN CONVERTING THE VALUES OF TABLE 2 TO NORMAL WORKING STRESSES

Species	Extreme Fiber in Bending or Tension parallel to Grain		Compression Parallel to Grain		Horizontal Shear		Compression Perpendicular to Grain		Modulus of Elasticity	
	Factor		Factor		Factor		Factor		Factor	
	Dry	Wet	Dry	Wet	Dry	Wet	Dry	Wet	Dry	Wet
Hickory, true and pecan	3.85	3.10	3.05	2.20	0.26	0.23	0.73	0.49	1.80	1.50
Beech, American	3.05	2.45	2.45	1.80	0.23	0.21	0.61	0.41		1.40
Birch, sweet and yellow	3.05	2.45	2.45	1.80	0.23	0.21	0.61	0.41	1.90	1.60
Elm, rock	3.05	2.45	2.45	1.80	0.23	0.21	0.61	0.41	1.40	1.30
Maple, black and sugar (hard maple)	3.05	2.45	2.45	1.80	0.23	0.21	0.61	0.41	1.70	1.40
Ash, commercial white	2.80	2.25	2.20	1.60	0.23	0.21	0.61	0.41	1.70	1.40
Oak, commercial red and white	2.80	2.25	2.05	1.50	0.23	0.21	0.61	0.41	1.60	1.30
Elm, American and slippery (white or soft elm)	2.20	1.75	1.60	1.15	0.19	0.17	0.31	0.21	1.40	1.20
Sweetgum (red or sap gum)	2.20	1.75	1.60	1.15	0.19	0.17	0.37	0.24	1.40	1.20
Tupelo, black (blackgum)	2.20	1.75	1.60	1.15	0.19	0.17	0.37	0.24	1.20	1.00
Tupelo, water	2.20	1.75	1.60	1.15	0.19	0.17	0.37	0.24	1.30	1.10
Ash, black	2.00	1.60	1.30	0.95	0.17	0.14	0.37	0.24	1.30	1.00
Yellow-poplar	2.00	1.60	1.45	1.05	0.15	0.13	0.27	0.18	1.50	1.20
Cottonwood, Eastern	1.55	1.20	1.20	0.90	0.11	0.10	0.18	0.12	1.20	1.00

TABLE 2

VALUES FOR USE IN COMPUTING WORKING STRESSES WITH THE FACTORS OF TABLE 1 TOGETHER WITH LIMITATIONS REQUIRED TO PERMIT THE USE OF SUCH STRESSES

Combination Symbol[a]	Ratio of size of maximum permitted knot to finished width of lamination	Number of laminations[b]	Extreme Fiber in Bending		Tension Parallel to Grain		Modulus of Elasticity in Bending	Compression Parallel to Grain		Maximum Longitudinal Shear Stress Module psi	Compression Perpendicular to Grain Stress Module psi	Tension Lamination Required for Members Greater than 16¼ in. in Depth
			Stress Module psi	Steepest grain slope	Stress Module psi	Steepest grain slope	Stress Module psi	Stress Module psi	Steepest grain slope			
A	0.1	4 to 14	800[c]	1:16	800[c]	1:16	1,000,000	970	1:15	1,000	1,000	301-26
	0.1	15 or more	800[c]	1:16	800[c]	1:16	1,000,000	970	1:15	1,000	1,000	301-26
B	0.2	4 to 14	770[c]	1:16	800[c]	1:16	1,000,000	920	1:15	1,000	1,000	301-26
	0.2	15 or more	800[c]	1:16	800[c]	1:16	1,000,000	930	1:15	1,000	1,000	301-26
C	0.3	4 to 14	600	1:12	750	1:15	900,000	860	1:14	1,000	1,000	301-24
	0.3	15 or more	660	1:12	780	1:16	900,000	870	1:14	1,000	1,000	301-24
D	0.4	4 to 14	450	1:8	590	1:10	800,000	780	1:12	1,000	1,000	301-20
	0.4	15 or more	520	1:8	650	1:12	800,000	810	1:12	1,000	1,000	301-20
E	0.5	4 to 14	300	1:8	410	1:8	800,000	690	1:10	1,000	1,000	301-20
	0.5	15 or more	380	1:8	490	1:8	800,000	730	1:10	1,000	1,000	301-20

[a]The tabulated combinations are applicable to arches, compression members, tension members and bending members less than 16¼ in. in depth. For bending members 16¼ in. or more in depth, the outermost tension laminations representing 5% of the total depth of the member shall meet all grading requirements as given in Table 2 for both the basic combination grading restrictions and the tension lamination requirements, whichever are more restrictive.

[b]When laminations of different thicknesses are used, divide the depth of the member by the thickness of the thickest lamination used and then assume the quotient to be the number of laminations in the member for use in determining the allowable stress.

[c]Stress modules for combinations A and B are identical in the cases of extreme fiber in bending and in tension parallel to grain because a slope of grain of 1:16 is a more restrictive limitation than knot size.

AMERICAN INSTITUTE
333 West Hampden Avenue

TIMBER CONSTRUCTION
Englewood, Colorado 80110

AITC 119-71
APPENDIX A
GRADING REQUIREMENTS FROM
AITC 301-20, 301-22, 301-24, 301-26
TENSION LAMINATION
RECOMMENDATIONS

Adopted as Recommendations October 7, 1971
Copyright 1972 by American Institute of Timber Construction

CONTENTS

A1. AITC 301-20 TENSION LAMINATION — MEMBERS IN BENDING (1,600, 1,800 and 2,000 psi)

A1.1 Growth rate requirements (including "dense" if required) shall apply to the full length of the piece. Pieces shall have near average or above average specific gravity for the species. (*Note:* Growth rate requirements are not applied in the grading of hardwoods.)

A1.2 Pieces containing wide-ringed or lightweight pith associated wood over $\frac{1}{8}$ of the cross section shall be excluded. (The next inch of wood outside the area of the pith associated wood shall meet the growth rate requirements of the grade including "dense" when dense laminations are required. The line along which measurement of this inch is made shall correspond to the line used in the standard grading rules for rate of growth and percentage of summerwood. If a distance of 1 in. is not available along this line, the measurement will be made over such lesser portion as exists.) *Note:* This requirement for limitation of pith associated wood is not applicable for hardwoods.

A1.3 Any cross section shall have at least 50% clear wood with a slope of grain not steeper than 1 : 12. However, knots shall not exceed the size permitted for the outermost laminations in the tension zone as specified in the laminating combinations.

A1.4   The general slope of grain shall not exceed 1 : 12.

A1.5   Knots shall not occur within 2 knot diameters of any finger joint.

A2. AITC 301-22 TENSION LAMINATION — MEMBERS IN BENDING (2,200 psi)

A2.1   In addition to the requirements of AITC 301-20, the following requirements shall apply:

A2.1.1   Knots shall not occupy more than $\frac{1}{4}$ of the cross section.

A2.1.2   The general slope of grain shall not exceed 1 : 16. Where more restrictive slope of grain requirements are required by the standard laminating specifications, these shall apply.

A2.1.3   Areas of local grain deviation steeper than 1 : 16 shall not occupy more than $\frac{1}{3}$ of the cross section.

A3. AITC 301-24 TENSION LAMINATION — MEMBERS IN BENDING (2,400 psi)

A3.1   In addition to the requirements of AITC 301-22, the following requirements shall apply:

A3.1.1   A 1 ft length of a lamination shall be considered as a cross section.

A3.1.2   Maximum size single strength-reducing characteristics when not in the same longitudinal projection of the section must be at least 2 ft apart, measured center to center.

A3.1.3   Knots shall not occupy more than $\frac{1}{5}$ of the cross section.

A3.1.4   Two-thirds of the cross section of the laminations must be free of strength-reducing characteristics and must have 1 : 16 or flatter slope of grain. (Knots plus associated localized cross grain, or knots plus associated localized cross grain plus localized cross grain not associated with knot, or localized cross grain not associated with a knot may occupy up to $\frac{1}{3}$ of the cross section.)

A4. AITC 301-26 TENSION LAMINATION — MEMBERS IN BENDING (2,600 psi)

A4.1   In addition to the requirements of AITC 301-24, the following requirements shall apply:

A4.1.1   Any cross section containing an edge knot must have 80% clear and straight-grained wood with a slope of grain not steeper than 1 : 16. (An edge knot is a knot that has any portion of itself or its associated localized cross grain at/or within $\frac{1}{2}$ in. of the edge of the piece. This $\frac{1}{2}$ in. is determined based on the average of the measurements on the 2 wide faces.)

AMERICAN INSTITUTE
333 West Hampden Avenue

TIMBER CONSTRUCTION
Englewood, Colorado 80110

AITC 120-71
STANDARD SPECIFICATIONS FOR STRUCTURAL GLUED LAMINATED TIMBER USING "E" RATED AND VISUALLY GRADED LUMBER OF DOUGLAS FIR, SOUTHERN PINE, HEM-FIR, AND LODGEPOLE PINE

Adopted as Recommendations August 26, 1971
Copyright 1971 by American Institute of Timber Construction

CONTENTS

1. GENERAL

1.1 Structural Glued Laminated Timber.

1.1.1 The term "structural glued laminated timber" as employed herein refers to an engineered, stress-rated product of a timber laminating plant, comprising assemblies of suitably selected and prepared wood laminations bonded together with adhesives. The grain of all laminations is approximately parallel longitudinally.

1.1.2 The separate laminations shall not exceed 2 in. in net thickness. They may be comprised of pieces end joined to form any length, of pieces placed or glued edge to edge to make wider ones, or of pieces bent to curved form during gluing.

1

1.1.3   This specification is applicable to laminated members of four or more laminations when the load is applied perpendicular to the wide face of the laminations. When members are designed with load applied parallel to the wide faces, a laminating combination in *Standard Specifications for Structural Glued Laminated Timber of Douglas Fir, Western Larch, Southern Pine and California Redwood*, AITC 117, should be selected.

1.1.4   The production of structural glued laminated timber under these specifications shall be in accordance with the current Voluntary Product Standard PS56-73, *Structural Glued Laminated Timber*.

1.1.5   These laminating specifications using "E" rated lumber are intended for members stressed principally in bending such as beams, girders, and purlins. When members are stressed primarily in axial tension or compression, the laminating specifications based on visual grades (AITC 117) may provide more economical sizes.

1.2   Lumber.

1.2.1   General. The "E" rated lumber used shall be lumber that has been nondestructively tested to sort it into "E" grades by measuring the modulus of elasticity (E) of each piece. In addition, the lumber must be visually graded to meet the visual grading requirements of this specification. Any method of nondestructive testing for determination of "E" may be used provided it meets the requirements of this specification. The accuracy of the method shall be such that the "E" value of not more than 5% of the pieces in a grade fall below the minimum "E" value specified in Table 1. In addition to the "E" rating, knot restrictions as given in Table 1 and as required in paragraphs 1.2.2, 1.2.3, 1.2.4, and 1.2.5 are applicable. For purpose of checking "E" values of nondestructively tested lumber, the average "E" value of a piece of lumber in flatwise bending determined in accordance with ASTM Standard D2915-70T shall be considered as the basis of reference (see Appendix B).

1.2.1.1   For that portion of the cross section that is not a structural part of the member, the strength provisions of this specification need not apply.

1.2.1.2   When a top or bottom lamination is specially selected to meet appearance requirements, the basic structural requirements of the required grade still apply.

1.2.1.3   Appearance requirements shall be in accordance with the current *Standard Appearance Grades for Structural Glued Laminated Timber*, AITC 110.

1.2.2   Douglas Fir. Reference herein to these species shall apply only to members laminated from Douglas fir grown within the states of Wyoming, Montana, Washington, Idaho, Oregon, and California since some allowable unit stresses shown are based on a statistical analysis of the growth characteristics of the lumber from these sources. The grade of all lumber used shall be no lower than the "L3" grade as described in the West Coast Lumber Inspection Bureau *Standard Grading Rules for West Coast Lumber, No. 16* or the Western Wood Products Association Special Product Rule 500.00, *Structural Laminations of Douglas Fir and Larch*.

1.2.3   Southern Pine. The grade of lumber used shall be no lower than No. 3 dimension as described in the 1970 *Standard Grading Rules for*

Southern Pine Lumber of the Southern Pine Inspection Bureau with the exception that it must be medium grain and the maximum knot size is limited to $\frac{1}{2}$ the cross section.

1.2.4 Hem-Fir. The hem-fir species combination may consist of any one or any combination of the following species: Western hemlock, Pacific silver fir, noble fir, grand fir, California red fir, and white fir as shown in the Western Wood Products Association 1970 *Standard Grading Rules for Western Lumber* and the West Coast Lumber Inspection Bureau *Standard Grading Rules for West Coast Lumber, No. 16.* The visual grade of lumber used shall be no lower than the "L3" grade of Douglas fir as described in Western Wood Products Association Special Products Rule 500.00, *Structural Laminations of Douglas Fir and Larch*, or the West Coast Lumber Inspection Bureau *Standard Grading Rules for West Coast Lumber, No. 16.*

1.2.5 Lodgepole Pine. Lodgepole pine is the species described in Western Wood Products Association 1970 *Standard Grading Rules for Western Lumber.* The grade of lumber used shall be no lower than the "L3" grade of Douglas fir as described in the Western Wood Products Association Special Products Rule 500.00, *Structural Laminations of Douglas Fir and Larch*, or the WestCoast Lumber Inspection Bureau *Standard Grading Rules for West Coast Lumber, No. 16.*

1.3   Adhesives.

1.3.1   Dry-use adhesives are those that perform satisfactorily when the moisture content of wood does not exceed 16% for repeated or prolonged periods of service and are to be used only when these conditions exist.

1.3.2   Wet-use adhesives will perform satisfactorily for all moisture conditions, including exposure to weather, marine use, and where approved pressure treatments are used either before or after gluing. They may be used for all moisture conditions of service, but are required when the moisture content exceeds 16% for repeated or prolonged periods of service.

1.3.3   Adhesives used shall comply with the specifications as contained in Voluntary Product Standard PS56-73, *Structural Glued Laminated Timber.*

2. DESIGN STRESSES

2.1   General.

2.1.1   For the allowable unit stresses given in Table 1, or modifications thereof, lumber satisfying the stiffness and visual grading required shall be assembled in accordance with the zone requirements indicated therein.

2.1.2   The allowable unit stresses given in Table 1 and the modifications required for other conditions of use and loading are applicable also to structural glued laminated members that have been pressure impregnated by an approved preservative process in accordance with *Treating Standard for Structural Timber Framing*, AITC 109.

2.1.3   The allowable unit stresses given in Table 1 are for normal conditions of loading. Modifications for other conditions of loading are given in Section 2.5.1.

2.1.4   The allowable unit bending stresses (F_b) given in Table 1 apply to a 12 in. deep member uniformly loaded with a span to depth ratio of

21 to 1. Modifications for other sizes and loading conditions are given in Section 2.5.4.

2.1.5 End joints may be plane scarf joints, finger joints, or other types that qualify for the allowable unit stress in accordance with the procedure recommended in Voluntary Product Standard PS56-73, *Structural Glued Laminated Timber*.

2.1.6 The design of glued laminated members and their fastenings shall be in accordance with the provisions of this specification and the AITC *Timber Construction Manual*.

2.2 Bending Stresses. Table 1 is based on an arrangement of laminations best suited for members where the principle stress is bending when the direction of loading is perpendicular to the wide face of the laminations.

2.3 Axial Compression and Axial Tension Stresses. The combinations given in this specification are intended primarily for members stressed in bending. The stress values for compression and tension parallel to grain are based primarily on the lower grades contained in the member and are conservative. They are intended to be used in design where secondary axial compression or tension stresses exist.

2.4 Condition of Use.

2.4.1 Dry condition of use stress values shall be applicable when the moisture content in service is less than 16%, as in most covered structures.

2.4.2 Wet condition of use stress values shall be applicable when the moisture content in service is 16% or more, as may occur in members not covered or in covered locations of high relative humidity.

2.5 Modification of Stresses.

2.5.1 Duration of Load.

2.5.1.1 Normal load duration contemplates fully stressing a member to the allowable unit stress by the application of the full design load for a duration of approximately 10 years (applied either continuously or cumulatively).

2.5.1.2 When a member is fully stressed by maximum design loads for long-term loading conditions (greater than 10 years applied either continuously or cumulatively), the allowable unit stresses shall be 90% of the values tabulated.

2.5.1.3 When the duration of full design load (applied either continuously or cumulatively) does not exceed the period indicated, increase the tabulated allowable unit stresses as follows:

> 15% for 2 months duration, as for snow
> 25% for 7 days duration
> $33\frac{1}{3}$% for wind or earthquake
> 100% for impact.

These increases are not cumulative.

2.5.1.4 The allowable unit stress for normal loading may be used without regard to impact if the stress induced by impact does not exceed the allowable unit stress for normal loading.

2.5.1.5 These adjustments do not apply to modulus of elasticity,

2.5.2 Curvature Factor.

2.5.2.1 For the curved portion of members, the allowable unit stress in bending shall be modified by multiplication by the following curvature factor:

$$C_c = 1 - 2{,}000 \left(\frac{t}{R}\right)^2$$

where t = thickness of lamination, in.
$\qquad R$ = radius of curvature of lamination, in.

and t/R should not exceed 1/125 for Douglas fir, hem-fir and lodgepole pine and 1/100 for Southern pine.

No curvature factor shall be applied to stress in the straight portion of an assembly, regardless of curvature elsewhere.

2.5.3   Radial Tension or Compression.

2.5.3.1   The radial stress (f_r) induced by a bending moment in a curved member of constant cross section is computed by the equation:

$$f_r = \frac{3M}{2Rbd}$$

where M = bending moment, in.-lb
$\qquad R$ = radius of curvature at centerline of member, in.
$\qquad b$ = width of cross section, in.
$\qquad d$ = depth of cross section, in.

This equation can also be used to estimate the radial stresses in members of varying cross section. For further information regarding more exact procedures for calculating radial stresses in curved members of varying cross section, contact AITC.

2.5.3.2   When M is in the direction tending to decrease curvature (increase the radius), the stress is tension across the grain. For this condition, the allowable tension stress across the grain (F_r) shall be limited to $\frac{1}{3}$ the allowable unit stress in horizontal shear for Southern pine for all load conditions and for Douglas fir, hem-fir, and lodgepole pine for wind or earthquake loadings. The limit shall be 15 psi for Douglas fir, hem-fir and lodgepole pine for other loading conditions. These values are subject to modifications for duration of load. If these values are exceeded, mechanical reinforcing shall be used and shall be sufficient to resist all radial tension stresses.

2.5.3.3   When M is in the direction tending to increase curvature (decrease the radius), the stress is compression across the grain and shall be limited to the allowable unit stress in compression perpendicular to the grain for all species included herein.

2.5.4   Size Factor.

2.5.4.1   When the depth of a rectangular beam exceeds 12 in., the tabulated unit stress in bending (F_b) shall be reduced by multiplying the tabulated stress by the size factor (C_F) as determined from the following relationship:

$$C_F = \left(\frac{12}{d}\right)^{1/9}$$

where C_F = size factor
$\qquad d$ = depth of member, in.

2.5.4.2   The size factor relationship given under 2.5.4.1 is applicable to a bending member satisfying the following basic assumptions: (*a*) simply supported beam, (*b*) uniformly distributed load, and (*c*) span to depth ratio (*L/d*) of 21. This factor can thus be applied with reasonable accuracy to most commonly encountered design situations. Where greater accuracy is desired for other sizes and conditions of loading, the percentage changes given in the following tables may be applied directly to the size factor calculated for the basic conditions as previously stated. Straight line interpolation may be used for other *L/d* ratios.

Span to Depth Ratio (*L/d*)	% Change
7	+6.3
14	+2.3
21	0
28	−1.6
35	−2.8

Loading Condition for Simply Supported Beams	% Change
Single concentrated load	+7.8
Uniform load	0
Third point load	−3.2

2.5.4.3   For a more detailed analysis of the size factor and its application to the design of bending members, contact AITC.

2.5.5   Lateral Stability.

2.5.5.1   The tabulated allowable unit bending stresses contained in this specification are applicable to members that are adequately braced. When deep, slender members not adequately braced are used, a reduction to the allowable unit bending stresses must be applied based on a computation of the slenderness factor of the member. In the check of lateral stability, the slenderness factor shall be applied in design as shown in the AITC *Timber Construction Manual*.

2.5.5.2   The reduction in bending stresses determined by applying the slenderness factor is not cumulative with a reduction in stress due to the application of size factor. In no case shall the allowable unit bending stress used in design exceed the stress as determined by applying the size factor.

3. DIMENSIONS

3.1   Standard Sizes. To the extent that other considerations will permit, the use of standard finished sizes constitutes recommended practice. These standard finished sizes are based on the widths of lumber and multiples of lamination thickness that can be used to best advantage for laminating.

3.2 Depth and Width

3.2.1 Straight and curved members shall be furnished in accordance with the depth dimensions required by the design.

3.2.2 Recommended standard finished widths are as follows:

Nominal Width, in.	Net Finished Width, in.
3	$2\frac{1}{4}$
4	$3\frac{1}{8}$
6	$5\frac{1}{8}$
8	$6\frac{3}{4}$
10	$8\frac{3}{4}$
12	$10\frac{3}{4}$
14	$12\frac{1}{4}$
16	$14\frac{1}{4}$

3.3 Radius of curvature. The recommended minimum radii of curvature for curved structural glued laminated timbers are 9 ft 4 in. for a lamination thickness (t) of $\frac{3}{4}$ in.; and 27 ft 6 in. for a lamination thickness of $1\frac{1}{2}$ in. Other radii of curvature may be used with these thicknesses and other radius-thickness combinations may be used provided the ratio t/R does not exceed 1/100 for Southern pine, nor 1/125 for other softwoods.

4. INSPECTION

4.1 Quality control. The assurance that quality materials and workmanship are used in structural glued laminated timber members shall be vested in the laminator's quality control in day-to-day operations. Visual inspections and physical tests of samples of production are also required to assure conformance with this specification and Voluntary Product Standard PS56-73. *Structural Glued Laminated Timber.* In addition, the laminator shall have a device for checking the modulus of elasticity (E). Such a device will be used to determine the "E" value of a piece of lumber. This device and its use is described in Appendix B.

5. MARKING

5.1 Straight or slightly cambered beams shall be stamped "TOP" on the top at both ends of the beam and on the wrapper of wrapped beams except that members which are fabricated in such a manner that they cannot be installed upside down need not be marked. The stamp shall contain letters approximately 2 in. in height.

6. PROTECTION DURING SHIPPING AND FIELD HANDLING

6.1 Protection shall be in accordance with *Recommended Practice for Protection of Structural Glued Laminated Timber During Transit, Storage and Erection*, AITC 111.

TABLE 1

GRADE REQUIREMENTS AND CORRESPONDING ALLOWABLE UNIT STRESSES (psi), FOR NORMAL CONDITIONS OF LOADING; MEMBERS STRESSED PRINCIPALLY IN BENDING, LOADED PERPENDICULAR TO THE WIDE FACE OF THE LAMINATIONS[a,b]

Part A Grade Requirements

Combination Symbol	Number of Laminations	Tension Zone—¼ of Depth				Compression Zone—¼ of depth					
		Outer Zone ⅛ of Depth		Intermediate Zone ⅛ of Depth		Outer Zone ⅛ of Depth		Intermediate Zone ⅛ of Depth		Inner Zone ½ of Depth	
		Minimum E	Edge Knot Restrictions[i]	Minimum E	Edge Knot Restrictions[i]	Minimum E	Knot Restrictions	Minimum E	Knot Restrictions	Minimum E	Knot Restrictions
Douglas fir											
22F-E[d]	4 or more	1,900,000	$\frac{1}{8}$	1,700,000	$\frac{1}{4}$	1,900,000	$\frac{1}{2}$	1,700,000	$\frac{1}{2}$	1,100,000	$\frac{1}{2}$
26F-E[e]	4 or more	2,300,000	$\frac{1}{6}$	1,900,000	$\frac{1}{8}$	2,300,000	$\frac{1}{2}$	1,900,000	$\frac{1}{2}$	1,100,000	$\frac{1}{2}$
Southern pine											
22F-E[d]	4 or more	1,900,000	$\frac{1}{6}$	1,700,000	$\frac{1}{4}$	1,900,000	$\frac{1}{2}$	1,700,000	$\frac{1}{2}$	1,100,000	$\frac{1}{2}$
26F-E[e]	4 or more	2,100,000	$\frac{1}{6}$	1,700,000	$\frac{1}{4}$	2,100,000	$\frac{1}{2}$	1,700,000	$\frac{1}{2}$	1,100,000	$\frac{1}{2}$
Hem-fir											
22F-E[d]	4 or more	1,700,000	$\frac{1}{6}$	1,400,000	$\frac{1}{4}$	1,700,000	$\frac{1}{2}$	1,400,000	$\frac{1}{2}$	1,100,000	$\frac{1}{2}$
26F-E[e]	4 or more	1,900,000	$\frac{1}{6}$	1,700,000	$\frac{1}{4}$	1,900,000	$\frac{1}{2}$	1,700,000	$\frac{1}{2}$	1,100,000	$\frac{1}{2}$

Combination	Laminations										
Douglas fir and hem-fir combined[h]											
26F-E[e]	4 or more	1,900,000	$\frac{1}{6}$	1,700,000	$\frac{1}{4}$	1,900,000	$\frac{1}{2}$	1,700,000	$\frac{1}{2}$	1,100,000	$\frac{1}{2}$
Lodgepole pine											
16F-E[f]	4 or more	1,400,000	$\frac{1}{3}$	1,200,000	$\frac{1}{3}$	1,400,000	$\frac{1}{2}$	1,200,000	$\frac{1}{2}$	900,000	$\frac{1}{2}$
20F-E[g]	4 or more	1,600,000	$\frac{1}{4}$	1,400,000	$\frac{1}{4}$	1,600,000	$\frac{1}{2}$	1,400,000	$\frac{1}{2}$	900,000	$\frac{1}{2}$

[a] The tabulated bending stresses are applicable to members 12 in. or less in depth. For members greater than 12 in. in depth, the requirements of Section 2.5.4 of this specification apply.

[b] The tabulated combinations are applicable to arches, compression members, tension members and bending members less than $16\frac{1}{4}$ in. in depth. For bending members $16\frac{1}{4}$ in. or more in depth, footnote c applies.

[c] The grading restrictions as contained in AITC 301-E16, 301-E20, 301-E22 and 301-E26 tension lamination requirements shall be followed for the outermost tension laminations representing 5% of the total depth of glued laminated bending members $16\frac{1}{4}$ in. or more in depth.

[d] AITC 301-E22 applicable in addition to minimum E values and edge knot restrictions required for outer tension zone.

[e] AITC 301-E26 applicable in addition to minimum E values and edge knot restrictions required for outer tension zone.

[f] AITC 301-E16 applicable in addition to minimum E values and edge knot restrictions required for outer tension zone.

[g] AITC 301-E20 applicable in addition to minimum E values and edge knot restrictions required for outer tension zone.

[h] This combination consists of hem-fir in the tension zone ($\frac{1}{4}$ of total depth of the member) and Douglas fir in the remainder of the member.

[i] Knots, knot holes, burls, distorted grain, or decay partially or wholly at edges of wide faces shall not occupy more of the net cross section than indicated in this column.

Table 1 (Continued)

Part B   Allowable Unit Stresses, psi

Dry Condition of Use

Combination Symbol	Extreme Fiber in Bending F_b	Tension Parallel to Grain F_t	Compression Parallel to Grain F_c	Compression Perpendicular to Grain $F_{c\perp}$	Horizontal Shear F_v	Modulus of Elasticity E
Douglas fir						
22F-E	2200	1600	1500	450	165	1,800,000
26F-E	2600	1600	1500	450	165	2,100,000
Southern pine						
22F-E	2200	1600	1500	450	200	1,700,000
26F-E	2600	1600	1500	450	200	1,900,000
Hem-fir						
22F-E	2200	1300	1200	245	155	1,600,000
26F-E	2600	1300	1200	245	155	1,800,000
Douglas fir and hem-fir combined						
26F-E	2600	1600	1500	245[J]	165	1,800,000
Lodgepole pine						
16F-E	1600	1100	1000	250	145	1,300,000
20F-E	2000	1100	1000	250	145	1,500,000

Wet Condition of Use

Combination Symbol	Extreme Fiber in Bending F_b	Tension Parallel to Grain F_t	Compression Parallel to Grain F_c	Compression Perpendicular to Grain $F_{c\perp}$	Horizontal Shear F_v	Modulus of Elasticity E
Douglas fir						
22F-E	1800	1300	1100	300	145	1,500,000
26F-E	2100	1300	1100	300	145	1,800,000
Southern Pine						
22F-E	1800	1300	1100	300	180	1,400,000
26F-E	2100	1300	1100	300	180	1,600,000
Hem-fir						
22F-E	1800	1000	900	165	140	1,300,000
26F-E	2100	1000	900	165	140	1,500,000
Douglas fir and hem-fir combined						
26F-E	2100	1300	1100	165[J]	145	1,500,000
Lodgepole pine						
16F-E	1300	900	700	165	130	1,100,000
20F-E	1600	900	700	165	130	1,300,000

[J]This value applies to the tension side only. $F_{c\perp}$ on the compression side is 450 psi for dry conditions of use and 300 psi for wet conditions of use.

AMERICAN INSTITUTE
333 West Hampden Avenue

TIMBER CONSTRUCTION
Englewood, Colorado 80110

AITC 120-71
APPENDIX A
GRADING REQUIREMENTS FOR
AITC 301-E26, AITC 301-E22, AITC 301-E20
AND AITC 301-E16
TENSION LAMINATION
RECOMMENDATIONS

Adopted as Recommendations August 26, 1971
Copyright 1971 by American Institute of Timber Construction

CONTENTS

A1. AITC 301-E26 TENSION LAMINATION — MEMBERS IN BENDING (2,600 psi)

A1.1 Pieces containing wide-ringed or lightweight pith associated wood over $\frac{1}{8}$ of the cross section shall be excluded. (The next inch of wood outside the area of the pith associated wood shall be of the same rate of growth and density of the remainder of the wood located away from the pith. The line along which measurement of this inch is made shall correspond to the line used in the standard grading rules for rate of growth and percentage of summerwood. If a distance of 1 in. is not available along this line, the measurement will be made over such lesser portion as exists.) All wood not included as pith associated wood must be of at least medium grain rate of growth.

A1.2 The general slope of grain shall not exceed 1:16 except where more restrictive slope of grain is required by the standard laminating specifications.

A1.3 Knots shall not occur within 2 knot diameters of the finger joints.

A1.4 A 1 ft length of a lamination shall be considered as a cross section.

A1.5   Maximum size single strength-reducing characteristics when not in the same longitudinal projection of the section must be at least 2 ft apart, measured center to center.

A1.6   Knots shall not occupy more than $\frac{1}{5}$ of the cross section.

A1.7   Two-thirds of the cross section of the lamination must be free of strength-reducing characteristics and must have 1:16 or flatter slope of grain. (Knots plus associated localized cross grain, or knots plus associated localized cross grain plus localized cross grain not associated with knot, or localized cross grain not associated with a knot may occupy up to $\frac{1}{3}$ of the cross section.)

A2. AITC 301-E22 TENSION LAMINATION — MEMBERS IN BENDING (2,200 psi)

A2.1   Pieces containing wide-ringed or lightweight pith associated wood over $\frac{1}{8}$ of the cross section shall be excluded. (The next inch of wood outside the area of the pith associated wood shall be of the same rate of growth and density of the remainder of the wood located away from the pith. The line along which measurement of this inch is made shall correspond to the line used in the standard grading rules for rate of growth and percentage of summerwood. If a distance of 1 in. is not available along this line, the measurement will be made over such lesser portion as exists.) All wood not included as pith associated wood must be of at least medium grain rate of growth.

A2.2   Knots shall not occupy more than $\frac{1}{4}$ of the cross section.

A2.3   The general slope of grain shall not exceed 1:16 except where more restrictive slope of grain is required by the standard laminating specifications.

A2.4   Areas of local grain deviation steeper than 1:16 shall not occupy more than $\frac{1}{3}$ of the cross section.

A2.5   Knots shall not occur within 2 knot diameters of the finger joints.

A3. AITC 301-E20 TENSION LAMINATION — MEMBERS IN BENDING (2,000 psi)

A3.1   Pieces containing wide-ringed or lightweight pith associated wood over $\frac{1}{8}$ of the cross section shall be excluded. (The next inch of wood outside the area of the pith associated wood shall be of the same rate of growth and density of the remainder of the wood located away from the pith. The line along which measurement of this inch is made shall correspond to the line used in the standard grading rules for rate of growth and percentage of summerwood. If a distance of 1 in. is not available along this line, the measurement will be made over such lesser portion as exists.) All wood not included as pith associated wood must be of at least medium grain rate of growth.

A3.2   Knots shall not occupy more than $\frac{1}{4}$ of the cross section.

A3.3   A 6 in. length of lamination shall be considered as a cross section.

A3.4   The general slope of grain shall not exceed 1:16 except where more restrictive slope of grain is required by the standard laminating specifications.

A3.5　Areas of local grain deviation steeper than 1 : 16 shall not occupy more than $\frac{1}{3}$ of the cross section.

A3.6　Knots shall not occur within 2 knot diameters of the finger joints.

A4. AITC 301-E16 TENSION LAMINATION — MEMBERS IN BENDING (1,600 psi)

A4.1　Pieces containing wide-ringed or lightweight pith associated wood over $\frac{1}{8}$ of the cross section shall be excluded. (The next inch of wood outside the area of the pith associated wood shall be of the same rate of growth and density of the remainder of the wood located away from the pith. The line along which measurement of this inch is made shall correspond to the line used in the standard grading rules for rate of growth and percentage of summerwood. If a distance of 1 in. is not available along this line, the measurement will be made over such lesser portion as exists.) All wood not included as pith associated wood must be of at least medium grain rate of growth.

A4.2　Knots shall not occupy more than $\frac{1}{3}$ of the cross section.

A4.3　A 6 in. length of lamination shall be considered as a cross section.

A4.4　The general slope of grain shall not exceed 1 : 12.

A4.5　Areas of local grain deviation (knots plus associated localized cross grain, or knots plus associated localized cross grain plus localized cross grain not associated with knot, or localized cross grain not associated with a knot) steeper than 1 : 12 shall not occupy more than $\frac{1}{2}$ of the cross section.

A4.6　Knots shall not occur within 2 knot diameters of the finger joints.

AMERICAN INSTITUTE
333 West Hampden Avenue

TIMBER CONSTRUCTION
Englewood, Colorado 80110

AITC 120-71
APPENDIX B
LAMINATOR'S QUALITY CONTROL
CHECK OF "E" RATED LUMBER

Adopted as Recommendations August 26, 1971
Copyright 1971 by American Institute of Timber Construction

B1. GENERAL

B1.1 In addition to the quality control equipment required by the *Inspection Manual*, AITC 200, each laminator producing glued laminated timber using "E" rated lumber shall have a static load testing device to measure the modulus of elasticity of lumber as shown in AITC Test 116.

B1.2 AITC Test 116 — Modulus of Elasticity of Lumber by Static Loading. This test is used for checking the modulus of elasticity in lumber that has been previously "E" rated either as an MSR grade or other acceptable means meeting the requirements of the laminating specifications for "E" rated lumber.

B1.2.1 Test Sample. The test sample shall consist of at least 20 samples picked at random from each 50,000 fbm or shipment of each size of lumber that is to be used in the outer $12\frac{1}{2}\%$ of the member and 20 samples for each 50,000 fbm or shipment used in the next $12\frac{1}{2}\%$ of the depth of the member. For purposes of this test, a shipment is defined as lumber received at one time by the laminator from a single source. When a shipment of a given size is less than 50,000 fbm, each shipment shall be checked. When a shipment exceeds 50,000 fbm, each 50,000 fbm or fraction thereof shall be sampled for testing. If more than 5% of the pieces are below the minimum E value specified, a second sampling of at least 40 additional test specimens shall be taken and if the number of pieces with E values less than the minimum E values is greater than 5% of the total number of pieces tested, the batch of lumber will not be used for the E level tested.

B1.2.2 Test Procedure. The E value used as a standard reference for this test is the average E for the total length of the piece. Any method of loading and span-depth ratio can be used provided corrections are applied in accordance with ASTM D2915-70 to convert the E value to the standard conditions listed below:

(*a*) Attitude of piece being tested — flatwise
(*b*) Span-depth ratio — 21

(c) Loading condition — uniform load on full span (see paragraph B2)

(d) Maximum bending stress during test — not to exceed 50% of proportional limit stress

(e) Deflection measurements used to determine E will be measured to nearest 0.001 in.

(f) Supports and loading methods shall conform to requirements in ASTM D198-67.

Any test procedure (see paragraph B3) meeting the above requirements can be used to check the E value.

B2. The E value determined by third point loading in the span-depth ratios most likely to be tested will be approximately $\frac{1}{10}$ of 1% less than that determined for uniform load. Therefore, test devices using third point loading can be considered equivalent to those using uniform loading. The E value determined by center point loading will be slightly less in span-depth ratios likely to be used than those determined by uniform loading. Since results are conservative, test devices using single point loading can be used at the option of the laminator without correction to uniform loading.

B3. One test device is the Western Wood Products Association's static stiffness tester. This device is used to determine deflection measurements on a fixed span of 4 ft resulting from third point loading. When this device is used, 3 deflection determinations will be made on each piece of lumber. The 3 loaded spans of the piece shall be spaced as far apart as practical. The E values for each loaded span shall be determined and the average of these values shall be considered as the E value of the piece. This value shall be further modified by multiplying by 0.980 when $1\frac{1}{2}$ in. thick lumber is tested to correct to the standard span-depth ratio of 21. When other thicknesses of lumber are tested, a similar multiplying factor developed by use of Table 2, ASTM D2915, shall be used.

INDEX

Boldface numbers indicate the Section numbers in Part I; three-digit numbers indicate Standards in Part II.